The P

MW01005689

This newly compiled and thoroughly up-to-date pocket-sized reference work is the companion volume to Dr. Brannen's popular *Practical English-Japanese Dictionary*, first published in 1991. Like its predecessor, it is designed to fill the gap between tourist phrasebooks, with their limited number of examples, and pocket dictionaries published for Japanese (and thus with many examples presented in Japanese script rather than romanized Japanese). All entries, definitions, and usage examples in *The Practical Japanese-English Dictionary* are rendered in romanized Japanese, as well as in Japanese script and English. The approximately 8,000 entries selected are both colloquial and useful, and the practical and natural Japanese usage examples are rendered into clear and common English equivalents, facilitating their use in conversation. A pronunciation guide assists those less familiar with romanized Japanese, while another section introduces the basics of Japanese grammar. Dr. Brannen's new dictionary will be a welcome volume for anyone learning or working in these two languages.

NOAH S. BRANNEN holds a doctoral degree in Far Eastern languages and literatures from the University of Michigan, and recently retired from his professorship at International Christian University in Tokyo. A resident of Japan for nearly four decades, he is also the author of *Everyday Japanese* and *Japanese by the Total Method*.

THE PRACTICAL
JAPANESE-ENGLISH
DICTIONARY

by

Noah S. Brannen

ノア・S・ブラネン

with the assistance of

Katsuhisa Yamaguchi

山口 勝久

WEATHERHILL
New York · Tokyo

First edition, 1998

Published by Weatherhill, Inc.
568 Broadway, Suite 705
New York, NY 10012

Library of Congress Cataloging-in-Publication Data
Brannen, Noah S.
    The Practical Japanese-English Dictionary. /
        Noah S. Brannen with the assistance of
Katsuhisa Yamaguchi. — 1st.ed.
        p.   cm.
ISBN 0-8348-0324-9 (soft: alk. paper)
1. Japanese language—Dictionaries—English.
I. Yamaguchi, Katsuhisa II. Title
    PL679.B72 1998
    495.6'321—dc21   97-9665
    CIP

Preface

Previously, we published *The Practical English-Japanese Dictionary*, designed for English speakers traveling, living, or doing business in Japan. The purpose of the dictionary was to fill a gap left between scanty tourist phrase books and the substantial pocket-size dictionaries prepared by Japanese *for* Japanese. Special features of this previous volume included printing all entries and illustrations both in Japanese and English letters; practical, natural English example sentences translated into natural, informal Japanese; a guide to pronunciation including accent and intonation notations not only for the entries but for illustrations as well; plus a capsule grammar and convenient appendices.

We now offer *The Practical Japanese-English Dictionary* with these same features to be used independently or as a companion volume to *The Practical English-Japanese Dictionary*. Special attention was paid to Japanese equivalents appearing in the English-Japanese version because we wanted to ensure that vocabulary selections reflected the practical needs of English speakers in Japan. All examples of entries in phrases and sentences were composed by native speakers of Japanese and the translations into English are my own. Effort was made to present examples in natural, contemporary, colloquial Japanese. The English translations, since they aim at the same goal, are not always what purists call "literal." These translations are *functionally equivalent*, which means the way one would say the equivalent in natural English, appropriate to the situation. To keep the dictionary compact we have eliminated foreign loan words *(gairaigo)* unless the meaning of the word has been significantly changed or restricted, such as the loan word *hômu*, which is an abbreviation of the English word 'platform.'

As the author, again I am at a loss to know where to begin to pay acknowledgments to the numerous friends and colleagues who have helped with the preparation of this dictionary. The students I have taught through the past thirty years at Japan Missionary Language Institute, International Christian University, University of California, and privately, together with dozens of Japanese language teachers with whom I have served as team member, have, of course, made the greatest contribution. In particular, I would like to thank and pay my respects to three vital contributors to the present volume: Yamaguchi Katsuhisa who selected and created the majority of illustrations and input the entire manuscript on the computer; Kevin Purell, specialist in layout and design; and Mary Onions, freelance editor and rewriter.

Acknowledgments

I will not attempt to acknowledge by name the numerous individuals, non-Japanese and Japanese, students, colleagues, and friends who have contributed in countless ways to the making of this dictionary, but, as the Japanese say, "Thanks to you" the imprint of your contributions may be found on every page. Thank you.

Noah

Japanese Grammar Basics

Simple Sentence Structure

In Japanese one can say the equivalent of: "Jack is a student," "The cars are new," "Children play," or "Jane teaches." In English each of these sentences contains a verb; i.e., 'is,' 'are,' 'play,' and 'teaches.' In the Japanese equivalents, however, only the last two sentences contain a verb; i.e., *asobu*, 'plays,' and *oshieru*, 'teaches.' The verb 'is' in the first sentence, is handled in Japanese sentence structure by a combination of a particle, *wa*, which marks the subject, and a final copula, *da*, to produce an equation-like sentence, A = B. Thus, *Jack wa gakusei* (student) *da*. For the second sentence, "The cars are new," in Japanese the subject is *kuruma* (the cars) while the remainder of the sentence is one word, an adjective: *atarashíi*. Thus, the four basic Japanese sentence types are:

1.	Jack wa gakusei da.	*Jack is a student.*
2.	Kuruma wa atarashíi.	*The cars are new.*
3.	Kodomo wa asobu.	*Children play.*
4.	Jane wa oshieru.	*Jane teaches.*

As in English, simple sentences can be expanded by adding modifiers and other sentence elements such as time, place, verb object, e.g.,

1	Jack wa <u>atarashíi</u> gakusei da.	*Jack is a <u>new</u> student.*
2.	<u>Jack no</u> kuruma wa atarashíi.	*<u>Jack's</u> car is new.*
3,	<u>Kono</u> kodomo wa <u>shízuka ni</u> asobu.	*<u>This</u> child plays <u>quietly</u>.*
4.	Jane wa <u>Getsuyōbi ni</u> (time)	*Jane, <u>on Monday</u>*
	<u>Yokohama de</u> (place)	*in Yokohama*
	<u>Eigo o</u> (object) oshieru.	*teaches <u>English</u>.*
	(Jane teaches English in Yokohama on Monday.)	

Observe the following in the above examples: 1) the predicate always comes last, i.e., (*gakusei da* [noun + da]; *atarashíi* [adjective]; *asobu* [*vi*, or intransitive verb, meaning that the verb does not take a direct object]; *oshieru* [*vt*, or transitive verb, meaning that the verb takes a direct object]) , 2) noun modifiers (*atarashíi; Jack no; kono*) come before the word they modify), 3) adverbs (*shízuka ni*) precede the verb they modify, 4) sentence elements have their distinctive particle markers which identify the grammatical function of the element (subject *wa*, time *ni*, place *de*, manner *ni*, object *o*).

Other grammatical features illustrated in the above examples are absence of articles ('a,' 'an' and 'the'); the lack of plural suffix for nouns (e.g., *kuruma* can mean both 'car' and 'cars,' and *kodomo* can mean both 'child,' and 'children'; and the absence of agreement in number between nouns and predicates (e.g., 'cars are,' 'car is').

Though this dictionary features short, simple sentences and phrases to illustrate the entries, it is, of course, possible to combine simple sentences to make longer, more complicated ones. Some example sentences demonstrate this. For example:

Amerika e ittára, hagaki o kudasái.	*When you go to America, send me a postcard.*
Kodomo wa terebi-gḗmu ni netchū-shite	*The children are absorbed in computer games*
iru <u>keredo</u>, dōse súgu akíru <u>kara</u>,	*<u>but</u> no doubt they'll tire of them right away,*
shibaráku hótte okó.	*<u>so</u> I'll let them alone.*
Seishin hírō ga tamatte shimattá <u>no de</u>,	*<u>Because</u> I had become so mentally exhausted,*
kū́ki no íi tokoró de kyūyō-shite iru.	*I am recuperating in a place where the air is good.*

Conversation and Styles of Speech

Everyday conversational styles, plain for personal, friendly conversation, and polite for more impersonal situations, are used throughout this dictionary, with occasional illustrations of words and phrases which may be used on formal occasions. Of course, plain talk and polite talk exist in every language, but attention should be called to certain features in the Japanese language which distinguish the two styles. In addition, the user should be aware of differences in feminine and masculine speech.

Plain and polite style are distinguished by the form of the predicate. Entries for the examples which are used above appear in this dictionary in plain style as follows:

>   **da** [*copula, plain form:* de wa (*or* ja) nai; datta]
>   **atarashí·i** [*adj* ataráshiku nái; ataráshikatta]
>   **asob·u** [*vi* asobanai; asonda]
>   **nár·u** [*vi* naránai; nátta] *become*
>   **arúk·u** [*vi* arukánai; arúita] *walk*
>   **tabé·ru** [*vt* tabénai; tábeta] *eat*
>   **This transitive verb (vt) may occur in sentences where the direct object is stated,* <u>O-sashimí</u> o tabemásu ka? *Do you eat <u>sashimi</u>?*
>   **oshie·ru** [*vt* oshienai; oshieta] *teach*
>   **This transitive verb may occur in sentences where both the direct object and the indirect object are stated, e.g.,* Jane wa <u>kodomo ni</u> wa <u>Eigo o</u> oshiemásen. *Jane doesn't teach <u>English to children.</u>*

A sentence which ends with the plain copula can be made polite by using the polite form of the copula; adjective-type sentences are made polite by adding desu; and verb-type sentences are made polite by suffixing *-masu* (or some form of *-masu*). Thus:

Plain Style

COPULA	da [*neg:* de wa (*or* ja) nai; *past:* datta]
ADJECTIVE	atarashí·i [*neg:* ataráshi-ku nái; *past:* ataráshi-katta]
VERB	asob·u [*neg:* asob-anai; *past:* ason-da]
	oshie·ru [*neg:* oshie-nai; *past:* oshie-ta]

Polite Style

COPULA	desu [*neg:* de wa (*or* ja) arimasén; *past:* deshita]
ADJECTIVE	atarashíi desu [*neg:* ataráshiku nái desu;
	past: ataráshikatta desu]
VERB	asob-imásu [*neg:* asob-imasén; *past:* asob-imáshita]
	oshie-mású [*neg:* oshie-masén; *past:* oshie-máshita]

To change the illustrations of this dictionary from plain style to polite style, follow the paradigms which appear above. To make these adjustments easier, we have inserted a raised period for adjective and verb entries to show where the various endings are to be attached. For adjective predicates, simply add *desu* to make the polite form.

In this dictionary a few illustrations where we felt the user should be cautioned are marked, <fem>, <masc>, <polite> or <formal>. By including these notations, we are not subscribing to sexist or social-conscious language usage, only reflecting the language as it is used in Japan today. For instance, unless she wishes to sound like a man, a Japanese woman does not end a sentence with the plain copula *da*. In a situation where a man would end his sentence with the abrupt plain-form *da*, a woman would attach the sentence-ending particle *wa* <fem>: e.g., *Kírei da wa!* (It's beautiful!). Though most of the examples are neutral, a few such sentences are included to give the user a more accurate picture of the way the language is used today. Sentences marked <polite> are for situations such as asking directions of a stranger or talking over the telephone. The inclusion of <formal> sample sentences is limited to situations where it is felt that the user might want to know the "proper" thing to say in formal situations.

English Equivalents of Entries and Illustrations

For the majority of entries, a number of English equivalents for the entry item are listed. Basic meanings are given first, extended and peripheral meanings follow. Illustrations are given to bring out these various meanings as far as space permits. When the Japanese sentence omits the subject, we have supplied a subject to fit the context. Occasionally adages, or idiomatic expressions, marked <set phrase> help to fill out the variety of extended meanings. At times we provide a literal translation of idiomatic expressions as well as a more natural English equivalent.

Conjugations

As has already been shown (in the dictionary entries for *da, atarashíi, asobu,* and *oshieru*), the copula, adjective, and verb are conjugated, i.e., suffixes are added to the stem to produce negative, past tense, and other forms in the same way that the suffix ' ed' is added to verb stems in English to indicate past tense, e.g., *hajime·ru* (start) → *hajime-ta* (start-ed). The idea that adjectives are declined seems strange to one thinking in terms of English grammar, but in Japanese, adjectives take the past tense suffix (*atarashí·i* 'is new' → *ataráshi-katta* 'was new') and a variety of other suffixes.

The conjugation of Japanese verbs is a bit complicated. With the exception of irregular *suru* (do) and *kuru* (come), verbs divide into those whose stem ends in a consonant and those whose stem ends in a vowel. To show this distinction, we have inserted a raised period in the entry, e.g., <u>asob</u>·u (consonant verb stem), <u>oshie</u>·ru (vowel verb stem). All suffixes are added to the stem (the underlined portion) to replace -*u* or -*ru*. To turn a plain-style sentence into a polite-style sentence, for consonant verbs add -*imasen* for negative and -*imashita* for past, and for vowel verbs add -*masen* and -*mashita*. (For detailed conjugation tables, see *The Practical English-Japanese Dictionary*.)

Pronunciation Guide

Japanese is not especially difficult to pronounce for the English speakers. As is often pointed out, the pronunciation of Japanese vowels is very close to that of Italian vowels, and, with very few exceptions, consonants correspond to similar consonants in English. The Japanese themselves, however, do not think in terms of consonant and vowel; rather, they conceive of a syllable as a distinct and indivisible unit formed either of a single vowel or a consonant followed by a vowel, for example *a, su, to,* and so on. There are exceptions to this consonant-plus-vowel rule. One is a series of syllables that, when romanized, feature a *y* immediately after a consonant. as in *kya, myu,* and *ryo.* Another is the series *cha, chi, cho, chu.* A further complication is the occurrence of the double and triple consonants *kk, mm, nn, pp, ss, ssh, tch, tt,* and *tts.* These can be understood by thinking of them as "long" consonants (as in long vowels) that are sounded twice as long as their corresponding single-element counterparts. An example in English of such a long consonant is the *kk* in book*k*eeper (compared with the *k* in bee *k*eeper). In addition, some syllables feature an *n* after a vowel as in *hon* (book). While this too may seem to be an exception, to the Japanese, *hon* is composed of the two syllables *ho* and *n, n* being the only consonant that functions as a syllable by itself.

The staccato delivery of spoken Japanese demonstrates its syllabic nature. This delivery strikes the English speaker as quite different from the large intonation contours and relatively melodic delivery that characterize English. The staccato effect of spoken Japanese is further emphasized by lack of stress on any particular part of a word in the manner of English. For emphasis, instead of stressing a particular syllable as we do in English, other devices, such as insertion of the particle *wa* for focus, are employed. (However, see the section below on pitch change and intonation.)

Vowels

Short	Long*
a as in mama	**ā**
i as in machine	**ī** (or **ii**)
u as in too	**ū**
e as in bet	**ē** (or **ei**)**ū**
o as in boat	**ōō**

*Long vowels have the same quality as the corresponding short vowels but are held roughly twice as long.

Consonants

b	as in bet	**n**	as in not
ch	as in chop	**p**	as in pot
d	as in dot	**r**	like *dd* in e**dd**y or *tt* in Be**tt**y
f*	as in foot	**s**	as in sot
g	as in got	**t**	as in tot
h	as in hot	**w**	as in watt
k	as in keep	**y**	as in yacht
j	as in jot	**z**	as in zero
m	as in meet		

*The consonant *f* is only followed by the vowel *u* in native Japanese words and is produced by bringing the lips close together to make friction. Words borrowed from English which begin with *f* may be pronounced in the same way as English.

Pitch Change in Words

The mark ´ is used throughout this dictionary to mark the syllable which precedes a fall in voice pitch or tone; it is not to be interpreted as a stress mark. In English, except for articles and prepositions, one syllable of every word is stressed. If the word is a long one, often there are primary and secondary stresses, as in *uncónstitútional*. In Japanese, in a straightforward sentence where no special intonation is employed, basically two tones are employed — high and low. The mark ´ over a vowel indicates that the tone of the next syllable is lower.

In the sentence *Kono kodomo wa shízuka ni asobu* (This child plays quietly), the fall from high tone to low tone occurs after the accented syllable, thus:

> Ko/no kodomo wa shí\zuka ni asobu.
> *This child plays quietly.*

The intonation contour line in the above example falls after the marked syllable *shí*. Notice that the tone of the first syllable of the utterance, *Ko*, is also low. This is because this syllable is the first syllable in the utterance and is like a "warm-up" syllable before the voice reaches the higher level. In a longer sentence, breaks occur marking "breath groups." After such breaks, the speaker "warms up" again, and the first syllable following the break is pronounced with the lower tone. For example:

> A/merika e ittá\ra, ha/gaki o kudasá\i.
> *When you go to America, send me a postcard.*

Intonation

In Japanese there are four basic intonation patterns: 1) falling, which marks the end of an utterance; 2) rising, which indicates a question or special emphasis; 3) level (neither falling nor rising), which means that the utterance is left incomplete; and 4) abrupt rising or falling, which indicates an emotional element such as excitement, anger, intense concern, or fear.

These intonation patterns are equivalent to the same patterns in English, but special attention should be paid to the second pattern; i.e., rising indication to indicate a question. As shown in the examples below, in English, the voice tone begins to rise early in the question, whereas in Japanese, the rise occurs at the end.

> Ko/domo wa shí\zuka ni a/sobimá\su/ka?
>
> *Does /your child play quietly?*

If one uses the English question intonation pattern when speaking Japanese, the sentence will sound strange to a native Japanese speaker.

Abbreviations and Symbols

abbr	abbreviation; abbreviated form	*pass*	passive
adj	adjective, i.e., a word that ends with ·*i* in the dictionary entry	*plu*	plural
		polite	polite style
adv	adverb or adverbial expression	*Prot*	Protestantism
		RR	railroad
aff	affirmative	*set phrase*	a saying, adage, or idiomatic expression
Anat	anatomy	*Tech*	technical term
attr	attributive, i.e., a word or phrase that can precede a noun to modify it	*US*	United States
		vb aux	verb auxiliary
		vi	intransitive verb
Biol	biology; biological	*vt*	transitive verb
Bot	botanical term	*W*	western (European and/or American) or western style
Br	Great Britain or British	[ ]	enclosure for grammatical notes
Budd	Buddhism		
Cath	Roman Catholicism	( )	optional; enclosure for clarifying information
caus	causative verb form		
Chr	Christianity	[ ]	optional (in entry)
Elec	electricity or electrical	< >	enclosure for style notes, or set phrase
fem	feminine		
formal	formal style of speech	·(ru / u)	point in a verb where the break between stem and ending occurs
Geo	geological		
Geom	geometry		
Gram	grammar	·*i*	point in an adjective where the break between stem and ending occurs
hon	honorific style		
hum	humble style		
J	Japanese or Japanese style	´	pitch change: the following syllable is lower in pitch
lit	literally		
masc	masculine	;	or
Math	mathematics	/	or
Med	medical term	,	and
neg	negative form	⸉	example
or	alternative reading		

The Practical Japanese-English Dictionary

A

ā iu ああいう *such a (person / thing)* ❽Ima máde ā iu hitó ni deátta koto ga nákatta. 今までああ言う人に出会ったことがなかった。*I had never met such a person before.*

abare·ru [*vi* abarenai; abareta] 暴れる *run wild; go on a rampage* ❽Ano yopparai ga abarete iru. あの酔っ払いが暴れている。*The drunk (person) is on a rampage.*

abekobe ni あべこべに *opposite; backwards; back-to-front* ❽Sono sandaru o abekobe ni haite iru yó. そのサンダルをあべこべに履いているよ。*You are wearing your sandals on the wrong feet.*

abi·ru [*vt* abinai; abita] 浴びる *pour water over (oneself); bathe in* ❽Máiasa shāwā o abimásu ká? 毎朝シャワーを浴びますか。*Do you take a shower every morning?*

abise·ru [*vt* abisenai; abiseta] 浴びせる *shower with; heap on; bombard with* ❽Minná ga káre ni warúkuchi o abiseta. みんなが彼に悪口を浴びせた。*Everyone heaped abuse on him.*

ábu 虻 *horsefly*

abumi 鐙 *stirrup*

abuna·i [*adj* abunaku nái; abunákatta] 危ない *(be) dangerous* ❽Abunái! 危ない！*Look out!*

abura 油 *oil*

abura 脂 *fat meat; (cooking) fat*

aburá e 油絵 *oil painting* ❽abura énogu 油絵の具 *oil paints*

aburakkó·i [*adj* aburakkóku nái; aburakkókatta] 脂っこい *(be) greasy* ❽Narubeku aburakkói monó o tabénai yō ni shite iru. なるべく脂っこいものを食べないようにしている。*As much as possible, I'm trying not to eat greasy foods.*

achíkochi あちこち *here and there*

achira あちら *that way; over there; that person*

adana 渾名; 仇名 *nickname; sobriquet*

afuré·ru [*vi* afurénai; afúreta] 溢れる *overflow* ❽Mizu ga afúrete iru. 水が溢れている。*The water is overflowing.*

agar·u [*vi* agaranai; agatta] 上がる *go up; rise; end; be finished; get nervous* ❽yáne ni agaru 屋根に上がる *go up on the roof* ❽Kónkai no genkō wa shimekiri máe ni agatta. 今回の原稿は締切前に上がった。*This time the manuscript was finished before the deadline.* ❽shikén de agaru 試験で上がる *get nervous at an exam*

age·ru [*vt* agenai; ageta] 上げる *give (to another: Caution: another verb,* **kureru** *is used to express the meaning "give to me")* ❽Awánaku natte kita fuku o tomodachi ni ageta. 合わなくなってきた服を友達に上げた。 *I gave the clothes that no longer fit me to a friend.*

[-te]age·ru [*v. aux.*: agenai; ageta] （〜て）あげる *do (something) for another* ❊Tanaka-san no tamé ni o-isha-san o yonde ageta. 田中さんのためにお医者さんを呼んであげた。 *I called a doctor for Mrs. Tanaka.*

age·ru [*vt* agenai; ageta] 上げる; 挙げる *increase; raise* ❊Shachō wa sháin no kyū́ryō o ageta. 社長は社員の給料を上げた。 *The boss raised the company employees' salaries.* ❊Kotáe ga wakáttara té o agete kudasái. 答えが分かったら手を挙げて下さい。 *If you know the answer, raise your hand.*

age·ru [*vt* agenai; ageta] 揚げる *(deep fat) fry*

agura 胡座 *cross-legged; tailor-fashion* ❊agura o káku 胡座をかく *sit tailor-fashion (on tatami)*

áhen 阿片 *opium*

ahiru 家鴨 *(domestic) duck*

ái 愛 *love* ——**ai-súru** [*vt*] 愛する *(to) love* ❊Watashi o áishite imásu ka? 私を愛していますか。 *Do you love me?*

áibu 愛撫 *a caress* ——**áibu-suru** [*vt*] 愛撫する *(to) caress*

aidagara 間柄 *relationship (between people)*

aida ni 間 に *between; an interval (of time / between objects)* ❊Níji kara sánji no aida ni ukagatté mo yoroshíi deshō ka? 二時から三時の間に伺ってもよろしいでしょうか。 *May I visit you between 2 and 3 o'clock? <formal>* ❊Toshókan wa yū́bínkyoku to eigákan no aida ni áru. 図書館は郵便局と映画館の間にある。 *The library is between the post office and the movie theater.*

aida ni tátsu 間に立つ *arbitrate* ❊Futarí no aida ni tátte, hanashí o matomete kuremasén ka? 二人の間に立って、話をまとめてくれませんか。 *Would you please arbitrate between those two and help them settle their differences?*

áiirenai 相容れない *be incompatible* ❊Furúi sedai to atarashíi sedai no kangaekata wa o-tagai ni áiirenai tokoró ga áru. 古い世代と新しい世代の考え方はお互いに相容れないところがある。 *There are points where the ideas of the older and younger generations are incompatible.*

aiiro 藍色 *indigo*

aijin 愛人 *lover*

aijō 愛情 *affection; love* ❊aijō no hyōgén 愛情の表現 *expression of love*

aikagi 合鍵 *duplicate key*

aikawarazu 相変わらず *as always; without change* ❊Shibarakuburi de átta keredo, káre wa aikawarazu isogáshikatta. しばらくぶりで会ったけれど、彼は相変らず忙しかった。 *It had been some time since I saw him; he was busy as always.*

aikókusha 愛国者 *patriot*

aikókushin 愛国心 *patriotism*

aikyō 愛嬌 *charm* ❽"Otokó wa dókyō, onná wa aikyō" to mukashi yóku iwareta monó desu. 「男は度胸、女は愛嬌」と昔よく言われたものです。 *People used to say that a man should be brave and a woman should be charming.*

aimai [na] 曖昧（な）*vague* ❽Kánojo wa sono tóki, aimai na henjí shika shinákatta. 彼女はその時、曖昧な返事しかしなかった。*At that time, she gave only a vague reply.*

aima ni 合間 に *in the interval; between (time only)* ❽Watashi wa shigoto no aima ni shiyō dénwa o káketa. 私は仕事の合間に私用電話をかけた。*I made a personal telephone call during my (work) break.*

ainiku 生憎 *unfortunately* ❽Ainiku, sono hí no káigi ni wa shusseki-dekimasén. 生憎、その日の会議には出席できません。*Unfortunately, I cannot attend the meeting on that day.*

airashí-i [adj airáshiku nái; airáshikatta] 愛らしい *(be) charming; sweet*

áisatsu 挨拶 *greetings; salutations* ❽shínnen no áisatsu 新年の挨拶 *New Year's greetings* ❽Sono káigi de wa saisho ni shusáisha kara no áisatsu ga átta.その会議では最初に主催者からの挨拶があった。*At the beginning of the meeting, there were greetings from the sponsor.* ——**áisatsu-suru** [vt] 挨拶する *greet; bring greetings*

aiseki 相席 *a shared seat; a shared table (in a crowded restaurant)*

aiseki 哀惜 *grief*

aishō 愛称 *nickname; pet name*

aishō 相性 *compatibility in temperament*

aishū 哀愁 *sorrow*

aisō no [or ga] íi 愛想の（*or* が）いい *amiable* ❽aisō no íi hito 愛想のいい人 *an amiable person* ——**aisōyóku-suru** [vi] 愛想よくする *be friendly*

aité 相手 *companion; partner; competitor; opponent; the opposite (or other) party* ❽Aité wa dónata desu ka? 相手はどなたですか。*Who is your companion?* ❽kyōsō áite 競争相手 *a rival* ❽Go no aité o sagashite iru. 碁の相手を探している。*I'm looking for an opponent for a game of go.*

aitsu あいつ *that fellow; that rascal; he* ❽Aitsu wa ōhei na yátsu da. あいつは横柄な奴だ。*He's stuck-up.* <masc>

áitsuide 相次いで *in succession; one after another* ❽Ryōshin wa áitsuide kono yó o sátta. 両親は相次いでこの世を去った。*My parents passed on one after the other.*

aiyoku 愛欲 *passion*

áizu 合図 *a signal* ——**áizu-suru** [vt] 合図する *signal* ❽Júmbi ga dékitara áizu-shite kudasai. 準備ができたら合図して下さい。*When you're ready, signal me.*

aizuchi 相槌 *chiming in (in a conversation)* **⑧**Tanaka-san wa ítsumo taimingu-yóku aizuchi o útsu. 田中さんはいつもタイミングよく相槌を打つ. *Tanaka always chimes in with something appropriate at the right moment.*

aji 味 *a taste; flavor; distinctiveness* **⑧**aji ga suru 味がする *taste; have a taste* **⑧** aji no áru 味のある *flavorful; interesting* **⑧**aji no nái 味のない *tasteless; uninteresting; dull* **⑧**Sore wa dónna aji (ga shimásu ka)? それはどんな味(がしますか)。 *What does that taste like?* **⑧**Anó hito wa mikake wa tómokaku, totemo aji no áru táipu desu. あの人は見かけはともかく、とても味のあるタイプです。 *He may not be much to look at, but he is a very interesting type of person.*

áji 鯵 *horse mackerel*

ajikená·i [adj ajikenáku nái; ajikenákatta] 味気ない *dull; insipid; wearisome* **⑧**Shigoto to ié to no ōfuku daké no seikatsu wa totemo ajikenái. 仕事と家との往復だけの生活はとても味気ない。 *It's a very dull life, doing nothing but commuting between home and work.*

ajisai 紫陽花 *hydrangea*

ajiwá·u [vt ajiwawánai; ajiwátta] 味わう *taste* **⑧**wáin o ajiwau ワインを味わう *taste wine*

áka 赤 *red (color)*

aká 垢 *dirt; filth; grime* **⑧**Erí ni aká ga tsúite iru. 襟に垢がついている。 *There's dirt on the collar.* **⑧**Séken no aká o otósu. 世間の垢を落す。 *Rid oneself of the grime of the world.*

akaáka [to] 赤々(と) *with a red appearance; brightly* **⑧**Dánro no hí ni akaáka to moete iru. 暖炉の火が赤々と燃えている。 *The fire in the fireplace is burning brightly.*

ákachan 赤ちゃん *baby*

akage 赤毛 *red hair*

aka·i [adj akaku nái; akákatta] 赤い *(be) red* **⑧**Akai kutsú ga hoshíi. 赤い靴がほしい。 *I want a pair of red shoes.*

akaji 赤字 *red figures; in the red* **⑧**akaji kókusai 赤字国債 *deficit-covering bond* **⑧**Uchi no kakéibo wa ítsumo akaji desu. うちの家計簿はいつも赤字です。 *Our household accounts are always in the red.*

akaku nár·u [vi akaku naránai; akaku nátta] 赤くなる *blush* **⑧**Hitomae de geppú-shite, hazukáshikute kao ga akaku nátta. 人前でげっぷして、恥ずかしくて顔が赤くなった。 *I belched in public and then blushed out of embarrassment.*

akami 赤み *redness*

akami 赤身 *lean meat* Maguro no sashimí wa akami yóri tóro no hō ga umái. 鮪の刺身は赤身よりトロの方が旨い。 *The fatty part of raw tuna tastes better than the lean meat.*

akambō 赤ん坊 *a baby*

akari 明かり *a light; lamp*

akaru·i [adj akaruku nái; akarúkatta] 明るい *(be) bright; light; cheerful* 🗲akarui heyá 明るい部屋 *a bright room* 🗲akarui hitó 明るい人 *a cheerful person* ——**akaruku** 明るく *cheerfully* 🗲Kánojo wa tsurai tóki, ítsumo akaruku furumátte ita. 彼女は辛い時、いつも明るく振舞っていた。 *Even in hard times, she always acted cheerful.*

akarumi ni déru 明るみに出る *come to the light; be exposed* 🗲Zōwai jíken ga akarumi ni déta. 贈賄事件が明るみに出た。 *The bribery case was exposed.*

aka-shíngō 赤信号 *red light (traffic signal)*

akatsuchi 赤土 *red soil*

akazátō 赤砂糖 *refined brown sugar*

akegata 明け方 *daybreak; dawn*

akekuré·ru [vi akekurénai; akekúreta] 明け暮れる *be absorbed in; spend all one's time (doing)* 🗲Káre wa máinichi shigoto de akekúreta. 彼は毎日仕事で明け暮れた。 *He spent all his time every day working.*

ake no 明けの *dawning; rising; morning* 🗲Kinsei wa ake no myōjō tó mo yoi no myōjō tó mo iwarete iru. 金星は明けの明星とも宵の明星とも言われている。 *Venus is called both the morning star and evening star.*

akeppanashi 開けっ放し *left open; free and open* 🗲Mádo o akeppanashi ni shináide kudasái. 窓を開けっ放しにしないで下さい。 *Don't leave the window open.* 🗲Yamada-san wa dare to demo akeppanashi de katariáu. 山田さんは誰とでも開けっ放しで語り合う。 *Yamada talks freely and openly with everyone.*

ake·ru [vt akenai; aketa] 開ける；明ける *open* 🗲Kono kán no futa o akete kuremasén ka? この缶の蓋を開けてくれませんか。 *Would you open this can for me?*

ake·ru [vt akenai; aketa] 空ける *vacate; make empty; make room for; empty out* 🗲Kabin no mizu o akete kudasái. 花瓶の水を空けて下さい。 *Please empty the water out of the vase.*

áki 秋 *fall; autumn*

aki 空き *vacancy; opening; space*

akichi 空き地 *vacant lot*

akínai 商い *business; trade*

akíraka [na] 明らか (な) *evident; plain* 🗲Kono kotó wa akíraka na jíjitsu desu. このことは明らかな事実です。 *This is a plain fact.* ——**akíraka ni** 明らかに *evidently; plainly; clearly* 🗲Kimi no sono jíken no kioku wa akíraka ni machigátte iru. 君のその事件の記憶は明らかに間違っている。 *Your recollection of that event is clearly mistaken.* ——**akíraka ni suru** 明らかにする *make plain; make clear* 🗲Higísha wa tōjitsu no aribai o akíraka ni shinákatta. 被疑者は当日のアリバイを明らかにしなかった。 *The suspect did not clearly establish an alibi for that day.*

akiramé·ru [vt akiraménai; akirámeta] 諦める *abandon; give up; resign (oneself) to* ❸Káre wa ryūgaku o akirámeta. 彼は留学を諦めた。 *He gave up studying abroad.*

akire·ru [vi akirenai; akireta] 呆れる *be astounded; dumbfounded; fed up with; disgusted with* ❸Káre ga amarí ni mo múchi na no de akirete shimatta. 彼があまりにも無知なので呆れてしまった。 *I was dumbfounded that he could be so ignorant.*

akí·ru [vi akínai; ákita] 飽きる *tire of; have enough of* ❸Musumé wa konki ga nákute náni o yatté mo súgu akíru. 娘は根気がなくて何をやってもすぐ飽きる。 *My daughter has no perseverance; no matter what she does, she soon tires of it.*

akishitsu 空き室 *vacant room; room for rent*

akiya 空き家 *vacant house; house for rent*

akka 悪化 *worsening* ——**akka-suru** [vi] 悪化する *become worse* ❸Sono kuni no seiji jōkyō wa masúmasu akka-shite iru. その国の政治情況はますます悪化している。 *The political situation in that country is growing worse and worse.*

akke ni toraréru 呆気にとられる *be taken aback; be amazed* ❸Kimi no itta koto ni odoróite, akke ni toráreta. 君の言った事に驚いて、呆気にとられた。 *I was taken aback at what you said.*

ákki 悪鬼 *demon; devil*

akogare 憧れ *longing*

akogare·ru [vi akogarenai; akogareta] 憧れる *long for; yearn; want passionately* ❸Musuko wa akushon sutá ni akogarete iru. 息子はアクションスターに憧れている。 *My son wants (passionately) to become an action (movie) star.*

ak·u [vi akanai; aita] 開く *open; be open* ❸Koshō ka na? Jidō dóa ga akanai na. 故障かな？ 自動ドアが開かないな。 *Is it out of order? The automatic door doesn't open.* <masc>

ak·u [vi akanai; aita] 空く *be (or become) vacant; be (or become) empty* ❸Hóteru no heyá wa aite iru. ホテルの部屋は空いている。 *The hotel room is vacant.*

áku 悪 *evil* ❸zén to áku 善と悪 *good and evil*

akubi 欠伸 *a yawn* ❸Omówazu akubi ga déte shimatta. 思わず欠伸が出てしまった。 *I couldn't help yawning.* ——**akubi-suru** [vi] 欠伸する *yawn*

akujúnkan 悪循環 *vicious circle*

ákuma 悪魔 *devil; Satan*

ákumu 悪夢 *nightmare*

akunin 悪人 *bad person; criminal*

akuru- 明くる〜 *the following (day / year, etc.)* ❸Watashítachi wa kekkón-shiki no akuru-ása, shinkon-ryókō ni shuppatsu-shita. 私たちは結婚式の明くる朝、新婚旅行に出発した。 *We started on our* *honeymoon the morning after our wedding.*

akushitsu [na] 悪質（な）*bad nature; evil characteristic*

ákushu 握手 *handshake* ——**ákushu-suru** [*vi*] *shake hands (with)* §Hajímete áu hitó to ákushu-suru. 初めて会う人と握手する。*I shake hands with someone I meet the first time.*

akushū 悪臭 *stench; bad smell*

akutai 悪態 *curse word* §akutai o tsúku 悪態をつく *curse*

aku-un 悪運 *bad luck*

akuyō-suru [*vt*] 悪用する *misuse; make wrong use of* §Kokyaku rísuto o akuyō-shité wa ikenai. 顧客リストを悪用してはいけない。*You mustn't misuse the customer (mailing) list.*

áma 尼 *nun (Budd)*

áma 海女 *woman diver*

amachua アマチュア *amateur*

amádo 雨戸 *rain shutters (J)*

amae·ru [*vi* amaenai; amaeta] 甘える *presume on the love or kindness (of someone); act like a baby; seek pampering; be dependent on* §Watashi wa háha ni amaetái. 私は母に甘えたい。*I want to be pampered by my mother.*

amágu 雨具 *rain gear*

amágutsu 雨靴 *rain shoes; rubbers*

ama·i [*adj* amaku nái; amákatta] 甘い *(be) sweet; lenient* §Satō wa amai. 砂糖は甘い。*Sugar is sweet.* §Eigo no senséi no tésuto no saiten wa amákatta. 英語の先生のテストの採点は甘かった。*The English teacher was lenient in grading the tests.*

amakuchi 甘口 *sweet; not dry (of alchoholic beverages)*

amámizu 雨水 *rainwater*

amámori 雨漏り *a leak (letting rain in)*

Ama-nó-gawa 天の川 *the Milky Way; the Galaxy*

amanójaku 天の邪鬼 *perversity; obstinate person* §Káre wa nán demo wázato hito ni sakaráu kara, amanójaku da. 彼は何でもわざと人に逆らうから、天の邪鬼だ。*He's contrary; he deliberately contradicts you, no matter what you say.*

amari 余り *remainder* §Jū waru nána wa ichi, amari san. 十割る七は一余り三. *Ten divided by seven equals one with a remainder of three.*

amari あまり *(not) very much* [*with neg*] §Amari o-kane o mótte inai. あまりお金を持っていない。*I don't have very much money.*

[no] ámari （の）あまり *to (such) an extent; at the extremity of* §Hinkon no ámari kánojo wa mízukara no ínochi o tátte shimatta. 貧困のあまり彼女は自らの命を断ってしまった。*Because of extreme poverty, she took her own life.*

amá·ru [*vi* amaránai; amátta] 余る *be left over; be extra* §Kongetsu wa dénki o setsuyaku-shitá no de o-kane ga amátta. 今月は電気を節約し

たのでお金が余った。*There's money left over because we saved on electricity this month.*

amattare 甘ったれ *spoiled child*

amma 按摩 *masseur; masseuse*

amayádori 雨宿り *shelter from the rain*

amayakás·u [*vt* amayakasánai; amayakáshita] 甘やかす *pamper; spoil* §kodomo o amayakásu 子供を甘やかう *spoil a child*

áme 雨 *rain* §Áme ga fútte iru. 雨が降っている。 *It's raining.*

ame 飴 *(hard) candy*

amí 網 *net* §amí o útsu 網を打つ *cast a net*

amíbō 編み棒 *knitting needle*

amímono 編み物 *knitting; crocheting; knitted (crocheted) goods*

amma 按摩 *massage; masseur; masseuse* §amma o tóru 按摩を取る *have (or get) a massage*

ammaku 暗幕 *black (out) curtain*

ámpi 安否 *safety; welfare*

Ampo Jōyaku 安保条約 *Japan-US Security Treaty*

ám·u [*vt* amánai; ánda] 編む *knit; crochet; braid* §sétā o ámu セーターを編む *knit a sweater*

án 餡 *sweet bean jam* §an pán 餡パン *bean jam bread*

án 案 *proposal; plan* §án o teishutsu-suru 案を提出する *present a plan* §án o tanaage ni suru 案を棚上げにする *shelve a plan* §án o tekkai-suru 案を撤回する *withdraw a plan*

aná 穴 *hole; opening* §aná o akeru 穴を開ける *make a hole* §Kutsúshita ni aná ga aite shimatta. 靴下に穴が開いてしまった。 *There is a hole in this sock.* §Sukéjūru ni aná ga aita. スケジュールに穴が開いた。 *There is an opening in the schedule.*

anadór·u [*vt* anadoránai; anadótta] 侮る *defy; despise; look down on* §hito o anadóru 人を侮る *look down on people*

anago 穴子 *sea eel* §anago no kabayaki 穴子の蒲焼き *barbecued eel*

anaguma 穴熊 *a badger*

anáta あなた *you* §Anáta wa dóko kara kimáshita ka? あなたはどこから来ましたか。 *Where are you from?*

anatagáta あなた方 *you* [*plu*]

anaúnsā アナウンサー *announcer*

anda 安打 *(base) hit*

ane 姉 *(one's own) older sister*

ángai 案外 *unexpected; surprisingly* §Jishin ga átta no ni, tensū wa ángai hikúkatta. 自信があったのに、点数は案外低かった。 *My grade was surprisingly low, and I was so confident.*

angō 暗号 *a code*

angura アングラ *underground (art, theater, etc.)*

áni 兄 *(one's own) older brother*

anime アニメ *animation; animated film*

anji 暗示 *a hint; suggestion* ——**anji-suru** [*vt*] 暗示する *(to) hint; suggest; indicate; forebode*

anji·ru [*vt* anjinai; anjita] 案じる *be anxious about* ⑧Háha no byōjō o anjite iru. 母の病状を案じている。 *I'm anxious about my mother's health.*

ánkēto アンケート *questionnaire; survey*

anki 暗記 *memorization* ⑧Anki wa rekishi no gakushū ni yakudátsu. 暗記は歴史の学習に役立つ。 *Memorization is helpful for the study of history.* ——**anki-suru** [*vt*] 暗記する *commit to memory; memorize*

ankoku 暗黒 *darkness* ⑧ankoku no sékai 暗黒の世界 *the underground; the dark side of society*

anna あんな *such; that kind of; that sort of* ⑧anna hitó あんな人 *such a person*

anna ni あんなに *to such an extent* ⑧Anna ni o-kane o tamete dố suru n darō? あんなにお金を貯めてどうするんだろう。 *What does he plan to do with all that money he's saving? <masc>* ⑧Anna ni okoránakute íi ja nai no? あんなに怒らなくていいじゃないの？ *You don't have to get so angry! <fem>*

annái 案内 *guiding; leading; showing around* ——**annái-suru** [*vt*] 案内する *guide; lead; show around* ⑧Kánojo o Kamakura ni annái-shita. 彼女を鎌倉に案内した。 *I showed my girlfriend around Kamakura.*

annai-gákari 案内係 *clerk at an information desk; guide*

annaijo 案内所 *information office*

ano あの *that (over there)* ⑧ano mise あの店 *that store* ⑧ano yo あの世 *the other world*

anraku 安楽 *ease; comfort* ⑧anrakú-isu 安楽椅子 *easy chair* ⑧anrákushi 安楽死 *euthanasia; mercy killing*

ansatsu 暗殺 *assassination* ——**ansatsu-suru** [*vt*] 暗殺する *assassinate* ⑧J.F. Kénedī wa ansatsu-sareta. J. F. ケネディーは暗殺された。 *J. F. Kennedy was assassinated.*

ansei 安静 *rest and quiet* ⑧ansei ryóhō 安静療法 *rest cure*

anshin 安心 *relief; peace of mind* ——**anshin-suru** [*vi*] 安心する *feel easy about; be relieved (not worried)* ⑧Sono shirase o kiite anshin-shita. その知らせを聞いて安心した。 *I was relieved to hear the news.*

anshitsu 暗室 *darkroom*

anshō bángō 暗唱番号 *personal secret identity number*

anshō-suru [*vt*] 暗唱する *recite from memory* ⑧Musuko wa Amerika no shū no namae o zémbu anshō-dekíru. 息子はアメリカの州の名前を全部暗唱できる。 *My son can recite from memory the names of all the states of America.*

antei 安定 *stability* ⑧antéikan 安定感 *sense of stability* ⑧antei séiryoku 安定勢力 *stabilizing power* ——**antei-suru** [*vi*] 安定する

be stabilized ❌antei-shita tsúka 安定した通貨 *stable currency* ❌antei-shita rōdṓryoku 安定した労働力 *stable workforce* ❌Nihon no seiji jṓkyo ga antei-surú no wa ítsu no kotó deshō ka? 日本の政治情況が安定するのはいつのことでしょうか。 *I wonder when the Japanese political situation will stabilize.* ——**antei-saseru** [*caus*] 安定させる *cause to stabilize* ❌bukka o antei-saseru 物価を安定させる *stabilize commodity prices*

anzan 暗算 *mental calculation; doing arithmetic in one's head*

anzen 安全 *security* ——**anzen [na]** 安全（な）*secure; safe* ❌anzén pin 安全ピン *safety pin* ❌Kokuren Anzen Hoshō Rijíkai 国連安全保障理事会 *United Nations Security Council* ❌anzen na shákai 安全な社会 *a safe society* ——**anzen ni** 安全に *safely; securely*

anzu 杏 *apricot*

áo 青 *blue; green* ❌aoiro 青色 *blue color* ❌ao shíngō 青信号 *green light*

aoáo [to] 青々（と）*with a green appearance* ❌Sono yamá ni wa kí ga aoáo to shigétte iru. その山には木が青々と茂っている。 *That mountain is covered with luxuriant growth.*

aó·i [*adj* áoku nái; áokatta] 青い *(be) blue; green; unripe; pale* ❌aói sora 青い空 *blue sky* ❌aói ringo 青いりんご *green apple* ❌Kao ga aói ne. 顔が青いね。 *You look pale.*

aóg·u [*vt* aogánai; aóida] 仰ぐ *look up at; look up to; respect* ❌sóra o aógu 空を仰ぐ *look up at the sky* ❌shí to aogaréru 師と仰がれる *be respected as a mentor*

aojáshin 青写真 *blueprint*

aojiró·i [*adj* aojíroku nái; aojírokatta] 青白い *pale, pallid*

aómono 青物 *greens; vegetables* ❌aomono yókochō 青物横町 *vegetable market (street)*

aomuke ni 仰向けに *facing up(ward); on one's back*

aonísai 青二才 *immature*

aozamé·ru [*vi* aozaménai; aozámeta] 青ざめる *be pale* ❌aozámeta kao 青ざめた顔 *a pale face*

apáto アパート *apartment (building / room)*

appaku 圧迫 *oppression; pressure* ❌appaku ni kussuru 圧迫に屈する *yield to pressure* ——**appaku-suru** [*vt*] 圧迫する *oppress; exert pressure* ❌Gakusei jichíkai wa daigaku tṓkyoku o appaku-shita. 学生自治会は大学当局を圧迫した。 *The student government exerted pressure on the school authorities.*

Ara! あらっ。[*exclamation*] <*fem*>

araióke 洗い桶 *dishpan*

araiotós·u [*vt* araiotosánai; araiotóshita] 洗い落とす *wash out* ❌doro yógore o kyōryoku sénzai de araiotósu 泥汚れを強力洗剤で洗い落とす *wash out dirt stains with an extra-strength detergent*

arakajime 予め *in advance* ❸Arakajime itte okimásu ga.... 予め言って おきますが… *Let me say in advance...*

aramashi あらまし *general (or main) outline; draft; gist* ❸Jíken no aramashi o kiita. 事件のあらましを聞いた。 *I heard the gist of the incident.*

arappó·i [adj arappóku nái; arappókatta] 荒っぽい *(be) rough; rude; wild* ❸arappói kotoba-zúkai 荒っぽい言葉遣い *rough language* ❸arappóku atsukau 荒っぽく扱う *handle roughly*

arare 霰 *hail* ❸Késa arare ga fútta. 今朝霰が降った。 *It hailed this morning.*

árashi 嵐 *storm* ❸Árashi ga fuite iru. 嵐が吹いている。 *There is a storm raging.*

arashíage 荒（or 粗）仕上げ *rough finish* ❸Kabe wa arashíage no hō ga soboku de íi. 壁は荒仕上げの方が素朴でいい。 *A rough finish on the wall is better because it's simple.*

arasoi 争い *contention; strife; war* ❸Minzoku dóshi no arasoi ga tahatsu- shite iru. 民族同士の争いが多発している。 *Ethnic strife is on the increase.*

arasó·u [vt arasowánai; arasótta] 争う *quarrel; contend (with / over); dispute (with / over); fight (for)* ❸shōbu o arasóu 勝負を争う *contend forvictory* ❸Minzoku dóshi ga arasótte iru. 民族同士が争っ ている。 *Ethnic groups are fighting each other.*

aras·u [vt arasanai; arashita] 荒らす *lay waste; ruin; harm* ❸Dorobō wa heya-jū o arashite nani mo torázu ni nígeta. 泥棒は部屋中を荒らして 何も盗らずに逃げた。 *The thief thrashed the entire room and fled without taking a thing.*

arasuji 粗筋；荒筋 *outline; plot (of a story)* ❸ shibai no arasuji 芝居の あらすじ *the plot of a play.*

aratamár·u [vi aratamaránai; aratamátta] 改まる *be changed* ❸Toshí ga aratamátta. 年が改まった。 *It's a new year.*

aratamátta [attr] 改まった *formal; serious* ❸aratamátta séki de 改まっ た席で *on formal occasions* ——**aratamátte** 改まって *formally; ceremoniously; seriously*

aratamé·ru [vt aratamＥnai; aratámeta] 改める *correct; revise* ❸Yosan o aratámenakereba naránai. 予算を改めなければならない。 *We'll have to revise the budget.*

arátámete 改めて *again; over again* ❸Mata nochi hodo arátámete o- dénwa shimasu. また後ほど改めてお電話します。 *I'll call you again later. <polite>*

ara·u [vt arawanai; aratta] 洗う *wash* ❸Yokusō o téinei ni aratte kudasái. 浴槽を丁寧に洗って下さい。 *Wash the bathtub well.*

árawa ni suru 露にする *disclose; reveal* ❸ikari o árawa ni suru 怒りを 露にする *bare (one's) anger*

araware 現れ *manifestation; expression*

arawaré·ru [*vi* arawarénai; arawáreta] 現れる *appear; make an appearance; come into view* §UFO ga arawáreta tte hontō desu ka? UFOが現れたって本当ですか。*Is it true that a UFO appeared?*

arawás·u [*vt* arawasánai; arawáshita] 現す *show; display; express* §súgata o arawásu 姿を現す *appear; put in an appearance* §Ninki háiyū ga puremiá-shō ni súgata o arawáshita. 人気俳優がプレミアショーに姿を現した。*A popular actor put in an appearance (or appeared) at the premier.*

arawás·u [*vt* arawasánai; arawáshita] 表す *express; manifest; show* §Shijin wa kono shi de dónna kanjō o arawasō to shita to omoimásu ka? 詩人はこの詩でどんな感情を表そうとしたと思いますか。*What feeling do you think the poet was trying to express in this poem?*

arawás·u [*vt* arawasánai; arawáshita] 著す *write; (to) author* §Gakúmon no Susume wa Fukuzawa Yukichi ga arawáshita. 「学問のすすめ」は福沢諭吉が著した。*Fukuzawa Yukichi wrote Gakumon no Susume (An Invitation to Learning).*

arayúru あらゆる *all; every; each and every; extensive* §arayúru shurúi no あらゆる種類の *an extensive assortment of* §Watashítachi wa arayúru shúdan o kokorómita ga, kotogótoku shippai ni owátta. 私たちはあらゆる手段を試みたが、ことごとく失敗に終わった。*We tried everything but failed completely.*

are あれ *that (over there)*

arechi 荒れ地 *wasteland* §Arechi o kaikon-shite kōsakúchi ni shita. 荒れ地を開墾して耕作地にした。*They reclaimed the wasteland and made it into cultivated land.*

Are má! あれ、まあ！ [*exclamation*] <*fem*>

are·ru [*vi* arenai; areta] 荒れる *be chapped; be rough; run wild* §Watashi wa té ga arete iru. 私は手が荒れている。*My hands are chapped.* §Taifū de úmi ga areta. 台風で海が荒れた。*The ocean became rough because of the typhoon.*

ari 蟻 *ant*

ariénai 有りえない *(it) cannot (possibly) be* §Káre ga úso o iú nante ariénai. 彼が嘘を言うなんて有りえない。*It's not possible that he would tell a lie.*

arifureta ありふれた *commonplace; very common; not at all unusual* §arifureta hanashí ありふれた話 *a very common story*

arigatá·i [*adj* arigatáku nái; arigatákatta] 有難い *(be) welcome; meriting gratitude*

arigatáku 有り難く *gratefully* §arigatáku chōdai-suru 有り難く頂戴する *receive gratefully*

Arígatō [gozaimasu]. 有難う（ございます）*Thank you.*

arinomama ありのまま *as is; in (its) untouched state* §Arinomama no shizen o hógo-suru no wa muzukashíi. ありのままの自然を保護するのは難しい。*It is difficult to keep nature in its pristine state.*

arísama 有様 *sight; scene; condition* ❧Jíko no arísama o shōsai ni obóete iru. 事故の有様を詳細に覚えている。*I remember the accident (or scene) in detail.*

ári to arayúru 有りとあらゆる *every conceivable* ❧Nyūyóku ni wa sekaijū kara ári to arayúru jinshu ga atsumátte iru. ニューヨークには世界中から有りとあらゆる人種が集まっている。*People of every conceivable race in the world are congregated in New York City.*

ár·u [vi nái; átta] ある *be; exist* [inanimate] ❧Tēburu no ué ni koppu ga áru. テーブルの上にコップがある。*There is a glass on the table.*

[-te] ar·u [vb aux: stative] 〜て ある ❧Dóa wa (or o) akete áru. ドアは (or を) 開けてある。*The door is open (because someone purposely opened it).*

áru ある *a certain* ❧Áru hi, áru tokoro de áru hito ga korosareta. ある日ある所である人が殺された。*On a certain day, at a certain place, a certain person was killed.*

arubáito アルバイト *part-time work; side job* ❧Ano gakusei wa arubáito ni owarete benkyō ni shūchū-dekínai. あの学生はアルバイトに追われて勉強に集中出来ない。*That student is so involved in part-time work she can't concentrate on study.*

arúiwa 或いは *or; perhaps*

arukōru アルコール *alcohol* ❧arukōru izon-shō アルコール依存症 *alcoholism* ❧arukōru izon-shō kánja アルコール依存症患者 *an alcoholic*

arúk·u [vi; vt arukánai; arúita] 歩く *walk* ❧Watashi wa arúite gakkō ni kayoimásu. 私は歩いて学校に通います。*I walk to school.*

áru teido made ある程度まで *to some extent; to a certain extent* ❧Rísuku ni tsúite wa áru teido kákugo ga dékite iru. リスクについてはある程度覚悟ができている。*To a certain extent I am prepared to take a risk.*

ása 朝 *morning* ❧ásaban 朝晩 *morning and evening*

asá 麻 *flax; linen*

aságao 朝顔 *morning glory (Bot)*

asagóhan 朝御飯 *breakfast*

ásahi 朝日 *morning sun; rising sun*

asa·i [adj asaku nái; asákatta] 浅い *(be) shallow* ❧asai nábe 浅い鍋 *a shallow pan* ❧Sono kangáe wa asai. その考えは浅い。*That thought (or idea) is shallow.*

asanébō 朝寝坊 *late riser; one who sleeps late*

asáne-suru [vi] 朝寝する *rise late; lie in bed until late* ❧Nichiyóbi wa asáne-surú no ga shūkan ni nátte iru. 日曜日は朝寝するのが習慣になっている。*It's my habit to sleep late on Sunday.*

asari 浅蜊 asari (small clam; Japanese species)

asátte 明後日 the day after tomorrow

áse 汗 perspiration ❦áse o káku 汗をかく perspire

asér·u [vi aseránai; asétta] 焦る be in a hurry; be impatient ❦Shimekiri ga semátte iru ga, genkō ga máda dékite inái no de, henshūsha wa asétte iru. 締切りが迫っているが原稿がまだ出来ていないので、編集者は焦っている。 The deadline is nearing, and the manuscript is still not ready, so the editor is impatient.

asér·u [vi asénai; asétta] 褪せる fade; discolor ❦Jínzu wa iró ga aseyasúi. ジーンズは色が褪せやすい。 Jeans fade easily.

áshi 葦 reed (Bot)

ashí 足；脚 foot; leg ❦ashí no tsume 足の爪 toenail ❦ashí no ura 足の裏 sole of the foot ❦ashí no yubi 足の指 toe ❦Hito wa nihón ashi de tátsu dōbutsu désu. 人は二本足で立つ動物です。 A human being is an animal that stands on two legs.

ashibaya ni 足早に at a quick pace

ashidai 足台 footstool

ashihire 足ひれ flippers; fins

ashika 海驢 sea lion

ashikúbi 足首 ankle ❦Ashikúbi o nenza-shita. 足首を捻挫した。 I sprained my ankle.

ashióto 足音 (sound of) footsteps ❦Ashióto ga kikoeru. 足音が聞こえる。 I (can) hear footsteps.

ashita 明日 tomorrow

ashimóto 足元 at one's feet ❦Ashimóto ni go-chūi kudasái. 足元に御注意下さい。 Watch your step.

asobi 遊び game; play; amusement; pastime; visit ❦omoshirói asobi 面白い遊び an interesting game ❦Asobi wa náni ga sukí desu ka? 遊びは何が好きですか。 What do you like to do for amusement? ❦Kinō, furúi tomodachi ga asobi ni kimáshita. 昨日、古い友達が遊びに来ました。 Yesterday, an old friend came for a visit.

asobiba 遊び場 playground

asobi tómodachi 遊び友達 playmate

asob·u [vi asobanai; asonda] 遊ぶ play ❦Kodomo no tóki, dónna kotó o shite asonda no? 子供の時どんなことをして遊んだの。 When you were a child, what (kind of games) did you play? <fem>

asoko あそこ over there

assári-shita [attr] あっさりした simple; light; uncomplicated ❦Kómban, assári-shita monó ga tabetái. 今晩、あっさりしたものが食べたい。 Tonight I'd like to eat something light. ❦Assári-shita seikaku no hitó wa tsukiaiyasúi. あっさりした性格の人は付き合いやすい。 It's easy to get along with someone who isn't complicated.

assen 斡旋 (job) recommendation

asu 明日 *tomorow* (see also **ashita**)

atae·ru [*vt* ataenai; ataeta] 与える *give; provide; allot* ❧Yasei no dōbutsu ní wa katte ni esá o ataenái de! 野生の動物には勝手に餌を与えないで！ *Don't give the wild animals food (indiscriminately)!* ❧hínto o ataeru ヒントを与える *give a hint*

atai 値 *value; worth*

átakamo あたかも *just like; just as if* ❧Sonó hito wa átakamo gemba ni itá ka no yō ni, sono jíken ni tsuite hanáshita. その人はあたかも現場にいたかのようにその事件について話した。 *He talked about the incident just like he had been there at the scene.*

atamá 頭 *head (Anat)* ❧atamá ga íi 頭がいい *be smart; intelligent* ❧Atamá ga itái. 頭が痛い。 *I have a headache.*

atamakin 頭金 *down payment* ❧Atamakin o ōku iremásu kara, bunkatsu-bárai no shiharai o yásuku shite kuremasén ka? 頭金を多く入れますから、分割払いの支払いを安くしてくれませんか。 *I will make a large down payment, so would you make the monthly payments lower?*

atarashí·i [*adj* ataráshiku nái; ataráshikatta] 新しい *(be) new; fresh* ❧atarashíi kuruma 新しい車 *a new car* ❧atarashíi yasai 新しい野菜 *fresh vegetables* ❧atarashíi kangae 新しい考え *a new (or fresh) idea*

átari 辺り *vicinity; surroundings* ❧Kono átari ni íi byōin ga arimásu ka? この辺りにいい病院がありますか。 *Is there a good hospital in this vicinity?*

atarí 当り *a hit; a win* ❧atarí kuji 当り籤 *a winning ticket* ❧Hitótsu wa atari, hitótsu wa hazure dátta. 一つは当り、一つは外れだった。 *One was a hit, and one was a miss.*

atarimae [no] 当たり前（の）*natural; usual; proper* ❧Hito o kizutsúketara, ayamáru no wa atarimae désu. 人を傷つけたら謝るのは当たり前です。 *It's only natural to apologize to someone when you have hurt them.* ——**atarimae ni** 当たり前に *naturally; usually; properly* ❧atarimae ni ikíru 当たり前に生きる *(to) live naturally (as one is expected to live)*

atar·u [*vi* ataranai; atatta] 当たる *hit; strike against; touch* ❧Ishí ga mádo ni atatte, garasu ga wareta. 石が窓に当たってガラスが割れた。 *The rock hit the window and the glass shattered.*

atashi あたし *I; me* <*fem*> (see also **watashi**)

atatáka [na] 暖か（な）*warm*

atataká·i [*adj* atatákaku nái; atátakakatta] 暖かい；温かい *(be) warm* ❧atatakái hi 暖かい日 *a warm day* ❧atatakái nomimono 温かい飲み物 *a warm drink* ❧atatakái kokoró 暖かい心 *a warm heart*

atatamár·u [*vi* atatamaránai; atatamátta] 暖まる；温まる *be heated; be warmed up* ❧Heyá ga yóku atatamátte iru. 部屋がよく暖まっている。 *The room is well heated.*

atatamé·ru [*vt* atataménai; atátameta] 温める *heat; warm up* ❧súpu o atataméru スープを温める *warm up soup* ❽kyūkō o atataméru 旧交を暖める *renew an old friendship*

ate 当て *aim; objective; hope; expectation* ❽ate ni suru 当てにする *expect; count on*

atehamár·u [*vi* atehamaránai; atehamátta] 当て嵌まる *be applicable to; be suitable; fit* ❽yoku atehamátta fūfu よく当て嵌まった夫婦 *a couple well suited to each other* ❽Yamakan de kotáe ga úmaku atehamátta. やまかんで答えがうまく当て嵌まった。 *I hit on the right answer by chance.*

atehamé·ru [*vt* atehaménai; atehámeta] 当て嵌める *apply to; adapt; fit (into)* ❽Kono búnshō no kasémbu ni tadashíi kotáe o kaitóran kara eránde atehámete kudasai. この文章の下線部に正しい答えを解答欄から選んで当て嵌めて下さい。 *Select the correct answer from the list and fit it into the underlined section of the sentence.*

atena 宛名 *address (on a letter)*

ate·ru [*vt* atenai; ateta] 当てる *hit; strike; place upon; assign; guess* ❽Watashi no toshí wa íkutsu da to omoú? Atete goran. 私の年はいくつだと思う？当ててごらん。 *How old do you think I am? See if you can guess.*

atesaki 宛先 *address (of the addressee)*

áto 跡 *remains; ruins* ❽shiro no áto 城の跡 *the ruins of a castle* ❽yake-ato 焼け跡 *remains from a fire* ❽kizu-ato 傷跡 *a scar*

áto 後 *remainder* ❽Áto wa o-makase shimásu. 後はお任せします。 *I'll leave the rest (or remainder) for you to take care of.*

áto あと *in addition; additional; further* ❽Áto dono gurai de shigoto ga owarimásu ka? あとどの位で仕事が終わりますか。 *How soon will you be finished with the work?* ❽Áto dono gurai chokin-suréba shinsha ga kaeru deshó ka? あとどのぐらい貯金すれば新車が買えるでしょうか。 *I wonder about how much more I need to save to be able to buy a new car?*

áto de 後で *later; after* ❽Áto de aimashó. 後で会いましょう。 *See you later.* ❽Áto de katazukéru. 後で片付ける。 *I'll clean up after.*

atokatázuke 後片付け *clean up; cleaning (of things); straightening up* ❽Atokatázuke o o-negai-shimásu. 後片付けをお願いします。 *Please straighten things up later.*

atomáwashi ni suru 後回しにする *put off; postpone; take up later* ❽Iyá na shigoto wa atomáwashi ni shigachi desu. 嫌な仕事は後回しにしがちです。 *I have a tendency to put off doing things I dislike.*

atomódori-suru [*vi*] 後戻りする *go back; turn back* ❽Kōshō ga ketsuretsu-shite kadai ga futatabi zéro made atomódori-shita. 交渉が決裂して課題が再びゼロまで後戻りした。 *Negotiations broke down and we had to start from scratch.* ❽Michi o machigáete atomódori-shita. 道を間違えて後戻りした。 *I went the wrong way and retraced* *my steps.* 8Mố atomódori-dekínai. もう後戻りできない。*You can't turn back now*

áto no matsurí 後の祭り *to be too late; lock the barn door after the horse has escaped <set phrase>*

atorie アトリエ *art studio*

atsú·i [*adj* átsuku nái; átsukatta] 暑い；熱い *(be) hot* 8Kinō wa átsukatta. 昨日は暑かった。*It was hot yesterday.* 8Atsúi furó ga sukí desu. 熱い風呂が好きです。*I like a hot bath.*

atsu·i [*adj* atsuku nái; átsukatta] 厚い *(be) thick* 8atsui kíji 厚い生地 *thick (or heavy) cloth material.*

atsukai 扱い *treatment; handling* 8Kánojo wa kodomo no atsukai ni nárete iru. 彼女は子供の扱いに慣れている。*She's used to handling children.*

atsuka·u [*vt* atsukawanai; atsukatta] 扱う *manage; treat; handle; use* 8Tốten de wa kompyútā wa atsukatte imasén. 当店ではコンピューターは扱っていません。*We don't handle computers at this store.* 8Kono kikái o dố atsukau ka oshiete kudasái. この機械をどう扱うか教えて下さい。*Teach me how to use this machine.*

atsukurushí·i [*adj* atsukurushíku nái; atsukurushíkatta] 暑苦しい *stuffy; sultry*

atsumarí 集まり *meeting; gathering*

atsumár·u [*vi* atsumaránai; atsumátta] 集まる *gather together; be collected* 8Mītingu ní wa kankéisha ga zen'in atsumátta. ミーテイングには関係者が全員集まった。*All persons involved were at the meeting.* 8Kóno bijutsúkan ní wa Góhho no hotóndo no sakuhin ga atsumátte iru. この美術館にはゴッホのほとんどの作品が集まっている。*In this art museum almost all of Van Gogh's works have been collected.* 8Nihon no jinkō no ichí-wari ga Tōkyō ni atsumátte iru. 日本の人口の一割が東京に集まっている。*Ten percent of the population of Japan is concentrated in Tokyo*

atsumé·ru [*vt* atsuménai; atsúmeta] 集める *collect* 8Kitté o atsuméru shúmi ga aru. 切手を集める趣味がある。*I have an interest in collecting stamps.*

atsurae [no] 誂え (の) *made-to-order*

atsúryoku 圧力 *pressure* 8atsuryoku nábe 圧力鍋 *pressure cooker* 8atsuryoku dántai 圧力団体 *pressure group* 8atsúryoku o kakéru 圧力をかける *apply pressure (to)* 8Séifu ni keizai dántai kara no atsúryoku ga kakátte iru. 政府に経済団体からの圧力がかかっている。*The government is under pressure from economic power groups.*

átsusa 暑さ；熱さ *temperature; heat*

atsusa 厚さ *thickness*

átto iu ma ni あっと言う間に *in an instant; all too soon* 8Shinkánsen kara míta késhiki wa átto iu ma ni kiete iku. 新幹線から見た景色はあ

っと言う間に消えて行く。*From the bullet train, the scenery flashes by in an instant.*

attō-suru [*vt*] 圧倒する *overcome; overwhelm* §Orimpíkku de no Ameriká-zei no kiroku wa tákoku o attō-shita. オリンピックでのアメリカ勢の記録は他国を圧倒した。*The record set by the American entrants in the Olympics overwhelmed the other countries.*

attōteki [na] 圧倒的（な）*overwhelming* §attōteki na daitasū́ 圧倒的な大多数 *an overwhelming majority* §attōteki na shṓri 圧倒的な勝利 *an overwhelming victory*

á·u [*vi* awánai; átta] 合う *match; fit* §Kono dóresu wa anáta no sáizu ni átte iru. このドレスはあなたのサイズに合っている。*This dress is (**or** fits) your size.*

á·u [(*v*) awánai; átta] 会う *meet; see* §Penfuréndo ni kyṓ hajímete áu. ペンフレンドに今日初めて会う。*I'm going to meet my pen pal today for the first time.*

-á·u [*compound verb suffix*] 合う *together; mutually* §tasuke-áu 助け合う *help each other* §hanashi-áu 話し合う *talk together*

awá 泡 *foam; bubble*

áwabi 鮑 *abalone*

awadatéki 泡立て器 *mixer; beater*

áware [na] 哀れ（な）*miserable; pitiful; pathetic* §Káre wa áware na sáigo o mukaeta. 彼は哀れな最期を迎えた。*He met a pathetic end.*

awaremi 哀れみ *pity*

awarém·u [*vt* awaremánai; awarénda] 哀れむ *pity; show compassion for* §Memoriaru kíruto wa Éizu de nakunatta hitó o awarému tame no mono de mo aru. メモリアルキルトはエイズで亡くなった人を哀れむためのものでもある。*Memorial quilts are also for the purpose of showing compassion for people who have died of AIDS .*

awasér·u [*vt* awasénai; awáseta] 合わせる *bring together; set (**or** adjust)* §Kóe o awásete kírei na hā́monī o tsukútta. 声を合わせてきれいなハーモニーを作った。*They joined their voices and made beautiful harmony.* §Térebi no channeru o yakyū bángumi ni awáseta. テレビのチャンネルを野球番組に合わせた。*I switched the TV channel to the baseball game.* ——**ma ni awaséru** 間に合わせる *make (something) do; manage with* §Kono kamí de ma ni awaséru koto ga dekimásu ka? この紙で間に合わせることが出来ますか。*Can you make do with this paper?*

awásete 併せて *taken together; joined together* §Kyṓ no kaimono wa zémbu de awásete íkura ni narimásu ka? 今日の買物は全部で併せていくらになりますか。*Altogether, how much did today's shopping come to?*

awatadashí·i [*adj* awatadáshiku nái; awatadáshikatta] 慌ただしい *(be) busy; confused; hurried* §awatadashíi seikatsu 慌ただしい生活 *a* *busy (hectic) life* ❀Awatadashíi ichinichi ga súgita. 慌ただしい一日が過ぎた。*A busy day ended.*

awate·ru [*vi* awatenai; awateta] 慌てる *be confused; be flustered; be in a flurry* ❀Totsuzen no supíchi no shimei ni awatta. 突然のスピーチの指名に慌てた。*I was flustered when I was designated to make a speech on the spur of the moment.*

ayafuya [na] あやふや（な）*uncertain; vague* ❀Kono mondai ni jishin ga nákatta no de, ayafuya na kotáe shika dekinákatta. この問題に自信がなかったので、あやふやな答しか出来なかった。*I had no confidence with this problem so I was only able to make a vague answer.*

ayamachi 過ち *mistake; fault; sin* ❀ayamachi o okasu 過ちを犯す *commit a sin*

ayamári 誤り *a mistake* ❀Ayamári ni kizúitara, teisei-shite kudasái. 誤りに気づいたら訂正して下さい。*If you find a mistake, please correct it.*

ayamár·u [*vt* ayamaránai; ayamátta] 誤る *make a mistake* ❀Musuko wa hándan o ayamátta. 息子は判断を誤った。*My son made a mistake in judgement.*

ayamár·u [*vt* ayamaránai; ayamátta] 謝る *apologize* ❀Musuko ni kawatte ayamarimásu. 息子に代わって謝ります。*I apologize for (or in place of) my son.*

ayamátte 誤って *mistakenly; accidently* ❀Kuruma o ayamátte gādorḗru ni butsukete shimatta. 車を誤ってガードレールにぶつけてしまった。*I accidently ran my car into the guardrail*

ayame 菖蒲 *iris (Bot)*

ayashi·i [*adj* ayáshiku nái; ayáshikatta] 怪しい *(be) doubtful; suspicious* ❀Káre no aribai ga ayashíi. 彼のアリバイが怪しい。*His alibi is suspicious.*

ayashím·u [*vt* ayashimánai; ayashínda] 怪しむ *suspect; be suspicious of* ❀Watashi wa káre no kyodō o ayashínde iru. 私は彼の挙動を怪しんでいる。*I am suspicious of his behavior.*

ayatsúr·u [*vt* ayatsuránai; ayatsútta] 操る *maneuver; manipulate* ❀hitó o ayatsúru 人を操る *manipulate people* ❀Kánojo wa rokkakokugo o jōzú ni ayatsútte iru. 彼女は六ヶ国語を自由に操っている。*She handles six languages skillfully.*

ayauku 危うく *almost; nearly*

áyu 鮎 *sweetfish*

azá 痣 *birthmark*

azaké·ru [*vt* azakénai; azáketa] 嘲る *deride* ❀Kánojo wa otto o uwaki mo dekínai nasakenái otoko to azaketa. 彼女は夫を浮気もできない情けない男と嘲た。*She derided her husband for being a pathetic man incapable of even having an affair.*

azamúk·u [*vt* azamukánai; azamúita] 欺く *deceive* ❀Hito o azamúku no wa ikenai kotó desu. 人を欺くのはいけないことです。 *One should not deceive people.*

azárashi あざらし *seal (mammal)*

azáyaka [na] 鮮やか（な）*brilliant* ❽azáyaka na iro 鮮やかな色 *a brilliant color* ❽azáyaka na udemae 鮮やかな腕前 *brilliant skill——* **azáyaka ni** 鮮やかに *brilliantly* ❽Barerína wa "Hakuchō no Mizuúmi"o azáyaka ni odorikítta. バレリーナは「白鳥の湖」を鮮やかに踊りきった。 *The ballerina danced Swan Lake brilliantly.*

azukár·u [vt azukaránai; azukátta] 預かる *keep; hold; look after* ❽Yokin tsúchō o azukátte kuremasén ka? 預金通帳を預かってくれませんか。 *Would you please keep my bank book?* ❽Chikáku ni ōkíi nímotsu o azukátte kureru tokoró wa arimasén ka? 近くに大きい荷物を預かってくれるところはありませんか。 *Is there some place near where I can check large luggage?*

azukeire 預け入れ *a deposit*

azuké·ru [vt azukénai; azúketa] 預ける *deposit; put in care of* ❽Ginkō ni yokin o azúketa hō ga íi desu. 銀行に預金を預けた方がいいです。 *One should deposit one's savings in the bank.* ❽Kodomo o ichinichi sóbo ni azúketa. 子供を一日祖母に預けた。 *I left my child in my grandmother's care for the day.*

azukí 小豆 *red bean*

B

ba 場 *place; occasion; time; scene*

-ba ～ば *if [provisional suffix]* ❽Homeraréreba dare demo ureshíi deshō. 褒められれば誰でも嬉しいでしょう。 *Anyone is happy if he's praised.*

baai 場合 *case; occasion; situation* ❽Áme ga fútta baai wa ikimasén. 雨が降った場合は行きません。 *If it rains, I'm not going.*

bachí 撥 *drumstick; plectrum (for shamisen)*

-bai ～倍 *double; twice; -times* ❽Kono zukei o nibai ni kakudai-shite kudasái. この図形を二倍に拡大して下さい。 *Make this drawing twice as big.*

-bai (see **-hai**)

báibai 売買 *buying and selling* ——**báibai-suru** [vt] 売買する *buy and sell* ❽Fudōsan-ya wa tochi ya ié o báibai-shimásu. 不動産屋は土地や家を売買します。 *A realtor buys and sells land and houses.*

báidoku 梅毒 *syphilis*

baikai 媒介 *mediation; transmission* ❽baikáisha 媒介者 *a mediator* ——**baikai-suru** [vt] 媒介する *transmit* ❽Byōki ní wa ka ga baikai-

suru monó mo arimásu. 病気には蚊が媒介するものもあります。
Some sicknesses are transmitted by mosquitoes.

baikin 黴菌 *bacillus; germ*

báikingu バイキング *smorgasbord; buffet*

baishakunin 媒酌人 *a go-between (in a marriage)*

baishin 陪審 *jury* §baishín-in 陪審員 *a juror* §baishin séido 陪審制度 *jury system*

baishō 賠償 *reparation(s)* ――**baishō-suru** [*vt*] 賠償する *compensate; indemnify; make reparation* §songai o baishō-suru 損害を賠償する *make reparation for damage*

baishū 買収 *a purchase; a bribe* ――**baishū-suru** [*vt*] 買収する *purchase; bribe* §Amerika wa Furansu kara Ruijiana ísei no hirói tochi o baishū-shita. アメリカはフランスからルイジアナ以西の広い土地を買収した。 *America purchased from France a large tract of land extending from Louisiana westward.* §Sono kōhósha wa senkyóku no yūkénsha o baishū-shimáshita. その候補者は選挙区の有権者を買収しました。 *The candidate bribed voters in his electoral district.*

baishun 売春 *prostitution* §baishun bōshi-hō 売春防止法 *anti-prostitution law* §baishun yádo 売春宿 *brothel; house of prostitution* §baishúnfu 売春婦 *a prostitute*

baiten 売店 *(news) stand; kiosk*

báiu 梅雨 *rainy (or wet) season*

bájin バージン *virgin*

báka 馬鹿 *a fool; idiot; foolishness* **báka na** 馬鹿な *foolish; stupid* §Báka na kotó o iú na! 馬鹿なことを言うな！ *Don't talk foolishness!*

bakabakashí·i [*adj*] bakabakáshiku nái; bakabakáshikatta] 馬鹿馬鹿しい *absurd; ridiculous*

bakágeta [*attr*] 馬鹿げた *foolish* §bakágeta hanashi 馬鹿げた話 *foolish talk*

bakarashí·i [*adj.* bakaráshiku nái; bakaráshikatta] 馬鹿らしい *(be) absurd; foolish* §Kyosei o hatte ikíru nante bakarashíi yo. 虚勢を張って生きるなんて馬鹿らしいよ。 *It's foolish to live by pretense.*

-bákari ばかり *only; just; merely* §Mochikin wa wazuka bákari da. 持ち金はわずかばかりだ。 *I have only a little money on me.* <masc> §Kánojo wa ryōri bákari shite iru wa! 彼女は料理ばかりしているわ！ *All she ever does is cook!* <fem>

-bákari de náku ばかりでなく *not only ... but also* §Kánojo wa utsukushíi-bákari de náku seikaku mo íi. 彼女は美しいばかりでなく性格もいい。 *Not only is she beautiful, she also has a good personality.*

bakemóno 化け物 *freak; monster; ghost*

baké·ru [*vi* bakénai; báketa] 化ける *take the form of; transform into* §Tánuki ga ningen ni bakéru to iu hanashí ga áru. 狸が人間に化けると言う話がある。 *It is said that a tanuki (a racoon-like animal) takes* *human form.*

bakkin 罰金 *a fine; penalty*

bakuchi 博打 *gambling* §**bakuchí-uchi** 博打打ち *gambler*

bakudai na 莫大な *enormous* §Chichí wa bakudai na shisan o súbete fukúshi no tamé ni tsukatte shimatta. 父は莫大な資産を全て福祉のために使ってしまった。*My father gave all of an enormous fortune to charity.*

bakudan 爆弾 *a bomb* §**genshi bákudan** 原子爆弾 *atomic bomb* §**suisō bákudan** 水素爆弾 *hydrogen bomb*

bákufu 幕府 *the shogunate; feudal government* §**Tokugawa bákufu** 徳川幕府 *Tokugawa shogunate; Tokugawa regime*

bakugeki 爆撃 *bombing attack*

bakuhatsu 爆発 *explosion* §**gasu bákuhatsu** ガス爆発 *gas explosion* §**jinkō bákuhatsu** 人口爆発 *population explosion* ——**bakuhatsu-suru** [vi] 爆発する *explode*

bákuro 暴露 *disclosure; exposure; exposé* ——**bákuro-suru** [vt] 暴露する *expose; disclose* §Sono yūméijin no puráibashī ga bákuro-sareta. その有名人のプライバシーが暴露された。*That famous person's private life was exposed.*

bakuyaku 爆薬 *an explosive*

bakuzen to 漠然と *vaguely; obscurely* ——**bakuzen to shita** [attr] 漠然とした *vague; obscure* §bakuzen to shita keikaku 漠然とした計画 *a vague plan*

bámbutsu 万物 *all things; everything*

bámen 場面 *scene; place; situation* §Ano eiga no kuraimákkusu no bámen wa sugókatta ne. あの映画のクライマックスの場面は凄かったね。*The climactic scene of that movie was terrific, wasn't it?*

-bamme ～番目 [suffix for ordinal numerals] §Anáta no mensetsu wa sanbammé desu. あなたの面接は三番目です。*Your interview is third.*

ban 晩 *night; evening* §Saikin ása to ban wa sukóshi suzúshiku nátte kimáshita. 最近、朝と晩は少し涼しくなってきました。*Lately it's gotten a bit cooler in the morning and evening.*

bán 番 *(one's) turn; keeping watch; guarding* §Kóndo wa watashi no bán da wa! 今度は私の番だわ！*It's my turn next!* <fem> ——**bán o suru** 番をする *keep watch over* §Tóire ni itte kúru aida, kono nímotsu no bán o shite kudasai. トイレに行ってくる間、この荷物の番をして下さい。*Please watch these bags while I go to the toilet.*

-ban ～番 No.- [number suffix] §**ichíban** 一番 No. 1 §**níban** 二番 No. 2 §**samban** 三番 No. 3 §Anó ko wa kúrasu de ichíban desu. あの子はクラスで一番です。*That student is No. 1 in her class.*

-ban (see **-han**)

-banchi 番地 *lot number* §Mitaká-shi, Ósawa, nana chốme, san-bánchi

三鷹市大沢七丁目三番地 *3, 7-chōme, Osawa, Mitaka City*

bando バンド *instrumental musical group* ❽Ano rokku-bándo wa íma ichiban ninki ga arimásu. あのロックバンドは今一番人気があります。 *That rock band is the most popular band today.*

báne ばね *(metal) spring*

bangṓ 番号 *number* ❽Watashi no denwa bángō wa zéro-yón-ní-sán no sán-sán no kyū-kyū-zéro-sán-ban desu. 私の電話番号は0423-33-9903番です。 *My telephone number is 0423-33-9903.*

bangóhan 晩御飯 *evening meal; supper*

bangumi 番組 *(radio / TV) program*

banken 番犬 *watchdog*

bánkoku 万国 *all the countries of the world* ❽bankoku hakuránkai (abbr bampaku) 万国博覧会 (万博) *world fair; world exposition*

bannen 晩年 *one's later years*

bannṓ [no] 万能（の） *all-around; versatile* ❽Yamamoto-san wa supótsu bannō desu. 山本さんはスポーツ万能です。 *Yamamoto is an all-around athlete.*

bansán[kai] 晩餐（会） *a feast; banquet; (formal) dinner*

-bansen 〜番線 *track No. -* ❽Chūōsen no tokubetsu káisoku wa ichi-bansen kara hassha-shimásu. 中央線の特別快速は一番線から発車します。 *The Chūō Line Special Rapid Express leaves from Track No. 1.*

bansō 伴奏 *(musical) accompaniment; arrangement* ❽Sopurano dokushṓkai dé wa yóku piano no bansō ga tsukimásu. ソプラノ独唱会ではよくピアノの伴奏がつきます。 *At soprano recitals there is often piano accompaniment.*

bansōkō 絆創膏 *a bandage; adhesive tape*

Banzái! 万歳。 *Hurrah!*

baputésuma バプテスマ *baptism* ❽baputésuma o ukéru バプテスマを受ける *be baptized*

bara 薔薇 *a rose*

barabara [na] ばらばら（な）*random; out of order* ❽barabara na shorui ばらばらな書類 *papers which are out of order* ——**barabara ni náru** ばらばらになる *come apart; become separate* ❽Shorui ga barabara ni naránai yō ni kuríppu de tomete óite kudasái. 書類がばらばらにならないようにクリップで留めておいてください。 *Fasten the documents with a clip so that they won't get separated.* ——**barabara ni suru** ばらばらにする *(to) separate; pull apart; cut in pieces*

baramá·ku [vt baramakánai; baramáita] ばら撒く *scatter; spread around* ❽Watashi wa hai o Taihéiyō ni baramakimáshita. 私は灰を太平洋にばら撒きました。 *I scattered the ashes in the Pacific Ocean.* Ano seijika wa wáiro no kane o baramaita. あの政治家は賄賂の金をばら撒いた。 *That politician spread bribes everywhere.*

barás·u [vt barasánai; barashíta] ばらす *reveal; expose* ❽himitsu o barásu 秘密をばらす *reveal a secret*

baré·ru [vi barénai; báreta] ばれる *be revealed; be divulged; be disclosed*

bariki 馬力 *horsepower*

barométā バロメーター *barometer*

[o-]básan (お) 婆さん *(another's) grandmother; old woman; Grandmother!* 🪶Sóbo wa nanajússai ni narimásu ga, anáta no o-básan wa o-ikutsu ni narimásu ka? 祖母は七十歳になりますが、あなたのお婆さんはおいくつになりますか。 *My grandmother's seventy. How old is your grandmother?*

básha 馬車 *horse-drawn carriage; horsecart*

basho 場所 *a place*

bassuru [vt basshinai; basshita] 罰する *punish; chastize; fine* 🪶tsúmi o bassuru 罪を罰する *punish for a crime* 🪶Nihón de wa miséinen ga kitsuen-suru to basseraremásu. 日本では未成年が喫煙すると罰せられます。 *In Japan, a minor can be fined for smoking.*

bátabata [to] ばたばた（と）*(with) rattling; clattering; thumping* 🪶Kánai wa ása ókite mó daidokoro de bátabata hataraite imásu. 家内は朝起きてもう台所でばたばた働いています。 *My wife has gotten up and is already clattering about in the kitchen.* 🪶Kono átsusa de hito ga bátabata taórete iru. この暑さで人がばたばた倒れている。 *People are falling like flies in this heat.*

batán [to] ばたん（と）*with a bang; with a slam* 🪶Dóa ga batán to shimátta. ドアがばたんと閉まった。 *The door slammed shut.*

batchíri ばっちり *right (on the button)* 🪶Kyó no shikén wa batchíri datta yo. 今日の試験はばっちりだったよ。 *I aced (or did very well on) today's test.*

bátsu 罰 *punishment; penalty* 🪶tsúmi to bátsu 罪と罰 *crime and punishment* 🪶bátsu o ataeru 罰を与える *punish* 🪶bátsu o ukéru 罰を受ける *receive punishment*

bátsu ばつ；*an "X"；mark; wrong; false* 🪶bátsu o tsukéru ばつをつける *mark (something) as wrong; mark with an "X"*

batsugun [no] 抜群（の）*outstanding* 🪶Tómu no seiseki wa batsugun de, Hābādo dáigaku no shōgakukin o moratte imáshta. トムの成績は抜群で、ハーバード大学の奨学金を貰っていました。 *Tom's grades were outstanding, and he received a scholarship to Harvard.*

batta ばった *grasshopper; locust*

battári [to] ばったり（と）*suddenly; abruptly; unexpectedly* 🪶Sákki éki de Tanaka-san ni battári átta yo. さっき駅で田中さんにばったり会ったよ。 *Just now I unexpectedly ran into Tanaka at the station.*

Béikoku- 米国 *America* 🪶Béi- 米 ～ *American-; US-* 🪶Bei-Chū káidan 米中会談 *US-China Conference* 🪶Béi-daitōryō kantei 米大統領官邸 *The White House* 🪶Béi-kokubō-shō 米国防省 *Pentagon; US National Defense Department*

-beki [*verb suffix*] 〜べき *necessary to...; must ...; should...* ❀Hito wa tsúne ni shōjíki de áru-beki desu. 人は常に正直であるべきです。*A person should always be honest.*

bekkan 別館 *(building) annex*

bekkō べっ甲 *tortoise shell* ❀bekkō no megane furému べっ甲の眼鏡フレーム *tortoiseshell eyeglass frames*

bempi 便秘 *constipation* ——**bempi-suru** [*vi*] 便秘する *be constipated*

bén 便 *excretion* ❀daibén 大便 *feces; stool* ❀shōben 小便 *urine* ❀bénki 便器 *toilet (bowl)*

bén 便 *convenience* ❀Uchi wa básu no bén ga íi. うちはバスの便がいい。*My house is easy to get to by bus.*

bén 弁 *valve*

béngi 便宜 *convenience; facilities; accommodations; negotiation; measure* ❀bengijō 便宜上 *as a matter of convenience* ❀béngi o hakáru 便宜を図る *determine the best measures*

béngo 弁護 *defense; justification* ❀jiko béngo 自己弁護 *self-justification* ——**béngo-suru** [*vt*] 弁護する *defend; plead for; justify* ❀yūjin o béngo-suru 友人を弁護する *defend a friend*

bengóshi 弁護士 *lawyer*

benibana 紅花 *safflower*

beniyá-ita ベニヤ板 *plywood*

benjo 便所 *toilet* ❀suisen bénjo 水洗便所 *flush toilet* ❀yōshiki bénjo 洋式便所 *western-style toilet*

benkai 弁解 *explanation; excuse; apology* ——**benkai-suru** [*vt*] 弁解する *explain; excuse oneself* ❀Beŋkai no yóchi ga nái yo. 弁解の余地がないよ。*There is no (room for) excuse.*

benkyō 勉強 *study* ❀benkyō-beya 勉強部屋 *study room* ——**benkyō-suru** [*vt*] 勉強する *study*

bénri [na] 便利（な）*convenient; useful; suitable* ❀Sono hóteru wa kankō ni bénri na tokoró ni áru. そのホテルは観光に便利なところにある。*That hotel is in a convenient location for sightseeing.*

benron 弁論 *debate; public speaking* ❀benrón-bu 弁論部 *debate club* ❀benron táikai 弁論大会 *speech contest* ——**benron-suru** [*vt*] 弁論する *debate; make a speech; plead* ❀Bengonin wa hōtei de hikoku no tamé ni benron-shimásu. 弁論人は法廷で被告のために弁論します。*In court the defense counsel pleads on behalf of the defendant.*

benshō 弁償 *compensation payment* ——**benshō-suru** [*vt*] 弁償する *pay for; recompense; make up for* ❀"A! Shimátta! Madogárasu o watchatta!" "Benshō-shinákereba naránai yo!" 「あっ、しまった！窓ガラスを割っちゃった！」「弁償しなければならないよ！」*"Oh! I've done it! I broke the windowpane!" "You'll have to pay for it!"*

benshōhō 弁証法 *dialectic(s)*

bentō 弁当 *box lunch* ❽eki-ben 駅弁 *box lunch (sold at a train station)* ❽bentō o motte iku 弁当を持って行く *take a lunch*

berabō [na] べらぼう（な）*unreasonable; absurd; extreme* ❽berabō na nedan べらぼうな値段 *unreasonable price*

bessō 別荘 *vacation cottage (or house)*

bēsuáppu ベースアップ *a raise; a salary increase* ❽Kotoshi wa fukéiki de bēsuáppu ga arimasén. 今年は不景気でベースアップがありません。*Because of the recession, there will be no pay raise this year.*

betsu [no/na] 別（の／な）*another; separate; different; special; distinctive* ❽sei betsu 性別 *sex distinction* ❽Betsu no hōhō mo kangáeta hō ga íi yo. 別の方法も考えた方がいいよ。*You should try thinking about (or doing) it another way.* ——**betsu [ni]** 別（に）*separately; not especially [with neg]* ❽Kore to kore o betsu ni tsutsúnde kudasái. これとこれを別に包んで下さい。*Please wrap this one and this one (or these) separately.* ❽Betsu ni yōji wa arimasén. 別に用事はありません。*I don't have any business (in coming) in particular.* ——**betsu to shite** 別として *apart from* ❽Híyō no mondai wa betsu to shite... 費用の問題は別として.... *Apart from the matter of expense...*

betsumei 別名 *different name; pseudonym; alias*

bí 美 *beauty*

bibún[gaku] 微分（学）*differential calculus* ❽bibun sekibúngaku 微分積分学 *calculus*

bígaku 美学 *aesthetics*

bihin 備品 *fixture(s)*

bíjin 美人 *beautiful woman*

bíjutsu 美術 *art* ❽bijutsúkan 美術館 *art museum*

-biki *(see* **-hiki***)*

bíkko o hik·u びっこをひく *be lame; walk with a limp*

bikkúri-suru [vi] びっくりする *be surprised; be astonished* ❽Watashi wa sono shirase o kiite bikkúri-shita wa. 私はその知らせを聞いてびっくりしたわ。*I was surprised when I heard the news.* <fem>

bikō 鼻孔 *nostril*

bíkubiku-suru [vi] びくびくする *be frightened; be afraid* ❽Kodomo wa itazura ga barénai ka to bíkubiku-shite iru. 子供は悪戯がばれないかとびくびくしている。*The child is afraid his mischief will be discovered.*

bímbō 貧乏 *poverty; want* ——**bímbō na** 貧乏な *poor* ——**bímbō-suru** [vi] 貧乏する *be poor; be in want*

bimyō [na] 微妙（な）*subtle; delicate; involved; touchy* ❽bimyō na aji 微妙な味 *a delicate flavor* ❽bimyō na mondai 微妙な問題 *a touchy problem* ❽bimyō na nyúansu o ríkai-suru 微妙なニュアンスを理解する *understand the subtle meaning*

bín 瓶 *bottle* 🞴kusuri no bín 薬の瓶 *medicine bottle*

bín 便 *(airline) flight; (scheduled) ship; (scheduled) train*

binánshi 美男子 *good-looking man*

binkan [na] 敏感 (な) *delicate; sensitive* 🞴ryūkō ni binkan na hitó 流行に敏感な人 *a person who is sensitive to latest fashions ——***binkan ni** 敏感に *delicately; sensitively* 🞴binkan ni hannō-suru 敏感に反応する *respond sensitively*

binsen 便箋 *letter-writing paper; stationery*

bira ビラ *leaflet; bill* 🞴bira o máku ビラをまく *distribute leaflets* 🞴bira o haru ビラを貼る *post bills*

bíri びり *last place; bottom rank*

birōdo ビロード *velvet*

bishobisho びしょびしょ *soaking wet; drenched* 🞴Áme ni furárete zenshin ga bishobisho désu. 雨に降られて全身がびしょびしょです。 *I got rained on and I'm completely soaked.*

bisshóri びっしょり *soaking wet; drenched* 🞴bisshóri ni náru びっしょりになる *become soaking wet*

biteki [na] 美的 (な) *aesthetic* 🞴biteki kánnen 美的観念 *aesthetic sense*

biwa 琵琶 *a Japanese lute*

bíwa 枇杷 *loquat*

biyaku 媚薬 *aphrodisiac*

biyṓin ; biyṓshitsu 美容院；美容室 *hairdresser's; beauty parlor*

bō 棒 *a stick*

bō- 防〜 *prevention from; defense from* 🞴bōsai 防災 *disaster defense*

bốbi 防備 *defense ——***bốbi-suru** [vt] 防備する *defend* 🞴genjū ni bốbi-suru 厳重に防備する *staunchly defend*

bóchi 墓地 *graveyard; burial ground* 🞴kyōdo bóchi 共同墓地 *common burial ground*

bōchō 膨張 *expansion; growth; swelling; increase* 🞴jinkō no bōchō 人口の膨張 *population growth ——***bōchō-suru** [vi] 膨張する *expand; grow; swell; increase* 🞴Yosan ga bōchō-shimásu. 予算が膨張します。 *The budget will increase.*

bōdai [na] 膨大 (な) *bulky; big; gigantic; enormous* 🞴bōdai na shíryō 膨大な資料 *a mass of documentation* 🞴bōdai na yósan 膨大な予算 *an enormous budget*

bōdō 暴動 *a riot* 🞴bōdō o okósu 暴動を起こす *start a riot* 🞴Bōdō ga ókita. 暴動が起きた。 *A riot occurred.*

bōei 防衛 *defense* 🞴Bōéi-chō 防衛庁 *Defense Agency* 🞴bōéi-hi 防衛費 *defense budget*

bōeki 貿易 *trade; commerce* 🞴bōeki kyốtei 貿易協定 *trade agreement* 🞴bōeki shūshi 貿易収支 *trade balance* 🞴bōeki fukínkō 貿易不均衡 *trade imbalance* 🞴bōeki hakuránkai 貿易博覧会 *trade fair* 🞴bōeki jiyūka 貿易自由化 *trade liberalization* ◊bōeki shōsha 貿易商社 *trading firm*——**bōeki-suru** [*vi*] 貿易する *trade* ◊Nihon wa Chūgoku to árata ni bōeki-suru kotó ni nátta. 日本は中国と新たに貿易することになった。 *Japan has resumed trade with China.*

bōenkyō 望遠鏡 *telescope*

bōen rénzu 望遠レンズ *telephoto lens*

bōfu 防腐 *preservation against decay* ◊bōfuzai 防腐剤 *an antiseptic* ◊bōfu-eki 防腐液 *antiseptic solution* ——**bōfuteki [na]** 防腐的（な）*antiseptic*

bōfū 暴風 *rainstorm; strong (or violent) wind* ◊bōfū-u 暴風雨 *hurricane*

bōgai 妨害 *obstruction; hindrance* ——**bōgai-suru** [*vt*] 妨害する *hinder; obstruct; disturb* ◊Fuhō chūsha wa tsūkō o bōgai-suru. 不法駐車は通行を妨害する。 *Illegal parking obstructs traffic.* ◊Henken wa ningen no jiyū o bōgai-shimasu. 偏見は人間の自由を妨害します。 *Prejudice obstructs people's freedom.*

bōgyaku 暴虐 *tyranny*

bōgyo 防御 *defense; protection* ——**bōgyo-suru** [*vt*] 防御する *defend* ◊Watashítachi no chímu wa aite chímu no kōgeki o hisshi ni bōgyo-shimáshita. 私たちのチームは相手チームの攻撃を必至に防御しました。 *Our team desperately defended itself against the opposition's attack.*

bōhan 防犯 *crime prevention*

bōhatei 防波堤 *breakwater*

boin 母音 *vowel*

bōju-suru [*vt*] 傍受する *intercept* ◊Watashítachi no fúne wa SOS no musen o gūzen ni bōju-shita. 私たちの船はSOSの無線を偶然に傍受した。 *By chance, our ship intercepted an SOS (radio) signal.*

bōka 防火 *fire prevention; fireproof* ◊bōka kénchiku 防火建築 *fireproof structure*

bōkan 傍観 *watching; observing (from the sidelines)* ◊bōkánsha 傍観者 *observer; spectator; onlooker; bystander* ——**bōkan-suru** [*vt*] 傍観する *observe; watch* ◊Wakamono ga bōkō-saréru no o atsumátta tsūkōnin wa bōkan-shite iru daké datta. 若者が暴行されるのを集まった通行人は傍観しているだけだった。 *A crowd of passersby simply looked on as the youth was attacked.* ◊Nihon séifu wa Námboku Chōsen káidan no yukue o bōkan-shite imásu. 日本政府は南北朝鮮会談の行方を傍観しています。 *The Japanese government is observing the course of the North and South Korean talks.*

bokás∙u [*vt* bokasánai; bokáshita] ぼかす *shade off; make fuzzy; be ambiguous* ◊henjí o bokásu 返事をぼかす *make an ambiguous reply* ◊iró o bokásu 色をぼかす *shade (a color) off*

bōken 冒険 *adventure; risk* ◊bōken-zuki na 冒険好きな *adventure-*

loving ——**bōkenteki [na]** 冒険的（な）*venturesome; adventurous*   ❧Káre wa nani ni de mo chōsen-suru bōkenteki na hitó desu. 彼は何にでも挑戦する冒険的な人です。*He's an adventurous person who'll challenge anything.*

boké·ru [*vi* bokénai; bóketa] 惚ける *be (or become) senile; be blurred; be out of focus*   ❧Saikin wa toshi no séi ka, atamá ga sukóshi bókete kimáshita. 最近は年のせいか、頭が少し惚けてきました。*I must be getting old; recently my head's a bit fuzzy.*   ❧Kimi wa ítsumo pinto ga bókete iru yo. 君はいつもピントが惚けているよ。*You're always slightly off target.*

bóki 簿記 *bookkeeping*   ❧bóki o tsukéru 簿記をつける *keep books*

bokki 勃起 *erection; erect penis* ——**bokki-suru** [*vi*] 勃起する *have (or get) an erection*

bókō 母校 *alma mater*

bōkō 膀胱 *bladder*   ❧bōkṓ-en 膀胱炎 *inflamation of the bladder*   ❧bōkō késseki 膀胱結石 *bladder stone*

bōkō 暴行 *assault; rape*   ❧bōkō o kuwáéru 暴行を加える *assault; rape*   ❧bōkōhan 暴行犯 *assailant; rapist*   ❧Sono otokó wa bōkō jíken no yógi de táiho-sareta. その男は暴行事件の容疑で逮捕された。*The man was arrested on suspicion of rape.* ——**bōkō-suru** [*vi*] 暴行する *assault; rape*   ❧bōkō-sareru 暴行される *be assaulted; be raped*

bókoku 母国 *motherland*   ❧bokokugo 母国語 *mother tongue*

bóku 僕 *I* [*masc, informal*]   ❧bókutachi 僕たち *we*

bokuchiku 牧畜 *stock farming; stock raising*

bokujō 牧場 *meadow; pasture; ranch*

bókun 暴君 *tyrant; autocrat*

bókushi 牧師 *pastor; minister*

bokusō 牧草 *grass (for grazing); pasturage*

bōmei 亡命 *exile; defection*   ❧bōméisha 亡命者 *refugee; defector*   ❧seiji bṓmei 政治亡命 *defection for political reasons* ——**bōmei-suru** [*vi*] 亡命する *go into exile; defect*

bon 盆 *tray*

bonchi 盆地 *basin (Geo)*   ❧Kōfu Bónchi 甲府盆地 *Kofu Basin*

bōnénkai 忘年会 *year-end party*

bonsai 盆栽 *bonsai; dwarf tree in a pot*

bon'yári [to] ぽんやり（と）*vague(ly); absent-minded(ly); unconsciously; purposelessly*   ❧bon'yári kangaekómu ぽんやり考えこむ *be lost in thought*   ❧bon'yári kurasu ぽんやり暮らす *live purposelessly*   ❧Bon'yári to shika obóete inai. ぽんやりとしか覚えていない。*I remember only vaguely.* ——**bon'yári-suru** [*vi*] ぽんやりする *be dim; be vague; be absent-minded*

bōrei 亡霊 *dead person's spirit; ghost*

bóro ぽろ *rag; scrap of cloth; imperfection*   ❧borokire ぽろ切れ *a rag;*

shreds   §Shaberi-súgite bóro ga déte-shimatta. 喋りすぎてぼろが出てしまった。 *I talked too much and exposed my ignorance.*

bōru ボール *mixing bowl*

bōru-bako ボール箱 *cardboard box*

bōru-gami ボール紙 *cardboard paper*

bōru pen ボールペン *ballpoint pen*

bóryoku 暴力 *violence; force*   §bōryokúdan 暴力団 *gangster organization*   §bóryoku o furuu 暴力をふるう *use force; show violence*

bosatsu 菩薩 *bodhisattva*

bōseki 紡績 *spinning*   §bōsekí-gyō 紡績業 *spinning industry*   §bōseki kójō 紡績工場 *(cotton) spinning mill*

bōshi 帽子 *hat; cap*

bōshi 防止 *prevention*   §hanzai bōshí-saku 犯罪防止策 *crime prevention measures* ——**bōshi-suru** [vt] 防止する *prevent*   §byōki man'en o bōshi-suru 病気蔓延を防止する *prevent the spread of a disease*

boshū 募集 *recruitment* ——**boshū-suru** [vt] 募集する *recruit; take applications for*   §Sadóbu wa buin o boshū-shite imásu. 茶道部は部員を募集しています。 *The tea ceremony club is recruiting members.*

bōshúzai 防臭剤 *deodorant*

bōsō 暴走 *reckless driving*   §bōsózoku 暴走族 *speed driving gang; motorcycle gang* ——**bōsō-suru** [vi] 暴走する *drive recklessly*   §Densha wa dassen-shite bōsō-shita. 電車は脱線して暴走した。 *The train derailed and ran wild.*

bōsui [no] 防水（の）*waterproof*

bótan 牡丹 *peony*   §botán yuki 牡丹 雪 *snow (falling in large flakes)*

bōtoku 冒涜 *profanity* ——**bōtoku-suru** [vt] 冒涜する *profane*   §Kámi no na o bōtoku-suru 神の名を冒涜する *profane God's name*

bótsubotsu ぼつぼつ *little by little*   §Sono hón wa bótsubotsu uredáshita. その本はぼつぼつ売れ出した。 *Little by little the book began to sell.*

bótsukí ame 棒付き飴 *lollipop; sucker*

bótto ぼうっと *faintly; dimly*   §Bōtto honóo ga moete iru. ぼうっと炎が燃えている。 *The flame is burning faintly.* ——**bōtto-suru** [vi] ぼうっとする *be listless; be in a fog; be in a daze*   §Átsusa de bōtto-shite imásu. 暑さでぼうっとしています。 *I'm listless in all this heat.*

boyaké·ru [vi boyakénai; boyáketa] ぼやける *grow dim; become uncertain; be blurred*   §Shōten ga boyákete iru. 焦点がぼやけている。 *The focus is blurred.*

bōzen to 茫然と; 呆然と *vacantly; at a loss; dumbfounded*   §bōzen to náru 茫然となる *be struck dumb*   §Háha no totsuzen no shí o kiite, watashi wa táda bōzen to shite-shimatta. 母の突然の死を聞いて、私はただ茫然としてしまった。 *I was stunned by the news of my* *mother's sudden death.*

bōzu 坊主 *Buddhist priest* ❊bōzu átama ni suru 坊主頭にする *shave one's head*

buai 歩合 *percentage; rate* ❊kōtei buái 公定歩合 *official bank rate* ❊buai-sei de 歩合制で *on a percentage basis* ❊buai o wakéru 歩合を分ける *give a commission*

buáisō [na] 無愛想（な）*curt; unfriendly; surly* ❊buáisō na musumé 無愛想な娘 *a surly girl*

búbū (to) ぶうぶう（と）[*mimetic for the grunting of a pig or the blowing of a car horn*] ❊búbū iu ぶうぶう言う *complain*

búbun 部分 *portion; part* ❊Kono búbun o teisei-shite kudasái. この部分を訂正して下さい。*Revise this part, please.*

buchō 部長 *division chief*

budō 葡萄 *grape* ❊budō-dana 葡萄棚 *grape arbor*

budōshu 葡萄酒 *wine*

budōtō 葡萄糖 *dextrose; glucose*

búgei 武芸 *military arts*

buhin 部品 *parts (for a machine)*

buji [na] 無事（な）*safe; well* ❊buji na ryokō 無事な旅行 *a safe trip* ——**buji ni** 無事に *safely; without mishap* ❊Kodomo wa buji ni tōchaku-shita. 子供は無事に到着した。*The children arrived safely*

bujoku 侮辱 *an insult* ——**bujoku-suru** [*vt*] 侮辱する *insult*

búka 部下 *a subordinate*

búki 武器 *arms; weapons* ❊búki dan'yaku 武器弾薬 *arms and ammunition*

bukimi [na] 不気味（な）*eerie; weird* ❊Kono yashikí wa shizumari-káette ite bukimi desu. この屋敷は静まり返っていて不気味です。*This mansion is so hushed and quiet it's eerie.*

bukíyō [na] 不器用（な）*awkward; clumsy* ❊bukíyō na hito 不器用な人 *an awkward person; a clumsy person*

bukka 物価 *commodity prices* ❊bukka ántei 物価安定 *price stability* ❊bukka héndō 物価変動 *price fluctuation* ❊bukka néage 物価値上げ *price hike* ❊bukka táisaku 物価対策 *price measures* ❊bukka yókusei 物価抑制 *price control* ❊Nihón wa nan démo bukka ga takái. 日本は何でも物価が高い。*In Japan, everything is expensive.*

Búkkyō 仏教 *Buddhism* ❊Bukkyóto 仏教徒 *Buddhist*

bumben 分娩 *(baby) delivery* ❊bumbén-shitsu 分娩室 *delivery room*

bumbetsu 分別 *division; classification* ——**bumbetsu-suru** [*vt*] 分別する *divide; distinguish; classify*

bumbōgu 文房具 *stationery and office supplies*

bummei 文明 *civilization; culture* ❊bumméi-koku 文明国 *a civilized nation* ❊seiō búmmei 西欧文明 *Western civilization*

búmon 部門 *branch; division; class* ❊eigyō búmon 営業部門 *business* *division*

bumpai-suru [vt] 分配する *distribute* §tómi o bumpai-suru　富を分配する　*distribute the wealth*

bumpō 文法　*grammar*

bumpu 分布　*distribution* ——**bumpu-suru** [vi / vt] *be distributed; range; be located* §Kōgyō-chítai wa umi ni sotte bumpu-shite iru. 工業地帯は海にそって分布している。 *The industrial belt is located along the ocean.*

bún 文　*a sentence (Gram)*

búngaku 文学　*literature* §Nihon búngaku　日本文学　*Japanese literature* §koten búngaku　古典文学　*classical literature*

bungaku hákase (or **hákushi**) 文学博士　*Doctor of Philosophy (Ph. D.)*

bungákushi 文学士　*Bachelor of Arts (B.A. / A.B.)*

bungaku shúshi 文学修士　*Master of Arts degree (M.A.)*

bungakuteki [na] 文学的（な）*literary* §bungakuteki na hyōgén 文学的な表現　*a literary expression*

bungo 文語　*literary language; written language*

bunjō 分譲　*parceling (or sub-division) of land* §bunjō jútaku 分譲住宅 *ready-built houses for sale* ——**bunjō-suru** [vt] 分譲する *sell (land) in lots* §Sono tochi wa bunjō-sarete iru. その土地は分譲されている。 *That land is being subdivided.*

búnka 文化　*culture* §Bunkáchō 文化庁 *The Agency for Cultural Affairs* §bunka ísan 文化遺産　*cultural heritage* §bunka kóryū 文化交流　*cultural exchange*

bunkai 分解　*taking apart; analysis* ——**bunkai-suru** [vt] 分解する *dismantle; take apart; analyze* §Anó ko wa omócha o ataerareru to súgu bunkai-shite shimau. あの子は玩具を与えられるとすぐ分解してしまう。 *Every time that kid is given a toy, he takes it apart immediately.*

bunkatsu-bárai 分割払い　*easy payment plan; installment plan*

bunken 文献　*(written) records; literature* §Watashi wa rombun sákusei no tamé ni bunken o atsumemáshita. 私は論文作成のために文献を集めました。 *I collected materials to write a paper.*

bunretsu 分裂　*division; splitting up* §saibō búnretsu 細胞分裂 *cell division* ——**bunretsu-suru** [vi] 分裂する *split; divide* §Sono sóshiki wa futatsú ni bunretsu-shimáshita. その組織は二つに分裂しました。 *That organization split into two.*

bunrui 分類　*classification* ——**bunrui-suru** [vt] 分類する *classify; catalogue* §Koko ni áru hón wa súbete sakusha-betsu ni bunrui-shite arimásu. ここにある本は全て作者別に分類してあります。 *The books that are here are catalogued according to author.*

bunseki 分析　*analysis; classification* ——**bunseki-suru** [vt] 分析する *classify; analyze* §Kono idó-mizu no sámpuru no séibun o bunsekishite kudasaimasén ka? この井戸水のサンプルの成分を分析して下さいませんか。 *Would you analyze the chemical content of this well-water sample?*

búnsho 文書 *a document*

búnshō 文章 *piece of writing; sentence; paper; composition*

buntan 分担 *allotment; apportionment* ——**buntan-suru** [vt] 分担する *allot (to); assign (to); divide* ⑧Nímotsu o buntan-shite hakobimasén ka? 荷物を分担して運びませんか。 *Why don't we divide up the baggage and carry it?*

buntsū 通 *correspondence* ——**buntsū-suru** [vi] 通する *correspond with; carry on a correspondence (with)* ⑧Musuko wa Amerikájin no yūjin to buntsū-shite imásu. 息子はアメリカ人の友人と通しています。 *My son corresponds with an American friend.*

bún'ya 分野 *area; field* ⑧semmon bún'ya 専門分野 *technical field; field of specialization*

búrabura ぶらぶら *hanging; swinging; idly* ⑧búrabura arúku ぶらぶら歩く *amble; stroll* ⑧búrabura kurasu ぶらぶら暮らす *live idly*

búranko ぶらんこ *a swing*

burasagar·u [vi burasagaranai; burasagatta] ぶら下がる *hang down; dangle* ⑧Gṓka na shandéria ga tenjō kara burasagatte iru. 豪華なシャンデリアが天井からぶら下がっている。 *A gorgeous chandelier is hanging from the ceiling.*

burasage·ru [vt burasagenai; burasageta] ぶら下げる *hang; suspend, carry (hanging from the hand)* ⑧Uwábaki-ire o burasage-nágara kodomótachi wa gakkō kara káette kimásu. 上履き入れをぶら下げながら子供たちは学校から帰ってきます。 *The children come home from school carrying their shoe bags (containing indoor shoes).*

búrei [na] 無礼（な） *impolite; rude* ⑧Áitsu wa búrei da. あいつは無礼だ。 *That guy's rude.* <masc> ⑧Sore wa búrei da wa! それは無礼だわ！ *That's rude!* <fem>

-buri 〜ぶり *after the lapse of* ⑧jūnen-buri ni áu 十年ぶりに会う *meet after ten years*

búri 鰤 *adult yellowtail (fish)*

búruburu ぶるぶる *shivering* ⑧sámusa de búruburu furueru 寒さでぶるぶる震える *shiver in cold weather* ——**búruburu-suru** [vi] ぶるぶるする *shiver* ⑧"Nán de búruburu-shite iru no?" "Dátte, kowái n da mono!" 「何でそんなにぶるぶるしているの？」「だって、怖いんだもの！」 *"Why are you shivering like that?"* <fem> *"Because I'm scared!"* <fem>

búryoku 武力 *armed force* ⑧buryoku shṓtotsu 武力衝突 *armed clash*

búshi 武士 *samurai; warrior*

bushō 無精; 不精 *laziness* ——**bushṓ na** 無精な; 不精な *lazy*

búshu 部首 *(kanji) radical*

busō 武装 *arms* §busō gérira 武装ゲリラ *armed guerilla* ——**busō-suru** [*vt*] 武装する *arm; take up arms* §Hán-seifu gérira wa busō-shite, kokkyō no machí o osoimáshita. 反政府ゲリラは武装して、国境の町を襲いました。 *The antigovernment guerilas took up arms and attacked border towns.*

bússhi 物資 *material goods; commodities*

busshitsu 物質 *matter; substance* §busshitsu búmmei 物質文明 *materialistic civilization* §busshitsu shúgi 物質主義 *materialism* §kagaku bússhitsu 化学物質 *chemical matter*

búsu 醜女 *ugly woman*

busű 部数 *quantity* §hakkō búsu 発行部数 *number of copies published; circulation*

buta 豚 *pig; hog* §butaniku 豚肉 *pork*

bútai 舞台 *stage*

bútai 部隊 *troops* §zen'ei bútai 前衛部隊 *advance troops; reconnaissance*

bútsubutsu iu ぶつぶつ言う *grumble; murmur* §bútsubutsu fuman o iu ぶつぶつ不満を言う *complain*

butsukar·u [*vi* butsukaranai; butsukatta] ぶつかる *strike; hit; collide with; crash into; run into* §Watashi wa tokidoki, kírei ni migakareta uindō ya dóa ni butsukaru kotó ga áru. 私は時々、きれいに磨かれたウインドーやドアにぶつかることがある。 *Sometimes I bump into highly polished windows or doors.* §Anáta wa iroiro na shōgai ni butsukatta tóki, soréra o kokufuku-suru kotó ga dekimásu ka? あなたは色々な障害にぶつかった時、それらを克服することができますか。 *Are you able to overcome various obstacles that you run up against?*

butsuke·ru [*vt* butsukenai; butsuketa] ぶつける *throw at and hit; strike; bump into* §Urusai néko ni ishi o butsuketa. うるさい猫に石をぶつけた。 *I threw a rock at the yowling cats.*

butsurí[gaku] 物理 (学) *physics* §butsuri ryōhō 物理療法 *physical therapy*

butsuzō 仏像 *Buddhist statue*

buttai 物体 *physical object*

butten 仏典 *Buddhist sutra*

búyo 蚋 *gnat*

byő 鋲 *a tack* §gabyō 画鋲 *thumbtack* §byő o útsu 鋲を打つ *(to) rivet; (to) tack*

-byő ～秒 *second* §Íppun wa rokujű-byō desu. 一分は六十秒です。 *One minute is sixty seconds.*

byōbu 屏風 *folding screen*

byōdō 平等 *equality* §dánjo byōdō 男女平等 *sex equality* ——**byōdō na** 平等な *equal* §Súbete no ningen wa umare-nágara ni shite byōdō desu. 全ての人間は生まれながらにして平等です。 *All people are born equal.*

byōin 病院 *hospital* §daigaku byōin 大学病院 *university hospital* §kojin byōin 個人病院 *private hospital; clinic* §sōgō byōin 総合病院 *general hospital* §semmon byōin 専門病院 *specialized hospital*

byōjaku [no / na] 病弱（の/な）*sickly*   Tsúma wa byōjaku de ítsumo nyūin-shite iru. 妻は病弱でいつも入院している。 *My wife is sickly; she's always in the hospital.*

byōki 病気 *illness* ——**byōki no** 病気の *ill; sick* §Miyuki-san wa i no byōki de chiryō o úkete imásu. 美由紀さんは胃の病気で治療を受けています。 *Miyuki is under treatment for a stomach illness.* §Hísho wa kono isshūkan, byōki de yasúnde imásu. 秘書はこの一週間、病気で休んでいます。 *My secretary is home sick this week.*

byōnin 病人 *sick person; invalid*

byōsha 描写 *description* §Kawabata Yasúnari wa josei no shinri byōsha ga umái. 川端康成は女性の心理描写がうまい。 *Yasunari Kawabata is skilled in his depiction of a woman's psychology.* ——**byōsha-suru** [vt] 描写する *describe; depict*

byōshitsu 病室 *sickroom*

byūbyū [to] びゅうびゅう（と）[mimetic for fiercely blowing; howling wind] §Kogárashi ga byúbyū fúite iru. 木枯らしがびゅうびゅう吹いている。 *The winter wind is howling.*

C

cha 茶 *tea; tea plant* §nihoncha 日本茶 *Japanese (green) tea* §kōcha 紅茶 *black tea* §úróncha ウーロン茶 *oolong tea* §O-cha wa dónna no ga íi desu ka? お茶はどんなのがいいですか？ *What kind of tea would you like?*

chairo [no] 茶色（の）*brown (color)*

chakás·u [vt chakasánai; chakáshita] 茶化す *make fun of; jest* §Káre wa watashi ga majime na hanashí o suru to ítsumo chakásu. 彼は私が真面目な話をするといつも茶化す。 *He always makes fun of me when I talk seriously.*

chakín-zushi 茶巾寿司 *sushi wrapped in egg*

chákku チャック *zipper; fastener*

-cháku 〜着 [classifier for suits, coats, jackets, etc.] §Natsumono no sútsu ga nánchaku arimásu ka? 夏物のスーツが何着ありますか？ *How many summer suits do you have?*

-cháku 〜着 *arrive at* §Yonhyaku mētorúsō no itcháku wa dáre desu ka? 400メートル走の一着は誰ですか？ *Who was first in the 400-meter race?* §Watashi wa shōgo-cháku no shinkánsen ni norimásu. 私は正

午着の新幹線に乗ります。 *I'm taking the bullet train that arrives at noon.*

chakujitsu [na] 着実（な）*steady; faithful* ——**chakujitsu ni** 着実に *steadily; faithfully* §Atarashíi katei kyōshi ni tsúite kara musuko no gakuryoku wa chakujitsu ni nóbite iru. 新しい家庭教師についてから息子の学力は着実に伸びている。 *My son has improved steadily since he's had the new home tutor.*

chakuriku 着陸 *(plane) landing* ——**chakuriku-suru** [vi] 着陸する *(to) land* §Kyōfū no náka, sono hikōki wa buji ni chakuriku-shita. 強風の中、その飛行機は無事に着陸した。 *The plane landed safely in the storm.*

chakuseki 着席 *taking a seat* ——**chakuseki-suru** [vi] 着席する *take a seat; sit down*

chambara ちゃんばら *sword fight; samurai movie* §chambara gókko ちゃんばらごっこ *playing sword fighting* §Kodomo no tóki, watashi wa yóku chambara o shite asonda monó desu. 子どもの時、私はよくちゃんばらをして遊んだものです。 *When I was a kid, I often played chambara.*

chamise 茶店 *tea stall; resting place*

-chan 〜ちゃん *[diminuitive noun suffix, used as an appellative and expressing familiarity; often attached to a child's name in place of -san]*

chanko nábe ちゃんこ鍋 *a stew eaten by sumo wrestlers*

chanoma 茶の間 *living room; parlor*

chanoyu 茶の湯 *tea ceremony* §Chanoyu wa Sen no Ríkyū ni yotte taisei-sareta. 茶の湯は千利休によって大成された。 *The tea ceremony was refined by Sen no Rikyū.*

chanto ちゃんと *precisely; just; neatly; properly; perfectly* §Genkan de kutsú o núide, chanto soróete kudasái. 玄関で靴を脱いで、ちゃんと揃えて下さい。 *Take your shoes off at the entrance and arrange them neatly, please.*

chashitsu 茶室 *tea ceremony room; tea house*

chawan 茶碗 *teacup (J); (rice) bowl* §gohan-jáwan 御飯茶碗 *rice bowl* §chanomi-jáwan 茶のみ茶碗 *teabowl*

chazuke 茶漬け *bowl of rice doused with tea*

chí 地 *earth; soil* §tén to chí 天と地 *heaven and earth* §chí no hate 地の果て *the ends of the earth* §chí-tai-kū misáiru 地対空ミサイル *surface-to-air missile*

chi 血 *blood* §chi o nagásu 血を流す *shed blood* §Chi ga déte iru yo! 血が出ているよ。 *You're bleeding!*

chian 治安 *safety; security; public peace* §Nihón wa chian ga íi to iwarete iru. 日本は治安がいいと言われている。 *They say Japan is a safe place.*

chíbusa 乳房 *(human) breast(s)*

chichí 父 *(one's own) father*

chichí 乳 *milk; woman's breast*

chídori 千鳥 *plover*   ❷chidorí-ashi de arúku 千鳥足で歩く *stagger (like a drunk)*

chié 知恵 *wisdom*   ❷chieókure no ko 知恵遅れの子 *mentally handicapped child*

chífusu チフス *typhus; typhoid (fever)*

chigai 違い *difference*   ❷Ningen to hoka no dōbutsu tó no chigai wa nán desu ka? 人間と他の動物との違いは何ですか？ *What is the difference between humans and other animals?*

[ni] chigainái ～に違いない *without doubt; I'm sure*   ❷Anó hito wa táshika Yamada-san ni chigainái. あの人は確か山田さんに違いない。 *Without doubt, that is Yamada.*

chiga·u [vt chigawanai; chigatta] 違う *be different; be wrong; be mistaken*   ❷Kyó no kánojo wa ítsumo to chigau. 今日の彼女はいつもと違う。 *She's different from her usual self today.*   ❷Chigaimásu. 違います。 *No.; That's wrong.*

chigír·u [vt chigiránai; chigítta] 千切る *tear (to pieces)*   ❷Kodomo wa pán o chigítte tábete iru. 子供はパンを千切って食べている。 *The child is tearing up her bread and eating it.*

chiheisen 地平線 *the horizon*

chíhō 地方 *locality; region*   ❷chihóshoku 地方色 *local color*   ❷chihō jichítai 地方自治体 *local autonomy; local government*   ❷chihózei 地方税 *local tax*

chíi 地位 *rank; status; place; position*   ❷Josei no shakaiteki chíi wa máda mada hikúi. 女性の社会的地位はまだまだ低い。 *Women's place in society is still quite low.*

chíiki 地域 *area; region*   ❷chiiki kénkyū 地域研究 *area study; regional studies*   ❷chiiki shákai 地域社会 *local society*

chíji 知事 *governor*   ❷to chíji 都知事 *governor of Tokyo*   ❷ken chíji 県知事 *prefectural governor*

chijimar·u [vi chijimaranai; chijimatta] 縮まる *shrink; contract; shorten*

chijime·ru [vt chijimenai; chijimeta] 縮める *shorten; cut down; squeeze (into)*   ❷Kono bún wa nagasugíru kara mótto chijimeta hō ga íi yo. この文は長すぎるからもっと縮めた方がいいよ。 *This sentence is too long; you should shorten it.*

chijim·u [vi chijimanai; chijinda] 縮む *shrink; shrivel*   ❷Kono sétā wa mizúarai suru to chijimimásu. このセーターは水洗いすると縮みます。 *This sweater will shrink if washed in water.*

chijire·ru [vi chijirenai; chijireta] 縮れる *be kinky; be wavy; be curly* ——**chijireta** 縮れた *kinky; curly*   ❷chijireta kami 縮れた髪 *kinky hair*

chijō de 地上で *on the earth*

chíka 地価 *land price(s)* 8takái chíka 高い地価 *high land prices* 8Chíka ga agaru ippō desu. 地価が上がる一方です。*The price of land only goes up.*

chiká 地下 *underground; basement* 8chikáshitsu 地下室 *basement (room)* 8chika sóshiki 地下組織 *underground organization*

chikádō 地下道 *underground passage; underpass*

chikágoro 近頃 *nowadays; lately; recently* 8Chikágoro, monowásure ga hídoku natte kita. 近頃、物忘れがひどくなってきた。*Lately, I've become very forgetful.*

chikai 地階 *basement floor* 8Shokuryōhin úriba wa chikai ni gozaimásu. 食料品売り場は地階にございます。*Foodstuffs are on the basement floor. <formal>*

chiká·i [adj chíkaku nái; chíkakatta] 近い *(be) near* 8Byōin wa ié kara chikái. 病院は家から近い。*The hospital is near my house.*

chikai 誓い *oath; vow; pledge* 8chikai no kotoba 誓いの言葉 *(marriage) vows*

chikájika 近々 *in the near future* 8Chikájika, sono byōki no tokkṓyaku ga kansei-suru rashíi. 近々、その病気の特効薬が完成するらしい。*It's seems that a cure for that disease will be perfected in the near future.*

chikáku [no] 近く（の）*near; nearby; close* 8Watashi no uchí wa éki no súgu chikáku desu. 私の家は駅のすぐ近くです。*My house is very near the station.* 8Yasai wa chikáku no misé de kaimásu. 野菜は近くの店で買います。*I buy vegetables at a nearby store.*

-chíkaku ～近く *around* 8Shōgo-chíkaku ni ukagaimásu. 正午近くに伺います。*I will come (or call) around noon. <formal>*

chikámichi 近道 *shortcut*

chikan 痴漢 *a pervert; molester*

chikará 力 *power; strength; energy* 8chikará o koméru 力を込める *muster (one's) strength* 8Chikará o awásete yarimashṓ. 力を合わせてやりましょう。*Let's work together and do it.*

chikarámochi 力持ち *physically strong person*

chikara-zuké·ru [vt -zukénai; -zúketa] 力づける *strengthen; cheer up* 8Tanaka-san wa ókusan o nakushite kiochi-shite irú no de, chikara-zúkete agemashṓ. 田中さんは奥さんを亡くして気落ちしているので、力づけてあげましょう。*Tanaka is feeling depressed since his wife died. Let's go and cheer him up.*

chikatetsu 地下鉄 *subway; metro; underground; tube*

chika·u [vt chikawanai; chikatta] 誓う *vow; pledge; take an oath; swear to; promise* 8Jíjitsu o shōjíki ni tsutaeru kotó o chikaimásu. 事実を正直に伝えることを誓います。*I swear to tell the truth.*

chikayór·u [vi chikayóranai; chikayótta] 近寄る *draw near (to); approach* 8Ayashii hitó ga chikayótte kita. 怪しい人が近寄って来

た。 *A suspicious person approached me.*

chikazuké·ru [*vt* chikazukénai; chikazuketa] 近づける *bring (something) close; bring near*

chikazúk·u [*vi* chikazukánai; chikazúita] 近づく *approach; draw near (to)* ❸Dḗto no hi ga chikazúite kita. デートの日が近づいて来た。 *The day of our date drew near.*

chikoku 遅刻 *tardiness; lateness* ──**chikoku-suru** [*vi*] 遅刻する *be late; be tardy* ❸Chikoku-shite gomen-nasái. 遅刻してご免なさい。 *I'm sorry to be late.*

chíku 地区 *district* ❸jūtaku chíku 住宅地区 *residential district* ❸shōgyō chíku 商業地区 *business district*

chíkuchiku [to] ちくちく（と）*prickly; stabbing* ❸Mōchō ga chíkuchiku itánde imásu. 盲腸がちくちく痛んでいます。 *My appendix hurts with a stabbing pain.*

chikudénchi 蓄電池 *storage battery*

chikunōshō 蓄膿症 *sinus headache; (Tech) empyema*

chikúrichikúri [to] ちくりちくり（と）*stinging; cutting* ❸Jōshi wa ítsumo watashi ni táishite chikúrichikúri to iyamí o iu. 上司はいつも私に対してちくりちくりと厭味を言う。 *My superior's always making cutting remarks about me.*

chikushō 畜生！*Hell!; Dang!; Shit!; Damn it!* ❸Chikushō! O-mae nánte shinde shimáe! 畜生！お前なんて死んでしまえ！*Damn you! Go to hell!* <masc>

chikyū 地球 *(planet) earth; the globe*

chimbotsu 沈没 *sinking (of a ship); submersion* ──**chimbotsu-suru** [*vi*] 沈没する *sink*

chiméishō 致命傷 *fatal wound*

chimeiteki [na] 致命的（な）*mortal; fatal; very serious* ❸Watashi wa chimeiteki na mísu o shite, sono kaisha o kubi ni nátta. 私は致命的なミスをして、その会社を首になった。 *I made a serious (or unforgivable) mistake and was fired from that company.*

chimmoku 沈黙 *silence; reticence* ❸chimmoku no sékai 沈黙の世界 *the silent world (the world of the hearing impaired)* ❸Chimmoku wa kin. 沈黙は金。 *Silence is golden.* <set phrase> ❸Káre wa chimmoku o mamótta. 彼は沈黙を守った。 *He kept his silence.*

chin'age 賃上げ *wage-hike; salary increase* ❸Kumiái-in wa kaisha ni táishite nipāsénto no chin'age o yōkyū-shite iru. 組合は会社に対して2パーセントの賃上げを要求している。 *The labor union is demanding a two percent raise in wages from the company.*

chinami ni 因に *incidentally; by the way; in relation to that* ❸Yoshida-san no shúmi wa ténisu desu. Chinami ni watashi no shúmi wa suiei désu. 吉田さんの趣味はテニスです。因に私の趣味は水泳です。 *Yoshida's hobby is tennis. And mine, by the way, is swimming.*

chindon-ya ちんどん屋 *street musical band (for publicity)*

chíngin 賃金 *wages; pay*   8takái chíngin 高い賃金 *high wages*   8chingin hikíage 賃金引き上げ *pay raise*   8chíngin yókusei 賃金抑制 *wage control*   8chíngin o morau 賃金を貰う *receive pay*   8chíngin o haráu 賃金を払う *pay wages*

chínō 知能 *intellect; mental ability*   8chinō shísū 知能指数 *IQ (intelligence quotient)*   8Iruka wa chínō no takái honyū dōbutsu desu. いるかは知能の高い哺乳動物です。 *Dolphins are mammals of high intelligence.*

chinretsu 陳列 *exhibiting; display*   8chinretsu-hin 陳列品 *item on exhibit*   8chinretsú-shitsu 陳列室 *showroom* —— **chinretsu-suru** [vt] 陳列する *exhibit; display*

chinséizai 鎮静剤 *sedative*   8chinséizai o nómu 鎮静剤を飲む *take a sedative*   8chinséizai o útsu 鎮静剤を打つ *inject sedatives*

chintsūzai 鎮痛剤 *painkiller; (Tech) anodyne*

chírachira [to] ちらちら（と）*shimmering; flickering; faintly; lightly*   8Hónoo ga chírachira hikátte iru. 炎がちらちら光っている。 *The flame is flickering.*   8Yukí ga chírachira fútte kita. 雪がちらちら降ってきた。 *A light snow has started to fall.*   8Sukáto no suso kara súrippu ga chírachira miéru. スカートの裾からスリップがちらちら見える。 *Your slip's showing (beneath your skirt) a little.* —— **chírachira-suru** [vi] ちらちらする *flicker; twinkle; glitter; glisten*

chirakar·u [vi chirakaranai; chirakatta] 散らかる *be scattered; be in disorder*   8Heyá ga chirakatte iru. 部屋が散らかっている。 *The room is messy.*

chirakas·u [vt chirakasanai; chirakashita] 散らかす *scatter*   8omócha o chirakasu 玩具を散らかす *scatter one's toys*   8Chirakashité wa ikemasén. 散らかしてはいけません。 *You mustn't scatter things about. (or You mustn't litter).*

chirashi ちらし *leaflet; handbill; pamphlet*   8chirashi o kubáru ちらしを配る *distribute pamphlets*   8chirashi o haru ちらしを貼る *post bills*

chirí 塵 *dust*   8chirí ga tamaru 塵が溜まる *dust collects*   8Chirí mo tsumóreba yamá to náru. 塵も積もれば山となる。 *If dust accumulates it makes a mountain (Little drops of water make the mighty ocean). <set phrase>*

chirigami 塵紙 *(coarse) toilet paper; tissue paper*   8Íma wa chirigami yóri tísshū o tsukaimásu. 今は塵紙よりティッシューを使います。 *Nowadays, tissues are used more (commonly) than chirigami.*

chiri-nabe チリ鍋 *a pot of fish and vegetables served with yuzu (Chinese lemon) juice*

chirígaku 地理学 *geography*

chirimen 縮緬 *crepe*

chirínchirin [to] ちりんちりん（と）*ringing (of a bell)* ❧ Jitensha wa chirín chirin to béru o narashinágara hodō o hashítta. 自転車はちりんちりんとベルを鳴らしながら歩道を走った。*A bicycle came running down the sidewalk ringing a bell.*

chiritóri 塵取り *dustpan*

chir·u [vi chiranai; chitta] 散る *fall* ❧ Sakura no haná ga chitte iru. 桜の花が散っている。*The cherry blossoms are falling.*

chiryō 治療 *(medical) treatment; therapy; remedy* ❧ chiryō o ukéru 治療を受ける *receive therapy* ❧ chiryō o suru 治療をする *give therapy*

chīsá·i [adj chísaku nái; chísakatta] 小さい *(be) small; little; young* ❧ Otōtó yori áni no hó ga chīsái. 弟より兄の方が小さい。*My older brother is smaller than my younger brother.* ❧ Musumé wa máda chīsái. 娘はまだ小さい。*My daughter's still young.*

chísa na 小さな *small* ❧ chísa na dekigóto 小さな出来事 *an insignificant event; a small happening*

chísei 知性 *intellect* ——**chiseiteki [na]** 知性的な *intellectual*

chíshiki 知識 *knowledge; information* ❧ hōfu na chíshiki 豊富な知識 *extensive knowledge* ❧ Watashi wa kágaku no chíshiki ga toboshíi. 私は科学の知識が乏しい。*I'm lacking in scientific knowledge.*

chishitsúgaku 地質学 *geology*

chissoku 窒息 *suffocation* ❧ chissokú-shi 窒息死 *death by suffocation* ——**chissoku-suru [vi]** 窒息する *suffocate* ❧ Chissoku-shisō desu. Mádo o akete kudasái. 窒息しそうです。窓を開けて下さい。*I'm about to suffocate. Open a window, please.*

chisuji 血筋 *lineage; heredity* ❧ chisuji ga íi 血筋がいい *good bloodline; good lineage* ❧ Uchi wa gakusha no chisuji o hiite iru. うちは学者の血筋を引いている。*There are scholars in our family line.*

chitai 地帯 *zone; area* ❧ anzen chítai 安全地帯 *safety zone* ❧ shin'yō jurin chítai 針葉樹林地帯 *coniferous forest zone*

chiteki [na] 知的（な）*intelligent; intellectual; rational; mental* ❧ chiteki na josei 知的な女性 *an intellectual woman*

chítsu 膣 *vagina* ❧ chitsúen 膣炎 *vaginitis*

chitsújo 秩序 *order; system; discipline* ❧ shūdan no chitsújo o mamóru 集団の秩序を守る *maintain group discipline*

chittómo ちっとも *(not) at all [with neg]* ❧ Kono hón wa chittómo omoshíroku nái. この本はちっとも面白くない。*This book is not at all interesting.*

chízu 地図 *a map*

chízu チーズ *cheese*

chó 腸 *intestines* ❧ dái-chō 大腸 *large intestines* ❧ shó-chō 小腸 *small intestines* ❧ jūnishí-chō 十二指腸 *the duodenum*

chó ; chóchō 蝶 ; 蝶々 *butterfly*

-chó 〜長 *head (of an organization)* ❧ káchō 課長 *section chief*

⑧kaichō 会長 *chairperson* ⑧shachō 社長 *company president; CEO*
⑧buchō 部長 *division head*

-chō ～庁 *government agency; government office* ⑧Bōeichō 防衛庁
Defense Agency ⑧Kokuzeichō 国税庁 *National Tax Administration
Agency*

-chō ～兆 *trillion* ⑧Bōeihi ga ni-chōen kíbo ni made fukuranda. 防衛費
が二兆円規模にまで膨らんだ。 *The defense budget (or expense)
expanded to two trillion yen.*

chō- 超～ *super-; beyond; above* ⑧chōkyṓha 超教派
interdenominational ⑧chōmán'in 超満員 *over-capacity crowd*
⑧chō-ónsoku 超音速 *supersonic speed* ⑧chōtṓha gaikō séisaku 超党
派外交政策 *nonpartisan foreign policy*

chōbo 帳簿 *account book; ledger* ⑧Zeimusho no kánsa ga áru no de
chōbo no séiri o shite okó. 税務署の監査があるので帳簿の整理をし
ておこう。 *The tax office audit is coming up right away, so I'll get the
account ledger in order.*

chōchín 堤灯 *paper lantern* ⑧bon-jṓchin 盆堤灯 *Bon festival lantern*
⑧chōchín gyṓretsu 堤灯行列 *a lantern procession (parade)* ⑧chōchín
o kakageru 堤灯を掲げる *hang a paper lantern*

-chṓchō ～長調 *major (key)* ⑧ha-chṓchō ハ長調 *C major* ⑧to-chṓchō
ト長調 *G major*

chōdái 頂戴！ *please (give it to me)* —— **chōdai-suru** [vt] 頂戴する *I
receive* <formal> ⑧Enryo náku chōdai-shimásu. 遠慮なく頂戴しま
す。 *Thank you; I'll accept (what you are offering me).* <formal>

chōdo 丁度 *precisely; exactly; just* ⑧Kono kutsu no sáizu wa chōdo íi.
この靴のサイズは丁度いい。 *This shoe size is just right.*

chōeki 懲役 *imprisonment; penal servitude* ⑧Káre wa chōeki naná-nen
no kéi o úketa. 彼は懲役七年の刑を受けた。 *He received a prison
sentence of seven years.*

chōhei 徴兵 *conscription; military draft* ⑧chōhei kíhi 徴兵忌避 *draft
evasion* ⑧chōhei kihísha 徴兵忌避者 *draft dodger* ⑧chōhei séido
徴兵制度 *conscription system*

chōhṓkei 長方形 *rectangle*

chōin 調印 *signature; signing; sealing* ⑧chōínkoku 調印国 *a signatory
power* ⑧chōín-shiki 調印式 *signing ceremony*

chōji 弔辞 *message of condolence* ⑧Watashi wa kokubetsú-shiki de chōji
o nobéru koto ni nátta. 私は告別式で弔辞を述べることになった。
I'm to give a condolence speech at the memorial service.

chójo 長女 *(one's own) oldest daughter*

chōjṓ 頂上 *(mountain) summit; climax*

chṓkaku 聴覚 *hearing; auditory sense*

chōkan 朝刊 *morning newspaper*

chokin 貯金 *savings; deposit* ⑧chokin tsúchō 貯金通帳 *bankbook* ——

chokin-suru [*vi*] 貯金する *save (deposit) money*

chokkaku 直角 *right angle*

chokkan 直観 *intuition*   §Chokkan wa hatsumei no motó ni náru. 直観は発明の基になる。 *Intuition is the source of invention.*

chokkei 直径 *diameter*

chokki チョッキ *vest; waistcoat*

chōkō 兆候 *symptom; indication; sign*   §keiki kaifuku no chōkō 景気回復の兆候 *indication (or sign) of economic recovery*

chōkō 聴講 *attendance (at a lecture)*   §chōkōsha 聴講者 *an attendant at a lecture; an auditor (US)* ——**chōkō-suru** [*vt*] 聴講する *audit a lecture (US)*   §Raigákki, watashi wa hikaku gengógaku no júgyō o chōkō-shimásu. 来学期、私は比較言語学の授業を聴講します。 *I'm going to audit the class in comparative linguistics next semester.*

chōkoku 彫刻 *sculpture; carving*   §chōkoku-ka 彫刻家 *a sculptor* ——**chōkoku-suru** [*vt*] 彫刻する *(to) sculpt*

chokón to ちょこんと *simply; briefly; (the appearance of something small)*   §chokónto o-jigi o suru ちょこんとお辞儀をする *bow slightly*   §Musumé wa zabúton ni chokón to suwatta. 娘は座布団にちょこんと座った。 *My little girl perched on the zabuton.*

chokubai 直売 *direct sale*

chokuryū 直流 *direct current (Elec)*   *(see also* **kōryū***)*

chokusen 直線 *straight line*

chokusetsu 直接 *direct; straight; immediate*   §chokusetsú ぜい 直接税 *direct tax*   §chokusetsu kǎinyū 直接介入 *direct interference; direct involvement*   §chokusetsu no renraku 直接の連絡 *direct contact* ——**chokusetsu ni** 直接に *directly; immediately*

chokutsū 直通 *straight through; direct*   §chokutsū dénsha 直通電車 *a through train*   §chokutsū dénwa 直通電話 *direct dial(ing)*

chokuyaku 直訳 *literal translation*   §Chokuyaku wa íi hon'yaku to wa ienai. 直訳はいい翻訳とは言えない。 *Literal translation cannot be called good translation.* ——**chokuyaku-suru** [*vt*] 直訳する *translate directly (or literally)*

chókuyu 直喩 *simile*

chōkyóri 長距離 *long-distance*   §chōkyóri dénwa 長距離電話 *long-distance telephone call*   §chōkyóri kyṓsō 長距離競争 *long-distance race*   §chōkyóri básu 長距離バス *long-distance bus*   §chōkyóri únten 長距離運転 *long-distance driving*

-chōme 〜丁目 *-chome* [*street address suffix*]   §Koko wa Marunóuchi itchōme desu. ここは丸の内一丁目です。 *This is Marunouchi, 1-chome.*

chṓmi 調味 *seasoning; flavoring*   §chōmíryō 調味料 *seasoning; spices* ——**chṓmi-suru** [*vt*] 調味する *(to) season*

chōnán 長男 *(one's own) oldest son*

chón to ちょんと *just; merely*

chō-ónkai 長音階 *major scale* §**tan'ónkai** 短音階 *minor scale*

chóri 調理 *cooking* ——**chóri-suru** [*vt*] 調理する *prepare food; cook* §Denshi rénji de chóri-suru to taihen bénri desu. 電子レンジで調理すると大変便利です。 *It's very convenient to cook with a microwave oven.*

chōrúigaku 鳥類学 *ornithology*

chōsa 調査 *investigation; survey; research; inquiry; census* §kokusei chōsa 国勢調査 *national census* §jitchi chōsa 実地調査 *field research* §ankēto chōsa アンケート調査 *questionnaire* ——**chōsa-suru** [*vt*] 調査する *investigate; examine*

chosák(u)ken 著作権 *copyright*

chōsei 調整 *regulation; limitation; adjustment* §koyō chōsei 雇用調整 *employment adjustment (or downsizing through attrition and hiring limits)* ——**chōsei-suru** [*vt*] 調整する *regulate; limit; adjust* §sukéjūru o chōsei-suru スケジュールを調整する *adjust the schedule*

chōsen 挑戦 *challenge* ——**chōsen-suru** [*vi*] 挑戦する *challenge; defy; attempt; dare* §Kóndo wa ano yamá ni chōsen-shiyō. 今度はあの山に挑戦しよう。 *I'm going to tackle (or try) that mountain next.*

Chōsén 朝鮮 *Korea* §Kita Chōsén 北朝鮮 *North Korea (abbr for Chōsén Minshu-shúgi Jimmin Kyōwákoku* 朝鮮民主主義人民共和国 *Democratic People's Republic of Korea)*

chōsetsu 調節 *adjustment; regulation* ——**chōsetsu-suru** [*vt*] 調節する *adjust; regulate* §kúrā no óndo o chōsetsu-suru クーラーの温度を調節する *adjust the temperature of the airconditioner*

chósha 著者 *author; writer*

chōshi 銚子 *sake bottle; sake container* §Chōshi no o-káwari o kudasái. 銚子のお代わりを下さい。 *Another bottle of sake, please.*

chōshi 調子 *musical pitch; key; manner; condition; disposition* §ippon chóshi; ippon-jóshi 一本調子 *unvarying (or monotonous) manner* §Chōshi ga íi. 調子がいい。 *I'm in good shape (physically).*

chōshin 長針 *the minute hand (on a clock)*

chōshínki 聴診器 *stethoscope* §chōshínki o muné ni ateru 聴診器を胸に当てる *put a stethoscope to the chest; listen with a stethoscope*

chósho 長所 *(one's) strong point; forte* §Watashi no chósho wa konki-zuyói kotó desu. 私の長所は根気強いことです。 *My strong point is my perseverance.*

chōshoku 朝食 *breakfast*

chōshū 聴衆 *audience*

chōtatsu 調達 *provision; supply*——**chōtatsu-suru** [*vt*] 調達する *provide; supply; raise (money)*

chōtei 朝廷 *dynasty; imperial court*

chōtei 調停 *mediation; arbitration* ❧chōtéi-an 調停案 *mediation plan*
——**chōtei-suru** [*vt*] 調停する *mediate; arbitrate*

chōten 頂点 *climax; peak; apex* ❧Bukka jōshō wa móhaya chōten ni tasshite iru. 物価上昇はもはや頂点に達している。*The rise in prices has already reached its peak.*

chōtsúgai 蝶番 *hinge*

chótto ちょっと *just; just a little; a little bit; a moment* ❧Chótto mátte kudasái. ちょっと待って下さい。*Just a moment, please.* ❧Chótto ukagaimásu ga... ちょっと伺いますが... *May I (just) ask——?* <*formal*>

chōwa 調和 *harmony* ——**chōwa-suru** [*vi*] 調和する *harmonize* ❧Iró to katachi ga chōwa-shite iru. 色と形が調和している。*The color and shape harmonize.*

chozóshitsu 貯蔵室 *storeroom* ❧wain chozóshitsu ワイン貯蔵室 *wine cellar*

chū 注 *annotation; (explanatory) note*

-chū (ni) ; -jū (ni) 〜中（に）*during; before the end of; in the course of* ❧kongetsu-chū ni 今月中に *during this month* ❧ni-san-nichi-jū ni 二、三日中に *in two or three days*

chúbu チューブ *tube* ❧jiténsha no chúbu 自転車のチューブ *bicycle tire tube*

chúchū [to] ちゅうちゅう（と）[*mimetic for a sucking, squeaking, chirping sound*] ❧Ákachan wa okásan no óppai o chúchu sutte iru. 赤ちゃんはお母さんのおっぱいをちゅうちゅう吸っている。*The baby is sucking at its mother's breast.* ❧Nezumi ga chúchū sawáide iru. 鼠がチューチュー騒いでいる。*Mice are squeaking noisily.*

chūdō 中道 *middle path* ❧chūdō séisaku 中道政策 *middle-of-the-road policy*

chúdoku 中毒 *poisoning; addiction* ❧shokuchúdoku 食中毒 *food poisoning* ❧terebi chúdoku テレビ中毒 *hooked on TV* ❧katsuji chúdoku ni náru 活字中毒になる *become a bookworm*

chūgákkō 中学校 *middle school; junior high school*

chūgákusei 中学生 *middle-school pupil*

[o-]chūgen （お）中元 *midsummer gift*

chúgi 忠義 *loyalty; devotion; fidelity* ❧Anáta wa dáre ni chúgi o shimeshimásu ka? あなたは誰に忠義を示しますか？*To whom do you show loyalty?*

Chúgoku 中国 *China* ——**Chūgokújin** 中国人 *a Chinese* ——**Chūgokugo** 中国語 *Chinese (language)*

Chūgoku-chíhō 中国地方 *the Chūgoku (central Japan) district; western Honshu*

chúi 注意 *attention; care* ❧chúi o hiku 注意を引く *draw attention (to)* ——**chúi-suru** [*vi/ vt*] 注意する *warn; caution; notify; pay attention* *(to)* 8Sénséi wa, jugyō-chū osháberi-shite iru séito o chūi-shita. 先生は、授業中お喋りしている生徒を注意した。 *The teacher cautioned students who were talking during class.*

chūi-buká·i [*adj* -búkaku nái; -búkakatta] 注意深い *(be) careful; cautious*——**chūi-búkaku** 注意深く *carefully* 8Watashi wa hoshi no ugokí o chūi-búkaku kansatsu-shite iru. 私は星の動きを注意深く観察している。 *I'm watching carefully the movement of the stars.*

chūjí-en 中耳炎 *middle-ear infection; (Tech) otitis media*

chūjitsu [na] 忠実（な） *faithful* 8Kono inú wa káinushi ni chūjitsu désu. この犬は飼い主に忠実です。 *This dog is faithful to its master.*——**chūjitsu ni** 忠実に *faithfully*

chūjun 中旬 *middle ten days of a month*

chūkai 仲介 *arbitration; mediation* 8chūkáisha 仲介者 *arbitrator; go-between* 8fudōsan toríhiki no chūkai o suru 不動産取り引きの仲介をする *act as an agent in a real estate deal*——**chūkai-suru** [*vt*] 仲介する *arbitrate; mediate*

chūkaku 中核 *kernel; core; center* 8Seiji no chūkaku wa kokumin no fukúshi no kōjō ni áru. 政治の中核は国民の福祉の向上にある。 *Promotion of the people's welfare is the core of government.*

chūkan [no] 中間（の） *middle; interim; intermediate* 8chūkan hōkoku 中間報告 *interim report* 8chūkan sénkyo 中間選挙 *off-year election; midterm election*

chūkei hōsō 中継放送 *relay broadcast (from the scene)*

Chūkíntō 中近東 *the Middle and Near East*

chūko 中古 *used; second-hand* 8chūkósha 中古車 *used car*

chūkō 昼光 *daylight*

chūkoku 忠告 *warning; advice*——**chūkoku-suru** [*vt*] 忠告する *warn; advise* 8Watashi wa shigoto no susumekata ni tsúite chūkoku-shita. 私は仕事の進め方について忠告した。 *I advised (him) concerning work procedure.*

chūmoku 注目 *attention*——**chūmoku-suru** [*vt*] 注目する *pay attention to; notice* 8Saikin, idéngaku de wa DNA no hataraki ni chūmoku-shite iru. 最近、遺伝学ではDNAの働きに注目している。 *Recently, attention in genetics has focused on the function of DNA.*

chūmon 注文 *order; requisition*——**chūmon-suru** 注文する *order; require* 8Hambágu sutéki o chūmon-shimáshita ga, máda desu ka? ハンバーグステーキを注文しましたが、まだですか？ *I ordered hamburger steak. Isn't it ready yet?*

chúnchun [to] ちゅんちゅん（と） *chirp-chirp* 8Kotori wa chúnchun to náku. 小鳥はちゅんちゅんと鳴く。 *Birds go "chirp-chirp."*

chūnen 中年 *middle age*

chūníkai 中二階 *mezzanine (floor)*

chūō 中央 *the center; median* 8chūō no 中央の *central* 8chūō bunritai 中央分離帯 *median strip (zone)* 🔹Chūō Jōhōkyoku 中央情報局 *(US) CIA (Central Intelligence Agency)*

chūritsu 中立 *neutrality* 🔹chūritsu chítai 中立地帯 *neutral zone* 🔹chūritsúkoku 中立国 *neutral power*🔹eisei chūritsúkoku 永世中立国 *permanent neutral country* ——**chūritsu no** 中立の *neutral* 🔹Tsúne ni chūritsu no táchiba o tóru kotó wa muzukashíi. 常に中立の立場をとることは難しい。 *It's difficult to always take a neutral position.*

chūryū káikyū 中流階級 *middle class*

chūsa 中佐 *Lieutenant Colonel (Army); Commander (Navy)*

chūsai 仲裁 *mediation; arbitration* 🔹rikon sóshō no chūsai ni háiru 離婚訴訟の仲裁に入る *mediate in a divorce case*

chū́sei 中世 *medieval times; the Middle Ages* 🔹chūsei Yōróppa 中世ヨーロッパ *medieval Europe*

chūsha 注射 *injection* 🔹chūsháki 注射器 *syringe* 🔹chūsha-bári 注射針 *hypodermic needle* 🔹hika chū́sha 皮下注射 *hypodermic (injection)* 🔹jōmyaku chū́sha 静脈注射 *intravenous injection*

chūsha 駐車 *parking* 🔹chūshajō 駐車場 *parking lot; parking space* 🔹yūryō chūshajō 有料駐車場 *paid parking lot* 🔹muryō chūshajō 無料駐車場 *free parking lot* 🔹chūsha íhan 駐車違反 *parking violation* ——**chūsha-suru** [vt] 駐車する *park (a vehicle)*

chūshaku 注釈 *(explanatory) notes; interpretation* 🔹"Genji Monogátari" wa tōji no jidai háikei ni tsúite no chūshaku náshi ni wa tadashíku rikai dekínai. 「源氏物語」は当時の時代背景についての注釈なしには正しく理解できない。 *One cannot understand the Tale of Genji without interpreting it against the background of the period in which it was written.*

chūshi 中止 *cessation; discontinuance* ——**chūshi-suru** [vt] 中止する *cease; stop; cancel* 🔹Berurin kōkyō-gákudan no Nihon tsúa wa Karáyan no kyūshi de chūshi-sareta. ベルリン交響楽団の日本ツアーはカラヤンの急死で中止された。 *The Japan tour of the Berlin Philharmonic Orchestra was canceled because of the sudden death of Karajan.*

chūshin 中心 *center* 🔹chūshin to suru 中心とする *make central*

chūshō 中小 *small-to-medium-sized* 🔹chūshō kígyō 中小企業 *small- and medium-sized enterprises; smaller businesses*

chūshō 中傷 *slander* 🔹chūshō gássen 中傷合戦 *a mud-slinging match*

chūshoku 昼食 *lunch; noon meal*

chūshōteki [na] 抽象的（な）*abstract* 🔹chūshōteki na é 抽象的な絵 *abstract painting* 🔹Káre no sekkyō wa ítsumo chūshōteki de yóku wakaránai. 彼の説教はいつも抽象的でよく分からない。 *His sermons are always so abstract I can't understand them.*

Chū́tō 中東 *Middle East*

chūto 中途 *halfway* ❀chūto hámpa 中途半端 *halfway; neither fish nor fowl; unfinished*

chūyu 注油 *lubrication (see also* **kyūyu***)*

chūzetsu 中絶 *interruption* ❀jinkō chūzetsu; ninshin chūzetsu 人工中絶；妊娠中絶 *surgical abortion*

D

da *[copula, plain form:* de wa *(or* ja) nai; datta] ❀Súmisu-san wa shitashíi tomodachi da. スミスさんは親しい友達だ。*Smith is a close friend (of mine).* <masc> *(see also* **desu***)*

dabudabu だぶだぶ *loose (-fitting); baggy* ❀Kono sétā wa dabudabu desu. このセーターはだぶだぶです。*This sweater's too baggy.*

dachō 駝鳥 *ostrich*

dága だが *but* ❀Ore wa karada wa chīsái. Dága ki wa ōkíi. 俺は身体は小さい。だが、気は大きい。*I may be small in stature, but I've got lots of spirit.* <masc>

dagáshi 駄菓子 *(cheap) sweets; candy*

dageki 打撃 *a blow; a setback; a strike* ❀Báburu ga hajíkete shōbai wa dageki o úketa. バブルが弾けて商売は打撃を受けた。*Business has taken a hit with the bursting of the (economic) bubble.*

dáha 打破 *breaking; defeat; crushing* ——**dáha-suru** [vt] 打破する *break down; overthrow* ❀taisei o dáha-suru 体制を打破する *overthrow the establishment* ❀furúi inshū o dáha-suru 古い因襲を打破する *break with old conventions*

dái 題 *title; subject; theme* ❀hón no dái 本の題 *title of a book*

dái 台 *table; stand*

dái- 第～ *No.-* ❀dai-ichi 第一 *number one* ❀dai-ichi nichiyőbi 第一日曜日 *the first Sunday (of the month)* ❀dai-niji sángyō 第二次産業 *secondary industry*

dái- 大～ *very; great* ❀dai-séikō 大成功 *a great success* ❀Dai-sánsei desu. 大賛成です。*I heartily approve.* ❀Aisukurímu ga dái-suki désu. アイスクリームが大好きです。*I like icecream very much.* ❀Watashi wa kímuchi no niói ga dáikirai desu. 私はキムチの臭いが大嫌いです。*I hate the smell of kimchi.*

-dái ～台 *[classifier for counting machines]* ❀Sono ié ni kuruma ga sán-dai mo áru. その家に車が三台もある。*That family has three cars.*

-dái ～代 *generation; age* ❀jűdai no hito 十代の人 *teenager* ❀onaji nendai no hitó 同じ年代の人 *a person of the same generation*

daibén 大便 *excrement; feces; stool*

daibu 大分 *rather; considerably; pretty much* ❀Sono kőji wa kansei máde ni daibu kakáru. その工事は完成までに大分かかる。*It'll take* *quite some time to complete that work.*

daibúbun 大部分 *the greater part; most* 🔸Shigoto no daibúbun ga súnda. 仕事の大部分が済んだ。 *Most of the work's done.*

daibutsu 大仏 *a giant Buddha image*

dáichi 大地 *the earth; Mother Earth*

daidái 橙 daidai *(a bitterorange)* 🔸daidai-iro 橙色 *deep orange (color)*

dáidai 代々 *generation after generation; from generation to generation* 🔸senzo dáidai no haka 先祖代々の墓 *ancestral grave* 🔸Kono tochi wa dáidai uketsugárete kita. この土地は代々受け継がれてきた。 *This land has been handed down from generation to generation.*

daidokoro 台所 *kitchen*

daigaku 大学 *university; college* 🔸daigakúsei 大学生 *college (or university) student* 🔸daigakúin 大学院 *graduate school* 🔸daigakuínsei 大学院生 *graduate student* 🔸tanki dáigaku 短期大学 *junior college* 🔸kokuritsu dáigaku 国立大学 *national university* 🔸shiritsu dáigaku 私立大学 *private university*

daigíshi 代議士 *member of the House of Representatives (J)*

daihon 台本 *play script; libretto; scenario*

daihyō 代表 *representation; representative* 🔸daihyōdan 代表団 *delegation* ——**daihyō-suru** [vt] 代表する *represent; act on behalf of* 🔸Watashi wa kyō, kaisha o daihyō-shite kono ba ni shusseki-shite orimásu. 私は今日、会社を代表してこの場に出席しております。 *I am attending today as a representative of my company* <formal>

daijí [na] 大事（な）*important; valuable* 🔸daijí ni suru 大事にする *prize; value; cherish; esteem* 🔸O-daijí ni! お大事に！ *Take care of yourself (her / him).*

dáijin 大臣 *cabinet minister* 🔸sōri dáijin 総理大臣 *prime minister* 🔸mombu dáijin 文部大臣 *minister of education*

daijóbu [na] 大丈夫（な）*all right; fine; OK* 🔸"Dóko ka guai ga warúi no desu ka?" "Íe, daijóbu desu." 「どこか具合が悪いのですか？」「いいえ、大丈夫です。」 *"Do you feel bad?" "No, I'm OK."*

dáika 代価 *price*

daikan 大寒 *coldest season of the year; heart of winter*

daikígyō 大企業 *big business*

daikin 代金 *price* 🔸daikin o haráu 代金を払う *pay the price*

daikon 大根 *(Japanese) radish* 🔸daikon yákusha 大根役者 *an unskilled actor*

dáiku 大工 *carpenter* 🔸funadáiku 船大工 *ship builder* 🔸miyadáiku 宮大工 *temple carpenter*

daimei 題名 *title*

daiméishi 代名詞 *pronoun*

daimyō 大名 *daimyo; feudal lord*

dainashi 台無し *ruination* 🔸dainashi ni suru 台無しにする *ruin; spoil*

§dainashi ni náru 台無しになる *be ruined; be spoiled*

dainingu-kítchin ダイニングキッチン *eat-in kitchen*

dainō 大脳 *cerebrum*

dairi 代理 *proxy; representation; deputy* §Watashi ga kesseki no bái wa dairi o tatemásu. 私が欠席の場合は代理を立てます。*When I cannot attend I will send a proxy.* <*formal*>

dairíseki 大理石 *marble*

dairíten 代理店 *agency* §ryokō dairíten 旅行代理店 *travel agency* §hoken dairíten 保険代理店 *insurance agency*

dái-rokkan 第六感 *the sixth sense*

daisáigai 大災害 *catastrophe*

daiséidō 大聖堂 *cathedral*

daisha 台車 *cart; pushcart*

daishō 代償 *compensation* §daishō o haráu 代償を払う *pay compensation*

daisū(gaku) 代数（学） *algebra*

daitai 大体 *in general; roughly; substantially* §Senséi no hanashí wa daitai wakátta. 先生の話は大体分かった。*I understood almost everything the teacher said.*

daitán 大胆 *daring; boldness* ——**daitán na** 大胆な *bold; courageous; daring* §daitán na dezáin 大胆なデザイン *a bold design* §daitán na hassō 大胆な発想 *a daring idea*

daitásū 大多数 *majority*

daitốryō 大統領 *president (of a country)*

dáiya ダイヤ *(train) schedule* §daiya káitei ダイヤ改訂 *a schedule change*

daizu 大豆 *soybean*

dajare 駄洒落 *joking; a pun; a gag*

dakai 打開 *breakthrough; development* ——**dakai-suru** [*vt*] *make a breakthrough; break* §nankan o dakai-suru 難関を打開する *break a deadlock*

dákara だから *so; therefore* [*sentence connective*] §Imōtó wa Amerika no íkita Eigo ga benkyō-shitái desu. Dákara Amerika e ryūgaku-shimásu. 妹はアメリカの生きた英語が勉強したいです。だからアメリカへ留学します。*My younger sister wants to learn English the way it's really spoken in America, so she's going to study in America.*

daké だけ *only; merely* §Yūhan wa yasai dáke desu. 夕飯は野菜だけで。*There's only vegetables for supper.*

dakiá·u [*vi* dakiawánai; dakiátta] 抱き合う *embrace*

dakiokós·u [*vt* dakiokosánai; dakiokóshita] 抱き起こす *lift (someone) up in (one's) arms*

dakishimé·ru [*vt* dakishiménai; dakishímeta] 抱き締める *hug; embrace; clasp (someone) in (one's) arms*

dakkai 脱会 *withdrawal from an organization; defection; apostasy* ——
   dakkai-suru [vt] 脱会する *leave an organization; apostatize*

dákko 抱っこ *carrying* ——**dákko-suru** [vi] 抱っこする *carry in one's
   arms* ❀ akambō o dákko-suru 赤ん坊を抱っこする *carry a baby in
   one's arms*

dakkyū 脱臼 *dislocation (med)* ❀ kokansetsu dákkyū 股関節脱臼
   dislocation of hip joint ——**dakkyū-suru** [vi] 脱臼する *be dislocated*

dak·u [vt dakanai; daita] 抱く *carry (a person); hold (in the arms)*

dakuon 濁音 *voiced sound (Gram)*

dakyō 妥協 *a compromise* ❀ dakyōan 妥協案 *a compromise plan* ——
   dakyō-suru [vt] 妥協する *compromise*

-dama 〜玉 *-coin* ❀ jūen-dama 十円玉 *a ten-yen coin*

damár·u [vi damaránai; damátta] 黙る *be quiet; be silent; shut up*
   ❀ Damátte! (*or* Damáre!) 黙って！（黙れ！）*Shut up!* <masc>
   ❀ Damari nasai! 黙りなさい！*Be quiet!* ——**damátte** 黙って
   silently; without speaking ❀ Damátte senséi no hanashí o kikinasái. 黙
   って先生の話を聞きなさい。*Be quiet and listen to the teacher.*

damás·u [vt damasánai; damáshita] 騙す *cheat; trick; deceive* ❀ Ōkami
   wa hahaoya ni bákete naná-hiki no koyagi o damáshita. 狼は母親に化
   けて七匹の子山羊を騙した。*The wolf disguised itself as their mother
   and tricked the seven little goats.*

dambō 暖房 *heating* ❀ Kono heyá wa dambō ga kikanai. この部屋は暖
   房が利かない。*This room doesn't have any heat. (or There is no heat
   in this room.)*

dambōrú-bako 段ボール箱 *cardboard box*

damé [na] 駄目（な）*no good; not good; useless* ❀ damé na keikaku 駄
   目な計画 *a useless plan* ❀ Iiwake shité mo damé da. 言い訳しては
   駄目だ。*It's no good making excuses.* <masc> —— **damé ni naru** 駄
   目になる *be ruined; become useless* ❀ Sentákki ga damé ni natta. 洗
   濯機が駄目になった。*The washing machine broke down.*

dampukā ダンプカー *dump truck*

dán 段 *step, rung; stage; column (of a text); act (of a play); grade; rank;
   belt* ❀ ichiban shita no dán 一番下の段 *tthe bottom step* ❀ shimbun
   no dán 新聞の段 ❀ gedan 下段 *lower berth*

dan'atsu 弾圧 *suppression* ❀ Seijiteki dan'atsu ni yori, bōmei-suru hitó
   ga fúete iru. 政治的弾圧により、亡命する人が増えている。
   *Because of political pressure, the number of people defecting has
   increased.*

danchi 団地 *housing development*

dandán [to] 段々（と）*gradually*

dandan-bátake 段々畑 *terraced fields*

dangai 弾劾 *impeachment* ——**dangai-suru** [vt] 弾劾する *impeach*
   ❀ saibánkan o dangai-suru 裁判官を弾劾する *impeach a judge*

dangan 弾丸 *bullet; projectile*

dangen 断言 *affirmation; assertion* ——**dangen-suru** [*vt*] 断言する *affirm; assert*

dango 団子 *dumpling; rice cake*

daní ダニ *mite; tick*

danjiki 断食 *fasting* ——**danjiki-suru** [*vi*] 断食する *fast; observe a fast*

dánjite 断じて (+ neg.) *absolutely (not)* ⑧Aitsu o dánjite yurusánai zo! あいつを断じて許さないぞ！ *I absolutely will not forgive him!* <*masc*> ⑧Dánjite shuchō o kaenákatta wa! 断じて主張を変えなかったわ！ *I absolutely refused to change my statement!* <*fem*>

dánjo 男女 *male and female* ⑧danjo dōken-shúgi 男女同権主義 *feminism* ⑧danjo kyōgaku 男女共学 *coeducation* ⑧dánjo byōdō 男女平等 *equality of the sexes*

dankai 段階 *grade; rank; step; stage; phase*

danketsu 団結 *unity; solidarity* ——**danketsu-suru** [*vi*] 団結する *unite; combine; band together*

dánko 団固 *firm resolve* ⑧dánko to shite 断固として *determinedly; emphatically*

dankō 団交 *collective bargaining* ⑧Keiei-gawa to kumiai-gawa tó de bēsuáppu no dankō o mótta. 経営側と組合側とでベースアップの団交を持った。 *Labor and management held a collective bargaining session on the wage increase issue.*

danna 旦那 *a patron; master* ⑧danna-sáma 旦那様 *(another's) husband*

danraku 段落 *paragraph; conclusion* ⑧ichi-dánraku tsukéru 一段落つける *settle (a matter) for now* ⑧Danraku no hajime wa ichíji ságete kakihajimemashō. 段落の初めは一字下げて書き始めましょう。 *At the beginning of a (new) paragraph, indent one character.*

dánro 暖炉 *fireplace*

danryoku 弾力 *elasticity; spring; resilience; flexibility* ⑧danryoku no nái wagomu 弾力のない輪ゴム *a rubber band with no elasticity* ——**danryokuteki [na]** 弾力的（な）*flexible* ⑧danryokuteki un'yō 弾力的運用 *flexible application (of a rule)*

dansei 男性 *man; male* ——**danseiteki [na]** 男性的（な）*masculine* ⑧danseiteki na seikaku 男性的な性格 *a masculine character (or personality)*

dánshaku 男爵 *baron*

dánshi 男子 *boy; man; gentleman*

danshō 談笑 *a chat* ——**danshō-suru** [*vi*] 談笑する *chat; talk freely*

danshō 男娼 *male prostitute*

dansui 断水 *cutting off of water; water stoppage* ——**dansui-suru** [*vi*] 断水する *cut the water supply*

dantai 団体 *group; organization* §dantai yakúin 団体役員 *an official of an organization* §seiji dántai 政治団体 *political organization*

danwa 談話 *discourse; conversation* ——**danwa-suru** [*vi*] 談話する *discourse; talk; converse*

danzen [to] 断然（と）*resolutely; decisively; absolutely; decidedly* §Watashi wa anáta no teian ní wa danzen to hantai-shimásu. 私はあなたの提案には断然と反対します。*I am decidedly against your proposal.* §Kono hón no hố ga danzen omoshirói yo! この本の方が断然面白いよ！*This book is definitely more interesting!*

danzetsu 断絶 *gap; rupture; rift; discontinuation* §kokkō danzetsu 国交断絶 *a rift in diplomatic relations* §óyako danzetsu 親子断絶 *parent-child (or generation) gap* ——**danzetsu-suru** [*vi*] 断絶する *become extinct; be severed; be cut off; be discontinued*

dappi 脱皮 *casting off skin (of reptiles); (Biol) ecdysis* ——**dappi-suru** [*vi*] 脱皮する *cast off skin (of reptiles); shed outer shell (of insects)*

dáradara [to] だらだら（と）*dripping; rambling; dragging on* §Kōshō wa dáradara nagabíite iru. 交渉はだらだら長引いている。*The negotiations are dragging on and on.*

-dárake [no] 〜だらけ（の）*covered with; full of* §doro-dárake 泥だらけ *covered with mud* §nukeana-dárake no hōritsu 抜け穴だらけの法律 *a law (which is) full of loopholes*

daraku 堕落 *degradation; degeneration; fall* ——**daraku-suru** [*vi*] 堕落する *degenerate; fall apart* §darakɯ-shita seikatsu 堕落した生活 *a life of degradation*

darashiná·i [*adj* darashináku nái; darashinákatta] だらしない *sloppy; slovenly* §darashinái seikaku だらしない性格 *a slovenly nature* §Káre no kikonashi wa ítsumo darashinái. 彼の着こなしはいつもだらしない。*He always dresses sloppily.*

dáre 誰 *who?* §Anó hito wa dáre desu ka? あの人は誰ですか？*Who is that person?*

dáre de mo 誰でも *anyone; anyone at all* §Sore wa dáre de mo dekíru yo! それは誰でもできるよ！*Anyone can do that!*

dáre ka 誰か *someone* §Koko ni Eigo no wakáru hito wa dáre ka imasén ka? ここに英語の分かる人は誰かいませんか？*Is there someone here who speaks English?*

dare mo [*with neg*] 誰も *no one* §Dare mo inákatta. 誰もいなかった。*There was no one there.*

darố だろう [*presumptive form of* **da** <*masc*>] §Mītingu wa ashita darố? ミーティングは明日だろう？*The meeting's tomorrow, isn't it?*

darú·i [*adj* dáruku nái; dárukatta] だるい *(be) sluggish; tired* §Késa kara karada ga darúi. 今朝から身体がだるい。*I've felt tired since this morning.*

Daruma 達磨 *Daruma doll (representing Bodhidharma, the founder of Zen*

Buddhism)

dásha 打者 *(baseball) batter*

dashí 出し *soup stock; broth*   §súpu no dashí o tóru スープの出しを取る *make stock for soup*

dashia·u [vt dashiawanai; dashiatta] 出し合う *pool; go together to buy*   §chié o dashiau 知恵を出し合う *pool (people's) wisdom*

dashímono 出し物 *theater program*

dasoku 蛇足 *(something) unnecessary; redundancy; superfluity*

dassen 脱線 *digression*   §Ano senséi no hanashí wa ítsumo dassen ga ói. あの先生の話はいつも脱線が多い。 *That professor's lectures are always full of digressions.* ——**dassen-suru** [vi] 脱線する *digress; go off the track; derail*   §Ressha ga dassen-shita. 列車が脱線した。 *The train derailed.*

dassui 脱水 *draining water (cycle on a washing machine)*   §dassúi-ki 脱水機 *spin-dryer (for washing machine)* ——**dassui-suru** [vt] 脱水する *dehydrate; evaporate*

dassō 脱走 *an escape* ——**dassō-suru** [vt] 脱走する *run away from; defect*   §keimúsho o dassō-suru 刑務所を脱走する *escape from prison*

dás·u [vt dasánai; dáshita] 出す *put out; pay (money); mail (a letter)*   §chié o dásu 知恵を出す *show wisdom*   §o-kane o dásu お金を出す *pay money*   §néko o sóto ni dásu 猫を外に出す *put out the cat*   §tegami o dásu 手紙を出す *mail a letter*

datai 堕胎 *abortion* ——**datai-suru** [vt] 堕胎する *abort*

datchō 脱腸 *hernia*

-date 〜建て *-story*   §nikai-date no ié 二階建ての家 *a two-story house*   §ikko-date no ié 一戸建ての家 *detached house; independent house*

datō [na] 妥当（な）*proper; right; appropriate; reasonable*   §Datō na kingaku de keiyaku ga seiritsu-shita. 妥当な金額で契約が成立した。 *The contract was signed at a reasonable figure.*

datsugoku 脱獄 *prison break* ——**datsugoku-suru** [vt] 脱獄する *break out of prison*

datsuraku 脱落 *omission; desertion*   §kókó datsurákusha 高校脱落者 *a highschool dropout* ——**datsuraku-suru** [vi] 脱落する *be omitted; be lacking (in); fall out; drop out (of school)*   §Káre wa kaisha no shusse kōsu kara datsuraku-shita. 彼は会社の出世コースから脱落した。 *He was passed over for promotion at his company.*

datsuzei 脱税 *tax evasion*   §Datsuzei to setsuzei wa chigaimásu. 脱税と節税は違います。 *Tax evasion and tax saving are different.*

dátta [*past form of* **da**]

dáttara [*conditional form of* **da**] (*see also* **-tara**)

dátte だって〜 *But...*   §Dátte shō ga nái ja nái. だって、しょうがないじゃない。 *But, it can't be helped, can it?*

datte だって *you (or they) say* 🔸Shiranái n datte! 知らないんだって。 *You mean (to say) you don't know!?*

dattō 脱党 *defection from a political party; leaving a political party* —— **dattō-suru** [vt] 脱党する *defect from (or leave) a political party* 🔸Kisei séitō o dattō-shite shíntō o kessei-shita. 既成政党を脱党して新党を結成した。 *They pulled out of the established political parties and formed a new party.*

de で *by; by means of* [particle: means *or* instrument marker] 🔸Hasamí de kamí o kítta. 鋏で紙を切った。 *I cut the paper with scissors.* 🔸Jiténsha de gakkō ni kayoimásu. 自転車で学校に通います。 *I commute to school by bicycle.*

de で *at; in* [particle: location marker] 🔸Sū́pā de kaimono o shimásu. スーパーで買い物をします。 *I shop at the supermarket.* 🔸Shitsunai pū́ru de oyogimásu. 室内プールで泳ぎます。 *I swim in an indoor pool.*

de で *with; because of* [particle: reason *or* cause marker] 🔸Musumé wa kaze de gakkō o yasúnde imásu. 娘は風邪で学校を休んでいます。 *My daughter is staying home from school with a cold.*

de で [-te *form of* **desu**] 🔸Musuko wa génki de, itazura-bákari shite imásu. 息子は元気で、悪戯ばかりしています。 *My son is high-spirited and is always getting into mischief.*

deai 出会い *an encounter; a meeting* 🔸omoigakenái deai 思いがけない出会い *a chance (or unexpected) encounter*

de áru である [literary form of **desu**] 🔸"Wagahai wa néko de áru." 「我が輩は猫である」 *I Am a Cat (title of a novel by Natsume Sōseki)*

deá·u [vi deawánai; deátta] 出会う *meet with; happen to meet; encounter* 🔸Saisho ni kimi to deátta no wa ítsu dakké? 最初に君と会ったのはいつだっけ？ *When was it I first met you? <masc>* 🔸Osana-tómodachi no Makoto-kun ni gūzen deátta wa. 幼友達の誠くんに偶然出会ったわ。 *I unexpectedly ran into my childhood friend, Makoto. <fem>*

debán 出番 *one's turn; shift; one's time (to go on stage)* 🔸Komátte iru hitó o míru to watashi no debán ga hajimaru. 困っている人を見ると私の出番が始まる。 *When I see someone in trouble I feel it's up to me to do something.*

débeso 出臍 *protruding navel* 🔸Omáe no káchan debeso! お前の母ちゃん出臍！ *Your mother's belly button sticks out! (children's taunt, usually chanted in a sing-song fashion)*

débu でぶ *fat person*

de gozaimásu でございます [humble form of **desu**] 🔸Watashi wa Tanaka de gozaimásu. 私は田中でございます。 *I am Tanaka. <formal>*

déguchi 出口 *exit*

de irasshaimásu でいらっしゃいます [*exalted form of* **desu**)
  §Mayúzumi-san wa Ningen Kókuhō de irasshaimásu. 黛さんは人間国宝でいらっしゃいます。 *Mr. Mayuzumi is a Living National Treasure.* <*formal*>

déiri 出入り *going in and out; frequent; regular* §deiri gyósha 出入り業者 *a regular client* ——**déiri-suru** [*vt*] 出入りする *go in and out; frequent* §Tanaka-kun wa saikin ore no uchí ni chókuchoku déiri-suru. 田中君は最近、俺の家にちょくちょく出入りする。 *These days Tanaka is in and out of my place a lot.* <*masc*>

deká·i [*adj* dékaku nái; dékakatta] でかい *huge; great; big* <*masc*>
  §Anó hito wa karada ga dekái. あの人は身体がでかい。 *He's big.*
  §Aitsu wa táido ga dekái. あいつは態度がでかい。 *He's conceited.*

dekake·ru [*vi* dekakenai; dekaketa] 出かける *go out (from one's home); leave* §Shūmatsu wa dókoka ni dekakemásu ka? 週末はどこかに出かけますか？ *Are you going somewhere on the weekend?* §Dóchira e dekakeraremásu ka? どちらへ出かけられますか？ *Where are you going?* <*formal*>

dekasegi 出稼ぎ *working away from home* §Nōka no hitó wa nōkánki ni wa tokai e dekasegi ni iku. 農家の人は農閑期には都会へ出稼ぎに行く。 *In the slack season, farmers go to the city to work.*

dekiagar·u [*vi* dekiagaranai; dekiagatta] 出来上がる *be completed; be finished* §Sakuhin ga dekiagatta. 作品が出来上がった。 *The novel (or work) is finished.*

dekiai [no] 出来合い（の） *ready-to-wear* §dekiai no sútsu 出来合いのスーツ *a ready-made suit*

dekígoto 出来事 *happening; event*

dekimóno 出来物 *a boil; a rash; a sore*

dekí·ru [*vi* dekínai; dekíta] 出来る *be able; can; be done; be ready* §unten ga dekíru 運転が出来る *be able to drive* §Shokuji ga dékita. 食事が出来た。 *Dinner's ready.* §Nihongo ga dekimásu ka? 日本語が出来ますか？ *Can you speak Japanese?* ——**kotó ga dekíru** ことが出来る *be able to; can* §Nihongo o yómu kotó ga dekimásu ka? 日本語を読むことが出来ますか？ *Can you read Japanese?*

dekiru dake 出来るだけ *if possible; as ... as possible* §Dekiru dake no kotó wa shitái. 出来るだけのことはしたい。 *I want to do as much (or as many things) as possible.*

dekitate [no] 出来立て(の) *freshly made; just finished*

dekoboko でこぼこ；凸凹 *uneven; rough; bumpy* §dekobokó-michi でこぼこ道 *a bumpy road*

dekunóbō 木偶の坊 *blockhead; dunce*

demae 出前 *(lunch / dinner) delivery service* §sóba no demae 蕎麦の出前 *soba delivery* §O-híru ni demae o torimashő. お昼に出前をとりましょう。 *Let's have lunch delivered (or brought in).*

démo でも *but* ❀Watashi wa kaoiro ga warúi. Démo génki nan desu yó. 私は顔色が悪い。でも、元気なんですよ。*I look sickly. But I'm healthy.*

-démo 〜でも *even* [*particle, emphatic*]; *for instance* ❀Muzukáshiku nái. Kodomo ni démo dekíru. 難しくない。子供にでも出来る。*It isn't difficult. Even a child can do it.*

démpa 電波 *radio wave*

dempō 電報 *telegram; cable* ❀keichō dempō 慶弔電報 *a telegram of congratulation or condolence*

dempyō 伝票 *tab; bill* ❀Dempyō o o-negai shimásu. 伝票をお願いします。*My bill, please? (or May I have my bill?)*

demukae 出迎え *going to meet (someone); reception* ❀Ashita, kūkō ni tomodachi o demukae ni ikimásu. 明日、空港に友達を出迎えに行きます。*Tomorrow, I'm going to the airport to meet a friend.*

demukae·ru [*vt* demukaenai; demukaeta] 出迎える *go to meet (someone)* ❀Tōkyō-eki no inaka kara kúru ryōshin o demukaeta. 東京駅で田舎から来る両親を出迎えた。*I went to Tokyo Station to meet my parents who are arriving from the country.*

den'atsu 電圧 *voltage* ❀kō-dén'atsu 高電圧 *high voltage*

dénchi 電池 *battery* ❀arukari dénchi アルカリ電池 *an alkali battery* ❀kan-dénchi 乾電池 *a dry battery* ❀kámera no dénchi カメラの電池 *a camera battery*

dendō 伝道 *missionary work; evangelism* ❀dendōsha 伝道者 *evangelist* ❀dendō shūkai 伝道集会 *evangelistic service (meeting)* ——**dendō-suru** [*vt*] 伝道する *engage in missionary work; evangelize*

den'en 田園 *country; rural district* ❀den'en chítai 田園地帯 *rural district* ❀den'en fūkei 田園風景 *a pastoral scene*

denki 伝記 *biography*

dénki 電気 *electricity* ❀denki séihin 電気製品 *electrical appliance* ❀denki sōjíki 電気掃除機 *electric vacuum cleaner* ❀dénki o tsúkeru 電気をつける *turn on a light* ❀Dénki ga tsúite iru. 電気がついている。*The light is on.*

denkyū 電球 *light bulb*

denrai 伝来 *introduction; transmission* ——**denrai-suru** [*vi*] 伝来する *be handed down; be transmitted; be introduced* ❀Jū wa Porutogaru kara denrai-shimáshita. 銃はポルトガルから伝来しました。*Guns were introduced (to Japan) from Portugal.*

densembyō 伝染病 *contagious disease; epidemic*

densen 電線 *electric line; electric wire; electric cord* ❀kōatsu dénsen 高圧電線 *high-voltage wire*

densetsu 伝説 *legend; tradition*

densha 電車 *(electric-powered) train* ❀densháchin 電車賃 *train fare*

dénshi 電子 *electron* ❀denshi rénji 電子レンジ *microwave oven*

§denshi sángyō 電子産業 *electronics industry*

dentō 伝統 *tradition; convention* §dentō búnka 伝統文化 *traditional culture* §dentō kṓgei 伝統工芸 *traditional arts and crafts* §dentō o mamóru 伝統を守る *preserve tradition*

dentō 電灯 *electric light*

denwa 電話 *telephone* §denwachō 電話帳 *telephone directory* §denwa kōkánshu 電話交換手 *telephone operator* §kōshū dénwa 公衆電話 *public telephone* §denwa o kakéru 電話をかける *(to) telephone; make a telephone call* ——**denwa-suru** [*vi*] 電話する *telephone* §Áto de denwa-shimásu. 後で電話します。 *I'll call you later.*

depáto デパート *department store*

déppa 出っ歯 *protruding teeth; bucktooth*

deppar·u 出っ張る *stick out; protrude* §Watashi wa chūnen ni nátte hará ga deppatte kíta. 私は中年になって腹が出っ張ってきた。*Since I've reached middle age I've developed something of a belly.*

dé·ru [*vi* dénai; déta] 出る *go out; leave; graduate; answer (the telephone)* §Watashi wa shṓgo ni uchi o déta. 私は正午に家を出た。*I left home at noon.* §Watashi wa kyónen daigaku o déta. 私は去年大学を出た。*I graduated from the university last year.* §Dáre ka denwa ni déte kudasái. 誰か電話に出て下さい。*Someone answer the phone, please.*

deshabár·u [*vi* deshabaránai; deshabátta] 出しゃばる *be pushy; meddle* §Deshabari-sugi wa méiwaku na tokí mo áru. 出しゃばりすぎは迷惑な時もある。*If one pushes too much, he can make a nuisance of himself.*

deshí 弟子 *disciple; pupil; apprentice* §shíshō to deshí 師匠と弟子 *master and disciple* §deshi-iri-suru 弟子入りする *become an apprentice*

déshita [*past form of* **desu**] でした §Kánojo wa rúsu déshita. 彼女は留守でした。*She wasn't home.*

deshṓ [*presumptive form of* **desu**] でしょう *probably* §Ano híto wa kóndo no mītingu ní wa shusseki-dekíru deshṓ. あの人は今度のミーティングには出席できるでしょう。*She probably will be able to attend the next meeting.*

desu [*copula, polite form: de wa (or ja) nai; deshita*] です [*The copula is used primarily in the sentence pattern,* N wa N desu: **Kore wa hon desu.** これは本です。*This is a book.*]

désu kara [*polite form of* **dákara**] ですから *therefore; so*

detarame [*na*] 出鱈目 *(na) nonsense; senseless* §Káre wa detarame bákari iu. 彼はでたらめばかり言う。*He talks nothing but nonsense.* ——**detarame** [*ni* 出鱈目（に）*at random; indiscriminately; haphazardly*] §Kono é wa detarame ni káite aru. この絵はでたらめ

に描いてある。 *This picture is haphazardly drawn.*

déte kuru [*vi* -konai; -kita] 出て来る *come out* ❊Ókusan ga génkan kara déte kita. 奥さんが玄関から出て来た。 *The woman come out of the front door.*

Dé wa...; Ja... では〜；じゃ〜 *Well then...* ❊Ja, matá! じゃ、又！ *Well, I'll see ya!* ❊Dé wa kyō wa dai-yónka kara benkyō o hajimemashō. では今日は第四課から勉強を始めましょう。 *Today we'll begin our study with Lesson Four.*

dé wa (or **ja**) **arimasén** [*neg polite form of* **desu**] では(or じゃ) ありません ❊Watashi wa Nihonjín de wa arimasén. 私は日本人ではありません。 *I'm not Japanese.*

de [wa] nai; ja nai [*neg form of* **da**] で（は）ない；じゃない

de [wa] nákatta; ja nákatta [*neg past form of* **da**] で（は）なかった；じゃなかった

dó 銅 *copper*

dó 胴 *torso*

dó? どう？ *how?* ❊Karada no guai wa dó desu ka? 身体の具合はどうですか？ *How are you? (lit: How's your condition?)* ❊Nyūyóku no ténki wa dó desu ka? ニューヨークの天気はどうですか？ *What's the weather like in New York?*

dōban 銅版 *copperplate* ❊dōban hánga 銅版画 *an engraving*

dobu 溝；どぶ *ditch; gutter* ❊dobu-nézumi 溝鼠 *gutter rat*

dobún to どぶんと *with a splash* ❊Kawá ni dobún to tobikónda. 川にどぶんと飛び込んだ。 *He jumped into the river with a splash.*

dōbutsu 動物 *animal* ❊honyū dōbutsu 哺乳動物 *a mammal*

dōbutsúgaku 動物学 *zoology*

dóchira どちら *which; which direction; which way; which alternative?* ❊Kono iró to sono iró to dóchira ga o-konomi désu ka? この色とその色とどちらがお好みですか？ *Which of these two colors do you like?* <*formal*>—**dóchira mo** どちらも *both* [with aff]; *neither* [with neg] ❊Anáta ní wa shíro mo kúro mo dóchira mo niáu. あなたには白も黒もどちらも似合う！ *Both white and black look good on you.*

dōdō to shita 堂々とした *magnificent; stately; splendid; admirable* ❊Anó hito wa ítsumo dōdō to shita táido de tanomoshíi. あの人はいつも堂々とした態度で頼もしい。 *You can depend on her; she does everything in grand form.*

dōfū-suru [*vt*] 同封する *enclose* ❊Kogítte o dōfū-shimásu. 小切手を同封します。 *I am enclosing a check.*

dógi 動議 *a motion (in parliamentary procedure); proposal*

dógi 道義 *public morals; morality*

dōgigo 同義語 *synonym*

dōgú 道具 *tool; instrument; furniture; equipment; gear* ❊daiku dógu 大工道具 *carpentry tools* ❊benkyō dógu 勉強道具 *study equipment*

dōhai 同輩 *a peer; an equal*

dōi 同意 *consensus; agreement; consent* ❧dōi o motoméru 同意を求める *seek agreement*

Dō itashimáshite. どういたしまして。 *Don't mention it!; Think nothing of it!; Not at all!*

Dóitsu ドイツ *Germany* ——**Doitsu-go** ドイツ語 *German (language)* ——**Doitsújin** ドイツ人 *a German*

dō iu どういう *what sort of?; what?* ❧Kono kotobá wa dō iu ími desu ka? この言葉はどういう意味ですか? *What is the meaning of this word?*

dō iu fū ni? どういう風に? *how?; in what way?; in what manner?* ❧Wáffuru wa dō iu fū ni tsukúttara oishíi desu ka? ワッフルはどういう風に作ったらおいしいですか? *How do you make delicious waffles?*

dóji どじ *blunder; goof* ❧Dóji o funda! どじを踏んだ。 *I goofed!*

dōji [ni] 同時（に）*at the same time; simultaneously* ❧dōji tsūyaku 同時通訳 *simultaneous interpretation* ❧Dáre ka ga génkan o nókku-surú no to dōji ni denwa ga natta. 誰かが玄関をノックするのと同時に電話が鳴った。 *The telephone rang at the same time that someone knocked on the front door.*

dōjídai no 同時代の *contemporary; of the same period* ❧dōjídai no sakka 同時代の作家 *contemporary writers*

dojin 土人 *native; aborigine*

dōjitsu 同日 *the same day* ❧Háwai ni wa jísa no kankei de dōjitsu no ása tōchaku-suru. ハワイには時差の関係で同日の朝到着する。 *Because of the time difference I arrive in Hawaii on the morning of the same day.*

dojō 泥鰌 *loach (fish)* ❧dojō-nábe どじょう鍋 *stewed loaches*

dōjō 道場 *training place (for martial arts); gym; hall* ❧karate dōjō 空手道場 *karate gym* ❧zazen dōjō 座禅道場 *Zen meditation hall*

dōjō 同情 *sympathy* ——**dōjō-suru** [vi] 同情する *sympathize (with)* ❧Kánojo wa káre no tsurai táchiba ni dōjō-shite iru. 彼女は彼の辛い立場に同情している。 *She sympathizes with him in his predicament.*

dóka 銅貨 *copper coin*

dóka どうか *please; somehow* ❧Dóka tasukéte kudasái. どうか助けて下さい。 *Please help me.*

dōkan 同感 *same feeling; agreement* ❧Watashi mo dōkan desu. 私も同感です。 *I feel that way too. (or I also agree.)*

Dō ka shimáshita ka? どうかしましたか? *What's the matter?; What happened?*

dōké 道化 *buffoonery; antics* ❧dōkemono 道化者 *a clown*

dōken 同権 *equal rights* ❧danjo dōken 男女同権 *equal rights for men and women*

dōki 動機 *motivation; motive; incentive* ❀satsujin no dōki 殺人の動機 *motive for murder*

dókidoki どきどき *palpitating; nervous; excited* ——**dókidoki-suru** [*vi*] どきどきする *palpitate; be nervous; be excited*

dokín to どきんと *with a start; with a jolt*

dokkóisho どっこいしょ [*exclamation, when exerting oneself physically*]

dóko どこ *where?* ❀Éki wa dóko desu ka. 駅はどこですか。*Where is the station?* ❀Ginkō wa dóko ni arimásu ka? 銀行はどこにあります か。*Where is there a bank?* ——**doko ni mo** [with neg.] どこにも *nowhere* ❀Mémo wa doko ni mo mitsukaranai. メモはどこにも見つ からない。*I can't find the memo anywhere.* ——**doko mo kámo** どこ もかも *everywhere* ❀Gōruden uíku wa doko mo kámo hito de ippai desu. ゴールデンウイークはどこもかも人でいっぱいです。 *During Golden Week there are crowds everywhere.*

dókoka どこか *somewhere* ❀Chikái uchi ni dókoka kúki no oishii tokoró ni ikitái. 近いうちにどこか空気のおいしいところに行きた い。*Sometime soon I'd like to go somewhere where the air is fresh and clean.*

-dókoro ka 〜どころか *anything but ...* ❀Kyónen no natsú wa atsúi dókoro ka samúi hi ga tsuzuita. 去年の夏は暑いどころか寒い日が続 いた。*Summer last year was anything but hot; there was a spell of cold days.*

dóko-soko どこそこ *such-and-such a place*

dōkō-suru [*vi*] 同行する *accompany; go together* ❀Otto no kaigai shútchō ni tsúma ga dōkō-shita. 夫の海外出張に妻が同行した。*The wife accompanied her husband on his overseas business trip.*

dokú 毒 *poison* ❀doku hebi 毒蛇 *poisonous snake* ❀dokuyaku 毒薬 *poisonous drug; poison* ——**doku [no]** 毒の *toxic; poisonous*

dok·u [*vi* dokanai; doita] 退く *move; get out of the way; step aside; stand back* ❀Sumimasén, soko o doite kudasaimasén ka? すみませ ん。そこを退いてくださいませんか。*Excuse me. Could you move out of the way?*

dokubō 独房 *solitary cell; solitary confinement; prison cell* ❀dokubō ni irerareru 独房に入れられる *be confined to a prison cell*

dokudanteki [na] 独断的（な）*dogmatic* ❀Tanaka-san wa ítsumo dokudanteki na íken bákari iu. 田中さんはいつも独断的な意見ばか り言う。*Tanaka always speaks his opinion dogmatically.*

dokugaku no 独学の *self-educated*

dókuji no 独自の *independent; personal; original* ❀dókuji no kenkyū 独自の研究 *independent research*

dokuritsu 独立 *independence* ❀dokuritsúkoku 独立国 *an independent country* ❀dokuritsu séngen 独立宣言 *declaration of independence* ——**dokuritsu-suru** [*vi*] 独立する *be separated from; be independent of*

dokusai 独裁 *despotism; autocracy* ⧫dokusai kúnshu 独裁君主 *dictator; despot* ⧫dokusáisha 独裁者 *a dictator* ——**dokusaiteki [na]** 独裁的（な）*dictatorial; despotic*

dokusen 独占 *monopoly* ⧫dokusen jígyō 独占事業 *monopolistic enterprise* ——**dokusen-suru** [vt] 独占する *monopolize* ⧫Yoshida-san wa tatta ichídai no kompyútā o dokusen-shite tsukatte iru. 吉田さんはたった一台のコンピューターを独占して使っている。*Yoshida is monopolizing the use of the only computer.*

dókusha 読者 *reader; one who reads*

dókushin 独身 *unmarried; single; celibacy*

dókusho 読書 *reading*

dokushō 独唱 *vocal solo*

dokusō 独奏 *instrumental solo*

dokutoku no 独特の *unique; peculiar; special* ⧫Teneshī Uíriamuzu no sakuhin ní wa dokutoku no sékai ga áru. テネシー．ウイリアムズの作品には独特の世界がある。*Tennessee Williams' plays present a unique world.*

dōkutsu 洞窟 *cave; den; lair; grotto*

dokuzen 独善 *self-righteousness* ——**dokuzenteki [na]** 独善的（な）*self-righteous* ⧫dokuzenteki na seikaku 独善的な性格 *a self-righteous disposition*

dókyō 度胸 *courage; pluck; guts* ⧫dókyō ga áru 度胸がある *have courage* ⧫dókyō ga nái 度胸がない *gutless*

dōkyúsei 同級生 *classmate*

domá 土間 *dirt-floor room*

domburi 丼 *(large) bowl* ⧫oyako dómburi 親子丼 *chicken and eggs served in a bowl on top of rice*

dómburiko どんぶりこ *sloshing and splashing*

-dome 〜度目 *-nth time* ⧫Sandomé no shōjíki. 三度目の正直。*(lit) The third time is honest. (The third time's a charm. / Third time does the trick.) <set phrase>*

dōmei 同盟 *alliance; union* ⧫heiwa dōmei o musubu 平和同盟を結ぶ *form a peace alliance*

dómo どうも *indeed; very much* ⧫Dōmo arígatō. どうも有難う。*Thank you very much.* ⧫Dōmo arígatō gozaimáshita. どうも有難うございました。*Thank you very much (for what you did).*

domór-u [vi domoránai; domótta] 吃る *stutter; stammer (preferred: kitsuon-shōgai)*

donár-u [vt donaránai; donátta] 怒鳴る *yell; shout* ⧫ōgóe de donáru 大声で怒鳴る *shout at the top of one's voice*

dónata どなた *who? (more polite than dáre)* ⧫Dónata desu ka? どなたですか。*Who are you. (or May I ask your name?)* ⧫Tanaka-san wa dónata desu ka? 田中さんはどなたですか。*Who is Mr. Tanaka? (or*

Which person is Mr. Tanaka?)

dóndon どんどん *rapidly*   ❊Sono shokúbutsu wa dóndon seichō-suru. その植物はどんどん成長する。 *That plant grows rapidly.*

dónguri 団栗 *acorn*

dónna どんな *what kind of?*   ❊Dónna éiga ga sukí desu ka? どんな映画が好きですか。 *What kind of movie do you like?*

dónna fū ni どんな風に *in what manner?; how?*   ❊Kore wa dónna fū ni shimásu ka? これはどんな風にしますか。 *How do you do this?*

dóno- どの〜 *which-*   ❊Dóno katá ga Yamamoto-san désu ka? どの方が山本さんですか。 *Which person is Mr. Yamamoto?*   ❊Dóno sakuhin ga sukí desu ka? どの作品が好きですか。 *Which work (of art / music / writing) do you like?*

dono gurai どのぐらい *about how much? / about how far?*   ❊Tōkyō-eki kara Hibiya Kōen made dono gurai kakarimásu ka? 東京駅から日比谷公園までどのぐらいかかりますか。 *About how long does it take from Tokyo Station to Hibiya Park?*

dontsū 鈍痛 *dull pain*

don'yoku 貪欲 *greed; covetousness*

don'yóri-suru [*vi*] どんよりする *be cloudy; be gray*   ❊Kyō wa sóra ga don'yóri-shite iru. 今日は空がどんよりしている。 *It's cloudy today (or The sky's gray today).*

dōnyū 導入 *introduction* ——**dōnyū-suru** [*vt*] 導入する *introduce; impose*   ❊Séifu wa shōhí-zei o dōnyū-shita. 政府は消費税を導入した。 *The government imposed a consumption tax.*

donzoko どん底 *the depths; very bottom*   ❊Káre no seikatsu wa donzoko ni áru. 彼の生活はどん底にある。 *His life is at rock bottom.*

dōon-igígo 同音異義語 *homonym*

dóre どれ *which (of three or more alternatives)?*   ❊Sukiyaki to tempura to tonkatsu no náka de anáta wa dóre ga sukí desu ka? すきやきと天ぷらと豚カツの中であなたはどれが好きですか。 *Of sukiyaki, tempura and pork cutlets, which do you like best?*

dorei 奴隷 *slave*   ❊dorei káihō 奴隷解放 *emancipation of slaves*

dōrí 道理 *reason; logic; rationality*   ❊dōrí ni kanáu 道理にかなう *be reasonable; be rational*

-dōri 〜通り *street; avenue*   ❊Ginza-dōri 銀座通り *Ginza Avenue*

doró 泥 *mud; dirt*   ❊dorómizu 泥水 *muddy water*   ❊Kutsú ni doró ga tsúite iru. 靴に泥がついている。 *There's mud on my shoes.*

dōro 道路 *road*   ❊kōsoku dōro 高速道路 *expressway*

dorobō 泥棒 *thief; burglar; robber*

dorodoro [no] どろどろ（の）*muddy; viscous; mushy*   ❊Namari ga dorodoro ni tókete iru. 鉛がどろどろに溶けている。 *The lead melted into a viscous mixture.* ——**dórodoro-suru** [*vi*] どろどろする *be muddy; be involved*   ❊Michi wa dórodoro-shite iru. 道はどろどろし

ている。 *The road is muddy.* ❽dórodoro-shita ningen kánkei どろど
ろした人間関係 *an involved personal relationship*

doronuma 泥沼 *bog; mire* ❽doronuma ni háiru 泥沼に入る *get
bogged down in a matter*

dōryō 同僚 *co-worker*

dóryoku 努力 *effort* ❽doryokuka 努力家 *a hard worker* ❽Anáta wa
dóryoku ga tarinai. 君は努力が足りない。 *You don't try hard enough.*
——**dóryoku-suru** [*vi*] 努力する *make an effort; try hard*

dósa 動作 *action; movement*

dóse どうせ *anyhow; after all; no doubt* ❽Kodomo wa terebi-gému ni
netchū-shite irú keredo, dōse súgu akíru kara, shibáraku hótte okó. 子供
はテレビゲームに熱中しているけれど、どうせ直ぐ飽きるから、
しばらく放っておこう。 *The children are abosorbed in computer
games, but no doubt they'll tire of them right away, so I'll let them
alone.*

Dosei 土星 *Saturn*

dōsei 同棲 *living together; cohabitation* ——**dōsei-suru** [*vi*] 同棲する
live together; cohabitate

dōséiai 同性愛 *homosexuality*

doshaburi どしゃぶり *heavy (pouring) rain; soaking (wet)*

dōshi 動詞 *verb (Gram)* ❽jidóshi 自動詞 *intransitive verb* ❽tadóshi
他動詞 *transitive verb*

dóshi 同士 *friend; fellow* ❽koibito dóshi 恋人同士 *lovers* ❽gakusei
dóshi 学生同士 *fellow students*

dóshi 同志 *comrade*

doshín [to] どしん（と）*with a thud; with a thump; heavily* ❽doshín to
ochíru どしんと落ちる *fall with a thud* ❽doshín to shirímochi o
tsuku どしんと尻餅をつく *fall heavily on one's buttocks*

dóshite どうして *why?; how?* ❽Dóshite chikoku-shitá no desu ka? どう
して遅刻したのですか? *Why were you late?*

dóshite ka どうしてか *for some reason (or other); why, I don't know*
❽Dóshite ka wakaránai. Démo nan to náku guai ga warúi. どうしてか
分からない。でも、何となく具合が悪い。 *I don't know why, but
somehow I don't feel good.*

dó shite mo どうしても *somehow; no matter what; no matter how* ❽Dó
shite mo kono sūgaku no mondai ga tokénai. どうしてもこの数学の
問題が解けない。 *I can't solve this math problem no matter how (I
try).*

dosō 土葬 *interment* ——**dosō-suru** [*vt*] 土葬する *bury (in the ground);
inter*

dōsōkai 同窓会 *alumni association; alumni meeting*

dossári どっさり *oodles; a lot* ❽Yasai o dossári kaikónda. 野菜をどっ
さり買い込んだ。 *I bought oodles of vegetables.*

dosshín to どっしんと *with a bang; with a thump*

dosshíri shita どっしりした *heavy; dignified* ❃dosshíri-shita taikaku どっしりした体格 *a heavy build*

dosún [to] *(see* **doshin to***)*

Dṓ suru kotó mo dekínai. どうすることもできない *nothing one can do.* ❃Íma to nátte wa dṓ suru kotó mo dekínai. 今となってはどうすることもできない。 *There's nothing anyone can do about it now.*

dṓtai 胴体 *body; trunk; fuselage* ❃hikṓki no dṓtai 飛行機の胴体 *airplane fuselage*

dótchi *(see* **dóchira***)*

dote 土手 *bank (of a river); dike*

dṓtei 童貞 *male virgin*

dṓtoku 道徳 *morals* ❃dōtoku-shúgi 道徳主義 *moralism*

dotto どっと *suddenly; all at once; with a rush* ❃Kekkónshiki ga owatte dotto tsukaré ga déta. 結婚式が終わってどっと疲れが出た。 *After the wedding ceremony I suddenly was (very) tired.*

dōwa 童話 *children's story; fairy tale; fable*

dóyadoya どやどや *noisily*

dṓ yara ... [yṓ desu] どうやら～（ようです） *somehow (it seems) ... ; for some reason or other (it seems) ...* ❃Dṓ yara ashitá wa áme ni náru yṓ desu. どうやら明日は雨になるようです。 *I have the feeling it's going to rain tomorrow.*

dōyō 動揺 *shaking; trembling* ——**dōyō-suru** [vi] 動揺する *shake; tremble*

dōyō 童謡 *nursery rhyme*

dōyō [no] 同様（の） *similar; like; the same* ——**dōyō ni** 同様に *in the same manner*

Doyṓbi 土曜日 *Saturday*

dṓzo どうぞ *(if you) please, go ahead* ❃Dṓzo yoroshiku. どうぞよろしく。 *How do you do? <set phrase>*

dōzoku 同族 *same family (line); tribe* ❃dōzoku-gáisha 同族会社 *family company*

E

e へ *to; toward* [*particle: direction marker*] ❃Watashi wa ashita Tōkyō e ikimásu. 私はあした東京へ行きます。 *I'm going to Tokyo tomorrow.*

e 柄 *a handle* ❃nokogíri no e 鋸の柄 *handle of a saw*

é 絵 *picture; drawing*

eakon エアコン *air conditioner*

ebi 海老 *shrimp* ❃ebi-fúrai 海老フライ *fried shrimp*

eda 枝 *branch; twig*   ✷kí no eda 木の枝 *tree branch*

edamame 枝豆 *green soybean*

Edo 江戸 *Edo (former name of Tokyo)*   ✷Edokko 江戸っ子 *"child of Edo" (a person whose personal characteristics identify him with "old Edo"); a Tokyoite*

Ée. ええ. *Yes; I agree.*

ee to… ええと… *[interjection, indicating hesitation]*

éfuda 絵札 *face card (a king, queen, or jack in a deck of cards)*

egák·u *[vt* egakánai; egáita*]* 描く *draw; paint; depict*   ✷jigázō o egáku 自画像を描く *paint a self-portrait*

égao 笑顔 *a smile; beaming face*   ✷Kánojo no égao wa suteki desu. 彼女の笑顔は素敵です。 *Her smile is charming.*

egatá·i *[adj* egátaku nái; egátakatta*]* 得難い *(be) hard to get; beyond reach; rare*   ✷egatái jinzai 得難い人材 *a person of rare ability*

e-hágaki 絵葉書 *picture postcard*

Éi! えい！ *[exclamation, said when exerting effort]*

eibin [na] 鋭敏（な） *sharp; keen; acute*

Eibúngaku 英文学 *English literature*

éichi 叡智；英知 *sagacity; wisdom; intelligence*

eien 永遠 *eternity*   ✷eien ni 永遠に *forever*   ✷Futarí no ái wa eien de áru. 二人の愛は永遠である。 *Their love is eternal. <formal>*

éiga 映画 *movie; film*   ✷eiga háiyū 映画俳優 *movie star*   ✷eigákan 映画館 *movie theater*

Eigo 英語 *English language*   ✷Eikáiwa 英会話 *English conversation*

eigyō 営業 *business; trade; commerce*   ✷eigyō jíkan 営業時間 *business hours*   ✷eigyō kőritsu 営業効率 *management efficiency*   ✷Káre wa eigyō kánkei no shigoto o shite irú no yo. 彼は営業関係の仕事をしているのよ。 *His business is commerce related. <fem>*——**eigyō-suru** *[vt]* 営業する *do business; trade*

éiki 鋭気 *spirit; vigor; energy; pep*   ✷Renkyū wa yukkúri yasúnde éiki o yashinaő. 連休はゆっくり休んで鋭気を養おう。 *I'm going to rest up during the holidays and get my energy back.*

eikō 栄光 *glory*

Eikoku 英国 *Britain; England; Great Britain*   ✷Ei-póndo 英ポンド *pound sterling*   ✷Ei-Bei 英米 *England and America*   ✷Ei-rémpō 英連邦 *British Commonwealth of Nations*

eikyō 影響 *influence; effect; repercussion*   ✷Chikyū no ondanka génshō no eikyō de ijō kíshō ga tsuzuite iru. 地球の温暖化現象の影響で異常気象が続いている。 *Global warming has resulted in continually strange weather.*——**eikyō o ataeru** 影響を与える *influence*   ✷Nihon no ukiyoe wa inshōha no gafū ni őkina eikyō o ataete iru. 日本の浮世絵は印象派の画風に影響を与えている。 *Japanese ukiyoe greatly influenced the paintings of the impressionists.*

eikyū 永久 *permanence; eternity* ❈eikyūsei 永久性 *permanency* ❈eikyúshi 永久歯 *permanent tooth* ——**eikyū no** 永久の *permanent; eternal; everlasting* ❈eikyū no ái 永久の愛 *everlasting love* —— **eikyū ni** 永久に *forever; eternally; permanently* ❈Anáta wa eikyū ni Nihón ni iru tsumori désu ka? 貴方は永久に日本にいるつもりですか。 *Do you plan to live in Japan permanently?*

eisei 衛星 *satellite* ❈eisei hōsō 衛星放送 *satellite broadcast* ❈eisei tóshi 衛星都市 *satellite city* ❈eisei tsūshin 衛星通信 *satellite communications*

eisei 衛生 *hygiene; sanitation* ❈eisei shísetsu 衛生施設 *sanitary facilities* ❈Eisei jōtai ga warúi. 衛生状態が悪い。 *Sanitary conditions are bad.* ——**eiseiteki [na]** 衛生的（な）*sanitary; hygienic* ❈eiseiteki na kankyō o totonoéru 衛生的な環境を整える *provide a sanitary environment*

eishácki 映写機 *movie projector*

Ei-yaku 英訳 *English translation*

éiyo 栄誉 *honor; distinction* ❈éiyo áru 栄誉ある *honorable*

eiyō 栄養 *nutrition* ❈eiyō shítchō 栄養失調 *malnutrition* ❈eiyóso 栄養素 *nutriment; nutritive element*

eiyū 英雄 *hero; great person.* ——**eiyūteki [na]** 英雄的（な）*heroic* ——**eiyūteki ni** 英雄的に *heroically*

eizō 映像 *image; reflection; shadow*

Éizu エイズ *AIDS (acronym for kōtensei men'eki fuzen shōkōgun* 後天性免疫不全症候群 *acquired immunodeficiency syndrome)*

ekaki 絵描き *artist; painter*

éki 駅 *depot; station* ❈shihatsú-eki 始発駅 *starting station* ❈shūchákú-eki 終着駅 *last station; terminus* ❈Tōkyō Eki 東京駅 *Tokyo Station*

éki 液 *liquid; fluid* ❈ekitai 液体 *liquid* ❈jokō-eki 除光液 *polish remover* ❈shūséi-eki 修正液 *correction fluid* ❈waipáeki ワイパー液 *windshield wiper fluid* ❈futóeki 不凍液 *antifreeze*

ekibyō 疫病 *epidemic; plague*

ekisha 易者 *fortune-teller*

ekitai 液体 *liquid* ❈ekitai chísso 液体窒素 *liquid nitrogen*

ekkusu kōsen エックス光線 *X-ray*

eko híiki 依怙贔屓 *favoritism; partiality* ——**eko híiki-suru** [vt] えこひいきする *be partial to; play favorites; favor* ❈Ano senséi wa seiseki no yói ko bákari ekohíiki-suru. あの先生は成績の良い子ばかりえこひいきする。 *That teacher favors only students who make good grades.*

ékubo えくぼ *dimple*

emban 円盤 *disc; discus*

émbun 塩分 *salt content; salinity*

empitsu 鉛筆 *pencil* ❈iro émpitsu 色鉛筆 *colored pencil*

én 円 *circle* §enchū 円柱 *column; shaft* §ensui 円錐 *cone* §daen 楕円 *oval; ellipse*

én 円 *yen (Japanese currency); a circle* §en shákkan 円借款 *yen credit* §én no kiriage 円の切り上げ *yen revaluation*

én 塩 *salt; saline* §enden 塩田 *salt field* §ensui 塩水 *salt water*

én 縁 *connection; relation; affinity* §enmúsubi 縁結び *marriage arrangement* §én ga áru 縁がある *have (a) connection*

en 縁 *porch; veranda*

enchō 延長 *extension; continuation* §enchō kókkai 延長国会 *extended Diet session* ——**enchō-suru** [vt] 延長する *extend; prolong* §taizai kíkan o enchō-suru 滞在期間を延長する *extend (one's) period of stay*

endómame 豌豆豆 *pea*

enérugī エネルギー *energy* §shō-ene 省エネ *(abbr for energy conservation)*

engan 沿岸 *the coast; shore* §engan gyógyō 沿岸漁業 *coastal fishing industry* §engan keibitai 沿岸警備隊 *Coast Guard (US)*

engawa 縁側 *porch; veranda (J)*

engei 園芸 *gardening; horticulture*

engei 演芸 *entertainment* §engéikai 演芸界 *the entertainment world*

engeki 演劇 *drama; play* §taishū éngeki 大衆演劇 *popular theater; popular drama*

éngi 演技 *(dramatic) performance* §engi-hō 演技法 *dramatic technique* ——**éngi-suru** [vt] 演技する *perform*

engi 縁起 *omen; portent* §engi ga íi 縁起がいい *(be) auspicious* §engi ga waruí 縁起が悪い *(be) inauspicious; ominous*

enji·ru [vt enjinai; enjita] 演じる *act (a part in a play)* §Káre wa shinu máde dórama o enjite ita. 彼は死ぬまでドラマを演じていた。*He acted in plays until his death.*

énjo 援助 *assistance; support; help* §keizai énjo 経済援助 *financial aid* §minkan enjo dántai 民間援助団体 *private support organization* ——**énjo-suru** [vt] 援助する *assist; aid; support*

enjuku-suru [vi] 円熟する *ripen; mature; develop; perfect* §Ano joyū wa ítsumo enjuku-shita éngi o mísete kureru. あの女優はいつも円熟した演技を見せてくれる。*That actress always gives a perfect performance.*

enkai 宴会 *banquet*

enki 延期 *postpone* §Kónkai mo mata, kokusan rokétto no uchiage ga enki ni nátta. 今回も又、国産ロケットの打ち上げが延期になった。*Again the launching of the Japanese rocket has been postponed.* ——**enki-suru** [vt] 延期する *postpone; put off; defer*

enogu 絵の具 *artist's paints* §suisai énogu 水彩絵の具 *watercolors* §abura énogu 油絵の具 *oils*

enryo 遠慮 *formality; reserve* §Enryo wa kimmotsu désu yo. 遠慮は禁

物ですよ。 *Formality (here) is forbidden.* ——**enryo-suru** [*vi*] 遠慮する *stand on ceremony; be reserved* ⑧enryo náshi ni 遠慮なしに *without (standing on) ceremony* ⑧Dōzo enryo-shináide. どうぞ遠慮しないで. *Please don't stand on ceremony.*

ensei 遠征 *expedition* ⑧enséigun 遠征軍 *expeditionary forces* ⑧kaigai énsei 海外遠征 *foreign expedition*

enshi 遠視 *farsighted(ness)* ⑧enshikyō 遠視鏡 *glasses for farsightedness*

enshō 炎症 *inflammation* ⑧enshō o okósu 炎症を起こす *become inflamed*

enshū 円周 *circumference* ⑧enshūritsu 円周率 *the ratio of the circumference of a circle to its diameter*

enshū 演習 *practice; maneuvers* ⑧Nihongo no sakubun énshū 日本語の作文演習 *composition exercise in the Japanese language*

enshutsu 演出 *(play) production* ——**enshutsu-suru** [*vt*] 演出する *produce; present (a play)*

énso 塩素 *chlorine*

ensō 演奏 *musical performance* ⑧ensōka 演奏家 *performer; artist* ——**ensō-suru** [*vt*] 演奏する *perform; play* ⑧Watashítachi wa suisōgaku de kōshínkyoku o ensō-shimáshita. 私たちは吹奏楽で行進曲を演奏しました。 *Our wind instrument section played a march.*

ensoku 遠足 *excursion; outing*

entaku 円卓 *round table* ⑧entaku káigi 円卓会議 *round-table conference*

entotsu 煙突 *chimney; smokestack*

enzetsu 演説 *speech* ——**enzetsu-suru** [*vt*] 演説する *deliver a speech*

era 鰓 *(fish) gill*

érā エラー *error (in games)*

eráb·u [*vt* erabánai; eránda] 選ぶ *choose; select* ⑧daitōryō o erábu 大統領を選ぶ *elect a president*

erá·i [*adj* éraku nái; érakatta] 偉い *great; famous; excellent* ⑧éraku náru 偉くなる *become famous* ⑧Yóku yatta! Erái! よくやった！偉い！ *You did a good job! Excellent!* <masc>

erebḗtā エレベーター *elevator*

erí 襟；衿 *collar; the neck* ⑧erí o tadásu 襟を正す *straighten oneself; be formal; be awestruck* ⑧Sháin wa minna erí o tadáshite shachō no hanashí ni mimí o katamúketa. 社員はみんな襟を正して社長の話に耳を傾けた。 *The company employees all sat up straight and listened to the president's speech.*

erímaki 襟巻 *scarf*

é·ru [*vt* énai; éta] 得る *receive* ⑧ikiói o éru 勢いを得る *gain momentum*

esá 餌 *feed; bait* ⑧Kíngyo ni esá o yarinasái. 金魚に餌をやりなさい。

Feed the goldfish.

éshaku 会釈 *greeting*

éso 壊疽 *gangrene*

etoku-suru [*vt*] 会得する *understand; grasp*

etsuran 閲覧 *perusal; reading* ◈**etsuránshitsu** 閲覧室 *reading room* ——**etsuran-suru** [*vt*] 閲覧する *read; peruse*

F

fú 封 *a seal* ◈**fú o kíru** 封を切る *break the seal* ◈**fú o suru** 封をする *seal (up)*

-fū ～風 *a la ; -style* ◈**chūka-fū** 中華風 *Chinese style* ◈**gendai-fū** 現代風 *modern style*

fuan 不安 *uneasiness; uncertainty; anxiety*

fuántei 不安定 *instability* ——**fuántei [na]** 不安定（な）*unstable* ◈**Sono kuní wa seiji jókyō ga máda fuántei desu.** その国は政治情況がまだ不安定です。*The political situation in that country is still unstable.*

fúben [na] 不便（な）*inconvenient* ◈**fúben na madori** 不便な間取り *an inconveniently arranged floor plan*

fúbo 父母 *father and mother; parents*

fúbuki 吹雪 *snowstorm*

fubyódō 不平等 *inequality* ——**fubyódō na** 不平等な *unequal; unfair* ◈**josei ni tótte fubyódō na séido** 女性にとって不平等な制度 *a system unfair to women* ——**fubyódō ni** 不平等に *unequally; unfairly*

fuchí 縁 *picture frame; hem; border* ◈**gaku-buchí** 額縁 *picture frame* ◈**mégane no fuchí** 眼鏡の縁 *eyeglass frames*

fuchúi 不注意 *carelessness; inattention* ◈**Jíko wa fuchúi de okíru kotó ga ói.** 事故は不注意で起きることが多い。*Most accidents are caused by carelessness.*

fuchújitsu 不忠実 *disloyalty* ——**fuchújitsu na** 不忠実な *disloyal* ◈**fuchújitsu na táido** 不忠実な態度 *a disloyal attitude*

fuda 札 *card; label; tag* ◈**fuda o kubáru** 札を配る *deal cards* ◈**haná-fuda** 花札 *playing cards (J)* ◈**(torámpu no) kirífuda** （トランプの）切り札 *trump card* ◈**nífuda** 荷札 *(baggage) tag; label*

fúdan 普段 *ordinary* ——**fúdan no** 普段の *usual; normal; everyday* ◈**fudángi** 普段着 *everyday clothes; casual dress*

fude 筆 *brush; writing brush*

fudósan 不動産 *real estate* ◈**fudósan'ya** 不動産屋 *real estate agent*

fudótoku 不道徳 *immorality* ——**fudótoku na** 不道徳な *immoral; wicked*

fue 笛 *flute* 　❽fue o fúku 笛を吹く *play a flute* 　❽yoko-bue 横笛 *horizontal flute* 　❽tate-bue 縦笛 *a recorder* 　❽kuchi-bue 口笛 *a whistle; whistling*

fué·ru [*vi* fuénai; fúeta] 増える *increase* 　❽Watashi wa taijū ga fúeta. 私は体重が増えた。*I've gained weight. (or My weight's increased).*

fúfu 夫婦 *married couple; husband and wife* 　❽fūfu-génka 夫婦喧嘩 *domestic quarrel*

fugókaku 不合格 *failure*

fugóri 不合理 *irrationality; absurdity* 　❽fugóri-geki 不合理劇 *theater of the absurd* ——**fugóri na** 不合理な *irrational; unreasonable* 　❽fugóri na kísoku 不合理な規則 *an unreasonable regulation*

fúgu 河豚 *blowfish; globefish*

fuhai 腐敗 *rottenness; decay; decomposition; corruption* ——**fuhai-suru** [*vi*] 腐敗する *be rotten; decay; decompose; be corrupt* 　❽Seiji wa fuhai-shikítte iru. 政治は腐敗しきっている。*Politics is totally corrupt.*

fuhei 不平 *complaint* 　❽fuhei o iu 不平を言う *complain*

fuhō [na] 不法（な）*illegal; unlawful* 　❽fuhō na kói 不法な行為 *an illegal act* 　❽fuhō kánkin 不法監禁 *illegal detention* 　❽fuhō sénkyo 不法占拠 *illegal occupation (of territory)* 　❽fuhō chúsha 不法駐車 *illegal parking*

fui ふい；不意 *suddenness; unexpectedness* 　❽fui uchi ふい打ち *a surprise attack* 　❽fui no kyaku 不意の客 *an unexpected visitor* 　❽teki no fui o tsúku 敵の不意を突く *take the enemy by surprise* ——**fui ni** 不意に *unexpectedly; suddenly* 　❽Tensai wa fui ni yatte kúru. 天災は不意にやってくる。*Calamities come unexpectedly.*

fuítchi 不一致 *disagreement; incompatibility* 　❽seikaku no fuítchi de rikon-suru 性格の不一致で離婚する *divorce because of incompatibility*

fuji 藤 *wisteria*

fúji 不時 *unscheduled; unexpected; emergency* 　❽fuji chákuriku 不時着陸 *emergency landing*

fujin 夫人 *Mrs.* 　❽Aoki-fújin 青木夫人 *Mrs. Aoki*

fujin 婦人 *lady; woman*

fujin-ka 婦人科 *gynecology* 　❽fujinká-i 婦人科医 *gynecologist*

fújiyū 不自由 *inconvenience; destitution; privation* ——**fújiyū na** 不自由な *uncomfortable; not free; inconvenient*

fújo 扶助 *aid; assistance* 　❽kōteki fújo 公的扶助 *public relief* 　❽bekkyo fujóryō 別居扶助料 *alimony*

fujújun [na] 不従順（な）*disobedient*

fuka 鱶 *shark*

fukái 不快 *displeasure; discomfort; unpleasantness* 　❽fukai shísū 不快指数 *discomfort index* ——**fukái na** 不快な *unpleasant; distasteful;*

displeased

fuká·i [*adj* fúkaku nái; fúkakatta] 深い *(be) deep; profound* ▥Kono púru wa fukái. このプールは深い。 *This pool is deep.* ——**fukáku** 深く *deeply* ▥fukáku kangáeru 深く考える *think deeply*

fukákai [na] 不可解 （な） *baffling; incomprehensible*

fukakujitsúsa 不確実さ *uncertainty*

fukamé·ru [*vt* fukaménai; fukámeta] 深める *deepen; strengthen; dig (down) into* ▥ríkai o fukaméru 理解を深める *deepen understanding* ▥Gíron o fukámete íi ketsuron o dasó. 議論を深めていい結論を出そう。 *Let's dig deeper into the matter and come up with a good solution.*

fukánō 不可能 *impossibility* ——**fukánō na** 不可能な *impossible*

fukánshō 不干渉 *nonintervention; noninterference*

fukanshō 不感症 *frigidity; apathy* ▥fukanshō ni náru 不感症になる *grow (or become) insensible to*

fukánzen [na] 不完全 （な） *deficient; incomplete* ▥fukanzen nénshō 不完全燃焼 *incomplete combustion (of fuel)*

fukanzénsa 不完全さ *imperfection*

fukáppatsu [na] 不活発 （な） *sluggish; languid* ——**fukáppatsu ni** 不活発に *inactively; sluggishly*

fukása 深さ *depth*

fukáshin 不可侵 *nonaggression; inviolability* ▥fukashin jóyaku 不可侵条約 *nonaggression treaty*

fuka-zara 深皿 *deep dish; casserole*

fuke 雲脂 *dandruff*

fúkei 風景 *scenery* ▥fūkei-ga 風景画 *a landscape painting*

fukéiki 不景気 *economic depression; recession; bad times*

fuké·ru [*vi* fukénai; fúketa] 老ける *grow (or become) old* ▥Chíchi wa mó fúkete shimaimáshita. 父はもう老けてしまいました。 *My father has grown old.*

fuketsu 不潔 *uncleanliness; impurity* ——**fuketsu na** 不潔な *dirty; unsanitary; impure*

fuki 蕗 *butterbur; bog rhubarb*

fukígen 不機嫌 *bad humor; sullenness* ——**fukígen na** 不機嫌な *ill-humored; bad-tempered; sullen*

fukikaké·ru [*vt* fukikakénai; fukikáketa] 吹きかける *breathe upon; blow on* ▥te ni íki o fukikakéru 手に息を吹きかける *blow on one's hands (to warm them)*

fukín 付近 *near; nearby; the neighborhood*

fukín 布巾 *cloth; dishcloth* ▥dai-búkin 台布巾 *wiping cloth*

fukínkō 不均衡 *disequilibrium; imbalance* ▥fukínkō no zesei 不均衡の是正 *correction of an imbalance*

fukísoku [na] 不規則 （な） *irregular* ▥fukísoku dóshi 不規則動詞 *irregular verb* ▥fukísoku na hénka 不規則な変化 *an irregular* *change*

fukitobás·u [*vt* fukitobasánai; fukitobáshita] 吹き飛ばす *blow away; scatter* ❀fuan o fukitobásu 不安を吹き飛ばす *get rid of anxiety*

fukkatsu 復活 *resurrection; rebirth* ❀Fukkatsúsai 復活祭 *Easter*

fukkō 復興 *rehabilitation; reconstruction; restoration; revival*

fukō 不幸 *unhappiness; misfortune* ❀fukōchū no saiwai 不幸中の幸い *fortune in the midst of misfortune* <*set phrase*> ——**fukō na** 不幸な *unfortunate; unhappy* ❀fukō na jínsei 不幸な人生 *an unhappy life*

fukōhei 不公平 *unfairness* ——**fukōhei na** 不公平な *unfair*

fukōsei 不公正 *injustice; unfairness* ❀fukōsei bōekíkoku 不公正貿易国 *unfair trade nation* ——**fukōsei na** 不公正な *unfair; unjust*

fukú 服 *clothing*

fuk·u [*vt* fukanai; fuita] 拭く *wipe* (*see also* **nugúu**)

fuk·ú [*vt* fukánai; fúita] 吹く *blow; breathe on* ❀kaze ga fukú 風が吹く *wind blows* ❀fue o fukú 笛を吹く *play a flute* ❀hóra o fukú ほらを吹く *brag; boast*

fuku- 副～ *vice-; deputy-* ❀fuku-sōri 副総理 *deputy prime minister*

fukuin 福音 *gospel* ❀Fukuinsho 福音書 (*one of the four*) *Gospels* ——**fukuin no** 福音の *evangelical*

fukujū 服従 *obedience; submission*

fukumé·ru [*vt* fukuménai; fukúmeta] 含める *include*

fukúm·u [*vt* fukumánai; fukúnda] 含む *include; imply; bear in mind*

fukurahagi ふくら脛 *calf* (Anat)

fukuram·u [*vi* fukuramanai; fukuranda] 膨らむ *swell; expand; get* (*or become*) *big* ❀Hará ga fukurande iru. 腹が膨らんでいる。 *My stomach's swollen.* ❀Káre no yumé ga fukuranda. 彼の夢が膨らんだ。 *His dream grew.*

fukure·ru [*vi* fukurenai; fukureta] 膨れる *swell; expand; get big; be sulky; be cross*

fukuró 袋 *sack; bag* ❀kami-búkuro 紙袋 *paper bag* ❀tesage-búkuro 手提げ袋 *carrying bag; shopping bag* ❀fukuro no nezumi 袋の鼠 *a trapped mouse; be in a tight* (*spot*) <*set phrase*>

fukurō 梟 *owl*

fukusámbutsu 副産物 *by-product*

fukusáyō 副作用 *side-effect*

fukusei 複製 *reprinting; reproduction; cloning* ❀fukuseiga 複製画 *a print; a replica* ——**fukusei-suru** [*vt*] 複製する *reproduce; reprint* ❀méiga o fukusei-suru 名画を複製する *reproduce a masterpiece*

fukushi 副詞 *adverb*

fukúshi 福祉 *welfare* ❀fukushi kókka 福祉国家 *welfare state* ❀shakai fúkushi 社会福祉 *social welfare*

fukusha 複写 *reproduction; duplication* ❀fukusháshi 複写紙 *duplicating paper* ❀fukusháki 複写機 *duplicator* ——**fukusha-suru**

[vt] 複写する *copy; duplicate*

fukushū 復習 *(lesson) review*

fukushū 復讐 *revenge; vengeance; vendetta* ——**fukushūteki [na]** 復讐 的（な）*retaliatory; vindictive* ——**fukushū-suru** [vi] 復讐する *avenge; get revenge*

fukusō 服装 *clothing; attire; dress*

fukusú 複数 *plural; multiple* ❧fukusú kakudántō 複数核弾頭 *multiple nuclear warheads*

fukutsū 腹痛 *stomachache; abdominal pain* ❧fukutsū o okósu 腹痛を 起こす *get (or have) a stomachache*

fukuzatsu [na] 複雑（な）*complex; complicated; involved* ❧fukuzatsu kóssetsu 複雑骨折 *compound fracture* ❧fukuzatsu na mondai 複雑な 問題 *complicated problem* ❧fukuzatsu ni náru 複雑になる *become complicated* ❧fukuzatsu ni suru 複雑にする *complicate*

fukyō 不況 *(economic) depression; recession*

fukyū 普及 *propagation; dissemination; spreading* ——**fukyū-suru** [vt] 普及する *diffuse; spread; propagate; disseminate* ❧Tadashíi chíshiki o fukyū-shinákereba naránai. 正しい知識を普及しなければならな い。*We must spread correct information.*

fumájime [na] 不真面目（な）*insincere; unsteady; not serious; frivolous* ❧fumájime na séito 不真面目な生徒 *a student who isn't serious*

fumánzoku 不満足 *dissatisfaction; discontent* ——**fumánzoku na** 不満 足な *dissatisfied; discontent; displeased* ❧fumánzoku na séika 不満 足な成果 *unsatisfactory result*

fúmbetsu 分別 *discretion; good sense* ——**fúmbetsu-suru** [vt] 分別する *judge; exercise discretion*

fumei 不明 *obscurity; incomprehensibility* ——**fumei na** 不明な *unknown; unclear; vague; incomprehensible* ❧yukue-fúmei 行方不明 *location unknown; lost*

fumetsu 不滅 *immortality; indestructibility* ——**fumetsu no** 不滅の *immortal; permanent; eternal*

fúmi 風味 *flavor; taste*

fumi-e 踏み絵 *(lit)* "picture to be trodden on"; *religious image used in seeking out Christians in Tokugawa Japan; loyalty test*

fumihazús·u [vt fumihazusánai; fumihazúshita] 踏み外す *miss (one's) step; lose (one's) footing*

fumikiri 踏切 *(railroad) crossing*

fumō 不毛 *barrenness; sterility (of land)* ——**fumō no** 不毛の *barren; sterile (land)* ❧fumō no chí 不毛の地 *barren land* ❧fumō no róngi 不毛の論議 *a sterile (fruitless) discussion*

fumotó 麓 *the foot (of); bottom (of a mountain)*

fum·u [vt fumanai; funda] 踏む *step on; tread on*

fún 糞 *excrement; feces*

fún (-pun) 分 *a minute*　§**gófun** 五分 *five minutes*　§**júppun** 十分 *ten minutes*

funánori 船乗り *sailor; seaman*

fúnare [na] 不慣れ（な）；不馴れ（な）*unfamiliar; inexperienced*　§Watashi wa sono shigoto ni fúnare desu　私はその仕事に不慣れです。*I'm unfamiliar with that work (or job).*

funayoi 船酔い *seasickness; nausea*

fúne 船 *boat; ship*

funésshin [na] 不熱心（な）*halfhearted; unenthusiastic*

fungai 憤慨 *indignation; resentment* ――**fungai-suru** [*vi*] 憤慨する *resent; be indignant*

fun'íki 雰囲気 *atmosphere*　§**katei no fun'íki** 家庭の雰囲気 *home atmosphere*　§**Koko wa fun'íki ga íi.** ここは雰囲気がいい。*The atmosphere here is nice.*

funka 噴火 *(volcanic) eruption*

funshoku 粉飾 *embellishment; gilding*　§**funshoku késsan** 粉飾決算 *window-dressing settlement (of accounts)* ――**funshoku-suru** [*vt*] 粉飾する *adorn; embellish; decorate*

funsō 紛争 *battle; struggle; dispute*　§**kokusai fúnsō** 国際紛争 *international dispute*

funsui 噴水 *fountain*

funwári ふんわり *gently; in an airy manner [onomatopoeia for lightness]*

fúrafura [to] ふらふら（と）*unsteadily; shakily; dizzy*　§**furafura ni náru** ふらふらになる *become dizzy*　§**fúrafura to okiagáru** ふらふらと起き上がる *stand up unsteadily* ――**fúrafura-suru** [*vi*] ふらふらする *be unsteady (on one's feet); be shaky; be dizzy*

fúrafura-shita ふらふらした *fluffy*

furai フライ *fried*　§**ebi-fúrai** 海老フライ *fried shrimp*　§**kaki-fúrai** 牡蛎フライ *fried oyster*　§**furai ni suru** フライにする *fry*

furai-pan フライパン *skillet*

furatsuk·u [*vi* furatsukanai; furatsuita] ふらつく *fluctuate; feel giddy*

fure·ru [*vi* furenai; fureta] 触れる *touch; feel; touch on; refer to*

fúri [na] 不利（な）*disadvantageous; unfavorable (to one)*

furí 振り *pretense; show*　§**Futarí wa tagai ni tanin no furí o shita.** 二人は互いに他人の振りをした。*They (or The two) pretended to be strangers.*

furikáer·u [*vi* furikaeránai; furikáetta] 振り返る *look back; look back over (one's) shoulder*

furikaké·ru [*vt* furikakénai; furikáketa] 振りかける *sprinkle over; splash (on)*

furikóm·u [*vt* furikománai; furikónda] 振り込む *transfer (money)*

furimawás·u [*vt* furimawasánai; furimawáshita] 振り回す *swing (something) about; brandish*　§**chíshiki o furimawásu** 知識を振り回

す *show off (one's) knowledge* ⑧gakureki o furimawásu 学歴を振り回す *parade (one's) academic credentials*

furimidás·u [vt furimidasánai; furimidáshita] 振り乱す *disarrange (one's) hair* ⑧kamí o furimidásu 髪を振り乱す *shake loose (one's) hair*

furimuké·ru [vt furimukénai; furimúketa] 振り向ける *turn; direct (a ship); assign (money) to*

fūrin 風鈴 *wind chime*

fúro 風呂 *bath* ⑧furoba 風呂場 *bathroom (J)*

furoa sutándo フロアスタンド *floor lamp*

furoku 付録 *appendix; supplement*

furonto フロント *front desk; reception desk*

furoshiki 風呂敷 *kerchief; large cloth (for bundling things to carry)* ⑧ōburóshiki o hirogeru 大風呂敷を広げる *talk big; brag* <set phrase>

fúr·u [vi furánai; fútta] 降る *precipitate; fall* ⑧Áme ga fútte iru. 雨が降っている。 *It's raining.*

fur·u [vt furanai; futta] 振る *wave; shake* ⑧kubi o furu 首を振る *shake (one's) head*

furubí·ru [vi furubínai; furúbita] 古びる *become old; have an antique look*

furue·ru [vi furuenai; furueta] 震える *tremble; quiver; shiver* ⑧ikarí ni furueru 怒りに震える *tremble with anger*

furuhon 古本 *used book; secondhand book* ⑧furuhon-ya 古本屋 *used-book store*

furui 篩 *sieve; sifter*

furú·i [adj fúruku nái; fúrukatta] 古い *(be) old; ancient*

furúku kara 古くから *from of old; for a long time*

furumai 振舞い *behavior; conduct; manner* ⑧kénkyo na furumai 謙虚な振舞い *modest behavior; humble manner* ⑧furumái-zake ni yóu 振舞い酒に酔う *getting drunk at another's expense* <set phrase>

furuma·u [vi furumawánai; furumátta] 振舞う *behave; entertain* ⑧shinshi ráshiku furumau 紳士らしく振舞う *behave like a gentleman* ⑧teryóri o furumáu 手料理を振舞う *treat someone to home cooking*

furúsato 故郷；古里 *hometown; place where one was born and raised*

furútsu フルーツ *fruit*

furu·u [vt / vi furuwanai; furutta] 振るう *display; wield; shake; thrive*

fúryo 不慮 *unexpected; unforeseen* ⑧fúryo no shí 不慮の死 *accidental death*

furyō 不良 *delinquent; bad; inferior* ⑧furyō shónen 不良少年 *juvenile delinquent* ⑧eiyō fúryō 栄養不良 *undernourishment*

fusá 房；総 *a bunch; a cluster; tassel*

fūsa 封鎖 *a blockade* ——**fūsa-suru** [vt] 封鎖する *blockade; seal off*

fusag·u [vt fusaganai; fusaida] 塞ぐ *close; cover; stop up*

fusai 負債 *debt; liability; dues*

fúsai 夫妻 *married couple; Mr. and Mrs.; husband and wife* ❊Tanaka-san gofúsai 田中さんご夫妻 *Mr. and Mrs. Tanaka <formal>*

fusaku 不作 *bad crop*

fusawashí·i [*adj* fusawáshiku nái; fusawáshikatta] 相応しい *(be) suitable; fitting; appropriate*

fuség·u [*vt* fusegánai; fuséida] 防ぐ *prevent; ward off* ❊Jíko o jizen ni fuségu kotó ga daiji desu. 事故を事前に防ぐことが大事です。 *It is important to prevent an accident before it happens.*

fusei 不正 *injustice; unfairness* ——**fusei na** 不正な *unjust; unfair*

fuséikaku 不正確 *inaccuracy; uncertainty* ——**fuséikaku na** 不正確な *inaccurate; imprecise; uncertain* ❊fuséikaku na kioku 不正確な記憶 *uncertain recollection*

fūsen 風船 *balloon*

fúsha 風車 *windmill*

fūshi 風刺 *satire; sarcasm* ❊fūshi mánga 風刺漫画 *a satiric cartoon*

fushigi [na] 不思議（な）*uncanny; strange; wonderful* ——**fushigi ni** 不思議に *uncannily; strangely; wonderfully*

fushin 不審 *suspicion; doubt; mistrust* ❊fushin na kōdō o suru 不審な行動をする *act suspiciously*

fushin 不信 *insincerity; faithlessness*

fushínnin 不信任 *nonconfidence* ❊fushinnín-an 不信任案 *nonconfidence bill* ❊fushinnin dṓgi 不信任動議 *nonconfidence motion* ❊fushinnin tṓhyō 不信任投票 *vote of nonconfidence*

fushínsetsu [na] 不親切（な）*unkind; unfriendly*

fushízen [na] 不自然（な）*unnatural* ❊fushízen na genshō 不自然な現象 *unnatural phenomenon* ❊fushízen na rónri 不自然な論理 *strained logic*

fushō 負傷 *injury* ❊fushō o manugaréru 負傷を免れる *escape unhurt* ——**fushō-suru** [*vi*] 負傷する *be wounded; be injured*

fusoku 不足 *insufficiency; shortage; deficit* ——**fusoku no** 不足の *insufficient* ——**fusoku-suru** [*vi*] 不足する *be deficient; be insufficient*

fūsoku 風速 *wind velocity*

fússo フッ素 *fluorine*

fusuma 襖 *sliding panel (partitions in Japanese-style houses)*

futa 蓋 *lid; cover* ❊futa o akeru 蓋を開ける *open; uncover*

futago 双子 *twins*

futan 負担 *burden; charge; dues* ——**futan-suru** [*vt*] 負担する *bear; shoulder*

futarí 二人 *two persons*

futáshika [na] 不確か（な）*uncertain* ❊futáshika na jōhō 不確かな情報 *uncertain information*

futatabi 再び *second time; again*

futatsú 二つ *two (when counting things)*

futéishi 不定詞 *infinitive (Gram)*

fúto ふと *by chance; suddenly; unintentionally* ❈**fúto míru** ふと見る *glance; cast a glance* ❈**fúto... omóu to** ふと〜思うと *it just occurred to me that...*

futō 不当 *injustice; unreasonableness; unfairness* ——**futō na** 不当な *unjust; unfair* ❈**futō rōdō kői** 不当労働行為 *unfair labor practices*

fūtō 封筒 *envelope*

futó·i [adj fútoku nái; fútokatta] 太い *thick; fat; big; brawny* ❈**futói ude** 太い腕 *brawny arm* ❈**futói míki** 太い幹 *thick (tree) trunk*

futóitsu 不統一 *inconsistency*

futokoro 懐 *space between one's kimono and breast; pocket*

futómei na 不透明な *opaque*

futon 蒲団; 布団 *quilt; bedding; cushion*

futór·u [vi futoránai; fútotta] 太る *become fat; gain weight* ——**fútotta** (attr) 太った *fat* ❈**fútotta otokó** 太った男 *a fat man*

futsuka 二日 *the second (of the month); two days*

futsuka-yoi 二日酔い *hangover*

futsū ni náru 不通になる *be cut off; suspended; blocked.* ❈**Jishin no tamé ni kōsoku dőro ga futsū ni natta.** 地震のために高速道路が不通になった。 *Because of the earthquake the expressway was closed.*

futsū no 普通の *usual; ordinary* ❈**futsū yókin** 普通預金 *ordinary savings account*

futtō 沸騰 *boiling* ❈**futtōten** 沸騰点 *boiling point* ——**futtō-suru** [vi] 沸騰する *come to a boil*

fuyás·u [vt fuyasánai; fuyáshita] 増やす *increase*

fuyō [no] 不用 (の) *useless*

fuyō [no] 不要 (の) *unnecessary*

fuyō kázoku 扶養家族 *dependent(s)*

fuyú 冬 *winter*

fuyúkai [na] 不愉快 (な) *unpleasant; distasteful; displeased*

fuzai 不在 *absence* ❈**fuzai shőmei** 不在証明 *alibi; proof of absence* ❈**fuzaisha tőhyō** 不在者投票 *absentee voting*

fuzaké·ru [vi fuzakénai; fuzáketa] ふざける *flirt; joke*

fuzoku 付属 *attached to* ❈**fuzoku giteisho** 付属議定書 *accompanying protocol* ❈**fuzoku kőkō** 付属高校 *a high school attached (to a university)*

fúzoku 風俗 *custom; manners*

G

ga 蛾 *moth*

ga が [*particle, subject marker*] ❸Sóra ga aói. 空が青い。*The sky is blue.* ❸Kono machí ni byōin ga mittsu áru. この町に病院が三つある。*There are three hospitals in this town.*

ga が *but* ❸Watashi wa Nihonjín desu ga, káre wa Kankokújin desu. 私は日本人ですが、彼は韓国人です。*I am Japanese, but he is Korean.* ❸Shitsúrei desu ga, dónata desu ka? 失礼ですが、どなたですか。*Excuse me, but who are you?*

gábugabu がぶがぶ *guzzle; drink heavily* ❸Nódo ga kawáite itá no de, mizu o gábugabu nónda. 喉が乾いていたので水をがぶがぶ飲んだ。*I was so thirsty I guzzled the water.*

gabyō 画鋲 *thumbtack*

gachán [to] がちゃん（と）*shatter; shatteringly* [*mimetic for the sound of breaking glass*] ❸Mado gárasu ga gachán to wareta. 窓ガラスががちゃんと割れた。*The window (glass) shattered.*

-gachi [no] 〜がち（の）*having a tendency to; apt to* ❸Ano séito wa byōki-shigachi désu. あの生徒は病気しがちです。*That student is often sick.*

gachigachi がちがち *clatteringly; noisily* [*mimetic for a crunching sound*] ――**gáchigachi-suru** [*vi*] がちがちする *be crunchy; clatter* ❸Fúruku nátta pán wa gáchigachi-suru. 古くなったパンはがちがちする。*The stale bread is crunchy.*

gachín [to] がちん（と）*sharply; rattlingly* [*mimetic for the sound of bottles hitting against each other*] ❸Atamá o gachín to naguráreta. 頭をがちんと殴られた。*I was hit sharply on the head.*

gachō 鵞鳥 *goose*

gádo ガード *elevated railway bridge*

gágā がーがー ; ガーガー [*mimetic for a duck's cry*]

-gai 〜外 *outside (of)* ❸kikakúgai 規格外 *nonstandard; substandard*

gái 害 *harm; injury; hurt; damage* ❸gái ni náru 害になる *be harmful* ――**gai-súru** [*vt*] 害する *harm; injure; hurt; damage* ❸kenkō o gai-súru 健康を害する *damage (one's) health*

gáibu 外部 *exterior; outside* ❸gáibu kara no hihan 外部からの批判 *criticism from the outside*

Gáigā-keisūkan ガイガー計数管 *Geiger counter*

gaijin (*abbr*) (*see* **gaikokújin**)

gáika 外貨 *foreign currency* ❸gaika jumbí-daka 外貨準備高 *foreign currency reserves*

gaikan 概観 *outward appearance; façade*

gaiken 外見 *in appearance; outwardly*

gaikō 外交 *foreign diplomacy* ❸gaikōkan 外交官 *foreign diplomat* ❸gaikō séisaku 外交政策 *foreign policy* ❸gaikō kánkei 外交関係

diplomatic ties ❧gaikō rúto 外交ルート *diplomatic channel* ❧gaikō no seijōka 外交の正常化 *diplomatic normalization* ❧gaikō kánkei o juritsu-suru 外交関係を樹立する *establish diplomatic relations*

gaikoku 外国 *foreign country* ——**gaikoku no** 外国の *foreign* ❧gaikoku no énjo 外国の援助 *foreign aid* ❧gaikoku kawase gínkō 外国為替銀行 *foreign exchange bank* ❧gaikoku kawase shíjō 外国為替市場 *foreign exchange market* ❧gaikokusen 外国船 *foreign ship*

gaikokugo 外国語 *foreign language*

gaikokújin 外国人 *foreigner*

gaimu dáijin 外務大臣 *foreign minister*

gaimúshō 外務省 *Ministry of Foreign Affairs*

gáinen 概念 *concept; general idea*

gairaigo 外来語 *foreign loanword*

gairai kánja 外来患者 *outpatient*

gáiro 街路 *avenue; street*

gairon *outline; general remarks* ❧Eigogaku gáiron 英語学概論 *introduction to the study of English*

gairyaku 概略 *outline; summary*

gaisha 外車 *foreign-made automobile*

gáishi 外資 *foreign capital (funds)* ❧gáishi dōnyū 外資導入 *introduction of foreign capital*

gaishoku 外食 *eating out* ——**gaishoku-suru** [vi] 外食する *eat out*

gaishutsu-suru [vi] 外出する *go out (from one's home)*

gaiteki 外的 *external; bodily* ❧gaiteki jōken 外的の条件 *external conditions* ❧gaiteki yókubō 外的の欲望 *carnal desires*

gaitō 街灯 *street light*

gaitō 外套 *overcoat*

gaitō [no] 該当（の） *pertinent; relevant* ❧gaitósha 該当者 *relevant parties* ——**gaitō** 該当 *pertinent; relevant* ——**gaitō-suru** [vi] 該当する *come under; apply to; correspond to*

gáka 画架 *easel*

gaka 画家 *painter; artist*

gake 崖 *cliff; precipice*

gakí 餓鬼 *small child; brat* ❧gaki-dáishō 餓鬼大将 *bully; cock of the walk*

gakka 学科 *school subject; subject of study*

gakka 学課 *lesson*

gakkai 学会 *academic society; academic organization; academic conference*

gakkári-suru [vi] がっかりする *be disappointed*

gakki 学期 *school term; semester*

gakki 楽器 *musical instrument*

gakkō 学校 *school*

gakkúri がっくり [*onomatopoeia for a feeling of complete collapse*]
 §gakkúri to kubi o taréru がっくりと首を垂れる *hang one's head in defeat* §tōsan-shite gakkúri-suru 倒産してがっくりする *be overcome by bankruptcy*

gaku 額 *sum (of money); picture frame*

-gaku 〜学 *study of; -logy* §gengogaku 言語学 *linguistics* §keizáigaku 経済学 *economics* §shinrígaku 心理学 *psychology* §tetsúgaku 哲学 *philosophy*

gakubu 学部 *department; (university) division* §bungakúbu 文学部 *literature department* §igakúbu 医学部 *medical department*

gakubuchi 額縁 *picture frame*

gakuchō 学長 *(college) president*

gakudan 楽団 *orchestra*

gakufu 楽譜 *musical score*

gakuhi 学費 *school expenses*

gákui 学位 *(academic) degree*

gakumen kákaku 額面価格 *face value*

gakúmon 学問 *learning; studies; academic discipline* §gakúmon no jiyú 学問の自由 *academic freedom* ——**gakumonteki [na]** 学問的（な） *academic*

gakunen 学年 *year in school; school year*

gakureki 学歴 *academic career*

gakuryoku 学力 *scholarly attainments; scholastic ability*

gakusei 学生 *(university; high school) student*

gakusetsu 学説 *theory; doctrine*

gakusha 学者 *a scholar; an academic (person)*

gákushi 学士 *baccalaureate; bachelor's degree holder*

gamagáeru 蒲蛙 *toad*

gáman 我慢 *endurance; patience* ——**gáman-suru** [vt] 我慢する *be patient; endure*

gambár·u [vi gambaránai; gambátta] 頑張る *persevere; stick it out* §Gambátte! 頑張って！ *Hang in there!*

gámen 画面 *screen (for movie / TV / computer)*

gán 癌 *cancer* §gán no shújutsu 癌の手術 *cancer operation*

gángan がんがん；ガンガン *aching; ringing; clanging* §burikikan o gángan tatáku ブリキ缶をがんがん叩く *make a clanging noise with a tin can.* §Atamá ga gángan-suru. 頭ががんがんする。 *I have a splitting headache.*

gángu 玩具 *a toy*

Ganjitsu 元日 *New Year's Day*

ganjō [na] 頑丈（な） *solid; strong; robust* §ganjō na hako 頑丈な箱 *strong box*

ganka 眼科 *department of opthalmology*   §ganká'i 眼科医 *ophthalmologist*

gánka ni 眼下に *right under (one's) eyes*   §shígai o gánka ni miorosu 市街を眼下に見下ろす *look down upon the street*

gánko [na] 頑固（な）*hardheaded; stubborn*   §ganko óyaji 頑固親父 *stubborn father*

gánrai 元来 *originally; from the beginning; by nature; essentially*

Gantan 元旦 *New Year's Day*

gan'yaku 丸薬 *pill (Med)*

gappei 合併 *combination; merger; union; amalgamation; consolidation*   §shichōson gáppei 市町村合併 *consolidation (or union) of towns and villages*   §gappéishō 合併症 *a (medical) complication* ——**gappei-suru** [vt] 合併する *combine; merge*   §futátsu no kaisha o gappei-suru 二つの会社を合併する *merge two companies*

gara 柄 *pattern; design; in view of*   §jimí na gara 地味な柄 *a plain (or nondecorative) pattern*   §gara ga warúi 柄が悪い *vulgar; unrefined*   §Shigoto-gara, zeikin ni kuwashíi desu. 仕事柄、税金にくわしいです。*In view of my work, I am knowledgeable about taxes.*

garakuta がらくた *clutter; rubbish; odds and ends*

garasu ガラス *window pane; glass; plate glass*

garátto がらっと [*mimetic for a rattling sound*]   §mádo o garátto akeru 窓をがらっと開ける *noisily open a window*

garigarimōja 我利我利亡者 *grasping fellow; self-centered person*

garō 画廊 *art gallery*

-gár·u [*verb-forming suffix attatched to adjectives, not used with first person*] ～がる *(another's) feel (for); desire*   §omoshirogáru 面白がる *enjoy*   §samugáriya 寒がり屋 *someone extremely sensitive to cold*   §Kowagaránai de! 怖がらないで！*Don't be afraid!*

gasshō 合唱 *singing in chorus; choral music; chorus*

gasshódan 合唱団 *chorus*

gásu ガス *gas; mist*   §gasu mḗta ガスメーター *gas meter*   §gasu more ガス漏れ *gas leak*   §gasu sutóbu ガスストーブ *gas heater*

gasú shitsu ガス室 *gas chamber*

-gata ～方 [*plural suffix*]   §anatagáta あなた方 *you* [*plu*]

gatagata がたがた *with a clatter* [*mimetic for a rattling sound*]   §Sóshiki ga gatagata ni nátte iru. 組織ががたがたになっている。*The organization has become shaky.* ——**gátagata-suru** [vi] がたがたする *rattle; clatter; be shaky*   §Gátagata-surú na! がたがたするな！*Don't clatter (about) so!* <masc>

-gatái ～難い *difficult; hard*   §wasure-gatái 忘れ難い *difficult to forget*

gatchíri [to] がっちり（と）*solid; substantial; tightly*   §gatchíri to tsukámu がっちりと掴む *grasp tightly* ——**gatchíri-suru** [vi] がっちりする *be solid; close-fisted; shrewd*   §gatchíri-shita otoko がっち

りした男 *a shrewd fellow*

gaten ga iku 合点がいく *be convincing* ❀gaten ga ikanai 合点がいかない *be unconvincing*

-gátera 〜がてら *while...; partly for...* Sampo-gátera chótto ojísan no yōsu o mí ni ikimáshita. 散歩がてらちょっとお祖父さんの様子を見に行きました。*While I was taking a walk I looked in on Grandfather to see how he was.*

-gawa 〜側 *-side* ❀soto-gawa 外側 *the outside* ❀uchi-gawa 内側 *the inside* ❀migi-gawa 右側 *right side* ❀hidari-gawa 左側 *left side*

gáyagaya がやがや *noisily; in an uproar; in a hubbub* ──**gáyagaya-suru** [vi] がやがやする *be in a great hubbub* ❀Kaijōnai wa gáyagaya-shite ita. 会場内はがやがやしていた。*The meeting hall was in a great hubbub.*

gayōshi 画用紙 *drawing paper*

gebabō ゲバ棒 *wooden stave (used for fighting)*

gedan 下段 *lower berth*

gedatsu 解脱 *salvation; liberation (Budd)*

gedokuzai 解毒剤 *antidote (for poison)*

gehín [na] 下品（な）*vulgar; indecent; unrefined*

geigō-suru [vi] 迎合する *flatter; curry favor with; ingratiate oneself with (someone)* ❀taishū ni geigō-suru 大衆に迎合する *curry favor with the public*

geijutsu 芸術 *art* ❀Geijutsúin 芸術院 *Academy of Arts* ❀geijutsuka 芸術家 *artist* ──**geijutsuteki [na]** 芸術的（な）*artistic*

geinō 芸能 *entertainment* ❀geinójin 芸能人 *an entertainer* ❀geinókai 芸能界 *entertainment world* ❀taishū géinō 大衆芸能 *entertainment for the masses*

geisha 芸者 *geisha (professional female entertainer)*

gejun 下旬 *last third of a month*

geka 外科 *department of surgery* ❀geká-i 外科医 *surgeon* ❀geka shújutsu 外科手術 *surgical operation*

géki 劇 *drama* ❀shingeki 新劇 *Shingeki; the New Theatre* ❀gekidan 劇団 *theatrical group* ❀gekijō 劇場 *theater* ❀gekisákka 劇作家 *playwright*

gekirei 激励 *encouragement; incitement* ──**gekirei-suru** [vt] 激励する *encourage; spur on; cheer up* ❀jishin no hisáisha o gekirei-suru 地震の被災者を激励する *encourage the earthquake victims*

gekizō 激増 *sudden (marked) increase* ──**gekizō-suru** [vi] 激増する *show a sudden increase; rise rapidly*

gekkan [no] 月刊（の）*(published) monthly* ❀gekkan zásshi 月刊雑誌 *monthly magazine*

gekkei 月経 *menstruation; a woman's period* ❀gekkei-tai 月経帯 *sanitary belt*

gekkei heishíki 月経閉止期 *menopause*

gekkéiju 月桂樹 *laurel tree*

gekkō 月光 *moonlight*

gekkyū 月給 *(monthly) salary*

gemba 現場 *site; scene (where something takes place)*

gembaku 原爆 *atom bomb*

gembun 原文 *original (text)*

gémmai 玄米 *brown rice*

gemmetsu 幻滅 *disillusionment*

gemmitsu [na] 厳密（な）*strict; close; exact; rigid* ——**gemmitsu ni** 厳密に *strictly; exactly; rigidly*

gén 弦 *string (on a musical instrument)* ⑧**gengákki** 弦楽器 *stringed instrument*

génchi 現地 *the locale; the spot* ⑧**genchi chósa** 現地調査 *on-the-spot survey*

géndai 現代 *the present; the present age*

géndo 限度 *limitation; limit; a ceiling*

gendóryoku 原動力 *generative power; motive power; driving force*

gen'ei 幻影 *phantom; specter; vision*

géngo 言語 *language; speech* ⑧**gengógaku** 言語学 *linguistics* ⑧**géngo ni zessuru** 言語に絶する *beyond words; inexpressable*

gen'in 原因 *cause; reason* ——**gen'in-suru** [*vi*] 原因する *be caused (by); originate in*

genjitsu 現実 *actuality; reality* ⑧**genjitsu shúgi** 現実主義 *realistic; realism* ——**genjitsu no** 現実の *actual; real* ——**genjitsuteki [na]** 現実的（な）*realistic* ——**genjitsuteki ni** 現実的に *realistically*

genjō 現状 *(present) circumstance*

genjū [na] 厳重（な）*strict; severe; stern* ——**genjū ni** 厳重に *strictly; severely; sternly; firmly*

genjúmin 原住民 *a native; indigenous people; aborigine*

genkai 限界 *limit; limitation*

genkaku [na] 厳格（な）*strict; severe* ——**genkaku ni** 厳格に *strictly; severely*

génkan 玄関 *entry hall; vestibule*

génki 元気 *energy; vitality; pep* ——**génki na** 元気な *energetic; lively; healthy* ⑧**génki na kodomo** 元気な子供 *healthy (or lively) child*

genkín 現金 *cash* ⑧**genkin wáribiki** 現金割引 *cash discount*

genkin 厳禁 *strict prohibition; a ban* ——**genkin-suru** [*vt*] 厳禁する *prohibit strictly*

genkō 原稿 *manuscript; draft*

génkon 現今 *at present; nowadays*

genkotsu 拳骨 *(clenched) fist; knuckles*

genkyū 言及 *reference* ——**genkyū-suru** [*vi*] 言及する *mention; refer to*

génri 原理 *principle; theory*

genrō 元老 *elder statesman*

genryō 原料 *(raw) materials*

gensaku 原作 *an original (work)*

gensen chōshūzei 源泉徴収税 *withholding tax*

génshi 原始 *primitive* ❊genshi jídai 原始時代 *prehistory*

génshi 原子 *atom* ❊genshíryoku 原子力 *atomic energy; nuclear power*
❊genshiryoku jídai 原子力時代 *atomic age* ❊genshi héiki 原子兵器
atomic weapons ❊genshí-kaku 原子核 *atomic nucleus*
❊genshiryoku kūbo 原子力空母 *nuclear aircraft carrier*
❊genshíryoku hatsudensho 原子力発電所 *nuclear power plant*

genshō 現象 *phenomenon*

genshō 減少 *reduction* ——**genshō-suru** [vi] 減少する *decrease*

genshoku 原色 *primary color*

gensō 幻想 *fantasy; illusion*

gensoku 原則 *principle; general rule* ——**gensoku to shite** 原則として
in principle; as a principle

gensoku 減速 *deceleration* ——**gensoku-suru** [vt / vi] 減速する
decelerate

gensúibaku 原水爆 *atomic and hydrogen bombs*

gentei 限定 *limitation* ❊gentei- 限定～ ❊gentei-ban 限定版 *limited
edition* ——**gentei-suru** [vt] 限定する *limit; restrict*

gen'yu 原油 *crude oil*

génzai 現在 *the present times; now* ❊génzai ni óite (wa) 現在において
（は） *at present*

genzaikei 現在形 *present tense (Gram)*

genzei 減税 *tax cut*

genzō 現像 *film developing* ——**genzō-suru** [vt] 現像する *develop film*

geppu げっぷ *a belch; a burp* ❊geppu ga déru げっぷが出る *belch;
burp*

geppu 月賦 *monthly installment payment*

géragera げらげら [mimetic for loud laughter] ❊géragera warau げら
げら笑う *guffaw; give a horselaugh*

gerende ゲレンデ *ski slope*

geri 下痢 *diarrhea* ❊geri-dome 下痢止め *a paregoric*

gésha 下車 *getting off (a train)*

geshuku 下宿 *boarding; staying overnight* ——**geshuku-suru** [vi] 下宿
する *lodge*

gessha 月謝 *monthly (lesson) fee*

gesshoku 月食 *lunar eclipse*

gesui 下水 *sewage* ❊gesui shorijō 下水処理場 *sewage disposal plant*
❊gesui shísetsu 下水施設 *sewage facilities; drainage system*

geta 下駄 *wooden clogs*

Getsuyōbi 月曜日 *Monday*

gezai 下剤 *laxative*

gíchō 議長 *the chair; chairperson*

gifutóken ギフト券 *gift coupon*

gíin 議員 *assemblyman; Diet assemblyman; congressman*

gíji 議事 *agenda*

gijutsu 技術 *technique* ❈gijutsu chíshiki 技術知識 *technical knowhow* ❈gijutsu énjo 技術援助 *technical assistance* ❈gijutsúsha 技術者 *technician*——**gijutsuteki [na]** 技術的（な）*technical*—— **gijutsuteki ni** 技術的に *technically*

gíkai 議会 *national assembly; Diet; Congress* ❈Gikai séiji 議会政治 *parliamentary government*

gikochiná·i [adj gikochináku nái; gikochinákatta] ぎこちない *(be) awkward; clumsy*

gikyoku 戯曲 *a drama; a play*

gimon 疑問 *a question*

gimón-fu 疑問符 *question mark*

gímu 義務 *obligation* ❈gimu kyóiku 義務教育 *compulsory education*

gín 銀 *silver*

Gínga 銀河 *the Milky Way; the Galaxy*

ginkō 銀行 *bank* ❈ginkōka 銀行家 *banker* ❈ginkō ríshi 銀行利子 *bank interest* ❈chihō gínkō 地方銀行 *regional bank* ❈shintaku gínkō 信託銀行 *trust bank* ❈toshi gínkō 都市銀行 *city bank*

ginnán 銀杏 *ginkgo nut (see also* ichō)

gípusu ギプス *plaster cast; rigid surgical dressing*

girí 義理 *obligation; duty* ❈girí to nínjō 義理と人情 *duty and compassion*

girigiri ぎりぎり *just barely* ❈Saishū dénsha ni girigiri ma ni átta. 最終 電車にぎりぎり間に合った。*I just made the last train.* ——**girigiri no** ぎりぎりの *just within the limit; just in time*

girí no 義理の *in-law* ❈Konó hito wa girí no áni desu. この人は義理の 兄です。*This is my brother-in-law.*

gíron 議論 *argument; discussion; controversy*——**gíron-suru** [vt] 議論 する *argue; discuss* ❈Watashítachi wa atarashíi purójekuto ni tsúite ása made tetteiteki ni gíron-shita. 私たちは新しいプロジェクトにつ いて朝まで徹底的に議論した。*We discussed the new project inside and out until morning.*

gisei 犠牲 *a sacrifice* ❈giséisha 犠牲者 *a victim; person sacrificed* ❈Jishin no giséisha wa gosen-nin o koshita. 地震の犠牲者は五千人を 越した。*(The number of) victims of the earthquake exceeded five thousand.* ❈gisei ni suru 犠牲にする *to sacrifice*

gíshi 技師 *engineer; technician*

gíshiki 儀式 *ceremony; rites*

gisō 偽装；擬装 *camouflage; disguise* §gisō sátsujin 偽装殺人 *a fake murder* ——**gisō-suru** [*vt*] 偽装する *camouflage; disguise*
gisshíri ぎっしり [*onomatopoeia for "packed tightly"*] §gisshíri umeru ぎっしり埋める *pack in; crowd* §Sono hako no náka ni wa garakuta ga gisshíri tsumátte iru. その箱の中にはがらくたがぎっしり詰まっている。*The box is packed full of odds and ends.*
giwaku 疑惑 *suspicion; misgivings*
gizō 偽造 *forgery; fabrication* §gizō shíhei 偽造紙幣 *counterfeit bill* ——**gizō-suru** [*vt*] 偽造する *forge; counterfeit*
gó 五；5 *five (the numeral)*
gó 碁 *(the game of)* go
go- 御～ [*hon noun prefix*] §goshújin 御主人 *(another's) husband* §Gokúrōsama. 御苦労様 *Thank you (for all your work).*
-gṓ ～号 *Number-* [*suffix, attached to room numbers in hotels, train names, ship names, etc.*] §níjūyongṓ shitsu 24号室 *Room No. 24* §Asamágō 浅間号 *The "Asama" (Express)*
goban 碁盤 *a go board; a checkerboard*
gōben jígyō 合弁事業 *joint venture*
gobusata 御無沙汰 *a long time* ——**gobusata-suru** [*vi*] 御無沙汰する *be remiss (in writing)* §Nagáraku gobusata-shite orimásu. 長らく御無沙汰しております。*I haven't seen (**or** been in touch with) you for some time. <formal>*
gochagocha ごちゃごちゃ *confusion; disorder* §gochagocha ni náru ごちゃごちゃになる *become entangled; become confused* §gochagocha ni suru ごちゃごちゃにする *mix up; confuse*
gochisō 御馳走 *a feast* §gochisō ni náru 御馳走になる *be treated (to a meal)* §gochisō-suru 御馳走する *treat (to a meal)* §Gochisō-sama déshita. 御馳走様でした。*Thank you (for the meal).*
góchō 伍長 *(military) corporal*
gōdō 合同 *combination; amalgamation* §gōdō iínkai 合同委員会 *joint council* —— **gōdō-suru** [*vt*] 合同する *combine; amalgamate; unite*
gofuku-ya 呉服屋 *clothier (seller of Japanese-style clothing)*
[go-]fúsai （御）夫妻 *husband and wife; Mr. and Mrs. <formal>* §Súmisu-san go-fúsai スミスさん御夫妻 *Mr. and Mrs. Smith <formal>*
gógaku 語学 *language study*
Gógatsu 五月 *May*
gogen 語源 *word origin*
gogéngaku 語源学；語原学 *etymology*
gógo 午後 *afternoon; P.M.* §gógo sánji 午後三時 *3:00 PM*
góhan 御飯 *rice; a meal*
gōhō 合法 *lawful* §gōhō séifu 合法政府 *legitimate government*
gói 語彙 *vocabulary; a word*

gōi 合意 *mutual agreement* 🔹gōi gijíroku 合意議事録 *agreed-upon minutes; official minutes*

goji 誤字 *misprint; erratum*

gójitsu 後日 *later on; another day later on* 🔹gojitsúdan 後日談 *sequel*

gōjō [na] 強情（な）*stubborn; obstinate* 🔹gōjō o haru 強情を張る *be obstinate; act stubbornly* —— **gōjōppari [na]** 強情張り（な）*pigheaded; stubborn*

gojū no tố 五重の塔 *five-storied pagoda*

gốka [na] 豪華（な）*splendid; gorgeous*

gokai 誤解 *misunderstanding* —— **gokai-suru** [vt] 誤解する *misunderstand*

gōkaku 合格 *passing an examination* —— **gōkaku-suru** [vi] 合格する *pass* 🔹nyūgaku shíken ni gōkaku-suru 入学試験に合格する *pass the entrance exam*

gokan 五感 *the five senses*

gōkei 合計 *total amount*

gokiburi ごきぶり *cockroach*

Gokigen yố! ご機嫌好う！ *How are you?; Goodbye. <formal>*

-gókko 〜ごっこ *imitative playing* 🔹oni-gókko 鬼ごっこ *playing "It"*

góku 極く *very* 🔹góku wázuka 極くわずか *very little* 🔹Góku jōtō da. 極く上等だ。*It's top class; It's excellent. <masc>*

Gokúrōsama! 御苦労様！ *Thank you (for your effort).*

goma 胡麻 *sesame; sesame seed* 🔹goma o íru 胡麻を煎る *toast sesame seeds* 🔹goma o súru 胡麻を摺る *flatter; curry favor (with)*

gomakashi 誤魔化し *deceit; manipulation*

gomakás·u [vt gomakasánai; gomakáshita] 誤魔化す *deceive; cheat; cover up; gloss over* 🔹toshí o gomakásu 年を誤魔化す *lie about one's age* 🔹otsuri o gomakásu おつりを誤魔化す *short-change (someone)*

gōman [na] 傲慢（な）*haughty; arrogant* 🔹gōman na táido 傲慢な態度 *arrogant attitude; stuck-up attitude*

gōman-sa 傲慢さ *arrogance; haughtiness*

Gomen dá! 御免だ！ *Excuse me!; Count me out!* 🔹Sore o surú no wa gomen da. それをするのは御免だ。*I'll have nothing to do with that. <masc>*

Gomen kudasái! 御免下さい！ *I beg your pardon! (an address used in place of knocking for admittance); Goodbye! (on the telephone)*

Gomen nasái. 御免なさい。 *I'm sorry; Pardon me.*

gomí ごみ *trash; dirt; filth* 🔹gomi-bako ごみ箱 *trash can* 🔹gomíya(-san) ごみ屋（さん）*garbage collector* 🔹Gomí o dáshite kudasái. ごみを出して下さい。*Take out the garbage, please.*

gōmon 拷問 *torture* —— **gōmon-suru** [vt] 拷問する *(to) torture*

gómu ゴム *rubber*

goraku 娯楽 *amusement; pastime*

[-te] goran 〜てごらん *try ...-ing [vb aux; hon]* ❧Anó hito ni kīite goran. あの人に聞いてごらん。 *Try asking her.* ❧Kore o tábete-goran. これを食べてごらん。 *Have some of this. (or Try [eating] this.)*

goran ni nár·u [*vt* -naránai; -nátta] ご覧になる *look at; see <formal>*

gōri 合理 *rationality* ❧gōrisei 合理性 *rationality* ❧gōrika 合理化 *rationalization* ——**gōriteki [na]** 合理的（な）*reasonable*

-góro 〜頃 *approximately (usually with time)* ❧Goji-góro ni wa kaerimásu. 五時頃には帰ります。 *I'll be home about five.*

górogoro ごろごろ；ゴロゴロ *rumbling [mimetic for the sound of thunder]; tumbling* ❧Kaminari ga górogoro natte iru. 雷がごろごろ鳴っている。 *It's thundering.* ❧Ishí ga górogoro korogatte iru. 石がごろごろ転がっている。 *Rocks are tumbling.*

gōryū 合流 *(traffic) converging; coming together* ——**gōryū-suru** [*vi*] 合流する *converge*

gōsei 合成 *synthetic* ❧gōsei sénzai 合成洗剤 *synthetic detergent* ——**gōsei-suru** [*vt*] 合成する *synthesize; compound*

gotagota ごたごた *trouble; difficulties; complications* ——**gótagota-suru** [*vi*] ごたごたする *be confused; be in a turmoil*

gōtō 強盗 *burglar; robber; housebreaker*

gōtto ごうっと *rumbling; thundering [mimetic for a rumbling, thundering sound]* ❧Jetto-kṓsutā ga gōtto otó o tátete sugói supído de hashítte iru. ジェットコースターがごうっと音を立てて凄いスピードで走っている。 *The jet coaster goes at a tremendous speed making a thundering sound.*

goyō 御用 *an order; business; errand* ❧Náni ka goyō desu ka? 何か御用 ですか。 *Do you have some business (here)?*

gozá ござ *straw mat*

gozár·u [*vi* gozaimasén; gozaimáshita] ござる *be; exist; have [<formal> for ar·u]* ❧Watakushi no kaisha wa Shinjukú Eki no minami-guchi no chikáku ni gozaimásu. 私の会社は新宿駅の南口の近くにございます。 *My company (or office) is near the south exit of Shinjuku Station. <fomal> (see also de gozár·u)*

gózen 午前 *morning; AM*

gozónji desu ご存じです *know [<formal> for shir·u]* ❧Anáta wa Tanaka-san o gozónji desu ka? あなたは田中さんをご存じですか。 *Do you know Ms. Tanaka? <formal>*

gu 具 *ingredients; condiments; topping (for pizza)*

guai 具合 *condition; disposition* ❧Guai ga íi. 具合がいい。 *I'm fine. (or I feel fine.)* ❧Guai ga warúi. 具合が悪い。 *I'm not doing so well.* ❧Karada no guai wa ikága desu ka? 身体の具合はいかがですか。 *How are you? (lit: What is your physical condition?)*

guchi 愚痴 *complaining; grumbling*

gúmbi 軍備 *armaments*   ⑧gumbi kákudai 軍備拡大 *arms increase*   ⑧gumbi shúkushō 軍備縮小 *arms reduction*   ⑧gumbi kyṓsō 軍備競争 *arms race*

gún 郡 *rural district; rural county*

gún 軍 *troops; army*   ⑧gúntai 軍隊 *military*   ⑧gun shiréibu 軍指令部 *military headquarters*   ⑧gunjin 軍人 *serviceman*   ⑧taieki gúnjin 退役軍人 *ex-serviceman*   ⑧gúnsō 軍曹 *(military) sergeant*

gunji 軍事 *naval and military affairs*   ⑧gunji dṓmei 軍事同盟 *military alliance*   ⑧gunji kíchi 軍事基地 *military base*   ⑧gunji kúnren 軍事訓練 *military exercise*   ⑧gunji shísetsu 軍事施設 *military facilities*

gunju 軍需 *munitions*

gunkan 軍艦 *warship*

gunshū 群衆 *crowd; large group of people*   ⑧gunshū kṓdō 群衆行動 *group behavior*   ⑧gunshū shínri 群衆心理 *mob psychology*

guntō 群島 *group of islands; archipelago*   ⑧Māsharu Gúntō マーシャル群島 *the Marshall Islands*

guragurátto ぐらぐらっと *in a shaking manner; unsteadily*   ⑧Jishin de ié ga guragurátto yureta. 地震で家がぐらぐらっと揺れた。 *The house shook terribly in the earthquake.*

gúrai 位 *extent; degree*   ⑧Gáman-dekínai gúrai itái. 我慢できないぐらい痛い。 *The pain is unbearable.*

-gúrai [-kúrai] ～位；～ぐらい *about*   ⑧jūnin-gúrai 十人ぐらい *about ten people*

gurátan グラタン *casserole*   ⑧makaroni gurátan マカロニグラタン *macaroni casserole*

gúrume グルメ *gourmet*

gúsha 愚者 *a fool*

gussúri ぐっすり *soundly*   ⑧Sakúya wa gussúri nemutta. 昨夜はぐっすり眠った。 *I slept soundly last night.*

gūsū 偶数 *an even (vs odd) number*

gutaiteki [na] 具体的（な）*concrete; definite*   ⑧Gutaiteki na hanashí ga shitái. 具体的な話がしたい。 *I'd like to talk about specifics (not in an abstract way).* ——**gutaiteki ni** 具体的に *concretely; definitely*

gūtara ぐうたら *a lazybones; a good-for-nothing*   ⑧gūtara téishu ぐうたら亭主 *a good-for-nothing husband*

gūtarasa ぐうたらさ *laziness*

guttári tsukarér·u [*vi* -tsukarénai; -tsukáreta] ぐったり疲れる *be dog tired*

gūzen 偶然 *coincidence*   ⑧gūzen no itchí 偶然の一致 *coincidental agreement* ——**gūzen ni** 偶然に *accidentally*   ⑧gūzen ni deáu 偶然に出会う *meet accidentally*

gūzō 偶像 *idol* ——**gūzōka-suru** [*vt*] 偶像化する *idolize*

gúzuguzu [to] ぐずぐず（と）*slowly; lazily; sluggishly*   ⑧gúzuguzu to shigoto o suru ぐずぐずと仕事をする *work slowly; goof off on the job* ◊Káre wa henjí o gúzuguzu hikinobáshite iru. 彼は返事をぐずぐず引き伸ばしている。*He keeps putting off his answer.* ——**gúzuguzu-suru** [*vi*] ぐずぐずする *shirk; fool around*

gyā́gyā ぎゃあぎゃあ [*mimetic for loud crying or squalling*] ◊Ákachan ga gyā́gyā naite iru yo. 赤ちゃんがぎゃあぎゃあ泣いているよ。*The baby's squalling!*

gyakkō 逆行 *retrogression; reverse movement*

gyakkṓka 逆効果 *adverse effect*

gyaku 逆 *the reverse; contrary* ——**gyaku ni** 逆に *on the contrary*

gyakusatsu 虐殺 *massacre; slaughter* ——**gyakusatsu-suru** [*vt*] 虐殺する *massacre; slaughter*

gyakushū-suru [*vi*] 逆襲する *counterattack*

gyakutai 虐待 *abuse* ◊jídō gyakutai 児童虐待 *child abuse* ——**gyakutai-suru** [*vt*] 虐待する *abuse*

gyakuten 逆転 *reversal; (termperature) inversion* ——**gyakuten-suru** [*vi / vt*] 逆転する *become reversed; become inverted*

gyṓ 行 *line (of text)*

gyōgi 行儀 *manners; behavior*

gyógyō 漁業 *fishing industry*

gyōji 行事 *planned event; a function*

gyōkan 行間 *between the lines*

gyokō 漁港 *fishing harbor*

gyōretsu 行列 *procession; parade; line*

gyōsei 行政 *public administration; management* ◊chihō gyṓsei 地方行政 *local administration* ◊gyōsei kíkan 行政機関 *administrative organ* ◊gyōsei tṓkyoku 行政当局 *administrative authorities* ◊gyōsei shídō 行政指導 *administrative guidance* ◊Gyōsei Kanríchō 行政管理庁 *Administrative Management Agency*

gyōsho 行書 *cursive style (of Japanese calligraphy)*

gyōshōnin 行商人 *traveling salesman; peddler*

gyoson 漁村 *fishing village*

gyotto-suru [*vi*] ぎょっとする *be startled; be shocked* ◊Sore o kiite gyotto-shita. それを聞いてぎょっとした。*I was shocked when I heard that*

gyūniku 牛肉 *beef*

gyūnyū 牛乳 *milk* ◊tei-shibō gyū́nyū 低脂肪牛乳 *low-fat milk*

gyutto ぎゅっと *firmly; tightly* ◊nawá de gyutto shibáru 縄でぎゅっと縛る *tie tightly with a rope*

H

ha 葉 *a leaf*

há 歯 *tooth; teeth* §háisha 歯医者 *dentist* §hamígaki 歯磨 *toothpaste*

há 刃 *edge; blade* §kamisorí no há 剃刀の刃 *razor blade*

haba 幅 *width; breadth; range*

habatsu; ha 派閥 ; 派 *faction; group; coterie* §sáha 左派 *leftists* §takaha 鷹派 *hawks*

hábu はぶ *a poisonous snake found in the Ryukyu Islands*

habúk·u [*vt* habukánai; habúita] 省く *remove; omit; exclude; save* §Kono bún de wa shúgo o habúite mo íi desu yo. この文では主語を省いてもいいですよ。*You may omit the subject in this sentence.*

habúrashi 歯ブラシ *toothbrush*

hachi 蜂 *bee; wasp; hornet* §hachi no su 蜂の巣 *a beehive*

hachí 鉢 *pot (for plants)* §hachiue 鉢植え *potted plant*

hachí 八 ; 8 *eight (the numeral)*

Hachigatsú 八月 *August*

hachímaki 鉢巻 *headband*

hachimitsu 蜂蜜 *honey*

hachū́rui 爬虫類 *reptile*

háda 肌 ; 膚 *the skin*

hadaka [no] 裸 （の） *naked; nude; bare*

hadashi 裸足 *barefoot*

hadé [na] 派手 （な） *gay; showy; bright; loud; noisy; garish; gaudy; flashy* §hadé na gara 派手な柄 *a showy pattern* §hade-gónomi 派手好み *be fond of show* ――**hadé ni** 派手に *loudly; gaudily* §hadé ni furumáu 派手に振舞う *behave in a flashy manner*

hadome 歯止め *a brake* §kū́ki hádome 空気歯止め *an air brake* §Séifu wa kyūgeki na en-daka ni hadome o kakéru seisaku o tótta. 政府は急激な円高に歯止めをかける政策をとった。*The government took measures to put a stop to the sudden rise in the value of the yen.*

hae 蝿 *fly (insect)* §hae tátaki 蝿叩き *fly swatter*

haé·ru [*vi* haénai; háeta] 生える *grow; spring up* §kí ga haéru 木が生える *trees grow* §Ákachan wa há ga háeta. 赤ちゃんは歯が生えた。*The baby has a tooth coming in.*

haé·ru [*vi* haénai; háeta] 映える *shine; excel; be popular* §haénai hito 映えない人 *a dull person; a person who doesn't stand out* §Sono fukú wa haéru. その服は映える。*That outfit will be a hit.*

hagaki 葉書 *postcard*

hagás·u [*vt* hagasánai; hagáshita] 剥がす *peel off; tear off*

hage-átama no 禿げ頭の *bald-headed*

hagemashi 励まし *encouragement*

hagemás·u [*vt* hagemasánai; hagemáshita] 励ます *encourage; cheer up*

&Háha wa hagemáshite kureta. 母は励ましてくれた。 *My mother encouraged me.*

hagém·u [vi hagemánai; hagénda] 励む *endeavor; strive; work hard*
&Musuko wa benkyō ni hagénde imásu. 息子は勉強に励んでいます。 *My son is working hard at his studies.*

hagé·ru [vi hagénai; hágeta] 剥げる *fall off (in layers); peel* &Penki ga hágeta. ペンキが剥げた。 *The paint peeled.*

hagé·ru [vi hagénai; hágeta] 禿げる *become bald* &Shújin wa dandan atamá ga hágete kimáshita. 主人はだんだん頭が禿げてきました。 *My husband has gradually become bald.*

hageshí·i [adj hagéshiku nái; hagéshikatta] 激しい *(be) fierce; violent; intense* &hageshíi áme 激しい雨 *a heavy rain* &hageshíi itami 激しい痛み *a severe pain* &hageshíi kishō 激しい気性 *a violent disposition* &hageshíi renshū 激しい練習 *hard practice; a hard workout*

hagewashi 禿鷲 *vulture*

hagoromo 羽衣 *robe of feathers; angel's robe*

hág·u [vt hagánai; háida] 剥ぐ *peel off; tear off; strip off*

háguki 歯茎 *gums; alveolar ridge*

hagúruma 歯車 *gear* &hagúruma no há 歯車の歯 *a gear tooth*

háha 母 *(one's own) mother* &hahaoya 母親 *mother (parent)*

hahen 破片 *broken piece; fragment* &garasu no hahen ガラスの破片 *a piece of broken glass*

hai 灰 *ash* &haizara 灰皿 *ashtray*

hai 肺 *the lungs*

Hái! はい！ *Yes!; I heard you.*

-hai; -bai; -pai 〜杯 *classifier for cupfuls, glassfuls, bowlfuls, spoonfuls*

háibi 配備 *arrangement; deployment* &haibi kéikaku 配備計画 *deployment plan* ——**háibi-suru** [vt] 配備する *deploy* &búki o háibi-suru 武器を配備する *deploy weapons*

haiboku 敗北 *a defeat* ——**haiboku-suru** [vi] 敗北する *be defeated; be beaten*

haibun 配分 *allotment; apportionment; distribution* &hirei háibun 比例配分 *proportional allotment* ——**haibun-suru** [vt] 配分する *allot; distribute*

haichaku 廃嫡 *disinheritance* ——**haichaku-suru** [vt] 廃嫡する *disinherit*

haichi 配置 *arrangement; placement* ——**haichi-suru** [vt] 配置する *arrange; place; distribute*

haiden 配電 *electric power distribution* &haidensho 配電所 *electric power (distribution) station* &haidemban 配電盤 *switchboard*

haiei 背泳 *backstroke*

haien 肺炎 *pneumonia*

háifun ハイフン *hyphen*

haiga 胚芽 *embryo; germ* §komugi no haiga 小麦の胚芽 *wheat germ* §haiga-mai 胚芽米 *whole rice (**or** embryo rice)*

haigū́sha 配偶者 *mate; spouse* §haigūsha téate 配偶者手当 *spouse's personal allowance*

háihai 這いはい *a crawl (term used for infants)* ——**háihai-suru** [*vi*] 這いはいする *crawl*

hai-iro 灰色 *gray*

háijo 排除 *exclusion; rejection* ——**háijo-suru** [*vt*] 排除する *exclude; reject; eliminate; remove* §Kidōtai ga barikḗdo o háijo-shita. 機動隊がバリケードを排除した。*The riot squad removed the barricade.*

haikankō 配管工 *plumber*

haikei 背景 *background; backdrop*

haiken-suru [*vt*] 拝見する *look at; see* *<formal>*

haiki 排気 *exhaust* §haiki gásu 排気ガス *exhaust (gas / fumes)* §haiki gásu kisoku kíjun 排気ガス規則基準 *emission gas standards*

haiku 俳句 *haiku (seventeen syllable poem)*

háikyo 廃墟 *ruins*

haikyū 配給 *a ration* ——**haikyū-suru** [*vt*] 配給する *ration (out); distribute*

haimawár·u [*vi* haimawaránai; haimawátta] 這い回る *crawl about; creep*

háir·u [*vi* hairánai; háitta] 入る *enter; join* §náka ni háiru 中に入る *go inside* §daigaku ni háiru 大学に入る *enter college* §o-fúro ni háiru お風呂に入る *take a bath* §kúrabu ni háiru クラブに入る *join a (school) club*

háiryo 配慮 *concern; consideration* §háiryo ni ireru 配慮に入れる *take into consideration*

haisen 敗戦 *defeat in war*

háisha 歯医者 *dentist*

haishaku-suru [*vt*] 拝借する *borrow* *<formal>*

haishi 廃止 *abolition; discontinuance* ——**haishi-suru** [*vt*] 廃止する *abolish; discontinue; abrogate*

haisui 排水 *drainage; waste water* §haisuikan 排水管 *drainpipe*

haisú·ru [*vt* haishínai; háishita] 拝する *worship* §butsuzō o haisúru 仏像を拝する *worship a Buddhist image*

haitateki [na] 排他的（な） *exclusive; cliquish; clannish*

haitatsu 配達 *delivery* ——**haitatsu-suru** [*vt*] 配達する *deliver*

haiyū 俳優 *actor; actress*

hají 恥 *shame; embarrassment*; *disgrace; dishonor*

hajimar·u [*vi* hajimaranai; hajimatta] 始まる *begin; start* §Gakkō wa kúji ni hajimarimásu. 学校は九時に始まります。*School begins at nine.*

hajime 初め *the beginning* §hajime kara yarinaósu 初めからやり直す

make a fresh start ❊hajime no uchi wa 初めのうちは *at first; in the beginning*

Hajimemáshite. 初めまして。 *I'm pleased to meet you.* <set phrase>

hajime·ru [vt hajimenai; hajimeta] 始める *begin; start* ❊Watashi wa kyónen kara atarashíi jígyō o hajimemáshita. 私は去年から新しい事業を始めました。 *I started a new business last year.*

-hajime·ru 〜始める *begin to (do)* ❊Sore o tsukuri-hajimeta bákari desu. それを作り始めたばかりです。 *I've just begun to make it.*

hajímete 初めて *for the first time* ❊Nihón wa hajímete desu ka. 日本は初めてですか。 *Is this your first time in Japan?*

haká 墓 *a grave; tomb* ❊haka-ishi 墓石 *tombstone; gravestone*

hakai 破壊 *destruction; wrecking; demolition* ❊hakai kátsudō 破壊活動 *subversive activities* ❊hakai kátsudō bōshi-hō 破壊活動防止法 *Anti-Subversive Activities Law* ——**hakai-suru** [vt] 破壊する *destroy; ruin; demolish*

hakamá 袴 *a divided skirt for men's traditional formal wear*

hakarí 秤 *a balance; scale*

hakár·u [vt hakaránai; hakátta] 測る *measure; gauge*

hakár·u [vt hakaránai; hakátta] 計る；図る *plan; project; design; plot; scheme* ❊keikaku o hakáru 計画を計る *make a plan*

hákase; hákushi 博士 *Doctor of Philosophy (Ph.D.)* ❊Jónzu-hakase ジョーンズ博士 *Dr. Jones* ❊hakasé-gō 博士号 *Ph.D. degree* ❊hakasé-gō o tóru 博士号をとる *earn a Ph.D.*

hakidas·u [vt hakidasanai; hakidashita] 吐き出す *vomit; throw up; spit out*

hakiké 吐き気 *nausea* ❊hakiké o moyōsu 吐き気を催す *feel like throwing up* ❊hakiké ga suru 吐き気がする *feel nauseous; feel like vomiting*

hakimono 履物 *footwear*

hakka 薄荷 *mint; pepperment; menthol*

hakken 発見 *discovery* ❊hakkénsha 発見者 *discoverer* ——**hakken-suru** [vt] 発見する *discover*

hakketsubyō 白血病 *leukemia*

hakki 発揮 *a display; show* ——**hakki-suru** [vt] 発揮する *exhibit; show; display* ❊jitsuryoku o hakki-suru 実力を発揮する *show (one's) ability*

hakkíri [to] はっきり（と） *clearly; distinctly* ❊Watashi wa jibun no íken o hakkíri itta. 私は自分の意見をはっきり言った。 *I expressed my opinion clearly.*

hakkō 発酵 *fermentation* ——**hakkō-suru** [vi] 発酵する *ferment* ❊Chízu wa gyūnyū o hakkō-sasete tsukurimásu. チーズは牛乳を発酵させて作ります。 *Cheese is made by fermenting milk.*

hakkō 発行 *publication; issue* ——**hakkō-suru** [vt] 発行する *publish*

hakkō-suru [vi] 発効する　*go into effect; become effective*　§Nikokú-kan de no heiwa jṓyaku ga shigatsu tsuitachí ni hakkō-suru kotó ni nátta. 二国間での平和条約が四月一日に発効することになった。*The peace agreement between the two countries is to go into effect on April 1.*

hakkyō 発狂　*madness; insanity* ――**hakkyō-suru** [vi] 発狂する　*become insane*

hako 箱　*box; case*

hakobidás·u [vt hakobidasánai; hakobidáshita] 運び出す　*haul; carry (or take) out (of a house / room)*　§Hikkoshi no nímotsu o zémbu hakobidáshita. 引っ越しの荷物を全部運び出した。*We've hauled all the articles that are to be moved.*

hakob·u [vt hakobanai; hakonda] 運ぶ　*carry; transport; haul*　§O-sara o ·daidokoro ni hakonde kudasái. お皿を台所に運んで下さい。*Please carry these dishes to the kitchen.*

hak·u [vt hakanai; haita] 履く　*wear; put on (trousers / shoes / etc.)*　§zubón o haku ズボンを履く　*put on (one's) trousers*　§kutsúshita o haku 靴下を履く　*put on (wear) socks*　§Kánojo wa sukáto o haite iru. 彼女はスカートを履いている。*She is wearing a skirt.*

hák·u [vt hakánai; háita] 掃く　*sweep; brush*　§hṓki de heyá o háku ほうきで部屋を掃く　*sweep the room with a broom*

hák·u [vt hakánai; háita] 吐く　*vomit; throw up; spit out; puff out*　§íki o háku 息を吐く　*blow (one's) breath*　§honne o háku 本音を吐く　*disclose (one's) real intention*

-haku; [-paku] 〜泊　*overnight stay*　§níhaku mikká 二泊三日　*two nights and three days*　§sámpaku yokká 三泊四日　*three nights and four days*

hakuai shugísha 博愛主義者　*humanitarian*

hakubutsúkan 博物館　*museum*　§Kokuritsu Hakubutsúkan 国立博物館 *the National Museum*

hakuchō 白鳥　*swan*

hakuchū 白昼　*broad daylight*　§hakuchū́mu 白昼夢 *a daydream*　§Hakuchū, gōtō ni hairáreta. 白昼、強盗に入られた。*Our house was burglarized in broad daylight.*

hakugai 迫害　*persecution; oppression* ――**hakugai-suru** [vt] 迫害する *persecute; oppress*　§takokúmin o hakugai-suru 他国民を迫害する *persecute foreign nationals*

hakuhyō 白票　*blank ballot*　§hakuhyō o tōjiru 白票を投じる　*cast a blank ballot (or refrain from voting)*

hakujin 白人　*Caucasian; white person*

hákujō 白状　*confession* ――**hákujō-suru** [vt] 白状する　*confess; acknowledge*

hakunaishō 白内障　*cataract (eye disease)*

hakuránkai 博覧会　*fair; exhibition*　§bankoku hakuránkai 万国博覧会

world fair

hakusái 白菜 *Chinese cabbage*

hakusei 剥製 *stuffed specimen (animal / bird)*

hakushaku 伯爵 *count (title of nobility)*

hakushi 白紙 *blank paper*   ❽hakushi ínin 白紙委任 *a carte blanche*   ❽hakushi no jōtai 白紙の状態 *a clean slate*   ❽hakushi ni modósu 白紙に戻す *start over again from scratch*

hákushu 拍手 *applause* —— **hákushu-suru** [vt] 拍手する *applaud*

hamá 浜 *beach*

hamachi はまち *yellowtail (fish)*

hamáguri 蛤 *clam (shellfish)*

hamar·u [vi hamaranai; hamatta] 填まる *fit; be suited to; fall into place*

hambágā ハンバーガー *hamburger*

hambai 販売 *selling; distribution*   ❽hambai sókushin 販売促進 *sales promotion*

hambáiki 販売機 *vending machine*

hambún 半分 *half*

-hamé ～羽目 *a fix; plight*   ❽kurushíi hamé ni ochiiru 苦しい羽目に陥る *get into a bad fix*

hame·ru [vt hamenai; hameta] 填める *put on; fit into*   ❽Jigusō pázuru no písu o koko ni hamete kudasái. ジグソーパズルのピースをここに填めて下さい。*Fit the jigsaw puzzle piece in here.*

hamidás·u [vi hamidasánai; hamidáshita] はみ出す *protrude; stick out*   ❽Nakámi ga hamidáshite iru yo! 中味がはみ出しているよ！*The contents are sticking out!*

hamígaki 歯磨 *toothpaste*

hámmā ハンマー *hammer*

hampatsu 反発 *rebellion; resistance; opposition; (negative) reaction* —— **hampatsu-suru** [vi] 反発する *rebel; resist; oppose; react against*   ❽Bōeki fukínkō de Amerika ga hampatsu-shite iru. 貿易不均衡でアメリカが反発している。*America is reacting against the trade imbalance.*

hán 判 *seal; stamp; chop*   ❽Koko ni hán o oshite kudasái. ここに判を押して下さい。*Please affix your seal here.*

han- 半～ *semi-; half*   ❽hambún 半分 *one half*   ❽hángetsu 半月 *half-moon*   ❽hantoshi 半年 *half a year*   ❽hambyónin 半病人 *a semi-invalid*   ❽hannichi 半日 *half a day*   ❽hangaku 半額 *half fare*   ❽hambiraki 半開き *half open*   ❽hanzúbon 半ズボン *short pants*   ❽hán'eikyūteki [na] 半永久的（な）*semipermanent*

-hán ～半 *half-past*   ❽rokuji hán 六時半 *half-past six*   ❽kōhan 後半 *the last half*

-han ～版 *edition*   ❽shohan 初版 *first edition (see also* **-ban***)*

haná 花 *flower*   ❽hanáya 花屋 *florist*   ❽hanawa 花輪 *floral wreath*

hana 鼻 *nose* §hana-gúsuri 鼻薬 *nose drops* §hana no aná 鼻の穴 *nostril* §hana ga takái 鼻が高い *high-bridged nose; be proud*

hánabi 花火 *fireworks* §uchiage hánabi 打ち上げ花火 *a skyrocket* §hanabi táikai 花火大会 *fireworks display*

hanabíra 花びら *petal*

hanahada 甚だ *very; awfully; terribly; exceedingly* §Anáta wa issho ni irassharánakute, hanahada zannén da wa. あなたは一緒にいらっしゃらなくて、甚だ残念だわ。*I'm terribly sorry you're not going!* *<fem>* §Konna kotó o saretara, hanahada méiwaka da. こんな事をされたら甚だ迷惑だ。*It's a great imposition on me to have you do such a thing. <masc>*

hanahadashí·i [*adj* hanahadáshiku nái; hanahadáshikatta] 甚だしい *(be) drastic; great; marked; serious* §hanahadashíi gokai 甚だしい誤解 *a serious misunderstanding.* ——**hanahadashíku** 甚だしく *drastically; extremely; markedly*

hanaji 鼻血 *nosebleed*

hanami 花見 *viewing cherry blossoms* §hanami ni iku 花見に行く *go to see the cherry blossoms*

hanamizu 鼻水 *nasal discharge; mucous; snot* §Hanamizu ga déru. 鼻水が出る *My nose is running.*

hanamízuki 花水木 *dogwood*

hanamúko 花婿 *bridegroom*

hanaréjima 離れ島 *remote island*

hanaré·ru [*vt* hanarénai; hanáreta] 離れる *leave; separate (from); quit* §oyamoto o hanaréru 親元を離れる *leave (one's) parents* §shoku o hanaréru 職を離れる *quit (one's) job* §té ga hanaréru 手が離れる *be free of (responsibility)* ——[*attr*] **hanáreta** 離れた *out-of-the-way; separated from*

hanashí 話 *a talk; speech* §Musume no endan no hanashí ga susunde iru. 娘の縁談の話が進んでいる。*The talks leading to arrangements for my daughter's marriage are proceeding.*

hanashiai 話し合い *conversation; talks* §Hanashiai no kekka o shirasete kudasái. 話し合いの結果を知らせて下さい。*Please let me know the outcome of the talks.*

hanashiá·u [*vi* hanashiawánai; hanashiátta] 話し合う *talk with one another; talk over*

hanashikaké·ru [*vi* hanashikakénai; hanashikáketa] 話しかける *speak to; address; accost*

hana-shṓbu 花菖蒲 *iris (Bot)*

hanás·u [*vt* hanasánai; hanáshita] 話す *speak; converse; talk*

hanás·u [*vt* hanasánai; hanáshita] 離す；放す *free; release; let go of; take off (of / from)* §mé o hanásu 目を離す *take (one's) eyes off* §té o handoru kara hanásu 手をハンドルから離す *take (one's) hands off*

the steering wheel　§kotori o kago kara hanásu　小鳥を籠から放す
free a bird from its cage

hanatába 花束 *bunch of flowers*

hanáya 花屋 *florist*

hanáyaka [na] 華やか（な）*bright; colorful; gorgeous*　§Sono
kekkónshiki wa hanáyaka datta wa!　その結婚式は華やかだったわ。
The wedding was gorgeous! <*fem*> §Kánojo wa hanáyaka na sonzai
da. 彼女は華やかな存在だ。*She is a gorgeous creature.* <*masc*>
——**hanáyaka ni** 華やかに *brilliantly; gorgeously*

hanáyome 花嫁 *bride*

hanazono 花園 *flower garden*

handa ハンダ *solder; pewter*

handō 反動 *reaction; counteraction*　§handō shugísha 反動主義者 *a
reactionary* ——**handōteki [na]** 反動的（な）*reactionary*
§handōteki na undō 反動的な運動 *reactionary movement* ——**handō-
suru** [*vi*] 反動する *react (to); counteract; rebound*

handoru ハンドル *steering wheel*

hane 羽；羽根 *feather*

hanechirás·u [*vt* hanechirasánai; hanechiráshita] 跳ね散らす *splash*

han'ei 繁栄 *prosperity* ——**han'ei-suru** [*vi*] 繁栄する *prosper; go well*

han'ei 反映 *reflection* ——**han'ei-suru** [*vt*] 反映する *reflect; be
reflected in*　§Fásshon wa sesó o han'ei-suru. ファッションは世相を
反映する。*Fashions reflect the times.*

hanekáe·ru [*vi* hanekaeránai; hanekáetta] 跳ね返る *rebound; splash*
§Mizu ga hanekáetta. 水が跳ね返った。*The water splashed.*　§Kabe
ni atatte bōru ga hanekáetta. 壁に当たってボールが跳ね返った。*The
ball bounced off the wall.*　§En-daka ga kakaku ni hanekáette iru. 円高
が価格に跳ね返っている。*The strong yen affects prices.*

hané·ru [*vi* hanénai; háneta] 跳ねる *leap; jump; hop*　§Usagi ga
pyónpyon hánete itta. 兎がぴょんぴょん跳ねていった。*The rabbit
hopped away.*

hané·ru [*vt* hanénai; háneta] 跳ねる *knock down; hit (with a car)*
§kuruma de hito o hanéru 車で人を跳ねる *hit a person with a car*

hanétsuki 羽根突き *shuttlecock and battledore (a game resembling
badminton)*

hanga 版画 *(woodblock) print*

hán'i 範囲 *scope; range; extent*　§Sore wa watashi no semmon hán'i ni
hairimásu. それは私の専門範囲に入ります。*That's in my field of
specialization.*　§kō-hán'i 広範囲 *wide range (scope; scale)*

hanikami はにかみ *shyness*　§hanikamiya はにかみ屋 *a bashful
person*　§hanikamiya no はにかみ屋の *bashful; self-conscious*

hanikám·u [*vi* hanikámanai; hanikánda] はにかむ *be embarrassed; be
shy*　§hanikánde utsumúku はにかんでうつむく *look down because*

(one) is shy

haniwa 埴輪 *an ancient clay funerary figure*

hanjuku 半熟 *half-ripe; half-done* ⑧hanjuku támago 半熟卵 *soft-boiled egg*

hankágai 繁華街 *downtown; busy shopping street*

hankan 反感 *antipathy; unfavorable feeling* ⑧hankan o kau 反感を買う *create antipathy*

hánkei 半径 *radius*

hanketsu 判決 *(legal) decision; verdict; judgment* ——**hanketsu-suru** [vt] 判決する *render a verdict*

hánki o kakageru 反旗を掲げる *fly an opposition flag; be opposed (to); protest*

hanko 判子 *(see* **hán***)*

hankō 反抗 *rebellion; resistance; opposition* ——**hankō-suru** [vi] 反抗する *rebel; resist; oppose*

hankyū 半球 *hemisphere* ⑧minami hánkyū 南半球 *southern hemisphere* ⑧kita hánkyū 北半球 *northern hemisphere*

han-Nichi 反日 *against Japan; anti-Japanese* ⑧Han-Nichi kánjō ga takamátte iru. 反日感情が高まっている。 *Anti-Japanese feelings are mounting.*

hánnin 犯人 *criminal; culprit* ⑧hánnin no zénka 犯人の前科 *criminal record*

hannō 反応 *reaction; response* ⑧kagaku hánnō 化学反応 *chemical reaction* ⑧kyozetsu hánnō 拒絶反応 *rejection (response)* ⑧Hánshin daishínsai ni taisúru Nihon séifu no hannō wa osókatta. 阪神大震災に対する日本政府の反応は遅かった。 *The Japanese government's reaction to the great Hanshin earthquake was slow.* ——**hannō-suru** [vi] 反応する *react; respond (to)*

hanran 反乱 *an uprising; rebellion* ⑧hanrángun 反乱軍 *rebel forces*

hansei 反省 *self-examination; introspection* ——**hansei-suru** [vt] 反省する *reflect (on one's behavior); reconsider; show contrition*

hansha 反射 *reflection* ——**hansha-suru** [vi / vt] 反射する *reflect*

hanshō 半焼 *partially destroyed by fire* ——**hanshō-suru** [vi] 半焼する *be partially destroyed by fire*

hanshoku-suru 繁殖する *propagate; increase*

hansú·ru [vi hanshínai; hánshita] 反する *be contrary to* ⑧Sore wa kísoku ni hánshite iru. それは規則に反している。 *That's against regulations.*

hansuto ハンスト *hunger strike*

hantai 反対 *against; opposed; objection; opposition* ⑧chōhei hantai úndō 徴兵反対運動 *anti-draft movement* ——**hantai-suru** [vi] 反対する *object (to); oppose; be against*

hantaigo 反対語 *antonym*

hantei 判定 *judgment; decision*

hantō 半島 *peninsula*

hanzai 犯罪 *crime; criminal offence* §hanzai bṓshi 犯罪防止 *crime prevention*

happa 葉っぱ *leaves; foliage*

happō 発砲 *gun discharge; a shot*

happyō 発表 *announcement; presentation* ——**happyō-suru** [vt] 発表する *announce; present* §kenkyū séika o happyō-suru 研究成果を発表する *present the results of (one's) research*

hára 原 *a plain; a field*

hará 腹 *stomach* §hara ga heru 腹が減る *(to) get (or feel) hungry* §hará ga ōkíi 腹が大きい *be generous* §hara no náka 腹の中 *at heart* §hará o watte hanásu 腹を割って話す *talk frankly* §hará ga tátsu (hará o tatéru) 腹が立つ（腹を立てる）*be / get angry* §Tabikasanaru seikai sukyándaru ni mínna ga hará o tátete iru. 度重なる政界スキャンダルにみんなが腹を立てている。*Everyone is angry at the successive scandals in the political world.*

haradatashí·i [adj haradatáshiku nái; haradatáshikatta] 腹立たしい *(be) maddening; incorrigible; infuriating* §Watashítachi wa bukkádaka de haradatashíi máinichi o okutte iru. 私たちは物価高で腹立たしい毎日を送っている。*We continue to be infuriated day by day by the high cost of living.*

[o-]harai （お）払い *exorcism; purification*

haraikóm·u [vt haraikománai; haraikónda] 払い込む *pay in; put money into a bank* §atamakin o haraikómu 頭金を払い込む *make a down payment on*

haraimodoshi 払い戻し *refund; reimbursement* §genkín no haraimodoshi 現金の払い戻し *cash refund*

hará·u [vt harawánai; harátta] 払う *pay; sweep (away); banish* §o-kane o haráu お金を払う *pay money*

haré 晴れ *clear (or fine) weather*

haremono 腫物 *tumor; abscess* §haremono ga dekíru 腫物ができる *have an abscess* §haremono ni sawaru 腫物に触る *touch (on) a sensitive matter*

harénchi [na] 破廉恥 （な）*shameless(ness); impudence*

haré·ru [vi harénai; hareta] 晴れる *clear up; stop (raining); be refreshed* §Sóra ga hárete iru. 空が晴れている。*The sky is clear.*

hare·ru [vi harenai; hareta] 腫れる *swell* §Rimpa-sen ga harete iru. リンパ腺が腫れている。*The lymph gland is swollen.*

haretsu 破裂 *bursting; explosion* ——**haretsu-suru** [vi] 破裂する *burst; rupture; explode* §Sámusa de suidōkan ga haretsu-shita. 寒さで水道管が破裂した。*The water pipe froze and burst.*

haréyaka [na] 晴れやか （な）*radiant; cheerful; fine* §haréyaka na égao 晴れやかな笑顔 *a radiant smiling face*

hári 針 *needle*

hari chíryō 鍼治療 *acupuncture*

harigami 貼紙 *poster; bill; pre-glued wallpaper*

harigane 針金 *(metal) wire*

haritsuké·ru [*vt* haritsukénai; haritsúketa] 張り付ける；貼り付ける *stick on; put on; post* §Shippúyaku o koshi ni shikkári to haritsúketa. 湿布薬を腰にしっかりと張り付けた。*I stuck a poultice (firmly) on my lower back.*

háru 春 *spring (season)*

har·u [*vt* haranai; hatta] 貼る *paste; affix* §Bira o haranáide kudasái. ビラを貼らないで下さい。*Post no bills.*

har·u [*vt* haranai; hatta] 張る *spread; stretch; strain* §himo o pín to haru 紐をぴんと張る *stretch a string* §Mizuúmi ni kóri ga hatte iru. 湖に氷が張っている。*The lake's iced over.* ——[*attr*] **hatta** 張った *strained*

harubáru [to] はるばる（と）*all the way (from)* §Kyūyū ga Amerika kara harubáru yatté kita. 旧友がアメリカからはるばるやって来た。*An old friend came all the way from America to see me.*

háruka [na] 遥か（な）*far away; distant* ——**háruka ni** 遥かに *by far; much more* §háruka ni ōkíi 遥かに大きい *bigger by far*

hasamí 鋏 *scissors; shears*

hasan 破産 *bankruptcy* ——**hasan-suru** [*vi*] 破産する *go bankrupt; declare bankruptcy*

hasé·ru [*vt* hasénai; háseta] 馳せる *run; gallop* §umá o haséru 馬を馳せる *gallop a horse* §rekishi ni na o haséru 歴史に名を馳せる *go down in history; become famous*

háshi 箸 *chopsticks*

hashi 端 *an end; edge; the extremity; corner*

hashí 橋 *bridge*

hashigo 梯子 *ladder* §hashigó-zake 梯子酒 *drinking from bar to bar; pub crawl*

hashiká 麻疹 *measles* §hashiká ni kakáru 麻疹にかかる *catch measles*

hashira 柱 *pillar; column; vertical beam*

hashír·u [*vi* hashiránai; hashítta] 走る *run; go to excess* §Ié made hashítte kita. 家まで走ってきた。*I ran all the way home.* §Kono shínsha wa sumúzu ni hashiru. この新車はスムーズに走る。*This new car runs smoothly.* §hikō ni hashíru 非行に走る *misdemeanor*

hashōfū 破傷風 *tetanus*

hashutsu kangófu 派出看護婦 *visiting (or day) nurse*

hason 破損 *damage; injury; breakdown* ——**hason-suru** [*vi*] 破損する *be damaged; be broken*

hassei 発生 *occurrence; outbreak* ——**hassei-suru** [*vi*] 発生する

happen; occur; break out; be generated ❽Doku gasu ga hassei-shita. 毒ガスが発生した。 *Poisonous gas was generated.*

hassha 発車 *departure; starting off* ——**hassha-suru** [vi] 発車する *depart; leave; start off* ❽Hikari jūsán-gō wa jūji sanjúppun ni hassha-shimásu. ひかり十三号は十時三十分に発車します。 *Hikari No.13 departs at 10:30.*

hassha 発射 *discharge; firing; shooting* ——**hassha-suru** [vt] 発射する *launch* ❽rokétto o hassha-suru ロケットを発射する *launch a rocket*

hasshín-on 発信音 *dial tone*

hasshin-suru [vt] 発信する *send; dispatch* ❽Mōrusu shíngō o hasshin-suru モールス信号を発信する *send Morse code*

hasu 蓮 *lotus* ❽hasu ike 蓮池 *lotus pond*

hatá 旗 *flag; banner*

hátachi 二十歳 *twenty years old*

hatake 畑 *cultivated field* ❽mikan-bátake 蜜柑畑 *mikan grove* ❽mugi-bátake 麦畑 *wheat field*

hatakí 叩き *duster*

hatamék·u [vi hatamekánai; hataméita] はためく *flutter; stir (or whip) in the wind* ❽Koinóbori ga kaze ni hataméite iru. 鯉のぼりが風にはためいている。 *The flying carp (banner) is whipping in the wind.*

hataraki 働き *work* ❽Musuko wa hataraki no nái kara, asonde bakari imásu. 息子は働きのないから、遊んでばかりいます。 *My son doesn't have a job, so all he does is play around.* ❽Kyō wa atama no hataraki ga warúi. 今日は頭の働きが悪い。 *My head's not working so well today.*

hataraki-sugi 働き過ぎ *overwork* ❽Káre wa hataraki-sugi de taórete shimatta. 彼は働き過ぎで倒れてしまった。 *He collapsed from overwork.*

hatarak·u [vi hatarakanai; hataraita] 働く *work; labor*

hatás·u [vt hatasánai; hatáshita] 果たす *carry out; perform; achieve; fulfill* ❽sekinin o hatásu 責任を果たす *fulfill (one's) responsibility*

hateshiná·i [adj hateshináku nái; hateshinákatta] 果てしない *boundless; endless*

háto 鳩 *dove; pigeon* ❽hato-ha to taka-ha 鳩派と鷹派 *(political) doves and hawks* ❽densho-báto 伝書鳩 *carrier pigeon*

hatoba 波止場 *wharf*

hatsubai 発売 *sale* ❽shin-hátsubai 新発売 *recently put on sale; just out; just released* ——**hatsubai-suru** [vt] 発売する *sell; put on sale* ❽hatsubai-sareru 発売される *go on sale* ❽Atarashíi bídeo ga hatsubai-sareta. 新しいビデオが発売された。 *A new video tape was put on sale.*

hatsudénki 発電機 *dynamo; generator* ❽suiryoku hatsudénki 水力発電機 *hydro generator* ❽karyoku hatsudénki 火力発電機 *thermo* *generator*

hatsugen 発言 *statement; utterance; pronouncement* ——**hatsugen-suru** [*vt*] 発言する *speak; make a speech; make a pronouncement*

hatsuka 二十日 *the twentieth (of the month); twenty days*

hatsuka dáikon 二十日大根 *radish*

hatsuka nézumi 二十日鼠 *mouse*

hatsukoi 初恋 *first love*

hatsumei 発明 *invention* ❧hatsumeika 発明家 *inventor* ——**hatsumei-suru** [*vt*] 発明する *invent* ❧Éjison wa denkyū o hatsumei-shita. エジソンは電球を発明した。 *Edison invented the light bulb.*

hatsunetsu 発熱 *attack of fever*

hatsuon 発音 *pronunciation* ——**hatsuon-suru** [*vt*] 発音する *pronounce*

hatsurei 発令 *official announcement* ——**hatsurei-suru** [*vt*] 発令する *announce officially* ❧Jirei o hatsurei-shita. 辞令を発令した。 *They announced officially the appointments.* ❧Nadare kéihō ga hatsurei-sareta. 雪崩警報が発令された。 *A landslide warning was announced.*

hátsuro 発露 *expression; manifestation* ——**hátsuro-suru** [*vi*] 発露する *express (itself); manifest (itself)*

hattatsu 発達 *development* ——**hattatsu-suru** [*vi*] 発達する *develop; progress; advance* ❧Bummei ga hattatsu-shitá to omoimásu ka? 文明が発達したと思いますか。 *Do you think civilization has advanced?*

hatten 発展 *growth; development* ❧hatten tojókoku 発展途上国 *developing country* ——**hatten-suru** [*vi*] 発展する *grow; develop; expand* ❧Kono tóshi wa kyūsoku ni hatten-shite iru. この都市は急速に発展している。 *This city is expanding rapidly.*

hatto はっと *with a start; in surprise* ——**hatto-suru** [*vi*] はっとする *be startled*

há·u [*vi* hawánai; hátta] 這う *crawl* ❧hátte arúku 這って歩く *crawl on all fours*

háya 早や *now; already* ❧Háya hi ga kureta. 早や日が暮れた。 *It's already dark.* ❧Íma wa háya teókure desu. 今は早や手遅れです。 *It's already too late.*

hayaashi 早足 *a trot; quick pace* ❧hayaashi de arúku 早足で歩く *walk at a quick pace*

hayabusa 隼 *falcon*

hayá·i [*adj* háyaku nái; háyakatta] 早い *(be) early* ❧ása hayái 朝早い *early in the morning* ——**háyaku** 早く *early* ❧Késa háyaku okita. 今朝早く起きた。 *I got up early this morning.*

hayá·i [*adj* háyaku nái; háyakatta] 速い *(be) fast; rapid; quick* ❧Shinkánsen wa totemo hayái. 新幹線はとても速い。 *The bullet train is very fast.* ——**háyaku** 速く *quickly; fast; hurriedly* ❧háyaku hashíru 速く走る *run fast*

hayakuchi kótoba 早口言葉 *tongue twister*

hayamé ni 早めに *early; in advance (of)* ❸Kono shigoto o yotei yóri hayamé ni katazukeyó. この仕事を予定より早めに片付けよう。 *Let's wind up this work in advance of the schedule.*

hayamé·ru [*vt* hayaménai; hayámeta] 早める *expedite; speed up; hasten* ❸ashí o hayaméru 足を早める *quicken (one's) pace* ❸shí o hayaméru 死を早める *hasten (one's) death* ❸yotei o hayaméru 予定を早める *speed up the schedule*

hayáne-suru [*vi*] 早寝する *go to bed early* ❸Kyó wa tsukáreta no de hayáne-shitái na! 今日は疲れたので早寝したいな！ *I'm tired today so I'd like to go to bed early.* <*masc*>

hayáoki 早起き *early rising* ——**hayáoki-suru** [*vi*] 早起きする *get up early*

hayár·u [*vi* hayaránai; hayátta] 流行る *be popular; be faddish; go around; circulate* ❸Íma hayátte iru kyoku wa nán desu ka? 今流行っている曲は何ですか。 *What songs are popular now?* ❸Kotoshi wa infuruénza ga hayátte iru. 今年はインフルエンザが流行っている。 *This year flu is going around.*

hayashi 林 *forest; grove*

-hazu ～筈 *should; ought to; is expected to* ❸Ashita, anó hito wa kúru hazu désu. 明日、あの人は来る筈です。 *She's expected to come tomorrow.* ❸Sonna hazu wa nái deshó. そんな筈はないでしょう。 *That's not likely, is it?*

hazukashí·i [*adj* hazukáshiku nái; hazukáshikatta] 恥ずかしい *(be) ashamed; embarrassed; shameful* ——**hazukashíku** 恥ずかしく *shamefully* ❸hazukashíku omóu 恥ずかしく思う *feel ashamed*

hazukashimé·ru [*vt* hazukashiménai; hazukashímeta] 辱める *shame (someone)* ❸chíi o hazukashiméru 地位を辱める *bromg shame to (one's) position*

hazukáshisa 恥ずかしさ *shyness; embarrassment; shamefulness*

hazum·u [*vi* hazumanai; hazunda] 弾む *bound; bounce* ❸chíppu o hazumu チップを弾む *tip well (or heavily)* ❸íki ga hazumu 息が弾む *pant; breathe hard* ❸Bóru ga hazunda. ボールが弾んだ。 *The ball bounced.* ❸Kokoró ga hazunda. 心が弾んだ。 *My heart leapt.* ❸chíppu o hazumu チップを弾む *tip well (or heavily)*

hazure·ru [*vi* hazurenai; hazureta] 外れる *come off; miss; be separated from* ❸hito no michi ni hazureru 人の道に外れる *stray from the path of humanity (or wander from the straight and narrow path)* ❸Yosó ga hazureta. 予想が外れた。 *It didn't happen as I expected.* ❸Shátsu no botan ga hazurete iru yo! シャツのボタンが外れているよ！ *Your shirt's unbuttoned.*

hazus·u [*vt* hazusanai; hazushita] 外す *disconnect; detach* ❸botan o hazusu ボタンを外す *unbutton (something)* ❸kikái o hazusu 機会を外す *miss an opportunity* ❸ménbā kara hazusu メンバーから外す

stop being a member   ❽Súmisu wa íma séki o hazushite imásu ga... スミスは今席をはずしていますが... *Smith isn't at his desk at the moment.*

hébi 蛇 *snake*

hedaté·ru [*vt* hedaténai; hedáteta] 隔てる *set apart; separate*   ❽michi o hedatéru 道を隔てる *be separated by a road*

hei 塀 *fence*

heian 平安 *peace*   ❽kokoro no heian o motoméru 心の平安を求める *seek peace of mind*

heibon [na] 平凡（な）*common; ordinary*

heichi 平地 *flat land; a plain*

heiei 兵営 *barracks*

heihō métoru 平方メートル *square meters*

heiin 兵員 *troops*

heijitsu 平日 *weekday; ordinary day*

heiki [na] 平気（な）*calm; unruffled; unafraid*   ❽heiki na kao de míru 平気な顔で見る *look on unconcerned*   ❽Bóku wa náni o iwareté mo heiki da. 僕は何を言われても平気だ。*I don't care, whatever people say to me.* <masc>

heikin 平均 *average*   ❽heikín-ten 平均点 *average score*   ❽heikin júmyō 平均寿命 *average life span*   ❽hinshitsu o heikin-saseru 品質を平均させる *standardize the quality*   ❽heikin shite 平均して *on the average*

heikō 平衡 *balance; equilibrium*   ❽heikō kánkaku 平衡感覚 *sense of balance*

heikō 平行 *parallel*   ❽heikōsen 平行線 *parallel lines*

heikō-suru [*vi*] 並行する *go side by side; run parallel*   ❽Sono gíron ga heikō-shite iru. その議論が並行している。*Those arguments run parallel (to each other)*

heimén 平面 *level; a plane (surface)*

héiryoku 兵力 *military power*

heiwa 平和 *peace*   ❽heiwa káidan 平和会談 *peace talks*   ❽heiwa iji bútai 平和維持部隊 *peace-keeping forces*   ❽heiwa jóyaku 平和条約 *peace treaty*   ❽heiwa shúgi 平和主義 *pacifism*   ❽heiwa shugísha 平和主義者 *pacifist*   ❽heiwa é no yūin 平和への誘因 *incentive for peace* ——**heiwa na** 平和な *peaceful*

heiya 平野 *a plain*   ❽Kantō héiya 関東平野 *Kanto Plain*

hékichi 僻地 *remote place; out-of-the-way place*

hekom·u [*vi* hekomanai; hekonda] 凹む *give in; be (or become) dented*

héma へま *a blunder; a goof; a mess* ——**héma o suru** へまをする *make a mess of*   ❽Matá hidói héma o shite shimatta! また酷いへまをしてしまった。*I made an awful mess of things again.*

hémpi [na] 辺鄙（な）*out-of-the-way*

hen 辺 *vicinity* ❽kono hen この辺 *nearby; this vicinity* ❽ano hen あの辺 *over there; in that area*

hen 偏 *left-hand radical (of a Chinese character)*

hén [na] 変（な）*strange; bizarre; weird* ❽hén na hito 変な人 *weird person* ❽hén na kangáe 変な考え *a strange idea* ❽Anó hito wa hén da. あの人は変だ。 *He's strange!*

henjí 返事 *a reply; an answer* ——**henjí-suru** [vi] 返事する *reply; answer*

hénka 変化 *change; variation; transition* ——**hénka-suru** [vi] 変化する *change; vary; alter*

henkei 変形 *transformation; metamorphosis; variation* ——**henkei-suru** [vi / vt] 変形する *be transformed; be changed; change (into); transform*

henken 偏見 *prejudice; biased view; bigotry* ❽Amerika de henken wa mádamada nezuyói. アメリカで偏見はまだまだ根強い。 *Prejudice is still deeply rooted in America.*

henkō 変更 *change; alteration; modification* ——**henkō-suru** [vt] 変更する *alter; change; modify*

henkyō [na/no] 偏狭（な／の）*narrow-minded; provincial*

hensan 編纂 *editing* ❽jiten no hensan o suru 辞典の編纂をする *edit a dictionary*

henshitsúsha 変質者 *a pervert; a degenerate*

henshoku 変色 *discoloration; fading* ——**henshoku-suru** [vi] 変色する *tarnish; fade; lose color*

henshū 編集 *editing* ❽henshūin 編集員 *editor* ——**henshū-suru** [vt] 編集する *edit*

hensō 変装 *a disguise* ——**hensō-suru** [vi] 変装する *disguise* ❽Shiritsu tántei wa bikō o suru tóki, hensō-suru kotó ga áru. 私立探偵は尾行する時、変装することがある。 *When a private detective tails (someone) he sometimes disguises himself.*

hentōsen 扁桃腺 *tonsils* ❽hentōsén'en 扁桃腺炎 *tonsillitis*

héra へら *spatula*

heras·u [vt herasanai; herashita] 減らす *diminish; decrease; reduce* ❽akaji o herasu 赤字を減らす *reduce a deficit* ❽hará o herasu 腹を減らす *become hungry* ❽sháin o herasu 社員を減らす *decrease (the number of) company employees*

herí 縁 *the edge; border (of tatami)* ❽Tatami no herí o fumanai yó ni! 畳の縁を踏まないように！ *Don't walk on the borders of the tatami!*

herikudátta kokoro 謙った心 *a humble heart*

her·u [vi heranai; hetta] 減る *diminish; decrease* ❽hará ga heru 腹が減る *be hungry* ❽Sono machi no jinkō ga hette kite iru. その町の人口が減ってきている。 *The population of that town has decreased.*

[o-]heso （お）臍 *navel; umbilicus* ❽heso o mageru へそを曲げる *be* *out of sorts; get cross*

hetá [na] 下手（な）*clumsy; unskillful* ❧Kánai wa ryóri ga hetá desu. 家内は料理が下手です。*My wife is not good at cooking.* ——**hetá ni** 下手に *clumsily; unskillfully*

heyá 部屋 *a room*

hi 日 *the sun* ❧Hi ga tétte iru. 日が照っている。*The sun's shining.*

hí 火 *fire* ❧hí ga tsúku 火がつく *catch fire* ❧hí ni kakéru 火にかける *put on the fire (or burner); cook* ❧hí o okósu 火を起こす *start a fire* ❧hí o tsukéru 火をつける *light (a match to); ignite* ❧hí o kesu 火を消す *put out a fire* ❧hi o aógu 火をあおぐ *fan the fire*

-hi ～費 *fee; expense* ❧gakuhi 学費 *tuition* ❧kōnetsusúihi 光熱水費 *utility expenses* ❧seikatsúhi 生活費 *living expenses* ❧un'éihi 運営費 *running (or operating) expenses*

híbachi 火鉢 hibachi *(charcoal brazier)*

hibakúsha 被爆者 *victim of bombing; victim of the atomic bomb*

híbana 火花 *a spark*

hibari 雲雀 *lark (bird)*

híbi 日々 *daily; day by day* ❧híbi no seikatsu 日々の生活 *daily life*

hibí ひび *a crack; fissure* ❧Kossetsu-shite inai kéredomo, honé ni hibí ga háitte imásu. 骨折していないけれども、骨にひびが入っています。*It isn't broken, but there is a fissure in the bone.*

hibík·u [vi hibikánai; hibíita] 響く *reverberate; echo; vibrate; affect* ❧muné ni hibíku 胸に響く *touch (one's) heart*

hibusó 非武装 *demilitarization* ❧hibusó chūritsu 非武装中立 *unarmed neutrality*

hída 襞 *a pleat; a fold* ❧yama-hida 山ひだ *mountain folds* ❧kokoro no hída o ukagau 心のひだを窺う *investigate (someone's) state of mind*

hidari 左 *left* ❧hidari-gawa 左側 *the left side* ❧hidari kiki 左利き *left-handed (person)* ❧hidarite 左手 *left hand*

hidénka 妃殿下 *Princess; Her Royal Highness; Her Imperial Highness*

hideri 日照り *drought; dry spell*

hidó·i [adj hídoku nái; hídokatta] 酷い *(be) severe; extreme; violent; cruel* ❧hidói áme 酷い雨 *violent (heavy) rain* ❧hidói shiuchi 酷い仕打ち *severe treatment* ——**hídoku** 酷く *cruelly; harshly; hard*

hidómei 非同盟 *non-alignment* ❧hidōméikoku 非同盟国 *non-aligned nation (or country)*

hidori 日取り *a date; (appointed) day* ❧Kekkónshiki no hidori o kimemáshita ka? 結婚式の日取りを決めましたか。*Have you fixed the date of the wedding?*

hiebíe 冷え冷え [onomatopoetic for cold] ——**hiebíe-suru** [vi] 冷え冷えする *be cold; feel chilly* ❧Kyó wa hiebíe-shite iru. 今日は冷え冷えしている。*It's chilly today.*

hi-eiriteki [na] 非営利的（な）*nonprofit*

hié·ru [vi hiénai; híeta] 冷える *become cold; cool off*   ❽Bíru ga híete iru. ビールが冷えている。*The beer's cold.* ❽Onaka ga hiénai yó ni harámaki o tsúkete iru. お腹が冷えないように腹巻をつけている。*I'm wearing a stomach-band to keep my stomach from getting cold.*

hífu 皮膚 *skin*   ❽hifu-ka 皮膚科 *department of dermatology*

higaeri 日帰り *day trip* ——**higaeri-suru** [vi] 日帰りする *make a day trip*

hígai 被害 *damage; harm*   ❽higáisha 被害者 *victim*   ❽hígai ga ókiku náru 被害が大きくなる *suffer great damage*

higán 彼岸 *equinox; the equinoctial week*   ❽higán-bana 彼岸花 *cluster amaryllis*   ❽higan-zákura 彼岸桜 *early-flowering cherry*   ❽háru no higán 春の彼岸 *the spring equinox*

higása 日傘 *parasol*

higashí 東 *east*

hige 髭 *beard; whiskers*   ❽agohige 顎髭 *beard (on the chin)*   ❽kuchihige 口髭 *moustache*   ❽higezura no 髭面の *heavily bearded*

hígeki 悲劇 *tragedy*

higure 日暮れ *dusk; sunset; nightfall*

hihan 批判 *criticism; a comment* ——**hihanteki [na]** 批判的（な）*critical (of)* ——**hihan-suru** [vt] 批判する *criticize; comment on*

híhi ひひ *baboon*

hihyō 批評 *comment; criticism; review*   ❽hihyōka 批評家 *a critic* ——**hihyō-suru** [vt] 批評する *review; criticize*

híiki [no] 晶屓（の）*favorite* ——**híiki-suru** [vt] ひいきする *favor; patronize; be partial to*   ❽séito o híiki-suru 生徒をひいきする *favor a student*

hijí 肘 *elbow*   ❽hiji-déppō 肘鉄砲 *a rebuff; elbowing*

hijō [no] 非常（の）*emergency; contingency; unusual; unexpected*   ❽hijō béru 非常ベル *alarm bell*   ❽hijó-guchi 非常口 *emergency exit*   ❽hijō jítai 非常事態 *state of emergency*   ❽hijōyō no 非常用の *for emergency* ——**hijō ni** 非常に *extremely; unusually*

hijun 批准 *ratification*   ❽hijúnken 批准権 *right of ratification*

hika chúsha 皮下注射 *hypodermic*

hikaeme 控えめ *moderate; temperate* ——**hikaeme ni** 控えめに *moderately; conservatively*

hikaé·ru [vt hikaénai; hikáeta] 控える *restrain; hold back*

hikage 日陰 *shade*

hikaku 比較 *comparison*   ❽hikaku- 比較〜 *comparative*   ❽hikaku búnka 比較文化 *comparative culture* ——**hikakuteki [na]** 比較的（な）*comparative* ——**hikakuteki ni** 比較的に *comparatively* ——**hikaku-suru** [vt] 比較する *compare*

hikaku chítai 非核地帯 *nuclear-free zone*

hikakuka 非核化 *denuclearization* §hikaku busō jṓyaku 非核武装条約 *denuclearization treaty* ——**hikakuka-suru** [*vt*] 非核化する *denuclearize*

hikan 悲観 *pessimism* §hikan shúgi 悲観主義 *pessimism* §hikan shugísha 悲観主義者 *pessimist* ——**hikanteki [na]** 悲観的（な）*pessimistic* ——**hikanteki ni** 悲観的に *pessimistically*

hikarí 光 *light; luster*

hikár·u [*vi* hikaránai; hikátta] 光る *shine; be bright*

hiketsu 否決 *voting down; negative vote* ——**hiketsu-suru** [*vt*] 否決する *vote down*

-hiki 〜匹 [*classifier for small four-legged animals, insects, and fish*] §koinu ippiki 小犬一匹 *one puppy* §konchū nîhiki 昆虫二匹 *two insects* §Iké ni sakana ga sámbiki iru. 池に魚が三匹いる。*There are three fish in the pond.*

hikiagé·ru [*vt* hikiagénai; hikiágeta] 引き上げる *raise; increase; pull out (of); leave* §chimbotsu-shita fúne o hikiagéru 沈没した船を引き上げる *raise (or salvage) a sunken ship* §Kyṓ wa bṓnasu ga déte sháin wa minna hayamé ni hikiágeta. 今日はボーナスが出て、社員はみんな早めに引き上げた。*Today we received our bonuses and everyone left the company early.*

hikidashi 引出し *drawer*

hikidás·u [*vt* hikidasánai; hikidáshita] 引き出す *draw on; withdraw* §o-kane o hikidásu お金を引き出す *withdraw money*

hikigane 引き金 *trigger* §hikigane o hiku 引き金を引く *pull the trigger* §Chîsa na gokai ga sono funsō no hikigane ni nátta. 小さな誤解がその紛争の引き金になった。*A simple misunderstanding was the trigger for (or triggered) the dispute.*

hikikaé·ru [*vt* hikikaénai; hikikáeta] 引き換える；引き替える *exchange; change*

hikikáes·u [*vi* hikikaesánai; hikikáeshita] 引き返す *come back; return; retrace (one's) steps*

hikinige 轢き逃げ *hit-and-run* §hikinige unténsha 轢き逃げ運転者 *hit-and-run driver*

hiki-niku 挽肉 *ground meat*

hikinobás·u [*vt* hikinobasánai; hikinobáshita] 引き伸ばす *extend; enlarge; lengthen* §káigi no shúryō jikan o hikinobásu 会議の終了時間を引き伸ばす *extend a meeting*

hikiokós·u [*vt* hikiokosánai; hikiokóshita] 引き起こす *give rise to; cause*

hikitomé·ru [*vt* hikitoménai; hikitómeta] 引き止める；引き留める *detain* §kyaku o hikitoméru 客を引き止める *detain a customer; keep a customer waiting*

hikitór·u [*vt* hikitoránai; hikitótta] 引き取る *take over; take charge of; look after*

hikitsúg·u [*vt* hikitsugánai; hikitsúida] 引き継ぐ *take over; succeed (to)* ❧chichí no shigoto o hikitsúgu 父の仕事を引き継ぐ *take over (one's) father's business*

hikitsuzúite 引き続いて *continuing; in succession; one after the other*

hikiuké·ru [*vt* hikiukénai; hikiúketa] 引き受ける *accept; take on; undertake; guarantee; vouch for* ❧shigoto o hikiukéru 仕事を引き受ける *take on a job* ❧mimoto o hikiukéru 身元を引き受ける *guarantee (a person's) character*

hikízan 引き算 *subtraction (Math)*

hikizur·u [*vt* hikizuranai; hikizutta] 引きずる *drag* ❧ashí o hikizuru 足を引きずる *drag (one's) feet* ❧Sono mondai wa nochinochi máde hikizutta. その問題は後々まで引きずった。 *The issue dragged on and on.*

hikkaké·ru [*vt* hikkakénai; hikkáketa] 引っ掛ける *hang; catch; trap*

hikkák·u [*vt* hikkakanai; hikkáita] 引っ掻く *scratch; claw*

hikkiri náshi ni ひっきりなしに *without interval; constantly; incessantly* ❧Hikkiri náshi ni hito ga deháiri-shite iru. ひっきりなしに人が出入りしている。 *People are coming and going constantly.*

hikkós·u [*vi* hikkosánai; hikkóshita] 引っ越す *move; change (one's) residence*

hikkuri-káer·u [*vi* -kaeránai; -káetta] ひっくり返る *turn over; turn upside down; capsize* ❧Fúne ga hikkuri-káetta. 船がひっくり返った。 *The boat overturned.* ❧Keisei wa sókuza ni hikkuri-káetta. 形勢は即座にひっくり返った。 *The situation suddenly turned topsy-turvy.*

hikkuri-káes·u [*vt* -kaesánai; -káeshita] ひっくり返す *upset; turn (something) over*

hikō bángō 飛行番号 *flight number*

hikóki 飛行機 *airplane*

hikokunin 被告人 *defendant*

hi-kóshiki [no] 非公式（の） *unofficial; informal*

hik·u [*vt* hikanai; hiita] 引く *drag; pull; draw; lead; subtract* ❧nigúruma o hiku 荷車を引く *pull a cart*

hik·u [*vt* hikanai; hiita] 弾く *play (the piano / organ / stringed instrument)* ❧piano o hiku ピアノを弾く *play the piano*

hik·u [*vt* hikanai; hiita] 轢く *run over (with a car)*

hik·u [*vt* hikanai; hiita] 挽く *grind* ❧kōhí-mame o hiku コーヒー豆を挽く *grind coffee beans*

hikú·i [*adj* híkuku nái; híkukatta] 低い *(be) low; short*

hikyó 卑怯 *cowardice* ——**hikyó na** 卑怯な *cowardly; mean* ❧hikyó na shúdan 卑怯な手段 *cowardly measure*

hima [na] 暇（な）*spare time; free*

hīmago 曾孫 *great-grandchild*

himashí-yu ひまし油 *castor oil*

himáwari 向日葵 *sunflower*

híme 姫 *princess*

himei 悲鳴 *a scream* §himei o ageru. 悲鳴を上げる *scream; shriek*

himitsu 秘密 *secret* §himitsu káidan 秘密会談 *secret talks* §himitsu kéisatsu 秘密警察 *secret police* ——**himitsu ni** 秘密に *secretly*

himo 紐 *band; cord; string* §himo o musubu 紐を結ぶ *tie a string* §himo de konímotsu o musubu 紐で小荷物を結ぶ *tie a package with a string* §himotsuki 紐つき *with strings attached* §himotsuki tóshi 紐つき投資 *a loan with strings attached*

himpan 頻繁 *frequency* ——**himpan na** 頻繁な *frequent* §himpan na kōtsū 頻繁な交通 *heavy traffic* ——**himpan ni** 頻繁に *frequently*

hímpu 貧富 *poverty and wealth* §hímpu no sa 貧富の差 *the gap between the wealthy and the poor*

hin 品 *grace; refinement; dignity* §hin no íi 品のいい *refined; elegant* §hin ga áru 品がある *be refined* §hin ga nái 品がない *be crude*

hína 雛 *chick; young bird*

hinágiku 雛菊 *daisy*

Hina Mátsuri 雛祭 *Doll Festival, or Girls' Festival (March 3)* §hina níngyō 雛人形 *hina dolls (for Doll Festival)*

hínan 非難 *blame; censure; criticism* ——**hínan-suru** [vt] 非難する *blame; censure; criticize*

hínan 避難 *evacuation* §hinanjo 避難所 *shelter; evacuation point* §hinanyō bóto 避難用ボート *lifeboat* ——**hínan-suru** [vi] 避難する *take refuge; flee (for safety)*

hinata 日向 *in the sunshine* §hinata bókko 日向ぼっこ *sunbathing*

hinekúreta ひねくれた *twisted; crooked; perverse*

hinér·u [vt hineránai; ninétta] 捻る *twist; twirl; wring; wrench* §sén o hinéru 栓を捻る *twist a stopper* §kubi o hinéru 首を捻る *twist (one's) neck; rack one's brains; think hard*

hinichi 日にち *the (appointed) date*

hiniku 皮肉 *sarcasm; cynicism; irony* ——**hiniku na** 皮肉な *sarcastic; cynical; ironical* §hiniku na warai 皮肉な笑い *a cynical laugh* §hiniku na úmmei 皮肉な運命 *ironic fate*

hinin 避妊 *contraception* §hiníngu 避妊具 *contraceptive device* §hinin-hō 避妊法 *contraceptive measure* §hinín-yaku 避妊薬 *contraceptive (medication)*

híningenteki [na] 非人間的（な）*inhuman*

hinjaku [na] 貧弱（な）*poor; scanty; meager*

hinketsu (shō) 貧血（症）*anemia*

hinkon 貧困 *poverty* ——**hinkon na** 貧困な *needy; poor* §hinkon bokumetsu úndō 貧困撲滅運動 *anti-poverty program*

Hinomaru 日の丸 *the Japanese national flag; (Rising-) Sun Flag*

hinómoto 火の元 *source of fire* §hinómoto yójin 火の元用心*

     precaution against fires

hinshitsu 品質 *quality* §hinshitsu séigen 品質管理 *quality control*

hippár·u [*vt* hipparánai; hippátta] 引っ張る *pull; tow; drag*

hiragána ひらがな；平仮名 *hiragana syllabary (J)*

hiraké·ru [*vi* hirakénai; hiráketa] 開ける *become civilized; become modernized; be opened (up)*

hirák·u [*vi / vt* hirakánai; hiráita] 開く *open; open up; uncover* §Densha no tobira ga hiráita. 電車の扉が開いた。 *The train doors opened.*

hirame 鮃；平目 *flounder; flatfish*

hiramék·u [*vi* hiramekánai; hiraméita] 閃く *flash; glitter* §Íi áidea ga hiraméita. いいアイデアが閃いた。 *A good idea just flashed into my mind.*

hiraóyogi 平泳ぎ *breaststroke*

hirashínto 平信徒 *layman; layperson; laity*

hirata·i [*adj* hirataku nái; hiratakatta] 平たい *flat; level*

hiraya 平屋；平家 *one-storied house*

hiré 鰭 *(fish) fin*

hiré ヒレ *fillet; tenderloin*

hirefús·u [*vi* hirefusánai; hirefúshita] 平伏す *bow; kneel; fall prostrate*

hirei 比例 ——**hirei-suru** [*vi*] 比例する *be in proportion to*

hiretsu [na] 卑劣（な） *mean; base; low-down*

hírihiri [to] ひりひり（と） *tingling; stinging; burning* ——**hírihiri-suru** [*vi*] ひりひりする *burn; sting* §kizuguchi ga hírihiri-suru 傷口がひりひりする *the wound stings*

híroba 広場 *open space; plaza*

hirogar·u [*vi* hirogaranai; hirogatta] 広がる *be spread (out); be widened; dilate*

hiroge·ru [*vt* hirogenai; hirogeta] 広げる *spread (out); widen*

hiró·i [*adj* híroku nái; hírokatta] 広い *(be) wide; broad; spacious* §hirói ie 広い家 *a big house* §hirói michi 広い道 *a wide street* ——**híroku** 広く *widely*

hiromé·ru [*vt* hiroménai; hirómeta] 広める *widen; extend; make known; diffuse; spread* §uwasa o hiroméru 噂を広める *spread a rumor*

hirónri 非論理 *illogic* ——**hironriteki [na]** 非論理的（な） *illogical*

hiro·u [*adj* hirowanai; hirotta] 拾う *pick up; gather*

hirú 昼 *noon; midday*

hirugóhan 昼御飯 *noon meal; lunch*

hiruma 昼間 *daytime*

hirune 昼寝 *a nap*

híryō 肥料 *fertilizer; manure; compost*

hisáisha 被災者 *victim of a disaster*

hisan 悲惨 *misery; wretchedness* ——**hisan na** 悲惨な *miserable;*

wretched; tragic   🔳hisan na sensō o fuségu 悲惨な戦争を防ぐ *prevent a tragic war*

hisashiburi 久しぶり *a long (elapse of) time*   🔳Hisashiburi (désu). 久しぶり (です). *It's been a long time (since I've seen you).* —— hisashiburi ni 久しぶりに *after a long time*   🔳Watashi wa hisashiburi ni yūjin ni átta. 私は久し振りに友人に会った。 *I met my friend after a long time.*

hishaku 柄杓 *dipper*

hísho 秘書 *private secretary*

híso 砒素 *arsenic*

hísohiso ひそひそ *secretively*   🔳hísohiso to hanásu ひそひそと話す *talk secretively*

hísoka ni 密かに *secretly*   🔳Yōgísha no aribai o hísoka ni sagutte iru. 容疑者のアリバイを密かに探っている。 *They are secretly investigating the suspect's alibi.*

hisshi ni 必死に *desperately; frantically*

hisshū [no] 必修（の）*required; essential*   🔳hisshū kámoku 必修課目 *a required subject (in school)*

hissóri-shita ひっそりした *quiet(ly); still* —— hissóri-suru ひっそりする *be quiet; hushed; deserted*   🔳Machí wa hissóri-shite iru. 町はひっそりしている。 *The streets are deserted.*

hissu 必須 *required; essential*

hisui 翡翠 *jade*

hitai 額 *brow; forehead*   🔳hitai ga hirói hito 額が広い人 *a person with a broad forehead*   🔳hitai o atsuméru 額を集める *go into a huddle; put heads together*

hitar·u [vi hitaranai; hitatta] 浸る *be soaked; be flooded with*   🔳kairaku ni hitaru 快楽に浸る *be filled with pleasure*

hitas·u [vt hitasanai; hitashita] 浸す *dip; immerse; soak*   🔳nuno o mizu ni hitasu 布を水に浸す *soak a cloth in water*

hitei 否定 *negation; denial*   🔳hiteikei 否定形 *negative form (gram)* —— **hiteiteki [na]** 否定的（な）*negative*   🔳Shōhí-zei no shinsetsu ní wa hiteiteki na íken ga ói. 消費税の新設には否定的な意見が多い。 *There are many negative opinions regarding the establishment of a consumer's tax.* —— **hitei-suru** [vt] 否定する *negate; deny; refute*

hito 人 *person; people; humankind*   🔳hitóbito 人々 *people*   🔳hito 人；他人 *other people; others*   🔳hito no go-shújin 他人のご主人 *another woman's husband*

hitó- 一 *one*   🔳hitókuchi 一口 *one mouthful; a bite*   🔳hitóban 一晩 *one night*   🔳hitófukuro 一袋 *one bag(ful)*   🔳hitófusa 一房 *one bunch*   🔳hitókoto 一言 *one word; a brief remark*   🔳hitósaji 一匙 *one spoonful*   🔳hitótsuki 一月 *one month*   🔳hitoshígoto 一仕事 *a bit of work*   🔳hitóyasumi 一休み *a rest; a break*

hitóase kák·u [*vi* -kakánai; -káita] 一汗かく *work up a sweat*
hitochígai 人違い *mistaken identity*
hitode 海星 *starfish*
hitode 人手 *workers; help; hands* §hitode-búsoku 人手不足 *short of hands; laxness* §hitode o kariru 人手を借りる *receive (someone's) help*
hito ga íi 人がいい *amiable; good-natured*
hitogara 人柄 *character; personality*
hitogomi 人ごみ *a crowd*
hitogoroshi 人殺し *homicide; murder*
hitojichi 人質 *hostage* §Sono tero-sóshiki wa ippan shímin o hitojichi ni shite iru. そのテロ組織は一般市民を人質にしている。*The terrorist organization is taking ordinary people hostage.*
hitomae de 人前で *publicly; in front of people* §hitomae de hají o kakásu 人前で恥をかかす *embarrass (someone) in public*
hitomáwari 一回り *once around* §hitomáwari ōkíi jímbutsu 一回り大きい人物 *a big (**or** gigantic) person* ——**hitomáwari-suru** [*vt*] 一回りする *go around once*
hitome-bore 一目惚れ *love at first sight*
hitomi 瞳 *pupil (of the eye)*
hitomúkashi mae 一昔前 *in the recent past; not long ago; awhile back*
hitonare-suru [*vi*] 人慣れする；人馴れする *be tamed; be accustomed to people* §hitinare-shite iru uma 人馴れしている馬 *a tamed horse* §Anó ko wa hitonare-shite iru. あの子は人馴れしている。*That child is used to (being around) people.*
hitonatsukkó·i [*adj* hitonatsukkóku nái; hitonatsukkókatta] 人懐っこい *(be) sociable; amiable; used to people* §Nara kṓen no shika wa hitonatsukkói. 奈良公園の鹿は人懐っこい。*The deer in Nara Park are used to people.*
hitóri 一人 *alone; one person* §hitori-bun 一人分 *one person's part; enough for one person*
hitoride ni ひとりでに *automatically; by itself* §Kuruma ga hitoride ni ugokidáshita. 車がひとりでに動き出した。*The car began to move by itself.*
hitorigoto o iu 独り言を言う *talk to oneself*
hitori hitóri 一人一人 *one by one* §hitori hitóri de 一人一人で *individually* §Seikaku wa hitori hitóri kotonátte iru. 性格は一人一人異なっている。*People's personalities differ one from another.*
hitorimono 独り者；一人者 *bachelor; unmarried person*
hitosashí-yubi 人さし指 *index finger*
hitoshí·i [*adj* hitóshiku nái; hitóshikatta] 等しい *be equivalent to; be tantamount to* §Ōkisa no ten de wa Nihón wa Karifórunia ni hóbo hitoshíi. 大きさの点では日本はカリフォルニアにほぼ等しい。*In*

size Japan is about the same as California.

hitótsu 一つ *one (when counting things)* §Sore o hitótsu kudasái. それを一つ下さい。 *Give me one of those, please.* §Hitótsu dốzo! 一つどうぞ！ *Have one!*

hitotsu hitótsu 一つ一つ *one by one; one at a time*

hitótsukami [no] 一掴み（の）*a handful; one scoop*

hitotsu-zútsu 一つづつ *one each*

hitsuji 羊 *sheep* §hitsujíkai 羊飼い *shepherd*

hitsujuhin 必需品 *necessities* §seikatsu hitsujuhin 生活必需品 *necessities of living; life's necessities*

hitsuyō [na] 必要（な）*necessary; essential* §hitsuyō saishốgen 必要最小限 *the absolute minimum necessary* §hitsuyō jốken 必要条件 *a necessary condition*

hiyakás·u [vt hiyakasánai; hiyakáshita] 冷やかす *make fun of; kid; scoff*

hiyake 日焼け *sunburn*

hiyás·u [vt hiyasánai; hiyáshita] 冷やす *make cool; chill* §bíru o hiyásu ビールを冷やす *cool the beer* §kűrā de heyá o hiyásu クーラーで部屋を冷やす *make a room cool with an air conditioner*

hiyố 費用 *cost; expense* §ryokố no hiyố 旅行の費用 *expenses of a trip*

hiyoke 日除け *awning; sunshade*

hiyoku [na] 肥沃（な）*fertile; rich; productive* §hiyoku na tochí 肥沃な土地 *fertile land*

hiyowa na ひ弱な *frailty; helplessness*

híyu 比喩 *metaphor; simile; figure of speech*

hiza 膝 *knee; lap* §hiza o mageru 膝を曲げる *bend (one's) knees* §hiza o óru 膝を折る *sit Japanese fashion* §hiza o útsu 膝を打つ *pat (one's) knee* §hiza o kuzúsu 膝を崩す *sit at ease (informally); cross (one's) legs* §hiza o tadásu 膝を正す *sit formally* §hiza no ue ni suwaru 膝の上に座る *sit on (someone's) lap*

hizamazúk·u [vi hizamazukánai; hizamazúita] 跪く *kneel*

hizashi 日差し；日射し *sunlight*

hizốbutsu 秘蔵物 *treasured article*

hizuke 日付 *the date* §Kono fūtố no hizuke wa kyónen no keshiin ni nátte iru. この封筒の日付は去年の消印になっている。*The cancellation date on this envelope is last year.*

hizume 蹄 *hoof*

hizumi 歪み *distortion; strain* §sekitsúi no hizumi 脊椎の歪み *distortion of the spinal column* §tómi no bunpai no hizumi 富の分配の歪み *unequal distribution of wealth*

hố 帆 *a sail*

hố 方 *direction; alternative* §kita no hố 北の方 *to the north* §Áni yhori otốto no hố wa se ga takái. 兄より弟の方は背が高い。*My younger brother's taller than my older brother.*

hoán 保安 *security; preservation of public peace* 　§hoánkan 保安官 *security officer; sheriff*

hōan 法案 *legislative bill*

hōbi 褒美 *a reward* 　§hōbi ni 褒美に *as a reward*

hōbo ほぼ *about; nearly; for the most part*

hōbō 方々 *everywhere*

hóchikisu ホチキス *stapler*

hōchō 包丁 *kitchen knife*

hochóki 補聴器 *hearing aid*

-hódai 〜放題 *to one's content; as much as (one) wants* 　§tabe-hódai 食べ放題 *all (one) can eat* 　§nomi-hódai 飲み放題 *all (one) can drink*

hodo 程 *about; limit; to the extent that; as much as* 　§Kyő wa kinő hodo átsuku nai. 今日は昨日ほど暑くない。*Today's not as hot as yesterday.* 　§Apáto wa éki ni chikákereba chikái hodo ii. アパートは駅に近ければ近いほどいい。*The closer the apartment (which I want to rent) is to the station the better.* 　§Jōdan ní mo hodo ga áru. 冗談にも程がある。*That's carrying a joke too far! (lit: There's a limit even to a joke!)*

hodō 歩道 *walkway; sidewalk* 　§hodōkyō 歩道橋 *pedestrian bridge; pedestrian overpass*

hōdō 報道 *reporting; news; report* 　§hōdō kíkan 報道機関 *the press (news media)*

hodohodo [ni] 程々（に）*in moderation*

hodók·u [vt hodokánai; hodóita] 解く *untie; unpack* 　§ní o hodóku 荷を解く *unpack (one's) bags (burden)*

hodoyó·i [adj] 程よい *good; favorable* 　§hodoyói yukágen 程よい湯加減 *just the right temperature (for bathwater)*

hoé·ru [vi hoénai; hóeta] 吠える *bark; roar*

hōfu 豊富 *abundance* ——**hōfu na** 豊富な *abundant* 　§Sono kuní wa chika shígen ga hōfu desu. その国は地下資源が豊富です。*That country has abundant underground resources.* ——**hōfu ni** 豊富に *abundantly*

hōfu 抱負 *ambition; aspiration* 　§Káre wa shőrai no hōfu o katatta. 彼は将来の抱負を語った。*He talked about his future aspirations.*

hōfuku 報復 *retaliation* 　§hōfuku shúdan 報復手段 *retaliatory measures* ——**hōfuku-suru** [vi] 報復する *retaliate*

hōgaku 方角 *direction; (one's) bearings*

hogáraka [na] 朗らか（な）*bright; clear; cheerful* ——**hogáraka ni** 朗らかに *brightly; cheerfully; merrily*

hōgén 方言 *dialect*

hógo 保護 *protection* 　§hogo bőeki 保護貿易 *protective trade* 　§hogósha 保護者 *guardian* ——**hógo-suru** [vt] 保護する *protect; guard; shield; conserve*

hṓhi 包皮 *foreskin (Anat)*

hōhō 方法 *method; manner; way of (doing)*

hohoemashí·i [adj hohoemáshiku nái; hohoemáshikatta] 微笑ましい *(be) pleasant; smile-provoking*

hohoemi 微笑み *a smile*

hohoém·u [vi hohoemánai; hohoénda] 微笑む *smile*

hoikúen 保育園 *nursery school*

hōji 法事 *memorial service (Budd)*

hójo 補助 *subsidy; assistance; aid* 8hojokin 補助金 *grant (of money)* ——**hójo-suru** [vt] 補助する *subsidize; assist; (give financial) aid*

hoka [no] 他（の）；外（の）*another; other* 8Hoka no séito wa minna káette shimatta. 他の生徒はみんな帰ってしまった。*The other students all returned home.* 8Hoka ni náni ka chūmon wa arimasén ka? 他に何か注文はありませんか。*Is there anything else you wish to order?*

hōka 放火 *arson* 8hōká-ma 放火魔 *arsonist*

hōka 砲火 *gunfire* 8hṓka o abiru 砲火を浴びる *be fired on*

hōkai 崩壊 *a collapse; a fall; crumbling* ——**hōkai-suru** [vi] 崩壊する *collapse; fall; crumble* 8Jishin de tatémono ga takusan hōkai-shita. 地震で建物が沢山崩壊した。*In the earthquake many buildings crumbled.* 8Kyū-taisei ga hōkai-shita. 旧体制が崩壊した。*The old system collapsed.*

hokan 保管 *custody* ——**hokan-suru** [vt] 保管する *save; keep; take into custody* 8shíryō o hokan-suru 資料を保管する *save / keep documents (in trust)*

hōkatsu 包括 *comprehensive; all-embracing* ——**hōkatsu-suru** [vt] 包括する *include; comprehend; comprise*

hoken 保険 *insurance* 8hokénryō 保険料 *insurance premium* 8seimei hóken 生命保険 *life insurance* 8kenkō hóken 健康保険 *health insurance* 8ryokō hóken 旅行保険 *travel insurance* 8kasai hóken 火災保険 *fire insurance* 8shōgai hóken 傷害保険 *accident insurance*

hōken 封建 *feudalism* 8hōken jídai 封建時代 *feudal times* ——**hōkenteki [na]** 封建的（な）*feudalistic*

hokenjo 保健所 *health center*

hoketsu 補欠 *a reserve (candidate / applicant / player)* 8hoketsu sénkyo 補欠選挙 *by-election*

hōki 箒 *broom* 8take-bṓki 竹ぼうき *bamboo broom (for garden)*

Hokkyoku 北極 *the Arctic; North Pole* 8Hokkyokukai 北極海 *Arctic Ocean* 8hokkyokukō 北極光 *northern lights; aurora borealis* 8hokkyokú-guma 北極熊 *polar bear*

hōkō 方向 *direction* 8hōkō shijíki 方向指示器 *turn signal* 8hōkō ténkan 方向転換 *change of direction* 8hōkō ónchi 方向音痴

lacking a sense of direction

hōkō 奉公 *duty; service; apprenticeship*

hōkoku 報告 *report; account* ——**hōkoku-suru** [*vt*] 報告する *report; inform*

hokori 埃 *dust*

hokorí 誇り *pride*

hokór·u [*vi* hokoránai; hokótta] 誇る *be proud of; boast*

hokósha 歩行者 *pedestrian* ⑧hokōsha téngoku 歩行者天国 *vehicle-free promenade*

hokusei 北西 *northwest*

hokutō 北東 *northeast*

hokorippó·i [*adj* hokorippóku nái; hokorippókatta] 埃っぽい *(be) dusty*

hokyū 補給 *supply; replenishment* ——**hokyū-suru** [*vt*] 補給する *supply; replenish* ⑧gasorin o hokyū-suru ガソリンを補給する *fill with (or replenish) gasoline*

hōkyū 俸給 *salary; pay*

homaré 誉れ *honor; credit; distinction*

hómbu 本部 *headquarters*

hōmén 方面 *direction; district; aspect; sphere*

homé·ru [*vt* homénai; hómeta] 褒める；誉める *praise; commend; extol*

hommono 本物 *the real thing* ⑧hommono no 本物の *real*

hōmon 訪問 *a visit* ——**hōmon-suru** [*vt*] 訪問する *visit; call on*

hómu ホーム *railroad platform*

hōmu dáijin 法務大臣 *minister of justice*

hōmúr·u [*vt* hōmuránai; hōmútta] 葬る *inter; bury* ⑧shísha o teatsuku hōmúru 死者を手厚く葬る *bury the dead carefully* ⑧Jíken wa yamí ni hōmúreta. 事件は闇に葬られた。 *The incident was buried in darkness (hushed up).*

hōmushíkku ホームシック *homesickness* ⑧hōmushíkku ni náru ホームシックになる *become homesick*

Hōmúshō 法務省 *Ministry of Justice*

hón 本 *book* ⑧hón'ya 本屋 *bookstore* ⑧hóntate 本立て *bookends* ⑧hómbako 本箱 *bookcase; bookshelf*

-hon (-bon; -pon) 〜本 [*classifier for long, cylindrical objects*] ⑧empitsu níhon 鉛筆二本 *two pencils* ⑧ninjin sámbon 人参三本 *three carrots* ⑧Nékutai o íppon katta. ネクタイを一本買った。 *I bought a tie.*

hóndo 本土 *mainland*

honé 骨 *bone* ⑧honetsugi 骨接ぎ *bone setting* ⑧honé o óru 骨を折る *break; fracture a bone; make efforts*

honeori 骨折り *hard work; pains; labor*

hón'i 本意 *real intent; motive; purpose*

honkakuteki [na] 本格的（な）*regular; full-scale; real; earnest; serious*

——**honkakuteki ni** 本格的に *in earnest; seriously*

honkan 本館 *main building*

honki 本気 *seriousness; earnestness* §honki de 本気で *seriously; in earnest*

honne 本音 *real intention; motive* §honne to tatemae 本音と建て前 *real vs. ostensible motive (or intention)*

hon no ほんの *a mere* §hon-no sukóshi ほんの少し *only a little*

hónnō 本能 *instinct* §Shokuyoku wa hónnō no hitótsu desu. 食欲は本能の一つです。 *Appetite is one of our instincts.*

hónoo 炎 *a flame; a blaze* §rōsóku no hónoo ろうそくの炎 *a candle flame* §hónoo ni tsutsumaréru 炎に包まれる *be engulfed in flames*

hōnō 包嚢 *cyst*

hónrai 本来 *originally; essentially; fundamentally* ——**hónrai no** 本来の *original; essential; natural; fundamental* §Sore wa hónrai no ími kara kakehanárete iru. それは本来の意味からかけ離れている。 *That's far removed from the original meaning.*

honrō-suru [vt] 翻弄する *toss about; trifle with* §úmmei ni honrō-sareru 運命に翻弄される *be trifled with by fate*

honshitsu 本質 *essence; substance* §jíken no honshitsu o tsúku 事件の本質をつく *grasp the essence of the matter* ——**honshitsuteki [na]** 本質的（な）*essential; substantial* ——**honshitsuteki ni** 本質的に *essentially; in essence*

hontō 本当 *real; true; actual* §Hontō? 本当？ *Really?* §Kekkon-shita tte hontō? 結婚したって本当？ *Is it true you got married?* §Hontō wa ... 本当は~ *The truth is ...; In fact ...* ——**hontō ni** 本当に *truly; really*

hon'yaku 翻訳 *translation* §hon'yákusha 翻訳者 *translator* ——**hon'yaku-suru** [vt] 翻訳する *translate*

honyū 哺乳 *suckling; nursing* §honyū dóbutsu 哺乳動物 *mammal* §honyū bin 哺乳瓶 *nursing bottle*

hóo; hóho 頬 *the cheek*

Hóra! ほら！ *Look!* §Hóra, míte goran! ほら、見てごらん！ *Hey, look!* §Hóra! Mégane wa koko ni átta yo! ほら！眼鏡はここにあったよ！ *Look! Your glasses were here (all the time)!*

horaana 洞穴 *cave; cavern; den*

hōrénsō ほうれん草 *spinach*

hore·ru [vi horenai; horeta] 惚れる *fall in love with* §Ore wa omae ni horeta. 俺はお前に惚れた。 *I fell (or I've fallen) in love with you. <masc>*

hōridás·u [vt hōridasánai; hōridáshita] 放り出す *throw out; quit; abandon; dismiss*

hōritsu 法律 *law; legislation* §hōritsu-jō 法律上 *legally* §hōritsujō no 法律上の *legal*

horobír·u [*vi* horobínai; horóbita] 滅びる *fall into decline; perish; become extinct* ▪Kodai búmmei ga horóbita. 古代文明が滅びた. *The ancient civilization perished.*

horobós·u [*vt* horobósanai; horobóshita] 滅ぼす *ruin; destroy; annihilate; exterminate* ▪áku o horobósu 悪を滅ぼす *exterminate evil* ▪kuni o horobósu 国を滅ぼす *destroy a country; bring about a nation; ruin* ▪mi o horobósu 身を滅ぼす *ruin oneself*

hór·u [*vt* horánai; hótta] 掘る *dig; excavate* ▪aná o hóru 穴を掘る *dig a hole* ▪ído o hóru 井戸を掘る *dig a well*

hór·u [*vt* horánai; hótta] 彫る *carve; engrave*

hóryo 捕虜 *prisoner of war* ▪hóryo ni náru 捕虜になる *be taken prisoner (of war)*

hosei 補正 *revision; supplement* ▪hosei yósan 補正予算 *supplementary budget* ——**hosei-suru** [*vt*] 補正する *revise; rectify*

hōseki 宝石 *jewel; jewelry; precious stone*

hōsha 放射 *radiation* ▪hōshánō 放射能 *radioactivity* ▪hōshajō [*no*] 放射状（の）*radial* ▪hōshajō ni 放射状に *radially* ▪hōshasei [*no*] 放射性（の）*radioactive*

hoshaku 保釈 *bail* ▪hoshaku o shuchō-suru 保釈を主張する *demand bail*

hoshi 星 *star*

hoshigár·u [*vt* hoshigaránai; hoshigátta] 欲しがる *want; covet* [*not used with first person*]

hoshí·i [*adj* hoshiku nái; hoshikatta] 欲しい *(be) desired; want* ▪hóshikute tamaranai 欲しくてたまらない *want so bad (one) can't stand it*

hōshiki 方式 *established form; method; formula*

hoshikusa 干し草 *hay; dry grass*

hōshin 方針 *a plan; course* ▪hōshin o tatéru 方針を立てる *plot a course; map out a plan* ▪hōshin o kaeru 方針を変える *change plans*

hōshin 疱疹 *cold sore; herpes*

hōshi-suru [*vi*] 奉仕する *serve; give (one's) services free*

hoshō 保証 *a guarantee; warranty* ▪hoshōnin 保証人 *guarantor* ——**hoshō-suru** [*vt*] 保証する *guarantee* ▪Kámera wa ichinénkan hoshō-sarete iru. カメラは一年間保証されている. *The camera is guaranteed for one year.*

hóshu 保守 *conservatism; conservativeness* ▪hoshu gíin 保守議員 *Tory dietman; a conservative diet member* ▪hoshu-tō 保守党 *conservative party* ▪hoshu náikaku 保守内閣 *conservative administration* ▪hoshu shúgi 保守主義 *conservatism* ——**hoshuteki** [**na**] 保守的（な）*conservative* ▪hoshuteki na kangae-kata 保守的な考え方 *a conservative way of thinking*

hōshū 報酬 *a reward; pay; remuneration* ▪hōshū o éru 報酬を得る

receive remuneration

hosō 舗装 *pavement* ——**hosō-suru** [*vt*] 舗装する *pave* §hosō dốro 舗装道路 *a paved road*

hōsō 放送 *a broadcast* §hōsốkyoku 放送局 *broadcasting station* —— **hōsō-suru** [*vt*] 放送する *broadcast*

hosó·i [*adj* hósoku nái; hósokatta] 細い *(be) thin; slender; narrow* §hosói íto 細い糸 *fine thread* §hosói michi 細い道 *a narrow road*

hosonagá·i [*adj* hosonágaku nái; hosonágakatta] 細長い *(be) long and narrow*

hosshin 発心 *awakening (Budd)*

hōtai 包帯 *a bandage; surgical dressing* ——**hōtai-suru** [*vi*] 包帯する *bandage; apply a bandage*

hótaru 蛍 *firefly*

hōtei 法廷 *court; courtroom; tribunal* §hōtei tốsō 法廷闘争 *litigation battle*

hōtō 放蕩 *dissipation; debauchery* §hōtō músuko 放蕩息子 *the prodigal son* ——**hōtō-suru** [*vi*] 放蕩する *dissipate (one's) fortune; live loosely*

hotoké 仏 *the Buddha; departed soul*

hotóndo 殆ど *nearly; almost (all)* §Hotóndo no hito ga jíjitsu o shiranai. 殆どの人が事実を知らない。 *Most people don't know the true facts.* §Hotóndo tabe-owátta. 殆ど食べ終わった。 *I finished eating almost all (of it).*

hótte ok·u [*vt* -okanai; -oita] 放っておく *leave (something) alone; let it stand*

hotto-suru [*vi*] ほっとする *be relieved; breathe a sigh of relief* §Kázoku no buji o kiite hotto-shita. 家族の無事を聞いてほっとした。 *I breathed a sigh of relief when I heard my family was OK*

hoyō 保養 *recuperation* §hoyốchi 保養地 *health resort* ——**hoyō-suru** [*vi*] 保養する *recuperate*

hoyū 保有 *possession* §hoyűken 保有権 *ownership* ——**hoyū-suru** [*vt*] 保有する *possess; own* §káku o hoyū-suru 核を保有する *possess nuclear power*

hozon 保存 *preservation* §hozón-saku 保存策 *preservation policy* §hozón-shoku 保存食 *keepable food* ——**hozon-suru** [*vt*] 保存する *preserve; keep; store* §bunka ísan o hozon-suru 文化遺産を保存する *preserve cultural heritage*

hōzuki ほおずき *Chinese lantern plant*

hyakka jíten 百科事典 *encyclopedia*

hyakú 百 *one hundred*

hyō 表 *table; schedule; chart*

hyő 雹 *hail; hailstone; hailstorm*

hyő 豹 *leopard; panther*

hyō 票 *a vote*

-hyō 〜表 *table; list* ⑧jikoku-hyō 時刻表 *timetable* ⑧nempyō 年表 *chronological table*

hyōban 評判 *reputation; opinion*

hyōga 氷河 *glacier* ⑧hyōgá-ki 氷河期 *glacial epoch; ice age*

hyōgén 表現 *expression; manifestation* ――**hyōgén-suru** [*vt*] 表現する *express; manifest*

hyōgi íinkai 評議委員会 *board of counselors; board of trustees*

hyōhakú-zai 漂白剤 *bleach*

hyōjó 表情 *(facial) expression; a look* ⑧akarui hyōjó 明るい表情 *a pleasant (**or** bright / cheerful) expression*

hyōjun 標準 *standard; norm*

hyōka 評価 *evaluation; appraisal* ⑧hyōka kákaku 評価価格 *appraised value* ――**hyōka-suru** [*vt*] 評価する *evaluate; appraise* ⑧seiseki o hyōka-suru 成績を評価する *evaluate the result*

hyōki 表記 *inscription* ――**hyōki-suru** [*vt*] 表記する *inscribe; write down*

hyōmén 表面 *surface* ⑧chikyū no hyōmén 地球の表面 *the earth's surface*

hyōnó 氷嚢 *ice bag; ice pack*

hyōron 評論 *critique; review* ⑧hyōron-ka 評論家 *literary critic* ⑧eiga hyōron 映画評論 *movie review* ――**hyōron-suru** [*vt*] 評論する *criticize; review*

hyōryū-suru [*vi*] 漂流する *drift about*

hyōsatsu 表札 *nameplate (on a house)*

hyōshí 表紙 *cover (of a book)*

hyōshí 拍子 *time; rhythm* ⑧yonbyóshi 四拍子 *4/4 time*

hyōshiki 標識 *road sign; marker* ⑧kōtsū hyóshiki 交通標識 *traffic sign*

hyōtán 瓢箪 *gourd*

hyotto-suru [*vi*] ひょっとする *perhaps; by some chance* ⑧Hyotto-shitára kyō watashi wa kaerénai ka mo shirenai. ひょっとしたら今日私は帰れないかもしれない。 *It just may be that I won't be able to come home today.*

hyōzan 氷山 *iceberg*

hyún [to] ひゅーん（と）[*mimetic for the sound of something rushing through the air, i.e., a whistling or whizzing sound*]

I

í 胃 *stomach*

ibara 茨 *thornbush; bramble*

ibár·u [*vi* ibaránai; ibátta] 威張る *boast; be proud (of); be haughty;*

swagger

ibikí 鼾 *a snore* §ibikí o káku 鼾をかく *snore*

íbo 疣 *wart*

ibutsu 遺物 *relic; remains; memento* §kódai no ibutsu 古代の遺物 *ancient remains*

ichí 一 *one (the numeral)*

íchi; íchiba 市；市場 *market (place)* §aomono íchiba 青物市場 *vegetable market* §uo íchiba 魚市場 *fish market*

íchi 位置 *situation; place; location; position*

ichíban 一番 *number one; #1; the first; the best* §kurásu de ichíban クラスで一番 *first in one's class* §ichiban yasúi 一番安い *cheapest*

ichíbu 一部 *one part; a portion; a section*

ichídan 一段 *a (or one) step; a stage*

ichidánraku 一段落 *a pause* ——**ichidánraku-suru** [vi] 一段落する *settle (a matter) temporarily; put a period to; stop (for now); have a let-up* §Kono shigoto ga ichidánraku-shitara, tsugí no shigoto ni torikakarṓ. この仕事が一段落したら、次の仕事に取りかかろう。 *When this job's done (or When this stage of the job's done), I'm going to start on the next project.* ——**ichidánraku-tsúk·u** [vi -tsukánai; -tsúita] 一段落つく *be settled; be completed* §Shigoto ga ichidánraku-tsúita. 仕事が一段落ついた。 *This completes one stage of the job.*

ichidó 一度 *one time; once* §ichidó ni 一度に *all at once*

ichidṓ 一同 *all; everyone* §sháin ichidṓ 社員一同 *all employees; the entire staff*

ichigai ni 一概に *summarily; generally; in general; unconditionally* §Dóchira ga warúi nante ichigai ní wa ienai. どちらが悪いなんて一概には言えない。 *One can't say in general which is bad.*

Ichigatsú 一月 *January*

ichigo 苺 *strawberry*

ichíichi 一々 *every single one; one-by-one* §Aitsu wa ore no itta kotó ni ichíichi mónku o tsukéru n dakara, atamá ni kúru yo. あいつは俺の言うことに一々文句をつけるんだから、頭に来るよ。 *He gets on my nerves the way he complains about every single thing I say. <masc>*

ichíji 一時 *temporarily; for a brief time* §ichiji ázukari 一時預り *temporary (baggage) check* §ichiji-kin 一時金 *lump-sum allowance; one-time allowance* §ichiji téishi 一時停止 *momentary stop* ——**ichijiteki [na]** 一時的（な）*temporary* ——**ichijiteki ni** 一時的に *temporarily* §Erebḗta wa ichijiteki ni koshō-shita. エレベーターは一時的に故障した。 *The elevator was temporarily out of order.*

ichíjiku 無花果 *fig*

ichijirushí·i [adj ichijirúshiku nái; ichijirúshikatta] 著しい *(be) remarkable; outstanding* ——**ichijirushíku** 著しく *markedly;*

appreciably; outstandingly

ichimen 一面 *the entire surface* §Sóto wa ichimen yuki-nóhara desu. 外は一面雪野原です。 *Outside, it's a solid expanse of snow.* ——**ichimenteki [na]** 一面的（な）*one-sided* ——**ichimenteki ni** 一面的に *one-sidedly*

ichimókusan [ni] 一目散（に）*at full speed; head over heels; as fast as (one's) legs can carry (one)* §Satsujínsha wa ichimókusan ni nigedashita. 殺人者は一目散に逃げ出した。*The murderer fled at full speed.*

ichininmae 一人前 *a full-fledged adult; serving for one person*

ichinin-suru [*vt*] 一任する *entrust; leave up to; commit (to)* §Sono kettei ni tsúite wa búka ni ichinin-shita. その決定については部下に一任した。*I left the decision on the matter to my subordinate.*

ichiō 一応 *once; for the time being; in a way* §Ichiō yatte miyṓ. 一応やってみよう。*I'll just try it.*

ichiranséi(ji) 一卵性（児）*identical twins*

ichiryṓjitsu 一両日 *a day or so* §ichiryṓjitsu ni 一両日に *in a day or two*

ichiryū no 一流の *top-rated; first-class*

ichiyō ni 一様に *uniformly; similarly; alike*

ichizuké·ru [*vt* ichizukénai; ichizúketa] 位置付ける *make a place for; locate*

ichō 銀杏；公孫樹 *ginkgo tree*

idai [na] 偉大（な）*great; grand; mighty*

iden 遺伝 *heredity* §idén-gaku 遺伝学 *genetics* §idénshi 遺伝子 *a gene* ——**iden-suru** [*vi*] 遺伝する *be inherited; be transmitted (from one's parents)*

ído 井戸 *well* §idó-mizu 井戸水 *well water* §ído o hóru 井戸を掘る *dig a well*

ído 緯度 *latitude*

idō 移動 *movement; tranfer*

idóm·u [*vi / vt* idománai; idónda] 挑む *confront; challenge; defy; take on; dare; tackle* §teki ni idómu 敵に挑む *confront the enemy* §ronsō o idómu 論争を挑む *dispute; challenge to an argument* §yamá ni idómu 山に挑む *take on a mountain; tackle (climbing) a mountain*

ié 家 *house*

iede-suru [*vi*] 家出する *run away from home*

iemoto 家元 *main branch (of a family); head (of a school of traditional arts)* §ikébana no iemoto 生け花の家元 *head of an* ikebana *school*

Iésu イエス *Jesus*

ífuku 衣服 *clothing; apparel*

igai 意外 *a surprise* ——**igai na** 意外な *unanticipated; unexpected* §igai na ketsumatsu 意な結末 *an unexpected outcome*

-ígai 〜以外 *beyond; outside of; except for* §Kankeisha-ígai tachiiri kinshí! 関係者以外立ち入り禁止。 *No entry, except for related personnel!*

ígaku 医学 *medical science; medicine*

igan 胃癌 *stomach cancer; gastric cancer*

igen 威厳 *dignity; stateliness* §Anó hito ni wa igen ga áru. あの人には威厳がある。 *That person has dignity.* ——**igen no** 威厳の *dignified; stately; commanding*

ígi 意義 *meaning; significance* §ígi aru jínsei 意義ある人生 *a meaningful life*

ígi 異議 *different meaning; dissent* §ígi o tonaéru 異議を唱える *raise an objection*

Igirisu イギリス *England; Great Britain: U.K.* ——**Igirisújin** イギリス人 *a British person; a Briton* (see also **Eikoku**)

-ígo 〜以後 *after this; from now (or then) on; henceforth; thereafter* §Sore ígo no ikisatsu wa shiranai. それ以後の経緯は知らない。 *I don't know the developments from that point on.*

ihai 位牌 *memorial tablet (Budd)* §Ihai o butsudan ni kazaru. 位牌を仏壇に飾る。 *We place the memorial tablet(s) in the Buddhist altar.*

ihan 違反 *violation (of the law)* ——**ihan-suru** [vi] 違反する *violate (or break) the law*

ihō 違法 *unlawful; against the law*

ihōjin 異邦人 *foreigner*

í·i [adj yóku nái; yókatta] いい；良い；善い；好い (be) good; nice; OK*

iiarawás·u [vt iiarawasánai; iiaráwashita] 言い表す *express; put into words* §Kánsha no kimochi o kotobá de iiarawásu kotó wa dekínai. 感謝の気持ちを言葉で言い表すことはできない。 *I cannot express in words my feeling of gratitude.*

iibun 言い分 *complaint; one's say; one's claim* §Iibun ga áru. 言い分がある。 *I have a complaint.* (or *I have something to say about that.*)

iidás·u [vi / vt iidasánai; iidáshita] 言い出す *bring up (a matter); broach (a subject)*

Iié. いいえ。 *No.*

iifurás·u [vt iifurasánai; iifuráshita] 言いふらす *spread; circulate* §warúkuchi o iifurásu 悪口を言いふらす *spread slander*

iigakari 言いがかり *accusation; imputation* §iigakari o tsukéru 言いがかりをつける *accuse falsely*

iikáereba 言い換えれば *in other words*

ii kagen [na] いい加減（な）*haphazard; irresponsible* §Aitsu wa kánari ii kagen da. あいつはかなりいい加減だ。 *He's rather haphazard (about things).* <masc> ——**ii kagen ni suru** いい加減にする *have done with (it); quit (it); stop (it)* <masc> §Báka na kotó o iú no wa ii kagen ni shinasai yo! 馬鹿なことを言うのはいい加減にしなさい

よ！ *Don't talk foolishness!* <fem>

iikaké·ru [vt iikakénai; iikáketa] 言いかける *speak to; address; accost*

iikata 言い方 *manner (or way) of saying*

iimawashi 言い回し *wording; manner of expression*

iín 委員 *committee member*   ❖iínkai 委員会 *committee*

iinikú·i [adj iiníkuku nái; iiníkukatta] 言いにくい *(be) difficult to say; delicate*   ❖Sore wa iinikúi. それは言いにくい。 *That's hard to say. (or I hesitate to say.)*

iisokoná·u [vt iisokonawánai; iisokonátta] 言い損なう *make a slip of the tongue*

iisugi 言い過ぎ *saying more than necessary; an exaggeration*

iisugí·ru [vt iisugínai; iisúgita] 言い過ぎる *speak too much; go too far*

iitsuke 言いつけ *an order; a command*   ❖iitsuke o mamóru 言いつけを守る *keep (follow) an order*

iitsuké·ru [vt iitsukénai; iitsúketa] 言いつける *order; instruct; tell (someone) to do (something); inform*   ❖yōji o iitsukéru 用事を言いつける *order (some) work done*   ❖jōshi ni iitsukéru 上司に言いつける *inform one's superior*

iitsukús·u [vt iitsukusánai; iitsukúshita] 言い尽くす *tell all; exhaust (telling something)*

iitsutae·ru [vt iitsutaenai; iitsutaeta] 言い伝える *hand down orally; convey; transmit*

iiwake 言い訳 *an excuse* ——**iiwake-suru** [vt] 言い訳する *apologize; offer an excuse*

ijí 意地 *willpower; backbone; pride; nature; temper*   ❖ijí o haru 意地を張る *be stubborn (or obstinate)*   ❖ijí o tṓsu 意地を通す *have (or insist on) one's own way*   ❖ijí ga warúi 意地が悪い *have a bad temper*   ❖ijí ga kitanái 意地が汚い *greedy; gluttonous*   ❖otoko no ijí 男の意地 *a man's pride* ——**ijipparí [na]** 意地っ張り（な）*stubbornness; stubborn*

iji 維持 *upkeep; maintenance*   ❖ijí-hi 維持費 *upkeep expense*   ❖genjō iji 現状維持 *keeping the status quo* ——**íji-suru** [vt] 維持する *maintain; keep up; preserve*

ijime 苛め *bullying*   ❖Gakkō dé wa ijime jíken ga tahatsu-shite iru. 学校では苛め事件が多発している。 *Cases of bullying at school are increasing.*   ❖ijimekko 苛めっ子 *(young) bully*   ❖ijimeya 苛め屋 *(adult) bully*

ijime·ru [vt ijimenai; ijimeta] 苛める *tease; harass; bully*

ijír·u [vt ijiránai; ijítta] 弄る *finger; fool with; tamper with; touch*   ❖kikái o ijíru 機械を弄る *tamper with a machine*   ❖niwa o ijíru 庭を弄る *work in the garden*   ❖kaisoku o ijíru 会則を弄る *revise membership rules*

ijiwáru [na] 意地悪（な）*mean; ill-tempered; crabby; spiteful; vexatious*

❸ijiwáru o suru 意地悪をする *do something mean (to a person / animal)*

ijō [na] 異状（な）*something wrong; extraordinary* ❸Ijō wa nái. 異状 はない。*There is nothing out of the ordinary*

ijō [na] 異常（な）*extraordinary; unusual; abnormal* ❸ijō na kōdō 異常 な行動 *abnormal behavior*

-íjō ～以上 *more than; above* ❸Gakushú-kai ni wa jūnin-íjō no kaiin ga atsumátta. 学習会には十人以上の会員が集まった。*More than ten members gathered at the study meeting.*

Íjō desu. 以上です。*That's all (meaning, "I have finished saying what I wanted to say").*

ijū 移住 *immigration; emigration; migration* ——**ijū-suru** [vi] 移住する *immigrate; emigrate; migrate* ❸Tanaka-san íkka wa Burajiru ni ijū-shita. 田中さん一家はブラジルに移住した。*The Tanaka family emigrated to Brazil.*

ika 烏賊 *squid; cuttlefish*

-íka ～以下 *less than; downward; below* ❸Gojutten-íka wa fugókaku desu. 五十点以下は不合格です。*(A score of) 50 or less is failing.* ❸Goman'en-íka no sútsu o sagashite imásu ga… ¥50,000以下のスー ツを探していますが… *I'm looking for a suit that costs less than ¥50,000.*

ikada 筏 *raft*

ikága 如何; 如何が *how about?; what?* ❸Kōhí wa ikága desu ka? コー ヒーは如何ですか。*How about some coffee?* ❸Shikei ni tsúite no go-íken wa ikága desu ka? 死刑についてのご意見は如何ですか。 *What is your opinion regarding the death penalty?*

ikáiyō 胃潰瘍 *stomach ulcer*

ikameshí·i [adj ikaméshiku nái; ikaméshikatta] 厳しい *(be) dignified; solemn; majestic* ❸ikameshíi táido 厳しい態度 *a dignified attitude* ❸ikameshíi mon-gámae 厳しい門構え *a majestic front gate*

ikan 遺憾 *regret* ❸ikan no í o hyō-súru 遺憾の意を表する *show regret* ❸ikan na 遺憾な *regrettable; lamentable; deplorable* ❸ikan ni omóu 遺憾に思う *(to) regret*

ikánaru 如何なる *whatever; whatever kind of* ❸ikánaru riyū de... 如何 なる理由で～ *for whatever reason...* ❸ikánaru jijō ga átte mo... 如何 なる事情があっても～ *no matter what the situation...*

ikari 錨 *anchor* ❸ikari o ageru 錨を上げる *pull up the anchor* ❸ikari o orósu 錨を下ろす *drop anchor*

ikarí 怒り *anger*

ikár·u [vt ikaránai; ikátta] 怒る *be (or become) angry (see also* **okór·u**)

ikás·u [vt ikasánai; ikáshita] 生かす *let stand; make good use of; make the most of* ❸hima o ikásu 暇を生かす *make (good) use of leisure time* ❸Kimi no púran o ikasō. 君のプランを生かそう。*Let's go with* *your plan.* <masc>

iké 池 *pond*

ikébana 生け花 *Japanese flower arranging*

ikegaki 生け垣 *a hedge*

íken 意見 *opinion; idea; view; advice* §jibun no íken o nobéru 自分の意見を述べる *express one's opinion* §Gyōsei káikaku ni tsuite, dónna íken o o-mochi desu ka? 行政改革について、どんな意見をお持ちですか。*What ideas do you have about administrative reform?* §Anó hito wa watashi no íken o kikanái. あの人は私の意見を聞かない。*He doesn't take my advice.*

Ikenai! いけない！ *That won't do!*

ikenie 生け贄；生贄 *victim; a sacrifice; sacrifical offering*

iké·ru [*vt* ikénai; íketa] 生ける *arrange (flowers)* §haná o ikéru 花を生ける *arrange flowers*

íki 息 *breath* §íki o suru 息をする *breathe* §íki o tomeru 息を止める *hold one's breath; stop breathing* §íki o kirásu 息を切らす *gasp*

-iki ;-yuki ～行き *bound for* §Hakata-yuki 博多行き *bound for Hakata*

ikichigai ; yukichigai 行き違い *cross (**or** pass) one another (on the way); misunderstanding* §Anáta to watshi lto wa ikichigai ni nátta. あなたと私とは行き違いになった。 *We missed each other in passing.* §Kimi to bóku to no íken ni wa dṓmo ikichigai ga áru yō da. 君と僕との意見にはどうも行き違いがあるようだ。*Our opinions seem to differ.* <masc>

ikidomari ; yukidomari 行き止まり *dead end; cul-de-sac*

ikidṓr·u [*vi* ikidōránai; ikidṓtta] 憤る *resent; get angry* §shákai no mujun ni ikidṓru 社会の矛盾に憤る *resent the contradictions (**or** inconsistencies) of society*

ikigai 生き甲斐 *reason to live; reason for living*

ikiíki-shita 生き生きした *full of life; lively*

ikikae·ru [*vi* ikikaeranai; ikikaetta] 生き返る *come back to life; revive; be resuscitated* §Mizu o máitara kusábana ga ikikaetta. 水を撒いたら草花が生き返った。*The plants revived after I watered them.*

ikíki 行き来 *comings and goings*

ikímono 生き物 *living creature*

ikinari いきなり *abruptly; all of a sudden; outright* §Mishiranu hitó ga ikinari tobikónde kita no! 見知らぬ人がいきなり飛び込んで来たの。*A stranger suddenly jumped out (at me)!* <fem>

ikinokór·u [*vi* ikinokoránai; ikinokótta] 生き残る *remain alive; survive* §Watashítachi wa hisan na sensō ni ikinokótta. 私たちは悲惨な戦争に生き残った。*We survived a tragic war.*

ikiói 勢い *force; power; spirit; vigor* §ikiói-yoku 勢いよく *spiritedly; vigorously*

ikí·ru [*vi* ikínai; íkita] 生きる *live; exist* §hitóri de ikíru 一人で生きる

live alone

ikisaki ; yukisaki 行き先 *destination*

ikisatsu 経緯 *circumstances; particulars; details* ◊komiitta ikisatsu 込み入った経緯 *complicated circumstances*

íkita *(attr)* 生きた *vital; live; living;* ◊íkita chié 生きた知恵 *vital resourcefulness* ◊íkita Eigo 生きた英語 *English as it is actually spoken (lit. living English)*

ikiume ni náru [*vi* -naránai; -nátta] 生き埋めになる *be buried alive*

ikizumari ; yukizumari 行き詰まり *blind alley; deadlock*

ikizumár·u [*vi* ikizumaránai; ikizumátta] 息詰まる *be choked; be oppressed; be stifled*

íkka 一家 *one (entire) family* ◊Kobayashi-san íkka 小林さん一家 *the Kobayashi family*

ikkái 一回 *once; one time* ◊ikkái ni 一回に *at one time; all at once* ◊ikkaibun 一回分 *a dose (of medicine)*

ikkan 一貫 *consistency; coherence* ——**ikkan-suru** [*vi*] 一貫する *be consistent; cohere* ◊ikkan-shita 一貫した *consistent* ◊ikkan-shita shuchō 一貫した主張 *a consistent claim (or assertion)*

ikkatsu 一括 *a bundle; a lump* ——**ikkatsu-suru** [*vt*] 一括する *summarize; lump together*

íkken 一軒 *one building; separate building* ◊ikkén'ya 一軒家 *a separate (independent) house* ◊ikken-góto ni 一軒毎に *from house to house; door-to-door*

íkki 一気 *one breath* ◊íkki ni 一気に *at a breath; in a breath* ◊íkki ni nómu 一気に飲む *swallow in one gulp; gulp down*

ikkō 一行 *a group; a party*

ikko-date [no] 一戸建て（の）*separate; detached; independent structure*

ikō 意向 *intention; inclination*

ikóru イコール *equal (to)*

ikotsu 遺骨 *remains (of a dead person)*

ik·u [*vi* ikanai; itta] 行く *go* ◊Watashi wa ráigetsu Yōróppa ni ikimásu. 私は来月ヨーロッパに行きます。 *I'm going to Europe next month.*

[-te] iku [*vb aux*]（～て）いく *(walk) out; go (on)... -ing* [*vb: aux*] ◊heyá kara déte iku 部屋から出ていく *go out of (or leave) a room* ◊Kyó wa obentō o motte iku. 今日はお弁当を持っていく。 *I'm taking a lunch today.* ◊Nihon no jinkō wa dandan fúete iku to omóu. 日本の人口はだんだん増えていくと思う。 *I think Japan's population is going to gradually increase.*

íkuji 育児 *infant care; child rearing*

íkunichi ka 幾日か *several days*

íkura いくら *how much?* ◊íkura ... té mo いくら～ても *no matter how much* ◊Íkura tabeté mo futoránai wa. いくら食べても太らないわ。 *I don't gain weight, no matter how much I eat.* <fem> ◊Íkura kimi no tanomí demo bóku ni wa kotaéru kotó ga dekínai. いくら君の頼みでも僕には応えることができない。*No matter how much you beg, I can't help you.* <masc>

íkutsu いくつ *how old?; how many?*

íkutsuka [no] いくつか（の） *some; several*

ikyō 異教 *heresy* §ikyṓto 異教徒 *heathen; pagan*

imá 居間 *living room*

íma 今 *now* ——**íma ni** 今に *right away; soon* ——**íma de wa** 今では *nowadays* ——**ima máde ni** 今までに *up until now* ——**íma ni mo** 今にも *at any moment*

imada 未だ *yet; as yet; so far; hitherto*

imadoki 今時 *nowadays; today; the present age*

ima hitótsu 今一つ *not quite (enough)* §Ima hitótsu, settokúryoku ga yowái. 今一つ説得力が弱い。*I'm still not quite convinced.*

ima hitótsu wa 今一つは *another; the second*

imaimashí·i [*adj* imaimáshiku nái; imaimáshikatta] いまいましい *(be) annoying; tiresome; vexing* §imaimashíi jíken いまいましい事件 *an annoying occurrence*

imasara 今更 *at this late hour; after so long*

imashime 戒め *admonition; lesson; precept*

imashimé·ru [*vt* imashiménai; imashímeta] 戒める *admonish; reprove; warn*

ími 意味 *meaning; signification* §imíron 意味論 *semantics* ——**ími-suru** [*vt*] 意味する *mean; signify*

imin 移民 *immigration; emigration; immigrant; emigrant* ——**imin-suru** [*vi*] 移民する *immigrate; emigrate*

imo 芋 *potato; sweet potator; taro*

imono 鋳物 *casting; article cast in metal*

imōtó 妹 *(one's own) younger sister*

ín 印 *a seal; stamp* §inkan 印鑑 *signature seal*

in 韻 *a rhyme* §in o fumú 韻を踏む *rhyme (with)*

ína 否 *no; nay*

inago 蝗 *locust*

-ínai ～以内 *within; less than; inside of* §Íma kara juppun-ínai ni anáta no tokoró ni ikimásu. 今から十分以内に貴方のところに行きます。*I'll be there in less than ten minues.*

inaka 田舎 *country; rural district* §inaká michi 田舎道 *rural road* §inakamono 田舎者 *country bumpkin* §inaka no 田舎の *rural; country*

inasaku 稲作 *rice cultivation; growing rice*

[ya] ínaya ～（や）否や *as soon as* §Yūshoku o tabéru ya ína ya musumé wa dḗto ni tobidáshite itta. 夕食を食べるや否や娘はデートに飛び出して行った。*As soon as she had eaten supper, my daughter* *rushed out on a date.*

inazuma 稲妻 *lightning*

ínchiki いんちき *cheating; fraud; trickery*

íne 稲 *rice plant; rice seedling*

inemúri 居眠り *a nap* ——**inemúri-suru** [*vi*] 居眠りする *nap; doze off*

infure インフレ *inflation* ⑧infure chōsei kéikaku インフレ調整計画 *inflation control program* ⑧infure o yokusei-suru インフレを抑制する *curb inflation* ⑧infure o norikoéru インフレを乗り越える *overcome inflation; come out of inflation*

ínga 因果 *cause and effect; karma; fate* ⑧inga kánkei 因果関係 *a causal sequence* ⑧ínga ōhō 因果応報 *consequence; retribution*

ínja 隠者 *hermit*

inki na 陰気な *depressing; gloomy; melancholy* ⑧inki na séikaku 陰気な性格 *a melancholy disposition* ⑧inki na heyá 陰気な部屋 *a gloomy room*

ínko いんこ *parakeet*

ínochi 命 *life*

inochigake no 命懸けの *risky; a matter of life and death*

inorí 祈り *prayer; a plea*

inór·u [*vt* inoránai; inótta] 祈る *pray*

inoshíshi 猪 *wild boar* ⑧inoshishi-doshi 猪年 *year of the wild boar*

ínryoku 引力 *gravity; attraction*

insatsu 印刷 *printing* ——**insatsu-suru** [*vt*] 印刷する *print*

inshi 印紙 *(revenue) stamp*

inshō 印象 *impression* ⑧daiichi ínshō 第一印象 *first impression* ⑧tsuyói inshō 強い印象 *strong impression*

íntā インター *interchange; ramp (for) expressway*

intai 引退 *retirement* ——**intai-suru** [*vi*] 引退する *retire*

interi インテリ *intellectual (person)*

inú 犬 *dog* ⑧inu-goya 犬小屋 *doghouse*

inujini-suru [*vi*] 犬死にする *die for no purpose; die like a dog*

in'yō 引用 *quotation* ——**in'yō-suru** [*vt*] 引用する *quote*

inyū 移入 *introduction; importation* ⑧kanjō ínyū 感情移入 *empathy* ——**inyū-suru** [*vt*] 移入する *introduce; import*

inzei 印税 *royalty (on a book)*

iō 硫黄 *sulfur*

ippai [no] 一杯 (の) *full* ⑧ippai ni suru 一杯にする *fill*

ippan [no] 一般 (の) *ordinary* ⑧ippan káikei 一般会計 *general account* ⑧ippan kaikei yósan 一般会計予算 *general budget* ——**ippan ni** 一般に *ordinarily*

ippen 一変 *complete (or drastic) change* ——**ippen-suru** [*vi*] 一変する *change completely*

íppo 一歩 *one step* ⑧íppo yuzutte 一歩譲って *give a bit; yield a little*

ippṓ 一方 *one side; one direction* ❽ippōteki na shṓri 一方的な勝利 *lopsided victory* ❽ippōteki na yunyū kísei 一方的な輸入規制 *unilateral import control* ❽ippō tsūkō 一方通行 *one-way traffic*

ippuku 一服 *breather; a rest; a smoke* ——**ippuku-suru** [*vi / vt*] 一服す る *take a break; rest*

iradatashí·i [*adj* iradatáshiku nái; iradatáshikatta] 苛立たしい *(be) impatient*

iradáts·u [*vi* iradatánai; iradátta] 苛立つ *be irritated; be exasperated; fret*

irai 依頼 *a request; a solicitation* ——**irai-suru** [*vi / vt*] 依頼する *request; solicit; entrust*

-írai 〜以来 *since; from then on*

íraira-suru [*vi*] 苛々する *grow impatient; be irritable*

Irasshaimáse! いらっしゃいませ！*Welcome!*

irasshár·u [*vi* irassharánai; irasshátta] いらっしゃる *be; come; go* <*formal*>

ire-bá 入れ歯 *false tooth; denture*

ire·ru [*vt* irenai; ireta] 入れる *put in; insert*

irezumi 入れ墨 *tattoo*

-iri 〜入り *containing*

iriguchi 入口 *entrance*

iró 色 *color* ❽irotorídori no 色とりどりの *colorful*

iroai 色合い *color tone; shade (of color)*

iroiro [no / na] 色々（の／な）*various* ——**iroiro ni** 色々に *variously*

iroppó·i [*adj* iroppóku nái; iroppókatta] 色っぽい *(be) sexy; romantic*

irori 囲炉裏 *fireplace; hearth*

i·ru [*vi* inai; ita] 居る；いる *be (of people and animals)* ❽Shújin wa íma imasén. 主人は今いません。*My husband isn't in now.*

i·ru [*vi* iranai; itta] 要る *require; need* ❽Káigai ni iku tóki wa pasupṓto ga irimásu. 海外に行く時はパスポートが要ります。*When you go abroad you need a passport.*

[-te] i·ru [*vb: aux, progressive*] （〜て）いる ❽Watashi wa íma, hón o yónde imasu. 私は今、本を読んでいます。*I'm reading now.*

ír·u [*vt* iránai; ítta] 射る *shoot (an arrow)* ❽yumí o íru 弓を射る *shoot with a bow*

írui 衣類 *clothing*

iruka 海豚 *dolphin; porpoise*

íryoku 威力 *power; force*

isamashí·i [*adj* isamáshiku nái; isamáshikatta] 勇ましい *(be) brave; courageous* ——**isamáshiku** 勇ましく *bravely; courageously*

isan 胃酸 *stomach acid; gastric juice*

isan 遺産 *inheritance; property*

isei 威勢 *vigor; spirit; power* ❽isei ga íi 威勢がいい *high-spirited*

íseki 遺跡 *ruins; remains; relics*

isha 医者 *medical doctor; physician*

isháryō 慰謝料 *consolation money; payment for anguish caused to a former lover, ex-wife, surviving family members, etc.*

íshi 医師 *doctor*

íshi 意志 *will; volition*

íshi 意思 *intention*

ishí 石 *small stone* 　§ishi-bei 石塀 *stone wall* 　§ishi-dőrō 石灯篭 *stone lantern*

íshiki 意識 *consciousness* 　§íshiki fumei 意識不明 *unconscious*

ishitsúbutsu toriatsukaijo 遺失物取扱所 *lost and found office*

ísho 遺書 *will (and testament)*

ishoku 移植 *a transplant; transplanting* 　§shinzō íshoku 心臓移植 *a heart transplant* ——**ishoku-suru** [*vt*] 移植する *transplant*

isogashí·i [*adj* isogáshiku nái; isogáshikatta] 忙しい *(be) busy; in a hurry* 　§isogashíi sukejúru 忙しいスケジュル *a busy schedule* 　§Kimura-san wa ítsumo isogashíi. 木村さんはいつも忙しい。 *Ms. Kimura is always busy.*

isogí 急ぎ *haste* 　§Isogí! 急ぎ！ *Urgent!*

isóg·u [*vi* isogánai; isóida] 急ぐ *hurry*

isóide 急いで *quickly; in a hurry*

isoshím·u [*vi* isoshimánai; isoshínda] 勤しむ *engage in* 　§bengaku ni isoshímu 勉学に勤しむ *engage in study*

íssai no 一切の *every; all; (not) at all* 　§issai gássai 一切合財 *all and every* 　§Sake wa íssai nománai. 酒は一切飲まない。 *I don't drink (alchohol) at all.*

issaku- (*lit*: "one before") 一昨 　§issakújitsu 一昨日 *day before yesterday* 　§issaku-nen 一昨年 *year before last*

issanka tánso 一酸化炭素 *carbon monoxide*

íssei 一世 *first generation*

issei ni 一斉に *all together* 　§issei ni sutáto-suru 一斉にスタートする *start all together*

isshín 一身 *oneself* 　§isshin-jō 一身上 *for personal reasons* 　§isshín ni hikiukéru 一身に引き受ける *take on by oneself*

isshitsú 一室 *one room*

issho [ni] 一緒（に） *together (with)*

isshō 一生 *a lifetime*

isshōkémmei [na] 一生懸命（な） *earnest; industrious* ——**isshōkémmei ni** 一生懸命に *with all (one's) might; industriously*

issō 一層 *still more; all the more* 　§Issō no dóryoku o sasagemásu. 一層の努力を捧げます。 *I will try even harder.*

ísshu 一種 *one kind of; one sort of* 　§Bájiru wa hábu no ísshu desu. バジルはハーブの一種です。 *Basil is a kind of herb.*

isu 椅子 *chair*

íta 板 *(wooden) board; plank*

itabásami 板ばさみ *dilemma*

itachi 鼬 *weasel* 🔸itachi-gókko いたちごっこ *a rat race*

Itadakimásu. 頂きます！ *(said before beginning to eat)* <*set phrase*>

itadak·u [*vt* itadakanai; itadaita] 頂く *receive (from a superior)* <*formal*> 🔸Kono kḗki wa o-tónari no ókusan ni itadakimáshita. この ケーキはお隣の奥さんに頂きました。*I received this cake from the lady next door.* <*formal*> 🔸Yamada-san ni tegami o káite itadakimáshita. 山田さんに手紙を書いていただきました。*Mr. Yamada wrote the letter for me (**or** I had Mr. Yamada write the letter for me).*

[-te] itadak·u [*vb: aux, benefactive*] <*formal*> （〜て）頂く *have (something) done for (oneself)*

itá·i [*adj* ítaku nái; ítakatta] 痛い *painful; hurt* 🔸Áshi ga itái. 足が痛 い。*My leg hurts.*

itai 遺体 *corpse; dead body*

itamí 痛み *an ache; a pain* 🔸I ni sukóshi itamí ga áru. 胃に少し痛みが ある。*I have a slight pain in my stomach.*

itám·u [*vi* itamánai; itánda] 痛む *hurt; be painful; suffer pain* 🔸há ga itámu 歯が痛む *have a toothache* 🔸kokoró ga itámu 心が痛む *suffer in (one's) heart*

itárutokoro [ni] 至る所（に）*everywhere*

itás·u [*vt* itasánai; itáshita] 致す *do* <*formal*>: *(applying to actions by the first person)*

itazura 悪戯 *mischief; prank* 🔸itazura dénwa 悪戯電話 *obscene phone call* 🔸itazura-gaki 悪戯書き *scribbling; doodling* 🔸kodomo no itazura 子供の悪戯 *a child's prank*

itazura ni 徒に *in vain; without purpose*

itchi 一致 *coincidence; correspondence; agreement* ——**itchi-suru** [*vi*] 一致する *agree; be in accord* 🔸-to itchi-shite 〜と一致して *be in line with*

íto 糸 *thread*

íto 意図 *intention; aim; purpose*

itóguchi 糸口；緒 *opening; beginning; way to unravel / solve* 🔸Mondai káiketsu no itóguchi ga mitsukatta. 問題解決の糸口が見つかった。*A way to solve the problem has been found.*

itóko 従姉妹；従兄弟 *cousin*

itómaki 糸巻 *spool (of thread)*

itonám·u [*vt* itonamánai; itonánda] 営む *engage in; work at* 🔸seikatsu o itonámu 生活を営む *build a life* 🔸hōyō o itonámu 法要を営む *hold a Buddhist service (for the dead)*

itósugi 糸杉 *(Italian) cypress*

ítsu 何時；いつ *when?*

ítsu demo いつでも *anytime*

itsuka 五日 *the fifth (of the month); five days*

ítsuka 何時か；いつか *someday; sometime; once*

ítsu made mo いつまでも *forever*

ítsumo いつも *always*   8**ítsumo nara** いつもなら *the usual (pattern)*   8**ítsumo no yō ni** いつものように *as always*

itsu no ma ní ka 何時の間にか *in no time at all; not knowing when*

itsútsu 五つ *five (when counting things)*

ittai (~ darō) 一体（〜だろう）*What!; How in the world!*   8**Ano otó wa ittai nán darō!** あの音は一体何だろう。 *What in the world's that sound!*

íttai 一体 *one body;*   8**ittaika** 一体化 *unification; integration*   8**Fūfu wa ittai to náru.** 夫婦は一体となる。 *A married couple become as one.*

ittan 一旦 *once*

ittei no 一定の *fixed; regular*

Itte (i)rasshái. 行っていらっしゃい。 *Goodbye (to one expected to be back shortly)*

Itte mairimásu. 行って参ります。 *Goodbye (by one who expects to return shortly)*

ittō 一等 *first place; first class*

ittoki 一時 *a short time*

i·u [*vt* iwanai; itta] 言う *say*

iwá 岩 *large rock; boulder*

iwába 言わば *that is to say; (the) so-called*

iwai 祝い *celebration*   8**tanjō íwai** 誕生祝い ¯*birthday celebration*

iwashi 鰯 *sardine*

iwá·u [*vt* iwawánai; iwátta] 祝う *celebrate; congratulate*   8**kekkon o iwáu** 結婚を祝う *celebrate (one's) marriage*

iwayúru いわゆる *so-called; what is called*

iyá [na] 嫌（な）*obnoxious; offensive; disgusting; distasteful* ——**iyá ni** 嫌に *disgustingly; offensively*

iyagár·u [*vt* iyagaránai; iyagátta] 嫌がる *dislike; hate (verb used of others' dislikes)*   8**Kodomo wa chūsha o iyagáru.** 子供は注射を嫌がる。 *Children hate (taking) shots.*

iyaiya nágara 嫌々ながら *unwillingly; grudgingly*

íyaku 医薬 *remedy; medication*

iyarashí·i [*adj* iyaráshiku nái; iyaráshikatta] 嫌らしい *(be) unpleasant; indecent; dirty*

iyashí 癒し *healing*

iyás·u [*vt* iyasánai; iyáshita] 癒す *heal; cure*   8**kokóro o iyásu** 心を癒す *heal the heart*

iyō [na] 異様（な）*strange* ——**iyō ni** 異様に *strangely*

iyóiyo いよいよ *at last; finally; more and more*

íza to náttara いざとなったら *in an emergency; just in case*

ízen 以前 *before* ——**-izen** 〜以前 *earlier than*

izen to shite 依然として *as always*

izumi 泉 *spring (of water)*

izure いずれ *sometime soon; sooner or later* ——**izure ni shité mo** いずれにしても *in any case*

izure mo いずれも *all*

J

ja... じゃ〜 *Well then...*

Ja né! じゃね！ *See ya!*

jábujabu じゃぶじゃぶ *splashing; vigorous(-ly)* ❈sentakumono o jábujabu arau 洗濯物をじゃぶじゃぶ洗う *vigorously wash clothes* ——**jábujabu-suru** [vi] じゃぶじゃぶする *splash*

jagaimo じゃが芋；馬鈴薯 *potato*

jaguchi 蛇口 *faucet; tap*

jáken [na] 邪険（な）*cruel; hardhearted; cold* ❈jáken na táido 邪険な態度 *a cruel attitude*

jakkan [no] 若干 *small amount, some*

-jáku 〜弱 *a little less than* ❈sémmei-jáku no hito 千名弱の人 *a little less than a thousand people*

jakutén 弱点 *weakness; weak point*

jakyō 邪教 *heresy; heretical religion*

jama 邪魔 *disturbance; hindrance; a bother* ❈Jama ga háitta. 邪魔が入った。*I was interrupted.* ——**jama-suru** [vt] 邪魔する *disturb; hinder; bother* ❈O-jama-shimáshita. お邪魔しました。*I'm sorry for having disturbed you.*

ja nái じゃない [neg of **desu**]

jankén じゃんけん *paper-scissors-stone game* ❈jankén o suru じゃんけんをする *play janken*

jari 砂利 *gravel; pebble*

jashū 邪宗 *false religion; heretical sect*

jí 字 *letter; (written) character; writing* ❈jí o káku 字を書く *write*

ji 痔 *hemorrhoids; piles*

-ji 〜時 *o'clock* ❈Íma nánji desu ka? 今、何時ですか。*What time is it (now)?* Níji desu. 二時です。*It's two o'clock.*

jiai 慈愛 *love; compassion; benevolence*

jiban 地盤 *foundation; base*

jíbi inkōka 耳鼻咽喉科 *ear, nose and throat department; (Tech) otorhinolaryngology*

jibun 自分 *self; oneself* ❈jibun de 自分で *by oneself* ❈jibun-jíshin 自

分自身 *oneself* §jibun-kátte [na] 自分勝手（な）*selfish; egoistic*
§jibun-kátte ni 自分勝手に *of one's own accord; of one's own free will*

jíchi 自治 *self-governing; autonomy*

jichi dáijin 自治大臣 *home affairs minister*

jidai 時代 *the times; period; era; generation* §Meiji jídai 明治時代 *the Meiji Period (1868–1912)* §jidái-geki 時代劇 *a period film* §jidai ókure 時代遅れ *behind the times*

jiden 自伝 *autobiography*

jídō 児童 *children* §jidō búngaku 児童文学 *children's literature* §jidō fukushihō 児童福祉法 *child welfare law*

jidō- 自動～ *automatic* §jidō hambáiki 自動販売機 *coin machine; automatic vending machine* §jidō séigyo 自動制御 *automatic control* §jidō káki 自動火器 *automatic firearms*

jidósha 自動車 *automobile*

jidóshi 自動詞 *intransitive verb (Gram)*

jiei 自衛 *self-defense* §Jieitai 自衛隊 *the Self-Defense Forces (J)*

jigazō 自画像 *self-portrait*

jigen 次元 *dimension* §sanjígen no 三次元の *three dimensional*

[o-]jigi 辞儀 *bowing* ——**[o-]jigi-suru** [vi] （お）辞儀する *bow*

jigoe 地声 *(one's) natural voice*

jigokú 地獄 *hell*

jígyō 事業 *enterprise; business* §jigyōka 事業家 *an entrepreneur; an enterprising person* §jígyō o okósu 事業を興す *start a business*

jihaku 自白 *confession* ——**jihaku-suru** [vt] 自白する *confess*

jihatsuteki [na] 自発的（な）*spontaneous; voluntary*

jihi 自費 *(one's) own expense; personal expense* §jihi de 自費で *at one's own expense* §jihi shúppan 自費出版 *publishing at one's own expense*

jihi 慈悲 *mercy*

jihyō 辞表 *resignation* §jihyō o dásu 辞表を出す *submit (one's) resignation*

jíin 寺院 *temple (Budd)*

[o-]jíisan （お）祖父さん；（お）爺さん *grandfather; old man [term of affection]*

jíishiki 自意識 *self-consciousness*

jíji 時事 *current events* §jiji móndai 時事問題 *current affairs*

jíjitsu 事実 *fact; reality; actuality* §jijitsujō no jinshu sábetsu 事実上の人種差別 *de facto segregation* §Jíjitsu wa shōsetsu yóri kí nari. 事実は小説より奇なり。 *Fact is stranger than fiction.* <set phrase>

jijō 事情 *state of affairs; condition; circumstances; (the) situation; consideration(s)*

jijóden 自叙伝 *autobiography*

jíka 自家 *(one's) own home*

jikaku 自覚 *self-awareness; self-consciousness* ——**jikaku-suru** [*vt*] 自覚する *realize; be aware of; be conscious of* §sekinin o jikaku-suru 責任を自覚する *be aware of one's responsibility*

jikan 時間 *time* §jikan-hyō 時間表 *time schedule; timetable* §jikán-kyū 時間給 *hourly wage* §jikan ga tátsu 時間が経つ *time passes*

jíkan 次官 *vice-minister; undersecretary*

-jíkan ～時間 [*classifier for counting hours*] §Ichijíkan mátte kudasái. 一時間待って下さい。 *Please wait for one hour.*

jikasén-en 耳下腺炎 *mumps; (Tech) paratitis*

jíken 事件 *event; incident; case*

jíki 時期 *opportunity; time; season; juncture*

jíki 磁器 *porcelain; china*

jíki 磁気 *magnetism*

jiki [ni] 直（に） *soon; right away; at once*

jikka 実家 *home; one's parents' home*

jikkan 実感 *gut feeling; realization* ——**jikkan-suru** [*vt*] 実感する *realize; experience personally*

jikken 実験 *an experiment; a test* ——**jikken-suru** [*vt*] 実験する *experiment (on); test*

jikkō 実行 *execution; practice* ——**jikkō-suru** [*vt*] 実行する *execute; put into practice; carry out*

jikkyō hősō 実況放送 *on-the-scene broadcast*

jíko 自己 *self; ego* §jiko béngo 自己弁護 *self-vindication* §jíko chūshin 自己中心 *self-centeredness* §jiko hítei 自己否定 *self-denial* §jiko mánzoku 自己満足 *self-satisfaction* §jiko shőkai-suru 自己紹介する *introduce oneself* §jíko o hokóru 自己を誇る *boast; brag about oneself*

jíko 事故 *accident; incident* §jidōsha jíko 自動車事故 *car accident*

jikō 事項 *matter; subject* §kentō jíkō 検討事項 *a matter for study*

jíkoku 時刻 *the hour; a point in time* §Jíkoku wa tadáima kúji desu. 時刻はただいま九時です。 *The time is now 9:00 o'clock.*

jikú 軸 *axis; spindle; scroll*

jikyō 自供 *confession* ——**jikyō-suru** [*vt*] 自供する *confess*

jikyū jisoku 自給自足 *self-sufficiency* §jikyū jisoku kéizai 自給自足経済 *self-sufficient economy*

jiman 自慢 *boasting; pride* §okuni jíman お国自慢 *pride in the place one comes from* ——**jiman-suru** [*vt*] 自慢する *brag; boast* §Aitsu wa ítsumo jiman-bákari shite iru. あいつはいつも自慢ばかりしている。 *He's always bragging.* <masc>

jímbutsu 人物 *character (persona) in a play; person*

jímejime-suru [*vi*] じめじめする *(feel) damp; moist; humid; clammy* §jímejime-shita ténki じめじめした天気 *humid weather* §jímejime-shita seikaku じめじめした性格 *sentimental character*

jímen 地面 *surface; the ground*

jimí [na] 地味（な）*quiet; conservative; plain; simple; restrained* &jimí na iro 地味な色 *a quiet color* &jimí na seikaku 地味な性格 *a conservative nature* ——**jimí ni** 地味に *quietly; simply; conservatively*

jimmáshin 蕁麻疹 *nettle rash; hives*

jimméiroku 人名録 *directory (of names); Who's Who*

jimmín 人民 *the people; the public*

jimmon 尋問 *questioning; inquiry; interrogation; cross-examination* ——**jimmon-suru** [vt] 尋問する *interrogate; question; cross-examine*

jimoto [no] 地元（の）*local* &jimoto no méishi 地元の名士 *a local celebrity*

jímu 事務 *clerical office work; business* &jimúin 事務員 *office worker* &jimúsho 事務所 *office* &jimúkyoku 事務局 *executive office; secretariat*

jín 陣 *military formation; encampment*

-jín ～人 [suffix indicating nationality] &Nihon-jín 日本人 *a Japanese*

jinárashi 地均し *ground leveling; grading; groundbreaking* &jinarashiki 地均し機 *a grader; bulldozer* &Hanron ga dénai yō ni jinárashi o shite óita. 反論が出ないように地均しをしておいた。*I did some (preliminary) groundbreaking so that there would be no opposition.*

jindōteki [na] 人道的（な）*humane*

jinin 辞任 *resignation* ——**jinin-suru** [vt] 辞任する *resign* &Watashi wa torishimariyaku o jinin-shita. 私は取締役を辞任した。*I resigned (my position) as director.*

jínja 神社 *Shinto shrine*

jínji 人事 *personnel* &jinji kōsa 人事考査 *personnel examination* &jinji ídō 人事異動 *personnel changes*

jínjifusei [no] 人事不省（の）*unconscious; loss of consciousness* &jínjifusei ni ochiíru 人事不省に陥る *become unconscious; pass out*

jinkaku 人格 *character; personality* &jinkakúsha 人格者 *a person of character* &jinkaku o mitomeru 人格を認める *respect (or recognize) character*

jinken 人権 *human rights; civil rights* &Jinken Séngen 人権宣言 *the Declaration of the Rights of Man* &jinken shíngai 人権侵害 *civil (human) rights violation* &jinken yōgo dántai 人権擁護団体 *civil (human) rights advocacy group*

jinkén-hi 人件費 *personnel expense*

jinkō 人口 *population* &jinkō misshū chítai 人口密集地帯 *densely populated area*

jinkō 人工 *man-made; mechanical; artificial* &jinkō éisei 人工衛星 *satellite* &jinkō júsei 人工受精 *artificial insemination* &jinkō kammíryō 人工甘味料 *artificial sweetener* &jinkō kókyū 人工呼吸 *artificial respiration*

jínrui 人類 *the human race; people* §jinrúi-ai 人類愛 *love of humanity; philanthropy* §jínrui no éichi 人類の英知 *the wisdom of humankind*

jinryoku 尽力 *endeavor; effect; assistance* §no jinryoku de 〜の尽力で *through the good offices of* ——**jinryoku-suru** [vi] 尽力する *endeavor; strive; exert (oneself)* §chikara no kágiri jinryoku-suru 力の限り尽力する *expend every effort*

jinsai 人災 *(man-made) disaster*

jínsei 人生 *human life* §jínsei no owari 人生の終り *the end of one's life* §Jínsei wa yumé no gotoshi. 人生は夢の如し。 *Life is like a dream.* <set phrase>

jinshu 人種 *(human) race* §jinshu sábetsu 人種差別 *racial discrimination*

jíntai 人体 *the human body* §jintai káibō 人体解剖 *autopsy; dissection of a human body* §jintai mókei 人体模型 *a model of the human body*

jinteki shígen 人的資源 *human resources*

jintsū 陣痛 *labor pains*

jinushi 地主 *land owner; landlord*

jinzō 腎臓 *kidney (Anat)*

jinzō [no] 人造（の） *artificial; synthetic* §jinzóko 人造湖 *man-made lake*

jion 字音 *pronunciation of a letter (word / Chinese character)*

jippi 実費 *actual expense; price; cost*

jirei 辞令 *written appointment; commission* §jirei o dásu 辞令を出す *commission (someone)* §jirei o ukéru 辞令を受ける *receive an appointment (to a post)*

jirettá·i [adj jirettáku nái; jirettákatta] じれったい *(be) irritating; exasperating; frustrating* §Jibun no kimochi ga aité ni tsutawaranákute jirettái. 自分の気持ちが相手に伝わらなくてじれったい。 *I'm frustrated because I can't communicate my feelings to others.*

jiriki de 自力で *by (one's) own effort*

jiritsu 自立 *independence; self-reliance* ——**jiritsu-suru** [vi] 自立する *stand on one's own feet; become independent* §Musuko wa mō jiritsu-shite iru. 息子はもう自立している。 *My son's on his own now.*

jiritsu 自律 *autonomy; self-restraint; self-control*

jírojiro [to] じろじろ（と） *fixedly* §jírojiro míru じろじろ見る *gawk; stare*

jísa 時差 *time difference* §jisaboke-suru 時差ぼけする *suffer from time lag* §jisa shúkkin 時差出勤 *staggered work (or office) hours*

jisan-suru [vt] 持参する *take (or carry) with oneself; keep on (one's) person*

jisatsu 自殺 *suicide* §jisatsu mísui 自殺未遂 *attempted suicide* §shūdan jísatsu 集団自殺 *group suicide* ——**jisatsu-suru** [vi] 自殺

する *commit suicide*

jisei 自制 *self-control; self-denial; continence* §jiséishin ga áru 自制心がある *have self-control* ——**jisei-suru** [vi] 自制する *control oneself; constrain oneself; hold oneself back*

jíshaku 磁石 *magnet* §den-íshaku 電磁石 *electromagnet*

jishin 自信 *self-confidence; confidence* §jishin sōshitsu 自信喪失 *loss of self-confidence* §jishin ga áru 自信がある *have self-confidence* §jishin ga nái 自信がない *have no self-confidence* §jishin kájō no 自信過剰の *overconfident*

jishin 地震 *earthquake* §jishin kansokujo 地震観測所 *seismographic station* §Késa ni-ji hachi-fun ni Miyakéjima ni daijishin ga okorimáshita. 今朝二時八分に三宅島に大地震が起こりました。*A major earthquake occurred on Miyake Island at 2:08 this morning.*

-jíshin 〜自身 *oneself* §Sore wa kimi jíshin no mondai da. それは君自身の問題だ。*That is your own problem.* <masc>

jísho 辞書 *dictionary*

jishoku 辞職 *resignation (from a job; position)* §jishoku kánkoku 辞職勧告 *advice to resign* ——**jishoku-suru** [vi] 辞職する *resign (from a job or position)*

jíshu 自主 *independence; autonomy* §jishu gáikō 自主外交 *independent diplomacy* §jishu kísei 自主規制 *voluntary restraint* §jishusei 自主性 *autonomy; independence*——**jishuteki [na]** 自主的（な）*independent; autonomous* §jishuteki na hándan 自主的な判断 *independent judgment* ——**jishuteki ni** 自主的に *independently; voluntarily*

jísoku 時速 *speed; mph; kph* §jísoku gohyaku máiru 時速五百マイル *a speed of five hundred mph*

jisónshin 自尊心 *self-respect; pride* §jisónshin ga áru 自尊心がある *have self-respect* §jisónshin ga nái 自尊心がない *have no self-respect* §jisónshin ga tsuyói 自尊心が強い *have a lot of self-respect* §jisónshin o kizutsukéru 自尊心を傷つける *wound one's pride*

jissai 実際 *the truth; fact* ——**jissai no** 実際の *real; actual* ——**jissai ni** 実際に *really; practically; actually*

jisséikatsu 実生活 *real life; actual living*

jissen 実践 *practice* ——**jissen-suru** [vt] 実践する *practice; put into practice*

jisshi 実施 *enforcement; operation; execution; implementation* ——**jisshi-suru** [vt] 実施する *enforce; execute; implement*

jisshitsu 実質 *quality; substance; essence* ——**jisshitsuteki [na]** 実質的（な）*substantial; material* §jisshitsu kéizai seichóritsu 実質経済成長率 *real economic growth rate*

jisshō 実証 *(actual) proof; evidence* ——**jisshōteki [na]** 実証的（な）*positive* ——**jisshōteki ni** 実証的に *positively* ——**jisshō-suru** [vt]

実証する *prove; demonstrate*

jisúberi 地滑り *landslide*

jítai 事態 *situation; state of affairs*

-jítai 〜自体 *itself*

jítai 辞退 *refusal; waiver* ——**jítai-suru** [*vt*] 辞退する *decline; refuse to accept* 🔊Káre wa bunka kúnshō no jushō o jítai-shita. 彼は文化勲章の受賞を辞退した。 *He declined the award of the Order of Cultural Merit.*

jitaku 自宅 *(one's own) home* 🔊jitaku no denwa-bángō 自宅の電話番号 *home telephone number*

jitchi 実地 *practice; actuality* 🔊jitchi no keiken 実地の経験 *practical experience*

jiten 辞典；事典 *dictionary* 🔊kokugo jíten 国語辞典 *a Japanese-Japanese dictionary* 🔊hyakka jíten 百科事典 *encyclopedia*

jiténsha 自転車 *bicycle*

jitsú wa 実は *actually; in fact; the truth is...*

jitsubutsu 実物 *the real thing (object); the genuine article*

jitsugen 実現 *realization; actualization* ——**jitsugen-suru** [*vi*] 実現する *be realized; come true; actualize*

jitsugyō 実業 *business; enterprise; industry* 🔊jitsugyō-ka 実業家 *business person; industrialist* 🔊jitsugyṓ-kai 実業界 *business circles*

jitsuin 実印 *(one's) registered (legal) seal (or chop)*

jitsujō 実情 *actual circumstances; actual state of affairs*

jitsuryoku 実力 *capability; competence* 🔊jitsuryoku kṓshi 実力行使 *display of force* 🔊jitsuryoku de shusse-suru 実力で出世する *rise by one's own ability*

jitsuyō 実用 *utility; practical use* ——**jitsuyṓteki [na]** 実用的（な） *practical; useful*

jitsuwa 実話 *true story; an authentic account*

jitto じっと *quietly; still; firmly; patiently* 🔊jitto gáman-suru じっと我慢する *endure patiently*

jíwajiwa [to] じわじわ（と） *slowly but steadily* 🔊Gán ga jíwajiwa to shinkō-shite iru. 癌がじわじわと進行している。 *The cancer is advancing steadily.*

jiyū 自由 *freedom; liberty* 🔊jiyū́sa 自由さ *freedom* ——**jiyū [na]** 自由（な）*free; liberal; unrestricted* 🔊jiyū kṓdō 自由行動 *free (independent) action* ——**jiyū́ ni** 自由に *freely; liberally; unrestrictedly*

jizen 慈善 *charity; benevolence* 🔊jizen dántai 慈善団体 *charity institution*

jizen 事前 *before the fact; prior* 🔊jizen shṓnin 事前承認 *prior approval*

jō 条 *article; clause; provision* 🔊daisánjō 第三条 *Article Three*

-jō 〜城 *castle* 🔊Matsumotójō 松本城 *Matsumoto Castle*

jō; jōmae 錠；錠前 *a lock; padlock*

jōba 乗馬 *horseback riding*

jōbu [na] 丈夫（な）*strong; durable; strong and healthy* §jōbu na kíji 丈夫な生地 *strong cloth (material)* §Otto wa karada ga jōbu désu. 夫は体が丈夫です。*My husband is strong and healthy.*

jōbutsu-suru [vi] 成仏する *enter nirvana; become Buddha*

jochō 助長 *encouragement; promotion* ——**jochō-suru** [vt] 助長する *foster; encourage*

jōcho; jōsho 情緒 *emotion; feeling* §jōcho fuántei 情緒不安定 *unstable emotions* §jōcho o arawásu 情緒を表わす *express (one's) feelings* ——**jōchoteki [na]** 情緒的（な）*emotional*

jōdai 上代 *ancient period; ancient times*

jōdán 冗談 *a joke; a jest*

jodōshi 助動詞 *verbal auxiliary (Gram)*

jōei-suru [vt] 上映する *show; put on the screen; screen; play*

joen 助演 *supporting performance* §joénsha 助演者 *supporting actor*

jōen 上演 *dramatic performance (or presentation)* ——**jōen-suru** [vt] 上演する *stage a performance; perform*

jogai 除外 *exception* ——**jogai-suru** [vt] 除外する *except; make an exception (of)*

jōge 上下 *top and bottom* ——**jōge-suru** [vi] 上下する *go up and down; rise and fall*

jogen 助言 *advice; counsel* ——**jōgen-suru** [vi] 助言する *advise; counsel*

jōgi 定規 *ruler* §T-jógi T 定規 *T square* §sankaku jōgi 三角定規 *triangle ruler*

jōgo 漏斗 *funnel*

jōhatsu 蒸発 *evaporation* ——**jōhatsu-suru** [vi] 蒸発する *evaporate*

jōhin [na] 上品（な）*refined; elegant*

jōhō 情報 *information; a report* §jōhōmō 情報網 *information network* §jōhō sángyō 情報産業 *information industry*

jōin 上院 *Upper House; Senate (US); House of Lords (Br)*

jōji 情事 *(love) affair*

jojíshi 叙事詩 *epic (poem)*

jójo ni 徐々に *gradually; slowly*

jōju 成就 *fulfillment; accomplishment* ——**jōju-suru** [vt] 成就する *complete; fulfill; accomplish*

jōjun 上旬 *the first ten days of a month; the early part of a month*

jojutsu 叙述 *narration; description* ——**jojutsu-suru** [vt] 叙述する *narrate; describe; depict*

jōkámachi 城下町 *castle town*

jōkei 情景 *scene; sight*

jōkén 条件 *condition; terms; requirements; stipulation*

jóki 蒸気 *steam; vapor*

jōkin 常勤 *full-time employment* ——**jōkin-suru** [*vi*] 常勤する *hold a full-time position*

jókki ジョッキ *mug; stein; tankard*

jokō 徐行 *going slow(ly)* ——**jokō-suru** [*vi*] 徐行する *go slow (ly)*

jōkoku 上告 *an appeal; final appeal* ——**jōkoku-suru** [*vt*] 上告する *appeal; make a (final) appeal*

jōkyaku 乗客 *passenger*

jōkyō 状況 *circumstances; situation; state of things*

jokyójju 助教授 *assistant professor*

jókyoku 序曲 *prelude; overture*

jōkyū 上級 *advanced level; advanced course (of study)* ❽**jōkyúsei** 上級生 *upper-class student* ❽jōkyū shōkō 上級将校 *ranking officer*

jomakúshiki 除幕式 *unveiling ceremony*

jōmu 常務 *regular business; daily routine* ❽jōmu torishimariyaku 常務取締役 *executive; managing director*

jōmúin 乗務員 *crewman; crew member*

jōmyaku 静脈 *vein (Anat)*

jōnetsu 情熱 *passion; enthusiasm*

jōnin iínkai 常任委員会 *standing committee*

joó 女王 *queen*

jōriku-suru 上陸する [*vi*] *go ashore; land*

jóro 如雨露 *watering can*

joron 序論 *introduction*

jōruri 浄瑠璃 *joruri; ballad drama (recitation for bunraku puppet plays)*

jōyokúju 常緑樹 *evergreen tree*

jōryū 上流 *upstream* ❽jōryū káikyū 上流階級 *upper class*

jōryū 蒸留 *distillation* ——**jōryū-suru** [*vt*] 蒸留する *distill*

josainá·i [*adj* josaináku nái; josainákatta] 如才ない *(be) tactful*

josainása 如才なさ *shrewdness; sharpness; tactfulness*

josámpu 助産婦 *midwife*

josei 女性 *woman; female*

josei 助成 *assistance; aid* ❽joseikin 助成金 *financial assistance; subsidy* ——**josei-suru** [*vt*] 助成する *foster; promote; assist; aid*

jōsen-suru [*vi*] 乗船する *get on a ship; board a ship*

josetsu 序説 *introduction*

josetsu 除雪 *snow removal* ❽josetsúsha 除雪車 *snowplow (train)*

jōsha 乗車 *boarding a vehicle* ——**jōsha-suru** [*vi*] 乗車する *board a vehicle*

joshi 助詞 *grammatical particle (J); e.g.,* **wa, ga, o, ni,** *etc.*

jóshi 女子 *girl; woman*

jóshi 上司 *(one's) superior(s); superior officer*

jōshiki 常識 *common knowledge*

joshu 助手 *assistant*

josō 女装 *woman's disguise* ——**josō-suru** [*vi*] 女装する *disguise (oneself) as a woman*

josōzai 除草剤 *weed killer; herbicide*

jōsui 上水 *waterworks; water supply*

jōtai 状態 *a state; condition*

jōtatsu 上達 *advancement; progress* ——**jōtatsu-suru** [*vi*] 上達する *advance; progress* ⊗Anáta no Nihongo wa jōtatsu-shite iru. あなたの日本語は上達している。 *You are making progress in Japanese.*

jōtō [no] 上等（の）*superior; first-rate; excellent*

jōto-suru [*vt*] 譲渡する *transfer (property); hand over*

jōyaku 条約 *treaty; pact; agreement* ⊗nikokukan jōyaku 二国間条約 *bilateral treaty* ⊗jōyaku o mamóru 条約を守る *abide by a treaty (agreement)*

jōyoku 情欲 *lust; sexual desire; passion*

joyū 女優 *actress*

jōzai 錠剤 *pill; tablet*

jōzú [na] 上手（な）*skillful; good at* ⊗Anáta wa ténisu ga jōzú da sō desu. あなたはテニスが上手だそうです。 *I hear you're good at tennis.* ——**jōzú ni** 上手に *skillfully*

jú 十 *ten (the numeral)*

jú 銃 *gun; rifle*

-jū ～中 *throughout* ⊗ichinichi-jū 一日中 *throughout one day; all day long*

jūbako 重箱 *set of square, stacking (lunch) boxes*

juban 襦袢 *under-kimono*

jūbún [na] 十(充)分（な）*enough; sufficient* ——**jūbún ni** 十分に *sufficiently* ⊗jūbún kóryo-suru 十分考慮する *take into full consideration* ⊗jūbún ni kentō-suru 十分に検討する *study thoroughly*

jūbyō 重病 *serious illness*

jūdai [no] 十代（の）*teenager*

jūdai [na] 重大（な）*important; serious*

jūdáisa 重大さ *importance*

judaku 受諾 *acceptance* ——**judaku-suru** [*vt*] 受諾する *accept; agree to* ⊗shímei o judaku-suru 使命を受諾する *accept a commission*

jūden 充電 *(battery) charge* ——**jūden-suru** [*vt*] 充電する *charge (a battery)*

judō 受動 *passiveness* ⊗judōtai 受動態 *passive (Gram)* ——**judōteki [na]** 受動的（な）*passive* ——**judōteki ni** 受動的に *passively*

júdō 柔道 *judo (Japanese martial art)*

jufun 受粉 *pollination* ——**jufun-suru** [*vt*] 受粉する *pollinate*

Jūgatsú 十月 *October*

jūgoya 十五夜 *full-moon night*

júgyō 授業 *class; lesson; lecture* ❈jugyṓryō 授業料 *tuition* ——**júgyō-suru** [*vi*] 授業する *teach; lecture*

jūgyṓin 従業員 *employee*

júi 獣医 *veterinarian*

Jūichigatsú 十一月 *November*

jūjika 十字架 *a cross*

jūjíro 十字路 *crossroad*

júji-suru [*vi*] 従事する *be engaged in; be occupied with*

jūjitsu 充実 *perfection; completeness* ——**jūjitsu-suru** [*vi*] 充実する *be perfect; fill up; be complete* ❈Watashi no seikatsu wa jūjitsu-shite iru. 私の生活は充実している。*My life is complete.*

jūjun [na] 従順（な）*meek; obedient*

jikasén-en 耳下腺炎 *mumps; (tech) parotitis*

jukéisha 受刑者 *a convict; inmate*

juken-suru [*vt*] 受験する *take an examination*

jūketsu 充血 *congestion (with blood)* ——**jūketsu-suru** [*vi*] 充血する *be bloodshot; be congested* ❈Mé ga jūketsu-shite iru yo! 目が充血しているよ！ *Your eyes are bloodshot!*

Jukkai 十戒 *the Ten Commandments*

jūkṓgyō 重工業 *heavy industry*

jūkon 重婚 *bigamy* ——**jūkon-suru** [*vi*] 重婚する *commit bigamy*

júku 塾 *private (cram) school*

jukugo 熟語 *phrase; idiom; kanji combination*

jukuren-suru [*vi*] 熟練する *become skilled; master*

júkushi-suru [*vt*] 熟視する *gaze at; look hard at*

jukús·u [*vi* jukusánai; jukúshita] 熟す *ripen* ❈Kono kudámono wa jukúshite iru. この果物は熟している。*This fruit is ripe.*

jukusui 熟睡 *sound sleep; deep sleep*

jukutatsu 熟達 *proficiency; mastery* ——**jukutatsu-suru** [*vi*] 熟達する *become proficient*

Júkyō 儒教 *Confucianism*

júkyo 住居 *housing* ❈jūkyó-hi 住居費 *housing expense*

jumban ni 順番に *in order; by turns; in rotation*

júmbi 準備 *preparation; provision* ❈jumbi iínkai 準備委員会 *preparatory committee* ——**júmbi-suru** [*vt*] 準備する *prepare; provide for*

jūmin 住民 *inhabitants; residents* ❈jūmin tṓroku 住民登録 *residential registration* ❈jūmín-zei 住民税 *resident tax*

jumyō 寿命 *life span*

jun 順 *order (of occurrence); turn* ❈jun ni 順に *in order; by turns*

jún [na] 純（な）*pure; innocent* ❈jun'eki 純益 *net profit* ❈junkin 純金 *pure gold* ❈jummen 純綿 *all cotton* ❈jummō 純毛 *all wool*

junan 受難 *suffering; ordeal*
jūnan [na] 柔軟（な）*supple; flexible*
junchō [na] 順調（な）*favorable; satisfactory* ——**junchō ni** 順調に *satisfactorily; smoothly; without a hitch*
jún'i 順位 *grade; order; ranking*
jūnibun [ni] 十二分（に）*more than enough*
Jūnigatsú 十二月 *December*
jūnin 住人 *inhabitant; resident*
jūníshi 十二支 *twelve signs of the Chinese zodiac*
jūnishí-chō 十二指腸 *(Tech) duodenum*
junji·ru [*vi* junjinai; junjita] 準じる *correspond to; be proportionate to*
junji·ru [*vi* junjinai; junjita] 殉じる *follow; sacrifice (for)* ₰kuni ni junjiru 国に殉じる *sacrifice (oneself) for (one's) country*
júnjo 順序 *order; sequence*
junjún ni 順々に *in order; in turn; one after another*
junkai-suru [*vt*] 巡回する *go round; make the rounds; tour* ₰junkai toshókan 巡回図書館 *library on wheels; circuit library*
junkan 循環 *circulation* ₰junkánki 循環器 *a circulatory organ (anat)* ₰ketsúeki no junkan 血液の循環 *blood circulation* ——**junkan-suru** [*vi*] 循環する *circulate*
junketsu 純潔 *purity; integrity* ₰junketsu shúgi 純潔主義 *chastity* ₰junketsu kyōiku 純潔教育 *education on sexual morality* ——**junketsu na** 純潔な *pure; clean; unspotted*
junkyṓsha 殉教者 *martyr*
junkyū 準急 *semi-express (train)*
junrei 巡礼 *pilgrimage* ₰junréisha 巡礼者 *pilgrim*
junsui [no] 純粋（の）*pure; genuine*
jū́rai no 従来の *up to the present time; formerly; hitherto*
jūrṓdō 重労働 *hard labor*
jūryṓ 重量 *weight*
jū́ryoku 重力 *gravity*
jūsatsu 銃殺 *execution by firing squad* ——**jūsatsu-suru** [*vt*] 銃殺する *execute (by shooting)*
jusei 受精 *fertilization*
júshi 樹脂 *resin*
jūshin 重心 *the center of gravity*
jū́sho 住所 *an (**or** one's) address*
jūshō 重傷 *serious injury* ₰jūshō o oú 重傷を負う *be seriously wounded*
jushō 受賞 *awarding a prize; recognition* ——**jushō-suru** [*vt*] 受賞する *win (a prize)*
jūsō 重曹 *bicarbonate of soda; baking soda*
jusshín-hō 十進法 *the decimal system*

jutai 受胎 *conception; pregnancy*

jūtai 重体；重態 *serious condition* ❂Sono kanja wa jūtai désu. その患者は重体です。 *The patient's condition is serious.*

jūtai 渋滞 *traffic jam* ——**jūtai-suru** [*vi*] 渋滞する *be delayed; be stalled* ❂Kōtsū ga jūtai-shite iru. 交通が渋滞している。 *The traffic is stalled.*

jūtaku 住宅 *residence; dwelling; house* ❂jūtakú-chi 住宅地 *residential area*

jútan 絨毯 *carpet*

jūten 重点 *important point* ❂jūtén o oku 重点を置く *place emphasis on; give importance to*

jūten 充填 *(tooth) filling; replenishment*

jutsugo 述語 *the predicate (Gram)*

juwáki 受話器 *telephone receiver*

jūyaku 重役 *director (of a company)* ❂jūyakú-kai 重役会 *board of directors*

juyō 需要 *demand (vs. supply)*

jūyō [na] 重要 （な） *important; principal*

jūyóshi-suru [*vt*] 重要視する *attach great importance to*

jūyu 重油 *heavy oil; crude petroleum*

jūzoku 従属 *subordination* ❂jūzoku kánkei 従属関係 *subordinate relation* ——**jūzoku-suru** [*vi*] 従属する *be subordinate to*

juzú 数珠 *prayer beads*

K

ka 蚊 *mosquito*

ka か [*sentence final particle: interrogative*] ❂Éki wa dóko desu ka? 駅はどこですか？ *Where is the station?* ❂Tsukaremáshita ka? 疲れましたか？ *Are you tired?*

ka か *or* ❂Sukéjūru wa kin'yóbi no gógo ka doyóbi no ása ga aite iru. スケジュールは金曜日の午後か土曜日の朝が空いている。 *My schedule's open on Friday afternoon or Saturday morning.* ❂Kōhí ka náni ka nomitái na. コーヒーか何か飲みたいな。 *I'd like (to drink) some coffee or something.* <*masc*>

-ká 〜課 *Lesson -; section; department* ❂dái-ĺkka 第一課 *Lesson One* ❂jinji-ka 人事課 *personnel section*

-ká 〜科 *section; department* ❂kaikeiká 会計科 *finance section* ❂gogakká 語学科 *language department*

kába 河馬 *hippopotamus*

kaban 鞄 *bag; handbag; briefcase*

kabá·u [*vt* kabawánai; kabátta] 庇う *protect; defend* ❂kodomo o kabáu

子供を庇う *protect a child*

kabayaki 蒲焼 *barbecued eel*

kabe 壁 *wall* ⑧kabe o nuru 壁を塗る *paint a wall* ⑧kabe ni tsukiatáru 壁につきあたる *come up against a wall.*

kabi 黴 *mold; mildew* ⑧kabi kusái かび臭い *moldy; smelling of mildew* ⑧Tsuyu no aida, kutsú ni kabi ga háete shimatta. 梅雨の間、靴にかびが生えてしまった。*During the rainy season the shoes mildewed.*

kabin 花瓶 *vase*

kabocha カボチャ; 南瓜 *pumpkin; squash*

kābónshi カーボン紙 *carbon paper*

kabu 株 *stump; root; stocks* ⑧kiríkabu 切り株 *a stump* ⑧kabu-ken 株券 *stock certificate* ⑧kabu-nushi 株主 *stockholder* ⑧kabushiki 株式 *shares* ⑧kabushiki-gáisha 株式会社 *(joint-stock) corporation*

kabu 蕪 *turnip*

kábu カーブ *a curve; a bend (in the road)*

kabuki 歌舞伎 *classical Japanese theater form*

kabúr·u [*vt* kaburánai; kabútta] 被る *wear; put on (the head)* ⑧bōshi o kabúru 帽子を被る *put on (or wear) a hat* ⑧hokori o kabúru 埃を被る *be covered with dust* ⑧sekinin o kabúru 責任を被る *accept responsibility*

kabusé·ru [*vt* kabusénai; kabúseta] 被せる *put on (the head); cover*

kábuto 兜 *helmet* ⑧kábuto o núgu 兜を脱ぐ *take off (one's) helmet; admit defeat*

kabutómushi 甲虫 *beetle*

káchi 価値 *value; worth* ⑧kachíkan 価値観 *sense of values* ⑧kachi hándan 価値判断 *value judgment* ⑧káchi ga áru 価値がある *have value*

kachí 勝ち *victory; a win*

kachiku 家畜 *domesticated animal; cattle*

kachínto かちんと *clinking [mimetic for the sound of bottles clinking against each other]*

kachō 課長 *section chief*

kadai 課題 *subject; topic; matter; problem* ⑧tōmen no kadai 当面の課題 *the matter at hand*

kádan 花壇 *flower bed*

kádo 角 *(outside) corner* ⑧Ano kádo o migi ni magatte kudasái. あの角を右に曲がってください。*Turn right at that corner, please.*

kádo no 過度の *excess; excessive* ⑧kádo no rōdō 過度の労働 *overwork*

kaede 楓 *maple (tree)*

kaekko-suru [*vi*] 変えっこする；替えっこする *exchange; take turns*

kaerí 帰り *return; returning home* ⑧Go-shújin no o-kaeri wa nánji desu ka? 御主人のお帰りは何時ですか？ *What time does your husband get home?* ——**kaerí ni** 帰りに *on (one's) way home* ❧Kaisha no kaerí ni sū́pā e yotte kurenai? 会社の帰りにスーパーへ寄ってくれない？ *Would you stop by the supermarket on your way home from the office?* *<fem>*

kaerimí·ru [*vt* kaerimínai; kaerimíta] 顧みる *look back on; take into consideration; turn around and look at*

kaeru 蛙 *frog*

kae·ru [*vt* kaenai; kaeta] 変える；替える *change; alter* ❧Káigi no nittei o kaeru kotó ga dekimásu ka? 会議の日程を変えることが出来ますか。 *Can we alter the schedule of the meeting?*

káer·u [*vi* kaeránai; kaetta] 帰る *return (home); leave (for home)* ❧Náni ni kaerimásu ka? 何時に帰りますか。 *What time are you coming home?*

káer·u [*vi* kaeránai; kaetta] 返る *return* ❧kodomo ni káeru 子供に返る *return to childish behavior (or act like a child)*

-kae·ru 〜換える *revise; change* ❧norikaeru 乗り換える *transfer; change (trains / buses)* ❧kakikaeru 書き換える *rewrite; revise*

káes·u [*vt* kaesánai; káeshita] 返す *return (something)* ❧Hón o toshókan ni káeshita no? 本を図書館に返したの？ *Did you return the book to the library?* *<fem>*

káette 却って *on the contrary; actually* ❧Asu wa káette tsugó ga íi. 明日は却って都合がいい。 *Actually tomorrow's more convenient .*

kafun 花粉 *pollen*

kagai 課外 *extracurricular*

kagáisha 加害者 *assailant; inflicter of harm*

kágaku 科学 *science* ❧shizen kágaku 自然科学 *natural science*

kágaku 化学 *chemistry* ❧kagaku híryō 化学肥料 *chemical fertilizer* ❧kagaku ryóhō 化学療法 *chemotherapy*

kagamí 鏡 *mirror*

kagam·u [*vi* kagamanai; kaganda] 屈む *crouch; stoop*

kagayakashí·i [*adj* kagayakáshiku nái; kagayakáshikatta] 輝かしい *(be) bright; brilliant*

kagayák·u [*vi* kagayakánai; kagayáita] 輝く *shine; glitter; sparkle; brighten* ❧Sóra ni hoshi ga kazoekirénai hodo kagayáite ita. 空に星が数え切れないほど輝いていた。 *Countless stars were shining in the sky.*

káge 影 *shadow; a trace* ❧káge o otósu 影を落とす *cast a shadow* ❧kagebóshi 影法師 *one's shadow* ❧Yōgísha no káge mo miénakatta. 容疑者の影も見えなかった。 *No trace of the suspect could be found.*

káge 陰 *shade; the area out of sight behind (something); behind a person's back*

kageki [na] 過激（な）*extreme; radical* ❧kageki-ha gurū́pu 過激派グル

ープ *extremist group* §kageki na shisō 過激な思想 *radical ideas*

-kágetsu 〜か月 [*classifier for counting months*] §ikkágetsu 一か月 *one month* §Áto sankágetsu de watashi wa jūnen Nihón ni imásu. 後三か月で私は十年日本にいます。*In three more months I will have been in Japan ten years.*

kagí 鍵 *key; lock* §dóa ni kagí o kakéru ドアに鍵をかける *lock the door*

kágiri 限り *a limit* §miwatasu kágiri. 見渡す限り *as far as the eye can see*

[ni] kagítte に限って *limited to; that particular* §Raishū ni kagítte hon'yaku no kúrasu o kyūkō ni shimásu. 来週に限って翻訳のクラスを休講にします。*I'm cancelling the translation class (just) next week.*

kago 籠 *basket; (bird) cage*

kágu 家具 *furniture*

kag·u [*vt* kaganai; kaida] 嗅ぐ *smell (something); sniff* §niói o kagu 匂いを嗅ぐ *smell an odor*

káhei 貨幣 *coin; currency*

kái 貝 *shellfish* §kaigára 貝殻 *seashell*

kái 会 *meeting; organization* §kaijō 会場 *meeting place; hall* §kaihi 会費 *membership dues* §kaiin 会員 *member of an organization* §Sono kái ni shusseki-suru tsumori désu ka? その会に出席するつもりですか？ *Do you intend to attend the meeting?*

-kái 〜階 [*classifier for floors or stories of a building*] §Nikai o o-negai shimásu. 二階をお願いします。*Second floor, please. (to an elevator operator)*

-kai 〜回 [*classifier for number of times*] §Sono éiga o sankai míta. その映画を三回見た。*I saw that movie three times.*

kaibatsu 海抜 *(elevation) above sea level* § kaibatsu sanzén métoru 海抜3,000m. *3,000 meters above sea level*

kaibō 解剖 *dissection; autopsy; (human) anatomy* §kaibōgaku 解剖学 *(study of) anatomy* ——**kaibō-suru** [*vt*] 解剖する *dissect* §shitai o kaibō-suru 死体を解剖する *dissect a corpse*

kaibutsu 怪物 *monster*

kaichō 会長 *chairperson; chair; president (of a company)*

kaichūdéntō 懐中電灯 *flashlight*

kaidan 会談 *talks; interview* §shunō káidan 首脳会談 *summit talks*——**kaidan-suru** [*vi*] 会談する *confer (with)*

kaidan 階段 *stair; stairway* §hijō káidan 非常階段 *fire escape (stairs)*

kaifuku 回復 *recovery*——**kaifuku-suru** [*vi*] *recover; improve* §kenkō ga kaifuku-suru 健康が回復する *recover one's health (or get well)*

káiga 絵画 *picture; painting*

káigai 海外 *overseas; foreign* §kaigai ryókō 海外旅行 *foreign travel* §kaigai shíjō 海外市場 *overseas market*

kaigan 海岸 *coast; seashore; waterfront*

káigi 会議 *conference; meeting*

káigun 海軍 *navy; naval forces* 　❊kaigun táishō 海軍大将 *admiral*

kaihatsu 開発 *development* 　❊kaihatsu tojókoku 開発途上国 *developing country*

kaihō 解放 *freedom; liberation*――**kaihōteki na** 解放的な *open; open-hearted; frank*――**káihō-suru** [vt] 解放する *release; set free* 　❊Seifúgun wa gérira kara hitójichi o kaihō-shita. 政府軍はゲリラから人質を解放した。 *The government forces freed the hostages from the guerrillas.*

kaihō-suru [vt] 開放する *open; leave open* 　❊Kaihō genkin! 開放厳禁。 *Keep closed!* ippan ni kaihō-suru 一般に開放する *open to the public.*

kaiin 会員 *member (of an association or club)*

kaijō 会場 *meeting place*

kaijū 怪獣 *monster*

kaikaku 改革 *reform; reformation* 　❊seiji káikaku 政治改革 *political reform* ――**kaikaku-suru** [vt] 改革する *reform; improve*

kaikan 会館 *(concert / convention) hall*

kaikan 快感 *pleasant sensation*

kaikatsu na 快活な *cheerful; merry; happy* 　❊kaikatsu na seikaku 快活な性格 *a cheerful disposition*

kaikei 会計 *accounts; finances* 　❊kaikei kánsa 会計監査 *an audit* 　❊kaikéishi 会計士 *accountant* 　❊kaikei néndo 会計年度 *fiscal year*

kaiketsu 解決 *solution; resolution; settlement* 　❊mondai káiketsu 問題解決 *solution of a problem*――**kaiketsu-suru** [vt] *solve; resolve; settle* 　❊Bōeki masatsu móndai wa emman ni kaiketsu-shita. 貿易摩擦問題は円満に解決した。 *The trade-friction problem has been settled amicably.*

kaikisen 回帰線 *tropic* 　❊Kita Kaikisen 北回帰線 *the Tropic of Cancer* 　❊Minami Kaikisen 南回帰線 *the Tropic of Capricorn*

káiko 蚕 *silkworm*

kaikyō 海峡 *strait; channel*

Káikyō 回教 *Islam*

kaikyū 階級 *rank; class* 　❊kaikyū séido 階級制度 *the class system* 　❊chishiki káikyū 知識階級 *intellectuals; the intelligentsia*

kaimen 海面 *surface of the ocean*

kaimono 買い物 *shopping* 　❊Kyó wa depáto de kaimono ga áru. 今日はデパートで買い物がある。 *Today I have some shopping to do at the department store.*

káin 下院 *Lower House; House of Representatives (J,US); House of Commons (Br)*

kairaku 快楽 *pleasure; enjoyment* 　❊kairaku shúgi 快楽主義

epicureanism; hedonism

káiri 海里 *nautical mile*

káiro 回路 *(electrical) circuit*

kairyō 改良 *improvement* ❸kairyō o kuwáeru 改良をくわえる *improve on (something); make improvements* ——**kairyō-suru** [vt] 改良する *improve*

kairyū 海流 *ocean current*

kaisai-suru [vt] 開催する *hold (an event)* ❸Tsugí no Orimpíkku wa dóko de kaisai-saremásu ka? 次のオリンピックはどこで開催されますか。 *Where will the next Olympic games be held?*

kaisan 解散 *dissolution; breakup* ——**kaisan-suru** [vt] 解散する *dismiss; break up; dissolve* ❸Náikaku wa gíkai o kaisan-shita. 内閣は議会を解散した。 *The Cabinet dissolved the Diet.*

kaisámbutsu 海産物 *marine products* ❸Kómbu wa Nihón no ómo na kaisámbutsu no hitótsu desu. 昆布は日本の主な海産物の一つです。 *Kombu (a kind of seaweed) is one of Japan's principal marine products.*

kaisatsúguchi 改札口 *(RR) ticket wicket*

kaisei 改正 *revision; amendment* ——**kaisei-suru** [vt] 改正する *revise; amend; improve*

kaisetsu 解説 *explanation; commentary* ❸kaisetsúsha 解説者 *commentator* ——**kaisetsu-suru** [vt] 解説する *explain*

kaisha 会社 *company; firm*

káishaku 解釈 *interpretation* ——**káishaku-suru** [vt] *interpret*

kaishi 開始 *beginning; start* ——**kaishi-suru** [vi] 開始する *begin; start*

kaisō 回想 *recollection* ❸kaisóroku 回想録 *reminiscences; memoirs* ——**kaisō-suru** 回想する *recollect; reflect on* ❸kodomo jídai o kaisō-suru 子供時代を回想する *recall one's childhood*

kaisoku 快速 *high speed* ❸kaisoku dénsha 快速電車 *rapid train*

kaisū 回数 *frequency; number of times*

kaisui 海水 *sea water* ❸kaisúiyoku 海水浴 *seabathing; swimming in the sea*

kaitaku 開拓 *development* ❸kaitákusha 開拓者 *a pioneer* ——**kaitaku-suru** [vt] 開拓する *develop; open up* ❸Nihón wa Tōnan Ájia ni atarashíi shijō o kaitaku-shite iru. 日本は東南アジアに新しい市場を開拓している。 *Japan is opening up new markets in Southeast Asia.*

kaitei 改訂 *revision* ——**kaitei-suru** [vt] 改訂する *revise*

kaiteki [na] 快適な *agreeable; pleasant; comfortable* ❸kaiteki na óndo 快適な温度 *a pleasant temperature* ——**kaiteki ni** 快適に *comfortably* ❸Chichi wa rōnen o kaiteki ni kurashíte iru. 父は老年を快適に暮らしている。 *Dad is living comfortably in his old age.*

kaiten 回転 *revolution; rotation* ❸kaiten dóa 回転ドア *revolving door* ——**kaiten-suru** [vi] 回転する *revolve; rotate; turn* ❸Kono énjin wa ippúnkan ni samman-káiten-suru. このエンジンは一分間に三万回転する。 *This engine runs at thirty thousand rpm.*

kaiten mókuba 回転木馬 *merry-go-round; carousel*

kaitō 解答 *solution; correct answer*

kaitō 回答 *a reply; an answer* ——**kaitō-suru** 回答する *reply; answer* ◊Sono ánkēto ni nanajuppāsénto no hitó ga kaitō-shita. そのアンケートに70％の人が回答した。 *Seventy percent (of the people) responded to the questionnaire.*

kaiwa 会話 *conversation* ◊Eikáiwa 英会話 *English conversation*

kaiyō 潰瘍 *ulcer*

kaiyō 海洋 *ocean* ◊kaiyōgaku 海洋学 *oceanography* ◊kaiyō seibutsúgaku 海洋生物学 *marine biology*

kaizen 改善 *improvement* ——**kaizen-suru** [vt] 改善する *improve* ◊Shigoto no taigū wa kaizen-sareta. 仕事の待遇は改善された。 *The terms of employment were improved.*

kaizō 改造 *reconstruction; reorganization* ——**kaizō-suru** [vt] 改造する *remodel; reconstruct* ◊shosai o kodomobeya ni kaizō-suru 書斎を子供部屋に改造する *convert a study into a children's room*

kaizu 海図 *(marine) chart*

káji 家事 *family affairs; housework*

káji 火事 *a fire; conflagration*

káji 舵 *rudder; helm* ◊káji o tóru 舵をとる *take the helm; steer*

kajiki máguro かじき鮪 *swordfish*

kajír·u [vt kajiránai; kajítta] かじる *nibble; gnaw; bite into* ◊ringo o kajíru りんごをかじる *bite into an apple* ◊Eigo o sukoshi kajitte iru. 英語を少しかじっている。 *I have a smattering of English.*

kajiya 鍛冶屋 *blacksmith*

kajō 過剰 *excess; surplus*

kakae·ru [vt kakaenai; kakaeta] 抱える *hold in the arms*

kakage·ru [vt kakagenai; kakageta] 掲げる *put up; hoist* ◊hatá o kakageru 旗を掲げる *hoist a flag* ◊risō o kakageru 理想を掲げる *hold up (high) ideals*

kakaku 価格 *price; value*

kákari 係り *person responsible* ◊annai-gákari 案内係り *information clerk; guide*

kakár·u [vi kakaránai; kakátta] かかる *take; require* ◊Koko kara soko máde dono kurai kakarimásu ka? ここからそこまでどのくらいかかりますか? *About how long does it take from here to there?*

kakár·u [vi kakaránai; kakátta] 掛かる *hang; be suspended* ◊Tokonoma ni kírei na kakéjiku ga kakátte ita. 床の間にきれいな掛軸が掛かっていた。 *There was a beautiful scroll hanging in the tokonoma.*

[byōki ni] kakáru （病気に）罹る *fall ill*

kakashi 案山子 *scarecrow*

kakato 踵 *heel*

[ni mo] kakawárazu 〜（にも）係わらず *in spite of; regardless of*
　§Áme ni mo kakawárazu, kása o motázu ni gaishutsu-shita. 雨にも係
　わらず、傘を持たずに外出した。 *In spite of the rain, he went out
　without an umbrella.*

kaké 賭け *a bet; gambling* §kaké o suru 賭けをする *bet; gamble*

kakebúton 掛け布団 *top futon; cover; duvet*

kakegae no nái 掛け替えのない *irreplaceable* §kakegae no nái tochi
　掛け替えのない土地 *irreplaceable land*

kakehanare·ru [vi kakehanarenai; kakehanareta] 掛けはなれる *be apart
　from; be different from; be separated from* §genjitsu to kakehanareta
　aidéa 現実と掛けはなれたアイデア *an idea that is far from reality*

kakéihi 家計費 *household expenses*

kakéizu 家系図 *family tree; genealogical chart*

kakéjiku 掛軸 *hanging scroll*

kakeorí·ru [vi / vt kakeorínai; kakeórita] 駆け降りる *run down (stairs)*
　§Kánojo wa éki no kaidan o kakeórite koronda. 彼女は駅の階段を駆
　け降りて転んだ。 *She ran down the station stairs and fell.*

kakera かけら *fragment; shard (of glass)*

kaké·ru [vi kakénai; káketa] 駆ける *run* §Rōka de kakénaide! 廊下で
　駆けないで！ *Don't run in the hall!*

kaké·ru [vt kakénai; káketa] 掛ける *hang; suspend* §mégane o kakéru
　眼鏡をかける *wear glasses* §Kốto o koko ni kákete okố. コートを
　ここに掛けておこう。 *I'll hang your coat here.*

kaké·ru [vt kakénai; káketa] 賭ける *bet; gamble*

kake·ru [vi kakénai; káketa] 欠ける *be (or become) chipped* §Kōhī-
　jáwan ga kakete iru yo! コーヒー茶碗が欠けているよ。 *This coffee
　cup is chipped!*

[denwa o] kaké·ru （電話を）かける *telephone*

kaketsu 可決 *approval* ——**kaketsu-suru** [vt] *approve (of); pass (a bill);
　adopt (a motion)*

kakézan 掛け算 *multiplication (Math)*

kaki 柿 *persimmon*

káki 牡蠣 *oyster*

kakiatsume·ru [vt kakiatsumenai; kakiatsumeta] 掻き集める *gather
　together* §shikín o kakiatsumeru 資金をかき集める *raise funds*

kakijun 書き順 *stroke order (of a Chinese character)*

kakimawas·u [vt kakimawasanai; kakimawashita] 掻き回す *stir*
　§Kogénai yố ni sore o kakimawashite! 焦げないようにそれを掻き回
　して！ *Stir it so it won't burn!*

kakimaze·ru [vt kakimazenai; kakimazeta] 掻き混ぜる *mix; blend*
　§Tamágo o tashite yóku kakimazete kudasái. 卵を足してよく掻き混
　ぜてください。 *Add an egg and blend well.*

kakíne 垣根 *hedge*

kakinaos·u [vt kakinaosanai; kakinaoshita] 書き直す *rewrite*

kakitome 書留 *registered (mail)* ❡Kono tegami o kakitome ni shite kudasái. この手紙を書留にしてください。 *Send this letter by registered mail, please.*

kakki 活気 *liveliness; vigor; spirit*

kakkiteki [na] 画期的（な）*epoch-making*

kákko 括弧 *parenthesis*

káko 過去 *the past* ❡kakokei 過去形 *past tense (Gram)*

kakō 加工 *processing* ❡kakō shókuhin 加工食品 *processed foods——*
  kakō-suru [vt] 加工する *process; work upon*

kakom·u [vt kakomanai; kakonda] 囲む *surround; enclose*
  ❡Watashítachi wa tēburu o kakonde hanashiátta. 私たちはテーブルを囲んで話し合った。 *We talked together around the table.*

káku 核 *nucleus* ❡kaku sénsō 核戦争 *nuclear war* ❡kaku héiki 核兵器 *nuclear weapon*

kaku 格 *rank; standing* ❡kaku ga sagáru 格が下がる *decline in rank* ❡shukaku 主格 *nominative case (Gram)*

kakú 角 *angle (Geom)* ❡chokkakú 直角 *right angle* ❡donkakú 鈍角 *obtuse angle* ❡eikakú 鋭角 *acute angle*

kák·u [vt kakánai; káita] 書く *write* ❡kakishirusu 書き記す *record* ❡kakitomeru 書き留める *jot down* ❡kakitori 書き取り *dictation*

kák·u [vt kakánai; káita] 描く *draw; paint*

kák·u [vt kakánai; káita] 掻く *scratch; rake* ❡Kayúi kara káite iru. かゆいから掻いている。 *I'm scratching because it itches.*

kak·u [vt kakanai; kaita] 欠く *lack; be short of* ❡níntai o kaku 忍耐を欠く *lack patience*

káku- 各〜 *each* ❡káku hőmen 各方面 *each area (or direction)* ❡káku kójin no shotoku 各個人の所得 *each individual's earnings*

kakū [no] 架空（の）*imaginary; fictitious* ❡kakū no jímbutsu 架空の人物 *a fictional person*

kakubetsu [na] 格別（な）*exceptional; particular ——***kakubetsu ni** 格別に *particularly; especially*

kakuchō 拡張 *extension; expansion ——***kakuchō-suru** [vt] 拡張する *extend; enlarge* ❡tatemóno o kakuchō-suru 建物を拡張する *extend a building*

kakudai 拡大 *magnification ——***kakudai-suru** [vt] 拡大する *enlarge; increase in scope; stretch* ❡J´no sáizu o jūyon póinto ni kakuda-shite kudasái. 字のサイズを十四ポイントに拡大して下さい。 *Enlarge the type size to fourteen points, please.*

kákudo 角度 *angle* ❡Iroiro na kákudo kara míru to... 色々な角度から見ると〜 *Looked at from various angles...*

kakugen 格言 *proverb; maxim*

kákugo 覚悟 *resolution; preparation; resignation* ——**kákugo-suru** [*vt*] 覚悟する *resolve; be ready to accept; resign oneself to*

kakujitsu [na] 確実な *certain; reliable* ⑧kakujitsu na jōhō 確実な情報 *reliable information*

kakumei 革命 *revolution* ⑧kakumei-ka 革命家 *a revolutionary*

kakunin 確認 *verification; certification; confirmation* ⑧kakuninsho 確認書 *a written confirmation* ——**kakunin-suru** [*vt*] 確認する *verify; certify; confirm* ⑧jōhō o kakunin-suru 情報を確認する *confirm a report*

kakuré·ru [*vi* kakurénai; kakúreta] 隠れる *hide; conceal (oneself)* ⑧kakurémbō 隠れん坊 *hide-and-seek*

kakuséizai 覚醒剤 *stimulant; amphetamine*

kakushin 確信 *conviction; certainty* ⑧Kore daké wa kakushin o mótte ieru. これだけは確信を持って言える。*I can say this with certainty.* ——**kakushin-suru** [*vi*] 確信する *believe firmly (in); be convinced (of)*

kakushin 革新 *reform*

kákushu [no] 各種（の）*various; all sorts (of)*

kakús·u [*vt* kakusánai; kakúshita] 隠す *conceal; hide*

kakutoku 獲得 *acquisition* ——**kakutoku-suru** [*vt*] 獲得する *acquire*

káma 鎌 *sickle*

kama 釜 *kettle; pot*

kamaboko 蒲鉾 *steamed fish paste*

kamado 竈 *furnace*

kamáe 構え *posture; appearance; style* ⑧kamáe o suru 構えをする *assume a stance*

kámakiri かまきり；蟷螂 *praying mantis*

kamá·u [*vi* kamawánai; kamátta] 構う *care about; mind; bother about* ⑧Kamaimasén. 構いません。*It doesn't matter.* ⑧Kamawánaide kudasái. 構わないで下さい。*Never mind. ; Please don't bother.; Please don't go to any trouble.*

kamban 看板 *billboard; sign*

kámben-suru [*vt*] 勘弁する *forgive; pardon*

kamboku 潅木 *bush; shrub*

kámbu 幹部 *executive branch; managerial staff*

kámbyō 看病 *nursing; caring for the sick* ——**kámbyō-suru** [*vt*] 看病する *nurse; take care of*

káme 亀 *turtle; tortoise*

kamé 瓶 *pot* ⑧mizu-gamé 水瓶 *water jar*

kamei 加盟 *participation; cooperating* ⑧kokuren no kaméi-koku 国連の加盟国 *a member nation of the United Nations* ——**kamei-suru** [*vi*] *join; participate in; associate with*

kamen 仮面 *mask* ⑧kamen o kabúru 仮面を被る *put on (or wear) a* *mask*

kamí 紙 *paper*

kamí 髪 *hair (of the human head)* ⑧kamí o tokásu 髪をとかす *comb (one's) hair*

kámi 神 *god; spirit* ⑧kamí-gami 神々 *the gods* ⑧Kámi-sama 神様 *God (Chr)*

kaminari 雷 *thunder; thunderbolt*

kaminóke 髪の毛 *hair (of the human head)*

kamisorí 剃刀 *razor* ⑧kamisorí no há 剃刀の刃 *razor blade*

kamitsuk·u [*vt* kamitsukanai; kamitsuita] 噛み付く *bite* ⑧Inú ga kodomo ni kamitsuita. 犬が子供に噛み付いた。 *A dog bit my child.*

kammuri 冠 *a crown; top radical (of a Chinese ideograph)* ⑧kammuri o kabúru 冠を被る *put on (or wear) a crown* ⑧kammuri o mageru 冠を曲げる *be out of sorts; be in a bad mood; have (one's) nose out of joint*

kámo 鴨 *wild duck*

kamoku 課目 *subject (for study)*

kamome 鴎 *seagull*

ká mo shirenai かもしれない *perhaps; it may (or might) be* ⑧Sore wa jíjitsu ka mo shirenai. それは事実かもしれない。 *It may be true.*

kámotsu 貨物 *freight; cargo* ⑧kamotsu réssha 貨物列車 *freight train*

kampan 甲板 *(ship) deck*

kampeki [na] 完璧 (な) *perfect*

kampóyaku 漢方薬 *Chinese herbal medicine*

kám·u [*vt* kamánai; kánda] 噛む *bite; chew*

[hana o] kam·u [*vt* kamanai; kanda] (鼻を) かむ *blow (one's) nose*

kán 缶 *a can* ⑧kankíri 缶切り *can opener*

kán 棺 *coffin*

kan 勘 *intuition; perceptiveness* ⑧kan ga íi 勘がいい *(one's) intuition is good*

-kan 〜感 *feeling; sense*

ka na *I wonder* <*masc*> ⑧Are o dóko ni oitá ka ná? あれをどこに置いたかな？ *I wonder where I put that.* <*masc*>

kanaé·ru [*vt* kanaénai; kanáeta] 叶える *grant; comply with* ⑧nozomi o kanaéru 望みを叶える *grant (one's) wish*

kanagu 金具 *metal fittings; metal parts (for furniture)*

kánai 家内 *(one's own) wife*

kaname 要 *a pivot; the point*

kanarazu 必ず *certainly; by all means; without fail* ⑧Suzuki-san wa kanarazu kimásu. 鈴木さんは必ず来ます。 *Suzuki will come without fail.*

kanarazúshimo [with neg] 必ずしも *(not) necessarily, (not) always*

kánari かなり *rather; fairly; to a considerable extent* ⑧Sore o naósu no

ni kánari kakáru deshō. それを直すのにかなりかかるでしょう。
*It'll take quite a lot (of time **or** money) to repair that.*

kanashi·i [*adj* kanashiku nái; kanáshikatta] 悲しい *(be) sad; sorrowful*

kanashimi 悲しみ *sadness; sorrow; grief*

kanashím·u [*vt* kanashimánai; kanashínda] 悲しむ *be sad; feel sorry for; grieve*

kaná·u [*vi* kanawánai; kanátta] 叶う *be fulfilled* ❸Yumé ga kanatta. 夢が叶った。*My dream was fulfilled.*

kaná·u [*vi* kanawánai; kanátta] 敵う；適う *meet (the requirements of); conform to; match; bear comparison with* ❸Reigi ni kanátte... 礼儀に適って~ *In conformance with etiquette...* ❸Ryōri de wa dare mo Yamáguchi-san ni kanawánai. 料理ではだれも山口さんにかなわない。*When it comes to cooking, no one is a match for Yamaguchi.*

kanchígai 勘違い *misunderstanding* ––**kanchígai-suru** [*vt*] 勘違いする *misunderstand*

kánchō 官庁 *government office*

kandai [na] 寛大（な）*broad-minded; generous; tolerant* ❸kandai na shóchi 寛大な処置 *a generous measure* ❸kandai na hitó 寛大な人 *a broad-minded person*

kandankei 寒暖計 *thermometer*

kandō 感動 *impression; emotion* ––**kandōteki [na]** 感動的（な）*impressive* ––**kandō-suru** [*vi*] 感動する *be impressed by; be moved by*

kane 金 *money; metal* ❸kanemóchi 金持ち *a wealthy person*

kánete kara 予てから *since some time ago; for some time*

kangáe 考え *idea; thought* ❸kangae-kata 考え方 *way of thinking*

kangaekóm·u [*vi* kangaekománai; kangaekónda] 考え込む *be lost in thought; brood (over); think hard (about)*

kangaenaós·u [*vt* kangaenaosánai; kangaenaóshita] 考え直す *reconsider*

kangáe·ru [*vt* kangáenai; kangáeta] 考える *think; consider* ❸Chótto kangaesásete kudasái. ちょっと考えさせて下さい。*Let me think about it a bit.*

kangei 歓迎 *a welcoming; reception* ❸kangeikai 歓迎会 *a welcoming party; a reception* ––**kangei-suru** [*vt*] 歓迎する *welcome*

kangeki 感激 *deep emotion; excitement* ––**kangeki-suru** [*vi*] 感激する *be deeply moved; be impressed (by)*

kangen gákudan 管弦楽団 *orchestra*

kángo 看護 *nursing; care (of the sick)* ❸kangófu 看護婦 *a nurse* ––**kángo-suru** [*vt*] 看護する *nurse; look after*

kani 蟹 *crab*

kanja 患者 *a patient*

kanji 漢字 *Chinese ideogram*

kanji 感じ *feeling; sensation; impression* ❸kanji ga warúi 感じが悪

い bad feeling 8kanji no íi hito 感じがいい人 an agreeable person 8Kánojo no kao o míte atatakái kanji ga shita. 彼女の顔を見て暖かい感じがした。 I got a warm feeling just seeing her face.

kanjin [na] 肝心 （な） important

kanji·ru [vt kanjinai; kanjita] 感じる feel; be aware of

kanjitór·u [vt kanjitoránai; kanjitótta] 感じ取る detect; feel 8hónshin o kanjitóru 本心を感じ取る sense another's real meaning (or intention)

kanjō 環状 ring; loop 8kanjō hachigōsen 環状 八号線 No. 8 Loop Road (around Tokyo)

kanjō 勘定 counting; calculation ——**kanjō-suru** [vt] 勘定する calculate 8Kanjō-shite kudasái. 勘定して下さい。 May I have my bill, please?

kanjō 感情 feeling; emotion ——**kanjōteki [na]** 感情的 （な） emotional ——**kanjōteki ni** 感情的に emotionally

kankaku 感覚 sense; sensation; feeling 8Musuko wa iró ni kankaku ga surudói. 息子は色に感覚が鋭い。 My son has a keen sense of color.

kankaku 間隔 space; interval

kankei 関係 relation; relationship; connection 8Nichi-Bei kánkei 日米関係 Japanese-American relations 8ningen kánkei 人間関係 human relations ——**kankei-suru** [vi] 関係する be related; be connected (with)

kanketsu [na] 簡潔 （な） brief; concise 8kanketsu na hyōgén 簡潔な表現 a concise expression

kanki 換気 ventilation 8kankisen 換気扇 exhaust fan ——**kanki-suru** [vt] 換気する ventilate

kankin-suru [vt] 監禁する block; stop; confine; imprison; restrict 8jitaku ni kankin-sareru 自宅に監禁される be placed under house arrest

kankitsúrui 柑橘類 citrus fruit

kankō 観光 sightseeing 8kankō básu 観光バス sightseeing bus 8kankőkyaku 観光客 sightseer; tourist 8kankőchi 観光地 tourist spot

kankō 刊行 publication 8kankőbutsu 刊行物 a publication ——**kankō-suru** [vt] publish

kankoku 勧告 advice 8kankoku chūsai 勧告仲裁 advisory arbitration ——**kankoku-suru** [vt] 勧告する advise 8Kasai wa wakai o kankoku-shita. 家裁は和解を勧告した。 The family court advised reconciliation.

Kánkoku 韓国 Republic of Korea (or South Korea) ——**Kankokugo** 韓国語 Korean language ——**Kankokújin** 韓国人 a Korean

kankyaku 観客 audience; spectator

kankyō 環境 environment; surroundings 8Kankyőchō 環境庁 Environment Agency 8kankyō hógo 環境保護 protection of the *environment* ◦kankyō ni tekiō-suru 環境に適応する *adapt to the environment*

kánnen 観念 *idea; concept* ◦kotei kánnen 固定観念 *fixed idea; stereotype* ◦chūshō-teki kánnen 抽象的観念 *an abstract concept* ◦Otto wa jikan no kánnen ga nái. 夫は時間の観念がない。*My husband has no concept of time.* ––**kannenteki [na]** 観念的（な） *ideal; ideological* ––**kannenteki ni** 観念的に *ideologically*

kánnin 堪忍 *patience; forebearance; pardon* ––**kánnin-suru** [vt] 堪忍する *pardon; forgive*

kanningu カンニング *cheating (on an exam)*

kanō [na] 可能（な）*possible*

kánojo 彼女 *she; her*

kan'óke 棺桶 *casket; coffin*

kanōsei 可能性 *possibility* ◦Kánojo to no kekkon wa kanōsei ga áru. 彼女との結婚は可能性がある。*There's a possibility I may marry her.*

kanránseki 観覧席 *stands; bleachers*

kanren 関連 *relation; connection; relevance* ––**kanren-suru** [vi] 関連する *be connected; be related (to)*

kánri 管理 *administration; management* ◦kanrísha 管理者 *administrator* ◦kanrinin 管理人 *custodian; caretaker* ––**kánri-suru** [vt] *administrate; manage; control*

kanrui 感涙 *tears of emotion* ◦kanrui ni musebu 感涙にむせぶ *choke with tears of emotion*

kanryō 完了 *completion* ––**kanryō-suru** [vi / vt] 完了する *complete; be completed; be finished* ◦Shigoto wa súbete kanryō-shita. 仕事はすべて完了した。*The work is all finished.*

kanryō 官僚 *bureaucrat; bureaucracy*

kánsa 監査 *an audit*

kansán-ritsu 換算率 *(currency) exchange rate* ◦Endaka de dóru e no kansán-ritsu ga íi. 円高でドルへの換算率がいい。*With the strong yen, the exchange rate to dollars is good.*

kansatsu 観察 *observation* ––**kansatsu-suru** [vt] 観察する *observe; watch closely*

kansei 完成 *completion* ––**kansei-suru** [vi / vt] 完成する *complete; be completed; be finished* –– **kansei-sasé·ru** [caus] 完成させる *finish; complete; cause to be completed*

kansen 感染 *infection* ––**kansen-suru** [vi] 感染する *be (or become) infected* ◦Kodomo wa infuruénza ni kansen-shita. 子供はインフルエンザに感染した。*My child has (or is infected with) influenza.*

kansetsu 関節 *a joint (Anat)* ◦kansetsúen 関節炎 *arthritis*

kansetsu [no] 間接（の）*indirect* ◦kansetsú-zei 間接税 *indirect tax* ––**kansetsuteki [na]** 間接的（な）*indirect* ––**kansetsuteki ni** 間接的に *indirectly*

kánsha 感謝 *thanks; appreciation*   ❊Kanshásai 感謝祭 *Thanksgiving*   ❊kanshájō 感謝状 *a letter of appreciation*   ❊kánsha no kimochi o arawásu 感謝の気持ちを表わす *express appreciation* ——**kánsha-suru** [*vi*] 感謝する *be grateful*

kanshi 監視 *watch; surveillance; observation* ——**kanshi-suru** [*vt*] 監視する *keep watch over; observe*   ❊Keisatsu wa yōgísha no kōdō o kanshi-shite iru. 警察は容疑者の行動を監視している。 *The police are watching the movements of the suspect.*

kanshin 感心 *admiration; wonder* ——**kanshin na** 感心な *praiseworthy; laudable* ——**kanshin-suru** [*vi*] 感心する *admire; wonder at; be impressed by*   ❊Watashi wa kono ryōri no úmasa ni kanshin-shite iru. 私はこの料理のうまさに感心している。 *I'm impressed by how good this food tastes.*

kanshin 関心 *interest in; feeling for*   ❊kanshin o shimésu 関心を示す *show an interest in*   ❊Tetsúgaku ni kanshin o mótte imasu ka? 哲学に関心を持っていますか? *Are you interested in philosophy?*

kanshō 環礁 *atoll*

kanshō 干渉 *interference; intervention* ——**kanshō-suru** [*vi*] *interfere (with); meddle (in)*   ❊Naisei ni kanshō-surú no wa kokusai-hō íhan desu. 内政に干渉するのは国際法違反です。 *Interfering in the internal affairs (of another nation) is a violation of international law.*

kanshō 鑑賞 *appreciation (of the arts)* ——**kanshō-suru** 鑑賞する *appreciate*

kanshū 慣習 *custom; convention*

kansō 感想 *thoughts; impression*   ❊Sono hón ni tsúite no kansō ga kikitái. その本についての感想が聞きたい。 *I'd like to hear your impression of that book.*

kánso [na] 簡素（な） *simple; plain*   ❊Watashítachi wa kánso na kekkón-shiki o agetái. 私たちは簡素な結婚式を挙げたい。 *We want to have a simple wedding ceremony.*

kansō 乾燥 *dryness; aridity* ——**kansō-suru** [*vi*] 乾燥する *be (or become) dry*

kansoku 観測 *observation; survey* ——**kansoku-suru** [*vt*] 観測する *observe; survey*   ❊tentai o kansoku-suru 天体を観測する *observe the celestial bodies*

kansui 冠水 *a flood* ——**kansui-suru** [*vi*] 冠水する *be submerged; be flooded*

kantan [na] 簡単（な） *simple; brief*   ❊Kono mondai wa kantan desu. この問題は簡単です。 *This problem is simple.* ——**kantan ni** 簡単に *simply; briefly*   ❊Yōtén o kantan ni setsumei-shite kudasái. 要点を簡単に説明してください。 *Explain the essential points briefly, please.*

kantan-suru [*vi*] 感嘆する *cry out (with admiration)*

Kántō 関東 *the Kantō area (includes Tōkyō and Yokohama)*

kantoku 監督 *supervision; control; direction* §eiga kántoku 映画監督 *movie director* ——**kantoku-suru** [*vt*] 監督する *supervise; direct*

kantsū 姦通 *adultery*

kantsū-suru [*vi*] 貫通する *penetrate; pass through* §Kaitei tónneru ga kantsū-shita. 海底トンネルが貫通した。 *The tunnel under the ocean has been completed.*

kan'yō [na] 肝要 （な） *important*

kanzei 関税 *customs tariff; duty*

kanzen 完全 *completeness; perfection* ——**kanzen na** 完全な *complete; perfect; whole* ——**kanzen ni** 完全に *completely*

kanzō 肝臓 *liver* (Anat)

kanzumé 缶詰 *canned goods; canning*

kao 顔 *face* §kao o arau 顔を洗う *wash (one's) face* §kaodachi 顔立ち *(physical) features* §kaoiro 顔色 *complexion* §kao o dásu 顔を出す *put in an appearance (at a gathering)* §aói kao o suru 青い顔をする *look pale* §hén na kao o suru 変な顔をする *look strange*

kaori 香り *aroma; scent; fragrance*

kappatsu [na] 活発 （な） *active; lively* §kappatsu na kodomo 活発な子供 *an active child* ——**kappatsu ni** 活発に *actively*

kará [no] 空 （の） *empty* §Hako no nakámi wa kará desu. 箱の中味は空です。 *The box is empty.* §Kokóro ga kará desu. 心が空です。 *My heart is empty.*

-kara 〜から *from; since* §Éki kara uchi máde tákushī ni notta. 駅から家までタクシーに乗った。 *I took a taxi home from the station.* §Nichiyóbi kara atamá ga itái. 日曜日から頭が痛い。 *I've had a headache since Sunday.*

-kara 〜から *because; so* §Nichiyóbi wa atamá ga itákatta kara, háyaku toko ni tsúita. 日曜日は頭が痛かったから早く床についた。 *I had a headache Sunday, so I went to bed early.*

karada 体；身体 *body* §karada (no guai) ga warúi 体 （の具合） が悪い *be in poor health*

kará·i [*adj* káraku nái; kárakatta] 辛い *(be) hot; spicy; peppery; severe* §karái ryōri 辛い料理 *spicy cooking* § karakuchi [no] 辛口 （の） *dry (wine); hot (curry)* § Ano senséi wa ten ga karái. あの先生は点が辛い。 *That teacher's a tough grader.*

karaká·u [*vt* karakawánai; karakátta] からかう *tease; make fun of*

karakuri níngyō からくり人形 *mechanical doll*

karaoke カラオケ *recorded songs with blank vocal track*

karashi 芥子 *mustard*

karate 空手 *karate (a Japanese martial art)*

kare·ru [*vi* karenai; kareta] 枯れる *wither; die* §kareki 枯木 *a dead tree* §Rúsu no aida, ueki ga zémbu karete shimátta. 留守の間、植木が全部枯れてしまった。 *While we were away, the potted plants all* *withered.*

kari [no] 仮り（の） *temporary; transient* ❽kari no súmai 仮りの住まい *temporary abode* ❽kari ménkyo 仮り免許 *a temporary (driver's) license*

kariiré·ru [vt kariirénai; kariíreta] 刈り入れる *harvest; reap*

kari·ru [vt karinai; karita] 借りる *borrow; rent; check out (a book)*

karō 過労 *overwork; excessive labor* ❽karōshi 過労死 *death from overwork*

karójite 辛うじて *barely; narrowly* ❽Karójite daigaku nyúshi ni gókaku-shita. 辛うじて大学入試に合格した。 *I barely passed the college entrance exams.*

kar·u [vt karanai; katta] 刈る *harvest; reap; mow; cut* ❽íne o karu 稲を刈る *harvest rice* ❽kami-nó-ke o karu 髪の毛を刈る *cut hair*

karu·i [adj karuku nái; karúkatta] 軽い *light; slight; minor* ❽karui byōki 軽い病気 *a minor illness* ❽karui kega 軽い怪我 *a slight injury* ❽Heriumu fúsen wa kúki yori karui. ヘリウム風船は空気より軽い。 *A helium balloon is lighter than air.*

káruta カルタ *playing cards* ❽iroha-gáruta いろはガルタ *Japanese alphabet cards*

karyū 下流 *downstream*

kása 傘 *umbrella* ❽higása 日傘 *parasol*

kasai 火災 *(destructive) fire; conflagration* ❽kasai hóken 火災保険 *fire insurance* ❽kasai hōchíki 火災報知器 *fire alarm*

kasanar·u [vi kasanaranai; kasanatta] 重なる *pile up; be (become) piled up; be close together*

kasane·ru [vt kasanenai; kasaneta] 重ねる *pile one thing on top of another* ❽tsúmi o kasaneru 罪を重ねる *commit more and more crimes (sins)* ❽Kasanete o-negai shimásu! 重ねてお願いします。 *Again I implore you. <formal>*

kaség·u [vt kasegánai; kaséida] 稼ぐ *work to earn money* ❽Saikin, ōku no shúfu wa arubáito de o-kane o kaséide iru. 最近多くの主婦はアルバイトでお金を稼いでいる。 *Nowadays, many housewives are working part-time to earn money.*

Kasei 火星 *the planet Mars*

kaséifu 家政婦 *housekeeper*

kaseki 化石 *fossil*

kasen 化繊 *synthetic fabric*

kasetsu 仮説 *hypothesis*

Káshi 華氏；カ氏 *Fahrenheit* ❽Káshi no sánjūnído ga Sésshi réido desu. 華氏の三十二度が摂氏零度です。 *32° Fahrenheit is 0° Centigrade.*

[o-]káshi 菓子 *sweets; candy*

kashigé·ru [vt kashigénai; kashígeta] 傾げる *lean; tilt* ❽kubi o kashigéru 首を傾げる *incline the head (in disbelief)*

kashikó·i [*adj* kashikóku nái; kashikókatta] 賢い *(be) clever; smart* —— **kashikóku** 賢く *cleverly*

Kashikomarimáshita. 畏まりました。*Certainly!* <*formal*>

kashimashí·i [*adj* kashimáshiku nái; kashimáshikatta] 姦しい *(be) noisy; boisterous*

kashira *I wonder* <*fem*> ❀Ashita áme ga fúru kashira? 明日雨が降るかしら? *I wonder if it will rain tomorrow.* <*fem*>

kashitsu 過失 *fault; mistake* ❀kashitsu chíshi 過失致死 *accidental homicide* ❀Dare ni demo kashitsu wa áru mono! 誰にでも過失はあるもの。*Everyone makes mistakes!* <*fem*>

káshu 歌手 *singer; vocalist*

kasō 火葬 *cremation* ❀kasōba 火葬場 *crematorium* ❀kasō ni suru 火葬にする *cremate*

kasō 仮想 *supposition; imaginary; hypothetical* ❀kasō tekíkoku 仮想敵国 *hypothetical enemy (country)* ❀kasō no teki to tatakáu 仮想の敵と戦う *fight windmills*

kassóro 滑走路 *(airport) runway*

kas·u [*vt* kasanai; kashita] 貸す *lend; rent* ❀Yamada-san ni sono hón o kashita. 山田さんにその本を貸した。*I lent that book to Yamada.* ——**kashite itadaku** 貸していただく *borrow* <*formal*> ❀Denwa o kashite itadakemásu ka? 電話を貸していただけますか。*May I use (or borrow) the telephone?* <*formal*>

kásuka [na] 微か（な）*faint; dim; vague; slight* ❀kásuka na hikari 微かな光 *a dim light* ❀Kásuka na otó ga kikoeru. 微かな音が聞こえる。*I can hear a faint sound.* ——**kásuka ni** 微かに *faintly; dimly; slightly; vaguely* ❀Sono jíken ni tsuite, kásuka ni obóete iru. その事件について微かに覚えている。*I remember the incident vaguely.*

kasumi 霞 *haze; mist* ❀kasumi ga déru 霞が出る *be (become) hazy* ❀Ano yamá ni kasumi ga kakátte iru. あの山に霞がかかっている。*There's mist hanging over that mountain.*

kasutera カステラ *sponge cake*

katá 方 *person* ❀Ano katá wa dónata desu ka? あの方はどなたですか。*Who is that person?* <*formal*>

katá 型 *mold; pattern; style; model* ❀katá ni ireru 型に入れる *put in a mold* ❀yōfuku no katá 洋服の型 *dressmaking pattern* ❀atarashíi katá no kompyútā 新しい型のコンピューター *a new model of computer* ❀katagami 型紙 *a (paper) pattern; stencil*

káta 肩 *shoulder* ❀katákori 肩こり *stiff shoulders* ❀káta o sukumeru 肩をすくめる *shrug (one's) shoulders*

-kata ～方 *way of (doing); how to (do)* ❀Anáta no kangaekata wa sukóshi hén desu yo. あなたの考え方は少し変ですよ。*Your way of thinking is a bit strange.* ❀Kono kompyútā no tsukaikata ga wakaránai. このコンピューターの使い方が分からない。*I don't know how to* *use this computer.*

kata- 片〜 *one side* ❚ **katate** 片手 *one hand* ❚ **katamichi** 片道 *one-way (train or airplane ticket)* ❚ **kataómoi** 片思い *unrequited love* ❚ **Tebúkuro no katáhō ga mitsukaranai.** 手袋の片方が見つからない。*I can't find one of my gloves.*

katachi 形 *shape; figure* ❚ **mono no katachi** 物の形 *the shape of a thing* ❚ **Anó hito wa kao-katachi ga íi.** あの人は顔形がいい。*That person has nice (facial) features.* ❚ **Yagate, purojékuto no katachi ga tsúita.** やがてプロジェクトの形がついた。*The project finally took shape.* ❚ **Kore wa hón no katachi bákari no orei desu.** これはほんの形ばかりのお礼です。*This is simply a token of (our) appreciation.* <formal>

kata·i [adj **kataku nái; katákatta**] 固い；堅い；硬い *(be) hard; solid; firm; tough* ❚ **katai mákura** 硬い枕 *a hard pillow* ❚ **katai kétsugi** 固い決議 *a firm decision* ❚ **Kono nikú wa katai.** この肉は硬い。*This steak is tough.* ——**kataku** 固く；堅く；硬く *solidly; firmly*

katakána カタカナ *one of the two Japanese syllabaries, used chiefly for foreign names and loanwords*

katakuna [na] 頑な（な）*firm; immovable* ——**katakuna ni** 頑なに *firmly; fixedly*

katakurushí·i [adj **katakurúshiku nái; katakurúshikatta**] 堅苦しい *(be) stiff; strict; formal* ❚ **Katakurushíí áisatsu wa kyó wa núki ni shiyó.** 堅苦しい挨拶は今日は抜きにしよう。*Today let's dispense with formal greetings.*

katamari 固まり；塊 *lump; mass; group; cluster* ❚ **shibō no katamari** 脂肪の固まり *a lump of fat* ❚ **nóka no katamari** 農家の塊 *a cluster of farm houses*

katamar·u [vi **katamaranai; katamatta**] 固まる *harden; become firm; solidify* ❚ **konkurīto ga katamaru** コンクリートが固まる *concrete hardens* ❚ **Kikaku ga sukkári katamatta.** 企画がすっかり固まった。*The plans have firmed up.*

katame·ru [vt **katamenai; katameta**] 固める *harden; make firm* ❚ **Zerī o reizóko de hiyashite katameru.** ゼリーを冷蔵庫で冷やして固める。*One hardens jelly by cooling it in the refrigerator.* ❚ **késshin o katameru** 決心を固める *stiffen (one's) resolve*

katami 形見 *keepsake; memento* ❚ **Kono kaichū-dókei wa chichí no katami desu.** この懐中時計は父の形見です。*This pocket watch is a memento of my father.*

katamuké·ru [vt **katamukénai; katamúketa**] 傾ける *lean (toward); tilt; slant* ❚ **mimí o katamukéru** 耳を傾ける *lend an ear; listen to*

katamúk·u [vi **katamukánai; katamúita**] 傾く *lean; list; incline; slant* ❚ **Fúne ga katamúite iru.** 船が傾いている。*The boat's listing.* ❚ **Káre wa kokusui shúgi ni katamúite iru.** 彼は国粋主義に傾いている。*He leans toward (ultra)nationalism.*

kataná 刀 *sword*

kataria·u [*vt* katariawánai; katariátta] 語り合う *talk together*   🔶Bóku wa aitsu to wa ítsumo jínsei o katariáu nakáma da. 僕はあいつとはいつも 人生を語り合う仲間だ。*He and I always talk over life's problems together.* <*masc*>

katar·u [*vt* kataranai; katatta] 語る *speak; talk; tell (a story)*

katatsúmuri 蝸牛 *snail*

katazuke 片付け *cleanup* 🔶ato-kátazuke 後片付け *the cleanup afterwards* 🔶Katazuke wa máda owaranai. 片付けはまだ終わらな い。 *We're not yet finished putting things in order.*

katazuké·ru [*vt* katazukénai; katazúketa] 片付ける *put in order; clear (away); clean up; straighten up* 🔶tsukue no ué o katazukéru 机の上を 片付ける *clean (or straighten) up the top of a desk*

katei 課程 *course; curriculum* 🔶shūshi kátei 修士課程 *master's course*

katei 家庭 *household; home; family* 🔶katei o mótsu otoko 家庭を持つ 男 *a family man* 🔶katei denki séihin 家庭電気製品 *household electric appliance* 🔶 katei kyōshi 家庭教師 *private tutor*

katei 仮定 *hypothesis; assumption; supposition* ——**kateiteki na** 仮定的 な *hypothetical* ——**kateiteki ni** 仮定的に *hypothetically* ——**katei-suru** [*vt*] 仮定する *assume; suppose*

káts·u [*vi* katánai; kátta] 勝つ *win; be victorious; dominate* 🔶sensō ni kátsu 戦争に勝つ *win a war* 🔶jibun ni kátsu 自分に勝つ *conquer oneself*

katsudō 活動 *activity* ——**katsudōteki [na]** 活動的（な）*active* 🔶Kánojo wa katsudōteki desu. 彼女は活動的です。*She is (very) active.* ——**katsudōteki ni** 活動的に *actively* ——**katsudō-suru** [*vi*] 活動する *be active (in)* 🔶Sono kaisha wa Tōnan Ájia de katsudō-shite iru. その会社は東南アジアで活動している。*That company is active in Southeast Asia.*

katsúg·u [*vt* katsugánai; katsúida] 担ぐ *shoulder; carry (on the shoulders)* 🔶mikoshi o katsúgu 御輿を担ぐ *carry a portable shrine* 🔶engi o katsúgu 縁起を担ぐ *be superstitious; believe in omens*

katsuji 活字 *printing type; print*

katsuo 鰹 *bonito (fish)* 🔶katsuobushi 鰹節 *dried bonito*

katsura 鬘 *wig; hairpiece*

katsuyaku 活躍 *activity* ——**katsuyaku-suru** [*vi*] 活躍する *be active (in)* 🔶Itō Mídori wa figyua sukéto de katsuyaku-shita. 伊藤みどりは フィギュアスケートで活躍した。*Itō Midori was active in figure skating.*

katte 勝手 *selfishness* 🔶Katte bákari iu hito wa kirai desu! 勝手ばかり 言う人はきらいです。*I don't like people who only think about themselves.* 🔶Kore wa watashi no katte deshō! これは私の勝手でし ょう。*I can do as I please! (or This is up to me!)* ——**katte na** 勝手

な *selfish; willful; arbitrary* §Kánojo wa katte na hitó desu. 彼女は勝手な人です。*She is a (very) selfish person.* ——**katte ni** 勝手に *as one pleases* §Katte ni shiro! 勝手にしろ！ *Do what you please!*

katteguchi 勝手口 *back (**or** kitchen) door*

ka·u [*vt* kawanai; katta] 買う *buy*

ká·u [*vt* kawánai; kátta] 飼う *keep; raise (a domestic animal)* §Inú o kátte imásu ka? 犬を飼っていますか。*Do you have (**or** keep) a dog?*

kawá 川 *river* §kawagishi 川岸 *riverbank* §kawakami 川上 *upstream*

kawá 革 *leather*

kawá 皮 *animal skin; tree bark; (orange) peel; (pie) shell*

kawaigár·u [*vt* kawaigaránai; kawaigátta] 可愛がる *love; dote (on); pet; cherish* §Háha wa magomúsume o totemo kawaigátte iru. 母は孫娘をとても可愛がっている。*Mother really dotes on her granddaughter.*

kawaí·i [*adj* kawáiku nái; kawáikatta] 可愛い *(be) cute; loveable; adorable* § kawaíi egao 可愛い笑顔 *a cute smile* §Dare de mo jibun no kodomo ga kawaíi. だれでも自分の子供が可愛い。*Everyone thinks their own children are adorable.*

kawairashí·i [*adj* kawairáshiku nái; kawairáshikatta] 可愛らしい *(be) cute; darling*

kawaisō [na] 可愛想（な）*pitiable; unfortunate; sad* §kawaisō na norainu 可愛想な野良犬 *a pitiable stray dog* §Yamamoto-san wa saikin go-ryōshin o tsuzukete nakushite, kawaisō desu ne. 山本さんは最近御両親を続けて亡くして、可愛想ですね。*I feel sorry for Yamamoto; he's lost both parents recently, one after the other.*

kawák·u [*vi* kawakánai; kawáita] 乾く；渇く *dry (out)* §Nódo ga kawáita. 喉がかわいた。*I'm thirsty.* ——**kawakás·u** [*caus* kawakasánai; kawakáshita] 乾かす *make dry; dry out* §Sentakumono o sóto de kawakáshite kudasái. 洗濯物を外で乾かして下さい。*Dry the wash outdoors.*

kawara 瓦 *(roof) tile*

[o-]káwari お代わり *a substitute; replacement* §O-káwari wa ikága desu ka? お代わりはいかがですか。*How about a second helping?*

kawaribánko ni 代わりばんこに *by turns; in rotation; alternately*

kawariyasú·i [*adj* kawariyásuku nái; kawariyásukatta] 変わりやすい *(be) changeable; easy to change* §Áki no ténki wa kawariyasúi. 秋の天気は変わりやすい。*Fall weather is uncertain.*

kawar·u [*vi/vt* kawaranai; kawatta] 代わる *change; exchange; take the place of; substitute for; replace* §Súmisu-san-tachi wa súmai ga kawatta. スミスさんたちは住まいが代わった。*The Smith's address has changed.* §Ashita no nijigen-mé no kúrasu o kawatte kuremasén ka? 明日の二時限目のクラスを代わってくれませんか。*Would you substitute for me for my second-period class tomorrow?*

kawar·u [*vi* kawaranai; kawatta] 変わる *change* ❅Jūnísai gúrai de otokó no ko wa kóe ga kawaru. 十二才ぐらいで男の子は声が変わる。*At about the age of twelve, a boy's voice changes.*

kawarugáwaru ni 代わる代わるに *by turns; alternately*

kawase 為替 *(monetary) exchange; (postal) money order* ❅kawase sóba 為替相場 *exchange rate* ❅kawase shíjō 為替市場 *foreign exchange market*

kawatta [*attr*] 変わった *different; odd; strange* ❅Kore wa kawatta dezáin ne. これは変わったデザインね。*This is an odd design, isn't it?* <*fem*> ❅Aitsu wa kawatta hitó da na. あいつは変わった人だな。*He's a strange guy.* <*masc*>

kayabuki yáne 茅葺き屋根 *thached roof*

Kayóbi 火曜日 *Tuesday*

kayókyoku 歌謡曲 *popular song*

kayo·u [*vi* kayowanai; kayotta] 通う *go to and from; commute* ❅Watashi wa máinichi nijíkan kákete, gakkō ni kayotte iru. 私は毎日二時間かけて学校に通っている。*I commute two hours to school every day.*

kayowá·i [*adj* kayowáku nái; kayowákatta] か弱い *(be) delicate; weak; frail* ❅Káre wa mikake ni yorazu, kayowái seikaku o shite iru. 彼は見かけによらず、か弱い性格をしている。*Despite his appearance, he is delicate.*

kayú·i [*adj* káyuku nái; káyukatta] 痒い *(be) itchy; itch* ❅Mushi ni sasárete, senaka ga kayúi. 虫にさされて背中が痒い。*I was stung by an insect and my back itches.*

kázan 火山 *volcano* ❅katsukázan 活火山 *an active volcano* ❅kyūkázan 休火山 *dormant volcano* ❅shikázan 死火山 *extinct volcano*

kazari 飾り *decoration* ❅kubi kázari 首飾り *necklace* ❅kazari no nái hito 飾りのない人 *an unpretentious person*

kazar·u [*vt* kazaranai; kazatta] 飾る *decorate; display* ❅heyá o kazaru 部屋を飾る *decorate a room* ❅uwabe o kazaru うわべを飾る *put on an outward show*

kaze 風 *wind; breeze* ❅kaze ga fúku 風が吹く *the wind blows* ❅Káre wa gakushákaze o fukáshite iru. 彼は学者風を吹かしている。*He has a scholar's air about him.* ❅Kaze no táyori ga tadóita. 風の便りが届いた。*A little bird told me (lit: News was delivered by the wind).* <*set phrase*>

kaze 風邪 *(common) cold* ❅Kaze o hiku. 風邪をひく *to catch (a) cold*

kazei 課税 *a tax; taxation*

kazoé·ru [*vt* kazoénai; kazóeta] 数える *count; enumerate*

kázoku 家族 *family* ❅kazoku kéikaku 家族計画 *family planning* ❅Go-kázoku to issho ni súnde imásu ka? 御家族と一緒に住んでいますか。*Do you live with your family?*

kázu 数 *a number* ❽kázu o kazoéru 数を数える *count numbers*
❽kázu őku 数多く *many* ❽Bóku mo kázu ni irete oite kuré yo. 僕も
数に入れておいてくれよ。*Count me in too!* *<masc>*

ke 毛 *hair; wool* ❽kamí no ke 髪の毛 *hair (of he head)* ❽wakige 脇
毛 *hair of the armpits* ❽ke no orimono 毛の織物 *wool cloth* ❽fude
no ke 筆の毛 *brush bristles* ❽tori no ke 鳥の毛 *bird feathers; down*

kéchi [na] けち（な）*stingy; miserly* ❽kéchi na kónjō けちな根性 *a
selfish nature* ❽Yamanaka-san wa kéchi desu, ne. 山中さんはけちで
すね。*Yamanaka's stingy, isn't he?*

kedamono 獣 *beast; animal*

kegá 怪我 *injury; wound* ❽kegá o suru 怪我をする *be injured*
❽keganin 怪我人 *casualty; injured person* ❽kegá no kōmyō 怪我の
功名 *a lucky hit; a fluke; a fortunate turn of events* *<set phrase>* ——
kegá-suru 怪我する *be injured*

kegawa 毛皮 *fur*

kegen [na] 怪訝（な）*dubious; questioning* ❽Sonó hito wa kegensō na
omomochi de setsumei o kiite ita. その人は怪訝そうな面持ちで説明
を聞いていた。*She listened to the explanation with a dubious
expression on her face.*

keiba 競馬 *horse racing*

keibetsu 軽蔑 *contempt; scorn* —— **keibetsu-suru** [vt] 軽蔑する
despise; scorn ❽Anó hito wa watashi o keibetsu-shite iru. あの人は
私を軽蔑している。*He despises me.*

kéibi 警備 *defense; guard* ❽keibitai 警備隊 *guard unit* ❽Terorísuto
no hanzai ga tahatsu-shite irú no de, kéibi ga kyőka-sareta. テロリスト
の犯罪が多発しているので、警備が強化された。*Terrorist attacks
are on the increase, so security has been strengthened.* —— **kéibi-suru**
警備する *defend; guard (against)*

kéidai 境内 *grounds; precincts* ❽tera (jínja) no kéidai 寺（神社）の境
内 *temple (or shrine) precincts*

kéido 経度 *longitude*

keiei 経営 *management* ❽keiéisha 経営者 *manager* ❽keiéigaku 経営
学 *business management* ❽keiéihi 経営費 *operating cost* ——**keiei-
suru** [vt] 経営する *manage; run*

keigo 敬語 *honorific level of speech*

keihatsu 啓発 *enlightenment* ❽jiko kéihatsu 自己啓発 *self-
enlightenment*

kéihi 経費 *expenses* ❽kéihi setsugen 経費節減 *cutting expenses*
❽hitsuyő kéihi 必要経費 *operating expenses*

keihō 警報 *caution; (official) warning* ❽keihō sőchi 警報装置 *alarm
system* ❽tsunami kéihō 津波警報 *tidal wave warning*

kéii 敬意 *respect* ❽kéii o haráu 敬意を払う *pay respect (to)* ❽kéii o
arawásu 敬意をあらわす *show respect (for)*

keiji 啓示 *revelation*

keiji 掲示 *notice; bulletin*   8keijiban 掲示板 *bulletin board*——**keiji-suru** [*vt*] *post (a notice)*

kéiji 刑事 *police detective*   8keiji jíken 刑事事件 *criminal case*

keika 経過 *progress; course; passage* ——**keika-suru** [*vi*] 経過する *pass; elapse*

keikai [na] 軽快(な) *light; light-hearted*   8keikai na rízumu 軽快なリズム *a light rhythm*   8keikai na ashidori 軽快な足取り *a light step*

keikai 警戒 *caution; precaution* ——**keikai-suru** [*vt*] 警戒する *guard (against); look out (for)*   8kiken o keikai-suru 危険を警戒する *look out for danger*

keikaku 計画 *a plan; a project*   8keikaku o tatéru 計画を立てる *make a plan*   8keikaku o jikkō-suru 計画を実行する *carry out a project*

keikan 警官 *police (person)*   8keikantai 警官隊 *the police (force)*

keiken 経験 *experience*   8keiken o tsumu 経験を積む *gain (have) experience*   8keiken no áru hitó 経験のある人 *a person with experience* ——**keiken-suru** [*vt*] 経験する *experience*

kéiki 契機 *turning point; opportunity*   8Kekkon ga seikatsu o kirikaeru kéiki ni nátta. 結婚は生活を切り替える契機になった。 *Marriage was the turning point in my life.*

keiki 景気 *(business) conditions; the economy; the times*   8keiki héndō 景気変動 *business fluctuation*   8keiki jōshō 景気上昇 *a rising trend (in business)*   8keiki kótai 景気後退 *business recession*   8keiki o tsukéru 景気をつける *liven up; brighten*   8Keiki ga warui. 景気が悪い。 *The economy is bad.*

kéiko 稽古 *lesson; practice (of one of the Japanese arts)*   8o-hana no kéiko お花の稽古 *an ikebana lesson*   8kéndō no kéiko 剣道の稽古 *kendo practice*

keikō 傾向 *tendency*   8Nihonjín wa hito to hanásu toki, aite no kao o mínai keikō ga áru. 日本人は人と話す時、相手の顔を見ない傾向がある。 *Japanese have a tendency not to look at people's faces when talking to them.*

keikō 経口 *oral*   8keikō hinin'yaku 経口避妊薬 *oral contraceptive*

keikoku 渓谷 *ravine; canyon; gorge*

keikoku 警告 *warning; caution*   8keikoku o hassuru 警告を発する *sound a warning* ——**keikoku-suru** [*vt*] 警告する *warn; caution*

keikōtō 蛍光灯 *flourescent light*

keimúsho 刑務所 *prison*

keireki 経歴 *career; educational and employment history; resumé*   8Nakata-san wa subarashíi keireki o mótte iru. 中田さんはすばらしい経歴を持っている。 *Ms. Nakata has a remarkable resumé.*

keiren 痙攣 *muscle cramp; muscle spasm*   8i-kéiren 胃痙攣 *stomach cramp*   8Fukurahagi no kínniku ga keiren o okóshite iru. ふくらはぎ

の 筋肉が痙攣を起こしている。*I have a cramp in the calf of my leg.*

kéiri 経理 *accounts* 🔹keiri tantṓsha 経理担当者 *accountant* 🔹Watashi wa kono kaisha de kéiri o tantō-shite imasu. 私はこの会社で経理を担当しています。*I'm in charge of accounts at this company.*

keirin 競輪 *bicycle racing*

kéiro 経路 *route; course; channel* 🔹Kónkai no ryokō wa dónna kéiro o torimásu ka? 今回の旅行はどんな経路をとりますか。*What route are you taking on your next trip?*

Keirō no Hi 敬老の日 *Respect-for-the-Aged Day (September 15)*

keiryō 計量 *weight; measurement*

keisan 計算 *calculation* 🔹keisánki 計算機 *calculator* ——**keisan-suru** [vt] 計算する *calcute; compute*

keisatsu 警察 *(the) police* 🔹keisatsusho 警察署 *police station*

keisha 傾斜 *slope; inclination* ——**keisha-suru** [vi] 傾斜する *lean (toward); be inclined (toward)* 🔹Káre wa sayoku shisṓ ni keisha-shite iru. 彼は左翼思想に傾斜している。*He has leftist tendencies.*

Keishíchō 警視庁 *Metropolitan Police Department*

keishiki 形式 *form; formality* 🔹sonata kéishiki ソナタ形式 *sonata form* ——**keishikiteki [na]** 形式的 (な) *formal* 🔹keishikiteki na tetsúzuki 形式的な手続き *a formal procedure* ——**keishikiteki ni** 形式的に *formally*

kéishi-suru 軽視する *take lightly; slight* 🔹Watashi no íken wa ítsumo kéishi-sareru. 私の意見はいつも軽視される。*My opinion is always taken lightly.*

keishókudō 軽食堂 *café; short-order restaurant*

keisotsu [na] 軽率 (な) *rash; reckless; careless*

keitai 携帯 *portable* 🔹keitai dénwa 携帯電話 *portable telephone; cellular phone* ——**keitai-suru** [vt] 携帯する *carry (with one); have (on one's person)* 🔹Gaikokújin wa tsúne ni gaikokújin tṓrokusho o keitai-shinákereba naránai. 外国人は常に外国人登録証を携帯しなければならない。*Foreigners must always carry their alien registration with them.*

keito 毛糸 *woolen yarn; wool*

keiyaku 契約 *contract; (written) agreement* 🔹keiyaku kíkan 契約期間 *the term of a contract* 🔹keiyakusho o torikawasu 契約書を取り交わす *make a contract*

keiyṓshi 形容詞 *adjective (Gram)*

-keiyu 〜経由 *by way of; via* 🔹UA happyaku-ichi-bin wa Honoruru keiyu, Sanfuranshisuko-yuki désu. UA 801便はホノルル経由、サンフランシスコ行きです。*United Airlines Flight 801 is bound for San Francisco via Honolulu.*

kéizai 経済 *economy; finance* 🔹keizai énjo 経済援助 *economic assistance* 🔹keizai seichṓ-ritsu 経済成長率 *economic growth rate*

keizoku 継続 *continuation* §keizoku shíngi 継続審議 *continued deliberations* §Keizoku wa chikará nari. 継続は力なり。 *In continuing there is strength.* <set phrase> ——**keizoku-suru** [vt] 継続する *continue; run on* §Jíken no sṓsa wa íma demo keizoku-shite iru. 事件の捜査は今でも継続している。 *Investigation of the case is continuing.*

keizu 系図 *genealogy* (see also **kakéizu**)

kejimé けじめ *(clear-cut) distinction; difference* §kejimé o tsukéru けじめをつける *draw a distinction between; wrap up* §Mondai wa, káre ni kṓshi no kejimé ga nái kotó da. 問題は彼に公私のけじめがないことだ。 *The problem is, he doesn't make a distinction between his private and public affairs.* <masc>

kekka 結果 *result; consequence; effect* §gen'in to kekka 原因と結果 *cause and effect* §Tésuto no kekka wa dṓ datta? テストの結果はどうだった？ *What was the result of the test?* ——**kekkateki ni** 結果的に *consequently; as a result*

kekkan 血管 *blood vessel* §mōsai kékkan 毛細血管 *capillary*

kekkō 欠航 *cancellation* ——**kekkō-suru** [vt] 欠航する *cancel (a flight / sailing)* §Pairótto no sutoráiki de kyō wa zembin kekkō ni nátta. パイロットのストライキで今日は全便欠航になった。 *All flights today have been cancelled because of a pilots' strike.*

kékkō [na] 結構（な） *good; fine; splendid* §Kékkō na o-temae désu ne. 結構なお手前ですね。 *You're very good at that (e.g., serving tea).* §Iie, kékkō desu. いいえ、結構です。 *No, thank you (I've had enough **or** it's all right the way it is).*

kekkon 結婚 *marriage* §miai kékkon 見合い結婚 *arranged marriage* §ren'ai kékkon 恋愛結婚 *marriage for love (not arranged)* §kekkónshiki 結婚式 *wedding ceremony* ——**kekkon-suru** [vi] *marry* §kekkon-shite iru 結婚している *be married* §Ákiko-san wa Yamákawa-san to kekkon-shita. 明子さんは山川さんと結婚した。 *Akiko married Yamakawa.*

kekkyoku 結局 *after all* §Kekkyoku, Yamanaka-san wa kimasén deshita. 結局、山中さんは来ませんでした。 *Ms. Yamanaka didn't come after all.*

kembikyō 顕微鏡 *microscope*

kembutsu 見物 *sightseeing* §kembutsu ni iku 見物に行く *go sightseeing* ——**kembutsu-suru** [vt] 見物する *see the sights of; look at; visit*

kemono 獣 *beast*

kémpō 憲法 *constitution* §Nihonkoku kémpō 日本国憲法 *the Constitution of Japan*

kemu·i [adj kemuku nái; kemúkatta] 煙い *(be) smoky*

kemuri 煙 *smoke* §tabako no kemuri 煙草の煙 *cigarette smoke*

kemushí 毛虫 *caterpillar*
kén 県 *prefecture* ❀Hiroshimá-ken 広島県 *Hiroshima Prefecture* ❀kénchō 県庁 *prefectural office* ❀ken-chíji 県知事 *prefectural governor*
kén 券 *ticket*
kenas·u [*vt* kenasanai; kenashita] けなす *speak ill of; criticize*
kenchiku 建築 *construction; building; architecture* ❀kenchikuka 建築家 *architect* ❀kenchikúgaku 建築学 *architecture* ——**kenchiku-suru** [*vt*] 建築する *build; construct; erect*
kéndō 剣道 *fencing (with bamboo swords) (J)*
ken'ekisho 検疫所 *quarantine station*
ken'etsu 検閲 *censorship* ——**ken'etsu-suru** [*vt*] 検閲する *censor*
kengaku 見学 *(school / class) inspection; a visit (for study)* ——**kengaku-suru** [*vt*] 見学する *inspect; visit (for study)*
kén'i 権威 *authority; power; prestige* ❀kén'i o furuu 権威を振るう *flaunt (one's) authority (**or** throw one's weight around)* ❀Yagi-senséi wa Nihon bíjutsu no kén'i desu. 八木先生は日本美術の権威です。*Professor Yagi is an authority on Japanese art.*
kenjō 謙譲 *humility; modesty*
kenka 喧嘩 *a quarrel; disagreement; dispute; argument; spat; a fight* ——**kenka-suru** [*vi*] 喧嘩する *argue; quarrel; fight*
kenketsu 献血 *blood donation*
kenkin 献金 *financial contribution; donation* ❀kyōkai kénkin 教会献金 *church offering*
kenkō 健康 *health* ❀kenkō hóken 健康保険 *health insurance* ❀kenkō shíndan 健康診断 *health examination* ❀kenkō o gai-súru 健康を害する *injure one's health; ruin one's helath* ❀kenkō ni íi 健康にいい *good for one's health* ❀kenkō o kaifuku-suru 健康を回復する *recover one's health* ——**kenkōteki [na]** 健康的（な）*healthful*
kenkyū 研究 *research; study* ❀kenkyū´sha 研究者 *a researcher* ——**kenkyū-suru** [*vt*] 研究する *research; do research on; study* ❀Yamanaka-hákase wa idenshi chíryō o kenkyū-shite iru. 山中博士は遺伝子治療を研究している。*Dr. Yamanaka is doing research on genetic therapy.*
kénri 権利 *a right* ❀kénri o mamóru 権利を守る *protect (one's) right* ❀kénri o hōki-suru 権利を放棄する *relinquish (one's) right*
kénryoku 権力 *authority; power* ❀kokka kénryoku 国家権力 *governmental authority; state power* ❀kenryoku séiji 権力政治 *power politics*
kénsa 検査 *inspection; examination; a check(-up)* ❀mé no kénsa 目の検査 *eye examination*
kensatsu 検察 *criminal investigation* ❀kensatsúkan 検察官 *public prosecutor* ❀kensatsúkyoku 検察局 *criminal investigation bureau*

kenson 謙遜 *modesty; humility* ——**kenson na** 謙遜な *modest; humble; unassuming*

kentō 見当 *an aim; an estimate; a guess* ❸kentō o tsukéru 見当をつける *target; take aim at* ❸Kása o dóko ni okiwasureta ka, sappári kentō ga tsukánai. 傘をどこに置き忘れたかさっぱり見当がつかない。*I don't have the slightest idea where I left my umbrella.*

kentō 検討 *a study; an investigation* ——**kentō-suru** [vt] 検討する *examine; inquire into* ❸Sono kotó ni tsúite wa jūbún kentō-shité kara o-kotae shimásu. そのことについては十分検討してからお答えします。*We will reply after we have looked into the matter thoroughly.* <formal>

kenzen [na] 健全（な）*solid; healthy; sound; wholesome* ❸kenzen na goraku 健全な娯楽 *wholesome entertainment.* ——**kenzen ni** 健全に *wholesomely* ❸kodomo o kenzen ni ikusei-suru 子供を健全に育成する *raise children wholesomely*

keppaku 潔白 *innocence; purity* ——**keppaku na** 潔白な *innocent; pure* ❸mi no keppaku o shōmei-suru 身の潔白を証明する *prove one's innocence*

kérai 家来 *vassal; follower*

kéredomo けれども *however; but* ❸Kónsāto ni ikitákatta. Kéredomo shigoto ga átta no de ikanákatta. コンサートに行きたかった。けれども仕事があったので行かなかった。*I wanted to go to the concert. But (or However) I had some work to do, so I didn't go.*

kér·u [vt keránai; kétta] 蹴る *kick*

késa 今朝 *this morning*

keshigomu 消しゴム *(pencil) eraser*

keshiin 消印 *postmark; stamp*

Keshikarán! 怪しからん！ *That's unforgivable!; That's disgraceful!*

késhiki 景色 *scenery; view* ❸Nán to utsukushíi késhiki nan deshō! 何と美しい景色なんでしょう！*What a beautiful view!*

keshō 化粧 *makeup* ❸keshōhin 化粧品 *cosmetics* ——**keshō-suru** [vi] 化粧する *apply makeup* ❸O-matsuri de háha wa kodomo no kao ni keshō-shita. お祭りで母は子供の顔に化粧した。*Mother made up the children's faces for the festival.*

késsan 決算 *account; settlement* ❸kessan hōkoku 決算報告 *statement of accounts* ——**késsan-suru** [vi] 決算する *settle accounts*

kesseki 欠席 *absence* ——**kesseki-suru** 欠席する *be absent from* ❸Ashitá wa musuko no kekkón-shiki de káigi o kesseki-shimásu. 明日は息子の結婚式で会議を欠席します。*I am going to be absent from the meeting tomorrow because of my son's wedding.*

kessen 決戦 *decisive battle; championship match*

késshin 決心 *determination; resolution; decision* ❸Musumé wa isha ni náru késshin o shita. 娘は医者になる決心をした。*My daughter has* *made a decision to become a doctor.* ——**késshin-suru** [*vt*] 決心する *decide; determine; make up (one's) mind*

kesshite 決して *by no means; never* [*with neg*] ❀Kore kará wa kesshite úso o iimasén. これからは決してうそを言いません。*I will never tell a lie again.*

kesshō 決勝 *title match*

kesshō 結晶 *crystal* ——**kesshō-suru** [*vi*] 結晶する *crystalize*

kesshū-suru 結集する *concentrate; gather together* ❀Chikará o kesshū-shite, kono nankyoku o norikirṓ. 力を結集して、この難局を乗りきろう。*Let's concentrate our efforts and surmount these difficulties.*

kes·u [*vt* kesanai; keshita] 消す *put out; extinguish; erase; cancel* ❀hí o kesu 火を消す *put out a fire* ❀kokuban o kesu 黒板を消す *erase the blackboard* ❀térebi o kesu テレビを消す *turn off the TV*

ketá 桁 *crossbeam; girder; number; figure; digit* ❀hashí no ketá 橋の桁 *a bridge girder* ❀ié no ketá to hari 家の桁と梁 *crossbeams and pillars of a house* ❀Ichí wa hitóketa, jū́ wa futáketa, hyakú wa sánketa desu. 一は一桁、十は二桁、百は三桁です。*1 is one digit, 10 is two digits, and 100 is three digits.*

ketsuatsu 血圧 *blood pressure* ❀kōkétsuatsu 高血圧 *high blood pressure* ❀Anáta wa ketsuatsu ga takái. あなたは血圧が高い。*Your blood pressure is high.*

ketsubō 欠乏 *lack; want; running short of* ❀bitámin A ketsubōshō ビタミンA欠乏症 *vitamin A deficiency* ——**ketsubō-suru** [*vi*] 欠乏する *lack; run short of; need* ❀Jinzai ga ketsubō shite iru. 人材が欠乏している。*There is a shortage of personnel.* (**or** *We're shorthanded.*)

ketsúeki 血液 *blood* ❀ketsueki-gata 血液型 *blood type* ❀ketsueki kénsa 血液検査 *blood test*

kétsugi 決議 *decision; resolution* ——**kétsugi-suru** [*vt*] 決議する *decide; resolve; adopt (a resolution)* ❀Káigi de rainéndo no yosán'an ga kétsugi-sareta. 会議で来年度の予算案が決議された。*At the meeting, the (proposed) budget for the next fiscal year was adopted.*

ketsumakúen 結膜炎 *conjunctivitis*

ketsumatsu 結末 *conclusion; outcome*

ketsuron 結論 *conclusion; decision* ❀ketsuron o dásu 結論を出す *make* (**or** *draw*) *a conclusion* ❀Ketsuron ga déta. 結論が出た。*A conclusion was reached.*

kettei 決定 *decision; conclusion; settlement* ——**ketteiteki [na]** 決定的(な) *conclusive; decisive* ❀Ketteiteki na shōko ga mitsukatta. 決定的な証拠が見つかった。*Conclusive evidence was found.* ——**kettei-suru** [*vi*] *decide; settle; fix (on)* ❀Rainen no kónsāto no sukejū́ru ga kettei-shita. 来年のコンサートのスケジュールが決定した。*The schedule for next year's concerts is fixed.*

kettén 欠点 *defect; fault; flaw; weak point* ❀ketten dárake no sakuhin 欠

点だらけの作品 *a work full of flaws* **8**Kánojo wa okorippói no ga kettén desu. 彼女は怒りっぽいのが欠点です。 *Her weak point is her short temper.*

kettō 血統 *blood; lineage; family line*

kewashí·i [*adj* kewáshiku nái; kewáshikatta] 険しい *(be) steep; severe* **8**Nihon no yamá wa kewashíi miné ga takusan áru. 日本の山は険しい嶺が沢山ある。 *Japan's mountains have many steep peaks.*

keyaki 欅 keyaki *tree (J); (Tech) Zelkova serrata*

kezur·u [*vt* kezuranai; kezutta] 削る *sharpen; whittle; cut; shave (off)* **8**náifu de empitsu o kezuru ナイフで鉛筆を削る *sharpen a pencil with a knife* **8**yosan o kezuru 予算を削る *cut (or whittle down) the budget*

kí 木 *tree* **8**kí o ueru 木を植える *plant a tree* **8**kígi 木々 *trees*

ki 気 *spirit; mind; heart; feeling* **8**ki ga kawaru 気が変わる *change (one's) mind* **8**ki ga nái 気がない *not be interested in* **8**ki ga omoi 気が重い *(be) heavy-hearted* **8**ki ga suru 気がする *feel; have a feeling (that)* **8**Watashítachi wa tōzakátte iru yō na ki ga suru. 私たちは遠ざかっているような気がする。 *I feel we're drifting apart.* **8**ki ga tōku náru 気が遠くなる *lose consciousness; faint* **8**ki ga tsúku 気が付く *notice; be aware of; be attentive to* **8**ki ni iru 気に入る *like; be pleased with* **8**Sono dezáin wa hitóme míte ki ni itta. そのデザインは一目見て気に入った。 *I liked that design the moment I saw it.* **8**ki ni náru 気になる *worry about; be anxious about* **8**Kodomo no byōki ga dómo ki ni nátte shikata ga nái. 子供の病気がどうも気になって仕方がない。 *I'm so worried about my sick child I don't know what to do.* **8**ki o tsukéru 気を付ける *be careful* **8**Ki o tsúkete! 気を付けて！ *Be careful!; Take care!*

kiatsu 気圧 *atmospheric pressure* **8**kōkíatsu 高気圧 *high atmopheric pressure* **8**teikíatsu 低気圧 *low atmospheric pressure*

kíba 牙 *fang*

kiban 基盤 *base; basis; foundation* **8**seikatsu no kiban o kizúku 生活の基盤を築く *establish a basis for living*

kibatsu [na] 奇抜 (な) *original; novel*

kibin [na] 機敏 (な) *quick; prompt; smart; alert* **8**kibin na hannō 機敏な反応 *quick reaction*

kibishí·i [*adj* kibíshiku nái; kibíshikatta] 厳しい *(be) hard; strict; severe* **8**kibíshii seikatsu 厳しい生活 *a hard life* **8**Ano senséi wa kibíshíi. あの先生は厳しい。 *That teacher's strict.* ——**kibishísa** 厳しさ *strictness; severity*

kíbo 規模 *scale; scope* **8**daikíbo ni 大規模に *on a big scale*

kibō 希望 *hope; desire; wish* **8**Kibō o ushinawanáide! 希望を失わないで。 *Don't give up hope!* **8**Bengóshi ni náru no ga watashi no kibō dátta. 弁護士になるのが私の希望だった。 *It was my wish to become* *a lawyer.* ——**kibō-suru** [vt] 希望する *hope for; wish for; desire*

kíbun 気分 *feeling; mood* 🔹Íi kíbun da! いい気分だ。*I feel good!* <masc> 🔹Kíbun ga yóku arimasén. 気分がよくありません。*I don't feel well.* 🔹Benkyō-suru kíbun ni narénai. 勉強する気分になれない。*I just can't get into the mood for studying.*

kíchi 基地 *(military) base* 🔹kūgun kíchi 空軍基地 *airforce base*

kichigái 気違い *madness; insanity* ——**kichigái no** 気違いの *mad; insane*

kichínto きちんと *precisely; exactly; neatly* 🔹Heyá wa kichínto katazúite ita. 部屋はきちんと片付いていた。*The room was in good order (i.e., things were neatly in place).*

kichō [na] 貴重 (な) *precious; valuable* 🔹kichōhin 貴重品 *valuables; precious item* 🔹kichō na taiken 貴重な体験 *a valuable experience*

kichōmen [na] 几帳面 (な) *exact; punctual; methodical; precise* 🔹Murata-san wa súbete ni kichōmen desu. 村田さんはすべてに几帳面です。*Murata is methodical about everything.*

kidō 軌道 *track; rail; orbit* 🔹kidō ni noseru 軌道に乗せる *put (something) on track* 🔹Uchiage rokétto wa kidō ni notte iru. 打ち上げロケットは軌道に乗っている。*The rocket is now in orbit.*

kidor·u [vi kidoranai; kidotta] 気取る *be affected; put on airs; be conceited* ——**kidotta** [attr] 気取った *conceited; affected* 🔹kidotta hanashikata 気取った話し方 *an affected manner of speaking*

kidōtai 機動隊 *riot (police) squad*

kie·ru [vi kienai; kieta] 消える *be extinguished; go out; vanish* 🔹Dénki ga kyū ni kieta. 電気が急に消えた。*The light suddenly went out.* 🔹Tantei ga áto o tsúkete ita hitó wa hitogomi ni kieta. 探偵が後を付けていた人は人ごみに消えた。*The person the detective was tailing vanished into the crowd.*

kífu 寄付 *contribution; donation* ——**kífu-suru** [vt] 寄付する *contribute; donate*

kigae 着替え *change of clothes* 🔹kigae o suru 着替えをする *change one's clothes*

kígai 危害 *injury; harm* 🔹kígai o kuwaeru 危害を加える *inflict an injury*

kigákari 気掛かり *anxiety; concern*

kigane 気がね *constraint* ——**kigane-suru** [vi] *feel hesitant (about); be ill at ease; be uncomfortable* 🔹Súmisu-san wa kigane-shite iru yōsu deshita. スミスさんは気がねしているようすでした。*Mr. Smith looked ill at ease.* 🔹Kigane-shinai aité ga hoshíi. 気がねしない相手がほしい。*I want a partner I can feel comfortable with.*

kigaru ni 気軽に *in a carefree manner; lightly ; readily* 🔹Ōyamá-shi wa watashi no tanomigoto o kigaru ni hikiúkete kureta. 大山氏は私の頼みごとを気軽に引き受けてくれた。*Mr. Ōyama readily accepted my* *request* .

kígeki 喜劇 *comedy* ——**kigekiteki [na]** 喜劇的（な）*comical*

kigen 機嫌 *health; mood; (one's) humor* ❈Kyō wa ákachan no kigen ga íi. 今日は赤ちゃんの機嫌がいい。*Today the baby's in a good mood.* ❈Go-kigen ikága desu ka? 御機嫌いかがですか。*How are you? <formal>*

kígen 期限 *time limit; term* ❈Kono shigoto o keiyakusho no kígen máde ni shiagéru yṓ ni dóryoku-shimasu. この仕事を契約書の期限までに仕上げるように努力します。*I will try hard to finish this job within the time limit of the contract.*

kígen 紀元 *era; epoch* ❈kígen-zén nisen-nen 紀元前2000年 *the year 2000 B.C.*

kígen 起源 *origin; beginning* ❈bummei no kígen 文明の起源 *the origin of civilization*

kigō 記号 *a mark; symbol* ❈hatsuon kígō 発音記号 *phonetic symbol* ❈kagaku kígō 化学記号 *chemical symbol* ❈kigṓron 記号論 *semiotics*

kígu 器具 *implement; utensil; appliance*

kígyō 企業 *business; enterprise; undertaking, industry* ❈daikígyō 大企業 *big business* ❈shōkigyō 小企業 *small business* ❈fukugō kigyōtai 複合企業体 *conglomerate*

kihan 規範 *a standard; the norm*

kiheitai 騎兵隊 *cavalry*

kihin 気品 *dignity; grace* ❈Anó hito wa kihin ga áru. あの人は気品がある。*That person has dignity. (or He has class.)*

kihon 基本 *base* ❈kihónkyū 基本給 *base salary* ——**kihonteki [na]** 基本的（な）*basic; fundamental* ❈kihonteki jinken 基本的人権 *fundamental human rights* ——**kihonteki ni** 基本的に *basically; fundamentally*

kiiro 黄色 *yellow* ——**kiiro·i** [adj kiiroku nái; kiirókatta] 黄色い *(be) yellow*

kíji 生地 *cloth; material; dough; pastry crust* ❈Kono kíji wa asetḗto desu. この生地はアセテートです。*This material is acetate.* ❈pan kíji パン生地 *bread dough*

kíji 記事 *article; (news) item*

kiji 雉子 *pheasant*

kijun 基準 *standard*

kijutsu 記述 *(written) description* ——**kijutsu-suru** [vt] 記述する *describe*

kíka 帰化 *naturalization* ——**kíka-suru** [vi] 帰化する *become a naturalized citizen*

kikágaku 幾何学 *geometry*

kikái 機会 *opportunity* ❈kikái kintō 機会均等 *equal opportunity*

§Kekkon no kikái o nogáshite shimatta. 結婚の機会をのがしてしまった。*I lost my chance at marriage.*

kikái 機械 *machine; machinery* §kikái o ugokásu 機械を動かす *operate a machine* ——**kikaiteki [na]** 機械的（な）*mechanical* —— **kikaiteki ni** 機械的に *mechanically*

kikaika 機械化 *mechanization* ——**kikaika-suru** [*vt*] 機械化する *mechanize*

kikaku 企画 *a plan*

kikaku 規格 *a standard* §Nihon kōgyō kíkaku 日本工業規格 *Japan Industrial Standards* ——**kikakuka-suru** [*vt*] 規格化する *standardize*

kikán 期間 *term; period* §Rṓn no hensai kíkan ga mijikasugíru. ローンの返済期間が短すぎる。*The period for loan repayment is too short.*

kikán 機関 *facility; organ; machine; engine* §hōdō kíkan 報道機関 *the press; news organ* §kōtsū kíkan 交通機関 *traffic facilities* §kin'yū kíkan 金融機関 *financial agency* §kikánsha 機関車 *a locomotive* §kikanjū 機関銃 *machine gun*

kikanshíen 気管支炎 *bronchitis*

kiken 棄権 *abstention (from voting)* ——**kiken-suru** [*vt*] 棄権する *abstain*

kíki 危機 *crisis* §kíki ni chokumen-suru 危機に直面する *face a crisis* §kíki o norikoéru 危機を乗り越える *overcome (**or** survive) a crisis*

kikiiré·ru [*vt* kikiirénai; kikiíreta] 聞き入れる *listen to; hear; accept* §Watshi no o-negai o kikiírete kudasátte arígatō. 私のお願いを聞き入れて下さってありがとう。*Thank you for accepting my request.*

kikime 効き目 *effect; efficacy* §Kono kusuri wa kikime ga áru. この薬は効き目がある。 *This medicine is effective.*

kikín 飢饉 *famine*

kikín 基金 *foundation; funding organization; fund* §kikín o atsumeru 基金を集める *raise funds*

kikkake きっかけ *opportunity; motivation* §kikkake o tsukámu きっかけをつかむ *seize an opportunity*

kikkári きっかり *just; exactly* §ichiman'en kikkári 一万円きっかり *exactly ten thousand yen* §ichiji kikkári 1時きっかり *one o'clock sharp* §kikkári to kúbetsu-suru きっかりと区別する *make a clear distinction*

kikō 気候 *climate; weather*

kikoe·ru [*vi* kikoenai; kikoeta] 聞こえる *be heard; can be heard* §Nami no otó ga kikoeru. 波の音が聞こえる。*You can hear the sound of the waves.* §Watashi no kóe ga kikoemásu ka? 私の声が聞こえますか。*Can you hear me?*

kik·u [*vt/vi* kikanai; kiita] 聞く *hear; listen to; ask* §óngaku o kiku 音楽を聞く *listen to music* §Musuko wa watashi no iu kotó o kikanai. 息子は私の言うことを聞かない。*My son doesn't listen to what I say.*

§Senséi ni kiite míte kudasái. 先生に聞いてみて下さい。*Ask the teacher.*

kik·u [*vi* kikanai; kiita] 効く；利く *be efficacious; have effect* §kusuri ga kiku 薬が効く *medicine has effect* §Burěki ga kikanákatta. ブレーキが利かなかった。*The brake didn't engage. (or The brake didn't work.)* §Hoken ga kikimásu ka? 保険が利きますか。*Will my insurance cover it?*

kikú 菊 *chrysanthemum*

kimari 決まり *a rule; conclusion; settlement* §kimari ga tsúku 決まりがつく *be settled* §kimari mónku 決まり文句 *fixed way of saying; hackneyed expression* §kimari ga warúi 決まりが悪い *feel embarrassed; feel awkward*

kimar·u [*vi* kimaranai; kimatta] 決まる *be decided; be settled* §Kekkónshiki no hidori ga kimatta. 結婚式の日取りが決まった。*The day of the wedding ceremony has been decided.*

kimben [na] 勤勉（な）*industrious; diligent*

kime·ru [*vt* kimenai; kimeta] 決める *decide; set*

kimi 君 *you (a familiar expression generally used to address intimates or people younger in age or rank) <masc>*

kimi 黄身 *egg yolk*

kímmu 勤務 *service; duty; work* §kimmu jíkan 勤務時間 *working hours* ——**kímmu-suru** [*vi*] 勤務する *work; perform a duty*

kimó 肝 *liver (Anat); courage; nerve* §kimó no chīsái hitó 肝の小さい人 *a timid person* §kimó ga suwatte iru hitó 肝がすわっている人 *a person with nerves of steel* §kimó o hiyásu 肝を冷やす *be struck with terror* §kimó o tsubusu 肝をつぶす *be amazed*

kimochi 気持ち *feeling; sensation; mood* §kimochi ga warúi. 気持ちが悪い *unpleasant* §sawáyaka de íi kimochi さわやかでいい気持ち *refreshing and pleasant feeling* §Aite no kimochi o taisetsu ni shiyő. 相手の気持ちを大切にしよう。*One should respect others' feelings.*

kimono 着物 *clothing; Japanese-style dress*

kimpatsu 金髪 *blond hair; a blonde*

kímyō [na] 奇妙（な）*strange; odd*

kín 菌 *bacillus; germ* §baikin ばい菌 *germ; bacillus* §saikin 細菌 *microbe*

kín 金 *gold* §kin'iro 金色 *gold color* §jūhachi kin 十八金 *18 karat gold* §kimpaku 金箔 *gold leaf*

kinchō 緊張 *tension; strain* §kinchō no omomochi 緊張の面持ち *a strained expression* §kinchō kánwa 緊張緩和 *alleviation of tension* ——**kinchō-suru** [*vi*] 緊張する *be tense* §Kinchō-shite nemurenai. 緊張して眠れない。*I'm so tense I can't get to sleep.*

kíndai 近代 *the modern age; recent times*

kindaika 近代化 *modernization* §kyūsoku na kindaika séisaku 急速な

近代化政策 *a policy of rapid modernization* ——**kindaika-suru** [*vt*] 近代化する *modernize*

kinémbi 記念日 *commemoration day; anniversary* ❸kekkon kinémbi 結婚記念日 *wedding anniversary*

kinénhi 記念碑 *monument; memorial*

kingaku 金額 *amount of money; sum; total*

kingan 近眼 *nearsighted* ❸Musuko wa kingan desu. 息子は近眼です。 *My son is nearsighted.*

kíngyo 金魚 *goldfish*

kinji·ru [*vt* kinjinai; kinjita] 禁じる *forbid; prohibit*

kínjo 近所 *neighborhood; vicinity* ❸ kínjo no misé 近所の店 *neighborhood store* ❸Kono kínjo ni kōban ga arimásu ka? この近所に交番がありますか。 *Is there a police box in this vicinity?*

kínko 金庫 *a safe; a vault*

kinkō 均衡 *a balance* ❸kinkō o tamótsu 均衡を保つ *maintain a balance*

kinkyō 近況 *recent conditions; developments* ❸Kinkyō o o-shirase kudasái. 近況をお知らせ下さい。*Inform me of (any) recent developments.*

kinkyū 緊急 *emergency* ❸kinkyū sóchi 緊急措置 *emergency measures* ❸kinkyū kyūsai 緊急救済 *emergency relief* ——**kinkyū no** 緊急の *urgent* ❸kinkyū no yōji 緊急の用事 *urgent business*

kínniku 筋肉 *muscle*

kinō 昨日 *yesterday*

kínō 機能 *function* ❸Shinzō no kínō ga otoróete iru. 心臓の機能がおとろえている。*(Your) heart's function(ing) is weak.* ——**kinōteki [na]** 機能的（な）*functional* ——**kinōteki ni** 機能的に *functionally*

kinodokú [na] 気の毒（な）*pitiable; miserable* ❸kinodokú ni omou 気の毒に思う *pity (someone)* ❸O-kinodoku-sama. お気の毒さま。*Too bad! (or I'm sorry (for you)!)* [Caution! *This expression may be used ironically.*]

kínoko 茸 *mushroom* ❸kinoko-gari 茸狩り *mushroom gathering*

kínome 木の芽 *a bud; young leaves of Japanese pepper*

kinrō 勤労 *labor; work* ❸kinrō káikyū 勤労階級 *the working class* ❸kinrósha 勤労者 *a laborer* ❸kinrō shótoku 勤労所得 *earned income* ❸Kinrō Kánsha no Hi 勤労感謝の日 *Labor Thanksgiving Day (J)*

Kinsei 金星 *the planet Venus*

kinshi 禁止 *forbidden* ❸Kin'en! 禁煙！*No Smoking!* ❸kinseihin 禁製品 *contraband* ——**kinshi-suru** [*vt*] *ban; forbid* ❸Nihón de wa jū no yunyū wa kinshi-sarete iru. 日本では銃の輸入は禁止されている。*In Japan, importing guns is forbidden.*

kinshi 近視 *shortsighted* ——**kinshiteki [na]** 近視的（な）*shortsighted;*

myopic &kinshiteki na seisaku 近視的な政策 *a shortsighted policy*

Kintō 近東 *the Near East*

kínu 絹 *silk* &kinu ito 絹糸 *silk thread*

Kin'yőbi 金曜日 *Friday*

kin'yoku 禁欲 *asceticism*

kin'yū 金融 *finance; financing* &kin'yū győkai 金融業界 *monetary circles* &kin'yū séisaku 金融政策 *monetary policy*

kinyū 記入 *written entry* ——**kinyū-suru** [vt] 記入する *make an entry; write in; record* **kínzoku** 金属 *metal* &kinzoku kőgyō 金属工業 *metalworking industry*

kioku 記憶 *memory* &kioku ga nái 記憶がない *have no memory of* ——**kioku-suru** [vt] 記憶する *remember* &Sono résutoran no namae o kioku-shite imásu ka. そのレストランの名前を記憶していますか. *Do you remember the name of that restaurant?*

kion 気温 *atmospheric temperature*

kippári [to] きっぱり（と）*flatly; definitely; clearly*

kippu 切符 *a ticket* &kippu úriba 切符売り場 *ticket office* &őfuku kíppu 往復切符 *round-trip ticket; return ticket* &supído íhan no kippu スピード違反の切符 *a speeding ticket*

kirai [na] 嫌い（な）*dislike; hate* &Kirai na tabemóno ga arimásu ka? 嫌いな食べ物がありますか. *Is there any food you dislike?* &Nattő ga kirai désu. 納豆が嫌いです. *I don't like nattō.*

kírakira [to] きらきら（と）*glistening; sparkling* &Yózora de hoshi ga kírakira to hikátte iru. 夜空で星がきらきらと光っている. *Stars are twinkling in the night sky.* ——**kírakira-suru** [vi] きらきらする *glisten; sparkle*

kiraku [na] 気楽（な）*easygoing; carefree* ——**kiraku ni** 気楽に *at ease; easily*

kira·u [vt kirawanai; kiratta] 嫌う *dislike; hate; despise* &Anó hito wa watashi o kiratte iru yő desu. あの人は私を嫌っているようです. *That person seems to dislike me.*

kiré 切れ *a cloth*

kírei [na] 奇麗（な）*pretty; nice-looking; beautiful; clean; neat* &kírei na haná 奇麗な花 *a beautiful flower* ——**kírei ni** きれいに *neatly; clean(ly)* &Heyá o kírei ni shite óita. 部屋をきれいにしておいた. *I left the room clean.*

kiré·ru [vi kirénai; kíreta] 切れる *cut off; run out; be exhausted; be out of (supplies);* &íki ga kiréru 息が切れる *be out of breath* &Gasorin ga kírete shimatta. ガソリンが切れてしまった. *I ran out of gasoline.* &Káre to wa mő én ga kírete iru. 彼とはもう縁が切れている. *I no longer have any relation to him.*

kiré·ru [vi kirénai; kíreta] 切れる *be sharp; cut well; shrewd* &Yóku kiréru hőchō ga arimásu ka? よく切れる包丁がありますか. *Do you* have a kitchen knife that cuts well? ▯Aitsu wa nakanaka kiréru otoko da. あいつはなかなか切れる男だ。 *He's very sharp.* <*masc*>

kiri 霧 *fog* ▯kiri ga kakáru 霧がかかる *fog gathers* ▯Kiri ga háreta. 霧が晴れた。 *The fog cleared.*

kiri 桐 *paulownia* ▯kiri dánsu 桐だんす *a chest of paulownia wood*

kirinuki 切り抜き *(newspaper) clipping*

kirinuk·u [vt kirinukanai; kirinuita] 切り抜く *cut out; clip* ▯Shimbun kara ryōri kíji o kirinuite iru. 新聞から料理記事を切り抜いている。 *I'm clipping cooking articles from the newspaper.*

Kirisutokyō キリスト教 *Christianity*

-kíro 〜キロ *kilograms; kilometers*

kiroku 記録 *record; documentation* ▯kiroku ni nokósu 記録に残す *put on record* ▯sekai shin kíroku 世界新記録 *a new world record* —— **kiroku-suru** [vt] 記録する *record*

kír·u [vt kiránai; kítta] 切る *cut; clip; punch (a ticket); turn off (electricity); drain off (water)* ▯kí o kíru 木を切る *fell a tree* ▯hasamí de kíru はさみで切る *cut with scissors* ▯Dénki o kítte kudasái. 電気を切って下さい。 *Turn off the light, please.*

ki·ru [vt kinai; kita] 着る *wear; put on (clothing)* ▯Ōbā o kita hố. ga íi yo. オーバーを着た方がいいよ。 *You ought to wear an overcoat.*

kiseki 奇跡 *miracle* ▯kiseki o okósu 奇跡を起こす *perform a miracle* —— **kisekiteki [na]** 奇跡的（な） *miraculous* —— **kisekiteki ni** 奇跡的に *miraculously*

kise·ru [vt kisenai; kiseta] 着せる *dress (someone); put (clothing) on (someone)* ▯Háha wa ítsumo kodomo ni ōbā o kiseta. 母はいつも子供にオーバーを着せた。 *Mother always put the children's overcoats on them.*

kisétsu 季節 *season (of the year)* ▯kisetsu ryōri 季節料理 *food in season*

kishá 記者 *news reporter; journalist* ▯kisha káiken 記者会見 *press conference*

kishá 汽車 *(non-electric) train*

kishí 岸 *shore; bank* ▯kawagishí 川岸 *river bank*

kishō 気象 *weather* ▯kishōchō 気象庁 *weather bureau; Meteorological Agency* ▯Koko no tokoro ijō kíshō ga tsuzuite iru. ここのところ異常気象が続いている。 *We've been having unusual weather lately.*

kisó 基礎 *foundation; fundamentals* ▯kiso kốji 基礎工事 *foundation construction* ▯Sūgaku no kisó o shikkári benkyō-shite óita. 数学の基礎をしっかり勉強しておいた。 *I studied the fundamentals of mathematics thoroughly.*

kisóku 規則 *rule; regulation* ▯kisóku o mamóru 規則を守る *keep a rule; abide by the regulations* ▯kisóku o yabúru 規則を破る *break a rule*

kissáten 喫茶店 *coffee shop; tea room*

kisū 奇数 *odd number (vs. even number)*

kitá 北 *north*

kitaé·ru [*vt* kitaénai; kitáeta] 鍛える *forge; build up through training* §ude o kitaéru 腕を鍛える *develop one's skill*

kitai 期待 *expectation; hope* §kitai ni kotaéru 期待に応える *fulfill an expectation* §kitai o uragíru 期待を裏切る *betray a hope* ——**kitai-suru** [*vt*] 期待する *expect; hope for; look forward to* §Kotoshi kóso, kachō shōshin o kitai-shite iru. 今年こそ課長昇進を期待している。 *This year (at last) I expect to be promoted to section chief.*

kitaku 帰宅 *returning home* ——**kitaku-suru** [*vi*] 帰宅する *return home*

kitaná·i [*adj* kitanáku nái; kitanákatta] 汚い *(be) dirty; soiled; foul* §kitanái fukú 汚い服 *dirty clothes* §kitanái kotoba-zúkai 汚い言葉遣い *foul language*

kitei 規定 *regulation; rule*

kitei 基底 *(philosophical) base*

kiten 起点 *starting point*

kitókai 祈祷会 *prayer meeting*

kitoku 危篤 *dangerously ill* §Kókyō no háha kara chichí ga kitoku to no shirase o úketa. 故郷の母から父が危篤との知らせを受けた。 *I received a letter from mother that my father is dangerously ill.*

kitsuen 喫煙 *smoking* §kitsuénseki 喫煙席 *smoking section* §Kitsuen Kínshi. 喫煙禁止。 *No Smoking.*

kitsu·i [*adj* kitsuku nái; kitsúkatta] きつい *(be) tight; stern; strong; intense; tough; rigorous* §kitsui kao o suru きつい顔つき *look stern; have a forbidding look (or expression) on one's face* §Kono kutsú wa sukóshi kitsui. この靴は少しきつい。 *These shoes are a little tight.* §Sono shigoto wa kitsúkute taerarénai. その仕事はきつくて耐えられない。 *The work is so hard I can't stand it.* ——**kitsuku** きつく *rigorously; sternly; intensely; severely* §Watashi wa kitsuku shikarareta. 私はきつく叱られた。 *I was severely scolded.*

kitsune 狐 *fox*

kitsuon shṓgai 吃音障害 *stuttering; stammering*

kitsútsuki 啄木鳥 *woodpecker*

kitte 切手 *postage stamp* §kitte shūshūka 切手収集家 *a stamp collector* §Hyaku-jūen kítte o ichímai kudasái. 百十円切手を一枚下さい。 *Give me a ¥110 stamp, please.*

kitto きっと *surely; certainly; without fail; undoubtedly* §Kánojo wa kitto kimásu. 彼女はきっと来ます。 *She'll come without fail. (or I'm certain she'll come.)*

kiwámete 極めて *exceedingly; extremely* §Kiwámete shinkoku na jítai ga hassei-shita. 極めて深刻な事態が発生した。 *An extremely serious condition has arisen.*

kíyō [na] 器用（な）*clever; skillful; dexterous* ▓Mákiko-san wa tesakí ga kíyō desu. まき子さんは手先が器用です。*Makiko has nimble fingers.* —**kíyō ni** 器用に *cleverly; skillfully*

kiyói [*adj* kíyoku nái; kíyokatta] 清い *(be) pure; clean; clear* ▓kiyói mizu 清い水 *clear water* ▓kiyói tsukiái 清い付き合い *a platonic relationship* ▓kiyói kokoro no hitó 清い心の人 *a person with a pure heart*

kiyomé·ru [*vt* kiyoménai; kiyómeta] 清める *purify; cleanse* ▓mi o kiyoméru 身を清める *purify oneself*

kíyosa 清さ *purity*

kizam·u [*vt* kizamanai; kizanda] 刻む *chop finely; mince; carve; inscribe; etch* ▓kyábetsu o kizamu キャベツを刻む *shred cabbage* ▓butsuzō o kizamu 仏像を刻む *carve a Buddhist statue* ▓tokí o kizamu 時を刻む *tick away the time* ▓Háha no omoide wa íma demo mábuta ni kizamarete iru. 母の思い出は今でもまぶたに刻まれている。*The memory of my mother is even now etched on my eyelids.*

kizetsu 気絶 *loss of consciousness* —**kizetsu-suru** [*vi*] 気絶する *faint; lose consciousness*

kízoku 貴族 *aristocrat; nobility* ▓kizoku káikyū 貴族階級 *the aristocracy; the aristocrat class* —**kizokuteki [na]** 貴族的（な）*aristocratic*

kizu 傷 *a wound; injury; a cut* ▓kizu o ou 傷を負う *suffer an injury* ▓kizu-ato 傷跡 *a scar*

kizúk·u [*vt* kizukánai; kizúita] 築く *build; construct* ▓seikatsu o kizúku 生活を築く *build a life* ▓Kono shiro wa daimyō ga kizúita. この城は大名が築いた。*A daimyo built this castle.*

kizúk·u [*vi / vt* kizukánai; kizúita] 気付く *notice; become aware* ▓Sono koto ni wa kizukánakatta. そのことには気付かなかった。*I didn't notice that.* ▓Jibun no machigai ni kizúita. 自分の間違いにきづいた。*I realized my mistake.*

kizutsuké·ru [*vt* kizutsukénai; kizutsúketa] 傷つける *injure; wound; damage; mar* ▓kokoró o kizutsukéru 心を傷つける *wound (someone's) heart* ▓méiyo o kizutsukéru 名誉を傷つける *damage (someone's) reputation* ▓Jiténsha de butsukatte hokōsha o kizutsúkete shimatta. 自転車でぶつかって歩行者を傷つけてしまった。*I hit a pedestrian with my bicycle and injured him.*

kizutsúk·u [*vi* kizutsukánai; kizutsúita] 傷つく *be injured; be wounded; be hurt* ▓Kánojo wa kizutsúku no ga kowái kara ren'ai o shinai. 彼女は傷つくのが恐いから恋愛をしない。*She doesn't want to fall in love because she's afraid of being hurt.*

ko 子 *child*

kō 香 *incense* ▓kō o taku 香を焚く *burn incense*

kō こう *thus; in this manner; such* ▓Kō shite mítara dō desu ka? こうし

てみたらどうですか。 *How about trying it this way?* 🔹Kō iu shitsumon ní wa kotaetáku nái. こういう質問には答えたくない。*I'd rather not answer such questions.*

kōan 公安 *public peace* 🔹kōan no íji 公安の維持 *maintenance of public peace*

kobám·u [*vt* kobamánai; kobánda] 拒む *refuse; reject*

kōban 交番 *police box*

kōbashí·i [*adj* kōbáshiku nái; kōbáshíkatta] 香ばしい *(be) fragrant; aromatic*

koboré·ru [*vi* koborénai; kobóreta] 零れる *spill; drop; fall* 🔹námida ga koboréru 涙がこぼれる *tears drop (or flow)*

kobós·u [*vt* kobosánai; kobóshita] 零す *spill* 🔹o-cha o kobósu お茶をこぼす *spill tea* 🔹guchi o kobósu 愚痴をこぼす *complain*

kobushi 拳 *fist* 🔹kobushi o furiagéru 拳を振り上げる *shake (one's) fist*

kōcha 紅茶 *black tea*

kōchaku-suru [*vi*] 膠着する *adhere; be cemented* 🔹Nikokúkan no kōshō wa kōchaku-shite iru. 二国間の交渉は膠着している。 *Negotiations between the two countries have reached a stalemate.*

kóchi コーチ *a coach (for sports)*

kochira こちら *this direction; this person* 🔹Kochira e dózo! こちらへどうぞ! *Please come this way!* 🔹Tóire wa kochira désu. トイレはこちらです。*The restroom is this way.* 🔹Kochira wa Tanaka-san désu. こちらは田中さんです。*This is Mrs. Tanaka.* <polite>

Kochira kóso. こちらこそ。 *How do you do? (as a response)* 🔹"Hajimemáshite, dózo yoroshiku." "Kochira kóso." 「始めまして、どうぞよろしく。」「こちらこそ。」*"How do you do?" "How do you do?"* <formal>

kochō 誇張 *exaggeration* ——**kochō-suru** [*vt*] 誇張する *exaggerate*

kōchō 校長 *principal (of a school)*

kōchū 甲虫 *beetle* 🔹Koganémushi ya hótaru o kōchū to iu. 黄金虫や蛍を甲虫と言う。*The gold bug and firefly are classified as beetles.*

kódachi 木立 *grove of trees*

kódai 古代 *ancient period* 🔹kodai íseki 古代遺跡 *ancient ruins* 🔹kodái-shi 古代史 *ancient history*

kōdai [na] 広大（な）*vast; extensive; grand* 🔹kōdai na shikichi 広大な敷地 *extensive grounds; a big plot* 🔹kōdai na kōsō 広大な構想 *a great concept* 🔹kōdai na kíbo ni 広大な規模に *on a grand scale*

kodama 木霊；谺 *echo*

kōdan 講談 *story; storytelling*

kōdo 高度 *altitude; height* 🔹Kono hikóki wa kódo samman fíto o tonde iru. この飛行機は高度30,000フィートを飛んでいる。*This aircraft is flying at an altitude of 30,000 feet.*

kōdō 講堂 *auditorium; hall*

kōdō 行動 *action; behavior; conduct* ⑧kōdō kágaku 行動科学 *behavioral science* ⑧Kodomo no kōdō hán'i wa semái. 子供の行動範囲は狭い。*A child's field of action is limited.* ⑧Kangáe o kōdō ni utsushinasái. 考えを行動に移しなさい。*Put your thoughts into action.* ——**kōdō-suru** [vi] 行動する *act; behave; conduct onself* ⑧katte ni kōdō-suru 勝手に行動する *act willfully*

kodomo 子供; 子ども *child* ⑧otona to kodomo 大人と子供 *adults and children* ⑧kodomo-dámashi 子供騙し *mere child's play; a childish trick* ⑧kodomo-rashíi 子供らしい *childlike* ⑧Tárō-kun wa kodomo rashíi kodomo desu. 太郎君は子供らしい子供です。*Taro is just like a child should be.*

kodomoppó·i [adj kodomoppóku nái; kodomoppókatta] 子供っぽい *childish* ⑧Yoshida-san wa sánjū nimo náru no ni kangáe ga imada ni kodomoppói. 吉田さんは30にもなるのに考えが未だに子供っぽい。*Yoshida is thirty years old, but his ideas are still childish.*

kóe 声 *voice* ⑧íi kóe いい声 *a good voice* ⑧ikari no kóe 怒りの声 *an angry voice* ⑧kóe o dásu 声を出す *speak* ⑧Kotori no kóe ga suru. 小鳥の声がする。*You can hear birds singing.* ⑧Tonari no ókusan wa ítsumo kigaru ni kóe o kákete kureru. 隣の奥さんはいつも気軽に声をかけてくれる。*The lady next door always greets me in a friendly manner.*

koeda 小枝 *sprig; twig*

kōei 光栄 *honor* ⑧O-me ni kakárete kōei désu. お目にかかれて光栄です。*I am honored to meet you. <formal>*

kōen 公園 *a park* ⑧kokuritsu kōen 国立公園 *national park* ⑧shizen kōen 自然公園 *nature park* ⑧jidō kōen 児童公園 *children's park*

kōen 講演 *a lecture* ——**kōen-suru** [vt] 講演する *lecture; give a lecture*

kōen 後援 *support* ⑧kōenkai 後援会 *supporting organization; fan club* ⑧Mombúshō no kōen o ukéru 文部省の後援を受ける *receive support from the Ministry of Education*

kōen 公演 *performance* ——**kōen-suru** [vt] 公演する *perform*

koe·ru [vt koenai; koeta] 越える *rise above; surmount* ⑧yamá o koeru 山を越える *cross over a mountain* ⑧kokkyō o koeru 国境を越える *cross a national boundary* ⑧Kodomo wa táion ga yonjúdo o koeta. 子供は体温が40度を越えた。*The child's temperature is over forty degrees Celcius.*

kōfuku 幸福 *happiness*

kofun 古墳 *ancient tomb; ancient burial mound* ⑧kofun jídai 古墳時代 *Tumulus Period (250—552 A.D.)*

kōfun 興奮 *excitement* ——**kōfun-suru** [vi] 興奮する *be excited* ⑧Kōfun-shite nemurenákatta. 興奮して眠れなかった。*I was so excited I couldn't sleep.*

kōgai 公害 *environmental pollution* ❈kōgai táisaiku 公害対策 *pollution countermeasure* ❈sōon kōgai 騒音公害 *noise pollution*

kōgai 郊外 *suburb* ❈Tōkyō no kōgai 東京の郊外 *a Tokyo suburb*

kogás·u [vt kogasánai; kogáshita] 焦がす *burn; scorch; singe* ❈Airon de kono shátsu o kogáshite shimatta. アイロンでこのシャツを焦がしてしまった。*I scorched this shirt with an iron.*

kogata [no] 小型（の）*small-sized* ❈kogata jísho 小型辞書 *pocket-size dictionary* ❈kogatá-jū 小型銃 *handgun* ❈kogatá-sha 小型車 *compact car*

kōgeki 攻撃 *the offensive; aggression; attack* ❈Ano barēbōru chímu wa kōgeki wa tokúi, da ga shúbi ga imáichi da. あのバレーボールのチームは攻撃は得意だが守備が今一だ。*That volleyball team is good on the offensive, but it lacks a little on the defensive.* <masc> ── **kōgekiteki [na]** 攻撃的（な）*aggresive* ❈kōgekiteki na seikaku 攻撃的な性格 *an aggressive nature* ── **kogekiteki ni** 攻撃的に *aggressively* ❈kōgekiteki ni tōron o shikakéru 攻撃的に討論を仕掛ける *argue aggressively* ── **kogeki-suru** [vt] 攻撃する *attack* ❈Gérira wa seifú-gun o kōgeki-shita. ゲリラは政府軍を攻撃した。*Guerillas attacked the government forces.*

kōgen 高原 *plateau; tableland; highlands*

kogé·ru [vi kogénai; kogeta] 焦げる *burn; scorch* ❈Náni ka kógeta niói ga suru. 何か焦げた臭いがする。*I smell something burning.*

kōgí 講義 *a lecture; a class* ❈kōgí o suru 講義をする *give a lecture; conduct a class*

kōgi 抗議 *complaint; protest* ── **kōgi-suru** [vi] 抗議する *complain; protest* ❈Jūmin wa gempatsu kéikaku ni kōgi-shite iru. 住民は原発計画に抗議している。*The citizens are protesting the plans for a nuclear power plant.*

kogítte 小切手 *bank draft; check* ❈ryokō kogítte 旅行小切手 *traveler's check* ❈Kogítte de shiharátte mo íi desu ka? 小切手で支払ってもいいですか。*May I pay by check?*

kōgó 口語 *the spoken language; colloquial language*

kōgo [no] 交互（の）*mutual; reciprocal* ── **kōgo ni** 交互に *alternately; by turns* ❈Watashítachi wa kōgo ni kuruma o unten-shita. 私たちは交互に車を運転した。*We took turns driving (the car).*

kōgō 皇后 *empress; queen* ❈Kōgō héika 皇后陛下 *Her Imperial Majesty, the Empress*

kogoe·ru [vi kogoenai; kogoeta] 凍える *become numb (from the cold)*

kóg·u [vt kogánai; kóida] 漕ぐ *row (a boat)* ❈Iké de bóto o kóida. 池でボートを漕いだ。*We rowed a boat in the pond.*

kōgyō 工業 *industry* ❈kōgyō chítai 工業地帯 *industrial belt* ❈kōgyō kōkō 工業高校 *technical high school* ❈kōgyō kókka 工業国家 *industrial country* ❈jū-kōgyō 重工業 *heavy industry*

kōhai 後輩 *(one's) junior (in grade or work)* ❊Támura-san wa watashi no ní-nen kōhai désu. 田村さんは私の二年後輩です。 *Tamura is two years my junior (in this company).*

kōhai 荒廃 *decline; waste; ruin; devastation* ❊Kínnen Nihón de wa kyóiku gémba no kōhai ga mondai ni nátte iru. 近年、日本では教育現場の荒廃が問題になっている。 *In recent years, the decline of the Japanese education system has become a major concern.* ――**kōhai-suru** [vi] 荒廃する *go to ruin; be laid waste* ❊Tatemóno ga kōhai-shita. 建物が荒廃した。 *The building has gone to ruin.*

kōhan 後半 *last part* ❊Kono hón wa zenhan yóri kōhan no hő ga omoshirói. この本は前半より後半の方が面白い。 *The last part of this book is more interesting than the first.*

kōhei [na] 公平（な）*fair; impartial* ❊Sáiban wa kōhei de nákereba naránai. 裁判は公平でなければならない。 *A court trial must be impartial.*

kōhí コーヒー *coffee*

kō-hisutamínzai 抗ヒスタミン剤 *antihistamine*

kőho 候補 *candidacy; candidature* ❊kōhósha 候補者 *candidate; nominee* ❊kōhóchi 候補地 *prospective site* ❊kőho ni tátsu 候補に立つ *be a candidate*

kōhyō 好評 *favorable comment; favorable review; popularity* ❊Shinkyoku wa wakamono no aida de kōhyō o hakúshite iru. 新曲は若者の間で好評を博している。 *The new song is popular (or has popularity) among young people.*

kōhyō 公表 *public announcement* ――**kōhyō-suru** [vt] 公表する *make public; announce publicly*

kói 鯉 *carp* ❊nishiki-gói 錦鯉 *a golden carp* ❊koinóbori 鯉のぼり *flying carp streamer*

kó·i [adj] kóku nái; kókatta] 濃い *(be) dark; deep; thick; strong* ❊kói iró 濃い色 *dark color* ❊kói kōhí 濃いコーヒー *strong coffee*

kói 行為 *an act; behavior; deed*

kói 好意 *goodwill; kindness* ❊kói o yoseru 好意を寄せる *feel affection for* ❊kói o mú ni suru 好意を無にする *fail to return a kindness*

kóji 孤児 *orphan* ❊kojín 孤児院 *orphanage*

kóji 工事 *work; construction* ❊Kōji-chū. 工事中。 *Under Construction.*

kojikí 乞食 *beggar*

kójin 個人 *an individual; private person* ❊kojín-sa 個人差 *individual differences* ❊kojin shúgi 個人主義 *individualism* ――**kojinteki [na]** 個人的（な）*individual; personal* ❊Kore wa kojinteki na kenkai désu. これは個人的な見解です。 *This is my personal view.*

kōjitsu 口実 *an excuse; pretext* ❊Hén na kōjitsu o mőkete wa ikenai. 変な口実を設けてはいけない。 *Don't make some lame excuse.*

kōjó 工場 *factory* ❊kōjō chítai 工場地帯 *industrial area* ❊garasu kőjó

ガラス工場 *glass factory* ❸jidōsha kŏjō 自動車工場 *automobile factory*

kŏka 硬貨 *coin* ❸hyaku-en kŏka 百円硬貨 *hundred-yen coin*

kŏka 効果 *an effect; result* ❸Terebi sénden no kŏka ga agatta. テレビ宣伝の効果が上がった。 *Television advertising got results.* ——**kōkateki [na]** 効果的（な）*effective* ❸Kŏkateki na Eigo gakushū-hō ga shiritái. 効果的な英語学習法が知りたい。 *I'd like to know an effective way to study English.*

kŏkai 航海 *navigation* ❸shojo kŏkai 処女航海 *maiden voyage* ——**kŏkai-suru** [vi / vt] 航海する *navigate* ❸Yótto de Taihéiyō o kŏkai-shita. ヨットで太平洋を航海した。 *They crossed the Pacific in a sailboat.*

kŏkai 後悔 *regret; repentance* ❸Kŏkai saki ni tátazu. 後悔先に立たず。 *It's too late to regret (It's no use crying over spilt milk). <set phrase>* ——**kŏkai-suru** [vt] 後悔する *regret; repent (of)* ❸Shōsetsu no shujínkō wa tatta ichidó no ayamachi o kŏkai-shi-tsuzúkete iru. 小説の主人公はたった一度の過ちを後悔し続けている。 *The hero of the novel continues to repent for his one single mistake.*

kōkai 公開 *open; public* ❸kōkaijō 公開状 *an open letter* ❸kōkai kŏza 公開講座 *open lecture* ❸kōkai tŏron 公開討論 *open debate* ——**kōkai-suru** [vt] 公開する *open to the public* ❸Sono teien wa ippan ni kōkai-sarete iru. その庭園は一般に公開されている。 *The garden is open to the general public.*

kōkaidō 公会堂 *community hall*

kōkan 交歓 *exchange (of courtesies); fraternization* ❸bunka kŏkan 文化交歓会 *cultural exchange.*

kōkan 交換 *exchange* ❸kōkan kyŏju 交換教授 *exchange professor* ❸kōkandai 交換台 *telephone switchboard* ❸kōkánshu 交換手 *telephone operator* ——**kōkan-suru** [vt] 交換する *exchange* ❸Pénparu to kitte o kōkan-shite iru. ペンパルと切手を交換している。 *I'm trading stamps with a pen pal.*

kōken 貢献 *contribution; support; services* ——**kōken-suru** [vt] 貢献する *contribute to; support* ❸Daitŏryō fujin wa geijutsu no hatten ni kōken-shita. 大統領夫人は芸術の発展に貢献した。 *The First Lady supported the development of the arts.*

kokeshi こけし *(Japanese traditional) wooden doll*

kŏki [na] 高貴（な）*high; noble; lofty* ❸kŏki na kao 高貴な顔 *a noble countenance* ❸Tanaká-shi wa kŏki no dé ná n desu yo. 田中氏は高貴の出なんですよ。 *Mr. Tanaka comes from the upper class.*

kōkíshin 好奇心 *curiosity* ❸kōkíshin ga tsuyói 好奇心が強い *full of curiosity* ❸Kōkíshin kara tsúi kiken na basho ni ashí o fumíirete shimatta. 好奇心からつい危険な場所に足を踏み入れてしまった。 *Curiosity led me to set foot on dangerous ground.*

kókka 国歌 *national anthem*

kókka 国家 *a state; country; nation* ❚kókka no anzen 国家の安全 *national security*

kokkai 国会 *Congress (US); Diet (J); Parliament (Br)* ❚kokkai gíin 国会議員 *Diet member* ❚Kokkai Gijidō 国会議事堂 *Diet Building* ❚Kokkai Toshōkan 国会図書館 *Diet Library*

kokkei [na] 滑稽（な）*funny; humorous* ❚Kokkei na hanashí ni tsúi waratte shimatta. 滑稽な話につい笑ってしまった。*I laughed at the humorous story in spite of myself.*

kokki 国旗 *national flag*

kokkō 国交 *diplomatic relations* ❚kokkō káifuku 国交回復 *restoration of diplomatic relations* ❚kokkō dánzetsu 国交断絶 *rupture of diplomatic relations* ❚Nihón to Chūgoku wa kokkō o juritsu-shita. 日本と中国は国交を樹立した。*Japan and China established diplomatic relations.*

kokkyō 国境 *national border* ❚kokkyō-sen 国境線 *national boundary line*

koko ここ *here* ❚Koko ni tóire ga arimásu ka?. ここにトイレがあります か。*Is there a restroom here?* ❚Koko ga watashi no uchí desu. こ こが私の家です。*This is my house.* ❚Koko wa dóko? ここはどこ。 *Where are we?* (**or** *Where is this?*)

kōkō *abbr for* **kótō gákkō**

kokochiyo·i 心地よい *[adj* kokochiyóku nai; kokochiyókatta] *(is) pleasant* ❚Yuágari wa kokochi-yói. 湯上がりは心地よい。*One feels good after a bath.*

kōkógaku 考古学 *archaeology* ❚kōkógakusha 考古学者 *archaeologist*

kōkoku 広告 *ad(vertisement); publicity* ❚kōkokúnushi 広告主 *sponsor; advertiser* ――**kōkoku-suru** *[vt]* 広告する *run an ad; post an advertisement; advertise*

kóko no 個々の *individual* ❚rōdōsha kóko no yōkyū ni kotaéru. 労働者 個々の要求に答える *respond to each individual worker*

kokonoká 九日 *the ninth (of the month); nine days*

kokónotsu 九つ *nine (when counting things)*

kokóro 心 *mind; heart; feeling* ❚kokóro to kárada 心と体 *body and soul* (**or** *spirit*) ❚kokóro no hirói hito 心の広い人 *a generous person* ❚kokóro ni kakéru 心にかける *bear in mind; take to heart* ❚kokóro o yómu 心を読む *read someone's thoughts* ❚kokóro o uchiakete hanásu 心を打ち明けて話す *have a heart-to-heart talk* ❚Kokóro ni nái koto o itte shimátta. 心にないことを言ってしまった。*I didn't mean what I said.* ❚Kokóro kara kansha-shimásu. 心から感謝しま す。*Thank you with all my heart.*

kokoroátari 心当たり *idea; clue; knowledge* ❚Kono Eigo no tegami o Roshia-go ni hon'yaku-shite kureru hitó ni kokoroátari ga arimasén ka?

この英語の手紙をロシア語に翻訳してくれる人に心当たりがありませんか。*Do you know someone (or have knowledge of someone) who can translate this English letter into Russian for me?*

kokorobosó·i [*adj* kokorobósoku nái; kokorobósokatta] 心細い *(be) uneasy; feel helpless; feel discouraged*

kokoroé·ru [*vt* kokoroénai; kokoróeta] 心得る *learn; know; understand*

kokoromí 試み *an attempt* **§**Saisho no kokoromí wa shippai ni owatta. 最初の試みは失敗に終わった。*The first attempt ended in failure.*

kokoromí·ru [*vt* kokoromínai; kokorómita] 試みる *attempt; try* **§**atarashíi hōhō o kokoromíru 新しい方法を試みる *try a new way*

kokoroyó·i [*adj* kokoroyóku nái; kokoroyókatta] 快い *(be) pleasant; agreeable; comfortable* ——**kokoroyóku** 快く *gladly; agreeably; happily; in good spirits* **§**Kánojo wa watashi no múri na negái o kokoroyóku úkete kureta. 彼女は私の無理な願いを快く受けてくれた。*She gladly accepted my unreasonable request.*

kokorozás·u [*vt* kokorozasánai; kokorozáshita] 志す *plan; intend; aspire to; aim at* **§**gakúmon ni kokorozásu 学問に志す *aspire to learning* **§**Ōkawa-san wa bengóshi o kokorozáshite iru. 大川さんは弁護士を志している。*Ōkawa is aiming at becoming a lawyer.*

koku- 国〜 *national* **§**kokusan 国産 *national product; made in (Japan)* **§**kokuzei 国税 *national tax* **§**kokubō 国防 *national defense* **§**kokuhō 国宝 *national treasure* **§**kokúnai 国内 *within the country; national; domestic*

kōkū 航空 *aviation; flight; air traffic*   **kōkūbin** 航空便 *air mail* **§**kōkū kíchi 航空基地 *air base* **§**kōkū uchū sángyō 航空宇宙産業 *aerospace industry*

kokuban 黒板 *blackboard*

kokubetsúshiki 告別式 *funeral; farewell service*

kokufuku 克服 *conquest; subjugation* ——**kokufuku-suru** [*vt*] 克服する *overcome; conquer* **§**byōki o kokufuku-suru 病気を克服する *overcome an illness*

kokuhaku 告白 *confession* ——**kokuhaku-suru** [*vt*] *confess; testify to* **§**tsumi o kokuhaku-suru 罪を告白する *confess one's guilt*

kokuhatsu 告発 *prosecution; indictment; accusation; charge* ——**kokuhatsu-suru** [*vt*] 告発する *prosecute; indict; accuse; charge (with)* **§**jíken o kokuhatsu-suru 事件を告発する *prosecute a case*

kokujin 黒人 *black person; a black; Negro*

kokumin 国民 *citizen; the people*

kokuó 国王 *king; monarch*

kokuritsu [no] 国立（の）*national; state* **§**kokuritsu dáigaku 国立大学 *national university* **§**kokuritsu kōen 国立公園 *national park*

kokúrui 穀類 *cereal; grain*

kokusai 国際 *international* **§**kokusai dénwa 国際電話 *international* *telephone call*   ❽kokusai kūkō 国際空港 *international airport*

  ❽kokusai kékkon 国際結婚 *international marriage* ——**kokusaiteki [na]** 国際的（な）*international*

Kokusai Réngō 国際連合 *United Nations*

kokusei chósa 国勢調査 *national census*

kokuseki 国籍 *nationality; citizenship*

kókuso 告訴 *accusation; lawsuit; complaint* ——**kókuso-suru** [vt] 告訴する *sue; accuse; charge* ❽Káre wa satsujin jíken de kókuso-sareta. 彼は殺人事件で告訴された。*He was accused of murder.*

kokutetsu (*abbr for* **kokuyū tétsudō**) 国(有)鉄(道) *national railroad*

kokuyūka 国有化 *nationalization* ——**kokuyūka-suru** [vt] 国有化する *nationalize*

kokyaku 顧客 *client; customer*

Kókyo 皇居 *Imperial Palace (Tokyo)*

kókyō 故郷 *(one's) native home; hometown* ❽Kókyō wa dóko desu ka? 故郷はどこですか。*Where is your home? (or Where are you from originally?)*

kōkyō gákudan 交響楽団 *symphony orchestra*

kōkyókyoku 交響曲 *symphony*

kokyū 呼吸 *breath; breathing* ——**kokyū-suru** [vi] 呼吸する *breathe*

kōkyū 高級 *high-class; top grade* ❽kōkyū kánryō 高級官僚 *senior official* ❽Miyamoto-kun wa kōkyūsha ni notte iru. 宮本くんは高級車に乗っている。*Miyamoto drives a luxury automobile.*

kōkyūteki [na] 恒久的（な）*permanent* ❽kōkyūteki na sétsubi 恒久的な設備 *permanent fixture*

komaká·i [adj komákaku nái; komákakatta] 細かい *very small; fine; minor; minute*

kōman [na] 高慢（な）*proud; arrogant* ❽kōman na táido 高慢な態度 *an arrogant attitude*

komár·u [vi komaránai; komátta] 困る *get into difficulty; get into a quandary; become troubled*

kómban 今晩 *tonight; this night*

Komban wá! 今晩は。*Good evening!*

komé 米 *(uncooked) rice*

kōmínkan 公民館 *community center*

kōmínken 公民権 *civil rights*

kómon 顧問 *consultant; adviser*

komóri 子守り *baby-sitting; nursing* ——**komóri-suru** 子守りする *baby-sit; look after children*

kốmori こうもり *a bat (animal)*

komponteki [na] 根本的（な）*basic; fundamental* ——**komponteki ni** 根本的に *basically; thoroughly; fundamentally* ❽Sono kikaku o komponteki ni henkō-shita. その企画を根本的に変更した。*I made* *basic changes to the plan.*

kóm·u [*vi* kománai; kónda] 込む *be crowded* §Densha wa jōkyaku de kónde ita. 電車は乗客で込んでいた。*The train was crowded (with passengers).*

komúgi 小麦 *wheat* §komugiko 小麦粉 *wheat flour*

kōmúin 公務員 *civil service; civil servant* §kokka kōmúin 国家公務員 *government employee; officeholder; national public official*

kón 紺 *navy blue*

kốnai 校内 *school grounds; campus*

kondánkai 懇談会 *discussion meeting; informal discussion*

kondate 献立 *menu*

kóndo *next time; this time* §Kóndo wa úmaku iki-sō da. 今度はうまくいきそうだ。*It looks like it's going to go well next time.* <*masc*> §Kóndo wa anáta ga iken o iu bán yo. 今度はあなたが意見を言う番よ。*Now it's your turn to express an opinion.* <*fem*>

kondō 混同 *confusion* ——**kondō-suru** [*vt*] 混同する *confuse; confound; mix up* §Kōshi o kondō-shite wa ikenai. 公私を混同してはいけない。*One mustn't confuse private with public matters.*

kōnénki 更年期 *menopause*

konéru [*vt* konénai; kóneta] こねる *knead* §pan kíji o konéru パン生地をこねる *knead bread* §néndo o konéru 粘土をこねる *knead clay*

kōnetsusúihi 光熱水費 *light, fuel and water expense; utilities expense*

kongen 根源 *origin; source*

kongetsu 今月 *this month*

kongo 今後 *from now; after this; in the future; next* §Kongo wa jūbún ki o tsukemásu. 今後は十分気をつけます。*I'll be very careful from now on.*

konímotsu 小荷物 *(small) baggage; luggage; parcel*

kónjō 根性 *nature; spirit; grit* §Anó hito wa kónjō ga áru. あの人は根性がある。*That person has spirit.*

konketsu 混血 *mixed blood* §konketsú-ji 混血児 *mixed-blood child*

konki 根気 *perseverance; patience; stamina* ——**konki yóku** 根気よく *patiently; with endurance*

kónkyo 根拠 *base; basis* §Hándan no kónkyo o akíraka ni shite kudasái. 判断の根拠を明らかにして下さい。*Please explain (lit: make clear) the basis of your decision.*

konna こんな *this kind; this sort (of)* §Konna mé ni áu nante, kangáete mo mínakatta! こんな目に会うなんて、考えてもみなかった！*I never thought something like this would happen to me!*

kónnan 困難 *difficulty; hardship; suffering* §arayúru kónnan ni uchikatsu あらゆる困難に打ち勝つ *overcome all difficulties* ——**kónnan na** 困難な *difficult; hard*

konnansa 困難さ *difficulty*

kónnichi 今日 *this day*

Konnichi wá! 今日は。 *Hello! (greeting used in the daytime)*

konnyakú こんにゃく *edible paste made from the konjac plant, a relative of taro*

kono- この *this-* ❈Kono pén wa dónata no desu ka? このペンはどなたのですか。 *Whose pen is this?*

kono aida この間 *the other day* ❈Kono aidá wa, dómo arígatō gozaimáshita. この間はどうもありがとうございました。 *Thank you for (what you did) the other day.*

kono goro この頃 *recently; these days* ❈Kono goro áni wa totemo isogashíi. この頃兄はとても忙しい。 *These days my brother is very busy.*

konomashí·i [*adj* konomáshiku nái; konomáshikatta] 好ましい *(be) agreeable; desirable* ❈Sháin no saiyō ni atatté wa keiken no áru hito ga konomashíi. 社員の採用に当たっては経験のある人が好ましい。 *In hiring company employees, people with experience are preferred.*

konomí 好み *liking; choice; taste* ❈Kono é wa watashi no konomí ni awánai. この絵は私の好みに合わない。 *This painting is not to my taste.*

konóm·u [*vt* konománai; konónda] 好む *like; have a preference for*

konran 混乱 *confusion* ❈konran jōtai 混乱状態 *a confused state* —— **konran-suru** [*vi*] 混乱する *be confused; be mixed up; be in disorder; be chaotic* ❈Kōtsū kíkan no súto de tsūkín-kyaku wa konran-shite iru. 交通機関のストで通勤客は混乱している。 *Commuters are in (a state of) confusion because of the transportation strike.*

kónsento コンセント *electrical outlet; plug*

konshū 今週 *this week*

konton 混沌 *chaos* —— **konton taru** (or **konton to shita**) 混沌たる *chaotic*

kon'yaku 婚約 *engagement; betrothal* —— **kon'yaku-suru** [*vi*] 婚約する *be engaged*

kónzatsu 混雑 *confusion; disorder* —— **kónzatsu-suru** [*vi*] 混雑する *be complicated; be in confusion; be disorderly; be crowded* ❈Depáto wa kyaku de kónzatsu-shite imáshita. デパートは客で混雑していました。 *The department store was crowded with customers.*

koppu コップ *(drinking) glass; tumbler*

Kóra! こら。 *Hey!; Watch it!*

koraé·ru [*vt* koraénai; koráeta] 堪える *bear; withstand; endure* ❈nemutása o koraéru 眠たさを堪える *withstand drowsiness*

kórai 古来 *from ancient times*

kore これ *this* ❈koréra これら *these* ❈Kore wa hón desu. これは本です。 *This is a book.* ❈Kore o kudasái. これを下さい。 *Give me* *this, please.* 🔸Kore wa watashi no shitashíi tomodachi no Éimī desu. これは私の親しい友達のエイミーです。*This is my close friend, Amy.*

kōrei 恒例 *established custom; common practice* 🔸Fasshon shó no gogatsu káisai ga kōrei ni nátte iru. ファッションショーの五月開催が恒例になっている。*It's an established custom to hold a fashion show in May.*

kōrei 高齢 *advanced age; old age*

kore kara これから *from now on*

kore máde これまで *until now; up to this point*

kōri 氷 *ice* 🔸kōrí mizu 氷水 *ice water* 🔸mizu de hiyásu *cool with ice* 🔸Mizuúmi ni kōri ga hatte iru. 湖に氷が張っている。*Ice has formed on the lake.*

kōritsu [no] 公立（の）*public* 🔸kōritsu gákkō 公立学校 *public school* 🔸kōritsu toshókan 公立図書館 *public library*

kóro 航路 *sea route* 🔸Yokohama-San Furanshisuko kōro no kamotsu-sen 横浜ーサンフランシスコ航路の貨物船 *a freighter on the Yokohama-San Francisco run*

korob·u [vi korobanai; koronda] 転ぶ *fall down; tumble* 🔸Kótta michi de subétte koronde shimatta. 凍った道で滑って転んでしまった。*I slipped on the icy road and fell.*

korogar·u [vi korogaranai; korogatta] 転がる *roll over; tumble* 🔸korogaru ishí 転がる石 *a rolling stone* 🔸Ishí ni tsumazuite korogatte shimatta. 石につまずいて転がってしまった。*I tripped on a rock and took a tumble.*

koromo 衣 *robe; garment; clothes; icing; coating; (cooking) batter* 🔸kísetsu no koromogae 季節の衣替え *changing of clothes for the season* 🔸Tempura no koromo wa karátto ageta hó ga oishíi. 天ぷらの衣はカラッと揚げた方がおいしい。*Tempura tastes best when the batter is crisply fried.*

koroshiya 殺し屋 *hired killer; hit man*

koros·u [vt korosanai; koroshita] 殺す *kill; put to death; murder* 🔸Hito o koroshité wa naránai. 人を殺してはならない。*Thou shalt not kill.* 🔸íki o korosu 息を殺す *hold one's breath* 🔸ikarí o korosu 怒りを殺す *contain one's anger* 🔸sainō o korosu 才能を殺す *squelch one's talent* 🔸akubi o korosu あくびを殺す *stifle a yawn*

kór·u [vi koránai; kótta] 凝る *be tight; concentrate on; be into* 🔸Káta ga kótte kubi ga mawaranai. 肩が凝って首が回らない。*My shoulders are stiff; I can't turn my head.* 🔸Musuko wa sáfin ni kótte iru. 息子はサーフィンに凝っている。*My son is into surfing.* ——**kótta** 凝った *elaborate; exquisite* 🔸Kono hóteru no róbī wa kótta dezáin desu. このホテルのロビーは凝ったデザインです。*This hotel lobby has exquisite decor.*

kōr·u [vi kōranai; kōtta] 凍る *freeze; be frozen* ⊗Sámukute semménki no mizu ga kōtte iru. 寒くて洗面器の水が凍っている。*It's so cold the water in the washbasin is frozen.*

kóryo 考慮 *consideration; reflection; deliberation* ⊗kóryo ni ireru 考慮に入れる *take into consideration* ⊗Kono kettei ni tsúite wa máda kóryo no yóchi ga nokótte iru. この決定についてまだ考慮の余地が残っている。*There still remain some things to consider before reaching a decision.* ——**kóryo-suru** [vt] 考慮する *consider; think over*

kóryoku 効力 *effect; efficacy; validity*

kōryū 交流 *alternating current; AC*

kōryū 拘留 *detention; custody*

kōsai 交際 *association; company; acquaintance* ⊗kōsái-hi 交際費 *expense account; entertainment allowance* ⊗Táshiro-san wa kōsai ga hirói desu. 田代さんは交際が広いです。*Tashiro has a wide circle of acquaintances.* ——**kōsai-suru** [vi] 交際する *associate with; keep company with*

kōsaku 耕作 *cultivation; farming* ——**kōsaku-suru** [vt] *cultivate; farm*

kōsaku 工作 *building; construction* ⊗kōsaku kíkai 工作機械 *machine tool* ⊗seiji kósaku 政治工作 *political maneuvering* ——**kōsaku-suru** [vt] 工作する *build; construct*

kosame 小雨 *a drizzle; light rain*

kōsan 降参 *a surrender; giving up* ——**kōsan-suru** [vi] 降参する *surrender; admit defeat; give up*

kōsaten 交差点 *crossing; intersection*

kósei 個性 *personality; individual character; idiosyncrasy* ⊗Anó hito wa kósei ga tsuyói. あの人は個性が強い。*That person has a forceful character.*

kōsei [na] 公正 （な) *fairness; impartiality; justice; fare; just* ⊗kōsei torihiki iínkai 公正取引委員会 *Fair Trade Commission* ⊗kōsei na hyóka 公正な評価 *a fair evaluation* ——**kōsei ni** 公正に *fairly; justly*

kōsei 更生 *rehabilitation; regeneration* ⊗kōsei shísetsu 更生施設 *facilities for rehabilitation (of criminals)* ——**kōsei-saseru** [vi: caus] 更生させる *rehabilitate; cause to reform*

kōsei bússhitsu 抗生物質 *antibiotics*

Kōséishō 厚生省 *Welfare Ministry; Ministry of Health and Welfare* ⊗kōsei dáijin 厚生大臣 *health and welfare minister*

koseki 戸籍 *family register* ⊗koseki shōmeisho 戸籍証明書 *birth certificate* ⊗koseki tóhon 戸籍謄本 *birth registration (J); a copy of one's family register*

kōseki 功績 *merit; service; achievement* ⊗Maeda-san wa kaisha no hatten ni óki na kōseki o ageta. 前田さんは会社の発展に大きな功績

をあげた。*Mr. Maeda made a great contribution to this company's development.*

kōsen 光線 *beam of light*　§rēzā kṓsen レーザー光線 *laser beam*

kōsha 後者 *the latter*　§Watashi wa zénsha yóri kṓsha no íken no hṓ ga ukeirerareru. 私は前者より後者の方が受け入れられる。*I can go along with the latter opinion more than the former.*

koshi 腰 *waist; lower back*　§koshi no hosói hito 腰の細い人 *a slim-waisted person*　§koshi ga karúi 腰が軽い *(be) agile; ready and willing (to work)*　§koshi ga hikúi 腰が低い *(be) modest*　§Koshi ga itái. 腰が痛い。*My back hurts.*

kṓshi 講師 *lecturer; instructor*　§sennin kṓshi 専任講師 *full-time instructor*　§jikan kṓshi 時間講師 *part-time lecturer*

Kōshi 孔子 *Confucius*

koshído 格子戸 *lattice-work (sliding) door*

koshikaké·ru [vi koshikakénai; koshikáketa] 腰掛ける *sit (on a chair)*

kōshiki [no] 公式 （の） *formality; official; formal*　§kōshiki hṓmon 公式訪問 *official visit* ——**kōshiki ni** 公式に *officially; formally*

kōshin 行進 *a march; a parade*　§kōshínkyoku 行進曲 *a march (music)* ——**kōshin-suru** [vi] 行進する *march; parade*

kōshin 更新 *renewal* ——**kōshin-suru** [vt] 更新する *renew*　§Menkyóshō o kōshin-shinákereba ikenai. 免許証を更新しなければいけない。*I have to renew my driver's license.*

koshirae·ru [vt koshiraenai; koshiraeta] こしらえる *make; manufacture; prepare*　§bentṓ o koshiraeru 弁当をこしらえる *prepare a lunch*　§kao o koshiraeru 顔をこしらえる *make up (one's) face*　§o-kane o koshiraeru お金をこしらえる *raise money; make money*

kōshitsu 皇室 *the imperial household*

koshitsu; koshū 固執 *adherence* ——**koshitsu-suru** [vi] 固執する *adhere to; stick to; insist on*　§Shushō wa ítsu made mo jibun no kangáe ni koshitsu-shite iru. 首相はいつまでも自分の考えに固執している。*The Prime Minister still sticks to his own idea.*

koshō 胡椒 *pepper*

koshō 故障 *breakdown; trouble; obstacle*　§Koshō-chū. 故障中 *Out of Order.* ——**koshō-suru** [vi] 故障する *break down; run into trouble*　§Sono kikái wa mata koshō-shite iru. その機械は又故障している。*That machine's out of order again.*

kōshō 交渉 *bargaining; negotiation* ——**kōshō-suru** [vi] 交渉する *negotiate (with); make an overture (to); bargain (with)*　§Kaisha keiéisha to rōdṓsha to ga chin'age ni tsúite kōshō-shite iru. 会社経営者と労働者とが賃上げについて交渉している。*Company management and labor are bargaining over a raise in wages.*

kōshoku 好色 *sensuality; amorousness; lust* ——**kōshoku no** 好色の *amorous; lustful*

kōshū 公衆 *the public* ――**kōshū no** 公衆の *public* §kōshū dénwa 公衆電話 *public telephone* §kōshū éisei 公衆衛生 *public sanitation*

kōshúkei 絞首刑 *death (penalty) by hanging*

kóso 酵素 *enzyme; yeast*

-kóso こそ *indeed; precisely* §Kore kóso tenkeiteki na réi desu. これこそ典型的な例です。*This (indeed) is a typical example.*

kōsō bíru 高層ビル *skyscraper*

kōsoku 拘束 *restriction; constraint; restraint* ――**kōsoku-suru** [vt] 拘束する *bind; restrain* §Higísha wa migara o kōsoku-sareta. 被疑者は身柄を拘束された。*The suspect was (physically) restrained.*

kōsoku dốro 高速道路 *expressway; limited-access highway*

kossetsu 骨折 *bone fracture* ――**kossetsu-suru** [vt] 骨折する *fracture; break*

kos·u [vt kosanai; koshita] 越す；超す *cross; go across; pass; exceed* §Bōru wa fénsu o koshite shimatta. ボールはフェンスを越してしまった。*The ball went over the fence.* §Nedan wa ichi-man-en o koshite iru. 値段は一万円を越している。*The cost exceeds ¥10,000.*

kōsui 香水 *perfume*

kosúr·u [vt kosuránai; kosútta] 擦る *rub; scrub; chafe* §mé o kosúru 目を擦る *rub one's eyes* §táoru de senaka o kosúru タオルで背中を擦る *scrub one's back with a towel*

kotaé·ru [vi kotáenai; kotáeta] 答える *answer; respond (to)* §Shitsumon ní wa hakkíri kotaeyố. 質問にははっきり答えよう。*Answer the questions clearly.*

kotaé·ru [vi kotáenai; kotáeta] 応える *respond; meet; live up to* §Minná no kitai ni kotáete gambarimásu. みんなの期待に応えてがんばります。*I'll do my best to live up to everyone's expectations.*

kōtai 交替；交代 *alternation; change; by turns* §kōtai de hataraku 交代で働く *work by turns; work in shifts* ――**kōtai-suru** [vi] 交替する；交代する *alternate; take turns* §Watashi wa otōtó to kōtai-shinágara inugoya o kansei-shita. 私は弟と交代しながら犬小屋を完成した。*My brother and I took turns and completed the dog house.*

kōtáishi 皇太子 *crown prince*

kotei 固定 *fixing; establishing* §kotei shísan 固定資産 *fixed assets* §kotei shíhon 固定資本 *fixed capital* ――**kotei-suru** [vt] 固定する *fix; settle; secure* §Kágu ga jishin de taorénai yō ni kotei-shita. 家具が地震で倒れないように固定した。*I secured the furniture so that it would not fall during an earthquake.*

kōtei 皇帝 *emperor* ――**kōtei no** 皇帝の *imperial*

kōtei 肯定 *affirmation; affirmative* §kōtéi-bun 肯定文 *an affirmative sentence (gram)* ――**kōteiteki [na]** 肯定的（な）*affirmative* §kōteiteki na táido 肯定的な態度 *an affirmative attitude* ――**kōtei-suru** [vt] *affirm; answer "yes"; acknowledge* §Shushō wa sono jíjitsu o súbete kōtei-shita. 首相はその事実を全て肯定した。*The prime minister acknowledged all the facts.*

kōtei kákaku 公定価格 *official price; ceiling price*

kōteki [na] 公的（な）*public*   §kōteki énjo 公的援助 *public support*   §kōteki séikatsu 公的生活 *public life*   §Anó hito wa kōteki na kao to shiteki na kao o mótte iru. あの人は公的な顔と私的な顔を持っている。*She has a public face and a private face.* ——**kōteki ni** 公的に *publicly*

koten 古典 *old book*   §koten búngaku 古典文学 *classical literature*

kōtetsu 鋼鉄 *steel*

kotó 事 *thing; event*   §Kyṓ wa suru kotó ga takusan áru. 今日はする事がたくさんある。*I have a lot of things to do today.*   §Sono kotó ni tsúite wa yóku wakarimasén. その事についてはよく分かりません。*I don't know much about that.*

-kotó 〜こと *(nominalizing suffix)*   §yómu kotó 読むこと *reading*   §tabéru kotó 食べること *eating*   §oyógu kotó 泳ぐこと *swimming*

kōtō 口頭 *verbal; oral*   §kōtō shímon 口頭試問 *oral examination*   §Jōshi wa kōtō de shíji o dáshita. 上司は口頭で指示を出した。*The boss gave oral instructions.*

kotobá 言葉 *word; language*   §Kotobá o kaete iéba... 言葉を換えて言えば〜 *In other words...*   §kotobá de arawásu 言葉で表わす *express in words*   §kotoba ásobi 言葉遊び *wordplay*   §Eigo wa sékai de tsūyō-suru kotobá desu. 英語は世界で通用する言葉です。*English is a language which is used throughout the world.*   §kotoba no fujiyū na hitó 言葉の不自由な人 *a mute*

kōtṓbu 後頭部 *the back of the head*   §Sugiyama-san wa sottō-shite kōtṓbu o kyṓda-shita. 杉山さんは卒倒して後頭部を強打した。*Sugiyama fainted and hit the back of his head hard.*

-koto ga dekíru ことが出来る *can (do)*   §Oyógu kotó ga dekimásu ka? 泳ぐことが出来ますか。*Can you swim?*

kōtō gákkō 高等学校 *high school*

kotogara 事柄 *a matter; affair; things*   §Watashi wa míte kita kotogara o seikaku ni hōkoku-shita. 私は見てきた事柄を正確に報告した。*I reported accurately on the things I had seen.*

kotonár·u [vi kotonaránai; kotonátta] 異なる *differ (from); be different*   §Sono kenkai wa jíjitsu to wa kotonátte iru. その見解は事実とは異なっている。*That point of view doesn't agree with the facts.*

kóto ni 殊に *especially*   §Imōtó wa óngaku, kóto ni póppusu ga dáisuki desu. 妹は音楽、殊にポップスが大好きです。*My younger sister likes music—especially pop music—very much.*

kotori 小鳥 *bird; small bird*

kotoshi 今年 *this year*

kotowár·u [vt kotowaránai; kotowátta] 断わる *decline; refuse*   §Ginkō wa shakkín no mōshide o kotowátta. 銀行は借金の申し出を断わった。 *The bank refused the loan.* ❽Tanaka-san no shōtai o kotowarō. 田中さんの招待を断わろう。 *I'm going to decline Tanaka's invitation.*

kotowaza 諺 *saying; proverb*

kotozuké 言付け *message (to be passed on)* ❽Anáta é no kotozuké ga arimásu. あなたへの言付けがありますよ。 *There's a message for you.* ❽Kotozuké o onegai-dekimásu ka? 言付けをお願いできますか。 *May I leave a message?*

kotsu こつ *skill; knack* ❽kotsu o tsukámu こつをつかむ *get the knack of* ❽Kore o surú ni wa kotsu ga áru. これをするにはこつがある。 *There's a knack to doing this.*

kōtsū 交通 *traffic; communication* ❽kōtsū íhan 交通違反 *traffic violation* ❽kōtsū jíko 交通事故 *traffic accident* ❽kōtsū jūtai 交通渋滞 *traffic jam* ❽kōtsū-hi 交通費 *travel expense* ❽kōtsū júnsa 交通巡査 *traffic policeman* ❽kōtsū shíngō 交通信号 *traffic signal* ❽Kono tōrí wa kōtsū ga hageshíi. この通りは交通が激しい。 *The traffic on this road is heavy.* ❽Sono murá wa ōyuki de kōtsū ga shadan-sare, koritsu-shite iru. その村は大雪で交通が遮断され、孤立している。 *Because of heavy snowfall, communications have been shut off and that village is (completely) isolated.*

kottōhin 骨董品 *antique; curio*

kōun 幸運 *good fortune* ❽Kōun o inorimásu. 幸運を祈ります。 *I pray for your good fortune. (or Good luck!)* ——**kōun ni** 幸運に *fortunately* ❽Kōun ní mo shiai ni kátta. 幸運にも試合に勝った。 *Fortunately we won the game.*

kouri 小売り *retail* ❽kourí ne 小売り値 *retail price* ——**kouri-suru** [vt] *sell; retail*

koushi 子牛 *calf* ❽koushí niku 子牛肉 *veal*

kowagár·u [vt kowagaránai; kowagátta] 怖がる *be afraid of; fear* [*not used with first person*] ❽Kodomo wa isha o kowagátte iru. 子供は医者を怖がっている。 *My child is afraid of the doctor.*

kowá·i [adj kówaku nái; kówakatta] 怖い *(be) fearful; frightening; afraid* ❽kowái yume 怖い夢 *a frightening dream* ❽Kowái wa! 怖いわ。 *I'm scared! <fem>*

kowaré·ru [vi kowarénai; kowáreta] 壊れる *be broken; be destroyed* ❽Tezukurí isu wa súgu kowárete shimatta. 手作り椅子はすぐ壊れてしまった。 *The handmade chair soon broke.*

kowás·u [vt kowasánai; kowáshita] 壊す *break; destroy* ❽furúi ié o kowásu 古い家を壊す *tear down an old house* ❽chawan o kowásu 茶碗をこわす *break a cup* ❽karada o kowásu 体を壊す *damage (one's) health* ❽onaka o kowásu お腹を壊す *get an upset stomach*

koya 小屋 *hut; shed; cabin* ❽yamá ni koya o tsukúru 山に小屋を作る

build a cabin in the mountains　§inu-goya　犬小屋　*doghouse*

kōyō 効用 *use; utility; effect; benefit*　§Kono kusuri no kōyō wa nán desu ka? この薬の効用は何ですか。 *What is this medicine for?*　§Hoka ni kōyō ga nái. 他に効用がない。 *It's not good for anything else.*

kōyō 紅葉 *autumn leaves; autumn colors* ——**kōyō-suru** [vi] 紅葉する *take on autumn colors*

koyomí 暦 *calendar*

koyū 固有 *characteristic; peculiarity* ——**koyū no** 固有の *peculiar; one's own*　§Nihón no koyū no búnka 日本の固有の文化 *Japan's unique culture*　§koyū méishi 固有名詞 *proper noun (Gram)*

kōyū 公有 *public*　§kōyúchi 公有地 *public land*

kōyū 交友 *companionship*　§kōyū kánkei 交友関係 *a friendly relationship*

koyubi 小指 *little finger*

kōza 口座 *bank account*　§kóza o hiráku 口座を開く *open a bank account*

kōza 講座 *lectureship; course (of lectures)*

kōzen [to] 公然（と）*openly; publicly*　§kōzen to hihan-suru 公然と批判する *openly criticize*　§kōzen no himitsu 公然の秘密 *an open secret*

kozeni 小銭 *small change; coins*　§kození-ire 小銭入れ *coin purse*　§Sumimasén. Kozeni no mochiawase ga arimasén ga. すみません。小銭の持ち合わせがありませんが。 *I'm sorry, I don't have any small change.*

kozō 小僧 *kid; child; brat; bonze (young Buddhist priest)*

kōzō 構造 *structure; organization*　§jōbu kōzō 上部構造 *superstructure*　§kabu kōzō 下部構造 *infrastructure*　§jíntai no kōzō 人体の構造 *structure of the human body*　§kōzō gengógaku 構造言語学 *structural linguistics*

kozue 梢 *treetop*

kōzui 洪水 *a flood*

kózukai 小遣い *personal allowance; pocket money*

kozútsumi 小包 *parcel; package*

kú 九 ; 9 *nine (the numeral)*

kú 苦 *suffering; worry; trouble*　§Kú wa raku no táne. 苦は楽の種。 *No pain, no gain. (lit: Suffering is the seed of joy.)* <set phrase>

-ku 〜区 *ward; district*

kū 空 *air; sky*　§kū tai kū misáiru 空対空ミサイル *air-to-air missile*　§kūbaku 空爆 *aerial bombardment*

kubár·u [vt kubaránai; kubátta] 配る *distribute; deal out; measure out*　§kokóro o kubáru 心を配る *be careful*　§torámpu o kubáru トランプを配る *deal cards*　§Senséi wa shiken móndai o kubarimáshita. 先生は試験問題を配りました。 *The teacher passed out the test* *questions.*

kúbetsu 区別 *distinction; difference* ❀Saikin wa fásshon daké de wa dansei to josei no kúbetsu ga tsukánai. 最近はファッションだけでは男性と女性の区別がつかない。 *These days one can't tell the difference betwen men and women on the basis of fashion alone.* —— **kúbetsu-suru** [*vt*] 区別する *distinguish; differentiate* ❀A to B o kúbetsu-suru A と B を区別する *distinguish A from B; differentiate between A and B*

kubi 首 *neck; head* ❀kubi o kashigéru 首を傾げる *incline the head (in doubt)* ❀kubi o yoko ni furu 首を横に振る *shake (one's) head* ❀Kubi no nagái josei ga urayamashíi. 首の長い女性が羨ましい。 *I envy women who have long necks.* ❀Musuko wa natsuyásumi o kubi o nágaku-shite mátte iru. 息子は夏休みを首を長くして待っている。 *My son can't wait for summer vacation (lit: My son is waiting with neck outstretched for summer vacation).*

kubikázari 首飾り *beads; necklace*

kubomi 窪み *hollow; depression*

kuchi 口 *mouth; opening; speech; taste; door; share* ❀Kuchi o ókiku akenasái. 口を大きく開けなさい。 *Open your mouth wide.* ❀iriguchi 入口 *entrance* ❀dé-guchi 出口 *exit* ❀shūshoku-guchi 就職口 *job opening* ❀Anó hito wa kuchi ga karúi. あの人は口が軽い。 *He can't keep a secret.* ❀Dôzo. O-kuchi ni áu ka dô ka wakarimasén ga. どうぞ。お口に合うかどうか分かりませんが。 *I don't know if it will suit your taste, but please try some.* ❀Kámpa wa hitó-kuchi ga ichiman-en désu. カンパは一口が一万円です。 *For the fund-raising drive, one share is ¥10,000.*

kuchibashi くちばし *(bird's) beak*

kuchibeni 口紅 *lipstick*

kuchibiru 唇 *lip(s)*

kuchibúe 口笛 *a whistle* ❀kuchibúe o fukú 口笛を吹く *whistle*

kuchíguchi ni 口々に *unanimously; one after the other* ❀Sono kaisha no sháin wa kuchíguchi ni kaisha no taisei no fúrusa o shiteki-shite iru. その会社の社員は口々に会社の体制の古さを指摘している。 *The employees unanimously point out how outmoded the company organization is.*

kuchinaoshi 口直し *a dish to clear one's palate*

kudámono 果物 *fruit* ❀kudamonoya 果物屋 *fruit store*

kudarana·i [*adj* kudaranaku nái; kudaranákatta] くだらない *(be) trifling; foolish; worthless* ❀Kudaranai kotó o iú na! くだらない事を言うな。 *Don't talk foolishness! <masc>* ❀Tanaka wa kudaranai yátsu da. 田中はくだらない奴だ。 *Tanaka's a jerk. <masc>* ❀Konna kudaranai monó o okurú no wa shitsúrei ja arimasén? こんなくだらないものを送るのは失礼じゃありません？ *Wouldn't it be rude to give such a* *trifle? <fem>*

kudari 下り *descent; the "down train" (away from the capital)* 🖉Koko kará wa nagái kudari ni narimásu. ここからは長い下りになります。 *From here there will be a long downward slope.* 🖉Kudari wa nánji desu ka? 下りは何時ですか。 *What time is the "down train"?*

kudar·u [*vi* kudaranai; kudatta] 下る *go down; descend; step down* 🖉kawá o kudaru 川を下る *go down a river*

kudasái [*vt: imperative*] 下さい *Please!; Give me!* 🖉Gyūniki o hyaku gúramu kudasái. 牛肉を百グラム下さい。 *Give me a hundred grams of beef, please.*

kudasár·u [*vt* kudasaránai; kudasátta] *give* [e.g., *a superior gives to me*] *<polite>* 🖉Kore o kudasáru no desu ka? これを下さるのですか。 *Are you giving this to me? <polite>* [te] **kudasár·u** [*vb aux*] (ーて) くださる *(someone) gives (me) the (favor of) doing (something) <formal>* 🖉Hayashi-san wa ocha o irete kudasaimáshita. 林さんはお茶を入れてくださいました。 *Mrs. Hayashi prepared tea for me.*

kuensan くえん酸 *citric acid*

kufū 工夫 *device; design; idea; plan* ——**kufū-suru** [*vt*] 工夫する *devise; contrive; design; plan* 🖉Máinichi no kondate o kufū surú no wa tanoshíi wa. 毎日の献立を工夫するのは楽しいわ。 *It's fun planning the menu every day. <fem>*

Kúgatsu 九月 *September*

kugi 釘 *nail; peg; spike* 🖉kugi-núki 釘抜き *pincer for pulling out nails* 🖉kugi o útsu 釘を打つ *drive a nail* 🖉kugi o sásu 釘を刺す *remind (or warn) someone*

kugír·u [*vt* kugíránai; kugítta] 区切る *partition; divide* 🖉tochi o futatsú ni kugíru 土地を二つに区切る *divide the land into two*

kūgun 空軍 *air force*

kugúr·u [*vi* kuguránai; kugútta] 潜る *pass through; pass under* 🖉Gádo o kugúttara usetsu-shite kudasái. ガードを潜ったら右折して下さい。 *Go through the underpass and turn right, please.*

kuichigai 食い違い *difference; disparity; discrepancy; conflict* 🖉Futarí no kangaekata ní wa kuichigai ga áru. 二人の考え方には食い違いがある。 *They don't think alike.*

kuichiga·u [*vi* kuichigawanai; kuichigatta] 食い違う *be contrary to; be in conflict; be contradictory* 🖉Kinō no komento to kyō no komento wa kuichigatte iru. 昨日のコメントと今日のコメントは食い違っている。 *Your comments yesterday and today are contradictory.*

kúiki 区域 *limit; district; zone; area* 🖉haitatsu kúiki 配達区域 *delivery zone*

kujaku 孔雀 *peacock; peahen*

kúji 籤 *lottery* 🖉kúji o hiku くじを引く *draw a lot* 🖉kúji ni ataru くじに当たる *win a lottery*

kujira 鯨 *whale*

kujō 苦情 *complaint; grievance* ❽kujō o iu 苦情を言う *complain*
❽Saikin wa gomi shūshū ni kansúru kujō ga fúete iru. 最近はゴミ収集
に関する苦情がふえている。 *Recently complaints about garbage
collection have been increasing.*

kūkan 空間 *space; room* ❽jikan to kūkan 時間と空間 *time and space*

kūki 空気 *air; atmosphere* ❽Máe no taiya no kūki ga tarinai. 前のタイ
ヤの空気が足りない。 *The air in the front tire is low.* ❽Tennyúsei
wa atarashíi gakkō no kūki ni najiménai. 転入生は新しい学校の空気
に馴染めない。 *The transfer student cannot get used to the atmosphere
of the new school.*

kūkō 空港 *airport*

kumá 熊 *bear (animal)*

kumadé 熊手 *bamboo rake*

kumánaku 隈無く *leaving no stone unturned; everywhere; universally*
❽Keisatsu wa yōgísha o tsuiseki-shite mori no náka o kumánaku
sagashita. 警察は容疑者を追跡して森の中を隈無く探した。 *The
police combed the woods in search of the suspect.*

kumiai 組合 *association; union; league* ❽rōdō kúmiai 労働組合 *labor
union*

kumitate 組み立て *structure; framework; pre-fab* ❽kumitate jútaku 組
み立て住宅 *prefabricated housing*

kumitaté·ru [*vt* kumitaténai; kumítateta] 組み立てる *assemble; put up;
put together* ❽jidósha o kumitatéru 自動車を組み立てる *assemble
an automobile*

kúmo 雲 *a cloud* ❽kúmo no ói hi 雲の多い日 *a cloudy day*

kúmo 蜘蛛 *spider*

kumorí 曇り *cloudy* ❽kumorí nochi haré 曇り後晴れ *cloudy, later
sunny* ❽Asú wa kumorí deshō. 明日は曇りでしょう。 *Tomorrow
will probably be cloudy.*

kumór·u [*vi* kumoránai; kumótta] 曇る *be cloudy* ❽Yúge ni mégane ga
kumótta. 湯気に眼鏡が曇った。 *The steam fogged up my glasses.*
❽Warúi shirase o kiite, háha no kao ga kumótta. 悪い知らせを聞いて、
母の顔が曇った。 *Hearing the bad news, mother's face became
downcast.*

kum·u [*vt* kumanai; kunda] 汲む *draw (water); ladle* ❽Tsurube de mizu
o kunda. 釣瓶で水を汲んだ。 *I drew water with the well bucket.*

kúm·u [*vi* kumánai; kúnda] 組む *braid; cross (one's legs); grapple (with);
join together (with); conspire (with)* ❽udé o kúmu 腕を組む *fold
(one's) arms* ❽Watashi wa ténisu de ítsumo kánai to péa o kúmu. 私
はテニスでいつも家内とペアを組む。 *In tennis, I always play
doubles with my wife as partner.*

kun 訓 *the kun (Japanese) reading of a Chinese character* ❽kun-yomi

訓読み *the kun reading*

-kun 〜君 *(name suffix, masc, familiar; also may be applied to a woman in school by a teacher or in an office by a superior)* §Yamada-kun 山田君 *Mr./ Ms. Yamada*

Kunáichō 宮内庁 *Imperial Household Agency*

kúnan 苦難 *hardship; suffering; distress* §kúnan o norikoeru 苦難を乗り超える *overcome hardships*

kuni 国 *country; nation*

kúnren 訓練 *training; drill* §Jidōsha shūri no kúnren o úkete iru. 自動車修理の訓練を受けている。 *I'm (receiving) training to be an automobile mechanic.* ――**kúnren-suru** [vi] 訓練する *train; drill*

kū́rā クーラー *air conditioner*

kurabe·ru [vi kurabenai; kurabeta] 比べる *compare; contrast* §Kono ringo to ano ringo, dóchira ga amái ka kurabete goran. このりんごとあのりんご、どちらが甘いか比べてごらん。 *Compare this apple and that one to see which is sweeter.*

kurage 水母 *jellyfish*

kurai 位 *rank; grade*

kura·i [adj kuraku nái; kurákatta] 暗い *(be) dark; gloomy; somber* §Sóto wa mő kurai yo! 外はもう暗いよ。 *It's already dark outside!* §Iyá na jíken bákari de kimochi ga kuraku nátte shimáu. 嫌な事件ばかりで気持ちが暗くなってしまう。 *With all these awful things happening, I feel depressed.*

-kúrai ; -gúrai 〜位 *about; approximately; to the extent that* §Shinsha wa ikura-gúrai surú no ka na? 新車はいくるぐらいするのかな。 *I wonder about how much a new car costs.* <masc> §Sore o suru-kúrai nara, shinda hő ga mashi yo. それをする位なら、死んだ方がましよ。 *I'd rather die than do that.* <fem>

kurákushon クラクション *(car) horn; klaxon*

kurashi 暮らし *living; livelihood; day-by-day life* §kurashi o tatéru 暮らしを立てる *make a living* §Máinichi no kurashi ni taikutsu-shite iru. 毎日の暮らしに退屈している。 *I'm bored with (my) life.*

kuras·u [vi kurasanai; kurashita} 暮らす *live; live (one's) life* §Ryőshin wa Tóyama de hissóri kurashite imásu. 両親は富山でひっそり暮らしています。 *My parents are living a quiet, simple life in Toyama.*

kurenái 紅 *red; crimson*

kure·ru [vi kurenai; kureta] 暮れる *be dark; grow dark; come to an end* §Mō súgu hi ga kureru. もうすぐ日が暮れる。 *It'll be dark soon.* §Kotoshi mo kuremáshita. 今年も暮れました。 *This year is over. (or Another year has passed.)*

kure·ru [vt kurenai; kureta] 呉れる *give (e.g., an equal or superior gives to me)* §Shújin ga kono nékkuresu o kuremáshita. 主人がこのネックレスを呉れました。 *My husband gave me this necklace.*

[te] kure·ru [*vb aux*] （ーて）くれる *(someone) gives (me) (the favor of) doing (something)* ❽Musume wa kono sḗtā o ánde kureta. 娘はこのセーターを編んでくれた。 *My daughter knit this sweater for me.*

kurí 栗 *chestnut*

kurikaeshi 繰り返し *repetition*

kurikáes·u [*vt* kurikaesánai; kurikáeshita] 繰り返す *repeat ; do over again* ❽Gógaku wa nándo mo kurikáeshite benkyō-suru shika nái. 語学は何度も繰り返して勉強するしかない。 *With languages, there's no other way but to study by repeating over and over again.*

kúro 黒 *black* ❽kuro-obi 黒帯 *black belt* ❽kuro-zátō 黒砂糖 *(unrefined) brown sugar*

kúrō 苦労 *trouble; hardship; labor* ❽kúrō no ói jinsei 苦労の多い人生 *a hard life* ——**kúrō-suru** [*vi*] 苦労する *suffer; endure hardships; labor hard* ❽Otṓtó wa shigoto o sagasú no ni kúrō-shimáshita. 弟は仕事を探すのに苦労しました。 *My brother had a hard time finding a job.*

kuró·i [*adj* kúroku nái; kúrokatta] 黒い *(be) black*

kúrōto 玄人 *an expert; a professional*

kúru [*vi irregular* kónai; kíta] 来る *come* ❽Ítsu Nihón ni kimáshita ka? いつ日本に来ましたか。 *When did you come to Japan?* ❽Asobi ni kíte kudásai. 遊びに来て下さい。 *Come over for a visit.*

[-te] kuru [*vb aux*] （ーて）くる *comes / starts (to be or to do)* ❽Kono machi no jinkō wa fúete kimáshita. この町の人口は増えてきました。 *The population of this town has grown.*

kuruma 車 *car; vehicle; wheel* ❽Kuruma no unten ga dekimásu ka? 車の運転が出来ますか。 *Can you drive a car?*

kurushí·i [*adj* kurúshiku nái; kurúshikatta] 苦しい *(be) painful; hard* ❽Íki ga kurushíi. 息が苦しい。 *It's hard to breathe.* ❽Kurushíi shigoto ni táete iru. 苦しい仕事に耐えている。 *I'm enduring the hard work.*

kurushimé·ru [*vt* kurushiménai; kurushímeta] 苦しめる *trouble; distress; harass; torment* ❽kokóro o kushiméru 心を苦しめる *worry about*

kurushimí 苦しみ *pain; anguish; suffering*

kurushím·u [*vi* kurushimánai; kurushínda] 苦しむ *suffer; feel pain; agonize* ❽Nihón wa jinkō kájō de kurushínde iru. 日本は人口過剰で苦しんでいる。 *Japan suffers from overpopulation.*

kurú·u [*vi* kuruwánai; kurútta] 狂う *go mad; go crazy; go wrong; go out of order* ❽Masao-san wa rókku ni kurútte iru. 正夫さんはロックに狂っている。 *Masao has gone crazy over rock music.* ❽Keikaku ga kurútte shimatta. 計画が狂ってしまった。 *The plans went awry.*

kusá 草 *grass; herb; weed* ❽kusá o karu 草を刈る *cut the grass* ❽kusá o tóru 草を取る *pull weeds* ❽kusa-karíki 草刈り機 *lawn* *mower*

kusahara 草原 *grassy field; plain; meadow*

kusá·i [*adj* kúsaku nái; kúsakatta] 臭い *(be) foul-smelling; stinking; malodorous* §Kono heyá wa tabako-kusái. この部屋はたばこ臭い。*This room smells of tobacco.* §Kusái monó ni futa o suru. 臭い物に蓋をする。*Cover up a foul odor (Sweep something under the rug).* *<set phrase>*

kusari 鎖 *chain*

kusár·u [*vi* kusaránai; kusátta] 腐る *spoil; go bad; rot* §Nikú ga kusátte shimatta. 肉が腐ってしまった。*The meat has gone bad.* §Kusátte mo tái. 腐っても鯛。*It may be spoiled but at least it's sea bream (It may not be what it once was, but it's still first class). <set phrase>*

kusé 癖 *habit; vice* §warúi kusé 悪い癖 *bad habit* §kusé ga tsuku 癖がつく *get into a habit* §kusé o naósu 癖をなおす *break a habit* §Imōtó wa kamí o ijíru kusé ga áru. 妹は髪をいじる癖がある。*My (younger) sister has a habit of playing with her hair.*

kushámi くしゃみ *a sneeze* §kushámi o suru くしゃみをする *sneeze* §kushámi ga déru くしゃみが出る *sneeze*

kushí 串 *a skewer; a spit* §kushiyaki 串焼 *skewered (meat)*

kushí 櫛 *a comb* §kamí ni kushí o ireru 髪に櫛を入れる *comb (one's) hair*

kushín 苦心 *effort; pains* §Isha no kushín wa mudá ni owatta. 医者の苦心は無駄に終わった。*The doctor's efforts were of no use.* ——**kushín-suru** [*vi*] 苦心する *take pains; work hard; expend effort* §Kono mondai o kaiketsu-surú no ni kushín-shimáshita. この問題を解決するのに苦心しました。*I worked hard to solve this problem.*

kūshū 空襲 *air raid* §kūshū kéihō 空襲警報 *air raid warning*

kusó 糞 *excrement* §Kusó! 糞！ *Shit!*

kūsō 空想 *dream; imagination; daydreaming* §Watashi wa ítsumo kūsō ni fukétte iru. 私はいつも空想に耽っている。*I'm always daydreaming.* ——**kūsō-suru** [*vi*] 空想する *imagine; fancy; dream*

kusugur·u [*vt* kusuguranai; kusugutta] くすぐる *tickle (someone)*

kusuguttá·i [*adj* kusuguttáku nái; kusuguttákatta] くすぐったい *(be) ticklish; feel ticklish* §Kusuguttái! くすぐったい！ *That tickles!*

kúsukusu wara·u [*vi*] くすくす笑う *giggle; titter*

kusúnoki 楠 *camphor tree*

kusuri 薬 *medicine; drug* §kusuriya 薬屋 *pharmacy; drugstore* §Ichinichi sankái kono kusuri o nónde kudasái. 一日三回この薬を飲んで下さい。*Take this medicine three times a day.*

kusuríyubi 薬指 *third finger; ring finger*

kutabiré·ru [*vi* kutabirénai; kutabíreta] くたびれる *tire; be fatigued; be exhausted; be worn out* §Undō-suru to, súgu kutabiréru. 運動すると直ぐくたびれる。*When I exercise I get tired right away.* §Kono kutsushitá wa mố kutabírete shimatta. この靴下はもうくたびれてしまった。 *These socks are worn out.*

kutakuta くたくた *utterly exhausted; worn out; worn to a frazzle* 🔸Kutakuta désu! くたくたです！ *I'm pooped!*

kutsú 靴 *shoes* 🔸kutsú o haku 靴を履く *put on (wear) shoes* 🔸kutsú o migaku 靴を磨く *polish shoes* 🔸kutsú himo 靴紐 *shoe lace* 🔸kutsú-zumi 靴墨 *shoe polish* 🔸kutsú issoku 靴一足 *a pair of shoes*

kutsū 苦痛 *pain; agony* 🔸seishinteki kutsū 精神的苦痛 *mental anguish* 🔸kutsū kara kaihō-sareru 苦痛から解放される *be freed (or released) from pain* 🔸Kóndo no projékuto wa kutsū da. 今度のプロジェクトは苦痛だ。 *The next project is going to be a pain. <masc>*

kutsugáes·u [*vt* kutsugaesánai; kutsugáeshita] 覆す *overturn; (cause to) capsize; reverse* 🔸fúne o kutsugáesu 船を覆す *overturn a boat* 🔸shōgen o kutsugáesu 証言を覆す *reverse (one's) testimony*

kutsujoku 屈辱 *an insult; indignity; humiliation*

kutsuróg·u [*vi* kutsurogánai; kutsuróida] 寛ぐ *relax; make (oneself) at home* 🔸Dốzo kutsuróide kudasái. どうぞ寛いで下さい。 *Please make yourself at home.*

kutsushitá 靴下 *socks; stockings*

kuttsuké·ru [*vt* kuttsukénai; kuttsúketa] くっ付ける *join; attach (firmly to); add on* 🔸Setchakúzai de kuttsúketa. 接着剤でくっ付けた。 *I attached it with glue.*

kuttsúk·u [*vi* kuttsukánai; kuttsúita] くっ付く *cling (to); adhere* 🔸Anó ko wa ítsumo okásan ni kuttsúite iru. あの子はいつもお母さんにくっ付いている。 *That child always clings to his mother.*

kú·u [*vt* kuwánai; kútta] 食う *eat <masc>* 🔸Meshi (o) kúu kai? めし（を）食うかい？ *Ya wanna eat? <masc>* 🔸Kono kuruma wa gásorin o kúu yo. この車はガソリンを食うよ。 *This car eats gasoline. <masc>*

kuwa 鍬 *a hoe*

kúwa 桑 *mulberry*

kuwadate 企て *a scheme; a plan; an attempt* ——**kuwadaté·ru** [*vt* kuwadaténai; kuwadáteta] 企てる *attempt; undertake*

kuwae·ru [*vt* kuwaenai; kuwaeta] 加える *add to; attach; supplement* 🔸Shió o mō sukóshi kuwaete kudasái. 塩をもう少し加えて下さい。 *Add a little more salt.* 🔸Watashi mo kuwaete kudasái. 私も加えて下さい。 *Count me in, too.*

kuwae·ru [*vt* kuwaenai; kuwaeta] くわえる *hold in the mouth* 🔸Hóra! Néko ga nánika kuwaete iru yo! ほら！猫が何かくわえているよ！ *Look! The cat's holding something in its mouth!*

kuwashí·i [*adj* kuwáshiku nái; kuwáshikatta] 詳しい *(be) detailed; well acquainted with* 🔸Kono chízu wa kuwashíi ne. この地図は詳しいね。 *This map is detailed, isn't it?* 🔸Háha wa Indo ryốri ni kuwashíi desu. 母はインド料理に詳しいです。 *Mother's an expert on Indian cuisine.* ——**kuwáshiku** 詳しく *in detail; minutely; at length* 8Senséi wa sono ími o kuwáshiku setsumei-shite kureta. 先生はその意味を詳しく説明してくれた。 *The teacher explained the meaning in detail.*

kuwawár·u [*vi* kuwawaránai; kuwawátta] 加わる *join; participate in; be added to* 8Gḗmu ni kuwawátte mo íi desu ka? ゲームに加わってもいいですか。 *May I join the game?*

kuyamí 悔やみ *condolence* 8kuyamí no dempō 悔やみの電報 *a telegram message of condolence* ——**kuyám·u** [*vt* kuyamánai; kuyánda] 悔やむ *be sorry about; regret*

kuyashí·i [*adj* kuyáshiku nái; kuyáshikatta] 悔しい *(be) vexing; frustrating; mortifying* 8Mata makete, kuyashíi! また負けて、悔しい。 *We lost again! It's so frustrating!*

kúzu 屑 *waste; scraps* 8kuzu kago 屑籠 *wastebasket* 8kami kúzu 紙屑 *waste paper* 8pan kúzu パン屑 *bread crumbs* 8ningen no kúzu 人間の屑 *the dregs of humanity*

kuzuré 崩れ *crumbling; collapse* 8gake kúzure がけ崩れ *landslide*

kuzuré·ru [*vi* kuzurénai; kuzúreta] 崩れる *crumble; collapse; go out of shape* 8Jishin de hashí ga kuzúreta. 地震で橋が崩れた。 *The bridge collapsed in the earthquake.*

kuzús·u [*vt* kuzusánai; kuzúshita] 崩す *demolish; tear down; destroy; break up* 8Sono tatemóno o kuzushimásu. その建物を崩します。 *We'll tear down that building.* 8Sen-én-satsu o kozeni ni kuzúshite kudasái. 千円札を小銭に崩して下さい。 *Change this ¥1000 bill into small change, please.*

kyakkan 客観 *the object (Tech)* 8kyakkansei 客観性 *objectivity* 8Gakumón no kenkyū ní wa tsúne ni kyakkansei ga hitsuyṓ desu. 学問の研究にはつねに客観性が必要です。 *In academic research objectivity is important at all times.* ——**kyakkanteki [na]** 客観的（な）*objective* 8kyakkanteki na íken 客観的な意見 *an objective opinion* ——**kyakkanteki ni** 客観的に *objectively* 8kyakkanteki ni míte... 客観的にみて *looking at it (or looked at) objectively....*

kyaku 客 *guest; customer* 8Gomen nasái. Íma o-kyaku-san ga kíte imásu.... ごめんなさい。お客さんが来ていますが。 *I'm sorry, I have a guest right now....*

kyṓ 今日 *today* 8Kyṓ wa nanyṓbi desu ka? 今日は何曜日ですか。 *What day (of the week) is it today?*

kyōchō 強調 *emphasis; stress* ——**kyōchō-suru** [*vt*] 強調する *emphasize; stress* 8Kono shṓhin no sḗrusu-póinto o nándo mo kyōchō-shita. この商品のセールスポイントを何度も強調した。 *I emphasized the sales points of this product over and over.*

kyṓdai 兄弟 *brothers and sisters; siblings* 8Kyṓdai ga imásu ka? 兄弟

がいますか。 *Do you have any brothers and sisters?*

kyodai na 巨大な *huge; gigantic; enormous* ❀Kyodai na dámu ga kensetsu-sarete iru. 巨大なダムが建設されている。 *A huge dam is being built.*

kyōdō 共同 *cooperation; common; joint* ❀kyōdō bókin 共同募金 *community chest* ❀kyōdō kénkyū 共同研究 *joint research (project)* ——**kyōdō-suru** [vi] 共同する *cooperate (with); work together (with)* ❀Sono gakkō no séito zen'in ga kyōdō-shite mozaiku héki-ga o kansei-saseta. その学校の生徒全員が共同してモザイク壁画を完成させた。 *All the students of the school joined together and completed a mosaic wall mural.*

kyōdōtai 協同体 *community; communal unit*

kyōfu 恐怖 *fear; terror; horror* ❀kyōfúkan 恐怖感 *feeling of fear* ❀kyōfu ni ononóku 恐怖におののく *tremble with fear*

kyōgi 協議 *conference; discussion; deliberation* ——**kyōgi-suru** [vt] 協議する *confer (with); discuss; deliberate* ❀Kokkai de kongo no bōsai táisaku ni tsúite kyōgi-shita. 国会で今後の防災対策について協議した。 *The Diet deliberated concerning a policy on disaster prevention.*

kyōgi 競技 *game; match* ❀kyōgíkai 競技会 *athletic meet* ——**kyōgi-suru** [vi] 競技する *have a game*

kyōgi 教義 *doctrine; dogma* ❀kyōgi móndō 教義問答 *catechism*

kyōhaku 脅迫 *threat; menace; harassment; intimidation* ——**kyōhaku-suru** [vt] 脅迫する *threaten; intimidate*

kyōhánsha 共犯者 *accomplice*

kyōhi 拒否 *denial; disapproval; rejection* ——**kyōhi-suru** [vt] 拒否する *reject; disapprove*

kyōi 驚異 *surprise; amazement* ❀Musuko no seichō no háyasa ni kyōi no mé o mihatta. 息子の成長の早さに驚異の目を見張った。 *We watched in amazement how fast our son grew.* ——**kyōiteki [na]** 驚異的（な）*surprising; amazing*

kyōiku 教育 *education* ❀gakkō kyōiku 学校教育 *schooling* ❀kyōiku séido 教育制度 *education system* ❀Áni wa Amerika de kyōiku o úketa. 兄はアメリカで教育を受けた。 *My older brother received his education in America.* ——**kyōiku-suru** 教育する *educate*

kyōin 教員 *teacher; instructor*

kyōju 教授 *instruction; professor* ❀jokyóju 助教授 *assistant professor*

kyōjū-suru [vi] 居住する *live; dwell* ❀Amerika Índian wa mukashi kono chíiki ni kyojū-shite ita. アメリカインデイアンは昔この地域に居住していた。 *Long ago, American Indians lived in this area.*

kyōka 許可 *permission; approval; license* ❀kyōka o éru 許可を得る *receive permission* ❀Kyōka ga órita. 許可がおりた。 *Permission was granted.*

kyōkai 教会 *church*

kyōkai 協会 *association*

kyōkai-sen 境界線 *boundary line; border*

kyōkásho 教科書 *textbook*

kyōken 狂犬 *mad (rabid) dog* ⸙**kyōken-byō** 狂犬病 *rabies*

kyōki 狂気 *insanity; madness*

kyoku 曲 *music; song* ⸙Dóno kyoku ga kikitái desu ka? どの曲が聞きたいですか。*What song do you want to hear?*

kyóku 局 *bureau; department* ⸙yūbínkyoku 郵便局 *post office* ⸙eiséikyoku 衛生局 *department of sanitation*

kyóku- 極～ *polar; extreme; complete* ⸙kyokutō 極東 *Far East* ⸙Hokkyoku 北極 *North Pole* ⸙kyokusa shúdan 極左集団 *extreme leftist group*

kyókubu 局部 *part; section; local; private parts* ⸙kyokubu másui 局部麻酔 *local anesthesia*

kyōkun 教訓 *lesson; teachings* ⸙Káko no ayamachi ga íma de wa yói kyōkun ni nátte iru. 過去の過ちが今では良い教訓になっている。*The mistakes of the past have become good lessons for the present.*

kyokután [na] 極端（な）*extreme; excessive* ⸙Sore wa kyokután na réi desu. それは極端な例です。*That's an extreme example.* —— **kyokután ni** 極端に *extremely; excessively; exceptionally*

Kyokutō 極東 *Far East*

kyōkyū 供給 *supply; service* ⸙kyōkyúsha 供給者 *supplier* ⸙juyō to kyōkyū 需要と供給 *supply and demand* ——**kyōkyū-suru** [vt] 供給する *supply; provide* ⸙kome o kyōkyū-suru 米を供給する *supply rice*

kyőmi 興味 *interest (in)* ⸙kottōhin ni kyőmi o mótsu 骨董品に興味を持つ *have interest in antiques* ⸙rekishi ni kyőmi ga áru 歴史に興味がある *be interested in history* ⸙kyőmi aru kámoku 興味ある科目 *an interesting (school) subject*

kyōmi-buká·i [adj -búkaku nái; -búkakatta] 興味深い *(be) of great interest* ⸙Kono shōsetsu wa totemo kyōmi-bukái desu. この小説はとても興味深いです。*This novel is very interesting.*

kyónen 去年 *last year*

kyōretsu [na] 強烈（な）*strong; intense; severe* ⸙kyōretsu na niói 強烈な臭い *a strong odor* ⸙Sore wa kyōretsu na inshō o nokóshita. それは強烈な印象を残した。*That left a strong impression.*

kyóri 距離 *distance*

kyōryoku 協力 *cooperation* ⸙Go-kyōryoku o arígatō. ご協力をありがとう。*Thank you for your cooperation.* ——**kyōryoku-suru** [vi] *cooperate* ⸙Kono shigoto wa minná de kyōryoku-shite gambátte kudasái. この仕事はみんなで協力して頑張って下さい。*Everyone please cooperate and put all you've got into this job.*

kyōsan shúgi 共産主義 *communism* ⸙kyōsan shugísha 共産主義者 *a* *communist* §Kyōsantō 共産党 *Communist Party*

kyōsei 強制 *compulsion* ——**kyōsei no** 強制の *compulsory* ——**kyōseiteki [na]** 強制的（な）*compulsory* ——**kyōseiteki ni** 強制的に *compulsorily; coercively* ——**kyōsei-suru** [*vt*] 強制する *compel; coerce; force* §Bokin o kyōsei-sareta. 募金を強制された。*I was forced to contribute to the fund.*

kyṓshi 教師 *teacher; tutor*

kyōshitsu 教室 *classroom*

kyōshū 郷愁 *homesickness; nostalgia* §Nihón o nágaku hanárete ite, kyōshū no nén ni kararete iru. 日本を長く離れていて郷愁の念にかられている。*I've been away from Japan a long time; I'm homesick.*

kyōsō 競争 *competition* §kyōsō ni kátsu 競争に勝つ *win (in) competition* ——**kyōsō no** 競争の *competitive* ——**kyōsō-suru** 競争する *compete*

kyōsō [na] 強壮（な）*strong; robust; athletic* §kyōsō na táikaku 強壮な体格 *a robust build*

kyōsṓkyoku 協奏曲 *concerto* §piano kyōsṓkyoku ピアノ協奏曲 *piano concerto*

kyōtsū [no] 共通（の）*common; shared* §kyōtsṹten 共通点 *(some)thing in common*

kyōyō 教養 *education; culture* §Míchino-san wa kyōyō no áru hitó desu. 道野さんは教養のある人です。*Ms. Michino is a well-educated person.*

kyōzai 教材 *curriculum materials*

kyozetsu 拒絶 *refusal; rejection; denial* ——**kyozetsu-suru** [*vt*] 拒絶する *refuse; reject; deny* §Watashi no yōkyū wa kyozetsu-sareta. 私の要求は拒絶された。*My request was denied.*

kyōzon 共存 *coexistence* ——**kyōzon-suru** [*vi*] 共存する *coexist*

kyṹ 九 *nine (the numeral)*

kyū 急 *suddenness; emergency; steepness* ——**kyū na** 急（な）*sudden; urgent; steep* §kyū na saka 急な坂 *a steep slope* §Kyū na yōji de dekakenákereba naránakatta. 急な用事で出かけなければならなかった。*I had to go out on urgent business.* ——**kyū ni** 急に*suddenly* §Kyū ni áme ga furidashita. 急に雨が降り出した。*It suddenly started to rain.*

kyūden 宮殿 *palace*

kyṹdō 弓道 *archery (J)*

kyūen 救援 *relief; rescue* §kyūen shíkin 救援資金 *relief funds* §Nammin ni kyūen o okurimáshita. 難民に救援を送りました。*We sent relief to the refugees.*

kyūgeki [na] 急激（な）*rapid; sudden; abrupt*

kyūgyō 休業 *business holiday; suspension of business (operation)*

kyūjitsu 休日 *holiday*

kyújo 救助 *rescue; relief* §kyūjo-tai 救助隊 *rescue party* ——**kyújo-suru** [*vt*] 救助する *rescue; save* §Watashi wa kawá de oborete iru kodomo o kyújo-shita. 私は川で溺れている子どもを救助した。 *I rescued a child who was drowning in the river.*

kyūka 休暇 *holiday; vacation* §Anáta wa nén ni nánnichi kyūka ga arimásu ka? あなたは年に何日休暇がありますか。 *How many days of vacation do you have in a year?*

kyūkei 休憩 *rest; recess* §kyūkei jíkan 休憩時間 *rest period* ——**kyūkei-suru** [*vi*] 休憩する *rest; take a break* §Sukóshi kyūkei-shimasén ka? 少し休憩しませんか。 *How about resting a bit?*

kyūkō 急行 *express train* §kyūkóken 急行券 *express ticket*

kyūkon 球根 *(plant) bulb* §kyūkon shokúbutsu 球根植物 *a bulbous plant*

kyūkon 求婚 *marriage proposal* ——**kyūkon-suru** [*vi*] 求婚する *propose marriage*

kyúkutsu [na] 窮屈（な）*tight-fitting; cramped*

kyūkyū 救急 *emergency aid* §kyūkyú-bako 救急箱 *first-aid kit* §kyūkyúsha 救急車 *ambulance*

kyūmei 救命 *lifesaving* §kyūméigu 救命具 *lifesaving equipment* §kyūmei dói 救命胴衣 *life jacket (vest)* §kyūmei bóto 救命ボート *lifeboat*

kyúryō 給料 *salary; pay* §Nihonjín no heikin no kyúryō wa íkura desu ka? 日本人の平均の給料はいくらですか。 *What is the average monthly salary for Japanese (or in Japan)?*

kyūsei- 急性〜 *acute* §kyūsei háien 急性肺炎 *accute pneumonia*

kyūshoku 給食 *school lunch (provided by the school)*

Kyúshū 九州 *Kyūshū (one of the four major islands of Japan)*

kyūshū 吸収 *absorption; assimilation* ——**kyūshū-suru** [*vt*] 吸収する *absorb; suck (take) in* §Kono suponji wa mizu o yóku kyūshū-suru. このスポンジは水をよく吸収する。 *This sponge absorbs water well.*

kyūsoku 休息 *a rest; a break* ——**kyūsoku-suru** [*vi*] 休息する *rest; take a break*

kyūsoku 急速 *swiftness; rapidity* ——**kyūsoku na** 急速な *swift; rapid* §Kompyútā sángyō wa kyūsoku na shímpo o togete iru. コンピュータ一産業は急速な進歩をとげている。 *The computer industry has made rapid progress.*

kyūsu 急須 *teapot*

kyúyo 給与 *allowance; salary* §kyūyo súijun 給与水準 *wage level*

kyūyō 急用 *urgent (pressing) business* §Chichí wa kyūyō de dekakete imásu. 父は急用で出かけています。 *My father has gone out on urgent business.*

kyūyō 休養 *rest; recuperation* ——**kyūyō-suru** [*vi*] 休養する *rest; recuperate* §Seishin hírō ga tamatte shimattá no de, kúki no íi tokoró de kyūyō-shite iru. 精神疲労がたまってしまったので、空気のいいところで休養している。 *I was experiencing a great deal of mental fatigue, so I am recuperating in a place where the air is refreshing.*

kyūyu 給油 *oil supply* ——**kyūyu-suru** [*vt*] 給油する *supply oil (gasoline)*

M

ma 間 *space; room; interval of time* ❧Sukóshi ma o oite ukagaimashố. 少し間を置いて伺いましょう。 *Let's wait a bit before we call on (him).*

má まあ *Well!; My!; [an interjection indicating hesitation]* ❧Mắ, nánte suteki nán deshô! まあ、なんて素敵なんでしょう！ *My! How nice!* <*fem*> ❧Sore wa ...mắ...nán to ittára íi deshô? それは…まあ…何と言ったらいいでしょう？ *That's ...uh...what should I say?*

maatarashí·i [*adj* ma-ataráshiku nái; ma-ataráshikatta] 真新しい *brand-new* ❧Watashi wa nyūgakú-shiki ní wa ma-atarashíi seifuku o kite ítta. 私は入学式には真新しい制服を着て行った。 *I went to the school entrance ceremony in a brand-new uniform.*

mabátaki 瞬き *a wink; a blink* ——**mabátaki-suru** [*vi*] 瞬きする *wink; blink* ❧Kodomo wa mabátaki mo sézu ni gámen ni kugi-zuke ni nátte shimatta. 子供は瞬きもせずに画面に釘付けになってしまった。 *Without blinking, the children's eyes were glued to the screen.*

mābōdốfu 麻婆豆腐 *Szechuan (spicy) tofu dish*

maboroshi 幻 *vision; phantom; illusion* ❧maboroshi o míru 幻を見る *see an illusion; have a vision* ❧maboroshi no meishu 幻の銘酒 *very rare saké*

mabushí·i [*adj* mabúshiku nái; mabúshikatta] 眩しい *(be) glaring; dazzling; radiant* ❧Táiyō ga mabushíi. 太陽が眩しい。 *The sun is glaring.*

mabushísa 眩しさ *a glare; dazzling light*

mábuta 瞼 *eyelid* ❧Mábuta ga omói. まぶたが重い。 *My eyelids are heavy.* ❧mábuta no háha まぶたの母 *the memory of (one's) mother*

machí 町；街 *street; town (administrative unit)* ❧chísa na machí 小さな町 *a small town* ❧machí o arúku 街を歩く *walk the streets*

machiáishitsu 待合室 *waiting room*

machiawase·ru [*vt* machiawasenai; machiawaseta] 待ち合わせる *wait for; meet (a person) by appointment*

máchibari 待ち針 *a straight pin*

machidōshí·i [*adj* machidōshíku nái; machidōshíkatta] 待ち遠しい *(be) impatient; await eagerly* ❧Watashi wa kikoku no hí ga machidōshíi. 私は帰国の日が待ち遠しい。 *I'm waiting eagerly for the day I get* *back (to my) home (country).*

machikado 街角；町角 *street corner*

machigáe·ru [*vt* machigaénai; machígaeta] 間違える *make a mistake*
❊kotáe o machigáeru 答えを間違える *make a mistake on the answer; miss the answer* ❊Machigáete imōtó no kása o mótte dekakete shimatta. 間違えて妹の傘を持って出かけてしまった。*When I left, I took my sister's umbrella by mistake.*

machigái 間違い *error; mistake* ❊Machigái ni kizúitara súgu teisei-shita hő ga íi. 間違いに気付いたら直ぐ訂正した方がいい。*If you notice a mistake, it's better to correct it right away.*

machigá·u [*vi / vt* machigawánai; machigátta] 間違う *be mistaken*
❊Sono kangáe wa machigátte iru. その考えは間違っている。*That idea is mistaken.*

machikamae·ru [*vt* machikamaenai; machikamaeta] 待ち構える *be ready and eager for; await eagerly* ❊Ōzéi no kísha ga Bei-daitőryő shūnin no áisatsu o machikamaete iru. 大勢の記者が米大統領就任の挨拶を待ち構えている。*A crowd of newspaper reporters is waiting eagerly for the inaugural address of the US president.*

machikane·ru [*vt* machikanenai; machikaneta] 待ちかねる *await impatiently* ❊Sóbo wa isha ga kúru no o íma ka íma ka to machikanete iru. 祖母は医者が来るのを今か今かと待ちかねている。*Grandmother is waiting impatiently for the doctor to come.*

machí ni mátta 待ちに待った *long-awaited* ❊Machí ni mátta kekkónshiki ga iyóiyo asú ni nátta. 待ちに待った結婚式はいよいよ明日になった。*Tomorrow's the day of the long-awaited wedding.*

machinozom·u [*vt* machinozomanai; machinozonda] 待ち望む *expect; look forward to; anticipate* ❊Watashi wa buchō shőshin o machinozonde imásu. 私は部長昇進を待ち望んでいます。*I'm looking forward to being promoted to division chief.*

máda 未だ *(not) yet; still* ❊Áme wa máda yamanai. 雨は未だ止まない。*The rain hasn't let up yet.* ❊"Shokuji wa mő sumimáshita ka?" "Iyá, máda desu." 「食事はもう済みましたか？」「いや、まだです。」*"Have you already finished eating?" "No, not yet."* ❊Yoshida-san wa máda wakái desu. 吉田さんはまだ若いです。*Yoshida is still young.*

mádamada まだまだ *still; still more; much more* ❊Mádamada wakái monó ni wa makenai zo! まだまだ若い者には負けないぞ！*I can still hold my own against these young guys.* <masc>

madara 斑 *spots; speckles* ——**madara no** 斑の *spotted; mottled; dappled* ❊madara no hébi 斑の蛇 *a spotted snake* ——**madara ni** 斑に *spotted; in spots* ❊Yama no yukí ga madara ni nokótte iru. 山の雪が斑に残っている。*Snow remains on the mountains in spots.*

máde まで *to; up to; until* ❊shichí-ji máde 七時まで *until 7:00 o'clock*

❦áme ga yamu máde 雨が止むまで *until it stops raining* ❦éki kara uchi máde 駅から家まで *from the station (to) home* ——**máde ni** までに *by* ❦Yūshoku máde ni káette kinasái. 夕食までに帰って来なさい。 *Be home by supper.*

mádo 窓 *window* ❦mado-kake 窓かけ *window curtain; blind* ❦mado-gárasu 窓ガラス *windowpane* ❦mado-giwa de 窓際で *at the window* ❦madó-guchi 窓口 *ticket window; reception desk* ❦Mádo o akete kudasái. 窓を開けて下さい。 *Open the window, please.*

máe 前 *in front of; before; ago; previous* ❦Ie no máe ni tákushī ga tomatta. 家の前にタクシーが止まった。 *A taxi stopped in front of the house.* ❦Máe ni sonó hito ni átta kotó ga áru. 前にその人に会ったことがある。 *I've met that person before.* ❦Jūnen-máe ni ókita jíken o íma de mo obóete iru. 10年前に起きた事件を今でも覚えている。 *Even now I remember what happened ten years ago.* ❦Watashi wa máe kara Tóshiko-san ga sukí datta. 私は前から寿子さんが好きだった。 *I've liked Toshiko for a long time.* <masc> ❦Kono máe no shikén wa yasáshikatta no ni... この前の試験は易しかったのに。 *The previous exam was easy, but....*

maegaki 前書き *preface; introduction; introductory remarks*

maekake 前掛け *apron*

maekin 前金 *advance payment*

maemuki no 前向きの *forward-looking; optimistic; a positive manner* ❦Sono mondai ni tsúite watashítachi wa maemuki ni torikunde iru. その問題について私たちは前向きに取り組んでいる。 *We're handling that problem in a positive manner.*

maeuríken 前売券 *advance (sale) ticket*

magamo 真鴨 *mallard; wild duck*

magar·u [vi / vt magaranai; magatta] 曲がる *bend; turn; be crooked; be inclined* ❦Tsugí no kádo o migi ni magatte kudasái. 次の角を右に曲がって下さい。 *Turn right at the next corner.* ❦Magatta kugi wa yakú ni tatánai. 曲がった釘は役に立たない。 *A bent nail is of no use.* <set phrase>

mage·ru [vt magenai; mageta] 曲げる *bend; distort* ❦hiza o mageru 膝を曲げる *bend the knee* ❦jíjitsu o mageru 事実を曲げる *distort the facts*

magirás·u [vi / vt magirasánai; magiráshita] 紛らす *distract* ❦taikutsu o magirásu 退屈を紛らす *relieve the tedium* ❦kanashimi o warai ni magirásu 悲しみを笑いに紛らす *take (one's) mind off sorrow by laughing*

magirawashí·i [adj magirawáshiku nái; magirawáshikatta] 紛らわしい *(be) confusing; ambiguous*

mágiwa ni 間際に *at the last moment* ❦Watashi wa shuppatsu mágiwa ni wasuremono ni kizúita. 私は出発間際に忘れ物に気付いた。 *Just at* *the moment I was leaving I noticed I had forgotten something.*

magó 孫 *grandchild*

magotsuk·u [*vi* magotsukanai; magotsuita] まごつく *be confused; be at a loss*

maguro 鮪 *tuna*

magusa まぐさ *hay*

máhi 麻痺 *paralysis* §shinzō máhi 心臓麻痺 *heart failure; heart attack* ——**máhi-suru** [*vi*] 麻痺する *be paralyzed* §Sámusa de ashi-no-saki ga máhi-shite iru. 寒さで足の先が麻痺している。 *My toes are numb from the cold.* §Jishin de kōtsū ga máhi-shite iru. 地震で交通が麻痺している。 *Because of the earthquake traffic is paralyzed.*

mahō 魔法 *magic; sorcery* §mahō-bin 魔法瓶 *thermos; vacuum bottle* §mahō-tsúkai 魔法使い *wizard; witch*

mai 舞 *dance (Japanese traditional)* §mai o maú 舞を舞う *dance a mai* §tsurugi no mai 剣の舞 *a sword dance*

mai- 毎〜 *every* §máiasa 毎朝 *every morning* §máiban 毎晩 *every night* §maido 毎度 *every time* §mainen 毎年 *every year* §máinichi 毎日 *every day* §maitsuki 毎月 *every month; monthly* §maishū kayóbi ni 毎週火曜日に *every Tuesday (or every week on Tuesday)*

-mai 〜枚 [*classifier for flat things such a paper*] §Kamí o nímai kudasái. 紙を二枚下さい。 *Give me two sheets of paper.* §Hachijūen kítte o jūmai kudasái. 八十円切手を十枚下さい。 *Give me ten ¥80 stamps, please.* §Máiasa tōsuto o sámmai tabemásu. 毎朝トーストを三枚食べます。 *I eat three pieces of toast every morning.*

-mái 〜まい [*neg presumptive verb suffix*] §Watashi wa mō zettai ni úso o tsukumái to omoimásu. 私はもう絶対に嘘をつくまいと思います。 *I'll never tell a lie again.*

maiagár·u [*vi* -agaránai; -agátta] 舞い上がる *whirl up (into the sky); mount; fly* §Tatami o tatáku to hokori ga maiagáru yo. 畳を叩くと埃が舞い上がるよ。 *If you beat the tatami, dust will fly up.* §Kimochi ga maiagátte iru. 気持ちが舞い上がっている。 *Emotions are mounting.*

máigo 迷子 *a lost child* §máigo ni náru 迷子になる *become lost* §Musumé wa Dizunīrándo de máigo ni nátte shimatta. 娘はディズニーランドで迷子になってしまった。 *My daughter got lost in Disneyland.*

máir·u [*vi* mairánai; máitta] 参る *go; come; visit (a shrine); be beaten; be overcome; be upset* §Míte mairimásu. 見て参ります。 *I'll go see.* <*polite*> §O-kúruma ga mairimáshita. お車が参りました。 *Your car has arrived.* <*polite*> §o-mairi-suru お参りする *visit a shrine* §Ore wa kánojo ni máitte iru. 俺は彼女に参っている。 *My girlfriend has me baffled.* <*masc*> §Karada ga máitte shimatta. 身体が参って

しまった。*I'm beat! (lit: My body is beaten.)* §**Máitta!** 参った！
You've got me there! (or Darn it!)

maisō 埋葬 *burial; interment* §maisō kyokáshō 埋葬許可証 *burial
certificate* ——**maisō-suru** [vt] 埋葬する *bury; inter* §Ikotsu o
sénzo-dáidai no haká ni maisō-shita. 遺骨を先祖代々の墓に埋葬し
た。*We buried his ashes in the family grave.*

maitoshi 毎年 *every year; annually* ——**maitoshi no** 毎年の *annual*

májan 麻雀 *mahjong*

májika ni 間近に *near by; close at hand* §Shimekiri ga májika ni
semátte iru. 締切が間近に迫っている。*The deadline is drawing near.*

majime [na] 真面目（な）*earnest; serious; sober* §majime na séito 真
面目な生徒 *an earnest student* §majime na kao 真面目な顔 *a
serious expression* ——**majime ni** 真面目に *earnestly; in earnest;
seriously* §majime ni benkyō-suru 真面目に勉強する *study
earnestly*

majinai まじない *magic ritual; fortune telling* §majinái-shi まじない
師 *fortune teller*

majir·u [vi majiránai; majítta] 混じる *be mixed* §Mizu to abura wa
majiránai. 水と油は混じらない。*Oil and water don't mix.*

majiwári 交わり *association (with friends); gathering; a get-together*

majiwár·u [vi majiwaránai; majiwátta] 交わる *mix; mingle (with);
associate (with); socialize; converge* §Háha wa hito to majiwáru no ga
hetá desu. 母は人と交わるのが下手です。*Mother doesn't socialize
well with people.* §Futatsú no sén wa kono ten de majiwarimásu. 二つ
の線はこの点で交わります。*The two lines converge at this point.*

májo 魔女 *witch*

májutsu 魔術 *magic*

makaná·u [vt makanawánai; makanátta] 賄う *furnish; provide; pay*
§Kakei wa súbete jibun de makanátte iru. 家計は全て自分で賄ってい
る。*I pay all household expenses myself.*

makasé·ru [vi / vt makasénai; makáseta] 任せる *leave (up to); entrust (to)*
§Watashi ni makásete kudasái. 私に任せて下さい。*Leave it to me.*
§Ún o tén ni makaséru shika nái. 運を天に任せるしかない。*There's
nothing one can do but leave one's fortune to heaven.* <set phrase>

makas·u [vt makasanai; makashita] 負かす *defeat; outdo; beat* §Ane o
ténisu de makashita. 姉をテニスで負かした。*I beat my older sister at
tennis.*

[o-]make ni （お）まけに *in addition; as a bonus; what's more* §Kánojo
wa sé ga tákakute sutáiru ga yókute, o-make ni atamá ga íi desu. 彼女は
背が高くてスタイルが良くて、おまけに頭がいいです。*She's tall,
she's got a good figure, and, what's more, she's smart.*

make·ru [vi makenai; maketa] 負ける *lose; be defeated* §sensō ni
makeru 戦争に負ける *lose a war* §shiai ni makeru 試合に負ける

lose a (sports) match

make·ru [vt makenai; maketa] 負ける *reduce (in price); discount*   8Kore o sen-en ni makete kudasaimasén ka. これを千円に負けて下さいませんか。 *Could you discount this to a thousand yen?*

maki 薪 *firewood*

makige 巻き毛 *curly hair; a curl*

makijaku 巻尺 *tape measure*

makikóm·u [vt makikómánai; makikónda] 巻き込む *involve*   8sharin ni makikomaréru 車輪に巻き込まれる *be run over (by the wheels of a car)*   8funsō ni makikomaréru 紛争に巻き込まれる *be involved in war*

makimodós·u [vt makimodosánai; makimodóshita] 巻き戻す *rewind*   8Tépu o makimodóshite oite kudasái. テープを巻き戻しておいて下さい。 *Rewind the tape, please.*

makká [na] 真っ赤（な）*bright red; scarlet*   8makká na sétā 真っ赤なセーター *a bright red sweater.*   8Senséi wa okótte kao ga makká ni natta. 先生は怒って顔が真っ赤になった。 *The teacher became angry and his face got bright red.*

makkúra [na] 真っ暗〔な〕 *pitch dark*   8makkúra na heyá 真っ暗な部屋 *a pitch dark room*   8Sóto wa makkúra datta. 外は真っ暗だった。 *It was pitch dark outside.*

makoto 誠 *sincerity; honesty; truth*   8Úso ka makoto ka wakaránai. 嘘か誠か分からない。 *I don't know whether it's a lie or the truth.* —— **makoto no** 誠の *real; true*   8makoto no hanashi 誠の話 *a true story*   8makoto no ái 誠の愛 *true love* —— **makoto ni** 誠に *really; sincerely*   8Makoto ni arígatō gozaimáshita. 誠にありがとうございました。 *My sincere thanks.*

makú 幕 *act (of a play); curtain*   8makú ga aku 幕が開く *the curtain opens*   8makú ga oríru 幕が降りる *the curtain falls*   8makú ga agaru 幕が上がる *the curtain rises*   8hitómaku 一幕 *one act*   8dai-ichí maku 第一幕 *Act One*

makú 膜 *membrane*   8komaku 鼓膜 *eardrum*   8mőmaku 網膜 *retina*   8némmaku 粘膜 *mucous membrane*   8saibőmaku 細胞膜 *cell membrane*   8shojómaku 処女膜 *hymen*

mak·u [vt makanai; maita] 巻く *wind; coil; twine; tie around; roll*   8tokei no néji o maku 時計のねじを巻く *wind the clock.*   8yubí ni hōtai o maku 指に包帯を巻く *tie a bandage around a finger*

mák·u [vt makánai; máita] 撒く *scatter; sprinkle; water*   8Sóbo wa máinichi shibafu ni mizu o makimásu. 祖母は毎日芝生に水を撒きます。 *My grandmother waters the lawn every day.*

mák·u [vt makánai; máita] 蒔く *sow; plant*   8táne o máku 種を蒔く *sow seed*

mákura 枕 *pillow*   8makura kábā 枕カバー *pillowcase*

makur·u [*vt* makuranai; makutta] 捲る *roll up (one's sleeves); tuck up*

-mamá 〜まま *as is; as it stands; unaltered* ❧Yoshida-san wa Nyūyŏku ni itta mamá désu. 吉田さんはニューヨークに行ったままです。 *Yoshida went to New York, and that's the last I've heard of him.* ❧O-fúro no tanebi wa tsúketa mamá ni shite óite kudasái. お風呂の種火はつけたままにしておいて下さい。 *Leave the pilot flame on for the bath.* ❧Dŏzo, kutsu no mamá de kamaimasén. どうぞ、靴のままで構いません。 *It's OK to come on in with your shoes on.*

mámā まあまあ *just so-so; not bad (and not good)*

mamagoto ままごと *playing house*

mamé まめ *bunion; blister* ❧mamé ga dekíru まめができる *get a blister*

mamé 豆 *bean(s); pea(s)*

mamónaku 間もなく *soon; right away; shortly* ❧Ma-mó-naku o-híru ni náru. 間もなくお昼になる。 *It will soon be noon (or lunchtime).* ❧Senséi wa ma-mó-naku tōchaku-shimásu. 先生は間もなく到着します。 *The teacher will arrive shortly.*

mamór·u [*vt* mamoránai; mamótta] 守る；護る *protect; keep; observe* ❧kodomo o kiken kara mamóru 子供を危険から守る *protect children from danger* ❧yakusoku o mamóru 約束を守る *keep one's promise* ❧hōritsu o mamóru 法律を守る *observe the law*

mampuku 満腹 *full stomach* ——**mampuku-suru** [*vi*] 満腹する *eat to (one's) heart's content*

mamushi まむし；蝮 *Japanese pit viper*

-mán 万 *multiple of ten thousand* ❧ichiman-en 一万円 *ten thousand yen* ❧hyakuman'en 百万円 *one million yen*

manab·u [*vt* manabanai; mananda] 学ぶ *study; be taught; learn (from)* ❧Watashi wa Ókawa-senséi kara rekishi o manande imásu. 私は大川先生から歴史を学んでいます。 *I am studying history under Prof. Ōkawa.* ❧Daigaku de gengógaku o manabitai. 大学で言語学を学びたい。 *I'd like to study linguistics in college.*

manaita まな板；俎 *cutting board (for kitchen)* ❧manaita no kói まな板の鯉 *(like) a carp on the cutting board (helpless)* <set phrase> ❧Sono jíken wa manaita ni noserareta. その事件はまな板に載せられた。 *The incident has been exposed (lit: placed on the cutting board).*

manchŏ 満潮 *flood tide; high tide*

mane 真似 *imitation; mimicry* ❧Tárō-san wa Maikeru Jákuson no mane ga umái. 太郎さんはマイケル・ジャクソンの真似がうまい。 *Tarō does a good imitation of Michael Jackson.* ❧Báka na mane wa yamenasái. 馬鹿な真似はやめなさい。 *Don't act foolish!* ——**mane o suru** 真似をする *imitate; mimic; pretend*

manegoto 真似事 *mimicry; pretending; make-believe; mockery*

manék·u [*vt* manekánai; manéita] 招く *invite; engage; incur (blame /*

misfortune) 8Áni wa kekkón-shiki ni Sátō go-fúsai o manekimáshita. 兄は結婚式に佐藤ご夫妻を招きました。 *My older brother invited Mr. and Mrs. Sato to his wedding.* 8Takáhashi-san no hatsugen wa ítsumo gokai o manéite shimau. 高橋さんの発言はいつも誤解を招いてしまう。 *Mr. Takahashi's remarks always invite misunderstanding.*

mane·ru [*vt* manenai; maneta] 真似る *imitate; copy; mimic* 8Sénsei no hatsuon o shikkári manete míte kudasái. 先生の発音をしっかり真似てみて下さい。 *Try imitating the teacher's pronunciation precisely.*

manga 漫画 *cartoon* 8manga-ka 漫画家 *cartoonist* 8mangabon 漫画本 *comic book*

mángetsu 満月 *full moon*

maniá·u [*vi* maniawánai; maniátta] 間に合う *be in time; be enough* 8Isóidara saishū dénsha ni maniáu yo. 急いだら最終電車に間に合うよ。 *If we hurry we'll make the last train.* 8Júnin no pátī de kono ryóri, maniáu kashira. 十人のパーティーでこの料理、間に合うかしら。 *I wonder if this is enough food for a party of ten.* <*fem*>

maniawasé·ru [*vt* ma-ni-awasénai; ma-ni-awáseta] 間に合わせる *make do* 8Katakuríko ga kírete iru. Kōnsutáchi de maniawaseyō. 片栗粉が切れている。コーンスターチで間に合わせよう。 *We're out of katakuriko. I'll make do with cornstarch.*

mán'ichi 万一 *in case* 8Mán'ichi óki na jishin ga okóttara, kono shiji-dóri ni kōdō-shite kudasái. 万一大きな地震が起こったら、この指示通りに行動して下さい。 *In case of a big earthquake, follow these instructions exactly.*

man'in 満員 *full of people; a full house* 8man'in dénsha 満員電車 *a crowded train*

manjō itchi no 満場一致の *unanimous* 8Sono gidai wa manjō itchi de kaketsu-sareta. その議題は満場一致で可決された。 *The motion passed by a unanimous vote.*

mannaka 真ん中 *middle; center*

mannénhitsu 万年筆 *fountain pen*

mansei 慢性 *chronicity* 8manseibyō 慢性病 *a chronic disease* 8mansei zénsoku 慢性喘息 *chronic asthma* ——**mansei [no]** 慢性の *chronic* 8Mansei shōjō ga áru. 慢性症状がある。 *There are chronic symptoms.* ——**manseiteki na** 慢性的な *chronic* 8manseiteki na jin'in-búsoku 慢性的な人員不足 *a chronic lack of personnel*

manseki 満席 *all seats taken; full house*

mansha 満車 *full (parking lot)*

mánshon マンション *apartment; condominium (owned or rented)*

mantén 満点 *perfect score*

manuke 間抜け *fool; stupid person* ——**manuke na** 間抜けな *foolish; stupid*

mánzoku 満足 *satisfaction; contentment* ——**mánzoku [na]** 満足（な）

satisfactory; gratifying ——**mánzoku-suru** [*vi*] 満足する *be satisfied* ❂Watashi wa shínkyo ni mánzoku-shite iru. 私は新居に満足してい る。 *I'm satisfied with my new place (or house).*

mappíra [na] 真っ平（な）*(not) by any means; absolutely (not)* ❂Sore wa mappíra da. それは真っ平だ。 *Nothing doing! <masc>* ❂Mappíra gomen. 真っ平御免。 *Count me out, absolutely!*

mappíruma 真っ昼間 *broad daylight*

maré na 稀な *rare; uncommon; unusual* ❂Kotoshi wa kínnen maré na átsusa ni mimawarete iru. 今年は近年稀な暑さに見舞われている。 *This year we are being hit by an unusual hot spell.* ——**mare ni** 稀に *rarely; uncommonly; unusually* ❂Musuko wa gógaku ni maré ni míru sainō o mótte iru. 息子は語学に稀に見る才能を持っている。 *My son has ability in languages that is rarely seen.*

maru 丸 *circle* ❂maru o káku 丸を書く *draw a circle* ❂maru-gao 丸 顔 *a round face*

marude...yố [na] まるで…様（な）*just like; just as if* ❂Sore wa marude yume no yố na dekígoto deshita. それはまるで夢のような出来事でし た。 *What happened was like a dream.*

maru·i [*adj* maruku nái; marúkatta] 丸い；円い *(be) round* ❂marui tēburu 丸いテーブル *a round table* ❂maruku nátte suwaru 丸くな って座る *sit in a circle*

maru-jírushi 丸印 *circle (mark)* ❂Gaitố-suru kōmoku ni maru-jírushi o tsúkete kudasái. 該当する項目に丸印を付けて下さい。 *Circle the pertinent data.*

marumáru [to] 丸々（と）*plump; entirely; such-and-such (a number)* ❂Sono ákachan wa marumáru to futótte iru. その赤ちゃんは丸々と太 っている。 *The baby is fat as a butterball.* ❂Marumáru mikka kákete sốsu o tsukútta. 丸々三日かけてソースを作った。 *It took an entire three days to make the sauce.*

maruta 丸太 *log* ❂maruta-goya 丸太小屋 *a log cabin*

mása ni 正に *precisely; just; exactly* ❂Mása ni anáta no itta tốri da wa. 正にあなたの言ったとおりだわ。 *It's just like you said. <fem>* ❂Anó hito wa mása ni meijín da. あの人は正に名人だ。 *That person is truly a master. <masc>* ❂Mása ni dekakeru tokoró da. 正に出かけ るところだ。 *I was just about to leave. <masc>*

masár·u [*vi* masaránai; masátta] 勝る；優る *exceed; pass; be better* ❂Jitsuryoku wa káre no hố ga masátte iru. 実力は彼の方が勝ってい る。 *He is more competent (i.e., compared to someone else).*

masatsu 摩擦 *friction* ❂bōeki másatsu 貿易摩擦 *trade friction*

mashốmen 真正面 *straight ahead; head on*

massatsu 抹殺 *erasure; obliteration* ——**massatsu-suru** [*vt*] 抹殺す る *erase; strike out; ignore*

masshíro [na] 真っ白（な）*pure (or snow) white*

masshurúmu マッシュルーム *mushroom (imported varieties)*

massúgu [na] 真直ぐ（な）*straight ; honest; upright* ——**massúgu ni** 真直ぐに *straight; frankly; straightforwardly*

masú 鱒 *trout* §niji-masu 虹鱒 *rainbow trout*

mas·u [vi masanai; mashita] 増す *increase; mount up* §Sono dénsha wa sókudo o mashita. その電車は速度を増した。*The train increased its speed.* §Nikóku-kan no kinchō ga mashite iru. 二国間の緊張が増している。*Tension between the two countries is mounting.*

masui 麻酔 *anesthesia* §masúi-yaku 麻酔薬 *an anesthetic* §kyokubu másui 局部麻酔 *local anesthesia* §zenshin másui 全身麻酔 *general anesthesia*

masukomi マスコミ *mass communications; the media*

masúmasu 益々 *more and more* §Saikin masúmasu átsuku nátte kimáshita. 最近益々暑くなってきました。*It's getting hotter and hotter these days.*

mata 又 *again; also* §Mata raishū aimashō. また来週、会いましょう。*I'll see you again next week.* §Dé wa, mata! では、又！*Well, see ya!* §Watashi wa káshu de mata haiyū désu. 私は歌手でまた俳優です。*I'm a singer and also an actor.*

matá 股 *crotch*

matagár·u [vi matagaránai; matagátta] 跨がる *straddle; span* §umá ni matagáru 馬にまたがる *straddle a horse* §Gonen ni matagátta daijígyō ga kansei-shita. 五年にまたがった大事業が完成した。*A big project spanning five years has been completed.*

matasé·ru [caus matasénai; matáseta] 待たせる *cause to wait; keep (someone) waiting* §Matásete gomen ne. 待たせてご免ね。*I'm sorry I kept you waiting.* <fem> §O-matase-shimáshita. お待たせしました。*I'm sorry to have kept you waiting.* <polite>

matatáku ma ni 瞬く間に *in the twinkling of an eye (lit: in the time it takes to bat an eyelash).*

matá to nái 又とない *none other; never again; once in a lifetime* §Nagái aida mátte itá ga, matá to nái shusse no chánsu ga mawatte kíta. 長い間待っていたが、又とない出世のチャンスが回ってきた。*I waited a long time, but finally I got the chance of a lifetime.*

matá wa 又は *or* §Raisu matá wa pán? ライス又はパン？*Rice? or bread?*

maténrō 摩天楼 *skyscraper*

mato 的 *target; mark; an object* §mato o nerau 的を狙う *aim at a target* §mato-házure 的外れ *off the target* §Tádashi-kun wa kono machí zentai no sonkei no mató desu. 匤君はこの町全体の尊敬の的です。*Tadashi is the object of respect of this entire town.*

matomar·u [vi matomaranai; matomatta] 纏まる *be gathered; collected; put in order; be settled; completed* §Minná no íken ga matomatta. み

んなの意見がまとまった。*Everyone has come to an agreement.*
❧Rombun ga iyóiyo matomatté kita. 論文がいよいよまとまってき
た。*My thesis is finally taking shape.*

matome·ru [*vt* matomenai; matometa] 纏める *settle; bring to a
conclusion; put (bring) together* ❧Gomí o matomete suteyő. ごみを
まとめて捨てよう。*Let's collect the garbage and put it out.* ❧Kōshō
o matomerú no ga nigate désu. 交渉をまとめるのが苦手です。*I'm
not good at settling negotiation problems.*

mátsu 松 *pine (tree)*

máts·u [*vt* matánai; mátta] 待つ *wait* ❧Chótto mátte kudasái. ちょっと
待って下さい。*Wait a moment, please.* ❧Henjí wa ashitá made
maténai. 返事は明日まで待てない。*I can't wait till tomorrow for the
answer.*

matsuba-zúe 松葉杖 *crutches*

mátsuge 睫毛 *eyelash*

matsuri 祭り *festival; feast day; celebration*

matsutake 松茸 *mushroom (edible fungus from red pines)*

mattakú 全く *quite; entirely; complete; really (not) at all* ❧Yoshínaga
wa mattakú ún ga íi. 吉永は全く運がいい。*Yoshinaga really has
good luck.* ❧Watashi wa mattakú suiei ga dekimasén. 私は全く水泳
が出来ません。*I can't swim at all.*

ma·u [*vi / vt* mawanai; matta] 舞う *whirl; dance* ❧mai o mau 舞いを舞
う *perform (traditional) dance* ❧Óchiba ga mainágara chitte iru. 落ち
葉が舞いながら散っている。*(Falling) leaves whirl (in the air) as
they fall.*

mawari [no] 回り（の）; 周り（の）*(one's) surroundings; around*
❧Mawari ní wa dare mo imasén. 周りには誰もいません。*There's no
one around.*

mawarikudó·i [*adj* mawarikúdoku nái; mawarikúdokatta] 回りくどい
(be) roundabout ❧mawarikúdói hanashi o suru 回りくどい話をする
beat around the bush

mawarimichi 回り道 *detour; round-about way*

mawar·u [*vi* mawaranai; mawatta] 回る *turn (around); revolve; rotate*
❧Chikyū wa táiyō no mawari o mawatte iru. 地球は太陽の周りを回っ
ている。*The earth revolves around the sun.* ❧Kyónen wa Yōróppa o
mawatté kita. 去年はヨーロッパを回って来た。*I traveled around
Europe last year.* ❧Mő jūichí-ji o mawatte irú no ni, musumé wa máda
káette inai. もう十一時を回っているのに、娘はまだ帰っていない。
It's already past 11:00 o'clock and my daughter still hasn't come home.

mawashi 回し *sumo wrestler's loincloth (or belt)*

mawas·u [*vt* mawasanai; mawashita] 回す *turn; spin; pass on; transfer*
❧kóma o mawasu こまを回す *spin a top* ❧Kono shorui o kákakari
no hito ni mawashite kudasái. この書類を係の人に回して下さい。

Please pass these papers on to the person in charge.

mayaku 麻薬 *narcotic drug*

mayónaka 真夜中 *midnight; the middle of the night*

mayó·u [*vi* mayowánai; mayótta] 迷う *hesitate; waver; wonder; be in doubt; be confused; be unable to make up one's mind* §michi ni mayóu 道に迷う *lose one's way* §Watashi wa máda mayótte ite, ketsuron ga dénai. 私はまだ迷っていて、結論が出ない。 *I'm still unable to make up my mind; I can't decide.*

máyuge 眉毛 *eyebrow*

mazé·ru [*vt* mazénai; mázeta] 混ぜる *mix* §mazegóhan 混ぜ御飯 *rice mixed with assorted foods*

mázu まず *first; first of all; to begin with* §Mázu sono mondai kara gíron-shiyó. まずその問題から議論しよう。 *Let's begin our discussion with that issue.*

mazú·i [*adj* mázuku nái; mázukatta] まずい *(be) unsavory; unskillful; inadvisable; not good* §Kono sŭpu wa mazúi. このスープはまずい。 *This soup tastes terrible. <masc>* §Ano kotó o hanáshite shimatta no? Sore wa mazúi wa! あのことを話してしまったの？ それはまずいわ！ *You talked to him about that? That was a bad idea! <fem>*

mazushí·i [*adj* mazúshiku nái; mazúshikatta] 貧しい *(be) poor; impoverished* §Támura-san wa mazushíi ié ni umareta. 田村さんは貧しい家に生まれた。 *Tamura was born in a poor family.* §Matsumoto-san wa kokoro-mazushíi hitó desu. 松本さんは心貧しい人です。 *Matsumoto is a mean-spirited (or spiritually impoverished) man.*

mé 芽 *bud; sprout* §mé ga déru 芽が出る *to sprout (lit. a sprout appears)* §mé o dásu 芽を出す *to sprout (lit: put out sprouts)* §Chŭrippu wa mé ga déru koro desu. チューリップは芽が出るころです。 *It's time for the tulips (or tulip bulbs) to sprout.* §Mó káshu ni náru no wa yameyó. Nakanaka mé ga dénai kara. もう歌手になるのはやめよう。なかなか芽が出ないから。 *I'm going to give up singing (professionally), because it seems I'll never make it.*

mé 目 *eye* §mé o hanásu 目を離す *take (one's) eyes off* §mé o mukeru 目を向ける *turn (one's) eyes toward* §mé o samásu 目を覚ます *open (one's) eyes; wake up* §mé o tojíru 目を閉じる *close (one's) eyes* §mé o tomeru 目を止める *let (one's) eyes rest upon* §mé o tōsu 目を通す *scan; read over hastily* §me no máe ni 目の前に *before (one's) (very) eyes* §mé ga saméru 目が覚める *wake up* §megúsuri 目薬 *eye drops (medicine)*

méate 目当て *goal; mark; guide*

mebaé·ru [*vi* mebaénai; mebáeta] 芽生える *bud; sprout*

mechakucha 滅茶苦茶 *incoherence; confusion; absurdity; nonsense* —— **mechakucha na** 滅茶苦茶な *incoherent; confused; absurd*

mechamecha 滅茶滅茶 *mess; ruin; wreck* ❀mechamecha ni náru 滅茶滅茶になる *become a mess*
medamayaki 目玉焼き *egg fried sunnyside up*
medáts·u [*vi* medatánai; medátta] 目立つ *be conspicuous* ——**medátta** [*attr*] 目立った *striking; noticeable*
medetá·i [*adj* medétaku nái; medétakatta] 目出度い；めでたい *(be) happy; joyous; auspicious* ❀medetái koto 目出度いこと *a happy event*
megaké·ru [*vi* megakénai; megáketa] 目がける *aim at; aspire to*
mégane 眼鏡 *glasses; spectacles*
megumare·ru [*vi: passive*] 恵まれる *be blessed*
megumi 恵み *grace; blessing*
meguriá·u [*vi* meguriawánai; meguriátta] 巡り会う *meet by chance; happen upon*
mei 姪 *niece*
méi 銘 *inscription* ❀méi o kizamu 銘を刻む *engrave an inscription*
meian 名案 *great idea; well-devised scheme*
meibo 名簿 *name list; roster*
meigí 名義 *name; title; registration* ❀kuruma no meigí 車の名義 *car registration*
meigo-san 姪御さん *(another's) niece*
meikai na 明快な *clear; plain; unequivocal*
meikaku 明確 *definiteness; clarity* ——**meikaku na** 明確な *definite; clear*
meiméi [no] 銘々（の） *each (and every) one; individual*
Meiṓsei 冥王星 *Pluto*
meirei 命令 *a command* ❀meirei-kei 命令形 *imperative (Gram)* ——**meireiteki na** 命令的な *imperative* ——**meirei-suru** [*vt*] 命令する *order; command*
méiro 迷路 *maze; labyrinth*
meisai 明細 *particulars; details* ❀meisai-sho 明細書 *(detailed) statement; specification* ——**meisai na** 明細な *minute; detailed*
meisaku 名作 *masterpiece*
meisan 名産 *well-known product; specialty* ❀Tsubaki-ábura wa Izu Ōshima no meisan désu. 椿油は伊豆大島の名産です。*Camelia oil is a noted product of Izu Ōshima.*
meisei 名声 *fame; good reputation; renown* ❀Okamura-san wa operá-kai de meisei o hakúshite iru. 岡村さんはオペラ界で名声を博している。*Mr. Okamura has achieved renown in opera.*
meishi 名刺 *business (calling) card* ❀meishi o dásu 名刺を出す *present one's card* ❀meishi o kōkan-suru 名刺を交換する *exchange cards*
meishi 名詞 *noun (Gram)* ❀futsū méishi 普通名詞 *common noun*

❘koyū méishi 固有名詞 *proper noun* ❘chūshō méishi 抽象名詞 *abstract noun* ❘dai méishi 代名詞 *pronoun*

meishin 迷信 *superstition* ❘meishin o shinjíru 迷信を信じる *believe a superstition*

meishó 名所 *famous sightseeing spot*

méiwaku 迷惑 *nuisance; trouble* ❘méiwaku o oyobosu 迷惑を及ぼす *make trouble* ❘Méiwaku o kákete sumimasén. 迷惑をかけてすみません。 *I'm sorry to have caused you trouble.*

méiyo 名誉 *reputation; honor* ❘Ōe Kenzaburō no Nōberu bungakú-shō no jushō wa Nihón ni totte mo méiyo na kotó desu. 大江健三郎のノーベル文学賞の受賞は日本にとって名誉な事です。 *Oe Kenzaburo's receiving the Nobel Prize in literature was an honor for Japan.* —— **méiyo no** 名誉の *honorary* ❘meiyo kyōju 名誉教授 *honorary professor* ❘meiyo hakushí-gō 名誉博士号 *honorary doctorate* ❘meiyo kíson 名誉毀損 *slander* ❘meiyo o tattóbu 名誉を尊ぶ *honor; esteem*

mejírushi 目印 *mark; landmark; identification mark* ❘mejírushi o tsukéru 目印をつける *mark (something)*

mekaké 妾 *mistress*

mekakushi 目隠し *blindfold; blindman's bluff* ❘mekakushi-oni 目隠し鬼 *'it' in blindman's bluff* ——**mekakushi-suru** 目隠しする *blindfold (someone)*

mekata 目方 *weight* ❘Kono békon wa mekata de urimásu. このベーコンは目方で売ります。 *We sell this bacon by weight.*

mekurá 盲 *blindness; blind; a blind person (preferred: mé no miénai hito)*

mekuru [*vt* mekuranai; mekutta] めくる *turn (pages)* ❘pēji o mekuru ページをめくる *turn pages*

memái 目眩；眩暈 *dizziness* ❘memái ga suru めまいがする *be (become) dizzy; giddy*

mémbō 麺棒 *rolling pin*

mémbō 綿棒 *cotton swab*

memboku 面目 *honor; face; dignity; reputation* ❘memboku o ushinau 面目を失う *lose face; humiliate oneself* ❘memboku o hodokósu 面目を施す *maintain (one's) reputation* ❘memboku ga tátanai 面目が立たない *be disgraced* ❘memboku nái 面目無い *be ashamed of oneself*

mén 面 *face; surface* ❘ mén to mukatte hanásu 面と向かって話す *talk face-to-face*

men 面 *mask* ❘o-men お面 *a mask* ❘kamen 仮面 *mask; disguise* ❘Nō men 能面 *a Noh mask*

mén 綿 *cotton* ❘ménka 綿花 *cotton boll; raw cotton*

mendó 面倒 *trouble* ——**mendó na** 面倒な *bothersome; troublesome* ❘Mendó na shigoto wa ítsumo watashi ni mawatte kúru. 面倒な仕事は

いつも私に回ってくる。 *I always get the troublesome jobs.* ——
mendó o míru 面倒を見る *look after*   🔹Ákachan no mendó o míte kuremasén ka? 赤ちゃんの面倒を見てくれませんか。 *Would you look after my baby for me, please?*

mendōkusá·i [*adj* mendōkúsaku nái; mendōkúsakatta] 面倒くさい *troublesome; a bother; tiresome*   🔹Bóku ni ryóri o tsukúre tte? Sonná no mendōkusái yo! 僕に料理を作れって？ そんなの面倒くさいよ！ *You want me to fix supper? What a drag!* <masc>

mendori 雌鶏 *hen*

men'eki 免疫 *immunity*   🔹men'ekitai 免疫体 *antibody*

ménjo 免除 *exemption; immunity* ——**ménjo-suru** [*vt*] 免除する *exempt (from); excuse*

menjō 免状 *diploma*

menkai 面会 *meeting; interview*   🔹menkai jíkan 面会時間 *visiting hours* ——**menkai-suru** [*vi*] 面会する *interview*

ménkyo 免許 *license*   🔹menkyóshō 免許証 *a license; a certificate*   🔹kyōin ménkyo 教員免許 *teacher's license*   🔹unten ménkyo 運転免許 *driver's license*

ménrui 麺類 *noodles; vermicelli*

ménseki 面積 *area (measure of a bounded region)*

mensetsu 面接 *interview; job interview*   🔹mensetsu shíken 面接試験 *oral examination; interview*   🔹mensetsu o ukéru 面接を受ける *be interviewed*

menshoku 免職 *dismissal; discharge; removal from office*   🔹Míkami-san wa fuhō kői o shite menshoku ni nátta. 三上さんは不法行為をして免職になった。 *Mikami was dismissed for illegal conduct.* ——**menshoku-suru** [*vt*] 免職する *dismiss; relieve from a job; fire*

ménsu メンス *menstruation*

menzei [no] 免税 (の) *tax-free; duty-free*   🔹menzéi-ten 免税店 *tax-free shop*   🔹menzei-hin 免税品 *tax-free goods* ——**menzei-suru** [*vt*] 免税する *exempt from tax*

meshiagar·u [*vt* meshiagaranai; meshiagatta] 召し上がる *eat* <formal>   🔹Náni o meshiagarimásu ka? 何を召し上がりますか。 *What will you have to eat?* <formal>

mesú 雌 *female (animal)*

metsubō 滅亡 *doom; downfall*   🔹Dai-Rōma téikoku no metsubō 大ロー マ帝国の滅亡 *the fall of the Roman Empire* ——**metsubō-suru** [*vi*] 滅亡する *fall; go to ruin; collapse*

métta [na] 滅多 (な) *rash; reckless; thoughtless*   🔹métta na kotó 滅多 なこと *something rash* ——**métta ni** 滅多に *seldom; rarely*   🔹Métta ni nái gūzen no meguriawase dátta. 滅多にない偶然の巡り合わせだ った。 *It was a chance meeting that rarely happens.*

mezamashi-dókei 目覚まし時計 *alarm clock*

mezamé·ru [*vi* mezaménai; mezámeta] 目覚める *wake up; awaken; become aware* ❀genjitsu ni mezaméru 現実に目覚める *wake up to reality*

mezás·u [*vt* mezasánai; mezáshita] 目指す *aim at; set a goal* ❀Watashi wa daigaku shíngaku o mezáshite imásu. 私は大学進学を目指しています。*My goal is to get into college.*

mezurashí·i [*adj* mezuráshiku nái; mezuráshikatta] 珍しい *(be) rare; unusual*

mi 身 *the body; (one's) person* ❀mi o mamóru 身を守る *protect oneself* ❀mi o yokéru 身を避ける *step aside (from)* ❀mi o kó ni suru 身を粉にする *work hard* ❀Ífuku o mi ni tsúkete kudasái. 衣服を身につけて下さい。*Put your clothes on.*

mi 実 *fruit; nut; berry; soup ingredient* ❀mi o musubu 実を結ぶ *bear fruit* ❀mi ga náru 実がなる *bear fruit* ❀Misoshíru no mi wa , kyó wa wákame ni suru. 味噌汁の実は、今日はわかめにする。*We're having misoshiru soup with wakame seaweed today.* ❀Nagái aida no dóryoku ga mi o musunda. 長い間の努力が実を結んだ。*A long period of effort brought results.*

miage·ru [*vt* miagenai; miageta] 見上げる *look up; look up (at); admire* ❀daibutsu o miageru 大仏を見上る *look up at the Great Buddha (statue)* ❀Tanaka wa miageta yátsu da. 田中は見上げた奴だ。*Tanaka is a person people look up to.* <*masc*>

miai kékkon 見合い結婚 *arranged marriage*

miatar·u [*vi* miataranai; miatatta] 見当たる *find; come across* ❀Saifu ga nakanaka miataranai. 財布がなかなか見当たらない。*I can't seem to find my wallet.*

mibáe ga suru 見栄えがする *make a good showing; show to advantage; look nice* ❀Kono dóresu wa mibáe ga surú wa. このドレスは見栄えがするわ。*This dress looks nice.* <*fem*>

mibójin 未亡人 *widow*

míbun 身分 *status; (one's) identity* ❀mibun shōmeisho 身分証明書 *identification papers; ID card* ❀mibun séido 身分制度 *status system*

míburi 身振り *a gesture; gesticulation* ❀míburi de (kimochi o) tsutaéru 身振りで（気持ちを）伝える *communicate (one's feelings) with gestures*

michi 道 *street; way* ❀michi-bata 道端 *roadside* ❀michi-haba 道幅 *road width* ❀michi-shírube 道標 *a guidepost; signpost* ❀michi o machigaéru 道を間違える *lose one's way* ❀Yūshō é no michi wa kewashíi. 優勝への道は険しい。*The road to victory is steep.* <*set phrase*>

míchi [no] 未知の *unknown* ❀Kono bún'ya wa máda míchi no ryóiki desu. この分野はまだ未知の領域です。*This field is still unknown territory.*

michi ánnai 道案内 *guidance; a guide*

michibík·u [*vt / vi* michibikánai; michibíita] 導く *lead; guide* ❽shippai ni michibíku 失敗に導く *lead to failure* ❽kuni o han'ei ni michibiku 国を繁栄に導く *steer a nation to prosperity*

michikusa o kúu 道草を喰う *loiter about on the way; dilly-dally*

michí·ru [*vi* michínai; míchita] 満ちる *rise; wax; be full* ❽tsukí ga michíru 月が満ちる *the moon waxes* ❽shió ga michíru 潮が満ちる *the tide comes in* ❽kiken ni míchite iru 危険に満ちている *be filled with danger*

midaré 乱れ *disorder; disarray; disturbance; confusion* ❽midaré-gami 乱れ髪 *tangled hair* ❽myaku no midaré 脈の乱れ *irregular pulse* ❽nṓha no midaré 脳波の乱れ *brain-wave disorder* ❽Watashi ní wa máda kokoro no midaré ga áru. 私にはまだ心の乱れがある。*My mind's still confused.*

midaré·ru [*vi* midarénai; midáreta] 乱れる *be in disaray; be in disorder; be confused; be in a chaotic state* ❽Kūdétá no hassei de sono kuni wa midárete iru. クーデターの発生でその国は乱れている。*With the outbreak of a coup d'etat the nation is in a chaotic state.*

midashi 見出し *headline; title; entry*

midásu [*vt* midasánai; midáshita] 乱す *disorder; disarrange; disturb* ❽chian o midásu 治安を乱す *disturb the peace*

mídori 緑 *greenery; verdure* ❽mídori (no) 緑 (の) *green* ❽mídori yútaka [na] 緑豊か (な) *rich in greenery; lush*

mienikú·i [*adj* mieníkuku nái; mieníkukatta] 見えにくい *hard to see; indistinct* ❽Kokuban wa mienikúi. 黒板は見えにくい。*It's hard to see the blackboard.*

mié·ru [*vi* miénai; míeta] 見える *can be seen; be visible; look like* ❽Fújisan ga miemásu ka? 富士山が見えますか。*Can you see Mt. Fuji?* ❽Ōyama-san wa geijutsuka ni miéru ne! 大山さんは芸術家に見えるね。*Ōyama looks like an artist, doesn't she?*

migaki 磨き *a polish* ❽migaki o kakéru 磨きをかける *polish; apply polish (to)*

migak·u [*vt* migakanai; migaita] 磨く *polish; shine* ❽kutsú o migaku 靴を磨く *polish shoes* ❽há o migaku 歯を磨く *brush (one's) teeth* ❽udé o migaku 腕を磨く *improve (one's) skill*

migi 右 *right* ❽migite 右手 *right hand* ❽migite ni 右手に *on the (or your) right* ❽migi kiki 右利き *right-handed* ❽migi no hṓ 右の方 *to the right*

mígoto [na] 見事 (な) *creditable; wonderful; outstanding; admirable; brilliant* ❽Kono é wa mígoto na dekibae désu ne! この絵は見事な出来映えですね。*This painting is a brilliant work (of art).*

migurushí·i [*adj* migurúshiku nái; migurúshikatta] 見苦しい *(be) shabby; indecent; ugly; disgraceful* ❽migurúshiku nái 見苦しくない

presentable; decent &Míkami-kun wa ítsumo migurushíi fūtei o shite iru. 三上君はいつも見苦しい風体をしている。*Mikami always has a shabby appearance.* &O-kane ni bákari shūchaku-shite ite, aitsu wa migurushíi yátsu da. お金にばかり執着していて、あいつは見苦しい奴だ。*It's disgraceful, the way he thinks only about money. <masc>*

miharashi 見晴らし *view; outlook* &Kono hóteru kara wa Kyōto shígai no miharashi ga íi. このホテルからは京都市街の見晴らしがいい。*From this hotel the view of Kyoto is good.*

mihar-u [*vt* miharanai; mihatta] 見張る *keep watch; guard* &Keikan wa higísha no ugokí o mihatte iru. 警官は被疑者の動きを見張っている。*The police are keeping watch over the movements of the suspect.*

mihon 見本 *a sample; specimen* &Kiji-míhon o íkutsu ka mísete kudasái. 生地見本をいくつか見せて下さい。*Show me several fabric samples, please.*

míira ミイラ；木乃伊 *mummy*

mijika [*na*] 身近 （な） *familiar; near (oneself)*

mijiká-i [*adj* mijíkaku nái; mijíkakatta] 短い *(be) short; brief* &Mijikái sukáto ga hayátte imásu. 短いスカートが流行っています。*Short skirts are in style.* &Kánojo wa mijikái isshō o oeta. 彼女は短い一生を終えた。*Her brief life ended.*

míjime [*na*] 惨め （な） *pitiful; wretched* &Konna míjime na súgata wa dare ni mo miraretáku nái. こんな惨めな姿は誰にも見られたくない。*I don't want anyone to see me looking so wretched.*

mijin [*no*] 微塵 （の） *abit; an iota; (not) in the least* &mijin-giri ni suru 微塵切りにする *cut fine; cut in tiny pieces* &Kimi o uragíru kimochi nánte mijin mo nákatta. 君を裏切る気持ちなんて微塵もなかった。*I didn't have the slightest intention of betraying you.*

mijuku [*na*] 未熟 （な） *immature; unripe; inexperienced* &mijuku na kudámono 未熟な果物 *unripe (green) fruit* &mijukú-ji 未熟児 *a premature baby* &mijukumono 未熟者 *an inexperienced person* &Yoshida wa máda kangáe ga mijuku désu. 吉田はまだ考えが未熟です。*Yoshida's way of thinking is still immature.*

mikáihatsu no 未開発の *undeveloped*

mikake 見掛け *outward appearance; show* &Hitó wa mikake ni yoranai. 人は見掛けによらない。*People cannot be judged by appearances.*

mikaku 味覚 *sense of taste*

míkan 蜜柑 *mandarin orange*

mikata 味方 *ally; friend; supporter* ——**mikata o suru** 味方をする *take sides* &Háha wa ítsumo imōtó no mikata o suru. 母はいつも妹の味方をする。*Mother always takes my little sister's side.*

mikazuki 三日月 *crescent moon; new moon*

miketsu [*no*] 未決 （の） *undecided; pending*

míki 幹 *trunk (of a tree)*

mikka 三日 *the third of the month; three days*

mikkō-suru [*vi*] 密航する *stow away; take passage in secret*

mikomi 見込み *expectation; prospect; hope* ❧Kaifuku no mikomi wa nái. 回復の見込みはない。*There is no hope for recovery.*

mikon no 未婚の *unmarried; single* ❧mikon no háha 未婚の母 *an unwed mother*

[o-]míkoshi (お) 御輿 *portable shrine*

[o-]mimai (お) 見舞い *expression of sympathy; visit to a sick person*

mimamor·u [*vt* mimamoranai; mimamotta] 見守る *keep watch over; watch; look at intently* ❧Nariyuki o jitto mimamorŏ. 成り行きをじっと見守ろう。*Let's watch and see how things go.*

mimawas·u [*vt* mimawasanai; mimawashita] 見回す *look around*

mimí *ear* ❧mimí o kasu 耳を貸す *lend an ear; listen to* ❧mimí o katamukéru 耳を傾ける *bend an ear; pay attention to* ❧mimi no kikoenai hitó 耳の聞こえない人 *deaf person*

mimizáwari [na] 耳障り (な) *rasping; harsh; offensive* ❧Zatsuon ga mimizáwari desu. 雑音が耳障りです。*The noise is harsh.* ❧Mimizáwari na hanashí wa kikitaku nái. 耳障りな話は聞きたくない。*I don't want to hear anything offensive.*

mimizu 蚯蚓 *earthworm; angleworm* ❧mimizu-bare みみず腫れ *a welt (on the skin)*

mimoto 身元 *(one's) identity; character* ❧mimoto kákunin 身元確認 *verification of (one's) identity* ❧mimoto fúmei 身元不明 *an unidentified person* ❧mimoto o shōmei-suru 身元を証明する *vouch for a person's character*

minami 南 *south*

minamoto 源 *source; fountainhead*

minaos·u [*vt* minaosanai; minaoshita] 見直す *look at anew; take another look at* ❧Ano kén de wa anáta o minaoshita. あの件では貴方を見直した。*Because of that of affair, I took a second look at you.*

minarai 見習い *apprenticeship; a trainee*

minare·ru [*vi* minarenai; minareta] 見慣れる *get used to; be accustomed to; be familiar (to one)* ❧Minarenu hitó ga ie no máe ni tátte iru. 見慣れぬ人が家の前に立っている。*An unfamiliar person is standing in front of (the) house.*

minásan 皆さん *everyone*

minas·u [*vi* minasanai; minashita] 見なす *regard; consider; think of* ❧A o B to minasu. AをBとみなす。*Consider A as B.*

minato 港 *port; harbor* ❧minató-machi 港町 *a port city* ❧Fúne ga minato ni teihaku-shite iru. 船が港に停泊している。*The ship is in harbor.*

mingeihin 民芸品 *folk art; handicraft* ❧mingéikan 民芸館 *folkcraft museum*

minikú·i [*adj* miníkuku nái; miníkukatta] 醜い *unattractive; ugly; unseemly* 🔹minikúi yṓshi 醜い容姿 *an unattractive appearance* 🔹minikúi arasoi 醜い争い *an ugly dispute*

minikúsa 醜さ *ugliness*

minkan 民間 *private; civilian; folk* 🔹minkánjin 民間人 *a civilian* 🔹minkan kígyō 民間企業 *private (nongovernment) enterprise* 🔹minkan kōkúki 民間航空機 *commercial aircraft*

minná みんな *everybody; everyone* 🔹Minná ga sono uwasa o shínjite iru. みんながその噂を信じている。 *Everyone believes the rumor.*

minogas·u [*vt* minogasanai; minogashita] 見逃す *fail to see; overlook* 🔹Yōgísha o tsuiseki-shitá ga minogashite shimatta. 容疑者を追跡したが見逃してしまった。 *They pursued the suspect but failed to find him.* 🔹Kónkai daké wa kimi no shippai o minogasṓ. 今回だけは君の失敗を見逃そう。 *I'll overlook your failure (or goof) this time.*

minór·u [*vi* minoránai; minótta] 実る *bear fruit* 🔹Kono míkan-no-kí wa yóku minótte iru. この蜜柑の木はよく実っている。 *This mikan tree bears a lot of fruit.* 🔹Kono dóryoku ga ítsuka minótte hoshíi. この努力がいつか実ってほしい。 *I hope this effort bears fruit someday.*

minoué 身の上 *(one's) lot; personal affairs* 🔹mi-no-ué sṓdan 身の上相談 *personal advice; counselling about personal matters*

mínshu 民主 *democracy* 🔹minshu-sei 民主制 *democratic system* 🔹minshu shúgi 民主主義 *democracy* 🔹Minshutṓ 民主党 *Democratic Party (US)*——**minshuteki [na]** 民主的（な） *democratic* 🔹Sekinínsha wa minshuteki na hōhō de erabaremáshita. 責任者は民主的な方法で選ばれました。 *The people in charge were all elected by democratic procedures.*

minshū 民衆 *the people; the masses*

minwa 民話 *folktale*

mínzoku 民俗 *folk custom(s)*

mínzoku 民族 *race; people; nation* 🔹minzokú-gaku 民族学 *ethnology; ethnography* 🔹minzoku íshō 民族衣装 *folk (or ethnic) costume* 🔹taminzoku kókka 多民族国家 *a multiracial country* 🔹minzoku shúgi 民族主義 *nationalism; racialism* 🔹minzoku sábetsu 民族差別 *racial discrimination* 🔹shōsū mínzoku 少数民族 *minority race*

mioboe 見覚え *recognition; remembrance; recollection* 🔹Mioboe ga nái. 見覚えがない。 *I don't recall.* 🔹Sonó hito ni mioboe ga áru. その人に見覚えがある。 *I recognize that person.*

miokuri 見送り *send-off* 🔹Tōkyō-eki made tomodachi o miokuri ni ikimásu. 東京駅まで友達を見送りに行きます。 *I'm going to Tokyo Station to see a friend off.*

miokur·u [*vt* miokuranai; miokutta] 見送る *send off; see off; let go* 🔹Watashi wa kūkō de Jónson-san o miokutta. 私は空港でジョンソンさんを見送った。 *I saw Johnson off at the airport.* 🔹Musuko wa

Amerika ryúgaku o miokutta. 息子はアメリカ留学を見送った。*My son let go (or gave up) an opportunity to study in America.*

mioros·u [vt miorosanai; mioroshita] 見下ろす *look down (at); take a bird's-eye view (of)* ⬧Tōkyō-táwā kara Tōkyō no machinami o miorosu kotó ga dekíru. 東京タワーから東京の街並を見下ろすことができる。*From Tokyo Tower you can get a bird's-eye view of the city.*

mírai 未来 *future* ⬧mirai-kei 未来形 *future tense (Gram)*

míren 未練 *attachment; affection*

mí·ru [vt mínai; míta] 見る *see; look at*

miryoku 魅力 *fascination; attraction; charm* ⬧Ano égao wa Tómoko-san no miryoku no hitótsu ni nátte imásu. あの笑顔は友子さんの魅力の一つになっています。*Her smile is one of Tomoko's charms.* —— **miryokuteki [na]** 魅力的（な）*attractive* ⬧miryokuteki na josei 魅力的な女性 *an attractive woman*

mísa ミサ *Mass (Cath)*

misáiru ミサイル *missile*

misaki 岬 *cape; promontory; point*

misé 店 *shop; store*

miséinen 未成年 *a minor; a juvenile*

misé·ru [vt misénai; míseta] 見せる *show; disclose; reveal* ⬧Kippu o mísete kudasái. 切符を見せて下さい。*Show your ticket, please.*

míshin ミシン *sewing machine*

misoshíru 味噌汁 *miso (femented soybean paste) soup*

missetsu [na] 密接（な）*intimate; close; near* ⬧Shitsugyō to hanzai wa missetsu na kankei ga áru. 失業と犯罪は密接な関係がある。*There is a close relation between unemployment and crime.*

misuborashí·i [adj misuboráshiku nái; misuboráshikatta] みすぼらしい *shabby; miserable*

misute·ru [vt misutenai; misuteta] 見捨てる *desert; forsake* ⬧Watashi wa komátte iru hitó o misuteru kotó wa dekínai. 私は困っている人を見捨てることはできない。*I could never desert someone in trouble.*

mítai [na] みたい（な）*(look) like; resembling; seem* ⬧Hárada-kun wa jitensha ni norenai mítai désu. 原田君は自転車に乗れないみたいです。*It seems Harada can't ride a bicycle.* —— **mitai ni** みたいに *as if; like* ⬧Ōta-senséi wa hahaoya mítai ni imōtó ni sesshite kudasaimásu. 太田先生は母親みたいに妹に接して下さいます。*Ms. Ota (a teacher) treats my sister like a daughter. <formal>*

mitás·u [vt mitasánai; mitáshita] 満たす *meet; fulfill; fill up* ⬧yokusō ni mizu o mitasu 浴槽に水を満たす *fill the bathtub* ⬧Watashi no kono mitasarénai kimochi wa ittai dōshite deshó? 私のこの満たされない気持ちは一体どうしてでしょう。*I wonder why it is I feel so empty?*

mitei 未定 *undecided; undetermined* ⬧Kekkón-shiki no hidori wa máda mitei désu. 結婚式の日取りはまだ未定です。*The date of the* *wedding is still undecided.*

mitome·ru [*vt* mitomenai; mitometa] 認める *recognize; admit; consider* ❸Íshi wa sono kanja no nō-shukketsu shōjō o mitomete iru. 医師はその患者の脳出血症状を認めている。 *The doctor recognizes symptoms of brain hemorrhage in the patient.* ❸Sono higísha wa hankō no jíjitsu o mitometa. その被疑者は犯行の事実を認めた。 *The suspect admitted to the crime.*

mitore·ru [*vi* mitorenai; mitoreta] 見とれる *be taken by; be enraptured with; be enthralled* ❸Watashi wa kánojo no utsukúshisa ni sukkári mitorete-shimatta. 私は彼女の美しさにすっかり見とれてしまった。 *I was completely enthralled by her beauty.*

mitōshi 見通し *prospect; view; outlook; visibility* ❸Mitōshi ga akarui. 見通しが明るい。 *The outlook is bright.* ❸Kiri de mitōshi ga kikanai. 霧で見通しがきかない。 *Visibility is impaired by fog.* ❸Sannen-saki máde no mitōshi ga tátte iru. 三年先までの見通しが立っている。 *We have forecast three years into the future.*

mítsudo 密度 *density*

mitsukar·u [*vi* mitsukaranai; mitsukatta] 見つかる *be found; be discovered* ❸Kuruma no kagí wa mitsukatta? 車の鍵は見つかった。 *Did you find the car key? (or Was the car key found?)*

mitsuke·ru [*vt* mitsukenai; mitsuketa] 見つける *discover; find* ❸Ichibán-boshi mitsuketa! 一番星見～つけた！ *I discovered the first star tonight!* ❸Kóntakuto o otóshita ga, áni ga mitsukete kureta. コンタクトを落としたが、兄が見つけてくれた。 *I dropped my contact lens, but my brother found it for me.*

mitsume·ru [*vt* mitsumenai; mitsumeta] 見つめる *stare at; gaze at* ❸Kánojo wa watashi no kao o ana no aku hodo mitsumete iru. 彼女は私の顔を穴の開くほど見つめている。 *She's staring at me (hard) enough to drill a hole in my face.*

mitsumori 見積り *an estimate* ❸mitsumori-sho 見積書 *a written estimate* ❸Atarashíi ié o tatetái no désu ga, kenchikú-hi no mitsumori ga máda déte imasén. 新しい家を建てたいのですが、建築費の見積りがまだ出ていません。 *I want to build a new house but the builder hasn't yet submitted an estimate.*

mitsumor·u [*vt* mitsumoranai; mitsumotta] 見積もる *estimate* ❸yósan o mitsumoru 予算を見積もる *estimate the budget*

mitsurin 密林 *dense forest; jungle*

mitsuzō 密造 *manufacturing (brewing) secretly; moonshining* ❸mitsuzōshu 密造酒 *moonshine (whisky)* ❸Pisutoru o mitsuzō-shite iru gurúpu ga tekihatsu-sareta. ピストルを密造しているグループが摘発された。 *A group illicitly manufacturing pistols was uncovered.*

mittsú 三つ *three (when counting things)* ❸Tamágo o mittsú tótte kurenai? 卵を三つ取ってくれない？ *Would you get me three eggs?*

miushina·u [vt miushinawanai; miushinatta] 見失う *lose sight of*
  §Watashi wa shōrai no mokuhyō o miushinatte iru. 私は将来の目標を
見失っている。 *I've lost sight of my goals for the future.*

miwakuteki [na] 魅惑的（な）*glamorous; fascinating; bewitching*
  §miwakuteki na josei 魅惑的な女性 *a glamorous woman*

miwatas·u [vt miwatasanai; miwatashita] 見渡す *look (out) over*
  §Miwatasu kágiri no yukigéshiki da. 見渡す限りの雪景色だ。 *It's a
snowscape as far as the eye can see. <masc>*

miya 宮 *Shinto shrine*   §o-miya máiri お宮参り *visiting a shrine*

[o-]miyage （お）土産 *a present; souvenir*   §miyagemonoya 土産物屋
a souvenir shop   §miyage-bánashi 土産話 *traveler's tale; story one
tells about one's trip*

miyako 都 *capital city*   §Súmeba miyako. 住めば都。 *Home is where
you make it. <set phrase>*

miyasú·i [adj miyásuku nái; miyásukatta] 見やすい *(be) obvious; readily
understandable*

mizo 溝 *ditch; gutter; gulf*   §dóro-waki no mizo 道路脇の溝 *roadside
gutters*   §Óyako no mizo ga fukamátte iru. 親子の溝が深まってい
る。 *The gulf between parents and children has deepened.*

mizore 霙 *sleet*

mizu 水 *water*   §mizu-déppō 水鉄砲 *water pistol*   §mizuwari 水割り
Scotch and water   §kórímizu 氷水 *ice water*   §mizu de usumeru 水
で薄める *water down*

mizubáshō 水芭蕉 *skunk cabbage*

mizubósō 水疱瘡 *chicken pox; (Tech) varicella*

mizu-búkure 水膨れ *blister*

Mizugame-za 水瓶座 *Aquarius*

mízukara [no] 自ら（の）*itself; oneself*   §mízukara té o kudasu 自ら手
を下す *do (something) oneself*

mizuke 水気 *moisture*

mizumakí-ki 水撒き機 *sprinkler*

mizumushi 水虫 *athlete's foot*

mizusashi 水差し *jug; pitcher*

mizutamari 水溜まり *puddle; pool (of stagnant water)*

mizuúmi 湖 *lake*

mizuyókan 水羊羹 *soft, watery, gelatin-like confection*

mo 喪 *mourning*   §mofuku 喪服 *mourning clothes*   §mo ni fukúsu 喪
に服す *go into mourning*   §mo ga akeru 喪が明ける *the mourning
period ends*

mo; -mo...mo も；も〜も *too; also; both...and; neither...nor*   §Kore mo
hitótsu kudasái. これも一つ下さい。 *Give me one of these, too.*
  §Yakyū mo ténisu mo sukí desu. 野球もテニスも好きです。 *I like
both baseball and tennis.*   §Eigo mo Furansugo mo wakarimasén. 英

語もフランス語も分かりません。*I understand neither English nor French.*

mo; -témo; -démo 〜も；〜ても；〜でも *even* §Áme no hi mo jiténsha de iku. 雨の日も自転車で行く。*Even on rainy days I go by bicycle.* §Káre wa chúi-shite mo kikanai. 彼は注意しても聞かない。*Even if you warn him he won't listen.*

mó もう *already* §Yūhan wa mó tabemáshita. 夕飯はもう食べました。*I've already eaten supper.* ——**mó** [*with neg*] もう *never* §Káre ni wa mó tanománai! 彼にはもう頼まない。*I'll never ask him for anything again!*

mochi 餅 *glutinous rice cake*

mochiage·ru [*vt* mochiagenai; mochiageta] 持ち上げる *lift (up); flatter* §Watashi wa hako o mochiageru kotó ga dekínakatta. 私は箱を持ち上げることが出来なかった。*I couldn't lift the box.* §Tanaka wa ítsumo mochiagerarete íi ki ni nátte iru. 田中はいつも持ち上げられていい気になっている。*Tanaka feeling good because he's been praised.*

mochidas·u [*vt* mochidasanai; mochidashita] 持ち出す *take out; remove; put out (or pay out) money*

mochihakob·u [*vt* mochihakobanai; mochihakonda] 持ち運ぶ *carry; convey; transport*

mochii·ru [*vt* mochiiranai; mochiitta] 用いる *use; utilize* §Mōshikomi ní wa shotei no yōshi o mochiite kudasái. 申し込みには所定の用紙を用いて下さい。*To make an application, use the prescribed forms.*

mochikaeri ryôri 持ち帰り料理 *carry-out food; take-away food*

mochínushi 持ち主 *owner*

mochíron 勿論 *of course; certainly* §Ichí tasu ichí wa mochíron ní desu 1足す1は勿論2です。*Of course one and one makes two.* §Mochíron sansei da yó. 勿論、賛成だよ。*Certainly I agree.* <*masc*>

môchō 盲腸 *appendix (Anat)* §mōchó-en 盲腸炎 *appendicitis* §môchō shújutsu 盲腸手術 *appendectomy*

modokashí·i [*adj* modokáshiku nái; modokáshikatta] もどかしい *(be) impatient; irritating; fretful* §Benkyō ni omóu yó ni mi ga hairázu totemo modokashíi. 勉強に思うように身が入らずとてももどかしい。*It's frustrating not to be able to concentrate on my studies.*

modór·u [*vi* modoránai; modótta] 戻る *return* §séki ni modóru 席に戻る *return to (one's) seat* §Nánji ni modorimásu ka? 何時に戻りますか。*What time will you return?* §Byōjō wa ízen no jōtai ni modótte shimatta. 病状は以前の状態に戻ってしまった。*Unfortunately, his condition reverted to its previous state.*

modós·u [*vt* modosánai; modóshita] 戻す *put back; return* §Yónda hón o móto no tana ni modóshite oite kudasái. 読んだ本を元の棚に戻して

おいて下さい。 *Return books to the shelf after reading.*

moe·ru [*vi* moenai; moeta] 燃える *burn*

mōfu 毛布 *blanket*

mogura 土竜 *mole (animal)*

mogúr·u [*vi* moguránai; mogútta] 潜る *go through; swim underwater; go underground*   ♧mizu ni mogúru 水に潜る *dive under water*   ♧chiká ni mogúru 地下に潜る *go underground.*

mohan 模範 *model; example*   ♧mohan káitō 模範解答 *example answers*   ♧mohan nṓjō 模範農場 *a pilot farm*   ♧Táyama-san wa watashítachi no mohan désu. 田山さんは私たちの模範です。 *Tayama is an example for us.* ——**mohanteki** [**na**] 模範的（な）*model; exemplary*   ♧mohanteki na seinen 模範的な青年 *a model youth* —— **mohanteki ni** 模範的に *exemplarily*

móhaya 最早 *already; [with neg] no longer*   ♧Móhaya yó mo fúketa. 最早、夜も更けた。 *It's already night.*

mō ichido もう一度 *once more*   ♧Mō ichido kuwáshiku hanáshite kuremasén ka? もう一度詳しく話してくれませんか。 *Would you go over the details once more for me?*

móji 文字 *letter (of the alphabet); Chinese character*   ♧ōmoji 大文字 *a capital letter*   ♧komoji 小文字 *a lower-case letter* ——**moji-dóri** 文字どおり *verbatim; literally*   ♧Watashi no komento wa moji-dóri de nan no urá mo arimasén. 私のコメントは文字通りで何の裏もありません。 *My comment is just what it says; there's nothing written between the lines.*

mō jiki もう直き *right away; in a jiffy*   ♧Mō jiki o-híru ni náru. もう直きお昼になる。 *It'll be noon (lunchtime) in no time.*

mójin 盲人 *blind person* (preferred: mé no miénai hito)

mōkár·u [*vi* mōkáranai; mōkátta] 儲かる *be profitable; make a profit; earn; make a gain*   ♧Súmisu-san wa kabu de mōkarimáshita. スミスさんは株で儲かりました。 *Mr. Smith made a profit on the stock market.*

mokei 模型 *model; pattern*   ♧mokei hikṓki 模型飛行機 *model airplane*

mōké·ru [*vt* mōkénai; mōkéta] 儲ける *make a profit; earn*

mokkin 木琴 *xylophone*

mokugekísha 目撃者 *eye witness*   ♧Satsujin jíken no mokugekísha ga arawaremáshita. 殺人事件の目撃者が現われました。 *An eye witness to the murder turned up.*

mokuhyō 目標 *target; objective; aim; goal; purpose*   ♧mokuhyō no kíjitsu 目標の期日 *target date*   ♧Ikíru mokuhyō ga mitsukaranai. 生きる目標が見つからない。 *I can't find my purpose in life.*

mokuji 目次 *table of contents*

mokumoku [to] 黙々（と）*silently; without talking*   ♧Kōjō jūgyṓin wa minná mokumoku to hataraite iru. 工場従業員はみんな黙々と働いて

いる。*The factory workers are all working silently.*

mókumoku [to] もくもく（と）*in puffs* §Entotsu kara kemuri ga mókumoku déte iru. 煙突から煙がもくもく出ている。*There's smoke puffing from the chimney.*

mokuteki 目的 *purpose; goal; target* §mokutekíchi 目的地 *destination* §Mokuteki no tamé no shúdan o kangaeyố. 目的のための手段を考えよう。*Let's consider the steps we'll need to accomplish our purpose.*

Mokuyốbi 木曜日 *Thursday*

mokuzō 木造 *made of wood; wooden* §Nára no Tốdai-ji wa sékai saidai no mokuzō kénchiku désu. 奈良の東大寺は世界最大の木造建築です。*The Todaiji Temple in Nara is the world's largest wooden building.*

mokuzō 木像 *wooden statue*

mómban 門番 *gatekeeper; porter; concierge*

Mombu dáijin 文部大臣 *Education Minister*

Mombúshō 文部省 *Ministry of Education*

momen 木綿 *cotton (material)*

mome·ru [*vi* momenai; mometa] 揉める *quarrel; be in discord; have trouble; be uneasy; be anxious (about)* §Kyố no káigi wa mesố desu. 今日の会議は揉めそうです。*Today's meeting looks like trouble.* §Musume no endan de ki ga momerú wa. 娘の縁談で気が揉めるわ。*I'm anxious about my daughter's marriage arrangements.* <fem>

momiá·u [*vi* momiawánai; momiátta] 揉み合う *jostle; struggle (with one another)* §Rốshi wa chin'age ni tsúite hagéshiku momiátte iru. 労使は賃上げについて激しく揉み合っている。*Labor and management are fighting over wage increases.*

mómiji 紅葉 *maple tree; fall foliage*

momo 桃 *peach; peach tree*

mōmoku no 盲目の *blind (preferred: mé no fujiyứ na)* ——**mōmokuteki [na]** 盲目的（な）*blind* §Háha no ái wa tokí ni wa mōmokuteki de sáe áru. 母の愛は時には盲目的でさえある。*At times a mother's love is blind.*

mom·u [*vt* momanai; monda] 揉む *massage; rub* §káta o momu 肩を揉む *massage (someone's) shoulders*

món 門 *gate*

mondai 問題 *problem; matter; trouble* §Kono sūgaku no mondai ga tokemásu ka? この数学の問題が解けますか。*Can you solve this math problem?* §Yoshímura wa matá onna no kotó de mondai o okóshita. 吉村はまた女のことで問題を起こした。*Yoshimura's in trouble over a woman again.*

mongén 門限 *curfew*

mónku 文句 *words; terms; phrase; complaint; grievance* §mónku o iu 文句を言う *complain* §kimari mónku 決まり文句 *a catch phrase;*

fixed expression ❀meimónku 名文句 *a clever phrase* ❀mónku o tsukéru 文句をつける *complain (about)*

monó 物 *an object; thing*

monó 者 *person* ❀Watashi wa Abé to iu monó desu. 私は阿部という者です。*I'm Abe.* ❀Sumimásén. Íma sono kotó ni kuwashíi monó wa séki o hazushite imásu. すみません。今そのことに詳しい者は席を外しています。*I'm sorry, the person who is familiar with that subject isn't in right now. <formal>*

-monó desu 〜ものです *used to (do)* — ❀Kodomo no kóro, watashi wa yóku kyōkai ni kayotta monó desu. 子供の頃、私はよく教会に通ったものです。*When I was a child I used to go to church.*

monogátari 物語 *story; tale* ❀Isoppu Monogátari イソップ物語 *Aesop's Fables* ❀Heike Monogátari 平家物語 *The Tales of the Heike*

monogoi 物乞い *begging*

monógoto 物事 *things* ❀Arayúru kákudo kara monógoto o kentō-shiyó. あらゆる角度から物事を検討しよう。*Let's look at things from all angles.*

monohoshí-zao 物干し竿 *bamboo pole for hanging laundry out to dry*

monomane 物真似 *mimicry* ❀monomané-shi 物真似師 *a mimic* ❀Watashi wa dōbutsu no monomane ga józu desu. 私は動物の物真似が上手です。*I'm good at mimicking animals.*

monomórai 物貰い *a sty (in one's eye)*

monookí 物置 *storehouse; shed*

monosáshi 物差し *ruler; a measure*

monosugó·i [*adj* monosúgoku nái; monosúgokatta] 物凄い *(be) wonderful; excellent; marvelous; terrific; terrible; awful; horrible* ❀Ano jíko wa monosúgokatta ne. あの事故は物凄かったね。*The accident was horrible!* ❀Kono kónsāto wa monosúgói. このコンサートは物凄い。*This concert's terrific!*

monózuki 物好き *curiosity; whim* ❀Monózuki de konna koto o yatte iru n ja nái. 物好きでこんなことをやっているんじゃない。*I'm not doing this just for the fun of it.* ——**monózuki na** 物好きな *curious; fanciful*

moppara 専ら *persistent; exclusive; totally* ❀moppara no uwasa 専らの噂 *a persistent (or wide-spread) rumor* ❀kénryoku o moppara ni suru 権力を専らにする *take exclusive power* ❀moppara benkyō ni uchikomu 専ら勉強に打ち込む *be totally engrossed in study*

morás·u [*vt* morasánai; moráshita] 漏らす；洩らす *let (information) leak out; express; give vent to* ❀Himitsu o moráshita no wa dáre desu ka? 秘密を漏らしたのは誰ですか。*Who is it that let the secret out?* ❀ikari o morásu 怒りを漏らす *express (or give vent to) anger*

mora·u [*vt* morawanai; moratta] 貰う *get; receive* ❀Tárō-san kara tegami o moratta. 太郎さんから手紙を貰った。*I got a letter from*

Tarō. **❀**Watashi wa maitsuki kánai kara goman-en kózukai o moratte iru. 私は毎月家内から五万円小遣いを貰っている。*I receive a ¥50,000 (personal) allowance from my wife every month.*

[-te] mora·u [vb aux, benefactive] （〜て）もらう *have (something) done (for one)* **❀**Yamáguchi-san ni sono tegami o dáshite moratta. 山口さんにその手紙を出してもらった。*I had Mr. Yamaguchi mail the letters. (or Mr. Yamaguchi mailed the letters for me).*

moré·ru [vi morénai; móreta] 漏れる *leak; escape* **❀**Gásu ga mórete iru yo! ガスが漏れているよ！*Gas is leaking!*

mōretsu [na] 猛烈（な）*violent; furious; terrible; intense* **❀**mōretsu na kōgeki 猛烈な攻撃 *a violent attack* ——**mōretsu ni** 猛烈に *terribly; violently*

mori 森 *forest*

moriagari 盛り上がり *climax; upsurge (of emotion)*

moriagár·u [vi moriagaránai; moriagátta] 盛り上がる *swell; rise; mount* **❀**Fuhei ga moriagátte iru. 不平が盛り上がっている。*Grievances are building up.*

moriagé·ru [vt moriagénai; moriágeta] 盛り上げる *heap (up); pile (up)* **❀**sara ni kudámono o moriagéru 皿に果物を盛り上げる *heap fruit on a dish* **❀**Kánojo wa pátī no fun'íki o moriagéru no ga umái. 彼女はパーティーの雰囲気を盛り上げるのがうまい。*She's a whiz at enhancing the mood of a party.* <masc>

morói [adj móruku nái; mórokatta] 脆い *(be) fragile; brittle; delicate; vulnerable* **❀**Kono kén wa há ga morói. この剣は刃が脆い。*The blade of this sword is fragile.* **❀**Watashi wa jō ni morói seikaku desu. 私は情に脆い性格です。*I'm the sentimental type.*

mór·u [vi moránai; mótta] 漏る *leak; escape* **❀**Tenjō kara áme ga mótte iru. 天井から雨が漏っている。*Rain is leaking through the ceiling.*

mor·u [vt moranai; motta] 盛る *serve; fill; put into* **❀**dokú o moru 毒を盛る *poison; add poison to* **❀**Jōbun ni kono kitei o morô. 条文にこの規定を盛ろう。*Let's add this provision to the text.*

móshi...-tára もし〜たら *if —; supposing that* **❀**Móshi watashi ga tori dáttara, ōzóra o tobimawaréru no ni! もし私が鳥だったら、大空を飛び回れるのに。*If I were a bird I could fly about in the sky, but...*

mōshi-dé·ru [vt -dénai; -déta] 申し出る *suggest; pose; volunteer; apply (for); register* **❀**Bunkasai no jumbí'in ni naritái katá wa mōshi-déte kudasái. 文化祭の準備員になりたい方は申し出て下さい。*Anyone wishing to serve on the preparation committee for the culture festival, please register.*

mōshikomisho 申込書；申し込み書 *application (in writing)*

mōshikom·u [vt mōshikomanai; mōshikonda] 申し込む *apply (for); propose; ask (for); sign up (for)* **❀**Masao wa Támiko ni kekkon o mōshikonda. 正男は民子に結婚を申し込んだ。*Masao proposed* *(marriage) to Tamiko.* §Sono shimbún-sha shusai no kōénkai ni mōshikonda. その新聞者主催の講演会に申し込んだ。*I signed up for the lectures sponsored by the newspaper company.*

Móshi-moshi! もしもし！ *Hello! (said on the telephone); Pardon! (said to attract someone's attention)*

mōshitsuke·ru [*vt* -tsukenai; -tsuketa] 申し付ける *inquire; ask (about); order* §kinshin o mōshitsukeru 謹慎を申し付ける *order (one) to be on good behavior* §Nan nári to o-mōshitsuke kudasái. 何なりとお申し付け下さい。*Please ask about anything at all. <formal>*

Mōshiwake arimasén [or **Mōshiwake gozaimasén**]. 申し訳ありません（or ございません）。*I'm sorry (I have no excuse). <formal>* §Osoku-nátte mōshiwake arimasén. 遅くなって申し訳ありません。*Excuse me for being late.* §Mōshiwake gozaimasén ga, mō shibáraku o-machi kudasaimásu ka? 申し訳ございませんが、もう暫くお待ち下さいますか。*I'm sorry, but would you please wait a bit longer? <formal>*

mṓs·u [*vt* mōsánai; mṓshita] 申す *say <formal>* §Watashi wa Buráun to mōshimásu. 私はブラウンと申します。*I'm Mrs. Brown. <formal>*

motarás·u [*vt* motarasánai; motaráshita] 齎す；もたらす *bring; bring about; cause to hold* §Zaiaku wa wazawai o motarásu. 罪悪はわざわいをもたらす。*Evil leads to disaster.*

motenashi 持て成し *entertainment; hospitality*

moté·ru [*vi* moténai; móteta] 持てる *be attractive; be made much of; be popular with* §Tágami-san wa onná no ko ni motéru né. 田上さんは女の子にもてるね。*Tagami is popular with the girls.*

motó 元 *source; origin* §hí no motó 火の元 *the source of a fire* §motó o tadóru 元を辿る *trace the origin (of something)* ——**móto no** 元の *original* §Kono seihin no móto no zairyṓ wa nán desu ka? この製品の元の材料は何ですか。*What is the original material of this product?* ——**móto wa** 元は *formerly* §Inoue káchō wa móto wa watashi no búka datta n désu yo! 井上課長は元は私の部下だったんですよ。*The section boss, Mr. Inoue, was once my subdordinate.*

motó; motoi 基 *foundation; basis* §Uno-san wa kaisha hatten no motó o tsukútta hitó desu. 宇野さんは会社発展の基を作った人です。*Mr. Uno laid the foundation for the development of the company.*

motochō 元帳 *ledger; account book*

motomé·ru [*vt* motoménai; motómeta] 求める *want; ask; demand; seek; search for* §Tomodachi ni tasuké o motómeta. 友達に助けを求めた。*I asked my friend for help.* §Watashi wa íma shoku o motómete iru. 私は今、職を求めている。*I'm now looking for a job.*

motomoto 元々 *originally; from the first* §Anó hito wa motomoto wasureppói. あの人は元々忘れっぽい。*He always forgets. (lit: He's forgetful from the start.)*

motozúk·u [*vi* motozukánai; motozúita] 基づく *be founded (on); be based (on)* 🔹Watashi no kono hándan wa ima máde no keiken ni motozúite imásu. 私のこの判断は今までの経験に基づいています。 *My judgment is based on my experience to date.*

móts·u [*vt* motánai; mótta] 持つ *have; own; hold; carry; endure; last* 🔹Íma, kozeni o mótte-imásu ka? 今、小銭を持っていますか。 *Do you have any change on you?* 🔹Piano o mótte imásu ka? ピアノを持っていますか。 *Do you have a piano?* 🔹Chótto kore mótte! ちょっとこれ持って。 *Hold this a minute!*

mottaibútta 勿体ぶった *pompous; haughty* 🔹Égawa-san wa ítsumo mottaibútta iikata o suru. 江川さんはいつも勿体ぶった言い方をする。 *Ms. Egawa always talks in a pompous manner.*

mottainá·i [*adj* mottaináku nái; mottainákatta] 勿体ない *(be) wasteful* 🔹Mátte iru jikan ga mottainái. 待っている時間が勿体ない。 *It's a waste of time waiting.* 🔹Takushī-dai ga mottainái kara arúite kaerṓ. タクシー代が勿体ないから歩いて帰ろう。 *It's a waste of money to take a taxi. Let's walk home.*

motte ik·u [*vt* -ikanai; -itta] 持って行く *carry; take* 🔹Kyṓ wa áme ga furisṓ dakara kása o motte itta hṓ ga íi yo! 今日は雨が降りそうだから傘を持って行った方がいいよ。 *Today it looks like it's going to rain, so you'd better take an umbrella.*

motte k·úru [*vt* -kónai; -kíta] 持って来る *bring* 🔹Né kimí, réi no shorui o motte kíte kurenái kai? ねえ君、例の書類を持って来てくれないかい。 *Say, would you bring me those documents? <masc>*

mótto もっと *more* 🔹Mótto migi no hṓ ni é o ugokáshite kudasái. もっと右の方に絵を動かして下さい。 *Move the picture more to the right.*

mottómo 最も *very; most; exceedingly* 🔹Anáta no mottómo tokúi na kamoku wa nán desu ka? あなたの最も得意な科目は何ですか。 *What is your best subject in school?*

móya もや *haze; mist* 🔹Yamá ni móya ga kakátte iru. 山にもやがかかっている。 *Mist hangs over the mountain.*

moyashí 萌やし *bean sprouts*

moyas·u [*vt* moyasanai; moyashita] 燃やす *burn; kindle* 🔹Kamikúzu o moyashite kurenai? 紙屑を燃やしてくれない？ *Would you burn this waste paper? <fem>*

moyō 模様 *pattern; design* 🔹Mizutama móyō no buráusu ga yóku niáu yo. 水玉模様のブラウスがよく似合うよ。 *That polka-dot (design) blouse looks good on you.*

moyōshimono 催し物 *entertainment*

mú 無 *nothingness* 🔹Mú kara yṹ ga umareru. 無から有が生まれる。 *Being is born from nothingness. (or From nothingness comes being.) (A Buddhist concept)*

mu- 無～ *not –* 🔹mu-jíhi 無慈悲 *mercilessness; cruelty* 🔹mu-kándō

無感動 *indifference; apathy*

múcha [na] 無茶（な）*absurd; reckless; excessive* §Múcha na kotó o iú na yo. 無茶なことを言うなよ。*Don't be absurd!* §Múcha o surú na. 無茶をするな。*Don't do anything rash! <masc>*

muchakucha [na] 無茶苦茶（な）*confused; unreasonable* —— **muchakucha ni** 無茶苦茶に *in disorder; pell-mell* §Kono shōsetsu no sutṓrī wa muchakucha ni komiitte iru. この小説のストーリーは無茶苦茶に込み入っている。*The plot of this novel is confused.*

múchi 無知 *ignorance; innocence* —— **múchi [na]** 無知な *ignorant; innocent* §Watashi wa rekishi ni múchi desu. 私は歴史に無知です。*I'm ignorant about history.* §Kánojo wa totemo múchi da. 彼女はとても無知だ。*She is very innocent. <masc>*

muchū [no] 夢中（の）*engrossed; absorbed (in); taken (with)* —— **muchū de** 夢中で *frantically; like mad* §Shimekiri ga chikazuite, sono sakka wa muchū de genkō o káite iru. 締切が近づいて、その作家は夢中で原稿を書いている。*The author is frantically writing to meet his deadline.*

muda 無駄 *futility; uselessness* §muda-bánashi 無駄話 *a gabfest; idle talk; gossip* —— **muda [na]** 無駄な *wasteful; futile; useless* §Imasara kṓkai shité mo mṓ muda désu yo. 今更後悔してももう無駄ですよ。*It's too late to be sorry now.* —— **muda ni** 無駄に *wastefully*

mudan de 無断で *without notice; without permission*

mufúmbetsu [na] 無分別（な）*indiscriminatory; thoughtless; reckless*

mugen no 無限の *limitless; unbounded; endless* §mugen no ái 無限の愛 *endless love*

múgi 麦 *wheat* §ōmúgi 大麦 *barley* §komúgi 小麦 *wheat* §raimúgi ライ麦 *rye*

múhi no 無比の *unrivaled; unequaled; unparalleled*

muhō 無法 *lawlessness; injustice* —— **muhō na** 無法な *unlawful; outrageous* §muhō na furumai 無法な振舞い *outrageous behavior* §muhōmono 無法者 *an outlaw* §muhō chítai 無法地帯 *lawless territory*

muika 六日 *the 6th (of the month); six days*

muími [na] 無意味（な）*nonsense; meaningless* §muími na kotó o iu 無意味なことを言う *talk nonsense* —— **muími ni** 無意味に *meaninglessly* §muími ni tokí o tsuiyásu 無意味に時を費やす *spend time meaninglessly*

mújaki 無邪気 *innocence; naiveté* —— **mújaki [na]** 無邪気（な）*innocent; naive; guileless* §Kénchan wa mújaki desu ne. 健ちゃんは無邪気ですね。*Ken is naive.* —— **mújaki ni** 無邪気に *innocently; guilelessly* §Kodomótachi wa mújaki ni asonde iru. 子供たちは無邪気に遊んでいる。*The children are playing innocently.*

mujin éisei 無人衛星 *unmanned satellite*

mujóken 無条件 *without stipulations*   §mujōken kófuku 無条件降伏 *unconditional surrender*

mujun 矛盾 *contradiction* —— **mujun na** 矛盾な *contradictory* —— **mujun-suru** 矛盾する *be contradictory* §Póru wa ítsumo mujun-shita kotó o heiki de iu. ポールはいつも矛盾したことを平気で言う。 *Paul often makes contradictory statements unabashedly.*

mukade 百足；蜈蚣 *centipede*

mukae ni ik·u [vt -ikanai; -itta] 迎えに行く *go to meet* §O-kyakusan o kūkō ni mukae ni itta. お客さんを空港に迎えに行った。 *I went to meet a client at the airport.*

mukae·ru [vt mukaenai; mukaeta] 迎える *meet; go to meet; welcome* §Kūkō de osana-nájimi o mukaeta. 空港で幼馴染みを迎えた。 *I went to meet a childhood friend at the airport.*

mukai 向かい *opposite* §mukai-gawa 向かい側 *the opposite side* §Ginkō wa gakkō no mukai ni arimásu. 銀行は学校の向かいにあります。 *The bank is opposite the school.*

mukánkaku na 無感覚な *insensible; numb; callous*

mukánshin 無関心 *indifference; unconcern* —— **mukánshin na** 無関心な *indifferent; unconcerned; have no interest in* §Íma, seijiteki ni mukánshin na wakamono ga fúete imásu. 今、政治的に無関心な若者が増えています。 *These days the number of young people who have no interest in politics is increasing.*

mukashi 昔 *ancient times; long ago* §mukashi mukashi 昔昔 *once upon a time* §mukashi-bánashi 昔話 *ancient stories; fairy tales*

mukáshitsu [na] 無過失（な） *strict; absolute* §mukáshitsu baishō sékinin 無過失賠償責任 *no-fault liability (for compensation)*

muka·u [vi mukawanai; mukatta] 向かう *face; confront; defy* §góru ni mukatte hashíru ゴールに向かって走る *run toward a goal* §Oyá ni mukatte kuchigotae-surú nante. 親に向かって口答えするなんて！ *What do you mean, talking back to your parents!*

mukei no 無形の *intangible* §mukei bunkázai 無形文化財 *intangible cultural property*

-muki ～向き *facing; suitable for* §minami-muki no heyá 南向きの部屋 *a room facing south* §omote-muki no kójitsu 表向きの口実 *the ostensible reason* §natsu-muki no ífuku 夏向きの衣服 *summer clothes*

múko 婿 *son-in-law* §o-múko-san おむこさん *bridegroom*

mukō 向こう *across; beyond* §yama no mukō 山の向こう *beyond the mountain* §Watashi wa mukō isshūkan isogashíku náru. 私は向こう一週間忙しくなる。 *I'm going to be busy a week from now.*

mukō no 無効の *ineffective; invalid* §Pasupóto wa sengetsu mukō ni nátte ita. パスポートは先月無効になっていた。 *My passport became invalid last month.*

mukōzune 向こう脛 *shin*

muk·u [*vt* mukanai; muita] 剥く *peel; pare* 8ringo no kawá o muku り
んごの皮を剥く *peel an apple*

muk·u [*vi* mukanai; muita] 向く *turn (the head) toward; look toward*

múkuchi na hito 無口な人 *a person of few words; a taciturn person*

mumenkyo únten 無免許運転 *driving without a license*

munashí·i [*adj* munáshiku nái; munáshikatta] 空しい *(be) empty;
fruitless; futile* ——**munáshiku** 空しく *vainly; fruitlessly*

muné 胸 *breast; chest* 8Kikuchi-san wa muné ga warui rashíi. 菊池さん
は胸が悪いらしい。*Kikuchi has a lung problem.* 8Watashi wa
muné ga dókidoki-shite iru. 私は胸がどきどきしている。*My heart's
going pitter-patter.*

muneyake 胸やけ *heartburn*

murá 村 *village* 8mura-yákuba 村役場 *village office* 8mura-házure
村はずれ *village outskirts*

murásaki [no] 紫（の）*purple*

muré 群れ *a herd* 8muré o násu 群れをなす *flock (together); form a
group* 8hito no muré 人の群れ *a crowd of people* 8hitsuji no muré
羊の群れ *a flock of sheep*

múri 無理 *unreasonableness* ——**múri [na]** 無理（な）*unreasonable*
8muri shínjū 無理心中 *forced double suicide* ——**múri ni** 無理に
unreasonably; forcibly

múryoku 無力 *impotence; powerlessness* ——**múryoku [na]** 無力（な）
impotent; powerless 8Taisei ni táishite kójin no chikará wa amarí ni
mo múryoku desu. 体制に対して個人の力はあまりにも無力です。
One person is powerless against the system.

musabór·u [*vt* musaboránai; musabótta] 貪る *devour* 8musabori-kúu
貪り喰う *eat ravenously* 8musabori-yómu 貪り読む *devour (by
reading)*

músei [no] 無性（の）*asexual* 8musei séishoku 無性生殖 *asexual
reproduction*

muséigen [no] 無制限（の）*unlimited* ——**muséigen ni** 無制限に
indefinitely; freely

musékinin 無責任 *irresponsibility*

musen 無線 *wireless; radio*

múshamusha [to] むしゃむしゃ（と）*gobbling down; devouring (ly)*
8Káre no múshamusha tabéru mánā ga dōshité mo gáman-dekínai. 彼の
むしゃむしゃ食べるマナーがどうしても我慢できない。*I can't
stand the way he gobbles down his food.*

mushi 虫 *bug; insect*

mushiatsú·i [*adj* mushiátsuku nái; mushiátsukatta] 蒸し暑い *(be) muggy;
humid and hot* 8Nihon no natsú wa totemo mushiatsúi. 日本の夏はと
ても蒸し暑い。*Summers in Japan are very hot and humid.*

mushiba 虫歯 *decayed tooth*

mushíkaku 無資格 *disqualification; not qualified* §mushikaku íshi 無資格医師 *unlicensed doctor*

mushiró 筵席 *straw mat* §hári no mushiró 針のむしろ *a bitter experience (lit: a mat made of needles)* <set phrase>

múshiro...[no] hō 寧ろ… *rather (than); better (than)* §Hazukashime o ukéru nara múshiro shí no hō o erábu. 辱めを受けるなら、むしろ死の方を選ぶ。 *I would choose death rather than dishonor.*

múshi-suru [vt] 無視する *disregard; ignore; defy* §Ōnami no keikoku o múshi-shite, wakamono wa úmi ni háitte itta. 大波の警告を無視して、若者は海に入っていった。 *Defying the warning of big waves, the young people went swimming in the ocean.*

mús·u [vi / vt musánai; múshita] 蒸す *steam; be sultry* §Kón'ya wa hídoku músu ne! 今夜はひどく蒸すね！ *It's very sultry tonight, isn't it?*

musubime 結び目 *a bow; knot*

musubitsuké·ru [vt musubitsukénai; musubitsúketa] 結び付ける *tie to; fasten* §kí ni musubitsukéru 木に結び付ける *tie to a tree* §gen'in to kekka o musubitsukéru 原因と結果を結び付ける *tie cause and effect*

musub·u [vt musubanai; musunda] 結ぶ *tie; bind; fasten; make a knot* §nékutai o musubu ネクタイを結ぶ *tie a necktie* §mi o musubu 実を結ぶ *bear fruit*

musuko 息子 *(one's own) son*

musumé 娘 *girl; (one's own) daughter*

mutónchaku [na] 無頓着 *(な) nonchalant; indifferent* §Chichí wa mínari ni mutónchaku desu. 父は身なりに無頓着です。 *Dad's indifferent about the way he dresses.*

mutto-suru むっとする *get angry; be offended; take offense; be stuffy; be stifling* §Mutto-suru kimochi o osáeru no ga taihen dátta. むっとする気持ちを抑えるのが大変だった。 *It was hard to keep from getting angry.* §Heyá ni háiru to mutto-shita. 部屋に入るとむっとした。 *When I entered the room I felt stifled.*

muttsú 六つ *six (when counting things)*

muyūbyō 夢遊病 *sleepwalking*

múzai 無罪 *innocence; without guilt* ——**múzai no** 無罪の *innocent; not guilty*

muzukashi·i [adj muzukashiku nái; muzukashíkatta] 難しい *(be) difficult; hard* §Kyō no tésuto wa muzukashíkatta. 今日のテストは難しかった。 *The test today was hard.* §Káre wa muzukashii hitó da. 彼は難しい人だ。 *He's a difficult person.* <masc>

myakú 脈 *pulse* §myakuhaku 脈拍 *pulse* §myakú o toru 脈をとる

　　take (one's) pulse 🕭Myakú ga hayái. 脈が早い。 *The pulse is fast.*
　　🕭Myakú ga midárete iru. 脈が乱れている。 *The pulse is irregular.*

myōgónichi 明後日 *the day after tomorrow*

myōji 名字；苗字 *last name; surname*

myōjō 明星 *morning star; Venus*

myō na 妙な *odd; strange; mysterious*　🕭Sore wa myṓ na hanashí desu. それは妙な話です。 *That's a strange story.*

myōnichi 明日 *tomorrow*

N

na な *[emphatic sentence-ending particle: masc]*　🕭Hara hetta na! 腹へった な。 *I'm hungry.* *<masc>* 🕭Tsukáreta na! 疲れたな。 *I'm tired! <masc>*

na な *[copular particle linking a noun of a certain class to a noun it modifies; such nouns are identified in this dictionary by* **[na]** *in the entry]*　🕭génki na kodomo 元気な子供 *a healthy child* 🕭shínsetsu na hitó 親切な人 *a kind person*

nā なあ *[sentence-ending particle: indicating longing; masc]*　🕭Ryokō ni ikitái nā. 旅行に行きたいなあ！ *Gee, I'd like to take a trip! <masc>*

nábe 鍋 *pan (for cooking)*　🕭nabe ryṓri 鍋料理 *stew of vegetables and fish or meat*

nadaká·i *[adj* nadákaku nái; nadákakatta*]* 名高い *(be) distinguished; famous; well-known*

nadáraka [na] なだらか（な） *gently-sloping; smooth*　🕭 nadáraka na sakámichi なだらかな坂道 *a gentle slope* ——**nadáraka ni** なだら かに *smoothly*

nadare 雪崩 *avalanche; snowslide*

nadé·ru *[vt* nadénai; nádeta*]* 撫でる *fondle; pet; stroke; pat*　🕭Chichí wa kodomo no atamá o nádete iru. 父は子供の頭を撫でている。 *Dad is stroking the child's head.*

-nádo ～など *and so forth; etc.*　🕭Súpā de nikú ya yasai nádo o katta. ス ーパーマーケットで肉や野菜などを買った。 *At the supermarket I bought meat and vegetables and such.*

náe 苗 *young plant; seedling*

nafuda 名札 *name tag*

nagabik·u *[vi* nagabikánai; nagabíita*]* 長引く *be prolonged; be delayed*　🕭Rōshi-kṓshō wa nagabíite iru. 労使交渉は長引いている。 *Labor-management negotiations are dragging on and on.*

nagagutsu 長靴 *boots*

nagá·i *[adj* nágaku nái; nágakatta*]* 長い *(be) long*　🕭Kirin wa kubi ga nagái. キリンは首が長い。 *The giraffe's neck is long.* ——**nágaku** 長

く *long; for a long time* 🔹nágaku suru 長くする *make long(er)*
🔹Nágaku machimáshita ka? 長く待ちましたか。*Did you wait long?*

nagaikí 長生き *long life; longevity* ——**nagaikí-suru** 長生きする *live long; last long*

nagaisu 長椅子 *couch; sofa; lounge*

nagamé 眺め *a view* 🔹Koko kará no nagamé wa saikō desu. ここから の眺めは最高です。*The view from here is great.*

nagamé·ru [*vt* nagaménai; nagámeta] 眺める *look (intently) at* 🔹Miyamoto-san wa mádo no sóto o nagámete imásu. 宮本さんは窓の 外を眺めています。*Miyamoto is looking intently out the window.*

-nágara 〜ながら *while...-ing* 🔹Watashi wa ítsumo óngaku o kikinágara benkyō-shimásu. 私はいつも音楽を聴きながら勉強します。*I always study while listening to music.*

nagaré 流れ *a stream; a flow; current* 🔹kawa no nagare 川の流れ *river current* 🔹hanashi no nagare 話しの流れ *flow of a conversation*

nagaré-boshi 流れ星 *shooting star*

nagaré·ru [*vi* nagarénai; nagáreta] 流れる *flow; float; drift; run (down); stream down* 🔹kawá ga nagaréru 川が流れる *a river flows* 🔹kaze ni nagaréru 風に流れる *float on the breeze* 🔹Áse ga karada zentai o nagárete iru. 汗が身体全体を流れている。*Perspiration is streaming down my entire body.* 🔹Ōmizu de hashí ga nagáreta. 大水で橋が流れ た。*The bridge was washed away by the swollen river.*

nágasa 長さ *length* 🔹Nágasa wa dono gurai desu ka? 長さはどのぐら いですか。*What is the approximate length?*

nagashí 流し *a sink*

nágashi 流し *strolling musician; cruising taxi*

nagás·u [*vt* nagasánai; nagáshita] 流す *let flow; let run (out); pour; drain; exile* 🔹námida o nagásu 涙を流す *shed tears* 🔹mizu ni nagásu 水に 流す *let bygones be bygones* <set phrase>

nagaya 長屋 *tenement house*

nagekí 嘆き *grief; sorrow*

nagék·u [*vt* nagekánai; nagéita] 嘆く *pine; grieve; mourn for; feel sad; lament* 🔹Mi no fúun o nagéite mo hajimaranai. 身の不運を嘆いても 始まらない。*It does no good lamenting one's bad luck.*

nagé·ru [*vt* nagénai; nágeta] 投げる *throw; toss; pitch* 🔹bōru o nagéru ボールを投げる *pitch a ball*

nagetsuke·ru [*vt* nagetsukenai; nagetsuketa] 投げつける *throw at (and hit)* 🔹inú ni ishí o nagetsukeru 犬に石を投げつける *throw a rock at a dog*

nagorí 名残り *parting; trace; vestige; relic* 🔹nagori oshíi 名残り惜しい *be sorry (sad) at parting (from someone)*

nagóyaka [na] 和やか（な）*quiet; mild; calm; gentle; amiable; agreeable; harmonious; congenial* ——**nagóyaka ni** 和やかに

amiably; genially; peacefully 　❸Watashítachi wa nagóyaka ni kondan-shimáshita. 私たちは和やかに懇談しました。*We had a friendly talk.*

naguri-korosu [*vt* -korosanai; -koroshita] *beat to death* ——**naguri-korosaré·ru** [*pass*] 殴り殺される *be battered (beaten) to death*

nagúr·u [*vt* naguránai; nagútta] 殴る *beat (with the fists); punch* 　❸Áni wa watashi no yokottsura o nagútta. 兄は私の横っ面を殴った。*My (older) brother punched me in the face.*

nagusame 慰め *consolation; comfort* 　❸Nagusame no kotobá ga mitsukaranai. 慰めの言葉が見つからない。*I can't find words of consolation.*

nagusamé·ru [*vt* nagusaménai; nagusámeta] 慰める *comfort; console; soothe* 　❸Híroshi-san wa kanashisō na kodomo o nagusámeta. 博志さんは悲しそうな子供を慰めた。*Hiroshi comforted the unhappy child.*

nái ない *is not* [*neg plain form of* **ar·u**; *neg ending for verbs, adjectives and* **desu**]

náibu 内部 *interior; inner* 　❸naibu sóshiki 内部組織 *inner organization*

náikaku 内閣 *(government) cabinet* 　❸naikaku kámbō 内閣官房 *cabinet secretariat* 　❸náikaku kambō chōkan 内閣官房長官 *chief cabinet secretary*

naimen 内面 *inside; interior*

nairan 内乱 *civil war; internal fighting*

naishin 内心 *(one's) innermost feelings; real intention* 　❸naishin o uchiakeru 内心を打ち明ける *confess one's innermost feelings* 　❸naishin, fukai o oboéru 内心、不快を覚える *experience inward displeasure*

naishó 内緒 *secret* 　❸Watashi wa oyá ni naishó de dísuko ni itta. 私は親に内緒でディスコに行った。*I went to a disco, keeping it a secret from my parents.* 　❸Naisho-bánashi desu. 内緒話です。*It's a secret.*

naishoku 内職 *side job; a sideline*

naiyō 内容 *content(s); subject matter; substance* 　❸naiyō to keishiki 内容と形式 *content and form* 　❸Murayama-san wa wájutsu wa umái ga naiyō wa nái. 村山さんは話術はうまいが内容はない。*Mr. Murayama is eloquent but (his speeches) lack substance.*

najimí [no] 馴染み（の）*familiar* 　❸najimí no nái aji 馴染みのない味 *an unfamiliar taste*

najím·u [*vi* najimánai; najínda] 馴染む *be familiar with; make friends with; become attached to* 　❸Yúta-kun wa atarashíi okásan ni mố najínde imásu. 雄太君は新しいお母さんにもう馴染んでいます。*Yūta has accepted (or become attached to) his new mother.*

náka 中 *inside* 　❸ie no náka 家の中 *inside the house* 　❸hako no náka 箱の中 *the inside of a box.*

nakabá 半ば *(the) middle; halfway* 　❸rokugatsu nakabá 六月半ば *the middle of June* 　❸hashi no nakabá ni tátsu 橋の半ばに立つ *stand in* *the middle of a bridge*

nakamá 仲間 *companion; partner; group; friend(s)* ❧gorufu nákama ゴルフ仲間 *golfing companion* ❧asobi nákama 遊び仲間 *playmate* ❧nakama házure 仲間外れ *alienated (from a group); ostracized*

nakámi 中味；中身 *contents* ❧Hako no nakámi wa nán darō? 箱の中味は何だろう。 *I wonder what's in the box.* ❧Hanashi no nakámi wa ítsumo onaji desu. 話の中身はいつも同じです。 *The content of (his) speeches is always the same.*

nakanaka なかなか *very [with aff]; hardly [with neg]* ❧Kono éiga wa nakanaka omoshirói. この映画はなかなか面白い。 *This is a very interesting movie.* ❧Hánako-san é no denwa wa nakanaka tsunagaranai. 花子さんへの電話はなかなかつながらない。 *One can hardly ever reach Hanako by phone.*

nakaniwá 中庭 *courtyard; inner garden*

náka no íi 仲のいい *close; intimate* ❧náka no íi tomodachi 仲のいい友達 *a close friend*

nákayoku 仲良く *like good friends; friendly; pleasantly; in harmony* ❧Kodomótachi wa nákayoku asonde imásu. 子供達は仲良く遊んでいます。 *The children are playing together happily.*

-nákereba (or nákute wa) ikenai 〜なければ（なくては）いけない *must (do / be); have to (do / be); ought to (do / be)* ❧Ashitá wa kaimono ni ikanákereba ikenai. 明日は買い物に行かなければいけない。 *I have to go shopping tomorrow.* ❧Kodomo wa génki ja nákereba ikenai. 子供は元気じゃなければいけない。 *Children ought to be spirited.*

nakigóe 泣き声 *a cry; sound of crying; animal call; bird song* ❧akambō no nakigóe 赤ん坊の泣き声 *a baby's cry*

nakiharás·u [vi nakiharasánai; nakiharáshita] 泣き腫らす *cry one's eyes out*

nak·u [vi nakanai; naita] 泣く；鳴く *bark; sing; call; cry (of animals); weep (of humans)* ❧Nakánaide! 泣かないで。 *Don't cry!*

nakunar·u [vi nakunaranai; nakunatta] 無くなる *run out; play out; be exhausted; be lost* ❧Keshigomu ga nakunatchatta. 消しゴムがなくなっちゃった。 *The eraser is used up. (or I lost my eraser.)* ❧Jikan ga nakunatta. 時間がなくなった。 *Time is up.*

nakunar·u [vi nakunaranai; nakunatta] 亡くなる *pass away; die* ❧Háha wa ninen máe ni nakunatta. 母は二年前に亡くなった。 *My mother died two years ago.*

nakus·u [vt nakusanai; nakushita] 無くす *lose* ❧záisan o nakusu 財産を無くす *lose one's fortune* ❧Saifu o nakushita. 財布を無くした。 *I lost my wallet!*

-nákute [mo] íi 〜なくて（も）いい *it's O.K. if (something) isn't...; it's O.K. if (one) doesn't...* ❧Daiyamóndo wa ōkiku nákutemo íi desu. ダ

イヤモンドは大きくなくてもいいです。 *A diamond doesn't have to be big.* ❽Ryṓri ga jōzú ja nákutemo íi. 料理が上手じゃなくてもいい。 *It's O.K. if (you're) not good at cooking.*

náma [no] 生（の） *uncooked; raw* ❽nama bíru 生ビール *draft beer* ❽nama chúkei 生中継 *live broadcast*

namae 名前 *name; first (given) name*

namakemonó 怠け者 *lazy person; a lazybones; a good-for-nothing*

namaké·ru [vi namakénai; namáketa] 怠ける *be lazy; be neglectful; shirk* ❽shigoto o namakéru 仕事を怠ける *shirk (one's) work*

namari 鉛 *lead (metal)*

namarí 訛り *dialect; accent* ❽Namarí wa kuni no tegata desu. 訛りは国の手形です。 *Dialect is the stamp of one's origin.*

namayake [no] 生焼け（の） *underdone; undercooked*

námbā [puréto] ナンバー（プレート） *license plate*

Nambei 南米 *South America*

námboku 南北 *north and south* ❽Namboku Sénsō 南北戦争 *US Civil War* ❽Nambokú Amerika 南北アメリカ *North and South America*

naméraka [na] 滑らか（な） *smooth; slippery; soft* ❽naméraka na shámen 滑らかな斜面 *a smooth slope* ❽Káre no benzetsu wa naméraka da. 彼の弁舌は滑らかだ。 *He has an eloquent tongue.* <masc>

namé·ru [vt naménai; naméta] 舐める *lick; lap* ❽aisukurímu o naméru アイスクリームを舐める *lick ice cream* ❽shinsan o naméru 辛酸を舐める *experience bitter trials (lit: taste bitters)* ❽Heya no sumízumi made naméru-yō ni sōji-shita. 部屋の隅々まで舐めるように掃除した。 *I cleaned the room spic-and-span, from corner to corner.*

namí 波 *a wave; waves* ❽úmi no namí 海の波 *ocean waves* ❽hitonamí 人波 *a crowd* ❽keiki no namí ni noru 景気の波に乗る *ride the crest of the economic boom*

nami no 並みの *mediocre; average* ❽hitonami no 人並みの *ordinary* ❽nami no seiseki 並みの成績 *an average score (grade)* ❽seken-nami no sōba 世間並みの相場 *a reasonable price*

námida 涙 *tear(s)* ❽námida ni nureta 涙に濡れた *wet with tears* ❽námida o fuku 涙を拭く *wipe (one's) tears* ❽námida o nagásu 涙を流す *weep tears* ❽namida-gúmu 涙ぐむ *be moved to tears* ❽námida o ukabenágara 涙を浮かべながら *with tears in one's eyes*

namiki 並木 *roadside trees; a row of trees*

nammin 難民 *refugee*

nampa 難破 *shipwreck* ❽nampa-sen 難破船 *a shipwrecked boat*

nán 何 *what?* ❽Kore wa nán desu ka? これは何ですか。 *What is this?*

nan- (+ counter) 何〜 *how many?; how much?* ❽nándai 何台 *how many machines?* ❽nánkai 何回 *how many times?* ❽námmai 何枚 *how many sheets (of paper)?* ❽námbai 何杯 *how many cups (of* coffee)?

nána 七；7 *seven (the numeral)*

nanáme [no] 斜め（の）*diagonal* ❸nanáme no sén o hiku 斜めの線を引く *draw a diagonal line* ——**nanáme ni** 斜めに *diagonally; on a slant* ❸Kyúri o nanáme ni kítte kudasái. きゅうりを斜めに切って下さい。*Cut the cucumbers on a slant.*

nanátsu 七つ *seven (when counting things)*

nándaka 何だか *somehow* ❸Kyó wa nándaka karada ga darúi. 今日は何だか体がだるい。*Today somehow I feel weary.*

nandémo 何でも *anything (at all)* ❸Uchi no ko wa nandémo tabemásu yo. 家の子は何でも食べますよ。*My child eats anything.*

nándomo 何度も *over and over; many times; any number of times* ❸Watashi wa daigakujúken ni nándomo shippai-shite shimatta. 私は大学受験に何度も失敗してしまった。*I failed college entrance exams over and over.*

náni 何 *what?* ❸"Ano, chótto!" "Náni?" 「あの、ちょっと！」「何？」*"Hey! Just a second!" "What?"* ❸Kómban náni o tabemashó? 今晩、何を食べましょう？*What'll we eat tonight?*

nanigenái [adj nanigenáku nái; nanigenákatta] 何気ない *(be) casual; unconcerned* ❸nanigenái táido 何気ない態度 *a casual attitude* ——**nanigenáku** 何気なく *casually; accidentally; inadvertently* ❸Watashi wa nanigenáku furikáetta. 私は何気なく振り返った。*I happened to look back.*

nanigoto 何事 *what; whatever* ❸Nanigoto ga ókita no ka na? 何事が起きたのかな？*I wonder if something happened.* <masc>

nánika 何か *something* ❸Nomimóno ga nánika hoshíi. 飲み物が何か欲しい。*I'd like something to drink.*

nanimo 何も [with neg] *nothing* ❸Sore ni tsúite watashi wa nanimo shiranai. それについて私は何も知らない。*I don't know anything about it.*

nanimono 何者 *who?; what?* ❸Anó hito wa nanimono ná no? あの人は何者なの？*Who is that person?* <fem>

nánji 何時 *what time?* ❸Íma nánji desu ka? 今、何時ですか。*What time is it now?*

nangyō kúgyō 難行苦行 *asceticism; the practice of religious austerities (Budd)*

nankai 難解 *difficult to understand* ❸Ōe Kenzaburō no sakuhin wa nankai désu. 大江健三郎の作品は難解です。*Oe Kenzaburō's works are difficult to understand.*

nankyoku 難局 *crisis; difficult situation* ❸Watashi wa nán to ka nankyoku o norikoeru kotó ga dékita. 私は何とか難局を乗り越えることができた。*Somehow I managed to overcome the difficult situation.*

nanoká 七日 *the seventh (of the month); seven days*

nanra ká no 何らかの *some kind of* ❧Mondai káiketsu no tamé ni, nanra ká no taisaku o taténakereba naránai. 問題解決のために何らかの対策を立てなければならない。*In order to solve the problem, we must take some kind of measure.*

nán toka iu 何とか言う *someone; what's-his-name; something-or-other; what-you-may-call-it*

nan to mo ienai 何とも言えない *inexpressible; indescribable; I can't say anything (about it)* ❧nan to mo ienai fushigi na aji 何とも言えない不思議な味 *a strange, indescribable taste* ❧Sono kotó ni tsúite wa watashi kará wa nan to mo iemasén. そのことについては私からは何とも言えません。*I can't say anything concerning that.*

nan to náku 何となく *somehow; vaguely* ❧Nan to náku anó hito ga sukí desu. 何となくあの人が好きです。*I don't know why, but somehow I like that person.*

náo 尚 *more; further; still more*

naór·u [vi naóránai; naótta] 治る *be cured; heal; get well; recover* ❧Chichí no zensoku wa sukkári naorimáshita. 父の喘息はすっかり治りました。*My father's asthma is completely cured.*

naór·u [vi naóránai; naótta] 直る *be repaired; be fixed* ❧Térebi no koshó wa naorimáshita ka? テレビの故障は直りましたか。*Is the TV fixed?*

naosara 尚更 *still more; all the more*

naós·u [vt naosánai; naóshita] 治す *cure; heal* ❧Négishi-senséi wa watashi no ikáiyó o naóshite kureta. 根岸先生は私の胃潰瘍を治してくれた。*Dr. Negishi cured my stomach ulcer.*

naós·u [vt naosánai; naóshita] 直す *repair; fix* ❧Sentakúki o naóshite moratta. 洗濯機を直してもらった。*I had the washing machine repaired.*

naozari なおざり *negligence* ——**naozari na** なおざりな *negligent*

nara なら *if* ❧Ashitá nara iku kotó ga dekíru. 明日なら行くことができる。*If it's tomorrow, I can go.*

narabe·ru [vt narabenai; narabeta] 並べる *arrange; line up; put in a row* ❧Isu o chanto narabenasái. 椅子をちゃんと並べなさい。*Arrange the chairs neatly in a row.*

narab·u [vi narabanai; naranda] 並ぶ *be lined up; line up; be in a row* ❧Dōro-zoi ni atarashíi bíru ga narande iru. 道路沿いに新しいビルが並んでいる。*New buildings line the street.* ❧Narande machinasái. 並んで待ちなさい。*Wait in line.* ❧Futári wa narande arúite imásu. 二人は並んで歩いています。*The two (of them) are walking side by side.*

naras·u [vt narasanai; narashita] 鳴らす *ring; cause to ring (or sound)* ❧Búzá o narashimáshita ka? ブザーを鳴らしましたか。*Did you push the* *buzzer?*

nará·u [*vt* narawánai; narátta] 習う *learn; be taught* 🔹Imōtó wa Yamákawa-san ni piano o narátte imásu. 妹は山川さんにピアノを習っています。 *My sister is learning to play the piano from Ms. Yamakawa.*

naré·ru [*vi* narénai; náreta] 慣れる *become accustomed (to)* 🔹"Nánshī-san wa mó Nihon no seikatsu ni naremáshita ka?" "É´, naremáshita." 「ナンシーさんはもう日本の生活に慣れましたか。」「ええ、慣れました。」 *"Nancy, have you become accustomed to life in Japan?" "Yes, I'm used to it."*

narihibík·u [*vi* narihibikánai; narihibíita] 鳴り響く *ring (out)*

narikanénai [*vi: neg*] 成り兼ねない *it is not inconceivable that; there is a possibility that...* 🔹Dáre dátte ítsuka futó no higáisha ni narikanénai. 誰だっていつか不当の被害者に成り兼ねない。 *One can never rule out the possibility of sometime becoming the victim of injustice.*

naritats·u [*vi* naritatanai; naritatta] 成り立つ *hold; form; be made of; consist of* 🔹Kono rombun wa itsútsu no shó kara naritatte iru. この論文は五つの章から成り立っている。 *This thesis consists of five chapters.*

nár·u [*vi* naránai; nátta] 成る *become; get to be* 🔹génki ni náru 元気になる *get well* 🔹Kodomo wa yattsú ni narimáshita. 子供は八つになりました。 *My child is eight.*

nar·u [*vi* naranai; natta] 鳴る *ring; sound; peal* 🔹Mimí ga naru. 耳が鳴る。 *My ears are ringing.* 🔹Kaminarí ga natta. 雷が鳴った。 *It thundered.* 🔹O-tera no kane ga natte iru. お寺の鐘が鳴っている。 *The temple bell is tolling.*

narubeku なるべく *as...as possible* 🔹Narubeku háyaku kíte kudasái. なるべく早く来て下さい。 *Come as early (or quickly) as possible.*

naruhodo なるほど *I see!; Of course!* 🔹Naruhodo kimi no íken wa mottómo da. なるほど君の意見は尤もだ。 *Of course, your view is understandable. <masc>*

-nasái 〜なさい [*v: imperative suffix*] 🔹Háyaku o-fúro ni hairinasái. 早くお風呂に入りなさい。 *Hurry and take a bath.*

nasakebuká·i [*adj* nasakebúkaku nái; nasakebúkakatta] 情深い *(be) compassionate; kind-hearted*

nasakená·i [*adj* nasakenáku nái; nasakenákatta] 情けない *(be) heartless; miserable; pitiable; regrettable* 🔹Konna kotó ga dekínai nante nasakenái. こんなことができないなんて情けない。 *It's a shame you can't do such a (simple) thing.*

nasár·u [*vi* nasaránai; nasátta] 為さる *do <formal>* 🔹"Náni o nasátte irasshaimásu ka?" 「何をなさっていらっしゃいますか?」 *"What are you doing (or What do you do)?" <formal>*

nashí 梨 *pear (J)* 🔹yōnashi 洋梨 *(western) pear*

-náshi ni ～無しに *without...* §kyóka náshi ni 許可なしに *without permission.*

nashitoge·ru [*vt* nashitogenai; nashitogeta] 成し遂げる *accomplish; finish; carry out; win* §Káre wa kōnnan na shigoto o nashitōgeta. 彼は困難な仕事を成し遂げた。*He accomplished a difficult task.*

nás·u [*vt* nasánai; náshita] 成す *make; do; perform* §Kári wa muré o náshite tobu. 雁は群れをなして飛ぶ。*Wild geese fly in a flock.*

násu 茄子 *eggplant; aubergine*

natsú 夏 *summer* §natsuyásumi 夏休み *summer vacation*

natsukashigár·u [*vt* natsukashigaránai; natsukashigátta] 懐かしがる *long for; feel homesick (for)* [*not used with first person*]

natsukashí·i [*adj* natsukáshiku nái; natsukáshikatta] 懐かしい *(be) longed for; nostalgic (for); miss* §Furúsato ga natsukashíi. 故郷が懐かしい。*I miss my home.*

natsukashím·u [*vt* natsukashimánai; natsukashínda] 懐かしむ *remember nostalgically* §Sénshu ga káko no eikō o natsukashínde iru. 選手が過去の栄光を懐かしんでいる *The player is looking back nostalgically on his days of glory.*

nattoku 納得 *consent; understanding; persuasion* ——**nattoku-suru** [*vt*] 納得する *consent (to); be convinced* §Dōmo anata no kangáe ga nattoku-dekínai. どうもあなたの考えが納得できない。*There's no way I can accept (or consent to) your idea.*

nawá 縄 *cord; rope* §nawatóbi 縄跳び *jump rope; skipping rope* §nawabari 縄張り *staking out (territory)*

nayamasaré·ru [*vi: caus-passive*] 悩まされる *be troubled (by)* §Ryōshin wa musuko no hikō ni nayamasárete iru. 両親は息子の非行に悩まされている。*The parents are troubled by their son's bad behavior.*

nayamí 悩み *worry; trouble; distress; anxiety* §Ítsu made mo nayamí ga taénai. いつまでも悩みが絶えない。*Troubles never end.*

nayám·u [*vi* nayamánai; nayánda] 悩む *worry; grieve; be troubled about* §Yōko-san wa ren'ai móndai de nayánde iru. 陽子さんは恋愛問題で悩んでいる。*Yoko is grieving over a love problem.*

náze 何故 *why?* §Náze kónakatta no? なぜ来なかったの。*Why didn't you come?* <*fem*>

náze ka to iú to... なぜかというと～ *The reason is that...* §Kono kikaku ní wa múri ga áru. Náze ka to iú to kéihi ga kakarisugíru kara desu yo. この企画には無理がある。なぜかというと経費がかかり過ぎるからですよ。*This plan is not feasible. The reason is that it will cost too much.*

nazo 謎 *riddle; conundrum; puzzle; enigma* §Sono jíken no nazo ga máda tokénai. その事件の謎がまだ解けない。*The enigma surrounding that incident still hasn't been solved.*

nazuké·ru [vt nazukénai; nazukéta] 名付ける *name; give a name (to)*

ne ね [*sentence-final particle: tag question, non-emphatic*] ▮Kyṓ wa atsúi desu ne. 今日は暑いですね。 *It's hot today, isn't it?*

né 根 *root* ▮né ga tsúku 根がつく *become rooted* ▮né o orósu 根をおろす *put down roots* ▮Kúrita-san wa né wa íi hito desu. 栗田さんは根はいい人です。 *Kurita is basically a good person.*

ne 音 *a sound; tone* ▮suzu no ne 鈴の音 *the sound of a bell* ▮mushi no ne 虫の音 *an insect's chirping* ▮ne o ageru 音を上げる *admit defeat; give up*

ne 値 *price* ▮neagari 値上がり *rise in price*

nébaneba ねばねば *stickiness* ▮Té no nebaneba o tótta. 手のねばねばを取った。 *I washed the stickiness from my hands.* ——**nébaneba-suru** [vi] ねばねばする *be sticky; be stringy; be gooey; be slimy* ▮Nattō wa nébaneba-shite iru. 納豆はねばねばしている。 *Nattō is stringy and slimy.*

nebari-zuyó·i [adj -zúyoku nái; -zúyokatta] 粘り強い *(be) tenacious; persevering; persistent* ——**nebari-zúyoku** 粘り強く *persistently; tenaciously; importunately* ▮nebari-zúyoku kōshō-suru 粘り強く交渉する *negotiate importunately*

nebari-zúyosa 粘り強さ *stick-to-itiveness; tenacity*

nebár·u [vi nebaránai; nebátta] 粘る *be sticky; stick to it* ▮Sáigo made nebaránakereba naránai. 最後まで粘らなければならない。 *You have to stick it out to the end.*

nebō-suru [vi] 寝坊する *oversleep; sleep late* ▮Watashi wa nebō-shite máta dénsha ni noriokuréte shimatta. 私は寝坊してまた電車に遅れてしまった。 *I overslept and missed my train again.*

nebúsoku 寝不足 *lack of sleep*

nechigaé·ru [vt nechigaénai; nechigaeta] 寝違える *strain; wrench (in one's sleep)* ▮kubi o nechigaéru 首を寝違える *wrench one's neck while sleeping*

nedan 値段 *price* ▮Kono jaketto no nedan wa íkura desu ka? このジャケットの値段はいくらですか。 *What is the price of this jacket?*

nedoko 寝床 *bed; sleeping place* ▮Nedoko o shiita. 寝床を敷いた。 *I laid out the bedding. (or I made the bed.)*

nefuda 値札 *price tag*

negái 願い *an appeal; supplication; request; wish* ▮Negái ga kanátta yo! 願いが叶ったよ。 *I got my wish!*

negaigotó 願い事 *a request* ▮Negaigotó ga áru. 願い事がある。 *I have a request (to make).*

negá·u [vt negawánai; negátta] 願う *hope; wish; desire* ▮Bóku wa kimi no shiawase o negátte iru yo. 僕は君の幸せを願っているよ。 *I hope you will be happy.* <masc>

négi 葱 *scallion; green onion*

negír·u [*vt* negiránai; negítta] 値切る *cut the price; discount* 🔹Nana-sen'en no buráuso o go-sen'en ni negítte kaimáshita. 七千円のブラウスを五千円に値切って買いました。*I bought a ¥7,000 blouse for (or discounted to) ¥5,000.*

negokochi 寝心地 *degree of comfort when lying down* 🔹negokochi no íi béddo 寝心地のいいベッド *a comfortable bed*

nehan 涅槃 *nirvana (Budd)*

néji 螺子；捻子 *a screw* 🔹néji de shiméru ねじで締める *screw (something) on; attach with a screw* 🔹néji o maku ねじを巻く *wind a watch (clock)*

nejimáwashi ねじ回し *screwdriver*

nejír·u [*vt* nejiránai; nejítta] 捻る *twist; wrench; screw*

nekase·ru [*vt* nekasenai; nekaseta] 寝かせる *put (someone) to bed*

nekkyōteki [na] 熱狂的（な）*enthusiastic; fanatic* 🔹Sono chímu wa nekkyōteki na fán ni sasaerarete iru. そのチームは熱狂的なファンに支えられている。*That team is supported by enthusiastic fans.*

néko 猫 *cat* 🔹nekojita 猫舌 *a cat's tongue (a tongue which is over-sensitive to hot things)*

nekóm·u [*vi* nekománai; nekónda] 寝込む *fall asleep; be laid up; be sick in bed* 🔹Yūjin no shí o kiite watashi wa isshūkan nekónde shimatta. 友人の死を聞いて私は一週間寝込んでしまった。*When I heard my friend had died I took to my bed for a week.*

nemaki 寝間着；寝巻 *pajamas; sleeping robe*

nemáwashi 根回し *laying the groundwork; preparing the way (for smooth deliberations)*

nembutsu 念仏 *Buddhist prayer of invocation*

nempai [no] 年配（の）*older (person); the elderly* 🔹Kyō no kaigō ní wa nempai no hitó ga óku atsumátte ita. 今日の会合には年配の人が多く集まっていた。*There were many elderly people at the meeting today.*

nemu·i [*adj* nemuku nái; nemúkatta] 眠い *(be) sleepy* 🔹Nemúkute mō ókite irarenai. 眠くてもう起きていられない。*I'm so sleepy I can't stay awake.*

nemuribyō 眠り病 *sleeping sickness*

nemur·u [*vi* nemuranai; nemutta] 眠る *sleep* 🔹súyasuya nemuru すやすや眠る *sleep peacefully.*

nén; -nen 年；〜年 *year* 🔹nenshū 年収 *annual income* 🔹nén ni nikai 年に二回 *twice a year*. 🔹Tsúma wa sen-kyūhyaku gojūsán-nen ni umaremáshita. 妻は1953年に生まれました。*My wife was born in 1953.*

nenchōjun 年長順 *seniority* 🔹Watashi no kaisha dé wa shōshin wa nenchōjun ni nátte iru. 私の会社では昇進は年長順になっている。*Promotions in my company are on the basis of seniority.*

néndo 年度 *(fiscal) year* 🔹kaikei néndo 会計年度 *fiscal year* 🔹Konnéndo no késsan ga owatta. 今年度の決算が終わった。*The accounts for this fiscal year are finished.*

néndo 粘土 *clay*

nengṓ 年号 *name of an era*

nénjū 年中 *all the year round* §nenjū gyṓji 年中行事 *an annual event*

nennen 年々 *yearly; year by year* §Koko no tokoro nennen kodomo no shusshṓritsu ga sagátte iru. ここのところ年々子供の出生率が下がっている。*In recent years the birth rate has been decreasing year by year.*

nenrei 年齢 *age* §nenrei séigen 年齢制限 *age limit* §heikin nénrei 平均年齢 *average age* §seishin nénrei 精神年齢 *mental age*

nenryṓ 燃料 *fuel*

nenza 捻挫 *a sprain* ——**nenza-suru** [vi] 捻挫する *sprain* §ashíkubi o nenza-suru 足首を捻挫する *sprain one's ankle.*

nerai 狙い *an aim; target* §nerai o sadaméru 狙いを定める *take aim*

nera·u [vt nerawanai; neratta] 狙う *aim (at); set (one's) sights on* §suki o nerau 隙を狙う *look for an opening; wait for a chance* §yūshṓ o nerau 優勝を狙う *aim at the championship*

neriko 練り粉 *dough; batter*

ne·ru [vi nenai; neta] 寝る *lie down; go to bed; sleep* §aomuke ni neru 仰向けに寝る *sleep on one's back* §utsubuse ni neru うつ伏せに寝る *sleep on one's stomach* §Shújin wa máda nete imásu. 主人はまだ寝ています。*My husband is still sleeping.*

nér·u [vt neránai; nétta] 練る *knead; train; drill; exercise* §wazá o néru 技を練る *exercise a skill* §keikaku o néru 計画を練る *think over and improve a plan*

nesage 値下げ *mark-down in price* ——**nesage-suru** [vt] 値下げする *lower the price* §Endaka de gaikoku séihin ga nesage-sareta. 円高で外国製品が値下げされた。*Because of the high value of the yen, foreign goods have been marked down in price.*

[o-]nésan （お）姉さん *(another's) older sister; young woman*

nésshin [na] 熱心（な）*enthusiastic; earnest; eager* §nésshin na séito 熱心な生徒 *an earnest student.* ——**nésshin ni** 熱心に *earnestly; eagerly; diligently* §nésshin ni benkyō-suru 熱心に勉強する *study diligently*

netakiri [no] 寝たきり（の）*shut-in; bedridden* §Jṓnzu-san no ókusan wa Arutsuháimā de kono jūnénkan netakiri désu. ジョーンズさんの奥さんはアルツハイマーでこの十年間寝たきりです。*Mr. Jones's wife has been bedridden with Alzheimer's disease for the past ten years.*

netám·u [vt netamánai; netánda] 妬む；嫉む *envy; be jealous of* §Tamotsu wa Námi no seikō o netánde iru. 保は奈美の成功を妬んでいる。*Tamotsu is jealous of Nami's success.*

netchū 熱中 *enthusiasm; zeal* ——**netchū-suru** [vi] 熱中する *be* *enthusiastic about; be engrossed in; immerse (oneself) in* ❀Háha wa patchiwǎku ni netchū-shite imásu. 母はパッチワークに熱中しています. *My mother is engrossed in patchwork.*

netsú 熱 *heat* ❀netsú o kuwaeru 熱を加える *apply heat*

netsú 熱 *fever* ❀netsú o hakáru 熱を計る *take (one's) temperature* ❀netsú ga áru 熱がある *have a fever*

netsujō 熱情 *fervor; ardor; zeal; passion*

netsúk·u [*vi* netsukánai; netsúita] 寝付く *go to bed; fall asleep; be confined to bed*

netsuretsu [na] 熱烈（な）*enthusiastic; passionate; ardent* ❀netsuretsu na kangei 熱烈な歓迎 *an enthusiastic welcome* ❀netsuretsu na shinkō 熱烈な信仰 *ardent faith*

nettai 熱帯 *tropics* ❀nettai chíhō 熱帯地方 *the torrid zone* ❀nettáiya 熱帯夜 *a sultry night* ❀nettáigyo 熱帯魚 *tropical fish* ——**nettai no** 熱帯の *tropical*

neuchi 値打ち *value; worth* ❀Kono kenkyū wa taméshite miru neuchi ga áru to omoimásu. この研究は試してみる値打ちがあると思います. *I think there is value in attempting this research.*

nezō 寝相 *sleeping position* ❀nezō ga warúi 寝相が悪い *toss in (one's) sleep; sleep awkwardly*

nezúk·u [*vi* nezukánai; nezúita] 根付く *take root* ❀Minshushúgi ga nezúite imásu. 民主主義が根付いています. *Democracy has taken root.*

nezumi 鼠 *mouse; rat* ❀nezumítori 鼠取り *mousetrap*

nezumiiro 鼠色 *(dark) gray; slate color*

nezuyó·i [*adj* nezúyoku nái; nezúyokatta] 根強い *deep-rooted; firmly rooted* ——**nezúyoku** 根強く *firmly; tenaciously*

ní 二 ; 2 *two (the numeral)*

ni に *to* [*particle marking direction*] ❀Tanaka-san wa Yōróppa ni ikimásu. 田中さんはヨーロッパに行きます. *Mr. Tanaka is going to Europe.*

ni に *to* [*particle marking indirect object*] ❀Watashi wa imōto ni tokei o purézento-shimáshita. 私は妹に時計をプレゼントしました. *I gave my sister a watch as a present.*

ni に *in; at* [*particle marking location*] ❀Sasaki-san wa íma, toshókan ni imásu. 佐々木さんは今、図書館にいます. *Mr. Sasaki is at the library.*

ni に *on; at* [*particle marking time element*] ❀Maruyama-san wa ashita no ása jǔji ni Nárita ni tsukimásu. 丸山さんは明日の朝十時に成田に着きます. *Mr. Maruyama will arrive at Narita at 10:00 o'clock tomorrow morning.*

ni に [*particle marking a verb complement*] ❀Musuko wa isha ni narimáshita. 息子は医者になりました. *My son became a doctor.*

ni に *by* [*particle marking agent*] ❽Musumé wa yóku senséi ni homeraréru. 娘はよく先生に褒められる。*My daughter is often praised by her teacher.*

ni に *from* [*particle marking source*] ❽Ōsutorária no yūjin ni tegami o moraimáshita. オーストラリアの友人に手紙をもらいました。*I received a letter from my Australian friend.*

ni に *and* [*conjunction*] ❽Ninjin ni kyúri ni jagaimo o katté kite kudasái. 人参にきゅうりにじゃがいもを買って来て下さい。*Buy some carrots, and cucumbers, and potatoes, please.*

ni に *for* [*particle marking purpose*] ❽Nakayama-san wa kaimono ni ikimáshita. 中山さんは買物に行きました。*Nakayama went shopping.*

ní 荷 *bundle; burden; load* ❽Kono shigoto wa watashi ní wa ní ga omoi. この仕事は私には荷が重い。*This work is a heavy burden for me.*

niá·u [*vi* niawánai; niátta] *be becoming (to one)* ❽Kimi wa bōshi ga yóku niátte iru. 君は帽子がよく似合っている。*That hat looks good on you.* <masc>

nibú·i [*adj* níbuku nái; níbukatta] 鈍い *(be) dull; blunt; sluggish; faint* ❽nibúi itamí 鈍い痛み *a dull pain* ❽nibúi otó 鈍い音 *a faint sound* ❽Yúkiko-san wa kan ga nibúi. 雪子さんは勘が鈍い。*Yukiko has slow perception. (or Yukiko is dull-witted.)*

nichijō [no] 日常（の）*routine; everday-; daily* ❽nichijō káiwa 日常会話 *everyday conversation*

níchiya 日夜 *day and night* ❽Watashi wa Amerika ryūgakuchū no musumé o níchiya ánjite imásu. 私はアメリカ留学中の娘を日夜案じています。*I worry day and night about my daughter who is studying in America.*

Nichiyóbi 日曜日 *Sunday*

nichiyō 日用 *daily* ❽nichiyō hitsujuhin 日用必需品 *daily necessities*

nie·ru [*vi* nienai; nieta] 煮える *boil; cook* ❽Daikon ga yóku niemáshita. 大根がよく煮えました。*The radishes are well cooked.*

nífuda 荷札 *a label; a tag*

nigá·i [*adj* nígaku nái; nígakatta] 苦い *(be) bitter* ❽Kono kusuri wa nigái. この薬は苦い。*This medicine is bitter.* ❽Nigái keiken ga wasurerarenai. 苦い経験が忘れられない。*One can't forget a bitter experience.* ❽nigawárai 苦笑い *a bitter smile*

nigás·u [*vt* nigasánai; nigáshita] 逃がす *set free; miss (a chance)* ❽Uráshima Tárō wa ijimekko kara káme o nigáshite yatta. 浦島太郎はいじめっ子から亀を逃がしてやった。*Urashima Taro rescued (or freed) the turtle from the children who were tormenting it.* ❽Chánsu o nigasánai yó ni! チャンスを逃がさないように！*Don't miss your chance.*

nigate 苦手 *not good at; not successful with* ❽Watashi wa ryóri ga nigate

da wa. 私は料理が苦手だわ。 *I'm not good at cooking. <fem>*
❽Watashi wa kánojo ga nigate da. 私は彼女が苦手だ。 *I can't deal with her. <masc>*

Nigatsú 二月 *February*

nigé·ru [vi nigénai; nígeta] 逃げる *flee; run away; escape* ❽Dorobō wa furobá kara nigemáshita. 泥棒は風呂場から逃げました。 *The thief escaped through the bathroom.*

nigesar·u [vi nigesaranai; nigesatta] 逃げ去る *run away; flee* ❽Hánnin wa kuruma de nigesatte shimatta. 犯人は車で逃げ去ってしまった。 *The criminal escaped by car.*

[o-]nígiri （お）握り *rice ball*

nigir·u [vt nigiranai; nigitta] 握る *grasp; hold in the fist* ❽Kodomo wa okásan no té o nigitte iru. 子供はお母さんの手を握っている。 *The child is holding fast to her mother's hand.* ❽kénryoku o nigiru 権力を握る *grasp power (authority)*

nigiwai 賑わい *hustle and bustle; prosperity* ❽Yóru no Shinjuku wa ítsumo nigiwai o mísete iru. 夜の新宿はいつも賑わいを見せている。 *Shinjuku at night is always alive with activity.*

nigiwá·u [vi nigiwawánai; nigiwátta] 賑わう *be prosperous; flourish; thrive*

nigíyaka [na] 賑やか（な） *merry and cheerful; jovial; busy; bustling* ❽nigíyaka na hitó 賑やかな人 *a jovial person* ❽nigíyaka na matsurí. 賑やかな祭り *a merry festival.* ——**nigíyaka ni** 賑やかに *busily; jovially*

nigór·u [vi nigoránai; nigótta] 濁る *become muddy; be cloudy; be contaminated* ❽Mizu ga nigótte iru. 水が濁っている。 *The water is muddy.* ❽Kōjō no haieki de kawá wa nigótte iru. 工場の廃液で川は濁っている。 *The river is contaminated with waste from the factory.*

nigós·u [vt nigosánai; nigóshita] 濁す *make muddy; dirty; contaminate* ❽o-cha o nigósu お茶を濁す *cloud the tea (or muddy the issue)* ❽kotobá o nigósu 言葉を濁す *equivocate; give a vague answer*

nigúruma 荷車 *wagon; cart*

Nihón 日本 *Japan* ——**Nihongo** 日本語 *Japanese language* —— **Nihónjin** 日本人 *a Japanese*

Nihonka-suru [vi] 日本化する *Japanize; adapt (something) to Japan*

nihonshu 日本酒 *saké*

niji 虹 *rainbow* ❽nijiiro 虹色 *rainbow colors* ——**nijiiro no** 虹色の *iridescent*

nijígen no 二次元の *two-dimensional*

nijimasu 虹鱒 *rainbow trout*

nijím·u [vi nijimánai; nijínda] 滲む *run; spread; ooze out; sweat* ❽Inku ga nijínde iru. インクがにじんでいる。 *The ink is oozing out.* ❽Hitai ni áse ga nijínde iru. 額に汗がにじんでいる。 *Sweat is running* *from my brow.*

níjū 二十；20 *twenty (the numeral or counter)*

nijū 二重 *double* §nijūmádo 二重窓 *double (storm) windows* §nijūjínkaku 二重人格 *double personality* §nijūshō 二重唱 *(vocal) duet* §nijūsō 二重奏 *(instrumental) duet*

níjūyokka 二十四日；24日 *the twenty-fourth (of the month); twenty-four days*

ni kagítte 〜に限って *limited to...* §konshū ni kagítte 今週に限って *this week only; limited to this week* §Káre ni kagítte sonna kotó o iu wáke wa nái. 彼に限ってそんなことを言う訳はない。*He, of all people, has no reason to say such a thing.*

nikai 二階 *upstairs; 2nd floor*

nikakokugo 二か国語 *bilingual; two languages*

ni kamáete 〜に構えて *in preparation for...*

nikawa 膠 *glue* §nikawa de tsukéru 膠でつける *fasten with glue*

nikayó·u [*vi* nikayowánai; nikayótta] 似通う *look alike; resemble* §Musumé wa chichí to nikayótta tokoró ga ói. 娘は父と似通ったところが多い。*The daughter resembles her father in many ways.*

níkibi 面皰 *pimple; blackhead*

nikkan [no] 日刊（の）*daily* §nikkan shímbun 日刊新聞 *daily newspaper*

Nikkei [no] 日系（の）*of Japanese ancestry* §Nikkei Amerikájin 日系アメリカ人 *an American of Japanese ancestry*

nikki 日記 *diary* §nikki o tsukéru 日記をつける *keep a diary*

níkkō 日光 *sunshine* §nikkóyoku 日光浴 *sunbathing*

nikkóri [to] にっこり（と）*smiling; laughing* §Namie-san wa watashi o míte nikkóri hohoénda. 浪江さんは私を見てにっこり微笑んだ。*Namie looked at me and smiled.*

nikokúkan 二国間 *bilateral* §nikokukan jóyaku 二国間条約 *bilateral treaty*

nikóm·u [*vt* nikománai; nikónda] 煮込む *cook (slowly); simmer* §Bīfu shíchū o nikónde iru. ビーフシチューを煮込んでいる。*I'm cooking beef stew.*

níkoniko-suru [*vi*] にこにこする *smile (continuously)* §Sono ákachan wa ítsumo níkoniko-shite imásu. その赤ちゃんはいつもにこにこしています。*The baby smiles all the time.*

ni kotáete 〜に答えて；〜に応えて *in reply to...; in response to; in answer to...* §Minná no kitai ni kotáete yūshō-shita. みんなの期待に応えて優勝した。*He won in response to everyone's expectations.*

nikóyaka [na] にこやか（な）*smiling; beaming* §Nikóyaka na égao ga mitái. にこやかな笑顔が見たい。*I want to see a smiling face.* —— **nikóyaka ni** にこやかに *smilingly; beamingly*

nikú 肉 *meat; flesh* §nikúya (-san) 肉屋（〜さん）*butcher; meat store*

nikú·i [*adj* níkuku nái; níkukatta] 憎い *(be) hateful; detestable* ❡Aitsu ga nikúi. あいつが憎い。 *I hate him.*

-níkui ～にくい *difficult to (do)* ❡Kono hón wa ríkai-shiníkui. この本は理解しにくい。 *The book is hard to understand.*

nikúm·u [*vt* nikumánai; nikúnda] 憎む *hate; detest; abhor* ❡Tóshiko-san wa íma demo Yóshiki-san o nikúnde iru. 敏子さんは今でも良樹さんを憎んでいる。 *Even now Toshiko hates Yoshiki.*

nikurashí·i [*adj* nikuráshiku nái; nikuráshikatta] 憎らしい *(be) detestable; hateful* ❡Nikurashíi kotó wa iwanaide kuré yo. 憎らしいことは言わないでくれよ。 *Don't say such hateful things! <masc>*

nikushimi 憎しみ *hate; hatred; enmity* ❡Miyuki é no nikushimi ga kienai. 美幸への憎しみが消えない。 *My hatred of Miyuki doesn't go away.*

nikutai 肉体 *(human) flesh; the body* ❡nikutai to séishin 肉体と精神 *body and soul* ❡nikutáibi 肉体美 *physical beauty* ❡nikutai rṓdō 肉体労働 *physical labor* ——**nikutaiteki [na]** 肉体的（な）*physical* ——**nikutaiteki ni** 肉体的（に）*physically*

nikuyoku 肉欲 *lust; carnal desire*

nimáijita 二枚舌 *duplicity; equivocation*

nimmei 任命 *appointment* ——**nimmei-suru** [*vt*] 任命する *appoint* ❡Sakamoto-san wa kaigai fúnin o nimmei-sareta. 坂本さんは海外赴任を任命された。 *Sakamoto was appointed to a post overseas.*

nímmu 任務 *duty; office* ❡nímmu ni tsúku 任務に就く *assume (one's) duties; take office*

ní mo kakawárazu ～にも拘わらず *in spite of...* ❡Imóto wa netsú ga áru ni mo kakawárazu dḗto ni dekaketa. 妹は熱があるにもかかわらずデートに出かけた。 *My sister went on a date in spite of having a fever.*

nímotsu 荷物 *baggage; bag; bundle; (light) freight; a load*

niná·u [*vt* ninawánai; ninátta] 担う *carry; bear; shoulder* ❡Níshi-san wa kaisha de jūseki o ninátte iru. 西さんは会社で重責を担っている。 *Mr. Nishi is shouldering a heavy responsibility in the company.*

ningen 人間 *human being* ❡ningen kánkei 人間関係 *human relations* ❡ningemmi 人間味 *a human touch* ❡ningensei 人間性 *humanity; human nature*

ningyō 人形 *doll* ❡ningyógeki 人形劇 *puppet theater*

ninjin 人参 *carrot* ❡Chōsen ninjin 朝鮮人参 *ginseng*

ninka 認可 *authorization; approval; sanction* ——**ninka-suru** [*vt*] 認可する *approve; authorize* ❡Sono minkan borantia dántai wa shakai fukushi hṓjin to shite ninka-sareta. その民間ボランティア団体は社会福祉法人として認可された。 *The citizen's volunteer group has been approved as a social welfare organization.*

ninki 人気 *popularity* ❡Ano terebi tárento wa wakái josei ni ninki ga áru.

あのテレビタレントは若い女性に人気がある。*That TV star is popular among young girls.*

ninniku 大蒜 *garlic*

ninshiki 認識 *understanding; cognition; knowledge* 🔸Ninshiki ga tarinai. 認識が足りない。 *My knowledge (concerning that) is insufficient.* **——ninshiki-suru** [vt] 認識する *understand; recognize* 🔸Fuhō taizáisha no jittai o séifu wa ninshiki-shite iru. 不法滞在者の実態を政府は認識している。 *The government is aware that there are illegal residents.*

ninshin 妊娠 *pregnancy* **——ninshin-suru** [vi] 妊娠する *conceive; become pregnant*

níntai 忍耐 *patience; endurance; perseverence*

nintai-bukái 忍耐深い [adj -búkaku nái; -búkakatta] *(be) very patient*

nintai-zuyói [adj -zúyoku nái; -zúyokatta] 忍耐強い *(be) patient; long-suffering*

niói 匂い；臭い *scent; smell; odor* 🔸íi niói いい匂い *good smell* 🔸niói ga suru 臭いがする *smell (of)* 🔸Gásu no niói ga suru yo! ガスの臭いがするよ！ *I smell gas!* 🔸Kono kōsui wa íi niói ga suru. この香水はいい匂いがする。 *This perfume has a good scent.*

nió·u [vi niowánai; niótta] 匂う；臭う *smell* 🔸Kono sakana wa nióu! この魚は臭う。 *This fish smells!*

nira 韮 *Chinese (or garlic) chives; (Tech) Allium tuberosum*

niramí 睨み *a glare; sharp look*

nirám·u [vt niramánai; niránda] 睨む *glare (at); stare (at); keep an eye on; watch* 🔸Tanómu kara bóku no kotó o nirámu na yo! 頼むから僕のことを睨むなよ！ *Please don't stare at me.* <masc> 🔸Teki no ugokí o niránde iru. 敵の動きを睨んでいる。 *They are keeping a sharp eye on the movements of the enemy.*

ni·ru [vi ninai; nita] 似る *resemble; look alike* 🔸Hayashi-san to Watanabe-san wa tanin-dōshi ná no ni kao ga yóku nite imásu. 林さんと渡辺さんは他人同士なのに顔がよく似ています。 *Hayashi and Watanabe are strangers to one another but they look very much alike.*

ni·ru [vt ninai; nita] 煮る *boil (in seasoned liquid)*

niryū [no] 二流（の） *inferior; second-class*

[o-]nísan （お）兄さん *(another's) older brother; boy or young man*

nise [no] 偽（の） *imitation* 🔸nisesatsu 偽札 *a counterfeit bill (bank note)*

nísei 二世 *second generation; the second; Jr.* 🔸Erizabesu nísei エリザベス二世 *Elizabeth II* 🔸Nikkei nísei 日系二世 *second-generation Japanese (American)*

nisemono 偽物 *phony; fake* 🔸Nishímura-san no yasashisa wa nisemono désu. 西村さんの優しさは偽物です。 *Nishimura's gentleness is a show.*

nishi 西 *west*

níshiki 錦 *brocade* ❧mómiji no níshiki 紅葉の錦 *bright fall foliage*

níshin 鰊 *herring*

ni shité wa 〜にしては *considering that...* ❧Támura-san wa Eibunka o déta ni shité wa Eigo ga jōzú de wa nái. 田村さんは英文科を出たにしては英語が上手ではない。 *Considering that she graduated from the English department, Ms. Tamura isn't very good in English!*

nisshabyō 日射病 *sunstroke*

nísu ニス *varnish*

nitaté‧ru [vt nitaténai; nitatéta] 煮立てる *boil; bring to a boil*

nitchū 日中 *daytime* ❧Nitchū wa hizashi ga tsúyokatta. 日中は日射しが強かった。 *During the daytime the sun's rays were intense.*

Nitchū 日中 *Sino-Japanese*

nitō 二等 *second-class*

niwa 庭 *garden*

níwaka [na] 俄（な） *sudden; unexpected* ❧niwaká ame 俄雨 *a sudden shower* ——**níwaka ni** 俄に *suddenly; unexpectedly; on the spur of the moment* ❧Níwaka ní wa kimi no teian ni sansei-shikanéru. 俄には君の提案に賛成しかねる。 *I cannot agree to your proposal on the spur of the moment.*

niwatori 鶏 *chicken*

nizúkuri 荷造り *packing; crating* ❧Watashi wa hikkoshi no nizúkuri ni isogashíi. 私は引っ越しの荷造りに忙しい。 *I'm busy packing for our move.* ——**nizúkuri-suru** [vt] 荷造りする *pack; crate*

no の [interrogative sentence-ending particle; informal; fem] ❧Watashi mo itta hố ga íi no? 私も行った方がいいの? *Should I go, too?* <fem>

no の [emphatic sentence-ending particle; informal; fem] ❧Watashi ní wa sonna kotó wa dekínai no! 私にはそんなことはできないの。 *I can't do such a thing!* <fem>

no の [possessive particle] ❧Gakkō no hón o nakushite shimatta. 学校の本を無くしてしまった。 *I lost one of the school's books.*

no の one [noun substitute] ❧Akai shátsu wa kimi ni niáu kedo, kiirói no wa niawánai yo. 赤いシャツは君に似合うけど、黄色いのは似合わないよ。 *The red shirt looks good on you, but the yellow one doesn't.* <masc>

no の [particle: attributive / appositional] ❧Bengóshi no Yoshínaga-san wa hyōban ga íi. 弁護士の吉永さんは評判がいい。 *Yoshinaga, who is a lawyer, has a good reputation.*

-no da; -no desu 〜のだ；〜のです [sentence ending: explanatory] ❧Sono monogátari wa happī-éndo de owattá no desu. その物語はハッピーエンドで終わったのです。 *That story had a happy ending.*

Nố 能 *No (Noh) drama*

nō 脳 *brain*　§**nṓha** 脳波 *brain waves*　§**nṓshi** 脳死 *brain death*　§**nōshúkketsu** 脳出血 *cerebral hemorrhage*　§**nōmakuen** 脳膜炎 *meningitis*

nō-áiron ノーアイロン *wash-and-wear*

nobás·u [*vt* nobasánai; nobáshita] 延ばす；伸ばす *extend; stretch; lengthen; put off*　§Kánai wa jikka dé no taizai o isshūkan nobáshita. 家内は実家での滞在を 1 週間延ばした。*My wife extended her stay at her folk's by a week.*　§Máchiko-san wa kami nó ke o nágaku nobáshite iru. 真智子さんは髪の毛を長く伸ばしている。*Machiko is letting her hair grow long.*

nobé·ru [*vt* nobénai; nóbeta] 述べる *relate; state; narrate; tell*

nobétsutae·ru [*vt* nobetsutaenai; nobetsutaeta] 述べ伝える *proclaim; preach*

nobí·ru [*vi* nobínai; nóbita] 延びる；伸びる *stretch; extend; grow*　§Tetsúdō wa kono machí made nóbita. 鉄道はこの町まで延びた。*The railroad has extended to this town.*　§Sé ga gosénchi nóbita. 背が五センチ伸びた。*I've grown five centimeters.*

nobor·u [*vi* noboranai; nobtta] 昇る *climb; rise*　§Higashi no sóra ni hi ga nobotte iru. 東の空に日が昇っている。*The sun's rising in the eastern sky.*

nobor·u [*vi* noboranai; nobtta] 上る *climb; go up*　§kawá o noboru 川を上る *go up the river*　§saká o noboru 坂を上る *climb a slope*　§wadai ni noboru 話題に上る *become a topic of conversation*

nobor·u [*vi* noboranai; nobtta] 登る *climb*　§yamá ni noboru 山に登る *climb a mountain*

nochí 後 *later; after*

nochi hodo 後ほど *afterwards*

-no de 〜ので *because...*　§Netsú ga átta no de gakkō o yasúnda. 熱があったので学校を休んだ。*I stayed home from school because I had a fever.*

nódo 喉；咽 *throat*　§Nódo ga kawáita. 喉が乾いた。*I'm thirsty (lit: my throat is dry).*　§Nódo ga itái. 喉が痛い。*My throat hurts.*　§Nódo kara té ga déru hodo hoshíi. 喉から手が出るほど欲しい。*I want it so badly I could taste it.*

nódo 濃度 *density*

nodobue 喉笛 *windpipe; voice box*

nōen 農園 *farm; plantation*

nōen 脳炎 *brain inflammation; (tech) encephalitis*

nōfu 農夫 *farmer; farm laborer*

nogaré·ru [*vi* nogarénai; nogáreta] 逃れる *flee; escape*　§Ayauku nán o nogáreta. 危うく難を逃れた。*We barely escaped a disaster.*

nōgu 農具 *farm machinery; farm equipment*

nṓgyō 農業 *farming; agriculture*

nōgyō kyōdō kúmiai 農業協同組合 *agricultural cooperative*

nōgyóson 農漁村 *farm and fishing villages*

noiróze [no] ノイローゼ（の）*neurotic*

nōjō 農場 *a farm*

nójuku 野宿 *camping out; sleeping outdoors* ——**nójuku-suru** [*vi*] 野宿する *sleep out in the open*

noke·ru [*vt* nokenai; noketa] 除ける；退ける *remove; take away* ❷ishí o nokeru 石を除ける *remove a stone*

noki 軒 *eaves (of a building)*

nokogirí 鋸 *saw (tool)* ❷nokogirí de hiku 鋸でひく *saw (wood)*

-nokórazu 〜残らず *without (any) left over* ❷Hyakupéji made no atarashíi tango wa hitotsu nokórazu anki-shita. 百頁までの新しい単語は一つ残らず暗記した。*I memorized every single new word up to page one hundred.*

nokorí 残り *remainder; leftover* ❷Píza no nokorí ga futákire áru. ピザの残りが2切れある。*There are two pieces of pizza left.*

nokorimonó 残り物 *leftovers*

nokór·u [*vi* nokoránai; nokótta] 残る *remain; be left over* ❷Shachō daké ga kaisha ni nokótte iru. 社長だけが会社に残っている。*Only the boss is at the company (remaining after everyone else has left).* ❷Kinō no kéki wa máda nokótte iru no? 昨日のケーキはまだ残っているの。*Is there some cake left over from yesterday? <fem>*

nokós·u [*vt* nokosánai; nokóshita] 残す *leave; let remain* ❷Ákachan wa míruku o hambun nokóshite nemutte shimatta. 赤ちゃんはミルクを半分残して眠ってしまった。*The baby left half his milk and fell asleep.*

nōkotsu 納骨 *the act of laying a person's bones to rest* ❷nōkotsútsubo 納骨壷 *funeral urn*

nombíri [to] のんびり（と）*relaxed; carefree* ——**nombíri-suru** [*vi*] のんびりする *be relaxed; be at leisure* ❷Kinō wa ichinichi nombíri-shite ita. 昨日は一日のんびりしていた。*I relaxed all day yesterday.*

nómi 鑿 *chisel*

nomí 蚤 *flea* ❷nomi no ichí 蚤の市 *flea market* ❷nomi no fúfu 蚤の夫婦 *a mismatched couple (i.e., the wife is bigger than the husband)*

nómi のみ *only* ❷Kane nómi ga jínsei no mokuteki dé wa nái. 金のみが人生の目的ではない。*Money is not the only purpose in life.*

nomikom·u [*vt* nomikomanai; nomikonda] 飲み込む *swallow; take in; grasp; understand* ❷Ireba o nomikonda! 入れ歯を飲み込んだ。*I swallowed my false tooth!* ❷Jijō wa yóku nomikonde iru yo! 事情はよく飲み込んでいるよ。*I understand the situation well.*

nōmin 農民 *farmer(s)*

nomímono 飲み物 *beverage*

nomíya 飲み屋 *(drinking) bar*

nóm·u [*vt* nománai; nónda] 飲む *drink* ❷Máiasa kōhí o námbai nomimasu ka? 毎朝コーヒーをを何杯飲みますか。 *How many cups of coffee do you drink every morning?* ❊Íppai nomimasén ka? 一杯飲みませんか。 *How about a drink*

nó ni のに *in spite of...* ❊Kyố wa samúi no ni kaisúiyoku ni ikú no? 今日は寒いのに海水浴に行くの? *Are you going to swim in the ocean today, in spite of the fact that it's cold?* <fem>

nónki [na] 暢気；呑気（な）*carefree; easygoing*

nonoshír·u [vt nonoshiránai; nonoshítta] 罵る *curse; blaspheme; abuse; call names* ❊Shachō wa ítsumo watashi o nonoshítte iru. 社長はいつも私を罵っている。 *The boss is always cursing me.*

noren 暖簾 *shop curtain (at the entrance)* ❊noren o dásu 暖簾を出す *open; hang out (one's) shingle* ❊noren o orósu 暖簾をおろす *close shop; take down (one's) sign* ❊noren ni udeoshi 暖簾に腕押し *meaninglessness; futile (lit: pushing a noren with one arm)* <set phrase>

norí 糊 *starch; paste*

nori 海苔 *edible seaweed*

noridás·u [vi noridasánai; noridáshita] 乗り出す *begin; set about* ❊Fúne wa taikai ni noridáshita. 船は大海に乗り出した。 *The ship set out to sea.*

norikaé·ru [vt norikaénai; norikáeta] 乗り換える *change; transfer (trains / buses)* ❊Tōkyố eki de shinkánsen ni norikáeta. 東京駅で新幹線に乗り換えた。 *I changed to the bullet train at Tokyo station.*

norikós·u [vt norikosánai; norikóshita] 乗り越す *ride beyond (one's) station* ❊Inemúri-shite shūten máde norikóshite shimatta. 居眠りして終点まで乗り越してしまった。 *I fell asleep and rode to the end of the line.*

norikumíin 乗組員 *(ship) crew*

norimono 乗り物 *vehicle*

Nōrin Suisánshō; 農林水産省 *Ministry of Agriculture, Foresty and Fisheries* ❊nōrin suisán dáijin 農林水産大臣 *minister for agriculture, forestry and fisheries*

nōritsu 能率 *efficiency* ❊nōritsúkyū 能率給 *salary based on performance* ❊Kyố wa dốmo nōritsu ga agaranai. 今日はどうも能率が上がらない。 *I'm not working up to par (or efficiency) today.* —— **nōritsuteki [na]** 能率的（な）*efficient* ❊nōritsuteki na dandori 能率的な段取り *efficient procedures* ——**nōritsuteki ni** 能率的に *efficiently*

noró·i [adj nóroku nái; nórokatta] 鈍い *(be) slow; dull; sluggish* ❊Básu ga norói. バスが鈍い。 *The bus is slow.* ❊Dōsa ga norói. 動作が鈍い。 *(His) movements are sluggish.*

noroi 呪い *a curse* ❊noroi o kakéru 呪いをかける *put a curse on* ❊noroi ga kakáru 呪いがかかる *be cursed*

nóronoro のろのろ *slow(ly)*   §noronoro únten のろのろ運転 *bumper-to-bumper driving*

noró·u [*vt* norowánai; norótta] 呪う *put a curse (spell) on*

nor·u [*vi* noranai; notta] 乗る *ride; get on board; concur in*   §densha ni noru 電車に乗る *ride the train*   §umá ni noru 馬に乗る *ride a horse*   §kuchi-gúruma ni noru 口車に乗る *be taken in by sweet talk*   §Shigoto ni ki ga noranai. 仕事に気が乗らない。 *I can't seem to concentrate on this job.*

nor·u [*vi* noranai; notta] 載る *be recorded; be mentioned; appear in*   §Watashi no éssei ga shimbun ni notta. 私のエッセイが新聞に載った。 *My essay appeared in the newspaper.*

nóryoku 能力 *capability; ability*   §Kimi wa hoka no hitó to wa chigau nóryoku o mótte iru ne. 君は他の人とは違う能力を持っているね。 *You have special abilities (or talents) other people don't have.*

nōsakúmotsu 農作物 *crop; farm produce*

nōsámbutsu 農産物 *agricultural products*

nose·ru [*vt* nosenai; noseta] 載せる *place upon*   §Tsukue no ué ni kono hón o nosete óite kudasái. 机の上にこの本を載せておいて下さい。 *Put this book out on top of the desk.*

nóshu 嚢腫 *cyst*

nōson 農村 *farm village*

nóto ノート *notebook*

nōyaku 農薬 *agricultural chemical*

nōzei 納税 *tax payment* ——**nōzei-suru** [*vi*] 納税する *pay taxes*

nozoite 除いて *except; with the exception of*   §Tómoko o nozoite minná tōkō-shita. 智子を除いてみんな登校した。 *Everyone came to school except Tomoko.*

nozokikóm·u [*vt* nozokikománai; nozokikónda] 覗き込む *peer; peek into*   §Dáreka ga watashi no heyá o nozokikónde iru. 誰かが私の部屋を覗き込んでいる。 *Someone's peeking into my room.*

nozok·u [*vt* nozokanai; nozoita] 除く *remove; get rid of; exclude*   §zassō o nozoku 雑草を除く *get rid of the weeds*   §Dansei wa nozoite kudasái. 男性は除いて下さい。 *Exclude males.*

nozok·u [*vt* nozokanai; nozoita] 覗く *peek at; peep*   §Han-biraki no dóa kara shitsúnai o nozoita. 半開きのドアから室内を覗いた。 *I peeped into the room through the partly open door.*

nozomashí·i [*adj* nozomáshiku nái; nozomáshikatta] 望ましい *(be) desirable; advisable*   §Sono kyámpu ni wa zen'in sánka ga nozomashíí. そのキャンプには全員参加が望ましい。 *It is hoped that all members will attend the camp.*

nozomi 望み *wish; expectation; hope; desire;*   §nozomi ga kanáu 望みが叶う *get one's wish.*   §Máda nozomi wa áru na! まだ望みはあるな。 *There's still hope.* <*masc*>

nozom·u [vt nozomanai; nozonda] 望む *wish (for); hope (for)*   §Sekaijū no hitó ga heiwa o nozonde iru. 世界中の人が平和を望んでいる。 *People all over the world wish for peace.*

núg·u [vt nugánai; núida] 脱ぐ *take off (clothing); remove*   §Hakimono o núide kudasái. 履物を脱いで下さい。 *Take off your shoes, please.*

nuguisár·u [vt nuguisaránai; nuguisátta] 拭い去る *wipe away*   §Madogárasu no shimon o kírei ni nuguisátta. 窓ガラスの指紋をきれいに拭い去った。 *I wiped the window pane clean of all fingerprints.*

nugú·u [vt nuguwánai; nugútta] 拭う *wipe (dry)*   §námida o nugúu 涙を拭う *dry (one's) tears*   §omei o nugúu 汚名を拭う *wipe out a false rumor*

nuigurumi 縫いぐるみ *stuffed toy*   §kuma no nuigurumi 熊の縫いぐるみ *teddy bear*

nuimé 縫い目 *seam*   §nuimé ga arai 縫い目が粗い *rough seam*   §nuimé ga nái 縫い目がない *seamless*

nuká 糠 *rice bran*

nukas·u [vt nukasanai; nukashita] 抜かす *omit*   §Kono pēji wa nukashite saki o yomó. この頁は抜かして先を読もう。 *Let's omit this page and go on to the next.*

nukeme 抜け目 *imprudence; oversight*   §nukeme no nai 抜け目のない *shrewd; clever*   §Masao wa nukeme ga nái. 正夫は抜け目がない。 *Masao is shrewd. (or Masao has his wits about him.)*

nuke·ru [vi nukenai; nuketa] 抜ける *come out; come loose; fall out; be omitted; be missing; avoid; pass through (a small opening)*   §Ókuba ga nukesō desu. 奥歯が抜けそうです。 *A molar is about to come out.*   §Ningyō no kubi ga nukete shimatta. 人形の首が抜けてしまった。 *The doll's head came off.*   §Kono pēji ga nukete iru. この頁が抜けている。 *This page is missing!*

nukigaki 抜き書き *excerpt*   §Atarashíi hōsoku no nukigaki ga shimbun ni déta. 新しい法則の抜き書きが新聞に出た。 *An excerpt from the new law appeared in the newspaper.*

nuk·u [vt nukanai; nuita] 抜く *extract ; draw out; remove; skip; omit; empty (of)*   §kataná o nuku 刀を抜く *draw a sword*   §furó no mizu o nuku 風呂の水を抜く *let out the bathwater*   §Haisha-san wa há o nuita. 歯医者さんは歯を抜いた。 *The dentist pulled a tooth.*   §Kono fukú no shimi o nuite kudasái. この服の染みを抜いて下さい。 *Please remove the stain from this garment.*

numá 沼 *swamp; marsh; bog*

nuras·u [vt nurasanai; nurashita] 濡らす *wet; moisten*   §fukín o nurasu 布巾を濡らす *wet a cloth*

nure·ru [vi nurenai; nureta] 濡れる *be wet; be damp*   §Áme ni nurete shimatta. 雨に濡れてしまった。 *I got wet in the rain.*

nuri-gúsuri 塗り薬 *ointment; salve*

nur·u [nuranai; nutta] 塗る *paint; spread* 🔸Tóire no kabe o shirói penki de nuru kotó ni shita. トイレの壁を白いペンキで塗ることにした。 *I decided to paint the walls in the bathroom white.* 🔸Pán ni jámu o nuru to oishíi. パンにジャムを塗るとおいしい。 *If you spread jam on bread it's delicious.*

nurú·i [adj núruku nái; núrukatta] 温い *(be) lukewarm; tepid* 🔸Kono kōhí wa núrukute noménai. このコーヒーは温くて飲めない。 *I can't drink this coffee; it's not hot.*

nurúm·u [vi nurumánai; nurúnda] 温む *be (or become) warm*

nusumí 盗み *theft*

nusúm·u [vt nusumánai; nusúnda] 盗む *rob; steal* 🔸Dáreka ga watashi no tokei o nusúnda. 誰かが私の時計を盗んだ。 *Someone stole my watch.*

nú·u [vt nuwánai; nútta] 縫う *sew; stitch* 🔸Háha wa kono kimono o nútta. 母はこの着物を縫った。 *My mother sewed this kimono.*

nyő 尿 *urine*

nyőbō 女房 *(one's) wife* 🔸Uchi no nyőbō wa totemo hatarakimono da. うちの女房はとても働き者だ。 *My wife's a hard worker.* <masc>

nyūgaku 入学 *enrollment in school* 🔸nyūgaku shíken 入学試験 *entrance examination* ——**nyūgaku-suru** [vi] 入学する *enroll in school*

nyūgyū 乳牛 *dairy cow*

nyūin 入院 *hospitalization* ——**nyūin-suru** [vi] 入院する *enter a hospital; be hospitalized* 🔸Chichí wa ikáiyō de nyūin-shite iru. 父は胃潰瘍で入院している。 *My father has been hospitalized for a stomach ulcer.*

nyūjóken 入場券 *entrance ticket; admittance ticket*

nyūkō 入港 *entering port* 🔸Sono kyakusen wa myőchō nyūkō yótei desu. その客船は明朝入港予定です。 *The passenger liner is scheduled to come into port tomorrow morning.* ——**nyūkō-suru** [vi] 入港する *dock; come into port*

nyūkoku 入国 *immigration; entering a country* 🔸nyūkoku tetsúzuki 入国手続き *immigration procedures* ——**nyūkoku-suru** [vi] 入国する *immigrate; enter a country*

nyūséihin 乳製品 *dairy products*

nyūshősha 入賞者 *prizewinner*

nyūwa [na] 柔和（な）*meek; gentle* 🔸Ōtaka-san wa nyūwa na kao o shite iru. 大高さんは柔和な顔をしている。 *Ōtaka has a meek countenance.* ——**nyūwa ni** 柔和に *meekly; gently* 🔸Tákano-san wa ítsumo hito to nyūwa ni hanashí o suru. 高野さんはいつも人と柔和に話をする。 *Takano always talks gently to people.*

O

ó 尾 *tail* ❊Inu ga ó o futte iru. 犬が尾を振っている。*The dog's wagging its tail.*

o を [*particle marking object*] ❊Watashitachi wa kinō Chūkaryóri o tabeta. 私たちは昨日中華料理を食べた。*We ate Chinese food yesterday.*

o- お～ [*hon noun prefix*] ❊o-kyaku-sáma お客さま *customer; guest* ❊o-tégami お手紙 *a letter*

ó; ōsama 王；王様 *king*

ōáwate 大慌て *in great confusion; in great haste* ❊Kyū ni raikyaku ga átte, tsúma wa ōáwate de ryóri o tsukútta. 急に来客があって、妻は大慌てで料理を作った。*We had unexpected guests, so my wife prepared a meal in great haste.*

oba 伯母；叔母 *(one's own) aunt* ❊oba-san 伯母さん；叔母さん；小母さん *(another's) aunt; older woman*

ōbā オーバー *overcoat*

obáke お化け *goblin; spook; ghost* ❊obáke yáshiki お化け屋敷 *spook house; haunted house*

obāsan お婆さん *(another's) grandmother; old lady; Grandmother!*

Ōbei 欧米 *Europe and America* ❊Ōbei shókoku 欧米諸国 *the countries of Europe and America*

óbi 帯 *sash; band (worn with kimono)* ❊óbi o shiméru 帯をしめる *tie an obi*

obie·ru [*vi* obienai; obieta] 怯える *be frightened (at); be startled; be intimidated (by)* ❊Shújin wa náni ni obiete iru no ka, yóku ákumu o míru. 主人は何に怯えているのか、よく悪夢を見る。*My husband seems to be frightened by something; he often has nightmares.*

ōbo 応募 *subscription; application* ——**ōbo-suru** [*vt*] 応募する *subscribe to; apply for*

oboegaki 覚書 *memo; memorandum*

oboé·ru [*vt* oboénai; obóeta] 覚える *memorize; remember* ❊Máinichi Supeingo no tango o jū-zútsu obóete imásu. 毎日、スペイン語の単語を十ずつ覚えています。*I memorize ten Spanish words every day.* ❊Anó hito no namae o máda obóete imásu ka? あの人の名前をまだ覚えていますか？ *Do you still remember her name?*

O-bón （お）盆 *Bon Festival* ❊Bonódori 盆踊り *Bon festival dance*

obore·ru [*vi* oborenai; oboreta] 溺れる *drown; drown (oneself) in* ❊Chīsái ko ga kawá de oboreta. 小さい子が川で溺れた。*A small child drowned in the river.* ❊Oboreru monó wa wára o mo tsukámu. 溺れる者は藁をも掴む。*A drowning man will clutch at a straw.* <set phrase>

oboreshín·u [*vi* oboreshinánai; oboreshínda] 溺れ死ぬ *drown; die by drowning* ❊Kodomo ga úmi ni óchite oboreshínda. 子供が海に落ち

て溺れ死んだ。*The child fell into the ocean and drowned.*

obōsan お坊さん *priest (Budd)*

ṓbun オーブン *oven*

o-cha（お）茶 *tea; tea ceremony*

ōcháku 横着 *dishonesty; cunning; impudence* ❽ōcháku o kimekómu 横着を決め込む *be dishonest* ——**ōcháku na** 横着な *crafty; sly; cunning; negligent; lazy* ❽ōcháku na táido 横着な態度 *an impudent attitude*

ochiir·u [*vi* ochiiranai; ochiitta] 陥る *fall into; be involved in* ❽aná ni ochiiru 穴に陥る *fall into a hole; fall into trouble* ❽jirémma ni ochiiru ジレンマに陥る *be caught in a dilemma* ❽Watashi wa teki no sakuryaku ni ochiitte shimatta. 私は敵の策略に陥ってしまった。 *I fell into the enemy's trap.*

ochí·ru [*vi* ochínai; óchita] 落ちる *fall; come down* ❽iró ga ochíru 色が落ちる *(to) fade* ❽Kodomo ga iké ni óchita. 子供が池に落ちた。 *The child fell into the pond.*

ochitsuk·u [*vi* ochitsukanai; ochitsuita] 落ち着く *be calm; be composed; be at ease; be settled down* ❽Sáwagi ga ochitsuita. 騒ぎが落ち着いた。 *The commotion has calmed down.* ❽Otōtó wa íma wa Kṓbe ni ochitsuite iru. 弟は今は神戸に落ち着いている。 *Now my younger brother's settled down in Kobe.* ——**ochitsuita** 落ち着いた *composed; at ease*

ōdan 黄だん *jaundice*

ōdan hódō 横断歩道 *pedestrian crossing*

odate·ru [*vt* odatenai; odateta] 煽てる *flatter* ❽Odateté mo muda da yo. 煽てても無駄だよ。 *Flattery will get you nowhere.*

odáyaka [na] 穏やか（な）*even-tempered; calm; mild* ❽odáyaka na ténki 穏やかな天気 *mild weather* ❽odáyaka na hitó 穏やかな人 *an even-tempered person* ❽Kyṓ no úmi wa totemo odáyaka desu. 今日の海はとても穏やかです。 *The ocean is very calm today.*

odéki おでき *boil (on the skin)* ❽odéki ga dekíru おできができる *get (or have) a boil*

odokas·u [*vt* odokasánai; odokashita] 脅かす *scare; frighten* ❽Ammari odokasú na yo! あんまり脅かすなよ。 *Don't scare me like that!* <*masc*>

odori 踊り *a dance; dancing* ❽odori-ko 踊り子 *dancing girl*

odorokás·u [*vt* odorokasánai; odorokáshita] 驚かす *amaze; surprise; startle* ❽Chichí kara no táyori wa watashi o odorokáshita. 父からの便りは私を驚かした。 *The letter from my father surprised me.*

odorók·u [*vi* odorokanai; odoróita] 驚く *be startled; be surprised; be frightened* ❽Sono nyūsu o kiite odoróita. そのニュースを聞いて驚いた。 *I was startled at the news.*

odor·u [*vi /vt* odoranai; odotta] 踊る *dance* ❽Odotte itadakemasén ka?

踊って頂けませんか。 *Shall we dance?*

ōen 応援 *support; aid; encouragement* §ōen énzetsu 応援演説 *a campaign speech; a speech in support of (something)* §ōén-dan 応援団 *cheering squad* ——**ōen-suru** [*vt*] 応援する *support; cheer on; encourage; aid; assist* §Shíkin o dáshite sono jígyō o ōen-shita. 資金を出してその事業を応援した。 *They put up the capital to support the enterprise.*

oe·ru [*vt* oenai; oeta] 終える *finish; end; complete* §Íma shigoto o oeta tokoró desu. 今、仕事を終えたところです。 *I've just now finished the work.*

ōfuku 往復 *return trip* §ōfuku kíppu 往復切符 *round-trip ticket*

ogakúzu おが屑 *sawdust*

ogám·u [*vt* ogamánai; ogánda] 拝む *worship; adore; bow (to)*

ōgata [no] 大型（の） *large size* §ōgatá-sha 大型車 *full-sized automobile* §ōgata yósan 大型予算 *jumbo budget*

ogawa 小川 *brook; stream*

ōgesa [na] 大袈裟（な） *exaggerated* §ōgesa na hanashí 大袈裟な話 *an exaggerated account* ——**ōgesa ni** 大袈裟に *overexaggerated; in excess* §ōgesa ni itagáru 大袈裟に痛がる *overexaggrate (one's) pain [not used with 1st pers]*

ōgí 扇 *folding fan*

oginá·u [*vt* oginawánai; oginátta] 補う *complement; add to; supplement* §ketsuin o ogináu 欠員を補う *fill a vacancy* §Kotobá o oginawánai to gokai o manéku osoré ga áru. 言葉を補わないと誤解を招く恐れがある。 *I'm afraid there may be some misunderstanding if I don't elaborate a bit more (on this).*

ogor·u [*vt* ogoranai; ogotta] 奢る *treat (someone to a meal); be extravagant* §Kyō wa watashi ga ogorimásu. 今日は私が奢ります。 *Today I'm treating.* §Iegara ga íi kara to itte ogotté wa ikenai 家柄がいいからと言って奢ってはいけない。 *Just because one is of a better family is no reason to be extravagant.*

ogyá [to] おぎゃあ（と） *"waah" [mimetic for the sound of a small infant crying]* §ogyá to naku おぎゃあと泣く *cry "waah"*

ōháshagi-suru [*vi*] 大はしゃぎする *be in high spirits* §Ákiko wa kyó ōhashagi-shite iru. 昭子は今日大はしゃぎしている。 *Akiko's in high spirits today.*

o-híru お昼 *noon; lunch* §Mō o-híru da. もうお昼だ。 *It's already noon. <masc>* §O-híru ni shimasén ka? お昼にしませんか。 *How about lunch? <fem>*

o-hitáshi お浸し *boiled greens with soy souce and shaved dried bonito*

o-hitóyoshi お人好し *good-natured person; a dupe; naive; credulous*

oi 甥 *(one's own) nephew* §oigo-san 甥子さん *(another's) nephew*

ói 王位 *the throne; crown*

Ói! お～い！ *Hey!*   **Ói, kore wa nán dai!** お～い、これは何だい！ *Hey! What is this?* <*masc*>

ó·i [*adj* óku nái; ókatta] 多い *(be) many or a large amount*   **Masao wa kyódai ga ói.** 正雄は兄弟が多い。 *Masao has many brothers and sisters.*   **Kyónen wa áme ga ókatta.** 去年は雨が多かった。 *There was a lot of rain last year.*

oihará·u [*vt* oiharawánai; oiharátta] 追い払う *chase away; drive out; repel; turn away*   **Shakkín-tori o oiharátta.** 借金取りを追い払った。 *I got rid of the bill collector.*

oikaké·ru [*vt* oikakénai; oikáketa] 追い掛ける *chase (after); run after*   **Inú wa bōru o oikákete itta.** 犬はボールを追い掛けて行った。 *The dog chased after the ball.*   **Naomi wa ítsumo ryūkō o oikákete iru.** ナオミはいつも流行を追い掛けている。 *Naomi is always running after the latest fad.*

oikaze 追い風 *tail wind; favorable wind*   **Jígyō wa endaka no oikaze ni notte junchō ni susunde iru.** 事業は円高の追い風に乗って順調に進んでいる。 *The business is proceeding smoothly, riding on the wave of the high value of the yen.*

oikós·u [*vt* oikosánai; oikóshita] 追い越す *pass; overtake; outrun*   **Musumé wa háha no sétake o súde ni oikóshite iru.** 娘は母の背丈を既に追い越している。 *The daughter has already overtaken her mother in height.*

oimotomé·ru [*vt* oimotoménai; oimotómeta] 追い求める *seek; search for; pursue*

ōin 押印 *stamp* ——**ōin-suru** [*vt*] 押印する *affix a seal; stamp*   **Kono shorui ni wasurezu ni ōin-shite kudasái.** この書類に忘れずに押印して下さい。 *Don't forget to put your stamp on this document.*

ói ni 大いに *very; much; greatly*

oí·ru [*vi* oínai; oíta] 老いる *grow old; age*   **Soko ni toshi-óita mátsu ga íppon tátte iru.** そこに年老いた松が一本立っている。 *There is a solitary old pine tree standing there.*   **Óite wa ko ni shitagae.** 老いては子に従え。 *Be guided by your child when you grow old.* <*set phrase*>

oishi·i [*adj* oishiku nái; oishíkatta] 美味しい *(be) tasty; good tasting; delicious*   **Koko no kéki wa oishii desu ne.** ここのケーキは美味しいですね。 *The cake here is delicious, isn't it?*

óisogi de 大急ぎで *in a great hurry*

oitsúk·u [*vi* oitsukánai; oitsúita] 追い付く *overtake; catch up with*   **Áto kara shuppatsu-shita watashítachi wa súgu ni sempatsutai ni oitsúita.** 後から出発した私達は直ぐに先発隊に追い付いた。 *We started after but we soon overtook the team that started ahead.*

oiyár·u [*vt* oiyaránai; oiyátta] 追いやる *chase off*

ója 王者 *king*

oji 叔父；伯父 *(one's own) uncle* €**ojisan** 伯父さん；叔父さん *(another's) uncle; middle-aged man*

ōji 王子 *prince*

ojigi お辞儀 *a bow; obeisance* €**ojigi o suru** お辞儀をする *(to) bow*

ōji·ru [vi ōjinai; ōjita] 応じる *answer; reply; comply with*

ojīsan おじいさん *Grandfather; (another's) grandfather; old man*

[-ni] ōjite (〜に) 応じて *in proportion to; corresponding to; befitting* €Sono misé wa kyaku no dónna chūmon ní mo ōjite kureru. その店は客のどんな注文にも応じてくれる。 *That store will take customers' orders for anything.* €Yamamoto-san wa míbun ni ōjita kurashi o shite iru. 山本さんは身分に応じた暮らしをしている。 *Yamamoto lives in a style befitting his status.*

ōjo 王女 *princess*

o-jōsan お嬢さん *(another's) daughter; young lady*

oka 丘 *hill*

o-kaeshi お返し *change; return gift* €Hyaku-nijūen no o-kaeshi de gozaimásu. 百二十円のお返しでございます。 *Your change is ¥120.* <formal> €Kodomo no shussan-íwai no o-kaeshi o máda shite imasén. 子供の出産祝いのお返しをまだしていません。 *I still haven't sent a return gift for the present we received when the baby was born.*

ōkami 狼 *wolf*

o-kami-san おかみさん *wife* €yaoya no o-kami-san 八百屋のおかみさん *the grocer's wife*

o-kane お金 *money*

o-kásan お母さん *(another's) mother; Mother!*

o-káshi お菓子 *sweets; cookies; candy*

okashí·i [adj okáshiku nái; okáshikatta] おかしい *(be) odd; strange; funny* €Dōmo chōshi ga okashíi. どうも調子がおかしい。 *I feel odd. (or I don't feel right.)* €Anó hito no shigusa ga okáshikute, omowazu warátte shimatta. あの人のしぐさがおかしくて、思わず笑ってしまった。 *His mannerisms were so funny I couldn't help laughing.*

okás·u [vt okasánai; okashita] 犯す *violate; commit* €hanzai o okásu 犯罪を犯す *commit a crime*

okás·u [vt okasánai; okashita] 冒す *risk; brave; face; defy* €Uno wa séimei no kiken o okáshite tanken o tsuzuketa. 宇野は生命の危険を冒して探検を続けた。 *Risking his life, Uno continued the expedition.*

okás·u [vt okasánai; okashita] 侵す *invade; encroach upon* €Puráibashī o okáshite wa naránai. プライバシーを侵してはならない。 *One mustn't invade another's privacy.*

o-kazu おかず *side dish (dish eaten with rice to make a meal)*

oki 沖 *offshore* €Ōgatasen ga oki ni teihaku-shite iru. 大型船が沖に停

泊している。*Large ships are anchored offshore.*

ōkí·i [*adj* ōkiku nái; ōkikatta] 大きい *(be) big; large; great* 8 Ōkíi heyá ga íkutsu mo áru. 大きい部屋がいくつもある。*There are several large rooms.* 8 Yoshida-san wa ōkíi hitó desu. 吉田さんは大きい人です。*Yoshida is a big man.* 8 Jishin no songai wa ōkikatta. 地震の損害は大きかった。*Damage from the earthquake was great.* ——
ōkiku-suru [*vt*] 大きくする *make bigger; make more spacious*
óki na 大きな *big; large*

-óki ni ～おきに *every other (one)* 8 Senséi wa séito hitori-óki ni shitsumon-shite itta. 先生は生徒一人おきに質問していった。*The teacher asked questions of every other student.* 8 Yojikan-óki ni kono kusuri o nónde kudasái. 四時間おきにこの薬を飲んで下さい。*Take this medicine every four hours.*

oki·ru [*vi* okínai; ókita] 起きる *awake; get up* 8 Watashi wa máiasa rokúji ni okimásu. 私は毎朝六時に起きます。*I get up at six o'clock every morning.* 8 Anáta, máda ókite imásu ka? あなた、まだ起きていますか。*Are you still awake? <fem>*

oki·ru [*vi* okínai; ókita] 起きる *arise; happen; occur* 8 Sono jíken wa áru asa totsuzen ókita. その事件はある朝突然起きた。*The incident happened all of a sudden one morning.*

ōkisa 大きさ *size; dimension; magnitude*

okiwasuré·ru [*vt* okiwasurénai; okiwasúreta] 置き忘れる *leave; forget* 8 Shokuba ni kása o okiwasúrete shimatta. 職場に傘を置き忘れてしまった。*I left my umbrella at work.*

okkū [na] 億劫（な） *troublesome; bothersome; annoying; tiresome* 8 Kyó wa gaishutsu-surú no ga okkū da. 今日は外出するのが億劫だ。*Going out today is such a pain. <masc>*

ōkoku 王国 *kingdom; monarchy*

okonai 行い *deed; act; action*

okona·u [*vt* okonawanai; okonatta] 行う *perform; conduct; do* 8 shikén o okonau 試験を行う *conduct (or give) an exam*

okorasé·ru [*caus* okorasénai; okoráseta] 怒らせる *anger (someone); make angry* 8 Nándo mo yakusoku o yaburi, tótō musuko wa chichí o okorásete-shimatta. 何度も約束を破って、とうとう息子は父を怒らせてしまった。*The son broke his promises over and over, until finally he made his father angry.*

okorippó·i [*adj* okorippóku nái; okorippókatta] 怒りっぽい *(be) irritable; easy to anger*　**okór·u** [*vi* / *vt* okoránai; okótta] 怒る *(be) angry (at)* ——**okótta** [*attr*] 怒った *(be) angry* 8 Kánojo wa okótta kao de tobikónde kita. 彼女は怒った顔で飛び込んで来た。*She came running (at me) with an angry expression on her face.*

okór·u [*vi* okoránai; okótta] 起こる *happen; occur* 8 Jíken ga okótta no wa ítsu dakke? 事件が起こったのはいつだっけ。*When did the* *incident occur? <masc>*

okó·su [*vt* okosánai; okóshita] 起こす *awaken; raise; start (up); begin; cause; establish* ❀Rokúji ni okóshite kudasái. 六時に起こして下さい。*Wake me at six, please.* ❀Kyōfū de taōreta jitensha o okósu no o tetsudatta. 強風で倒れた自転車を起こすのを手伝った。*I helped upright the bicycles that were blown over in the gale.* ❀hí o okósu 火をおこす *make (or kindle) a fire*

okós·u [*vt* okosánai; okóshita] 興す *revive; resuscitate* ❀sangyō o okósu 産業を興す *revive an industry*

okotar·u [*vt / vi* okotaranai; okotatta] 怠る *neglect; be negligent; be lazy; be remiss* ❀Shigoto o okotatté wa ikenai. 仕事を怠ってはいけない。*You mustn't neglect your work.*

óku 奥 *the interior; innermost part; depths* ❀shōgi no óku o kiwaméru 将棋の奥を究める *master the art of Japanese chess* ❀Yamaóku ni yáshiro ga áru. 山奥に社がある。*There is a Shinto shrine in the recesses of the mountain.* ❀Hijōguchi wa óku no hō ni arimásu. 非常口は奥の方にあります。*The emergency exit is at the rear.*

óku 億 *one hundred million*

ok·u [*vt* okanai; oita] 置く *lay; place; put; keep* ❀tēburu no ué ni oku テーブルの上に置く *place (or put) on the table* ❀Watashi no ié de wa geshukunin o oite iru. 私の家では下宿人を置いている。*I keep boarders (at my house).*

[-te] ok·u 〜おく *(do) in advance; (do) in preparation (for)* [*vb aux*] ❀Ashita no pátī no júmbi o kyō no uchí ni shite-okó. 明日のパーティーの準備を今日のうちにしておこう。*Let's prepare today (in advance) for tomorrow's party.*

okubyō [na] 臆病 (な) *timid; cowardly; faint-hearted* ❀okubyō na hitó 臆病な人 *a cowardly person*

okúgai 屋外 *outdoors* ❀okúgai no bābekyū pátī 屋外のバーベキューパーティー *an outdoor barbecue*

ókugi; ōgi 奥義 *hidden mysteries; precepts*

okujō 屋上 *on the roof* ❀okujō téien 屋上庭園 *a roof garden*

óku no 多くの *many* ❀Séisho wa óku no kuní de yomárete iru. 聖書は多くの国で読まれている。*The Bible is read in many countries.*

okurase·ru [*caus* okurasenai; okuraseta] 遅らせる *cause to be late; delay; defer* ❀Hijō jítai de gekijō wa ópera no kaien o okuraseta. 非常事態で劇場はオペラの開演を遅らせた。*Because of an emergency, the theater delayed the commencement of the opera.*

Ōkuráshō 大蔵省 *Ministry of Finance* ❀ōkura dáijin 大蔵大臣 *minister of finance*

okure·ru [*vi* okurenai; okureta] 遅れる *be late; be tardy; be behind time* ❀Nebō-shite, gakkō ni okurete shimatta. 寝坊して、学校に遅れてしまった。*I overslept and was late to school.* ❀Tokei wa yómpun okurete iru. 時計は四分遅れている。 *The clock is four minutes slow.*

okurimono 贈り物 *present; gift*

okur·u [vt okuranai; okutta] 送る *ship; send; transmit; see off*
   §kozútsumi o okuru 小包を送る *send a package*   §Éki made okuró ka? 駅まで送ろうか。 *Shall I take you to the station? <masc>*

okur·u [vt okuranai; okutta] 贈る *present; give (a present); bestow (upon)*
   §Shinrō shímpu wa ryōshin ni hanatába o okutta. 新郎新婦は両親に花束を贈った。 *The bride and groom presented bouquets to their parents.*

ókusan; ókusama 奥さん; 奥様 *(another's) wife*

okuyukashí·i [adj okuyukáshiku nái; okuyukáshikatta] 奥ゆかしい *(be) refined; modest; graceful*

ōkyū 応急 *emergency*   §ōkyū téate 応急手当 *emergency treatment; first aid*   §ōkyū shóchi 応急処置 *emergency measure*

o-mae お前 *you (address to an inferior)*   §O-mae wa nánte wakaránai yatsú na n da! お前は何て分からない奴なんだ！ *You don't understand anything! <masc>*

o-make おまけ *free gift; giveaway; premium; discount*   §Kono gámu wa o-make ni moratta yo. このガムはおまけに貰ったよ。 *I got this chewing gum as a prize.*   §Ano misé de wa ichíwari o-make shite kureta. あの店では一割おまけしてくれた。 *They gave me a ten percent discount at that store.* ——**omake-suru** [vt] おまけする *discount; lower in price*

o-make ni おまけに *in addition; making matters worse*

o-máwari-san お巡りさん *policeman; police person*

O-medetō gozaimásu. おめでとうございます。 *Congratulations!*

o-me ni kakáru お目にかかる *see; meet <formal>*   §O-me ni kakárete kōei désu. お目にかかれて光栄です。 *It's a pleasure to meet you. <formal>*

o-miai お見合い *formal interview with a prospective marriage partner*

Ōmísoka 大晦日 *New Year's Eve*

ómo [na] 主（な） *chief; principal; main; most*   §Sono pátī ni wa Nihon no ómo na seijika ga atsumarimáshita. そのパーティーには日本の主な政治家が集まりました。 *The principal politicians of Japan gathered at that party.* ——**ómo ni** 主に *mainly; chiefly; mostly*

omócha おもちゃ *toy*

omo·i [adj omoku nái; omókatta] 重い *(be) heavy; weighty; serious*   §omoi nímotsu 重い荷物 *heavy baggage*   §omoi bátsu 重い罰 *a severe penalty*   §omoi byóki 重い病気 *a serious illness*

omoidás·u [vt omoidasánai; omoidáshita] 思い出す *recall; recollect; remember; think of*   §Anó hito no namae ga omoidasénai. あの人の名前が思い出せない。 *I can't recall that person's name.*

omoide 思い出 *memory; reflection; reminiscence; remembrances*   §kichō na omoide 貴重な思い出 *cherished memory*   §Kore wa omoide ni náru. これは思い出になる。*This will be something to remember.*

omoigakénai 思いがけない *(be) unexpected; unforeseen; unanticipated*
§Omoigakénai kotó ga ókita. 思いがけない事が起きた。*Something unanticipated happened.* ——**omoigakenáku** 思いがけなく *unexpectedly; accidentally*

omoikiri 思いきり *to (one's) heart's content; decisively; vigorously; hard*
§omoikiri ga íi 思いきりがいい *(be) resolute; decisive* §omoikiri yóku 思いきりよく *resolutely; decisively*

omoikítte 思い切って *decisively; resolutely; with a burst of courage*
§Tákeshi wa omoikítte Yúkiko ni puropózu o shita. 健は思い切って友紀子にプロポーズをした。*With a burst of courage, Takeshi proposed to Yukiko.*

omoinayám·u [*vt* omoinayámánai; omoinayánda] 思い悩む *be troubled; worry about* §Míchiko wa tabikasanaru shitsuren ni shórai o omoinayánde iru. 道子は度重なる失恋に将来を思い悩んでいる。*Michiko has been disappointed in love so often she's worried about her future.*

omoitsúk·u [*vt* omoitsukánai; omoitsúita] 思い付く *conceive; think of; come to mind* §Meian o omoitsúita. 名案を思い付いた。*I thought of a good plan.*

omoiukabe·ru [*vt* omoiukabenai; omoiukabeta] 思い浮かべる *call to mind; think of*

omoiukab·u [*vi* omoiukabanai; omoiukanda] 思い浮かぶ *come to mind; think of* §Ano résutoran no namae ga omoiukabanai. あのレストランの名前が思い浮かばない。*I can't recall the name of that restaurant.*

omoiyari 思い遣り *thoughtfulness; sympathy; consideration for*
§omoiyari ni kakeru hitó 思い遣りに欠ける人 *an inconsiderate person* §Ákiko-san wa tanin ni táishite omoiyari ga áru. 章子さんは他人に対して思い遣りがある。*Akiko is considerate of others.*

ōmoji 大文字 *capital letter*

omokage 面影 *(person's) face; visage; trace* §Watashi no kokoro no náka ni íma de mo háha no omokage ga áru. 私の心の中に今でも母の面影がある。*I can still see my mother's face in my mind.*

omomuki 趣 *meaning; tenor; drift; air; appearance*

omomúk·u [*vi* omomúkánai; omomúita] 赴く *go; proceed; head for*
§kokoro no omomúku mamá ni kōdō-suru 心の赴くままに行動する *follow (one's) heart* §Watashi wa Kyúshū ni omomúita. 私は九州に赴いた。*I went on to Kyūshū.*

omomuro ni 徐に *slowly; gradually; without haste* §Kóshi wa shussekísha zen'in o mimawashite, omomuro ni kuchi o hiráita. 講師は出席者全員を見回して、徐に口を開いた。*The speaker looked around the audience and without hurrying began to speak.*

omoni 重荷 *heavy burden; encumbrance* ⧙Nōryoku íjō no sekinin o motasaréru no wa omoni desu. 能力以上の責任を持たされるのは重荷です。 *To be made to take more responsibility than one is capable of is a heavy burden.*

omonjí·ru [*vt* omonjínai; omonjíta] 重んじる *respect; honor; value; esteem* ⧙taimen o omonjíru 体面を重んじる *respect (one's) honor*

omori 錘 *weight; sinker*

omosa 重さ *weight* ⧙Kono kaban no omosa wa nánkiro desu ka? この鞄の重さは何キロですか。 *What's the weight of this bag?*

omoshirogár·u [*vt* omoshirogaránai; omoshirogátta] 面白がる *enjoy; be amused; take delight in* [*not used with first person*] ⧙tanin no fukṓ o omoshirogáru 他人の不幸を面白がる *to take delight in other's misfortunes*

omoshiró·i [*adj* omoshíroku nái; omoshírokatta] 面白い *(be) interesting; amusing* ⧙Kono hón wa totemo omoshirói. この本はとても面白い。 *This book is very interesting.*

omoté 表 *front side; surface; exterior* ⧙Fūtō no omoté ni atena to atesaki o káite kudasái. 封筒の表に宛名と宛先を書いて下さい。 *Please write the name and address of the addressee on the front of the envelope.* ⧙Kodomo wa omoté de asonde iru. 子供は表で遊んでいる。 *The children are playing out front.* ⧙omotedóri 表通り *main street* ⧙omoteguchi 表口 *front door; front entrance*

omó·u [*vt* omowánai; omótta] 思う *think; consider; believe* ⧙Kyṓ wa isogashíku náru to omoimásu. 今日は忙しくなると思います。 *I think we're going to be busy today.* ⧙Kono keikaku o anáta wa dṓ omoimásu ka? この計画をあなたはどう思いますか。 *What do you think of this plan?* ⧙Kekka wa omoú tóri datta. 結果は思う通りだった。 *The result was just as I thought it would be.* ⧙Keikaku wa omóu yō ni susumanai. 計画は思うように進まない。 *The plan is not going the way I thought it would.*

omówazu 思わず *unconsciously; involuntarily; unintentionally; in spite of oneself* ⧙Watashi wa daijí na kaigichū ni omówazu nemutte shimatta. 私は大事な会議中に思わず眠ってしまった。 *In spite of myself, I fell asleep during an important meeting.*

ómoya 母屋 *main building*

ómpa 音波 *sound wave*

ompu 音符 *musical note*

ōmu おうむ *parrot* ⧙ōmu-gáeshi おうむ返し *parroting; mimicking; repeating*

omútsu おむつ *diaper*

on 音 *Chinese reading of a character*

onáidoshi 同い年 *same age (as)* ⧙Watashi to ítoko wa onáidoshi desu. 私と従姉妹は同年です。 *My cousin and I are the same age.*

onaji 同じ *same; identical*   ❀onaji gakkō no séito 同じ学校の生徒 *a student at the same school*   ❀Denwa to fákkusu no bangō wa onaji desu. 電話とフアックスの番号は同じです。 *The telephone and fax number are the same.*

o-naka お腹 *stomach; abdomen*   ❀o-naka ga itái お腹が痛い *have a stomachache*   ❀o-naka o kowásu お腹をこわす *have an upset stomach*   ❀Íma wa o-naka ga ippai désu. 今はお腹がいっぱいです。 *My stomach's full.*   ❀O-naka ga suita! お腹がすいた。 *I'm hungry!*

onara おなら *a fart*   ❀onara o suru おならをする *fart; break wind*

onchō 恩寵 *grace; favor*

onchō 音調 *tone*

ondan [na] 温暖（な）*mild (temperature)*

óndo 温度 *temperature; heat*   ❀Nihón wa óndo wa sésshi de hakarimásu. 日本は温度は摂氏で測ります。 *In Japan temperature is measured on the centigrade scale.*

ondokei 温度計 *thermometer*

óndo o tóru 音頭をとる *take the lead (in a song); call the tune (in negotiations)*   ❀kampai no óndo o tóru 乾杯の音頭をとる *make a toast*

ondori 雄鶏 *rooster*

óneji 雄ねじ *(male) screw; bolt*

óngaku 音楽 *music*   ❀ongakuka 音楽家 *a musician*

oní 鬼 *demon; ogre*

onjin 恩人 *benefactor; patron; person to whom one is indebted*   ❀Anó hito wa watashi no ínochi no onjin desu. あの人は私の命の恩人です。 *I owe my life to that person.*

onkei 恩恵 *benefit; favor*

onkyū 恩給 *pension*

onná 女 *female; woman*   ❀onná no ko 女の子 *girl*   ❀onna no hitó 女の人 *woman*   ❀onnatárashi 女たらし *lady killer*   ❀onna-zákari 女盛り *in the bloom of womanhood*

onnade 女手 *woman's hand; feminine (writing) style*   ❀Watashi wa onnade hitótsu de gonín no kodomo o sodatemáshita. 私は女手一つで五人の子供を育てました。 *I raised five children as a single woman.*

onnappó·i [adj onnappóku nái; onnappókatta] 女っぽい *(be) effeminate*

onnarashíi [adj -ráshiku nái; -ráshikatta] 女らしい *(be) feminine*

onnaráshisa 女らしさ *femininity*   ❀Sóbo wa hachijússai ni náru keredo, máda onna ráshisa o ushinatte imasén. 祖母は八十歳になるけれど、まだ女らしさを失っていません。 *My grandmother is eighty but she still hasn't lost her femininity.*

óno 斧 *axe; hatchet*

onó ono 各々 *each; each and every*   ❀Séito wa onó ono íken o nóbete-imasu. 生徒は各々意見を述べています。 *The students each give* *their own opinions.*

onore 己 *self; oneself* §onore no hómbun o tsukúsu 己の本分を尽くす *do one's duty*

onozu to 自ずと *spontaneously; naturally; of its own accord* §Dóryoku áru nómi. Onozu to michi ga hirákete kuru deshó. 努力あるのみ。自ずと道が開けてくるでしょう。 *All you have to do is try your best and a door will open.*

onryō 音量 *volume (of sound)* §Onryō o ságete kudasái. 音量を下げて下さい。 *Lower the volume, please.*

onsen 温泉 *hot spring; spa*

onsetsu 音節 *syllable*

onshitsu 音質 *tone quality*

onshitsu 温室 *greenhouse; hothouse*

onsoku 音速 *speed of sound* §chōónsoku 超音速 *supersonic*

ontai 温帯 *temperate zone*

onwa [na] 温和（な）*mild; gentle; temperate (climate)* §onwa na hitó 温和な人 *a gentle person* §onwa na seikaku 温和な性格 *a mild disposition* §onwa na kikō 温和な気候 *a temperate climate*

óppai おっぱい *woman's breasts; breast milk; mother's milk* §Ákachan wa óppai o nónde iru. 赤ちゃんはおっぱいを飲んでいる。 *The baby is nursing.* §Óppai ga yóku demásu ka? おっぱいがよく出ますか？ *Do you have enough breast milk?*

ōppira ni おおっぴらに *openly; in public* §ōppira ni furumáu おおっぴらに振る舞う *carry on in public* §Jíjitsu ga ōppira ni nátte shimatta. 事実がおおっぴらになってしまった。 *The truth came to light.*

Oranda オランダ *Holland; the Netherlands* ——**Oranda-go** オランダ語 *Dutch (language)* ——**Orandájin** オランダ人 *Dutch (person)*

ore 俺 *I <masc>*

orenji-iro オレンジ色 *orange (color)*

oré·ru [*vi* orénai; óreta] 折れる *break; be broken* §Há ga órete shimatta. 歯が折れてしまった。 *The tooth broke (off).* §Kono kása no honé ga íppon órete iru. この傘の骨が一本折れている。 *A rib of this umbrella is broken.*

orí 檻 *cage (for large animals)*

orígami 折り紙 *paper folding (folk art)*

oríkara [no] 折りから（の）*just at that time* §Oríkara no áme de yakyū no shiai wa chūshi ni nátta. 折りからの雨で野球の試合は中止になった。 *Because it started to rain (at just that time) the baseball game was cancelled.*

orikasanar·u [*vi* orikasanaranai; orikasanatta] 折り重なる *lie one upon another; overlap* §Éki no kaidan de jōkốkyaku ga orikasanatte taóreta. 駅の階段で乗降客が折り重なって倒れた。 *On the stairs at the* *station, boarding and detraining passengers fell over one another.*

orimono 織物 *textile goods* 8kinuorímono 絹織物 *silk goods*
8keorímono 毛織物 *woolen goods*

orí·ru [*vt / vi* orínai; órita] 降りる *get off (a vehicle); go down; step down* 8densha o oríru 電車を降りる *get off a train* 8yamá o oríru 山を降りる *go down a mountain* 8kyóka ga oríru 許可が降りる *be granted permission*

oritatamí isu 折り畳み椅子 *folding chair*

oritatam·u [*vt* oritatamanai; oritatanda] 折り畳む *fold (up)* 8Íma kása o oritatande iru tokoró desu. 今、傘を折り畳んでいるところです。 *I'm (just) folding up my umbrella.*

óroka [na] 愚か（な）*foolish; stupid* 8Kimi no kangáe wa óroka da. 君の考えは愚かだ。 *Your idea is foolish. <masc>*

[wa] óroka... （は）おろか～ *not only....but...* 8Hánnin wa higáisha no kane wa óroka, ínochi made ubátta. 犯人は金はおろか命まで奪った。 *Not only did the criminal take the victim's money, he took his life as well.*

orokása 愚かさ *foolishness* 8Kimi no orokása ga hana ni tsúku. 君の愚かさが鼻につく。 *I've had enough of your foolishness! <masc>*

órooro [to] おろおろ（と）*falteringly; unsure of what to do [mimetic of quavering and nervousness]* **——órooro-suru** [*vi*] *falter; quaver; be unsure of what to do* 8Kodomo wa ítsumo chichí ni donaráreto óroorosuhite iru. 子供はいつも父に怒鳴られておろおろしている。 *Yelled at by their father, the children are wailing all the time.*

oroshí *wholesale* 8oroshíshō 卸商 *wholesale merchant* 8oroshiuri o suru 卸売りをする *carry on a wholesale trade*

oroshi dón'ya 卸問屋 *discount house; wholesaler*

oroshigane 卸し金 *grater*

orós·u [*vt* orosánai; oróshita] 降ろす；下ろす *put down; let off (a vehicle); unload* 8kuruma kara ní o orósu 車から荷を降ろす *unload baggage from a car* 8né o orósu 根を下ろす *put down roots* 8ko o orósu 子を降ろす *abort; have an abortion*

orós·u [*vt* orosánai; oróshita] 卸す *sell at wholesale*

ór·u [*vi* oránai; ótta] 居る（*formal; humble*）8Chichí wa íma orimasén. 父は今居りません。 *My father is not at home right now. <formal>*

ór·u [*vt* oránai; ótta] 折る *break; bend; fold* 8eda o óru 枝を折る *break a limb (from a tree)* 8kamí o óru 紙を折る *fold paper* 8yubí o ótte kazoéru 指を折って数える *(to) count; total (up) (lit: count, bending the fingers)* 8Watashi wa sukí ni itte, ashi no honé o ótta. 私はスキーに行って足の骨を折った。 *I broke my leg skiing.*

ór·u [*vt* oránai; ótta] 織る *weave* 8hata o óru 機を織る *weave (on a loom)*

orugóru オルゴール *music box*

ōryō 横領 *misappropriation (of funds); embezzlement* ——**ōryō-suru** [vt] 横領する *embezzle; usurp; seize*

osáe·ru [vt osaénai; osáeta] 押さえる；抑える *press down; keep under control* ❂kizuguchi o osaéru 傷口を押さえる *put pressure on a wound* ❂bōdō o osaéru 暴動を抑える *suppress violence*

ōsaji 大匙 *tablespoon*

osamár·u [vi osamaránai; osamátta] 収まる；納まる *be governed; be controlled* ❂Genkō wa sanpḗji de osamátta. 原稿は三頁で納まった。 *I kept the manuscript to within three pages.* ❂Infure ga osamátta. インフレが収まった。 *Inflation was kept under control.*

osamé·ru [vt osaménai; osámeta] 収める；納める *put in; put away; gather; collect; pay; deliver; dedicate* ❂gessha o osaméru 月謝を納める *pay a monthly (lesson) fee* ❂dōyō-suru kokoró o osaméru 動揺する心を収める *calm (one's) excitement* ❂zeikin o osaméru 税金を納める *pay taxes* ❂Senden ga kḗka o osaméru. 宣伝が効果を納める。 *Advertising gets results.*

osamé·ru [vt osaménai; osámeta] 治める *rule* ❂kuni o osaméru 国を治める *rule a country; reign over a kingdom*

osaná·i [adj osánaku nái; osánakatta] 幼い *(be) very young; childish; immature* ❂Watashi no kangáe wa osanái deshō ka? 私の考えは幼いでしょうか。 *Do you think my idea is childish?*

osen 汚染 *contamination; pollution* ❂kankyō ósen 環境汚染 *environmental pollution*

ōsetsuma 応接間 *parlor; reception room*

osháburi おしゃぶり *pacifier*

oshi [no] 唖（の）*mute; dumb (preferred:* kotoba no fujiyū na hitó)

o-shíbori お絞り *moist, hot towel*

oshídori 鴛鴦 *mandarin duck*

oshie·ru [vt oshienai; oshieta] 教える *instruct; teach; give information* ❂Watanabe-san wa gaikokújin ni Nihongo o oshiete imásu. 渡辺さんは外国人に日本語を教えています。 *Watanabe teaches Japanese to foreigners.* ❂Namae o oshiete kudasái. 名前を教えて下さい。 *Please tell me your name.*

oshiire 押し入れ；押入れ *closet*

oshikomi 押込み *forcing (one's) way in* ❂oshikomi gótō 押込み強盗 *burglary; breaking and entry* ——**oshikóm·u** [vi/vt oshikománai; oshikónda] 押し込む *push in; stuff (into); crowd into* ❂Futon o oshiire ni oshikónda. 布団を押入れに押し込んだ。 *I stuffed the futon into the closet.*

oshím·u [vt oshimánai; oshínda] 惜しむ *begrudge; be sorry; regret; mourn; mind* ❂Watashi wa háha no shí o oshínde iru. 私は母の死を惜しんでいる。 *I mourn my mother's death.* ❂Kyōryoku o oshimimasén. 協力を惜しみません。 *I don't mind cooperating.*

oshinoké·ru [*vt* oshinokénai; oshinóketa] 押し退ける *push out of the way*
   §Watashi wa hito o oshinókete máe ni demáshita. 私は人を押し退け
て前に出ました。 *I pushed people aside and went to the front.*

oshiroi 白粉 *face powder*

oshitsuké·ru [*vt* oshitsukénai; oshitsúketa] 押し付ける *press (push)
against; force; compel*   §Tanaka wa watashi ni sekinin o oshitsúketa.
田中は私に責任を押し付けた。 *Tanaka forced the responsibility on
me.*

oso·i [*adj* osoku nái; osókatta] 遅い *(be) slow; late*   §Chichi wa ashí ga
osói. 父は足が遅い。 *My father walks slowly.*   §Musumé no kaerí ga
osoi. 娘の帰りが遅い。 *My daughter's late getting home.*

osóraku 恐らく *perhaps; probably; no doubt*   §Abe wa osóraku kónai
daró. 阿部は恐らく来ないだろう。 *Abe probably won't come.*

osoré 恐れ *dread; fear; anxiety; concern*   §Óame no osoré ga áru. 大雨
の恐れがある。 *There's fear of heavy rain.*

osoré·ru [*vt* osorénai; osóreta] 恐れる *dread; fear; be anxious about*
  §Kokumin wa bókun o osórete iru. 国民は暴君を恐れている。
People fear a despot.   §Reigai no hassei o osórete iru. 冷害の発生を
恐れている。 *We are anxious about what damage may have been
caused by the cold spell.*

osoroshí·i [*adj* osoróshiku nái; osoróshikatta] 恐ろしい *(be) fearful;
frightening; afraid*   §Kurai yómichi wa osoroshíi. 暗い夜道は恐ろし
い。 *I'm afraid of dark streets at night.*

osoru ósoru 恐る恐る *fearfully; with trepidation*   §Kodomo wa osoru
ósoru chichí no máe ni déta. 子供は恐る恐る父の前に出た。
Fearfully the child faced his father.

oso·u [*vt* osowanai; osotta] 襲う *attack; assail; set upon*   §Kumá ga
ryóshi o osotta. 熊が猟師を襲った。 *A bear attacked the hunter.*
  §Machí ga yógánryū ni osowareta. 町が溶岩流に襲われた。 *The town
was swept over by a pyroclastic flow.*

osowar·u [*vi / vt* osowaranai; osowatta] 教わる *receive instruction; be
taught*   §Kánai wa Amerikajin ryūgakúsei ni Eigo o osowatte iru. 家内
はアメリカ人留学生に英語を教わっている。 *My wife is being
taught English by an American overseas student.*

osshár·u [*vt* ossharánai; osshátta] おっしゃる *say <formal>*

osú 雄；牡 *male (of animals)*

os·u [*vt* osanai; oshita] 押す *push; shove; press*   §Génkan no búzā o
oshite kudasái. 玄関のブザーを押して下さい。 *Press the front door
buzzer, please.*

os·u [*vt* osanai; oshita] 押す *stamp; impress (on)*   §Shorui ni ín o oshita.
書類に印を押した。 *I stamped (a seal on) the documents.*

otafukúkaze お多福風邪 *mumps; (Tech) parotitis (see also **jikasén-en**)*

o-taku （お）宅 *(another's) house; home; you* ❊Otaku no keiki wa dố desu ka? お宅の景気はどうですか。*How's business at your place? (or How are things going for you?)*

otamajákushi お玉杓子 *tadpole; (written) music note*

otemba おてんば *tomboy; saucy girl*

oten 汚点 *a stain; a blot*

o-tétsudai[-san] （お）手伝い（さん）*maid*

otó 音 *a sound* ❊otó o tatéru 音を立てる *make a sound; make a noise*

ōto 嘔吐 *vomiting* ——**ōto-suru** [*vt*] 嘔吐する *vomit; throw up*

ōtóbai オートバイ *motorcycle; motorbike*

otogibánashi おとぎ話 *fairy tale; nursery tale*

otokó 男 *male* ❊otoko no ko 男の子 *a boy* ❊otoko no hitó 男の人 *a man* ❊otoko dốshi to shite 男同士として *man-to-man* ❊íi otoko いい男 *a regular guy* ❊Otoko ráshiku sé yo! 男らしくせよ! *Act like a man!*

otokode 男手 *masculine hand (style of writing); maleworkers* ❊Wágaya ni wa otokode ga tarinai. わが家には男手が足りない。*There aren't enough men (workers) in our house.*

otóme 乙女 *girl; maiden; virgin*

otona 大人 *adult* ❊otona no sékai 大人の世界 *the adult world* ❊otona ni náru 大人になる *grow up; become an adult*

otonagenái [*adj* otonagenáku nái; otonagenákatta] 大人げない *(be) childish; unbecoming of an adult* ❊Yoshie wa ítsumo otonagenái táido o tótte iru. 良恵はいつも大人げない態度をとっている。*Yoshie always has a childish attitude.*

otonashí·i [*adj* otonáshiku nái; otonáshikatta] おとなしい *(be) tame; gentle; meek; submissive; well-behaved* ❊Káre wa otonáshiku hikisagátta. 彼はおとなしく引き下がった。*He meekly withdrew.* ❊Sonó ko wa totemo otonashíi. その子はとてもおとなしい。*That child is very well-behaved.*

otoroé·ru [*vi* otoroénai; otoróeta] 衰える *decline; fade; decay; become weak* ❊Táiryoku ga otoróete kita. 体力が衰えてきた。*I've become weak.*

otór·u [*vi* otoránai; otótta] 劣る *be inferior (to)* ❊Kono kíshu wa sukóshi seinō ga otorimásu. この機種は少し性能が劣ります。*This machine is a bit inferior in efficiency.*

otốsan お父さん *(another's) father; Father!*

o-toshidama お年玉 *New Year's gift*

otoshimono 落とし物 *lost article*

otós·u [*vt* otosánai; otoshita] 落とす *drop; let fall; omit; lose* ❊Saifu o otoshita rashíi. 財布を落としたらしい。*I seem to have lost my wallet.* ❊Supído o otóshite kudasai. スピードを落として下さい。*Reduce the speed, please. (or Slow down, please).*

otōtó 弟 *(one's own) younger brother* ⚐otōto-san 弟さん *(another's) younger brother*

ototói 一昨日 *day before yesterday*

otótoshi 一昨年 *year before last*

ōtotsu 凹凸 *unevenness*

otozuré·ru [*vi / vt* otozurénai; otozúreta] 訪れる *visit; call on* ⚐Hisashiburi ni bókō o otozúreta. 久しぶりに母校を訪れた。*I visited my alma mater for the first time in many years.*

otto 夫 *(one's own) husband*

o·u [*vt* owanai; otta] 追う *chase; drive away; run after* ⚐risō o ou 理想 を追う *pursue an ideal* ⚐Kodomo wa háha no áto o otte imásu. 子供 は母の後を追っています。*The child is running after her mother.*

o·u [*vt* owanai; otta] 負う *take; assume; sustain (an injury)* ⚐sekinin o ou 責任を負う *take responsibility* ⚐Kánai wa jíko de kegá o otta. 家 内は事故で怪我を負った。*My wife sustained an injury in the accident.*

ō·u [*vt* ōwanai; ōtta] 覆う *cover; veil; overlay* ⚐Naedoko o biníru de ōimáshita. 苗床をビニールで覆いました。*I covered the seedbed with a plastic sheet.*

óushi 牡牛；雄牛 *ox; bull*

owari 終わり *the end*

owar·u [*vi* owaranai; owatta] 終わる *finish; end* ⚐Shigoto ga owatta. 仕事が終わった。*The work is finished.*

-owaru 〜終わる *finish (doing something)* ⚐Kono hón wa mō yomi-owatta yo! この本はもう読み終わったよ。*I've already finished reading this book.*

oyá 親 *parent* ⚐óyako 親子 *parent and child* ⚐oyakókō 親孝行 *filial piety*

ōya[-san] 大家（さん）*landlord; landlady*

ōyake no 公 *public* ——**ōyake ni** 公に *publicly* ⚐Jíken ga ōyake ni nátta. 事件が公になった。*The incident was made public.*

o-yakusho shígoto お役所仕事 *red tape*

oyashírazu [no há] 親知らず（の歯）*wisdom tooth*

O-yasumi [-nasái]! お休み（なさい）. *Good night!*

oyátsu おやつ *snack* ⚐O-yátsu ni kḗki o tábeta. おやつにケーキを食 べた。*We had cake for a snack.*

oyayubi 親指 *thumb; big toe*

ōyō- 応用〜 *applied* ⚐ōyō kágaku 応用科学 *applied science* ⚐ōyō gengógaku 応用言語学 *applied linguistics* ——**ōyō-suru** [*vt*] 応用す る *apply; practice*

oyob·u [*vi* oyobanai; oyonda] 及ぶ *reach to; extend to* ⚐Kono go ni oyonde máda tamerátte iru. この期に及んでまだためらっている。*Even now I'm still hesitating.*

oyóg·u [*vi* oyogánai; oyóida] 泳ぐ *swim* ❅Watashi wa máinichi pū́ru de go-hyaku mḗtoru oyóide imasu. 私は毎日プールで五百メートル泳いでいます。 *I swim 500 meters in the pool every day.*

oyoso 凡そ *approximately; generally (speaking)* ❅Oyoso no tokoró wa konna monó da. 凡そのところはこんなものだ。 *That's about it.*

ōzáppa na 大雑把な *rough; sketchy; general* ——**ōzáppa ni** 大雑把に *roughly; generally; approximately*

ōzéi [no] 大勢（の）*many (people)* ❅Ōzéi no hitó ga oshiyósete iru. 大勢の人が押し寄せている。 *Many people are pushing their way in.*

P

pachín [to] ぱちんと [*mimetic of a snapping sound*] ❅yubí o pachínto narasu 指をぱちんと鳴らす *snap (one's) fingers* ❅Jaketto no hókku o pachín to tomenasái. ジャケットのホックをぱちんと留めなさい。 *Snap up your jacket.*

pachinko パチンコ *pachinko (a vertical pinball game)*

páchipachi [to] パチパチ（と）*snap; blink; crackle* [*mimetic*] ❅shátta o páchipachi to osu シャッターをパチパチと押す *snap the shutter (of a camera)* ❅mé o páchipachi saseru 目をパチパチさせる *blink one's eyes* ❅Páchipachi to híbana ga chitta. パチパチと火花が散った。 *Sparks scattered with a crackling sound.*

pā́ma パーマ *permanent wave*

pán パン *bread* ❅pán ni bátā o nuru パンにバターをぬる *spread butter on bread*

panku パンク *puncture* ——**panku-suru** [*vi*] パンクする *go flat* ❅Táiya ga pánku-shita. タイヤがパンクした。 *A tire went flat.*

pántsu パンツ *underpants; pants; trousers*

pán'ya パン屋 *bakery* ❅pán'ya-san パン屋さん *baker*

páripari パリパリ *crisp* [*mimetic for a crunching sound*] ——**páripari-suru** [*vi*] パリパリする *crisp* ❅Páripari-shita piza kíji ga sukí da. パリパリしたピザ生地が好きだ。 *I like the pizza crust to be crisp.* <*masc*>

pásapasa パサパサ *dry* ——**pásapasa-suru** [*vi*] パサパサする *be dry* ❅Kono supagétī wa pásapasa-shite óishiku nái. このスパゲティはパサパサしておいしくない。 *This spaghetti is too dry; it doesn't taste good.*

patán [to] ぱたん（と）*with a snap (bang / thump / slam)* [*mimetic*] ❅Káre wa patán to hón o tójita. 彼はぱたんと本を閉じた。 *He slammed the book shut.*

pátapata パタパタ *pitter-patter; flip-flap* [*mimetic for a flapping or pattering sound*] ❅Rōka o pátapata hashíru suríppa no otó ga kikoeru.

廊下をパタパタ走るスリッパの音が聞こえる。*I can hear the pitter-patter of slippers running in the hall.*

patchíri-suru ぱっちりする *bright; wide-eyed*

páto パート *part-time work*

patoká パトカー *patrol car*

pechánko ぺちゃんこ *flattened out; flat* ——**pechánko ni suru** ぺちゃんこにする *crush* §Akikan o pechánko ni shite suteta. 空缶をぺちゃんこにして捨てた。*I crushed the empty cans and discarded them.*

pékopeko-suru ぺこぺこする *be hungry; bow (the head)* §Hará ga pekopeko de shinisō da. 腹がぺこぺこで死にそうだ。*I'm so hungry I'm about to die. <masc>* §Aitsu wa dáre ni demo pékopeko-suru. あいつは誰にでもぺこぺこする。*He bows and scrapes to everyone! <masc>*

penki ペンキ *paint* §Watashi wa kabe ni penki o nutta. 私は壁にペンキを塗った。*I painted the wall.*

pénshon ペンション *small home-like hotel; Western-style inn*

perapera ぺらぺら *fluently; eloquently* §Ikégami-san wa Eigo ga perapera desu. 池上さんは英語がぺらぺらです。*Ms. Ikegami speaks English fluently.*

píero ピエロ *clown*

pikapika ピカピカ；ぴかぴか *glittering(-ly)* ——**píkapika-suru** [vi] ピカピカする *glitter; shine; glisten* §Yuka wa píkapika-shite iru. 床はピカピカしている。*The floor glistens.*

píke ピケ *picket; picket line*

píman ピーマン *green pepper*

pin [to] ぴん（と）*taut; stretched tight; with a snap; with a flash* §Íto o pin to hatte kudasái. 糸をぴんと張って下さい。*Stretch the thread taut.* §Chokkan ga pin to hataraite, atarashíi kōshiki o hakken-suru kotó ga dékita. 直観がぴんと働いて、新しい公式を発見することができた。*With a flash of intuition he discovered a new formula.*

pinto ピント *focus* §pinto o awaséru ピントを合わせる *set the (lens) focus* §Pinto ga hazurete iru ne. ピントが外れているね。*It's out of focus, isn't it?*

píripiri-suru [vi] ぴりぴり（ピリピリ）する *smart (with pain); sting; be hot; become keyed up* §Nyūshi ga hajimaru jikan ga chikazuite kíte, shínkei ga píripiri-shité kita. 入試が始まる時間が近づいてきて、神経がぴりぴりしてきた。*As the time for the entrance exams approached, my nerves became keyed up.*

pirítto-shita ぴりっとした *sharp (flavor / taste); spicy; pungent* §pirítto-shita hitó ぴりっとした人 *a sharp person* §Tōgárashi wa pirítto-shita aji ga suru. 唐辛子はぴりっとした味がする。*Red pepper has a sharp (pungent) taste.*

pittári ぴったり *just; exactly* §Futarí no chīmu-wáku wa pittári da. 二

人のチームワークはぴったりだ。*Those two work perfectly together.* <*masc*>

pói-suru ポイする *toss aside; throw out* 🔊Sono gomí o pói-shite kurenái? そのごみをポイしてくれない？ *Would you take out the garbage?* <*fem*>

pombiki ポン引き *pimp; swindler*

pori yőki ポリ容器 *plastic container (for oil or water)*

póroporo ぽろぽろ *streaming; spilling* 🔊Góhan o póroporo kobóshita. 御飯をぽろぽろこぼした。*I spilled the rice.*

pósuto ポスト *mailbox*

potsún to tátsu ぽつんと立つ *stand all alone* 🔊Yama no náka ni ié ga íkken potsún to tátte iru. 山の中に家が一軒ぽつんと建っている。*There's a house standing all alone in the mountains.*

púnpun-suru ぷんぷんする *be angry; smell strongly* 🔊Kyő wa kánai wa ása kara púnpun-shite iru. 今日は家内は朝からぷんぷんしている。*My wife's been angry since this morning.*

pusshúfon プッシュフォン *touch-tone telephone*

pyómpyon ぴょんぴょん *hopping; skipping* 🔊Asoko de usagi ga pyómpyon hanemawatte iru. あそこで兎がぴょんぴょん跳ね回っている。*A rabbit is hopping around over there.*

R

-ra 〜ら [*pronoun plural suffix*] 🔊warera 我ら *we; us* 🔊kárera 彼等 *they; them*

ráigetsu 来月 *next month*

raikō-suru [*vi*] 来航する *dock; call at port*

raikyaku 来客 *visitor; guest; caller*

rainen 来年 *next year* 🔊rainéndo 来年度 *the next fiscal year*

rainichi 来日 *visit to Japan* ——**rainichi-suru** [*vi*] 来日する *come to (or visit) Japan* 🔊Béi-Daitőryō ga rainichi-shite iru. 米大統領が来日している。*The US President is visiting Japan.*

raishū 来週 *next week*

raiten 来店 *visiting a store* ——**raiten-suru** [*vi*] 来店する *come to a store* 🔊Matá, go-raiten kudasái. また、ご来店下さい。*Please visit our store again.* <*formal*>

ráiu 雷雨 *thunderstorm*

rakkan shúgi 楽観主義 *optimism* 🔊rakkan shugísha 楽観主義者 *optimist*

rakkanteki [na] 楽観的（な）*optimistic* ——**rakkanteki ni** 楽観的に *optimistically* 🔊Yoshínaga-shi wa ítsumo rakkanteki ni monógoto o kangáeru koto ga dékite urayamashíi. 吉永氏はいつも楽観的に物事

を考えることができて羨ましい。*I envy Yoshinaga; he is always able to think optimistically about things.*

rakkásan 落下傘 *parachute*

rakú [na] 楽（な）*easy; comfortable* §rakú na isu 楽な椅子 *a comfortable chair* §rakú ni náru 楽になる *be at ease; become comfortable* §Kono fukú wa rakú da wa. この服は楽だわ。*These clothes are comfortable.* <fem> §Kyō no shigoto wa rakú da. 今日の仕事は楽だ。*Today's job is easy.* <masc> ——**rakú ni** 楽に *easily* §Konna mondai wa rakú ni tokéru yo. こんな問題は楽に解けるよ。*This sort of problem is easily solved.*

rakuda 駱駝 *camel*

rakudai-suru [vi] 落第する *fail; flunk* §shíken ni rakudai-suru 試験に落第する *fail an examination*

rakuen 楽園 *paradise*

rakugaki 落書き *scribbling; graffiti* §Tóire no kabe tte dōshite rakugaki ga ói no deshō? トイレの壁ってどうして落書きが多いのでしょう。*Why is there so much graffiti on toilet walls?* ——**rakugaki-suru** [vt] 落書きする *scribble*

rakugo 落語 *traditional Japanese humorous storytelling*

rakutan 落胆 *dejection; discouragement; despondency* ——**rakutan-suru** [vi] 落胆する *be dejected; be discouraged; be despondent* §Gán no kokuchi o úkete shíbashi rakutan-shita. 癌の告知を受けてしばし落胆した。*When I heard I had cancer I was despondent for a while.*

rakuten 楽天 *optimism* §rakutenka 楽天家 *optimist* ——**rakutenteki na** 楽天的な *optimistic* §rakutenteki na seikaku 楽天的な性格 *optimistic disposition* ——**rakutenteki ni** 楽天的に *optimistically*

rambō 乱暴 *violence; rudeness; roughness* ——**rambō na** 乱暴な *violent; rough; rude; wild* §rambō na seikaku 乱暴な性格 *a violent nature* ——**rambō ni** 乱暴に *violently; roughly; rudely*

rán 蘭 *orchid*

rán 欄 *newspaper column*

ranshi 乱視 *astigmatism*

ran'yō 乱用；濫用 *abuse; misuse* §shokken no ran'yō 職権の濫用 *misuse of authority; (Tech) malfeasance* ——**ran'yō-suru** [vt] 濫用する *abuse; misuse*

ranzatsu 乱雑 *disorder; confusion* ——**ranzatsu na** 乱雑な *disordered; confused* §Kono heya no náka ga ítsumo ranzatsu ni nátte iru. この部屋の中がいつも乱雑になっている。*This room is always in disorder.*

rappa-zúisen らっぱ水仙 *daffodil*

-rashí·i [adj -ráshiku nái; -ráshikatta] ～らしい *seem like; appear (to be)* §Asú wa ténki ni náru rashí. 明日は天気になるらしい。*It looks like it'll be good weather tomorrow.* §Natsu rashíi átsusa desu. 夏らしい暑さです。*It's hot as you'd expect in summer.* §Anó ko wa totemo kodomo rashíi. あの子はとても子供らしい。*That child is very much a child.*

rashimban 羅針盤 *compass*

réi 霊 *spirit* §Koko ni réi ga yadóru ここに霊が宿る。*A spirit dwells here.*

réi 例 *example* §Kore wa íi réi da. これはいい例だ。*This is a good example.* <*masc*> §Réi o agerú to... 例を挙げると～ *To give an example...* ――**réi ni yotte** 例によって *as usual; following (fixed) procedure; following precedent* §Réi ni yotte, sono kái wa kaichō no áisatsu de hajimatta. 例によって、その会は会長の挨拶で始まった。*Following regular procedure, the meeting began with greetings from the chairman.*

réi 零 *zero*

[o-]rei (お) 礼 *courtesy; a bow; return gift; thank-you gift; payment* §O-rei ni kore o uketotte kudasái. お礼にこれを受け取って下さい。*In return (for your kindness) please accept this.* <*formal*>

reibō 冷房 *air conditioning* §reibō sốchi 冷房装置 *air-conditioning unit*

reidámbō [no] 冷暖房 (の) *air conditioned (cold & hot)* §reidámbō kámbi 冷暖房完備 *completely air-conditioned*

réido 零度 *zero degrees (temperature)*

reifuku 礼服 *formal dress*

reigai 例外 *exception (to the rule)* §Eigo ní wa hatsuon no reigai ga ối. 英語には発音の例外が多い。*In English there are many exceptions to pronunciation rules.* ――**reigaiteki [na]** 例外的 (な) *exceptional* ――**reigaiteki ni** 例外的に *exceptionally*

reigí 礼儀 *courtesy; manners* ――**reigi-shírazu [na]** 礼儀知らず (な) *ill-mannered*

reihai 礼拝 *worship* §reihaidō 礼拝堂 *chapel*

réiji 零時 *noon; midnight*

reijō 令状 *warrant; writ* §kataku sōsaku réijō 家宅捜索令状 *search warrant* §taiho réijō 逮捕令状 *an arrest warrant*

reikyaku 冷却 *cooling-off* §reikyaku kíkan 冷却期間 *cooling-off period* §Rikon chốtei ni wa reikyaku kíkan mo tokí ni wa hitsuyō desu. 離婚調停には冷却期間も時には必要です。*In divorce settlements, at times a cooling-off period is necessary.*

reireishí-i [*adj* reireishíku nái; reireishíkatta] 麗々しい *(be) ostentatious; pretentious; conspicuous* ――**reireishíku** 麗々しく *ostentatiously; conspicuously* §Sono zaidan no hokkinin ní wa choméijin no na ga reireishíku tsuraneráreru iru. その財団の発起人には著名人の名が麗々しく連ねられている。*Among the promoters of the foundation there is a conspicuous list of well-known people.*

reisei [na] 冷静 (な) *calm; cool; composed* ――**reisei ni** 冷静に

calmly; cooly; composedly

reisen 冷戦 *cold war*

reitán [na] 冷淡（な）*cold; indifferent* §Kimura-san wa watashi ni reitán desu. 木村さんは私に冷淡です。*Kimura is cool toward me.*

reiten 礼典 *sacrament; ceremony; rite*

reitō 冷凍 *freezing; refrigeration; cold storage* §reitō-gyo 冷凍魚 *frozen fish* §reitō hózon 冷凍保存 *cold storage* §reitō shókuhin 冷凍食品 *frozen foods* ——**reitō-suru** [vt] 冷凍する *freeze* §Kono nikú wa reitō-shite okó. この肉は冷凍しておこう。*I'll freeze this meat.*

reitóko 冷凍庫 *freezer*

reizóko 冷蔵庫 *refrigerator*

réji レジ *cash register*

rekishi 歴史 *history* §rekishi-ka 歴史家 *historian* ——**rekishiteki [na]** 歴史的（な）*historical* ——**rekishiteki ni** 歴史的に *historically*

rekkásha レッカー車 *tow truck*

remmei 連盟 *federation; league*

rempō 連峰 *series of peaks; mountain range*

ren'ai 恋愛 *love* §ren'ai kékkon 恋愛結婚 *a "love" marriage (vs an arranged marriage)*

rengō 連合 *union; federation* §rengō séifu 連合政府 *federal government* §rengōkoku 連合国 *allied powers* §Kokusai Réngō 国際連合 *United Nations*

rénji レンジ *range* §gasu-rénji ガスレンジ *gas range* §denshi-rénji 電子レンジ *microwave oven*

renkyū 連休 *successive holidays* §Kotoshi wa go-rénkyū ga nikái mo áru. 今年は五連休が二回もある。*This year there are two 5-day holidays.*

renraku 連絡 *connection; contact* §renrakusen 連絡船 *a ferry* §renraku o tóru 連絡をとる *(make) contact* ——**renraku-suru** [vi] 連絡する *get in touch with* §Atarashíi jūsho o áto de denwa de renraku-shimásu. 新しい住所を後で電話で連絡します。*I'll let you know my new address later by telephone.* §Ériotto-kyōju ni renraku o toritái no desu ga... エリオット教授に連絡をとりたいのですが... *I'd like to contact Professor Elliott.* §Kono básu wa tokkyū ni renraku-shite iru. このバスは特急と連絡している。*This bus makes connections with the limited express train.*

rensa hánnō 連鎖反応 *chain reaction*

renshū 練習 *practice; training* §piano no renshū ピアノの練習 *piano practice* ——**renshū-suru** [vt] 練習する *practice* §Watashi wa máinichi nijíkan táipu o renshū-shite iru. 私は毎日二時間タイプを練習している。*I'm practicing typing two hours each day.*

rensō 連想 *association; connection* ——**rensō-suru** [vt] 連想する *make* *(an) association with* ▪'Shirói,' 'tsumetai,' 'rokkakúkei,' kore kara rensō-suru monó wa nán desu ka? 「白い」「冷たい」「六角形」、これから連想するものは何ですか? *'White,' 'cold,' 'hexagonal'— what do you associate with these?*

rentogen レントゲン *X-rays*

renzoku 連続 *continuation; succession; sequence* ▪renzoku no 連続の *serial* ——**renzoku-suru** *[vi]* 連続する *continue; be continuous*

réssha 列車 *a train* ▪tokkyū-réssha 特急列車 *limited express train* ▪kyūkō-réssha 急行列車 *express train*

rétsu 列 *line; row* ▪gyō to rétsu 行と列 *rows and columns* ▪rétsu o tsukúru 列を作る *make a line* ▪rétsu ni náru 列になる *be lined up*

retteru レッテル *a label* ——**retteru o haru** レッテルを貼る *to label (something)* ▪Sono wakamono wa "furyō" no retteru o hararete iru. その若者は「不良」のレッテルを貼られている。 *Those youths have been labeled "delinquents."*

rettőkan 劣等感 *inferiority complex*

ríeki 利益 *benefit; gain; profit; advantage* ▪ríeki o éru 利益を得る *gain a profit* ▪ríeki o ageru 利益を上げる *make a profit* ▪shákai no ríeki 社会の利益 *a benefit to society* ▪Kónki no ríeki wa amari agatte inai. 今期の利益はあまり上がっていない。 *We haven't made much profit during this period.*

rígai 利害 *advantages and disadvantages; interests; concern* ▪rigai kánkei 利害関係 *matter of concern* ▪rígai tokushitsu 利害得失 *advantages and disadvantages*

rígaku 理学 *physical science* ▪rigakúshi 理学士 *Bachelor of Science (B.S.)* ▪rigaku shúshi 理学修士 *Master of Science (M.S.)*

ríkai 理解 *comprehension; understanding* ▪ríkai ni kurushímu 理解に苦しむ *have difficulty understanding* ▪ríkai no aru oyá 理解のある親 *parent(s) with understanding* ▪ríkai o shimésu 理解を示す *show comprehension* ——**ríkai-suru** *[vt]* 理解する *comprehend; understand*

rikishi 力士 *sumo wrestler*

rikkőho 立候補 *candidacy* ▪rikkōhósha 立候補者 *candidate* ——**rikkőho-suru** *[vi]* 立候補する *declare candidacy; run (for an office)*

rikō [na] 利口（な）*smart; clever; sensible* ▪rikō na kodomo 利口な子供 *a smart child* ——**rikō ni** 利口に *cleverly* ▪rikō ni tachimawaru 利口に立ち回る *be tactful; be shrewd*

rikon 離婚 *divorce* ▪rikónritsu 離婚率 *divorce rate* ——**rikon-suru** *[vi]* 離婚する *divorce; be divorced*

riko shúgi 利己主義 *egoism; egotism* ▪riko shugísha 利己主義者 *egoist* ——**rikoshúgi [na]** 利己主義（な）*selfish; egotistic* ▪Nishiyama-kun wa riko shúgi na yátsu da. 西山君は利己主義な奴だ。 *Nishiyama is an egotistic guy.* <masc>

riku 陸 *land*

rikutsu 理屈 *reason; rationality; theory*   §Sore wa rikutsu ni áu. それは理屈に合う。 *That stands to reason.*   §rikutsu ni awánai 理屈に合わない *irrational; against reason*   §rikutsu o konéru 理屈をこねる *argue*

rikutsuppó·i [*adj* rikutsuppóku nai; rikutsuppókatta] 理屈っぽい *argumentative*

rimbyō 淋病 *gonorrhea*

rimpasen リンパ腺 *lymph(atic) gland*   §rimpasén'en リンパ腺炎 *inflammation of the lymph gland*

ringo 林檎 *apple*

rinji [no] 臨時（の） *acting; extraordinary; temporary; emergency*   §rinji kókkai 臨時国会 *extraordinary Diet session*   §rinji réssha 臨時列車 *special (seasonal) train*   §rinji kyúgyō 臨時休業 *special holiday*   §rinji shokúin 臨時職員 *temporary employee*

rinsetsu-suru [*vi*] 隣接する *be near; be close; adjoin*

rippa [na] 立派（な） *splendid; exceptional; fine*   §rippa na ié 立派な家 *a splendid house*   §rippa na seiseki 立派な成績 *an exceptional grade*   §rippa na táido 立派な態度 *a fine attitude*

rippō 立法 *legislation*   §rippóken 立法権 *legislative power*   §rippó-fu 立法府 *legislative body*

rippótai 立方体 *cube (Geom)*

rippuku 立腹 *anger; offense* ——**rippuku-suru** [*vi*] 立腹する *be angry; be offended (by)*

ríra リラ *lilac*

rirekisho 履歴書 *(one's) personal history; curriculum vitae; dossier; resumé*

ririku 離陸 *(plane) take-off* ——**ririku-suru** [*vi*] 離陸する *take off*

ririshí·i [*adj* riríshiku nái; riríshikatta] 凛々しい *(be) gallant; manly; dignified*

ríron 理論 *theory*   §ríron to jissen 理論と実践 *theory and practice*   §ríron butsurígaku 理論物理学 *theoretical physics* ——**rironteki [na]** 理論的（な）*theoretical* ——**rironteki ni** 理論的に *theoretically*

risáisha 罹災者 *victim; sufferer (of a calamity)*

risei 理性 *reason; reasoning*   §Kanjō ni hashítte risei o ushinatté wa ikenai. 感情に走って理性を失ってはいけない。 *One mustn't give in to emotion and lose one's ability to reason.*

ríshi 利子 *interest (on money)*

risō 理想 *ideal*   §riso shúgi 理想主義 *idealism*   §risō shugísha 理想主義者 *idealist*   §risōkyō 理想郷 *Utopia*   §Káre wa risō ga takái. 彼は理想が高い。 *He has high ideals.* ——**risōteki [na]** 理想的（な）*ideal*   §Kore wa risōteki na ié desu. これは理想的な家です。 *This is an ideal house.* ——**risōteki ni** 理想的に *ideally*

risoku 利息 *interest (on money)* ❽risokúritsu 利息率 *interest rate*

rísshin shusse 立身出世 *success; career*

risshun 立春 *beginning of spring*

rísu りす *squirrel*

rítsu 率 *rate; percentage* ❽daritsu 打率 *batting average* ❽hanzáiritsu 犯罪率 *crime rate* ❽tohýóritsu 投票率 *turnout (of voters)*

riyō 利用 *use; utilization* ——**riyō-suru** [*vt*] 利用する *use; utilize; manipulate*

riyū 理由 *reason; cause; grounds* ❽riyū ga tatánai 理由が立たない *unjustifiable; not reasonable*

ro 炉 *fireplace (J)* ❽robata 炉端 *fireside* ❽robata ryōri 炉端料理 *cooking on an open fire*

rố ろう *wax* ❽rốgami ろう紙 *wax paper*

rōá(sha) 聾唖(者) *deaf-mute*

róba 驢馬；ロバ *donkey*

robō 路傍 *along the road; by the wayside* ❽robō déndō 路傍伝道 *street evangelism* ❽robō no hitó 路傍の人 *a passerby*

róbo 老母 *(one's) aged mother*

rōdō 労働 *manual labor; toil* ❽rōdō dáijin 労働大臣 *Labor Minister* ❽rōdō jóken 労働条件 *labor conditions* ❽Rōdō Kijunhō 労働基準法 *Labor Standards Law* ❽rōdō kyốyaku 労働協約 *labor agreement (convention)* ❽rōdō kúmiai 労働組合 *labor union; trade union* ❽rōdō móndai 労働問題 *labor issues* ❽rōdốryoku 労働力 *workforce; manpower; labor force* ❽rōdō sốgi 労働争議 *labor dispute* ❽rōdō úndō 労働運動 *labor movement*

rōdốsha 労働者 *worker*

rōhi 浪費 *a waste* ❽rōhika 浪費家 *a wastrel; a spendthrift*——**rōhi-suru** [*vt*] 浪費する *waste; squander* ❽jikan o rōhi-suru 時間を浪費する *waste time*

róji 路地；露地 *alley; lane*

rōjin 老人 *the elderly; an old person* ❽rōjinbyốgaku 老人病学 *geriatrics* ❽rōjíngaku 老人学 *gerontology* ❽Rōjin Fukushihō 老人福祉法 *Welfare Law for the Aged* ❽rōjin hốmu 老人ホーム *old people's home*

rōka 廊下 *hall*

rokkotsu 肋骨 *rib (Anat)*

rokotsu [na] 露骨（な）*plain; blunt; undisguised* ❽rokotsu na kójin kōgeki 露骨な個人攻撃 *an undisguised personal attack* ——**rokotsu ni** 露骨に *plainly; openly; bluntly* ❽rokotsu ni chūshō-suru 露骨に中傷する *slander openly*

rokú 六；6 *six (the numeral)*

rokuga 録画 *video recording* ——**rokuga-suru** [*vt*] 録画する *videotape; record (a video)*

Rokugatsú 六月 *June*

rokuon 録音 *recording; taping* &rokuon sṓchi 録音装置 *recording equipment* &gaitō rókuon 街頭録音 *a man-in-the-street interview* &jikkyō rókuon 実況録音 *documentation* ——**rokuon-suru** [vt] 録音する *record; tape*

rombun 論文 *dissertation; academic paper; thesis* &gakui rómbun 学位論文 *master's thesis* &sotsugyō rómbun 卒業論文 *graduation thesis* &rombun o happyō-suru 論文を発表する *present a paper*

rondai 論題 *topic*

ronji·ru [vt ronjinai; ronjita] 論じる *discuss; debate*

ronjitaté·ru [vt -taténai; -táteta] 論じ立てる *argue; make an argument* &Káre wa jíko no seitōsei o tsúyoku ronjitátета. 彼は自己の正当性を強く論じ立てた。 *He strongly argued that he (or his view) was right.*

rónri 論理 *logic; reason* &ronrígaku 論理学 *(the study of) logic* &jūmin úndō no rónri 住民運動の論理 *the reason behind the citizens' movement*

ronsō 論争 *controversy; dispute*

róshi 労使 *labor and capital; labor and management*

roshutsu 露出 *exposure (camera setting)* &roshutsukei 露出計 *exposure meter; light meter*

rōsóku ろうそく；ローソク *candle* &rōsokútate ろうそく立て *candlestick*

rozário ロザリオ *rosary*

rōzome ろう染め *batik*

rúi 類 *kind; sort; class* &rúi o mínai 類を見ない *unequaled* &Rúi wa tómo o yobú. 類は友を呼ぶ。 *Birds of a feather flock together (Like attracts like).* <set phrase>

ruigo jíten 類語辞典 *thesaurus*

ruiji 類似 *resemblance* ——**ruiji-suru** [vi] 類似する *resemble; be similar to*

rúsu [na] 留守（な）*not at home* &rusuban 留守番 *caretaker; house-sitting* &rusuban dénwa 留守番電話 *telephone answering machine* &rúsu ni suru 留守にする *leave (one's) home; be away from home* &rúsu o mamóru 留守を守る *watch a home in the owner's absence*

ryáku 略 *abbreviation* &ryakugo 略語 *abbreviation; abbreviated word* &ryakushiki 略式 *informality* &ryakuzu 略図 *rough sketch* ——**ryakús·u** [vt ryakusánai; ryakushita] 略す *abridge; revise; abbreviate* &Pāsonaru kompyúta wa pasokon to ryakúshite tsukau kotó ga ōi. パーソナルコンピューターはパソコンと略して使うことが多い。 *The word "personal computer" is often abbreviated to "pasokon" (in Japanese).*

ryō 量 *amount; quantity* &ryō ga ōi 量が多い *a large amount*

ryō 寮 *dormitory* &gakuséiryō 学生寮 *student dormitory*

§dokushínryō 独身寮 *bachelors' quarters*   §shaínryō 社員寮 *employees' dormitory*

ryóchi 領地 *domain*   §Mukashí, daimyő wa őku no ryőchi o mótte ita. 昔、大名は多くの領地を持っていた。*In former days, feudal lords owned vast domains.*

ryohi 旅費 *carfare; travel expense*

ryōhō 療法 *medical treatment; therapy*   §butsuri ryōhō 物理療法 *physical therapy*   §kagaku ryōhō 化学療法 *chemotherapy*   §shinri ryōhō 心理療法 *psychotherapy*

ryōhő 両方 *both; neither*   §Kánai wa Eigo mo Doitsugo mo ryōhő tomo hanaséru. 家内は英語もドイツ語も両方とも話せる。*My wife can speak both English and German.*   §Watashi wa piano mo gítā mo ryōhō hikenai. 私はピアノもギターも両方弾けない。*I can't play either the piano or the guitar.*

ryōiki 領域 *territory; range*

ryóji 領事 *consul*   §ryōjíkan 領事館 *consulate*

ryōkai 了解 *understanding; acceptance; consent*   §ryōkaijíkō 了解事項 *terms of agreement*   §ryōkai o éru 了解を得る *receive consent*   §ammoku no ryōkai 暗黙の了解 *silent consent* ——**ryōkai-suru** [vt] 了解する *understand; accept; consent*

ryokan 旅館 *(Japanese-style) inn*

ryőkin 料金 *charge; fee*   §ryōkinjo 料金所 *tollhouse*   §denki ryőkin 電気料金 *electricity charge*   §chūsha-ryōkin 駐車料金 *parking fee*

ryokő 旅行 *trip; journey*   §ryokősha 旅行者 *traveler*   §dantai ryókō 団体旅行 *group tour*   §kaigai ryókō 海外旅行 *overseas trip; overseas travel*   §pakku ryókō パック旅行 *package tour*   §shinkon ryókō 新婚旅行 *honeymoon*   §shūgaku ryókō 修学旅行 *school excursion* ——**ryokō-suru** [vi] 旅行する *travel; take a trip*

ryokyaku; ryokaku 旅客 *traveler*

ryőri 料理 *cooking; cuisine* ——**ryóri-suru** [vt] 料理する *cook; prepare food*

ryőritsu-suru [vi] 両立する *be combined (in harmony); be compatible*

ryōsei [no] 両性 (の) *bisexual*   §ryōséiai 両性愛 *bisexuality*

ryőshi 漁師 *fisherman*

ryőshin 良心 *conscience*   §Ryőshin ga togaméru. 良心が咎める。*My conscience is troubling me.* ——**ryōshinteki [na]** 良心的 (な) *conscientious*   §ryōshinteki heieki kyohísha 良心的兵役拒否者 *conscientious objector* ——**ryōshinteki ni** 良心的に *conscientiously*

ryőshin 両親 *both parents*   §Ryőshin tomo ni kenzai désu. 両親ともに健在です。*Both my parents are in good health.*

ryōshíron 量子論 *quantum theory*

ryőshu 領主 *lord of a manor*

ryōshūsho 領収書 *receipt*

ryotei 旅程 *itinerary*

ryōyōjo 療養所 *sanatorium*

ryú 竜；龍 *dragon*

ryúchō [na] 流暢（な）*fluent*   ⑧Amerikájin no Súmisu-san wa ryúchō na Nihongo o hanashimásu. アメリカ人のスミスさんは流暢な日本語を話します。*The American, Ms. Smith, speaks fluent Japanese.* ——**ryúchō ni** 流暢に *fluently*

ryūdō 流動 *a flow; flowing*   ⑧ryūdōtai 流動体 *a fluid*   ⑧ryūdō shísan 流動資産 *liquid assets; current assets* ——**ryūdōteki [na]** 流動的（な）*fluid; mobile*   ⑧ryūdōteki na jōsei 流動的な情勢 *a fluid situation*   ⑧ryūdōshoku 流動食 *a liquid diet* ——**ryūdō-suru** [vi] 流動する *flow; run; circulate*

ryūgaku 留学 *studying abroad* ——**ryūgaku-suru** [vi] 留学する *study abroad*

ryūketsu jíken 流血事件 *bloody incident*

ryūkō 流行 *popularity; fashion* ——**ryūkō-suru** 流行する *be popular; come into fashion*

ryūkōsei kámbō 流行性感冒 *influenza* (*abbr* **ryūkan**)   ⑧ryūkan ni kakáru 流感にかかる *come down with influenza*   ⑧ryūkan ga hayáru 流感が流行る *influenza is going around*

ryūmachi リュウマチ *rheumatism*

ryúrei [na] 流麗（な）*smooth and elegant*   ⑧Sakka no Kawabata-san wa ryúrei na búnshō o káku. 作家の川端さんは流麗な文章を書く。*The writer Kawabata had a smooth and elegant style.*

ryūsei 流星 *shooting star*

ryūtsū 流通 *circulation; distribution*   ⑧ryūtsū kíkō 流通機構 *distribution structure; marketing system*   ⑧Kúki no ryūtsū ga warúi. 空気の流通が悪い。*The air circulation is bad.* ——**ryūtsū-suru** [vi] 流通する *circulate; distribute*

ryúzan 流産 *miscarriage* ——**ryúzan-suru** [vi] 流産する *have a miscarriage*

S

sa 差 *difference; variation*   ⑧kojínsa 個人差 *individual difference(s)*   ⑧kotáisa 個体差 *individuality*   ⑧A to B no aida ni sa ga nái. AとBの間に差がない。*There is no difference between A and B.*

sá... さあ～ *well...* [interjection]   ⑧Sá, hitoshígoto shiyó ka! さあ、一仕事しようか！*Well, I guess I'll get to work!* <masc>

saba 鯖 *mackerel*   ⑧saba o yómu 鯖を読む *misrepresent (one's age); cheat (with numbers)*

sábaki 裁き *manipulation; judgment*

sabaku 砂漠 *desert*

sabák·u [vt sabakánai; sabáita] 捌く *sell; dispose of; deal with; handle*
   ❊Keisatsu ga kōtsū jūtai o sabáku. 警察が交通渋滞を捌く。 *The police deal with traffic congestion.* ❊todokōtta shigoto o sabáku 滞った仕事を捌く *take care of work that has piled up*

sabák·u [vt sabakánai; sabáita] 裁く *judge; settle*   ❊kenka o sabáku 喧嘩を裁く *settle a quarrel*

sábetsu 差別 *discrimination*   ❊jinshu sábetsu 人種差別 *racial discrimination*   ❊sei sábetsu 性差別 *discrimination on the basis of sex*   ❊sabetsu táigū 差別待遇 *discriminatory treatment* ——**sábetsu-suru** [vt] 差別する *discriminate (against); discriminate (between)*

sabi 寂 *(an aesthetic term meaning "beauty in stillness," "beauty in simplicity," "beauty in antiquity")*

sabí 錆 *rust*

sabí·ru [vi sabínai; sábita] 錆びる *to rust*   ❊Kugi ga minna sábite shimatta. 釘がみんな錆びてしまった。 *All the nails are rusted.*

sabishí·i [adj sabíshiku nái; sabíshikatta] 寂しい *(be) lonely; deserted*

sábisu サービス *free (of charge)*

sabór·u [vt saboránai; sabótta] サボる *loaf on the job; cut class*   ❊Anó hito wa shigoto o sabótte bákari iru. あの人は仕事をサボってばかりいる。 *He's always loafing on the job.*

sabotáju サボタージュ *a slow-down; a go-slow strike; cutting class* ——**sabotáju-suru** [vt] サボタージュする *cut class*   ❊Kyō wa ichi-jigemme no júgyō o sabotáju-shiyó. 今日は1時限目の授業をサボタージュしよう。 *Let's cut the first period class.*

saboten サボテン *cactus*

sadamár·u [vi sadamaránai; sadamátta] 定まる *be fixed; be settled; be decided*

sádō; chádō 茶道 *tea ceremony*

-sáe 〜さえ *even* [emphatic]   ❊Konó ko wa namae sáe kakénai. この子は名前さえ書けない。 *This child can't even write his name.*

saegír·u [vt saegiránai; saegítta] 遮る *obstruct; cut off; interrupt; interfere*   ❊Hanashí o saegítte sumimasén. 話を遮ってすみません。 *Excuse me for interrupting your conversation.*   ❊Kono shōji wa gaikō o úmaku saegítte kureru. この障子は外光をうまく遮ってくれる。 *This shoji cuts out the (glare of the) outside light very well.*

saé·ru [vi saénai; sáeta] 冴える *be clear; be serene*   ❊sáeta iro 冴えた色 *a bright color*   ❊Nishímoto-san wa ítsumo atama ga sáete imásu. 西本さんはいつも頭が冴えています。 *Nishimoto's always clear-headed.*   ❊Kíbun ga saénai. 気分が冴えない。 *I feel depressed.*

saezúr·u [vi saezuránai; saezútta] さえずる *sing; chirp; twitter*   ❊Kotori ga kí no ué de saezútte iru. 小鳥が木の上でさえずっている。 *A bird is singing in the top of the tree.*

ságan 砂岩 *sandstone*

sagár·u [*vi* sagaránai; sagátta] 下がる *fall; go down; dangle; be lowered* §Taremaku ga sagátte iru. 垂れ幕が下がっている。*The curtain is down.* §Saikin sukoshi-zútsu bukka ga sagátte iru yố da. 最近少しづつ物価が下がっているようだ。*Recently prices seem to have come down.*

sagas·u [*vt* sagasanai; sagashita] 探す；捜す *search; look for* §heyá o sagasu 部屋を探す *look for a room*

sagé·ru [*vt* sagénai; ságeta] 下げる *lower; bring down* §nedan o sagéru 値段を下げる *lower the price* §atamá o sagéru 頭を下げる *bow (one's) head*

sagi 鷺 *heron; egret*

sági 詐欺 *fraud; a swindle* §sagíshi 詐欺師 *a swindler; an imposter*

sagur·u [*vt* saguranai; sagutta] 探る *feel around in; grope around in; spy; investigate secretly; to try to find out; to try to discover* §pokétto o saguru ポケットを探る *feel around in one's pocket (for something)* §teki no yōsu o saguru 敵の様子を探る *spy on the enemy* §gen'in o saguru 原因を探る *try to find out the cause*

ságyō 作業 *work; working* §sagyōba 作業場 *workshop*

sáha 左派 *the Left; left-wing faction*

sáhō 作法 *etiquette; manners*

sái 犀 *rhinoceros*

sai- 最〜 *(the) most (superlative degree)* §saiaku 最悪 *the worst* §saitei 最低 *the lowest* §saishō 最少 *the least* §saikeikoku táigū 最恵国待遇 *most-favored nation treatment*

-sai 〜歳 *years old* §Kánai wa íma sánjūgó-sai desu. 家内は今35歳です。*My wife is now 35 years old.*

saibai 栽培 *growing; cultivation* ——**saibai-suru** [*vt*] 栽培する *grow; cultivate*

sáiban 裁判 *trial; justice; hearing* §saibansho 裁判所 *court* §saibánkan 裁判官 *a judge*

saibō 細胞 *cell (Biol)* §saibō sóshiki 細胞組織 *cellular tissue* §saibō búnretsu 細胞分裂 *cell division*

saidáigen [no] 最大限（の）*maximum* §Káre wa nőryoku o saidáigen ni hakki-shita. 彼は能力を最大限に発揮した。*He demonstrated his ability to the full.*

saifu 財布 *pocketbook; billfold; purse*

saigai 災害 *calamity; disaster* §shizen sáigai 自然災害 *natural calamity* §saigai kyūjo 災害救助 *disaster relief* §rōdō sáigai 労働災害 *occupational hazard* §saigáichi 災害地 *disaster area*

saigen 再現 *reappearance; revival* ——**saigen-suru** [*vt*] 再現する *reappear; revive; reconstruct* §jiko no jōkyō o saigen-suru 事故の状況を再現する *reconstruct the scene of an accident*

sáigo [no] 最後（の）*last; ultimate; final; end* ——**sáigo ni** 最後に *lastly; finally; in conclusion*

saihō 裁縫 *sewing; needlework; tailoring* §Tsúma wa saihō ga jōzu da. 妻は裁縫が上手だ。*My wife is good at sewing. <masc>*

saijitsu 祭日 *holiday*

saikai 再会 *reunion* ——**saikai-suru** *[vi]* 再会する *meet again; reunite*

saikai 再開 *resumption; beginning again*

saiken 債権 *credit; a claim* §furyō sáiken 不良債権 *bad loans*

saiken 債券 *bond; debenture* §kokko sáiken 国庫債券 *treasury bond*

saiken 再建 *reconstruction; rehabilitation* §saiken jígyō 再建事業 *reconstruction work*

sáiketsu-suru *[vt]* 採決する *take a vote; take a poll*

saikin 最近 *recently* ——**saikin no** 最近の *recent; the latest* §saikin no táyori 最近の便り *the latest news*

saikin 細菌 *bacteria; bacillus; microbe*

saikō [no] 最高（の）*maximum; the highest; excellent* §Yūmei na shinise hóteru de saikō no motenashi o úketa. 有名な老舗ホテルで最高のもてなしを受けた。*I received excellent hospitality at a famous old hotel.*

saikóro 賽子；骰子 *dice*

saikú 細工 *handiwork; device; trick; tactic* §káge de saikú o suru 陰で細工をする *work behind the scenes*

saimínjutsu 催眠術 *hypnotism*

sáin サイン *signature; signal* §hóshu no sáin 捕手のサイン *a catcher's signal* ——**sáin-suru** *[vt]* サインする *sign* §Osóre irimásu ga, koko ni sáin-shite itadakemásu ka? 恐れ入りますが、ここにサインして頂けますか？*Pardon me, but would you please sign here? <formal>*

sainán 災難 *disaster; misfortune; calamity*

sainō 才能 *talent; ability; gift* §kakúreta sainō 隠れた才能 *a hidden talent* §sainō no áru hito 才能のある人 *a talented person*

sainyū 歳入 *(annual) revenue; income*

sainyǔkoku 再入国 *reentry (into a country)* §sainyūkoku kyokásho 再入国許可書 *reentry permit*

saisei 再生 *resuscitation; reclamation; rebirth* ——**saisei-suru** *[vt]* 再生する *regenerate; reproduce; play back* §Tokage no shippó wa kítte mo saisei-shite kúru. とかげの尻尾は切っても再生してくる。*If you cut off a lizard's tail it will grow back.* §Bídeo o saisei-shite miyǒ. ビデオを再生してみよう。*Let's play the video.*

saisei 再製 *reclamation; recycling* ——**saisei-suru** *[vt]* 再製する *reclaim; recycle*

saiséiki 最盛期 *peak period; golden age*

saisen 賽銭；お賽銭 *offering; oblation (Budd)* §saisén-bako 賽銭箱

offering box   🔹saisen o nagéru 賽銭を投げる *make (lit: throw in) an offering*

sáishi 祭司 *priest*

saishin [no] 最新（の）*up-to-date; the latest*   🔹saishin-gata no kompyútā 最新型のコンピュータ *the latest-model computer*

saishin 細心 *carefulness; circumspection* ――**saishin no** 細心の *scrupulous; minute; circumspect*   🔹saishin no chúi o haráu 細心の注意を払う *pay careful attention to*

saisho 最初 *(at) first; (at) the beginning* ――**saisho no** 最初の *the first; original* ――**saisho ni** 最初に *in the first place*

saishoku shúgi 菜食主義 *vegetarianism*   🔹saishoku shugísha 菜食主義者 *a vegetarian*

saishū [no] 最終（の）*the last ; final; ultimate*   🔹Saishū réssha ni ma ni átta. 最終列車に間に合った。*I made the last train.* ――**saishūteki [na]** 最終的（な）*eventual; final* ――**saishūteki ni** 最終的に *in the end; finally; eventually*   🔹Kibishíi shiai dátta ga, saishūteki ni watashítachi no chímu ga yūshō-shita. 厳しい試合だったが、最終的に私たちのチームが優勝した。*It was a close game, but in the end our team won.*

sáisoku 催促 *a demand; urging*   🔹shakkín no (hensai no) sáisoku o suru 借金の（返済の）催促をする *demand (payment of) a loan* ――**sáisoku-suru** [vt] 催促する *urge; press; demand*

saiteki [na] 最適（な）*most suitable; most appropriate; optimum*   🔹Kodomo ni tótte saiteki na kankyō tte nán darō? 子供にとって最適な環境って何だろう？*What is the most suitable environment for children?*

saiwai 幸い *happiness; good fortune*   🔹fukō-chū no saiwai 不幸中の幸い *one consolation in the midst of misfortune or sadness* <set phrase>――**saiwai na** 幸いな *happy; fortunate* ――**saiwai ni** 幸いに *fortunately*   🔹Kótsū jíko o okóshita ga, saiwai ni táishita hígai wa nákatta. 交通事故を起こしたが、幸いに大した被害はなかった。*I had a traffic accident, but fortunately no one was badly hurt.*

saiyō 採用 *adoption; acceptance* ――**saiyō-suru** [vt] 採用する *adopt; make use of; employ*   🔹Watashi no kikaku ga saiyō-sareru kotó ni nátta. 私の企画が採用されることになった。*My plan was adopted.*

saizen 最善 *the best*   🔹saizen o tsukúsu 最善を尽くす *do (one's) best*

sají 匙 *spoon*   🔹kosaji 小匙 *teaspoon*   🔹ōsaji 大匙 *tablespoon*   🔹hitósaji 一匙 *one spoonful*   🔹sají o nagéru 匙を投げる *give up; throw in the towel* <set phrase>

sajikágen 匙加減 *dose; amount; prescription*   🔹Sajikágen hitótsu de dō ni de mo náru. 匙加減一つでどうにでもなる。*Just a slight adjustment sometimes is all that's needed.*

saká 坂 *slope; incline; hill*

sakadachi 逆立ち *handstand* ——**sakadachi-suru** [*vi*] 逆立ちする *stand on (one's) hands (head)* ❧Sakadachi-shité mo Ōta-san ní wa kanawánai. 逆立ちしても大田さんにはかなわない。*I'd be no match for Ōta even if I stood on my head.*

sakaé·ru [*vi*] sakaénai; sakáeta] 栄える *prosper; thrive* ❧Kono machí wa mukashi wa sakaéte ita rashii. この町は昔は栄えていたらしい。*It seems that this town was thriving in the past.*

sakái 境 *boundary; border* ❧sakái ishi 境石 *boundary stone* ❧sakaime 境目 *border; boundary line* ❧séishi no sakái o samayóu 生死の境を彷徨う *linger on the border of life and death*

sakan [na] 盛ん（な）*prosperous; thriving; flourishing; vigorous; energetic; enthusiastic* ❧íki sakan na wakamono 意気盛んな若者 *high-spirited youth* ❧sakan na hákushu 盛んな拍手 *enthusiastic applause* ❧Kuni ga sakan ni náru to omoimásu. 国が盛んになると思います。*I think the country will prosper.*

sakana 魚；肴 *fish; hors d'oeuvre (eaten with saké)* ❧sakanaya 魚屋 *fishmonger; fish store* ❧Sake no sakana ní wa edamame ga áu. 酒の肴には枝豆が合う。*Green soybeans make good hors d'oeuvre for saké.*

sakanobór·u [*vi* sakanoboránai; sakanobótta] 遡る *go upstream; go back (to); retrace the past* ❧Kawá o sakanobóru to taki ga áru. 川を遡ると滝がある。*If you go upstream there's a waterfall.* ❧Íma o rikai-suru tamé ni rekishi o sakanobóru kotó mo taisetsu désu. 今を理解するために歴史を遡ることも大切です。*In order to understand the present it is important retrace the past.*

sakan'ya 左官屋 *mason; plasterer*

sakará·u [*vi* sakarawánai; sakarátta] 逆らう *go against; oppose; counter* ❧shio no nagaré ni sakaráu 潮の流れに逆らう *go against the current* ❧Oyá ni sakaráu nante watashi ní wa dekínai. 親に逆らうなんて私にはできない。*It's not possible for me to oppose my parents.*

sakasa; sakasama 逆さ；逆さま *upside down*

sakaya 酒屋 *liquor store*

sake 酒 *saké (Japanese rice wine); alcoholic beverage* ❧Sake wa nónde mo sake ní wa nomaréru na. 酒は飲んでも酒には飲まれるな。*Drink, but don't be a slave to drink. <set phrase>*

sáke; sháke 鮭 *salmon*

sakebí 叫び *exclamation; outcry; shout*

sakéb·u [*vt* sakebánai; sakénda] 叫ぶ *shout; cry out; exclaim* ❧Sono murá no jūmin wa gempatsu kénsetsu hantai o sakénde iru. その村の住民は原発建設反対を叫んでいる。*The villagers are crying out against the construction of a nuclear power plant.*

saké·ru [*vi* sakénai; sáketa] 裂ける；割ける *split; be torn* ❧Kono kíji wa súgu sakéru. この生地は直ぐ裂ける。*This material tears easily.*

saké·ru [*vi/vt* sakénai; sáketa] 避ける *avoid; dodge* 🔸hitome o sakéru 人目を避ける *avoid the public eye* 🔸kiken o sakéru 危険を避ける *avoid danger*

saki 先 *point; tip; future; ahead; beyond* 🔸pensaki ペン先 *pen point* 🔸yubisaki 指先 *fingertips* 🔸Anó hito wa nínen saki ni kekkon-shisō désu. あの人は二年先に結婚しそうです。 *It looks like she's getting married two years from now.* 🔸Ginkō no saki ni eigákan ga arimásu. 銀行の先に映画館があります。 *Beyond the bank there is a movie theater.*

sakka 作家 *author; writer*

sakkaku 錯覚 *illusion*

sákki さっき *just now; just a minute ago* 🔸Sákki Hánako-san kara denwa ga átta yo. さっき花子さんから電話があったよ。 *You had a call from Hanako a minute ago.*

sakkin 殺菌 *sterilization; disinfection* 🔸sakkinhō 殺菌法 *pasteurization*——**sakkin-suru** [*vt*] 殺菌する *sterilize; disinfect; pasteurize*

sakkyokuka 作曲家 *songwriter; composer*

sakoku 鎖国 *closed country* ——**sakoku-suru** [*vi*] 鎖国する *close the country (to foreigners)* 🔸Nihón wa nagái aida sakoku-shite ita. 日本は長い間鎖国していた。 *For a long time Japan closed its doors to foreigners.*

sak·u [*vi* sakanai; saita] 咲く *bloom*

sák·u [*vt* sakánai; sáita] 裂く；割く *rend; rip; separate; split* 🔸kínu o sáku 絹を裂く *rip silk* 🔸Koibito no náka o sáku nante, Yamada wa hidói yo. 恋人の仲を裂くなんて、山田はひどいよ。 *Yamada's terrible—tearing lovers apart like that!* 🔸Jikan o sáite kudasátte arígatō gozaimasu. 時間を割いて下さってありがとうございます。 *Thank you for sparing your time. <formal>*

sakúban 昨晩 *last evening; last night*

sakubun 作文 *composition; essay; paper*

sakuhin 作品 *a work; production; opus*

sakuin 索引 *index*

sakújitsu 昨日 *yesterday*

sákujo 削除 *deletion* ——**sákujo-suru** [*vt*] 削除する *delete*

sakura 桜 *cherry (blossoms / tree)* 🔸sakura no kí 桜の木 *cherry tree* 🔸sakurambo 桜ん坊；桜桃 *cherry (fruit)*

sakuran-suru [*vi*] 錯乱する *be distracted; go mad; be mentally deranged* 🔸Káre wa shippai tsúzuki de séishin ga sakuran-shite shimatta. 彼は失敗続きで精神が錯乱してしまった。 *Because of repeated failures he became mentally deranged.*

sakusei-suru [*vt*] 作成する *make out; draw up; frame; prepare* 🔸Shorui o kyō-jū ni sakusei-shimásu. 書類を今日中に作成します。 *I'll finish* *preparing the documents today.*

sakusen 作戦 *maneuvers; strategy; (military) operation* ⑧sakusen kṓdō 作戦行動 *military maneuvers*

sakushika 作詞家 *lyricist; writer of song lyrics*

sákushu 搾取 *exploitation* ——**sákushu-suru** [vt] 搾取する *exploit*

sakúya 昨夜 *last night*

sakyū 砂丘 *sand dune*

samás·u [vt samasánai; samáshita] 冷ます *cool (down); make cold* ⑧O-yú o samáshite oite! お湯を冷ましておいて。*Cool down the bath! (lit: Cool down the hot water!)*

samás·u [vt samasánai; samáshita] 覚ます *awake; wake (someone)* ⑧mé o samásu 目を覚ます *wake up; awaken; open (one's) eyes* ⑧yoi o samásu 酔いを覚ます *sober up*

samatagé 妨げ *interference; obstacle*

samatagé·ru [vt samategénai; samatágeta] 妨げる *block; interfere with; prevent*

samayó·u [vt samayowánai; samayótta] 彷徨う *roam; wander* ⑧sabaku o samayóu 砂漠を彷徨う *wander about in the desert*

samázama [na] 様々（な）*all sorts of; various; diverse* ⑧Samázama na hitó ga atsumátte iru. 様々な人が集まっている。*All sorts of people are gathered.*

sambashi 桟橋 *dock; pier*

sámbi 賛美 *praise* ⑧sambika 賛美歌 *a hymn* ——**sámbi-suru** [vt] 賛美する *praise*

sambun no ichí 三分の一 *one-third*

sambutsu 産物 *product; produce; production* ⑧nōsámbutsu 農産物 *farm produce* ⑧suisámbutsu 水産物 *marine products* ⑧kōsámbutsu 鉱産物 *mine products* ⑧fukusámbutsu 副産物 *by-product* ⑧kenkyū no sambutsu 研究の産物 *research output* ⑧dóryoku no sambutsu 努力の産物 *the fruit of (one's) labor*

same 鮫 *shark*

samé·ru [vi saménai; sámeta] 冷める *be (or become) cool; be (or become) cold* ⑧Súpu ga sámete shimatta yo. スープが冷めてしまったよ。*The soup has gotten cold!* ⑧Watashi wa kágaku e no jōnetsu ga sámete shimatta. 私は科学への情熱が冷めてしまった。*My passion for science has cooled down.*

samé·ru [vi saménai; sámeta] 覚める *wake up* ⑧mé ga saméru 目が覚める *wake up; open the eyes* ⑧yoi ga saméru 酔いが覚める *sober up*

samé·ru [vi saménai; sámeta] 褪める *fade; discolor* ⑧Kón wa iró ga same-yasúi. 紺は色が褪めやすい。*Indigo (color) fades easily.*

sammyaku 山脈 *mountain range*

sámonai to さもないと *if not (then); otherwise* ⑧Mótto benkyō-

shinasái. Sámonai to nyūshi ni ukaránai yo! もっと勉強しなさい、さ
もないと入試に受からないよ！ *You will have to study harder.
Otherwise, you won't pass the entrance exam.*

sampatsu 散髪 *haircut; barber; barber shop* ——**sampatsu-suru** [*vt*]
散髪する *have (one's) hair cut*

sampo 散歩 *a stroll; a walk* ——**sampo-suru** [*vi / vi*] 散歩する *take a
stroll (walk)*

samú·i [*adj* sámuku nái; sámukatta] 寒い *(be) cold; chilly* ❧Nihon no
fuyú wa totemo samúi. 日本の冬はとても寒い。*Winters in Japan are
very cold.* ❧Futokoro ga samúi. 懐が寒い。 *I'm low on money. (lit:
My chest [referring to the place inside the kimono where the purse was
traditionally kept] is chilly.)* <set phrase> ❧O-samúi shísetsu da wa.
お寒い施設だわ。*(The place has) skimpy furnishings!* <fem>

samuké 寒気 *a chill* ❧Kinō kara nán da ka samuké ga shite iru. 昨日か
ら何だか寒気がしている。 *I don't know why, but I've had a chill
since yesterday.*

samurai 侍 *samurai; warrior*

sámusa 寒さ *cold; coldness* ❧Koko no tokoro kibishíi sámusa ga tsuzuite
iru. ここのところ厳しい寒さが続いている。 *Lately we've been
having a severe cold spell.*

sán 酸 *acid* ❧sansei 酸性 *acidity; sour taste* ❧Kono ryōri wa sán ga
tsuyói. この料理は酸が強い。 *This food is high in acid.*

[o-]san (お) 産 *childbirth* ❧o-san o suru お産をする *give birth to a
baby*

-san 〜さん *Mr.; Mrs.; Ms. (title of respect, attached to personal names)*

sandánjū 散弾銃 *shotgun*

san-dī-kéi 3DK; *apartment or condominium having three rooms, a
combined kitchen-dining room, a toilet, and a bath*

sanfujinka 産婦人科 *obstetrics and gynecology*

Sángatsu 三月 *March*

Sangíin 参議院 *House of Councillors (J)* ❧Sangiin gíin 参議院議員
member of the House of Councillors

sángo 珊瑚 *coral* ❧sangóju 珊瑚樹 *a coral formation* ❧sangodama
珊瑚珠 *coral beads* ❧sangóshō 珊瑚礁 *coral reef*

sangyō 産業 *industry* ❧sangyō kákumei 産業革命 *industrial revolution*
❧sangyō kúmiai 産業組合 *industrial union* ❧sangyō kōzō 産業構造
industrial structure

sánji 惨事 *disaster; disastrous accident*

sanji séigen 産児制限 *birth control*

sanka 参加 *participation; adherence* ——**sanka-suru** [*vi*] 参加する
participate; adhere (to) ❧Sono shūkai ni sanka-suru kotó ni shita. そ
の集会に参加することにした。 *I decided to participate in (or attend)
the meeting.*

sanka; sankágaku 産科；産科学 *obstetrics* ❦sanká'i 産科医 *obstetrician*

sánkaku 三角 *triangularity* ❦sankakuhō 三角法 *trigonometry* ❦sankakúsu 三角州 *a delta* ❦sankákkei 三角形 *a triangle* ❦sankaku kánkei 三角関係 *love triangle* ——**sánkaku no** 三角の *triangular* ——**sánkaku ni suru** 三角にする *make triangular* ❦mé o sánkaku ni suru 目を三角にする *look daggers*

sankō 参考 *reference* ❦sankōsho 参考書 *reference book* ❦sankō ni suru 参考にする *refer to; consult* ❦sankō ni náru 参考になる *be instructive; be helpful*

sanrínsha 三輪車 *tricycle; three-wheeled vehicle*

sansei 賛成 *agreement; approval; concurrence* ❦Bóku wa kimi no íken ni sansei da. 僕は君の意見に賛成だ。*I'm in agreement with your opinion.* <masc> ——**sansei-suru** [vi] 賛成する *agree (with); approve*

sanshō 参照 *reference* ——**sanshō-suru** [vt] 参照する *refer to* ❦Kono rombun o matomerú no ni, iroiro na bunken o sanshō-shita. この論文を纏めるのに、いろいろな文献を参照した。*I referred to a number of written sources to write this paper.*

sanshutsu 産出 *production* ——**sanshutsu-suru** [vt] 産出する *produce; yield* ❦Ano kōzan wa takusán no kín o sanshutsu-shita. あの鉱山は沢山の金を産出した。*That mine yielded a great amount of gold.*

sánso 酸素 *oxygen* ❦sanso bómbe 酸素ボンベ *oxygen tank* ❦sanso másuku 酸素マスク *oxygen mask*

sansú 算数 *arithmetic*

saó 竿 *pole* ❦monohoshí-zao 物干し竿 *laundry pole (for drying laundry)* ❦tsuri-zaó 釣り竿 *fishing pole*

sappári さっぱり *clean; simple; not at all [with neg]* ❦Ano hitó ga sappári wakaránai. あの人がさっぱり分からない。*I don't understand her at all.* ——**sappári-suru** [vi] さっぱりする *be refreshed; feel clean; be straightforward* ❦sappári-shita seikaku さっぱりした性格 *an open (frank) nature* ❦sappári-shita ají さっぱりした味 *lightly seasoned (taste)* ❦Mázu wa shawā o abite sappári-shite kúru yo. まずはシャワーを浴びてさっぱりしてくるよ。*First I'll go and take a shower and freshen up.*

sarainen 再来年 *year after next*

sára ni 更に *again; anew; in addition* ❦Sono mondai o sára ni kentō-shimashō. その問題を更に検討しましょう。*Let's study that problem further.*

sáru 猿 *monkey* ❦sarumane 猿真似 *aping; copying* ❦sarujie 猿知恵 *wily; crafty* ❦Sáru mo kí kara ochíru. 猿も木から落ちる。*Even monkeys fall from trees.* <set phrase>

sár·u [vi / vt saránai; sátta] 去る *leave; depart; go by* ❦furúsato o sáru

故郷を去る *leave (one's) native home* ❸shoku o sáru 職を去る *quit (one's) job* ❸yó o sáru 世を去る *leave this world; die*

sasae·ru [*vt* sasaenai; sasaeta] 支える *support; back up* ❸íkka no seikatsu o sasaeru 一家の生活を支える *support a family* ❸karada o sasaeru 体を支える *take care of (one's) health*

sasage·ru [*vt* sasagenai; sasageta] 捧げる *present; offer; dedicate; give* <*formal*> ❸inorí o sasageru 祈りを捧げる *offer a prayer* ❸Éjison wa hatsumei ni isshō o sasageta. エジソンは発明に一生を捧げた。 *Edison dedicated his entire life to invention.*

sasáyaka [na] ささやか（な）*tiny; small; insignificant* ❸sasáyaka na ié ささやかな家 *a humble abode* ❸sasáyaka na ryōri ささやかな料理 *simple fare* ❸sasáyaka na okurimono ささやかな贈り物 *a small gift*

sasayakí 囁き *a whisper* ❸kibō no sasayakí 希望の囁き *a whisper of hope*

sasayák·u [*vt* sasayakánai; sasayáita] 囁く *whisper* ❸mimimoto de sasayáku 耳元で囁く *whisper in (someone's) ear*

sase·ru [*vt*] させる *cause to do; allow to do; make (someone) do* ❸Háha wa musuko o isha ni saseta. 母は息子を医者にさせた。 *The mother made her son (become) a doctor.* ❸Chichi-oya wa musumé ni máiasa génkan no sōji o saseta. 父親は娘に毎朝玄関の掃除をさせた。 *The father made his daughter clean the entrance every morning.*

-sase·ru ～させる [*causative suffix*] *cause (to do); allow (to do); make (someone do)* ❸Kodomo ni góhan o tabesásete, hachíji ni nekásete kudasai. 子供にご飯を食べさせて、八時に寝かせてください。 *Give the children their supper (lit: Cause the children to eat the meal) and put them in bed (lit: cause them to go to bed) at eight.*

sasetsu 左折 *left turn* ——**sasetsu-suru** [*vi / vt*] 左折する *turn left* ❸Kóndo no shingó o sasetsu-shite kudasái. 今度の信号を左折して下さい。 *Turn left at the next traffic light.*

sashiagé·ru [*vt* sashiagenái; sashiágeta] 差し上げる *give* <*formal*>

sashiatari 差し当たり *for the present; for the time being* ❸Káre wa sashiatari hitsuyō na o-kane o mótte ié o déta. 彼は差し当たり必要なお金を持って家を出た。 *Taking what money he needed for the present, he left home.*

sashidashinin 差し出し人 *addresser (of a letter)*

sashie 挿絵 *illustration*

sashíhiki 差し引き *subtraction; deduction* ❸sashihiki kánjō 差し引き勘定 *balance sheet*

sashikomi 差し込み *electric plug; spasm* ❸Kono heyá ni sashikomi ga arimásu ka? この部屋に差し込みがありますか？ *Is there an electric plug in this room?* ❸Kyū ni i no sashikomi ga átta. 急に胃の差し込みがあった。 *Suddenly I had a stomach spasm.*

sashikom·u [*vi / vt* sashikomanai; sashikonda] 差し込む *plug in; insert;*

pour into; have a spasm ❧ Yūhi ga shinshitsu ni sashikomimásu. 夕日が寝室に差し込みます。 *The evening sun pours into my bedroom.*

[o-]sashimí （お）刺身 *sliced raw fish* ❧ maguro no sashimí 鮪の刺身 *tuna sashimi*

sashitsukaená·i [adj sashitsukaenáku nái; sashitsukaenáku nákatta] 差し支えない *(be) all right; justifiable* ❧ sashitsukaenákereba... 差し支えなければ〜 *If it's all right (with you)...* ❧ Sashitsukaenákereba, ashita o-taku ni ukagátte mo yoroshíi deshō ka? 差し支えなければ、明日お宅に伺ってもよろしいでしょうか? *If it's all right may I call on you at your home tomorrow?* <formal>

sáshizu 指図 *directions; orders; instructions* ❧ Kōchi no sáshizu ni chīmu zentai ga shitagau. コーチの指図にチーム全体が従う。 *The entire team follows the instructions of the coach.* ——**sáshizu-suru** [vt] 指図する *direct; order; instruct*

sasoi 誘い *invitation* ❧ sasoi o kakéru 誘いをかける *extend an invitation (to)* ❧ sasoi ni noru 誘いに乗る *accept an invitation*

sasori 蠍 *scorpion*

saso·u [vt sasowanai; sasotta] 誘う *invite; ask* ❧ Bóku wa Yoshie-san o déto ni sasotta. 僕は良恵さんをデートに誘った。 *I asked Yoshie for a date.* <masc>

sássa [to] さっさ（と）*quickly; promptly* ❧ Sássa to katazuke-nasái! さっさと片付けなさい。 *Be quick and clean (things) up!*

sassoku 早速 *promptly; right now; right away* ❧ Sassoku dekakete miyó. 早速出かけてみよう。 *Let's go right now.*

sassur·u [vt sasshinai; sasshita] 察する *perceive; understand; see through; guess* ❧ sassuru tokoro... 察するところ〜 *as near as I can guess...* ❧ Kánojo no kimochi wa jūbún sasshite iru tsumori da. 彼女の気持ちは十分察しているつもりだ。 *I'm sure I understand her feelings perfectly.* <masc>

sás·u [vt sasánai; sáshita] 刺す *stab; pierce; stick; sting* ❧ udé ni chūsha-bári o sásu 腕に注射針を刺す *stick a hypodermic needle into the arm* ❧ Ka ni sasáreta. 蚊に刺された。 *I was bitten by a mosquito.*

sás·u [vt sasánai; sáshita] 差す；指す；挿す *point at; aim at; stick into; hold up (an umbrella); wear (a sword)* ❧ kása o sásu 傘をさす *put up an umbrella* ❧ kanzashi o sásu かんざしを挿す *wear a hair ornament* ❧ kabin ni haná o sásu 花瓶に花を挿す *put flowers in a vase*

sasuga 流石；さすが *indeed; as expected* ——**sasuga no** 流石の [with aff] *as one (indeed) is;* [with neg] *though one may be* ❧ Kono mondai wa sasuga no shūsai ni mo tokénai kurai muzukashíi. この問題はさすがの秀才にも解けないくらい難しい。 *This problem is so difficult even a genius couldn't solve it.* ——**sasuga ni** 流石に *as may be expected* ❧ Kono resútoran wa oishisa de yūmei de, dóre o tábete mo sasuga ni umái. このレストランはおいしさで有名で、どれを食べても流石に旨い。 *This restaurant is famous for (the taste of) its food, so, as one might expect, no matter what you eat here it's delicious.* <*masc*>

satchúzai 殺虫剤 *insecticide*

sáte さて *well; then; now* §Sáte, kyő wa dóko kara hanaső kashira? さて、今日はどこから話そうかしら。 *Now then, where shall we begin (our talk) today?* <*fem*>

satō 砂糖 *sugar* §akazátó 赤砂糖 *brown sugar* §kurozátó 黒砂糖 *unrefined brown sugar* §konazátó 粉砂糖 *powdered sugar* §satóire 砂糖入れ *sugar bowl*

satōdáikon 砂糖大根 *sugar beet*

satōgóromo 砂糖衣 *frosting; icing*

satōkíbi 砂糖黍 *sugarcane*

satori 悟り *understanding; comprehension; enlightenment (Budd)* §Miyata-san wa satori ga hayái, démo Múraki-san wa nibúi. 宮田さんは悟りが早い、でも村木さんは鈍い。 *Miyata is quick to understand, but Muraki is slow.* §Satori no kyőchi ni tassurú no wa mádamada desu. 悟りの境地に達するのはまだまだです。 *I still have a long way to go before I reach (the state of) enlightenment.*

sator·u [*vt* satoranai; satotta] 悟る *understand; perceive* §géngai no í o satoru 言外の意を悟る *understand beyond the words* §Imbő o satori, kárera wa sakú o nétta. 陰謀を悟り、彼等は策を練った。 *Perceiving a plot, they took steps (to deal with it).*

satsu 〜札 *paper money* §ichiman'én satsu 一万円札 *a ten-thousand yen bill* §nisesatsu 偽札 *a counterfeit bill*

-satsu 〜冊 [*classifier for counting volumes, books, etc.*] §Hón o nánsatsu mótte imásu ka? 本を何冊持っていますか。 *How many books do you have?*

satsuei 撮影 *photography* ——**satsuei-suru** [*vt*] 撮影する *photograph*

satsúire 札入れ *pocketbook; billfold*

satsujin 殺人 *murder; homicide* §satsujin jíken 殺人事件 *a murder case* §satsujínhan 殺人犯 *a homicide* ——**satsujinteki [na]** 殺人的（な）*hectic; deadly; smothering* §Koko no tokoro satsujinteki na sukejúru ga tsuzuite iru. ここのところ殺人的なスケジュールが続いている。 *My schedule recently has been hectic.*

satsuma imo 薩摩芋 *sweet potato*

satto さっと *suddenly* §Tőríma ga satto kiritsukete kíta. 通り魔がさっと切りつけてきた。 *A purse-snatcher (or slasher) suddenly attacked me.*

sattō 殺到 *a rush; a stampede* ——**sattō-suru** [*vi*] 殺到する *rush; stampede; throng; pour* §Kodomótachi wa atarashíi bideo-shóppu ni sattō-shita. 子供たちは新しいビデオショップに殺到した。

Children flocked to the new video store.

sawagashí·i [*adj* sawagáshiku nái; sawagáshikatta] 騒がしい *(be) noisy; vociferous; clamorous; uproarious; confused; hectic* §Saikin wa yonónaka ga dómo sawagashí. 最近は世の中がどうも騒がしい。 *The world nowadays is turbulent.* ——**sawagáshiku** 騒がしく *noisily; vociferously; clamorously* §Sawagáshiku shinai yó ni! 騒がしくしないように! *Don't be (so) noisy!*

sáwagi 騒ぎ *commotion; ado; racket* §ōsáwagi 大騒ぎ *big commotion* §sawagi o okósu 騒ぎを起こす *raise a racket*

sawág·u [*vi* sawagánai; sawáida] 騒ぐ *create noise; raise a racket; be uproarious* §Byōin no náka de wa sawáide wa ikemasén. 病院の中では騒いではいけません。 *One must not make noise in a hospital.*

sawáyaka [na] 爽やか（な） *refreshing; invigorating; stimulating* §sawáyaka na ása o mukaeru 爽やかな朝を迎える *greet a refreshing morning*

saya íngen 莢隠元 *string beans*

sáyō 作用 *process; action; effort* §fukusáyō 副作用 *side effect* §hansáyō 反作用 *reaction* ——**sáyō-suru** [*vi*] 作用する *have (produce) an effect; act (on); affect*

sáyoku 左翼 *left wing* §sayokushu 左翼手 *left fielder*

Sayōnára さようなら。 *Goodbye.*

sázae 栄螺 *top shell; turbo (shellfish)* §sázae no tsuboyaki 栄螺のつぼ焼き *sazae cooked in the shell*

sazuké·ru [*vt* sazukénai; sazúketa] 授ける *bestow upon; give <formal>* §Shishō wa deshí ni hiden o sazúketa. 師匠は弟子に秘伝を授けた。 *The master gave his disciples the esoteric teachings. <formal>*

sé 背 *height; the back* §senaka 背中 *the back (Anat)* §isu no sé 椅子の背 *chair back* §sebone 背骨 *the spine; backbone* §sé o mukeru 背を向ける *turn (one's) back (to)* §Kánai wa bóku yori sé ga takái. 家内は僕より背が高い。 *My wife is taller than I.*

sebamár·u [*vi* sebamaránai; sebamátta] 狭まる *be (or become) narrow; contract*

sebamé·ru [*vt* sebaménai; sebámeta] 狭める *make narrow; contract; obstruct* §Máchiko-san wa jibun de shínro o sebámete iru. 真智子さんは自分で進路を狭めている。 *Machiko is standing in her own way.*

sédai 世代 *generation* §sédai no danzetsu 世代の断絶 *generation gap* §wakái sédai 若い世代 *the younger generation* §dōsédai 同世代 *same generation; contemporary*

séi 姓 *family name; name*

séi せい；所為 *fault; blame; consequence; result* §Sore wa watashi no séi ja nái. それは私のせいじゃない。 *That's not my fault.* §hito no séi ni suru 人のせいにする *blame (something) on someone (else)*

séi 性 *gender; sex; nature* §josei 女性 *female* §dansei 男性 *male*

§seikyóiku 性教育 *sex education*   seikói 性行為 *sex (sex act)*
§seikan 性感 *sexual feeling*   §seiyoku 性欲 *sexual desire*
§seisábetsu 性差別 *sex discrimination* ——**seiteki [na]** 性的（な）
sexual

séibi 整備 *maintenance; servicing*   §seibíshi 整備士 *repairman;
mechanic* ——**séibi-suru** [vt] 整備する *repair; maintain* §Watashi
wa kuruma o séibi-shite moratta. 私は車を整備してもらった。*I had
my car tuned up.*

séibun 成分 *ingredient; component*

séibutsu 生物 *living thing; life* §seibutsúgaku 生物学 *biology* §Tsukí
ni séibutsu ga imásu ka? 月に生物がいますか？*Is there life on the
moon?*

seichō 成長 *development; growth* §keizai séichō 経済成長 *economic
growth* §Kodomo wa seichō ga hayái. 子供は成長が早い。*Children
grow up quickly.* ——**seichō-suru** [vi] 成長する *develop; grow*

seidai [na] 盛大（な）*prosperous; magnificent; grand* ——**seidai ni** 盛
大に *prosperously; splendidly*

seidénki 静電気 *static electricity*

séido 制度 *system; organization* §nenkin séido 年金制度 *pension plan*
§shakai séido 社会制度 *social system* §gikai séido 議会制度
parliamentary system

seidō 青銅 *bronze* §seidōki jídai 青銅器時代 *the bronze age*

séieki 精液 *semen; sperm*

séifu 政府 *government* §Nihon séifu 日本政府 *the Japanese
government* §séifu shunō 政府首脳 *government leaders*

seifuku 制服 *uniform (clothing)*

seifuku 征服 *conquest; mastery* §seifukúsha 征服者 *conqueror* ——
seifuku-suru [vt] 征服する *conquer; overcome*

seigén 制限 *limit; restriction* §sokudo séigen 速度制限 *speed limit*
§jūryō séigen 重量制限 *weight limit* §nenrei séigen 年齢制限 *age
limit* §seigen jíkan 制限時間 *time limit* ——**seigén-suru** [vt] 制限
する *regulate; restrict* §Tenímotsu wa nijúkkiro máde ni seigén-sarete
iru. 手荷物は二十キロまでに制限されている。*Hand luggage is
limited to twenty kilograms.*

séigi 正義 *justice; righteousness* §shakai séigi no tamé ni tatakau 社会
正義のために戦う *fight for social justice*

seihántai 正反対 *exactly opposite* §Káre wa watashi to wa seihántai no
íken o iu. 彼は私とは正反対の意見を言う。*He always gives an
opposite opinion to mine.*

seihin 製品 *manufactured good(s); product(s)*

seihókei 正方形 *square (Geom)*

seiiku 生育；成育 *growth; development* ——**seiiku-suru** [vi] 成育する
grow; develop §Íne wa junchō ni seiiku-shite iru. 稲は順調に成育し

ている。*The rice is growing well.*

seiin 成員 *regular member* ❦Kono kái wa gojúnin no seiin de kōsei-sarete iru. この会は五十人の成員で構成されている。*This group is made up of fifty regular members.*

séii no nái 誠意のない *insincere* ❦Káre kara séii no nái hénji ga káette kita. 彼から誠意のない返事が返ってきた。*We received an insincere reply from him.*

seiji 政治 *politics; government* ❦seijika 政治家 *politician* ❦seijígaku 政治学 *politics; statecraft* ❦minshu séiji 民主政治 *democratic government* ❦seiji bōmei 政治亡命 *political asylum* ❦seiji bōméisha 政治亡命者 *political refugee* ❦seiji kénkin 政治献金 *political contribution* ——**seijiteki [na]** 政治的（な）*political* ❦seijiteki hándan 政治的の判断 *political judgment* ❦seijiteki kaiketsu 政治的解決 *political settlement*

seijin 聖人 *saint; sage*

seijin 成人 *a grown-up; an adult* ❦Seijin no Hí 成人の日 *Coming-of-Age Day (J)* ❦seijínshiki 成人式 *coming-of-age ceremony (J)* ❦seijin muki no 成人向きの *aimed at adults; for adults* ——**seijin-suru** [vi] 成人する *grow up; reach adulthood*

seijitsu 誠実 *sincerity; fidelity; honesty* ——**seijitsu na** 誠実な *sincere; faithful; honest* ❦seijitsu na táido 誠実な態度 *a sincere attitude* ——**seijitsu ni** 誠実に *sincerely; in good faith* ❦seijitsu ni kotaéru 誠実に答える *answer sincerely*

seijō 正常 *normality* ——**seijō na** 正常な *normal* ❦seijō búmben 正常分娩 *a normal (baby) delivery* ——**seijō ni** 正常に *normally* ❦Sono saibō wa seijō ni bunretsu-shite iru. その細胞は正常に分裂している。*Those cells are dividing normally.*

seijuku 成熟 *maturity; ripeness* ——**seijuku-suru** [vi] 成熟する *mature; ripen* ❦seijuku-shita táido 成熟した態度 *a mature attitude* ❦Kono kudámono wa máda seijuku-shite inai. この果物はまだ成熟していない。*This fruit isn't ripe yet.*

seijunsa 清純さ *purity* ❦kokóro no seijunsa 心の清純さ *purity of the heart*

séika 成果 *result; fruit; outcome* ❦Naganen no kenkyū wa subarashíi séika o ageta. 永年の研究は素晴しい成果を上げた。*Years of research brought spectacular results.*

seikágaku 生化学 *biochemistry*

seikai 政界 *political circles* ❦seikai to zaikai 政界と財界 *political and financial circles*

seikai 正解 *correct answer; correct interpretation* ❦Seikai wa hitótsu to wa kagiránai. 正解は一つとは限らない。*There may be more than one correct answer.*

seikaku 性格 *character; personality; nature*

seikaku [na] 正確 (な) *correct; accurate; precise* ❽Kono tokei wa seikaku desu ka? この時計は正確ですか. *Is this clock accurate?* ——**seikaku ni** 正確に *accurately; precisely; exactly* ❽Dóko kara in'yō-shita ka seikaku ní wa obóete imasén. どこから引用したか正確には覚えていません. *I don't remember exactly where I got that quotation.*

seikatsu 生活 *life* ❽seikatsúhi 生活費 *living expense* ❽seikatsu súijun 生活水準 *living standard* ❽seikatsu yṓshiki 生活様式 *lifestyle* ❽seikatsúku 生活苦 *life's hardships* ——**seikatsu-suru** [vi] 生活する *live* ❽Rōgo wa hissóri to seikatsu-suru tsumori da. 老後はひっそりと生活するつもりだ. *I plan to live a quiet life after I reach old age.*

seikei 生計 *livelihood* ❽Toshi óita ryṓshin wa hosobóso to seikei o tátete imásu. 年老いた両親は細々と生計を立てています. *In their old age my parents have managed to eke out a livelihood.*

seiken 政権 *political power* ❽seiken kṓtai 政権交代 *transfer of political power* ❽seiken íji 政権維持 *maintenance of political power*

seiketsu [na] 清潔 (な) *clean; sanitary* ❽Daidokoro wa seiketsu ni shite okṓ. 台所は清潔にしておこう. *Let's keep the kitchen sanitary.*

séiki 世紀 *century* ❽nijūisséiki 21世紀 *21st century* ❽seikímatsu 世紀末 *end of the century*

seikyūsho 請求書 *bill; debit note* ❽Getsumatsu ní wa seikyūsho ga okurarete kúru. 月末には請求書が送られてくる. *Bills come at the end of the month.*

seimei 声明 *public declaration; proclamation* ❽seimeisho 声明書 *a public statement; manifesto* ——**seimei-suru** [vt] 声明する *proclaim* ❽Nihón wa árata na Nichi-Bei kánkei no arikáta o seimei-shita. 日本は新たな日米関係の在り方を声明した. *Japan proclaimed a new approach to Japanese-American relations.*

séimei 生命 *life* ❽seimei hóken 生命保険 *life insurance* ❽seimei dói 生命胴衣 *life jacket* ❽Káre no seiji séimei wa tsúkite shimatta. 彼の政治生命は尽きてしまった. *His political life is over.*

seimitsu [na] 精密 (な) *minute; close; detailed; precise* ❽seimitsu kōgyō kikái 精密工業機械 *precision machine tool* ❽Kono kikái wa totemo seimitsu desu. この機械はとても精密です. *This machine is very precise.* ——**seimitsu ni** 精密に *minutely; precisely; in detail* ❽Kōin wa kikái o seimitsu ni kumitátete iru. 工員は機械を精密に組み立てている. *The factory workers assemble machines in minute detail.*

seimon 正門 *front gate; main entrance*

seinen 青年 *a youth; young person*

seinen gáppi 生年月日 *date of birth; year, month, and day of birth*

Seiō 西欧 *Western Europe*

Seirei 聖霊 *Holy Spirit (Chr)*

seireki 西暦 *A.D. (in the Christian era)*

séiri 生理 *menstruation; physiology* ❖seiríbi 生理日 *a woman's period* ❖seirítai 生理帯 *a sanitary belt* ❖seiriyō nápukin 生理用ナプキン *sanitary napkin*

séiri 整理 *adjustment; sorting; arranging* ❖jin'in séiri 人員整理 *adjustment of personnel* ——**séiri-suru** [*vt*] 整理する *sort out; arrange* ❖funkyū-shita gíron o séiri-suru 紛糾した議論を整理する *sort out a confused argument*

seiritsu 成立 *materialization; coming into being* ——**seiritsu-suru** [*vi*] 成立する *materialize* ❖Rainendo yósan ga kokkai de seiritsu-shita. 来年度予算が国会で成立した。 *The Diet finalized (or passed) next year's budget.*

seiryō ínryō 清涼飲料 *refreshments*

séiryoku 勢力 *power; influence* ❖séiryoku kinkō 勢力均衡 *balance of power* ❖Sono seitō wa seiji séiryoku o nobáshite iru. その政党は政治勢力を伸ばしている。 *That political party is extending its sphere of influence.*

seisai 精彩；生彩 *vividness; brilliance* ❖seisai o hanátsu 精彩を放つ *be vivid* ❖seisai o kaku 精彩を欠く *be lacking in brilliance* —— **seisai na** 精彩な *vivid; brilliant*

seisaku 政策 *policy* ❖gaikō séisaku 外交政策 *foreign policy* ❖fukushi séisaku 福祉政策 *welfare policy*

seisámbutsu 生産物 *produce; products (agricultural / industrial / mining)*

seisan 生産 *product* ❖seisánhi 生産費 *cost of production* ——**seisan-suru** [*vt*] 生産する *produce*

seisan [na] 凄惨 (な) *gruesome* ❖seisan na kōkei 凄惨な光景 *a gruesome sight* ❖seisan o kiwaméru 凄惨を極める *too gruesome for words*

seisan-suru [*vt*] 精算する *total up; keep an accurate account; pay the difference on fare* ❖Norikoshi ryókin o seisan-shimáshita ka? 乗り越し料金を精算しましたか？ *Did you pay the extra fare?*

seiséi dōdō 正々堂々 *fair and square* ❖Káre wa ítsu dónna toki de mo seiséi dōdō to shita táido o tótte iru. 彼はいつどんな時でも正々堂々とした態度をとっている。 *No matter when or where, he always displays a fair and square attitude.*

seiseki 成績 *grade(s); achievement* ❖seisekihyō 成績表 *report card*

seishiki [no / na] 正式 (の／な) *formal* ❖Seishiki no kettei ga déru made happyō-dekimasén. 正式の決定が出るまで発表できません。 *We cannot make an announcement until a formal decision has been made.* ——**seishiki ni** 正式に *formally*

séishin 精神 *spirit; soul; psyche; mind* ❖seishin bunretsushō 精神分裂症 *schizophrenia* ❖seishin búnseki 精神分析 *psychoanalysis* ❖seishinbyō 精神病 *mental disease; psychosis; insanity* ❖seishin byōrígaku 精神病理学 *psychiatry* ⬥seishin chítai 精神遅滞 *mental retardation* ⬥seishin nénrei 精神年齢 *mental age* ⬥seishin rṓdō 精神労働 *mental work* ⬥seishin ryṓhō 精神療法 *psychotherapeutic treatment* ⬥seishínryoku 精神力 *spiritual strength* ⬥seishin sákuran 精神錯乱 *delirium* ⬥seishin séikatsu 精神生活 *spiritual life; mental life* ⬥seishin shúgi 精神主義 *spiritualism* ——**séishin [no]** 精神（の）*mental* ——**seishinteki [na]** 精神的（な）*spiritual*

seishinká'i 精神科医 *psychiatrist*

seishitsu 性質 *nature; disposition* ⬥yasashii seishitsu 優しい性質 *a gentle disposition* ⬥Mizu to abura wa seishitsu ga kotonátte iru. 水と油は性質が異なっている。 *Water and oil are of different nature.*

Séisho 聖書 *The Bible* ⬥Shin'yaku Séisho 新約聖書 *New Testament* ⬥Kyūyaku Séisho 旧約聖書 *Old Testament*

seishoku 生殖 *reproduction* ⬥seishókuki 生殖器 *reproductive organ(s); genitals* ⬥seishoku kínō 生殖機能 *reproductive function*

seishókusha 聖職者 *clergy; minister*

seishun 青春 *youth; the springtime of life* ⬥seishun jídai 青春時代 *period of youth; youthful years* ⬥seishúnki 青春期 *puberty*

seisṓken 成層圏 *stratosphere*

seitai 生体 *living body; organism* ⬥seitáigaku 生体学 *somatology* ⬥seitai káibō 生体解剖 *vivisection*

seitai 声帯 *vocal cords* ⬥seitai mósha 声帯模写 *vocal mimicry; ventriloquy*

seitai 生態 *mode of life; ecology* ⬥seitaikei 生態系 *an ecosystem* ⬥seitáigaku 生態学 *ecological science; bionomics*

seitetsujo 製鉄所 *ironworks*

séito 聖徒 *saint; apostle*

séito 生徒 *pupil; student; private student*

seitō 政党 *political party* ⬥seitō séiji 政党政治 *party politics* ⬥seitō náikaku 政党内閣 *a party cabinet*

seitō [na] 正当（な）*just; proper; legal; lawful* ⬥seitōka 正当化 *justification* ⬥seitō bṓei 正当防衛 *legitimate self-defense* ⬥seitō na kénri o shuchō-suru 正当な権利を主張する *insist on (one's) lawful rights* ——**seitō ni** 正当に *justly; rightfully; properly*

seiuchi セイウチ；海象 *walrus*

seiyaku 制約 *restriction; limitation* ⬥Kónkai no keiyaku kōshin dé wa árata na seiyaku ga kuwawátta. 今回の契約更新では新たな制約が加わった。 *New restrictions were added when the contract was renewed.* ——**seiyaku-suru** [vt] 制約する *restrict; limit*

seiyaku 誓約 *oath; a vow* ⬥seiyakusho 誓約書 *a (written) pledge* ——**seiyaku-suru** [vt] 誓約する *make a vow; pledge* ⬥Himitsu génshu o seiyaku-saserareta. 秘密厳守を誓約させられた。 *I was made to pledge strict secrecy.*

Séiyō 西洋 *the West; the Occident* ❸Seiyō búmmei 西洋文明 *Western civilization* ❸Seiyőjin 西洋人 *a Westerner; an Occidental* ❸Seiyō ryőri 西洋料理 *Western cooking*

seiyō 静養 *rest; recuperation* ――**seiyō-suru** [vi] 静養する *take a rest; rest and recuperate*

Seiyō négi 西洋葱 *leek*

seiza 正座 *sitting formally (J)* ――**seiza-suru** [vi] 正座する *sit Japanese style*

seiza 星座 *constellation*

seizen 生前 *before death; while alive; during (one's) lifetime* ❸Háha ga seizen-chū wa iroiro o-séwa ni narimáshita. 母が生前中はいろいろお世話になりました。*Thank you for all your kindnesses to my mother during her lifetime.*

seizō 製造 *manufacturing; production* ❸seizō kőgyō 製造工業 *manufacturing industry* ――**seizō-suru** [vt] 製造する *manufacture; produce; make*

seizon 生存 *existence* ――**seizon-suru** [vi] 生存する *exist; live; survive*

seizu 製図 *drafting; cartography* ❸seizukō 製図工 *draftsman*

sékai 世界 *world* ❸kodomo no sékai 子供の世界 *children's world* ❸yume no sékai 夢の世界 *dream world* ❸sekai gínkō 世界銀行 *world bank* ❸sekai héiwa 世界平和 *world peace* ❸sékai isshū ryókō 世界一周旅行 *round-the-world trip* ❸sekai kíroku 世界記録 *world record* ❸sekáishi 世界史 *world history* ――**sekaiteki [na]** 世界的（な）*global* ❸sekaiteki kanshínji 世界的関心事 *a global affair; a matter of global concern*

seken-bánashi 世間話 *small talk; gossip*

séki 席 *a seat* ❸jiyűseki 自由席 *unreserved seat* ❸shitéiseki 指定席 *reserved seat* ❸Kono séki aite imásu ka? この席空いていますか？*Is this seat occupied?*

sekí 咳 *a cough* ❸sekí ga déru 咳が出る *have a cough* ❸sekí o suru 咳をする *cough* ❸seki-bárai 咳払い *clearing (one's) throat* ❸seki-dome 咳止め *cough drops; cough medicine*

sekidō 赤道 *equator*

Sekijűji 赤十字 *Red Cross* ❸Nihón Sekijűjisha 日本赤十字社 *Japan Red Cross*

sekikóm·u [vi sekikománai; sekikónda] 咳込む *cough; have a coughing attack*

sekinin 責任 *responsibility; liability* ❸sekinínkan 責任感 *sense of responsibility* ❸sekinin o hatásu 責任を果たす *fulfill one's responsibility.*

sekiryō 寂寥 *loneliness; desolation* ❸sekiryőkan 寂寥感 *a feeling of loneliness*

sekitán 石炭 *coal*

sekitei 石庭 *rock garden*

sekitome·ru [*vt* sekitomenai; sekitometa] 塞き止める *dam; dam up*

sekitsui 脊椎 *backbone; spine*   ❅sekitsui dṓbutsu 脊椎動物 *a vertebrate*   ❅sekitsui sónshō 脊椎損傷 *a spinal injury*   ❅sekitsui shiatsu chiryṓsha 脊椎指圧治療者 *chiropractor*

sekiyu 石油 *gasoline; petroleum*   ❅sekiyu-gáisha 石油会社 *oil company*   ❅sekiyu kombináto 石油コンビナート *oil refinery*   ❅sekiyu kagaku kṓgyō 石油化学工業 *petrochemical industry*

sékkai 石灰 *lime (mineral)*

sékkai 切開 *surgical operation; section; incision* ——**sékkai-suru** [*vt*] 切開する *do surgery; operate on*   ❅Isha wa kámbu o mésu de sékkai-shita. 医者は患部をメスで切開した。 *The doctor cut away the diseased part with a scalpel.*

sekkaku 折角 *with much trouble; specially; on purpose; deliberately*   ❅Sekkaku no dóryoku ga muda ni nátta. 折角の努力が無駄になった。 *All my effort went to waste.*   ❅Sekkaku kíte kuretá no ni rúsu ni shite gomen. 折角来てくれたのに留守にしてごめん。 *I'm sorry I was out when you called.*

sekkei 設計 *a plan; a design* ——**sekkei-suru** [*vt*] 設計する *plan; design*   ❅Kono tatemóno wa Ráito ga sekkei-shita. この建物はライトが設計した。 *(Frank Lloyd) Wright designed this building.*

sekken 石鹸 *soap*   ❅sekkén-bako 石鹸箱 *soap dish*   ❅sekkén-sui 石鹸水 *liquid soap*   ❅sentaku sékken 洗濯石鹸 *laundry soap*

sekkin 接近 *proximity* ——**sekkin-suru** [*vi*] 接近する *approach; draw near*   ❅Ōgata taifū ga Kyūshū ni sekkin-shite iru. 大型台風が九州に接近している。 *A major typhoon is approaching Kyūshū.*

sekkyō 説教 *sermon; preaching; moral lecture* ——**sekkyō-suru** [*vt*] 説教する *preach; reprimind; lecture (to)*   ❅Mongen ni okurete watashi wa háha ni sekkyō-sareta. 門限に遅れて私は母に説教された。 *I was lectured to by my mother for getting home after my curfew.*

sekkyoku 積極 *positive; active*   ❅sekkyokusei 積極性 *positiveness*   ❅sekkyokúsaku 積極策 *positive policy* ——**sekkyokuteki[na]** 積極的（な） *aggressive; positive; active; constructive* ——**sekkyokuteki ni** 積極的に *aggressively; positively; actively*   ❅Nóriko-san wa jínsei o sekkyokuteki ni íkite iru. 教子さんは人生を積極的に生きている。 *Noriko lives her life positively (energetically).*

sekuhara セクハラ *sexual harrassment*

semá·i [*adj* sémaku nái; sémakatta] 狭い *(be) small; narrow*   ❅Nihon no ié wa semái. 日本の家は狭い。 *Japanese houses are small.*   ❅Semái dṓro o ốki na kuruma ga hashítte iru. 狭い道路を大きな車が走っている。 *Large cars run on the narrow streets.*

sembatsu 選抜 *selection; choice*   ❅sembatsu shíken 選抜試験 *multiple-choice exam*   ❅sembatsu chímu 選抜チーム *a select team* ——

sembatsu-suru [*vt*] 選抜する *select; pick out; choose* 🎇Watashi wa kaigai hakéndan no mémbā ni sembatsu-sareta. 私は海外派遣団のメンバーに選抜された。*I was chosen to be a member of the overseas mission.*

sembetsu 餞別 *a send-off; parting present*

semé·ru [*vt* seménai; sémeta] 責める *urge; press; censure; reproach* 🎇shippai o seméru 失敗を責める *censure (a person) for failure* 🎇otto no uwaki o seméru 夫の浮気を責める *charge (one's) husband with infidelity*

semé·ru [*vt* seménai; sémeta] 攻める *attack* 🎇teki o seméru 敵を攻める *attack the enemy*

sémete せめて *at most; at least; at the very least* 🎇Sémete mō ichido kánojo ni aitái. せめてもう一度彼女に会いたい。*I'd like to see her at least once more.*

semí 蝉 *cicada*

semmen 洗面 *washing (one's) face* 🎇semmendai 洗面台 *washbasin; sink* 🎇semménki 洗面器 *washbasin* 🎇semmenjo 洗面所 *washroom*

semmon 専門 *specialty; profession* 🎇semmonka 専門家 *specialist; technician* 🎇semmon búnya 専門分野 *academic major (field); specialty* 🎇semmon gákkō 専門学校 *professional school; (technical) college* 🎇Anáta no semmon wa nán desu ka? あなたの専門は何ですか？ *What is your profession (or specialty)?*

sempai 先輩 *(one's) superior; (one's) elder* 🎇Inoue-san wa daigaku no sempai désu. 井上さんは大学の先輩です。*Inoue was ahead of me at my university.*

sempúki 扇風機 *electric fan* 🎇sempúki o kakéru 扇風機をかける *turn on the electric fan* 🎇sempúki o tomeru 扇風機を止める *turn off the electric fan*

semushí 傴僂 *hunchback*

sén 線 *line; railway line; route* 🎇denwasen 電話線 *telephone line* 🎇heikōsen 平行線 *parallel line* 🎇kokusaisen 国際線 *international airline* 🎇sén o hiku 線を引く *draw a line*

sén 栓 *stopper; cork* 🎇sennúki 栓抜き *bottle opener* 🎇Wáin no sén o núite kudasái. ワインの栓を抜いて下さい。*Uncork the wine, please.*

sén 千 *thousand*

senaka 背中 *the back* 🎇senaka áwase ni 背中合わせに *back-to-back* 🎇Senaka ga itái. 背中が痛い。*My back hurts.*

sénchō 船長 *ship's captain*

senden 宣伝 *propaganda; publicity; advertisement* 🎇senden bira 宣伝ビラ *a handbill* 🎇senden pósutā 宣伝ポスター *advertising poster* ——**senden-suru** [*vt*] 宣伝する *publicize; advertise*

sengén 宣言 *declaration; proclamation* ——**sengén-suru** [*vt*] 宣言する

declare; proclaim; officially announce   ❊Daitṓryō wa shin-kémpō no kṓfu o sengén-shita. 大統領は新憲法の公布を宣言した。 *The president made an official announcement of the promulgation of a new constitution.*

sengetsu 先月 *last month*

sengo 戦後 *after the war; postwar*   ❊Sengo no fukkō wa susamajíi. 戦後の復興はすさまじい。 *The postwar recovery is phenomenal.*

sén'i 繊維 *textiles; fiber*   ❊sen'i kṓgyō 繊維工業 *textile industry*   ❊sen'i séihin 繊維製品 *textile goods*   ❊gōsei sén'i 合成繊維 *synthetic fiber*   ❊kagaku sén'i 化学繊維 *chemical fiber*   ❊shokumotsu sén'i 食物繊維 *plant fiber*   ❊tennen sén'i 天然繊維 *natural fiber*

sen'in 船員 *sailor; crew*

senjitsu 先日 *the other day*   ❊Senjitsu wa o-séwa ni narimáshita. 先日はお世話になりました。 *Thank you for your help the other day.*

senjō 戦場 *battlefield*

senjo 洗浄 *washing; cleaning* ——**senjō-suru** [*vt*] 洗浄する *wash; rinse*

senjutsu 戦術 *tactics*   ❊gyūho sénjutsu 牛歩戦術 *delaying tactics (lit: ox-pace tactics)*

senkō 専攻 *(academic) major* ——**senkō-suru** [*vt*] 専攻する *major in*

sénkō 線香 *incense*   ❊sénkō o tatéru 線香を立てる *burn incense*

senkoku 宣告 *declaration; verdict* ——**senkoku-suru** [*vt*] 宣告する *declare; pass sentence on; condemn*   ❊Íshi wa sono kanja ni gán o senkoku-shita. 医師はその患者に癌を宣告した。 *The doctor informed the patient she had cancer.*   ❊Saibánkan wa satsujin hánnin ni shikéi o senkoku-shita. 裁判官は殺人犯人に死刑を宣告した。 *The judge sentenced the defendant to death.*

senkyaku 船客 *(boat / ship) passenger*

sénkyo 選挙 *election*   ❊senkyóken 選挙権 *suffrage; right to vote*   ❊senkyonin 選挙人 *electorate; voter*   ❊senkyonin méibo 選挙人名簿 *a voting register*   ❊senkyóku 選挙区 *electoral district* ——**sénkyo-suru** [*vt*] 選挙する *vote for; elect*

senkyṓshi 宣教師 *missionary*

sennyū́kan 先入観 *preconception*   ❊Sennyū́kan ga hándan o ayamaraséru kotó mo áru. 先入観が判断を誤らせることもある。 *Sometimes preconceptions can cause a mistake in judgment.*

senrei 洗礼 *baptism (Chr)*   ❊senrei o hodokósu 洗礼を施す *baptize*   ❊senrei o ukéru 洗礼を受ける *be baptized*

senren 洗練 *polishing; refinement* ——**senren-suru** [*vt*] 洗練する *refine*   ❊Kono seihin no dezáin wa nánkai mo henkō-shite senren-sarete kíte iru. この製品のデザインは何回も変更して洗練されてきている。 *The design of this product has been refined through a number of alterations.*

senritsu 戦慄 *a thrill; a shiver; a shudder* ——**senritsuteki** [*na*] 戦慄的

（な）*shuddering; frightful* ——**senritsu-suru** [vi] 戦慄する *thrill; shiver; shudder*

sénro 線路 *railroad track*

senryō 占領 *occupation; possession* 🔹senryṓchi 占領地 *occupied territory* 🔹senryṓgun 占領軍 *occupation forces* ——**senryō-suru** [vt] 占領する *occupy (a country)*

senryō 染料 *dyes; dyestuffs* 🔹tennen sénryō 天然染料 *natural dye* 🔹kagaku sénryō 化学染料 *chemical dye*

senséi 先生 *teacher* 🔹gakkō no senséi 学校の先生 *school teacher* 🔹sūgaku no senséi 数学の先生 *math teacher*

senséijutsu 占星術 *astrology*

senséngetsu 先々月 *the month before last*

sénsha 戦車 *(military) tank*

senshi 戦死 *death in battle* ——**senshi-suru** [vi] 戦死する *die in war*

senshin 専心 *undivided attention* ——**senshin-suru** [vi] 専心する *devote (oneself) to* 🔹Musuko wa máinichi idenshi kénkyū ni senshin-shite iru. 息子は毎日、遺伝子研究に専心している。 *My son devotes every day to research on genetics.*

senshínkoku 先進国 *advanced country* 🔹senshínkoku to kōshínkoku 先進国と後進国 *advanced and developing countries*

senshitsu 船室 *stateroom; cabin*

senshoku 染色 *dyeing* ——**senshoku-suru** [vt] 染色する *dye*

senshokutai 染色体 *chromosome*

sénshu 選手 *athlete; player on a team* 🔹suiei sénshu 水泳選手 *swimmer* 🔹yakyū sénshu 野球選手 *baseball player*

sensō 戦争 *war; battle; hostilities* 🔹kokunai sénsō 国内戦争 *civil war* 🔹kyokuchi sénsō 局地戦争 *limited warfare* 🔹sekai sénsō 世界戦争 *world war* 🔹sensō hṓki 戦争放棄 *renunciation of war* 🔹sensō baishōkin 戦争賠償金 *war reparations* 🔹sensō no shūketsu 戦争の終結 *cessation of hostilities* ——**sensō-suru** [vi] 戦争する *make (wage) war; fight (with)*

sensu 扇子 *folding fan*

sensúifu 潜水夫 *diver*

sensuikan 潜水艦 *submarine*

sentaku 洗濯 *washing; laundry* 🔹sentakumono 洗濯物 *laundry* 🔹senták(u-)ki 洗濯機 *washing machine* 🔹sentaku-básami 洗濯挟み *clothespin* ——**sentaku-suru** [vt] 洗濯する *launder; do the washing*

sentaku 選択 *choice; option; selection* 🔹sentaku kámoku 選択課目 *elective course* 🔹sentakúken 選択権 *option; right to choose* 🔹Sentaku no yóchi wa mṓ nái. 選択の余地はもうない。 *There is no longer any room for choice.* ——**sentaku-suru** [vt] 選択する *choose; select; opt (for)* 🔹Watashítachi ni wa shokúgyō o jiyū ni sentaku-suru kénri ga arimásu. 私たちには職業を自由に選択する権利がありま

す。*We have the right to freely choose our occupation.*

sentei-básami 剪定鋏 *pruning shears*

sentō 先頭 *the lead; the head; the first* 8sentō ni tátsu 先頭に立つ *lead; go first* 8Amerika no sénshu ga rḗsu no sentō o kítta. アメリカの選手がレースの先頭を切った。*The American athlete took the lead in the race.*

sen'yō 専用 *exclusive (or private) use* 8kankéisha sen'yō no chūshajō 関係者専用の駐車場 *a parking lot for the exclusive use of related personnel* 8Hijōji sen'yō. 非常時専用。*For emergency use only.* ——**sen'yō-suru** [vt] 専用する *use exclusively; use privately*

senzai 洗剤 *detergent; cleaning material* 8gōsei sénzai 合成洗剤 *synthetic detergent*

sénzo 先祖 *ancestor*

seó·u [vt seowánai; seótta] 背負う *bear; carry (on the back); take on; shoulder* 8ryukkusákku o seóu リュックサックを背負う *carry a knapsack on one's back* 8Michiyo-san wa ano wakása de íkka o seótte iru. 美智代さんはあの若さで一家を背負っている *Michiyo, young as she is, is supporting a family.*

seppaku 切迫 *urgency; immediacy; threatening* ——**seppaku-suru** [vi] 切迫する *be imminent; draw near; be urgent* 8Nichi-Bei kánkei wa seppaku-shita jōsei ni nátte iru. 日米関係は切迫した情勢になっている。*Japanese-American relations have reached a state of urgency.* 8Shakkín hensai no kígen ga seppaku-shite iru. 借金返済の期限が切迫している。*The time limit for paying back the loan is near.*

serifu 台詞 *lines (in a play)* 8serifu o oboéru 台詞を覚える *learn one's lines (in a play)* 8serifu máwashi 台詞回し *theatrical elocution; histrionics*

serifuda 競り札 *trumps (in bridge)*

seríne 競り値 *a bid*

seriuri 競り売り *an auction*

séron 世論 *public opinion* 8seron chósa 世論調査 *opinion poll* 8Gyōsei káikaku o motoméru séron ga moriagátte iru. 行政改革を求める世論が盛り上がっている。*Public opinion calling for administrative reform is mounting.*

serotḗpu セロテープ *Scotch tape; cellophane tape*

sésse to せっせと *assiduously; diligently* 8Sésse to hataraki-nasái. せっせと働きなさい。*Work diligently.*

sésshi 摂氏；セ氏 *centigrade; Celsius*

sesshō 折衝 *negotiation* ——**sesshō-suru** [vi] 折衝する *negotiate with*

sesshoku 接触 *connection; contact* 8Denki no sesshoku ga warúi. 電気の接触が悪い。*The electrical connection is bad.*

sessuru [vi: irr sesshinai; sesshita] 接する *border on; touch; make contact with*

setchakú-zai 接着剤 *glue*

setomono 瀬戸物 *chinaware; porcelain; crockery; pottery*

Seto Náikai 瀬戸内海 *Inland Sea of Japan*

sétsu 説 *explanation; theory* ▫gakusetsu 学説 *theory; doctrine* ▫Nihongo no kígen ni tsúite íkutsu ka no sétsu ga áru. 日本語の起源についていくつかの説がある。 *There are a number of theories concerning the origin of the Japanese language.*

-setsu 〜節 *section; verse* ▫Dai ísshō no sánsetsu o yōyaku-shite kudasái. 第一章の三節を要約して下さい。 *Summarize section three of chapter one.*

sétsubi 設備 *equipment; conveniences* ▫bōka sétsubi 防火設備 *fire-prevention equipment* ▫kūchō sétsubi 空調設備 *air-conditioning unit* ▫onkyō sétsubi 音響設備 *sound equipment*

setsumei 説明 *explanation; exposition; interpretation* ——**setsumei-suru** [vt] 説明する *explain; expound; interpret* ▫Pākínson no hōsoku ni tsúite mótto kuwáshiku setsumei-shite kuremasén ka? パーキンソンの法則についてもっと詳しく説明してくれませんか？ *Would you explain Parkinson's Law in more detail?*

sétsuri 摂理 *providence; dispensation* ▫Kámi no sétsuri ni yotte... 神の摂理によって... *By the providence of God...*

setsuritsu 設立 *establishment; founding* ——**setsuritsu-suru** [vt] 設立する *establish; set up* ▫Musumé wa hōseki hambai-gáisha o setsuritsu-shita. 娘は宝石販売会社を設立した。 *My daughter established a jewelry marketing company.*

setsuyaku 節約 *economy; saving; conservation* ▫enérugī no setsuyaku エネルギーの節約 *energy conservation* ——**setsuyakuteki [na]** 節約的（な）*thrifty; economic* ——**setsuyaku-suru** [vt] 節約する *save; conserve; economize* ▫jikan o setsuyaku-suru 時間を節約する *conserve time* ▫ŕoryoku o setsuyaku-suru 労力を節約する *conserve effort*

setsuzoku 接続 *connection; joining* ▫setsuzokúeki 接続駅 *a railroad junction* ▫setsuzokúshi 接続詞 *conjunction; connective (Gram)* ——**setsuzoku-suru** [vi] 接続する *join; connect* ▫Kono dénsha wa Nágoya de shinkánsen ni setsuzoku-shimásu. この電車は名古屋で新幹線に接続します。 *This train connects with the bullet train at Nagoya.*

séttai 接待 *entertainment; reception* ▫settáihi 接待費 *entertainment expense* ▫settai-gákari 接待係 *receptionist* ——**séttai-suru** [vt] 接待する *entertain; welcome* ▫Watashi wa gaikoku kará no taisetsu na o-kyakusáma o séttai-surú no ga amari sukí de wa arimasén. 私は外国からの大切なお客様を接待するのはあまり好きではありません。 *I don't enjoy entertaining VIP's from abroad.*

settei 設定 *establishment; fixing; setting* ▫Sono SF sákka wa shinsaku shippitsu ni atari, jidai-séttei o nisén-júnen no Ōsaka to shita. そのSF作家は新作執筆にあたり、時代設定を2010年の大阪とした。 *The science fiction writer chose Osaka in the year 2010 as the setting for his new novel.* ——**settei-suru** [*vt*] 設定する　*establish; set up* ❽Reibō o jáku ni settei-shite kudasái. 冷房を弱に設定して下さい。 *Set the air conditioner on low.*

settō 窃盗 *theft* ❽settōhan 窃盗犯 *larceny* ❽Yūjin wa nándo mo settō o hataraita. 友人は何度も窃盗を働いた。 *A friend of mine has committed theft several times.*

settoku 説得 *persuasion* ❽settokúryoku 説得力 *power of persuasion* ——**settoku-suru** [*vt*] 説得する　*persuade*

sewá o suru 世話をする　*assist; aid; serve; look after; care for* ❽Káre wa máinichi bonsai no sewá o shite imásu. 彼は毎日盆栽の世話をしています。 *He tends to his bonsai every day.* ❽Ane wa kodomo no sewá o surú no ga sukí desu. 姉は子供の世話をするのが好きです。 *My older sister likes looking after children.*

[o-]shábéri お喋り *chit-chat; talk; a talkative person* ——**o-shábéri-suru** [*vi*] お喋りする　*talk; chat; gab; prattle* ❽Séito wa senséi no hanashí o kikazu ni o-shábéri bákari shite iru. 生徒は先生の話を聞かずにお喋りばかりしている。 *The students are always talking to each other; they don't listen to the teacher.*

shabér·u [*vt*] shaberánai; shabétta] 喋る *talk; chat*

shabon-dama シャボン玉 *bubble; soap bubble*

shabur·u [*vt* shaburanai; shabutta] しゃぶる *suck on*

shachō 社長 *company head; boss; president*

shadan hójin 社団法人 *corporate juridical person; corporation*

shagam·u [*vi* shagamanai; shaganda] しゃがむ *squat; sit on (one's) heels* ❽Sono rōjin wa ítsu made mo kokage ni shagande ita. その老人はいつまでも木陰にしゃがんでいた。 *The old man sat on his haunches in the shade of a tree for hours.*

sháin 社員 *company employee; staff member*

Shaka 釈迦 *Buddha; S(h)akyamuni*

shákai 社会 *society; the world* ❽shakai fúkki 社会復帰 *(social) rehabilitation* ❽shakai fúkushi 社会福祉 *social welfare* ❽shakáigaku 社会学 *sociology* ❽shakai hóken 社会保険 *social insurance* ❽shakai hóshō 社会保障 *social security* ❽shakai kágaku 社会科学 *social science* ❽shakáijin 社会人 *a full-fledged member of society* ❽shakai móndai 社会問題 *social issue* ❽shakai shúgi 社会主義 *socialism* ❽shakai shugísha 社会主義者 *socialist* ❽Shakaitō 社会党 *Socialist Party* ❽kyōdō shákai 共同社会 *a community*

shakkín 借金 *debt; borrowings; loan* ❽Shakkín wa mố kaeshimáshita ka? 借金はもう返しましたか？ *Have you already paid back the loan?* ❽Máda shakkín ga nokótte iru. まだ借金が残っている。 *I still have* *some debts.* ——**shakkín-suru** [*vi*] 借金する *be in debt; owe*

shákkuri しゃっくり *hiccups; hiccough* ❧Shákkuri ga déte iru. しゃっくりが出ている。 *I have the hiccups.*

shakō 社交 *social intercourse* ❧shakō-gírai no 社交嫌いの *antisocial* ——**shakōteki** [na] 社交的（な）*social; sociable* ❧Shújin wa shakōteki désu. 主人は社交的です。 *My husband is (very) sociable.*

shaku 癪 *a fit; an annoyance* ❧shaku ni sawaru 癪にさわる *be irritating; be provoking*

shákudo 尺度 *measurement; scale; gauge; yardstick* ❧shákudo o hakáru 尺度を計る *measure* ❧shákudo o meikaku ni suru 尺度を明確にする *make clear what yardstick is (to be) used*

shakushi 杓子 *a ladle; dipper* ❧shakushi jógi 杓子定規 *formalism; a hard-and-fast rule.*

Shákuson 釈尊 *Shakyamuni (Buddha)*

shakuya; shakka 借家 *rented house* ❧shakkanin 借家人 *tenant*

shámen 斜面 *a slope*

share 洒落 *pun; play on words* ❧share o iu 洒落を言う *pun; make a play on words*

sharei 謝礼 *gratuity; honorarium; a thank-you gift*

share·ru [*vi* sharenai; shareta] 洒落る *get dressed up; dress stylishly* ——**shareta** 洒落た *swanky; stylish; chic; tasteful* ❧shareta ié 洒落た家 *a swanky (or plush) house* ❧shareta dóresu 洒落たドレス *a stylish (or chic) dress*

sharyō 車輛 *vehicles; cars; rolling stock*

shasatsu 射殺 *fatal shooting* ——**shasatsu-suru** [*vt*] 射殺する *shoot to death*

shasei 写生 *sketching; a sketch* ——**shasei-suru** [*vt*] 写生する *sketch; draw*

shasetsu 社説 *editorial*

shashin 写真 *photograph* ❧shashin sátsuei 写真撮影 *photography* ❧shashin fúkusha 写真複写 *photocopy*

shashō 車掌 *(train) conductor*

shataku 社宅 *company housing*

shí 四 *four (the numeral)*

shí 死 *death*

Shī! しっ！；シイツ。 *Hush!*

shi し *and* [*connective between sentences*] ❧Háwai wa kikō mo íi shi, késhiki mo íi shi, úmi mo kírei da. ハワイは気候もいいし、景色もいいし、海もきれいだ。 *In Hawaii the climate is good, the scenery is good, and the ocean is beautiful.* <*masc*>

-shi ～氏 *Mr.; Mrs.; Ms.* <*formal*> ❧Tanaká-shi o go-shōkai-sasete itadakimásu. 田中氏をご紹介させて頂きます。 *Let me introduce Ms. Tanaka.* <*formal*>

-shi 市 *city* §Mitaka-shi 三鷹市 *Mitaka City*

shiagár·u [*vi* shiagaránai; shiagátta] 仕上がる *be completed*
  §Sentakumono ga shiagatta. 洗濯物が仕上がった。*The laundry's done.*

shiage 仕上げ *finish; finishing touch; completion* §arashíage 荒仕上げ
rough finish §Shiage wa banzen da wa. 仕上げは万全だわ。*The finishing touch is perfect.* <*fem*>

shiagé·ru [*vt* shiagénai; shiágeta] 仕上げる *finish; complete*

shiai 試合 *sports meet; match* §ténisu no shiai テニスの試合 *tennis match*

shian kábutsu シアン化物 *cyanide*

shiasátte 明々後日 *two days after tomorrow; three days from now*

shiawase 幸せ *fortune; happiness* ——**shiawase na** 幸せな *happy*

shibafu 芝生 *lawn; grass* §Shibafu ni hairánaide kudasái. 芝生に入らないで下さい。*Keep off the grass.*

shibai 芝居 *a play; drama* §Ano nakigoto mo aitsu no shibai da yó. あの泣き言もあいつの芝居だよ。*That crying of his is all an act.* <*masc*>

shibakarí 芝刈り *gathering (fire) wood; cutting grass* §shibakaríki 芝刈り機 *lawn mower*

shibáraku 暫く *a short time; awhile; (for) a period of time* §shibáraku shite 暫くして *after a while; for a while* §Shibáraku o-machi kudasái. 暫くお待ち下さい。*Wait a moment, please.* §Yá, shibáraku da né. やあ、暫くだね。*Hi! It's been awhile!* <*masc*>

shibár·u [*vt* shibáranai; shibátta] 縛る *bind; tie* §furushímbun o tabánete shibáru 古新聞を束ねて縛る *tie up old newspapers in bundles* §shukketsu kásho o himo de shibáru 出血個所を紐で縛る *tie a cord (tourniquet) at the point of bleeding* §jikan ni shibararéru 時間に縛られる *be bound by time*

shíbashiba しばしば *frequently* §Watashi wa kodomo no tóki, shíbashiba shikarareta monó desu. 私は子供の時、しばしば叱られたものです。*When I was a kid, I was scolded frequently.*

shibiré·ru [*vi* shibirénai; shibíreta] 痺れる *be numb; have (one's) circulation cut off; be paralyzed* §Seiza-shite ashí ga shibírete shimatta. 正座して足が痺れてしまった。*My legs have gone to sleep from sitting in (Japanese) formal posture.*

shibō 脂肪 *fat; grease; suet* §Shibō no torisugi wa kenkō ni yóku nái. 脂肪の摂り過ぎは健康に良くない。*It's not healthy to consume too much fat.*

shibō 志望 *a wish; a desire; an aspiration* §shibósha 志望者 *an applicant* —— **shibō-suru** [*vt*] *wish; desire*

shibō 死亡 *death* §shibō tódoke 死亡届け *death report* §shibō shōmeisho 死亡証明書 *death certificate* §shibō kíji 死亡記事

obituary ❧shibóritsu 死亡率 *mortality rate* ❧shibósha 死亡者 *fatalities; dead people; the deceased* ——**shibō-suru** [*vi*] 死亡する *die*

shibom·u [*vi* shibomanai; shibonda] 萎む；凋む *wither; deflate; fade* ❧haná ga shibomu 花が萎む *flowers wither* ❧fúsen ga shibomu 風船が萎む *a balloon deflates* ❧kibō ga shibomu 希望が萎む *hope fades*

shiboríki 絞り機 *wringer*

shibór·u [*vt* shiboránai; shibótta] 絞る *wring out; squeeze*

shibutó·i [*adj* shibutoku nái; shibútokatta] しぶとい *(be) tenacious; stubborn; strong-willed* ❧Shibutói yátsu da! しぶとい奴だ。*Man, he's stubborn!* <*masc*> ——**shibutóku** しぶとく *tenaciously; stubbornly; daringly* ❧Shibutóku ikíru kotó mo tokí ni wa taisetsu désu. しぶとく生きることも時には大切です。*There are times when it's important to live daringly.*

shichí 七；7 *seven (the numeral)*

Shichigatsú 七月 *July*

shichimenchō 七面鳥 *turkey*

shichíya 質屋 *pawnshop*

shichō 市長 *mayor*

shichōkaku 視聴覚 *audio-visual*

shída 羊歯 *fern*

-shídai 〜次第 *as soon as...; depending on...* ❧Ténki ni nari shídai, shuppatsu-shiyó 天気になり次第、出発しよう。*As soon as the weather clears, let's go.* ❧Seikō wa doryoku shídai desu. 成功は努力次第です。*Success depends on effort.*

shidai ni 次第に *eventually; gradually* ❧Ténki ga shidai ni kaifuku-shite kíta. 天気が次第に回復してきた。*The weather has gradually improved.*

shidō 指導 *guidance; leading* ❧shidóin 指導員 *instructor* ❧shidó-ryoku 指導力 *leadership ability* ❧shidósha 指導者 *leader* ——**shidō-suru** [*vt*] 指導する *guide; lead* ❧Tsúma wa kodomo ni suiei o shidō-shite iru. 妻は子供に水泳を指導している。*My wife is guiding children swimming.* (**or** *My wife is teaching children to swim.*)

shígai 市街 *street; city; town* ❧shigaisen 市街戦 *street fighting*

shigaisen 紫外線 *ultraviolet ray*

shigamitsúk·u [*vi* shigamitsukánai; shigamitsúita] しがみつく *hold fast to; cling to; hold onto* ❧dáijin no isu ni shigamitsúku 大臣の椅子にしがみつく *hold onto a cabinet post*

shígan 志願 *a desire; wish; volunteering* ❧shigansho 志願書 *application form* ——**shígan-suru** [*vt*] 志願する *desire; apply for; volunteer*

Shigatsú 四月 *April*

shigeki 刺激 *stimulus; incentive; excitement* ⧈Kono éiga wa shigeki ga tsuyói. この映画は刺激が強い。*This movie is filled with excitement.* ——**shigeki-suru** [*vt*] 刺激する *stimulate; provide incentive*

shígen 資源 *resources; capital* ⧈chika shígen 地下資源 *underground resources* ⧈tennen shígen 天然資源 *natural resources* ⧈jinteki shígen 人的資源 *human resources* ⧈shakai shígen 社会資源 *social resources*

shigér·u [*vi* shigeránai; shigétta] 茂る；繁る *be dense; grow thickly* ⧈Akichi ní wa zassō ga shigétte iru. 空き地には雑草が茂っている。*Weeds are thick on the vacant lot.*

shígoku 至極 *very; quite; exceedingly* ⧈méiwaku shigoku 迷惑至極 *too much of a nuisance* ⧈zannén shigoku 残念至極 *too bad* ⧈Shígoku omoshirói. 至極面白い。*It's very interesting.*

shigósen 子午線 *meridian; prime meridian*

shigoto 仕事 *work; task; job; occupation* ⧈shigoto o sagasu 仕事を探す *look for a job* ⧈shigotoba 仕事場 *workplace; workshop* ⧈Anáta no shigoto wa nán desu ka? あなたの仕事は何ですか？*What is your occupation?* ⧈Abe-san wa shigoto de Sapporo ni imásu. 阿部さんは仕事で札幌にいます。*Mr. Abe is in Sapporo on business.*

shíhai 支配 *management; control* ⧈shiháinin 支配人 *manager* ⧈shihai káikyū 支配階級 *the ruling class* ⧈shiháisha 支配者 *ruler* ——**shíhai-suru** [*vt*] 支配する *manage; rule; control* ⧈Sono kuní wa gunji séiken ga shíhai-shite imásu. その国は軍事政権が支配しています。*That country is ruled by a military regime.*

shihan gákkō 師範学校 *school for training teachers; normal school*

shiharai 支払い *payment* ⧈shiharáibi 支払い日 *payment due date* ⧈Shiharai wa genkín de o-negai shimásu. 支払いは現金でお願いします。*Please make your payment in cash.*

shihará·u [*vt* shiharawánai; shiharátta] 支払う *pay (a bill)*

shihatsu 始発 *the first departure* ⧈shihatsú eki 始発駅 *the starting station* ⧈shihatsu dénsha 始発電車 *the first train*

shihon 資本 *capital; capital resource; a fund* ⧈shihonka 資本家 *a capitalist; financier* ⧈shihonkin 資本金 *capital* ⧈shihon shúgi 資本主義 *capitalism* ⧈shihon shugísha 資本主義者 *capitalist* ⧈shihon shugi kókka 資本主義国家 *a capitalist country* ⧈shihon tōshi 資本投資 *capital investment*

shíika 詩歌 *poetry*

shíite 強いて *by force; forcibly* ⧈shíite iwasete moraéba... 強いて言わせてもらえば... *If I'm forced to say...* ⧈shíite ikaseru 強いて行かせる *force (someone) to go*

shíji 指示 *instructions; directions* ⧈Watashi no shíji ni shitagatte kudasái. 私の指示に従って下さい。*Follow my directions.* ——**shíji-suru** [*vt*] 指示する *instruct; give directions*

shijin 詩人 *poet*

shijō 市場 *market* §shijō chōsa 市場調査 *marketing research*

shijū 始終 *from beginning to end; all the time* §Uchi no kodomo wa shíjū asonde iru. 家の子供は始終遊んでいる。*My child plays all the time.*

shika 鹿 *deer*

shíka 歯科 *dental department*

-shika [nai] ～しか（ない）*only; nothing but* [with neg] §Kono karē ní wa yasai shika háitte inai. このカレーには野菜しか入っていない。*There are only vegetables in this curry.*

shikaeshi 仕返し *revenge; retaliation* §Bōryoku-dan kará no shikaeshi ga kowái. 暴力団からの仕返しが恐い。*Retaliation from gangster groups is frightening.* ——**shikaeshi-suru** [vi] 仕返しする *take revenge*

shikai 司会 *chairmanship* §shikáisha 司会者 *chairperson; the chair; emcee* §Watashi wa yūjin no kekkónshiki no shikai o tanomáreta. 私は友人の結婚式の司会を頼まれた。*I was asked to be emcee at my friend's wedding.* ——**shikai-suru** [vt] 司会する *chair a meeting; preside; officiate* §Sawázaki-san wa sono shimpojíumu o shikai-suru kotó ni nátta. 沢崎さんはそのシンポジウムを司会することになった。*Mr. Sawazaki is to chair the symposium.*

shika ígaku 歯科医学 *dentistry*

shikaku 資格 *license; certification; qualification; eligibility* §shikaku shōmeisho 資格証明書 *a certificate* §bengóshi no shikaku 弁護士の資格 *a lawyer's license; certification to practice law*

shikaku 視覚 *eyesight; vision*

shikakú [no] 四角（の）*square*

shikakú·i [adj shikákuku nái; shikákukatta] 四角い *(be) square*

shikamettsura しかめっ面 *a frown; a scowl* §Kánai wa késa kara shikamettsura o shite iru. Náni o okótte irú no darō. 家内は今朝からしかめっ面をしている。何を怒っているのだろう？*My wife has had a scowl on her face since this morning. I wonder what she's mad about?*

shikámo しかも *moreover; besides* §Yamamoto-san wa sōmei de shikámo bíjin desu. 山本さんは聡明でしかも美人です。*Ms. Yamamoto is intelligent; moreover, she's beautiful.*

shikar·u [vt shikaranai; shikatta] 叱る *scold; reprimand; lecture (at)* §Oyá wa yóku kodomo o shikaru. 親はよく子供を叱る。*Parents often scold their children.*

shikáshi 然し *but; however* §Yoshínaga-kun wa totemo shigoto ga hayái. Shikáshi zatsu da. 吉永君は仕事が早い。然し雑だ。*Mr. Yoshinaga works fast, but he's sloppy.* <masc>

shikata 仕方 *way of doing* §Uchi no ko wa áisatsu no shikata o shirimasén. 家の子は挨拶の仕方を知りません。 *My child doesn't know how to greet people.* ——**shikata ga nái** 仕方がない *there's no help for it* 🔹Kyṓ wa sámukute shikata ga nái. 今日は寒くて仕方がない。 *It's so cold today I don't know what to do.* ——**shikata náku** 仕方なく *without choice; helplessly* 🔹O-kane ga nái no de shikata náku ichinichi uchi ni ita. お金がないので仕方なく一日家にいた。 *I didn't have any money so I had no choice but to stay home all day.*

shikéi 死刑 *capital punishment; death penalty* 🔹shikei séido 死刑制度 *capital punishment system* 🔹shikéi haishíron 死刑廃止論 *argument for abolishing the death penalty* 🔹shikei hánketsu 死刑判決 *death sentence*

shikén 試験 *examination; test* 🔹shikén o suru 試験をする *give a test; examine* 🔹shikén o ukéru 試験を受ける *take a test* 🔹shiken bénkyō 試験勉強 *studying for an exam* 🔹nyūgaku shiken 入学試験 *entrance exam* 🔹chūkan shíken 中間試験 *mid-term exam* 🔹kimatsu shíken 期末試験 *final exam* ——**shikenteki [na]** 試験的（な） *pilot; test* ——**shikén-suru** [vt] 試験する *examine; give a test*

shikenkan 試験管 *test tube* 🔹shikenkan bébī 試験管ベビー *test-tube baby*

shike·ru [vi shikenai; shiketa] 時化る *be stormy; be choppy* 🔹Taifū de úmi ga shikete iru. 台風で海が時化ている。 *Because of the typhoon the ocean is choppy.*

shiké·ru [vi shikénai; shíketa] 湿気る *get soggy; lose crispness (from absorbing moisture in the air)*

shikí 式 *ceremony; function; observance* 🔹shikijō 式場 *ceremony site* 🔹kaikáishiki 開会式 *opening ceremony* 🔹heikáishiki 閉会式 *closing ceremony* 🔹sotsugyṓshiki 卒業式 *graduation ceremony* 🔹jomakúshiki 除幕式 *unveiling ceremony*

shikí 指揮 *leading; directing; conducting; command* 🔹shikíkan 指揮官 *a commander* 🔹shikísha 指揮者 *conductor (of an orchestra)* 🔹shikíbō 指揮棒 *a baton* 🔹shikí o tóru 指揮を執る *take the lead* ——**shikí-suru** [vt] 指揮する *lead; direct; conduct; command*

-shiki ～式 *in the style of; fashion* 🔹Nihon-shiki ni suwaru kotó ga dekimásu ka? 日本式に座ることができますか？ *Can you sit Japanese style?*

shikibúton 敷布団 *under-futon; mattress (J)*

shikii 敷居 *threshold; door sill* 🔹Shikii ga takái. 敷居が高い。 *I wouldn't feel comfortable there. (lit: The threshold is too high.) <set phrase>*

shikimono 敷物 *carpet; rug; matting*

shikín 資金 *capital; funds; a fund* 🔹shikin kámpa 資金カンパ *fund-raising campaign* 🔹seiji shíkin 政治資金 *political campaign funds* 🔹kekkon shíkin 結婚資金 *a wedding fund (money set aside for* *wedding expenses)* §shikin-guri 資金繰り *capital management*

shikiri [ni] 頻り（に） *frequently; repeatedly; often*

shikkaku 失格 *disqualification* §Nomura senséi wa kyṓshi to shite shikkaku desu 野村先生は教師として失格です。 *Nomura is not qualified to be a teacher.* ——**shikkaku-suru** [*vi*] 失格する *be disqualified (for); be eliminated (from); be not qualified (for)*

shikkári [to] しっかり（と） *secure; steady; strongly; substantially* §Shikkári benkyō shinasái. しっかり勉強しなさい。 *Study good and hard.* §Shikkári to kagí o káketa. しっかりと鍵をかけた。 *I locked it securely.* ——**shikkári-suru** [*vi*] しっかりする *be solid; sturdy; stable* §Wakabáyashi-san wa shikkári-shite iru. 若林さんはしっかりしている。 *Ms. Wakabayashi is stable.* ——**shikkári-shita** しっかりした *solid; sturdy; stable*

shikke; shikki 湿気 *humidity; moisture* §Nihon no natsú wa shikke ga ṓi. 日本の夏は湿気が多い。 *In Japan, summers are high in humidity.*

[o-]shíkko （お）しっこ *pee; urine* ——**o-shíkko-suru** [*vi*] おしっこする *pee; pass urine*

shikkō 執行 *execution; performance; enforcement* §shikkō yṻyo 執行猶予 *postponement of execution (of a decision)* §shikkō kíkan 執行機関 *executive agency; executive department* ——**shikkō-suru** [*vt*] 執行する *execute; carry out; enforce* §shikei o shikkō-suru 死刑を執行する *carry out a death sentence*

shikkui 漆喰 *plaster* §shikkuí kabe 漆喰壁 *a plaster wall*

shikō 思考 *thinking* §shikṓryoku 思考力 *cognitive ability* ——**shikō-suru** [*vt*] 思考する *think; consider; conceive*

shikō sákugo 試行錯誤 *trial and error*

shik·u [*vt* shikanai; shiita] 敷く *spread; lay (out)* §tatami ni kā̃petto o shiku 畳にカーペットを敷く *spread a carpet on the tatami floor*

shikujír·u [*vt* shikujiránai; shikujítta] しくじる *fail at; fail to do*

shíkushiku [to] しくしく（と） *sharp abdominal pains; sobbing* §Onaka ga shíkushiku to itái. お腹がしくしくと痛い。 *I'm having sharp stomach pains* §Kodomo ga shikúshiku naite imásu. 子供がしくしく泣いています。 *The child is sobbing.*

shíkyo-suru [*vi*] 死去する *die*

shikyū 子宮 *uterus; womb* §shikyūnai hiníngu 子宮内避妊具 *intrauterine contraceptive device*

shikyū [no] 至急（の） *pressing; urgent* ——**shikyū ni** 至急に *urgently; right away* §Shikyū kyōmuka ni go-renraku kudasái. 至急、教務課にご連絡下さい。 *Contact the educational affairs department right away, please.*

shimá 島 *island* §shimaguni kónjō 島国根性 *insularity (lit: island country complex)*

shimá 縞 *stripe* §shimamóyō 縞模様 *striped pattern* §shimauma 縞

馬 *zebra*

shímai 姉妹 *sisters*   ❀kyódai shímai 兄弟姉妹 *brothers and sisters*   ❀shimaihin 姉妹品 *a related product*   ❀shimai-gáisha 姉妹会社 *an affiliated company*   ❀shimai tóshi 姉妹都市 *sister city*

shimár·u [*vi* shimaránai; shimátta] 閉まる *be shut; closed*   ❀To ga shimátte iru. 戸が閉まっている。*The door is closed.*

shimár·u [*vi* shimaránai; shimátta] 締まる *be firm; be solid; be tight*   ❀Néji ga shimátte ugokánai. ネジが締まって動かない。*The screw is frozen; it won't budge.*

shímatsu 始末 *result; the state of things; settlement; handling*   ❀shimatsusho 始末書 *a written explanation*   ❀shímatsu o tsukéru 始末をつける *finish off; wind up (one's) affairs*   ❀shímatsu ga warúi 始末が悪い *hard to deal with*   ❀shímatsu ni oenai 始末に負えない *be out of control; out of hand*

shimátta! しまった。*Drat it!; I've done it now!; Oops!*   ❀Shimátta! Kí o sáshita mama, kuruma no dóa ni kagí o kákete shimatta. しまった！キーを挿したまま、車のドアに鍵をかけてしまった。*I've done it now! I locked the car door with the key inside.*

shima·u [*vt* shimawanai; shimatta] 仕舞う *put away; store; finish*   ❀Kyó no shigoto o shimai ni suru. 今日の仕事を仕舞いにする。*I'm through with today's work.*   ❀Tsukatta dōgu o shimatte okó. 使った道具を仕舞っておこう。*Put away the tools you used.*

[-te] shima·u [*vb aux*] （～て）しまう *finish off; accidentally (do); irrevocably (do)*   ❀Tómasu-san wa Amerika ni káette shimaimáshita. トーマスさんはアメリカに帰ってしまいました。*Mr. Thomas returned to America for good.*

shímbō 辛抱 *perseverance; endurance; persistence; patience* —— **shímbō-suru** [*vt*] 辛抱する *persevere; endure; persist; be patient*

shimboku 親睦 *fellowship; friendship*   ❀shimbokúkai 親睦会 *fellowship meeting; party; mixer*   ❀shimboku o hakáru 親睦を図る *cultivate friendship*

shimbun 新聞 *newspaper*   ❀shimbun kísha 新聞記者 *newspaper reporter*   ❀shimbúnsha 新聞社 *newspaper company*

shímbutsu 神仏 *gods and buddhas*

shimégu 締め具 *ski binding*

shiméi 使命 *mission; calling; motivation*   ❀shiméikan 使命感 *a sense of mission; a calling*   ❀shímei o hatásu 使命を果たす *fulfill (one's) mission*   ❀shímei o obíru 使命を帯びる *be charged with a mission*

shimei 指名 *designation; nomination; appointment*   ❀shimei o ukéru 指名を受ける *receive an appointment* —— **shimei-suru** [*vt*] 指名する *designate; name; nominate*   ❀Watashi wa káigi no shikai ni shimei-sareta. 私は会議の司会に指名された。*I was designated chairperson for the meeting.*

shimekiri 締め切り *deadline* §Genkō no shimekiri ga semátte iru. 原稿の締め切りが迫っている。*The deadline for the manuscript is close at hand.*

shimekir·u [*vt* shimekiranai; shimekitta] 締め切る *close; shut (up / down)*

shímen 紙面 *(news) space* §Sono áidoru no kekkonshiki ga shimbun no shímen o nigiwásete iru. そのアイドルの結婚式が新聞の紙面を賑わせている。*Articles concerning that pop star's wedding are monopolizing newspaper space.*

shimeppó·i [*adj* shimeppóku nái; shimeppókatta] 湿っぽい *(be) moist; damp* §Futon ga shimeppói. 布団が湿っぽい。*The futon is damp.*

shimé·ru [*vt* shiménai; shímeta] 閉める *close; shut* §mádo o shímeru 窓を閉める *shut the window*

shimé·ru [*vt* shiménai; shímeta] 締める *fasten; bind; tie (up)* §Anzen-béruto o shímete kudasái. 安全ベルトを締めて下さい。*Fasten your seat belt, please.*

shimé·ru [*vt* shiménai; shímeta] 絞める *choke; throttle* §kubi o shiméru 首を絞める *strangle*

shimer·u [*vi* shimeranai; shimetta] 湿る *be damp; wet; moist* §shimetta fukín 湿った布巾 *a damp cloth*

shimés·u [*vt* shimesánai; shiméshita] 示す *show; demonstrate; denote* §hōkō o shimésu 方向を示す *show the direction* §mohan o shimésu 模範を示す *demonstrate* §séii o shimésu 誠意を示す *show sincerity*

shimetsu-suru [*vi*] 死滅する *die out; become extinct*

shimí 染み *spot; stain; blot* §shiminuki 染み抜き *spot remover* §inku no shimí インクの染み *an ink blot*

shimikomasé·ru [*vt* shimikomasénai; shimikómaseta] 染み込ませる *saturate (with)*

shimikóm·u [*vi* shimikómanai; shimikónda] 染み込む *permeate; infiltrate* §shōyúaji de shimikómu 醤油味が染み込む *be permeated with the taste of soy sauce*

shímin 市民 *citizen (of a city)* §shimín-ken 市民権 *citizenship*

shimi·ru [*vi* shiminai; shimita] 染みる *stain* §Shátsu ni inku ga shimite shimatta. シャツにインクが染みてしまった。*Ink stained my shirt.*

shimi·ru [*vi* shiminai; shimita] 凍みる *penetrate; sink into* §mi ni shimiru 身に凍みる *penetrate to the bone* §Há ga hírihiri shimimásu. 歯がひりひり凍みます。*I have a throbbing pain in my tooth.* §Kono kusuri wa sukóshi shimirú kamo shirenai. この薬は少し凍みるかも知れない。*This medicine may sting a bit.*

shimó 霜 *frost* §shimoyake 霜焼け *frostbite*

shimon 指紋 *fingerprint* §shimon ga tsúku 指紋が付く *leave fingerprints* §shimon o tóru 指紋を採る *take fingerprints*

shimpai 心配 *anxiety; worry; concern* §Háha no byōki ga shimpai dá wa. 母の病気が心配だわ。*I'm worried about my mother's health.* *<fem>* ——**shimpai-suru** [*vt*] 心配する *be worried about; be anxious about* §Musuko no juken o shimpai-shite irú no. 息子の受験を心配しているの。*I'm anxious about my son's entrance exams.* *<fem>*

shímpi 神秘 *mystery* ——**shímpi no** 神秘の *mysterious* ——**shimpiteki [na]** 神秘的（な）*mysterious*

shímpo 進歩 *progress* §shimpo-shugísha 進歩主義者 *a progressive* §kagaku gíjutsu no shímpo 科学技術の進歩 *progress in science and technology* ——**shimpoteki [na]** 進歩的（な）*progressive* §Kánai wa watashi yóri shimpoteki na kangaekata o mótte iru. 家内は私より進歩的な考え方をもっている。*My wife has more progressive ideas than I.* ——**shímpo-suru** [*vi*] 進歩する *make progress; improve* §Póru-san no Nihongo wa shímpo-shite iru. ポールさんの日本語は進歩している。*Paul's Japanese is improving.*

shímpu 神父 *priest (Cath)*

shín 芯 *wick; core* §rōsoku no shín ろうそくの芯 *candlewick* §ringo no shín りんごの芯 *apple core*

shinagire 品切れ *out of stock* §Shinséihin wa súde ni shinagire ni narimáshita. 新製品は既に品切れになりました。*The new product has already sold out.*

shínai 市内 *within the city limits* §Shínai ni wa meisho ga takusan arimásu. 市内には名所が沢山あります。*There are many famous sites in the city.*

shin'ai [na/no] 親愛（な／の）*affection; love; dear* §shin'ai no jō 親愛の情 *an expression of affection*

shinamono 品物 *merchandise; wares; goods*

shináyaka [na] しなやか（な）*limber; limp; flexible; pliable; graceful* §shináyaka na eda しなやかな枝 *a flexible branch* ——**shináyaka ni** しなやかに *flexibly; pliantly; lithely; gracefully*

shinchintáisha 新陳代謝 *metabolism*

shinchō 身長 *stature; height* §Shinchō wa dono kurai arimásu ka? 身長はどのくらいありますか? *How tall are you?*

shinchō 慎重 *caution; prudence; discretion* §shinchō o kisúru 慎重を期する *exercise caution* ——**shinchō na** 慎重な *cautious; prudent; careful; discreet; deliberate; serious* §shinchō na táido 慎重な態度 *a cautious attitude.* ——**shinchō ni** 慎重に *carefully; gingerly* §Gokai-sarenai yố ni shinchō ni kotaemáshita. 誤解されないように慎重に答えました。*I answered carefully so as not to be misunderstood.*

shinchū 真鍮 *brass*

shinchúgun 進駐軍 *occupation forces*

shindáisha 寝台車 *sleeping car*

shindan 診断 *diagnosis* §shindansho 診断書 *medical certificate* §Íshi wa sono kanja ni gán no shindan o kudashita. 医師はその患者に癌の診断を下した。 *The doctor rendered a diagnosis of cancer for that patient.* ——**shindan-suru** [vt] 診断する *diagnose*

shindénzu 心電図 *cardiogram* §shindenzukei 心電図計 *cardiograph*

shíndo 進度 *progress* §gakushū no shíndo wa dő deshō ka? 学習の進度はどうでしょうか? *How's your progress in school?*

shíndo 震度 *seismic scale; seismic intensity* §shíndo nána no gekishin 震度七の激震 *a severe earthquake of seven on the seismic scale*

shindō 振動 *tremor; vibration; oscillation*

shingai 侵害 *violation; trespassing; encroachment* §jinken shíngai 人権侵害 *a violation of human rights* §puráibashí no shingai プライバシーの侵害 *an encroachment on (one's) privacy*

shingaku 神学 *theology* §shingákkō 神学校 *theological school; seminary* ——**shingakuteki na** 神学的な *theological*

Shingeki 新劇 *the New Theater; modern theater*

shingénchi 震源地 *seismic center; epicenter; earthquake center*

shíngi 審議 *deliberations; discussion* §shíngi o kasaneru 審議を重ねる *continue discussion* ——**shíngi-suru** [vt] 審議する *deliberate; consider; discuss*

shingō 信号 *signal; traffic signal* §shingőki 信号機 *traffic signal; traffic light* §tebata shíngō 手旗信号 *semaphore*

shíngu 寝具 *bedding*

shinimono-gúrui de 死物狂いで *desperately* §Másako wa rikongo, shinimono-gúrui de hataraite kodomo o sodátete iru. 正子は離婚後、死物狂いで働いて子供を育てている。 *Since her divorce, Masako has been working desperately to raise her children.*

shinin 死人 *dead person; the dead* §Shinin ni kuchi nashi. 死人に口なし。 *The dead have no mouths (Dead men tell no tales).* <set phrase>

shínjin 信心 *belief; faith* ——**shínjin-suru** [vt] 信心する *believe*

shinjí•ru [vt shinjínai; shínjita] *believe* §Anáta wa kámi no sonzai o shínjite imásu ka? あなたは神の存在を信じていますか? *Do you believe in the existence of God?* ——**shinjirarénai** 信じられない *incredible; unbelievable* §Hísako-san ga sonna kotó o surú nante shinjirarénai! 寿子さんがそんなことをするなんて信じられない。 *It's unbelievable that Hisako would do a thing like that!*

shínjitsu 真実 *truth* ——**shínjitsu no** 真実の *truthful*

shinju 真珠 *pearl*

shínka 進化 *evolution* §shinkáron 進化論 *theory of evolution* ——**shínka-suru** [vi] 進化する *evolve* §Ningen wa sáru kara shínka-shita tte hontō kashira? 人間って猿から進化したって本当かしら。 *Is it true that humans evolved from monkeys?* <fem>

shinkánsen 新幹線 *the bullet train*

shínkei 神経 *a nerve* §shinkéigaku 神経学 *neurology* §shinkeika 神経科 *department of neurology* §shinkei kéitō 神経系統 *nervous system* §shinkei súijaku 神経衰弱 *nervous breakdown* ——
shinkéishitsu [na] 神経質（な）*nervous; high-strung* §Watanabe-san wa ā míete mo totemo shinkéishitsu desu yo. 渡部さんはああ見えてもとても神経質ですよ。*Watanabe may not look it, but he has a very nervous temperament.*

shinken [na] 真剣（な）*earnest; serious* ——**shinken ni** 真剣に *seriously; earnestly*

[o-]shinko （お）新香 *pickles; pickled vegetables (J)*

shinkō 進行 *progress; advance; onward movement* ——**shinkō-suru** [vi/vt] 進行する *proceed; progress; advance* §Keikaku wa junchō ni shinkō-shite iru. 計画は順調に進行している。*The plan is proceeding well.*

shinkō 信仰 *belief; faith*

shinkoku [na] 深刻（な）*serious; grave; keen* §Otto wa shinkoku na kao o shinágara káette kita. 夫は深刻な顔をしながら帰ってきた。*My husband came home with a serious expression on his face.* ——
shinkokuka-suru [vi] 深刻化する *become serious; become worse* §Kokkai no yo-yátō tairitsu wa shinkokuka-shite iru. 国会の与野党対立は深刻化している。*The conflict between the government party and opposition parties is becoming serious.*

shinkon fúfu 新婚夫婦 *newlyweds*

shinkon ryókō 新婚旅行 *honeymoon*

shinkūkan 真空管 *vacuum tube*

shínnā シンナー *paint thinner* §shinnā chúdoku シンナー中毒 *addiction to paint thinner (fumes)* §shinnā ásobi シンナー遊び *paint thinner sniffing*

shín no 真の *actual; real; true* §shín no yūjō 真の友情 *true friendship*

shinnyū 侵入 *invasion; aggression* §fuhō shínnyū 不法侵入 *breaking and entry* ——**shinnyū-suru** [vi] 侵入する *break into; invade; trespass* §Keisatsu wa gérira no himitsu ájito ni shinnyū-shita. 警察はゲリラの秘密アジトに侵入した。*The police raided the guerrillas' secret hideout.*

shinób·u [vt shinobánai; shinónda] 忍ぶ *endure; bear; tolerate; hide* §tsurasa o jitto shinóbu 辛さをじっと忍ぶ *silently endure hardship* §monokage ni shinóbu 物影に忍ぶ *conceal oneself in the shadows*

shinóg·u [vt shinogánai; shinónda] 凌ぐ *endure; bear; stand; exceed; surpass; outstrip; avoid; take shelter from*

shinrai 信頼 *confidence; trust; faith in* §Shinrai o kachitorú no wa muzukashíi. 信頼を勝ち取るのは難しい。*To gain (someone's) confidence is difficult.* ——**shinrai-suru** [vt] 信頼する *put trust in; rely on* §Minná ga kantoku o shinrai-shite iru. みんなが監督を信頼

している。 *Everyone has faith in the director.*

shínri 真理 *truth; indisputable fact*

shinrígaku 心理学 *psychology* ⑧rinshō shinrígaku 臨床心理学 *clinical psychology* ⑧shinrigákusha 心理学者 *psychologist*

shinrō shímpu 新郎新婦 *bride and groom*

shinryaku 侵略 *invasion; aggression* ⑧shinryaku sénsō 侵略戦争 *a war of aggression* ⑧shinryakúsha 侵略者 *invader* —— **shinryakuteki [na]** 侵略的（な） *aggressive* ——**shinryaku-suru** [vt] 侵略する *invade; raid; conquer*

shinryốhō 鍼療法 *acupuncture*

shinryoku 新緑 *fresh verdure; new green leaves* ⑧Háru no júmoku wa shinryoku de mizumizushíi. 春の樹木は新緑でみずみずしい。 *The trees in spring look young and fresh with the new green leaves.*

shinryōsho; shinryōjo 診療所 *medical clinic*

shínsa 審査 *inspection; examination; judgment* ⑧shinsáin 審査員 *a judge (in a contest)* ⑧shinsa iínkai 審査委員会 *screening committee* ——**shínsa-suru** [vt] 審査する *examine; judge*

shinsatsu 診察 *medical examination* ⑧shinsatsúryō 診察料 *doctor's fee* ⑧shinsatsu o ukéru 診察を受ける *be examined by a doctor* —— **shinsatsu-suru** [vt] 診察する *examine (a patient)*

shinsei [na] 神聖（な） *divine; holy; sacred*

shinseisho 申請書 *(written) application*

shinsen [na] 新鮮（な） *fresh; new* ⑧shinsen na yasai 新鮮な野菜 *fresh vegetables*

shínsetsu 親切 *kindness; goodness; a favor* ——**shínsetsu na** 親切な *kind; kindhearted* ⑧Tonari no ókusan wa totemo shínsetsu desu. 隣の奥さんはとても親切です。 *The next-door lady is very kind.* —— **shínsetsu ni** 親切に *kindly; kindheartedly; obligingly* ⑧shínsetsu ni suru 親切にする *be kind (to); show kindness (to)*

shínshi 紳士 *gentleman*

shinshitsu 寝室 *bedroom*

shinshoku 侵食 *erosion; corrosion* ⑧shinshoku sáyō 侵食作用 *erosive action* ⑧Kono kaigan wa shinshoku ni yotte dékita. この海岸は侵食によってできた。 *This coast was formed by erosion.* ——**shinshoku-suru** [vt] 侵食する *erode; encroach upon; gain* ⑧ryódo o shinshoku-sareru 領土を侵食される *have (one's) territory encroached upon*

shinshutsu 進出 *an advance; a march* ——**shinshutsu-suru** [vi] 進出する *advance; go (into); branch (out)* ⑧Sono kaisha wa káigai ni shinshutsu-shite iru. その会社は海外に進出している。 *That company is branching out overseas.*

shíntai 身体 *body* ⑧shintai kénsa 身体検査 *medical check; physical examination* ⑧shintai shōgáisha 身体障害者 *physically handicapped* *person*

shíntai 神体 *god; the god-presence (Shinto)*

shíntai 進退 *advance or retreat; movement* ⑧shíntai kiwamáru 進退極まる *be in a dilemma; be up against it; be cornered*

shintaku 信託 *trust* ⑧shintaku gínkō 信託銀行 *a trust bank* ⑧shintaku tōchi 信託統治 *trusteeship*

Shíntō 神道 *Shinto (religion indigenous to Japan; lit: "The Way of the Gods")*

shintō 浸透 *osmosis; permeation* ——**shintō-suru** [vi] 浸透する *permeate; infiltrate* ⑧Kono kuní de wa máda minshu-shúgi ga jūbún shintō-shite inai. この国ではまだ民主主義が十分浸透していない。 *Democracy still hasn't completely permeated this country.*

shin·u [vi shinanai; shinda] 死ぬ *die; pass away*

shin'wa 神話 *myth* ⑧Girisha shín'wa ギリシャ神話 *Greek myth*

Shin'yaku Séisho 新約聖書 *New Testament*

shin'yō 信用 *trust; belief in; confidence in* ⑧shin'yō ga áru 信用がある *have confidence in* ⑧shin'yō kúmiai 信用組合 *credit union* ——**shin'yō-suru** [vt] 信用する *trust; place confidence in; believe in*

shin'yū 親友 *close friend*

shinzen 親善 *friendship; amity; goodwill; rapprochement* ⑧shinzen gáikō 親善外交 *goodwill diplomacy* ⑧shinzen táishi 親善大使 *goodwill ambassador* ⑧kokusai shínzen 国際親善 *international friendship* ⑧shinzen o hakáru 親善を図る *seek amity*

shinzō 心臓 *heart (Anat)* ⑧shinzōbyō 心臓病 *cardiac disease* ⑧shinzō hóssa 心臓発作 *heart attack* ⑧shinzō ishoku shújutsu 心臓移植手術 *heart transplant operation*

shió 塩 *salt* ⑧shióaji 塩味 *salty taste* ⑧shióire 塩入れ *saltshaker*

shió 潮 *tide; current* ⑧hikishio 引き潮 *low tide* ⑧michishio 満ち潮 *high tide* ⑧shió ga hiite iru 潮が引いている *the tide's out* ⑧Shió ga míchite iru. 潮が満ちている。 *The tide's coming in.*

shiokará·i [adj shiokáraku nái; shiokárakatta] 塩辛い *(be) salty* ⑧Kono tarakó wa shiokarái. この鱈子は塩辛い。 *This cod roe is (very) salty.*

shiókaze 潮風 *sea breeze*

shíon 紫苑 *aster*

shiore·ru [vi shiorenai; shioreta] 萎れる *wither; droop; wilt* ⑧shioreta hana 萎れた花 *a withered flower*

shiori 枝折; 栞 *bookmark*

shiosai 潮騒 *the sound of waves*

shippai 失敗 *failure* ⑧Shippai wa seikō no háha. 失敗は成功の母。 *Failure is the mother of success.* <set phrase> ——**shippai-suru** [vi] 失敗する *fail; abort*

shippó 尻尾 *tail*

shippōyaki 七宝焼 *cloisonné*

shirabé·ru [*vt* shirabénai; shirábeta] 調べる *examine; investigate; inspect* ❧kiroku o shirabéru 記録を調べる *examine records* ❧Denwa bángō o shirabeyó. 電話番号を調べよう。*I'll look up the phone number.*

shírafu 素面；白面 *sober (not drunk)*

shiragá 白髪 *gray hair*

shirakaba 白樺 *white birch*

shiraké·ru [*vi* shirakénai; shiráketa] 白ける *become uninteresting; lose it's pleasant atmosphere*

shirasagi 白鷺 *egret*

shirase 知らせ *a notice; message* ❧"Háha kitoku" no shirase ga todóita. 「母、危篤」の知らせが届いた。*I got a message saying, "Mother's condition serious."*

shirase·ru [*vt* shirasenai; shiraseta] 知らせる *notify; inform; tell* ❧Mushi ga shiraseta. 虫が知らせた。*A little bird (lit: insect) told me.* <set phrase> ❧Isshūkan ínai ni kénsa no kekka o shirasemásu. 一週間以内に検査の結果を知らせます。*I'll inform you of the result of the (medical) examination within a week.*

shirei chōkan 司令長官；指令長官 *commander in chief*

shíren 試練 *trial; ordeal; test* ❧shíren ni taéru 試練に耐える *endure an ordeal*

shirewatár·u [*vi* shirewataránai; shirewatátta] 知れ渡る *become widely known*

[o-]shiri 尻 *buttocks*

shiriai 知り合い *acquaintance* ❧Tágami-kun to wa shiriai désu. 田上君とは知り合いです。*Mr. Tagami is an acquaintance of mine.*

shiriá·u [*vt* shiriawánai; shiriátta] 知り合う *know each other* ❧Kinóshita-san to wa ekimáe no aka-chóchin de shiriátta. 木下さんとは駅前の赤堤灯で知り合った。*I got to know Mr. Kinoshita at a bar by the station.*

shiritorí 尻取り *shiritori (a word game)*

shíritsu [no] 市立（の）*municipal* ❧shiritsu kōen 市立公園 *municipal park* ❧shiritsu toshókan 市立図書館 *city library*

shirizoké·ru [*vt* shirizokénai; shirizóketa] 退ける *repel; drive back; send away* ❧Watashítachi wa teki no kōgeki o shirizóketa. 私たちは敵の攻撃を退けた。*We repelled the enemy attack.* ❧Tsúma wa watashi no íken o shirizóketa. 妻は私の意見を退けた。*My wife brushed aside my opinion.*

shirizók·u [*vi* shirizokánai; shirizóita] 退く *retreat; draw back; pull away (from)* ❧Káre wa teinen de dáiissen o shirizóita. 彼は定年で第一線を退いた。*Reaching retirement age, he withdrew from the front lines.*

shíro 白 *white (color)*

[o-] shiro （お）城 *castle*

shiró·i [*adj* shíroku nái; shírokatta] 白い *(be) white*

shirómi 白身 *egg white; white meat*

shíróto 素人 *amateur* §Kono kotó ni kanshite wa, watashi wa máda shíróto desu.. この事にかんしては私はまだ素人です。*I'm still an amateur at this.*

shir·u [*vt* shiranai; shitta] 知る *know* §Sono kotó o shitte imáshita ka? その事を知っていましたか。*Did you know that?* §Watashi wa Yoshimura-san o shitte imásu. Démo Yoshímura-san wa watashi o shirimasén. 私は吉村さんを知っています。でも、吉村さんは私を知りません。*I know Ms. Yoshimura but she doesn't know me.*

shíru 汁 *juice; soup* §miso-shíru 味噌汁 *miso soup*

shirushi 印 *mark; sign; signal; symbol* §shirushi o tsukéru 印を付ける *affix a mark* §Kore wa hon no o-shirushi daké desu. これはほんのお印だけです。*This is only a token (of my gratitude).*

shirus·u [*vt* shirusanai; shirushita] 記す *write; down; note; mention*

shíryō 資料 *data; (research) materials* §Tsugí no kikaku ni hitsuyō na shíryō o atsúmete imásu. 次の企画に必要な資料を集めています。*We are gathering necessary data for the next project.*

shiryoku 視力 *eyesight; vision* §Watashi wa amari shiryoku ga yóku nái. 私はあまり視力が良くない。*My eyesight is not very good.*

shiryū 支流 *branch; tributary*

shisan 資産 *property; fortune; assets* §shisanka 資産家 *a person of property (means)* §shisan kōkai 資産公開 *public declaration (or offering) of property* §kotei shísan 固定資産 *fixed assets* §ryūdō shísan 流動資産 *floating assets*

shisatsu 視察 *inspection; observation* §shisatsu ryókō 視察旅行 *an inspection tour* ——**shisatsu-suru** [*vt*] 視察する *inspect; visit (in order to inspect)* §Shushō wa hisáichi o shisatsu-shite imásu. 首相は被災地を視察しています。*The prime minister is visiting the disaster area.*

shisei 施政 *administration; government* §shiséiken 施政権 *administrative right*

shisei 姿勢 *posture*

shiséiji 私生児 *illegitimate child; bastard; child born out of wedlock.*

shiséikatsu 私生活 *(one's) private life*

shiseki 史跡 *historical site*

shisen 視線 *a glance; a look* §shisen o sosogu 視線を注ぐ *fix one's gaze* §shisen o mukeru 視線を向ける *turn one's eyes* §Watashítachi wa shisen ga átta. 私たちは視線が合った。*Our eyes met.* §Watashi wa atsúi shisen o kanjite iru. 私は熱い視線を感じている。*I feel hostile eyes on me.*

shísetsu 施設 *facilities; equipment* §kōkyō shísetsu 公共施設 *public facilities* §yōgo shísetsu 養護施設 *(child) care facilities*

shísetsu 使節 *envoy* §shisetsúdan 使節団 *an envoy; entourage*

§shinzen shísetsu 親善使節 *goodwill ambassador*   §shísetsu o haken-suru 使節を派遣する *send an envoy*

shísha 使者 *messenger*   §shísha o tatéru 使者を立てる *send a messenger*

shísha 死者 *the dead; deceased person*   §shísha o tomuráu 死者を弔う *mourn the dead*

shísha gonyū 四捨五入 *round off to the nearest whole number*

shishin 指針 *compass needle; guideline*

shishó-bako 私書箱 *post-office box*

shishôsha 死傷者 *casualties; the dead and wounded*

shishū 刺繡 *embroidery*

shishū 詩集 *anthology of poetry*

shishúnki 思春期 *adolescence; puberty*

shishutsu 支出 *expenditure*   §Shūnyū to shishutsu no baransu ga warúi. 収入と支出のバランスが悪い。 *The balance of receipts and expenditures is not good.*

shisō 思想 *thought; ideology*   §shisōka 思想家 *a thinker*

shíson 子孫 *posterity; descendent*

shisshin 湿疹 *a rash; eczema*

shisshin-suru [vi] 失神する *faint*

shisshoku 失職 *unemployment* ——**shisshoku-suru** [vi] 失職する *lose (one's) job*   §Watashi wa fukéiki de shisshoku-shite shimatta. 私は不景気で失職してしまった。 *I lost my job because of the recession.*

shita [ni] 下（に） *below; down; under(neath); beneath*   §Tsukue no shita ni néko ga imásu. 机の下に猫がいます。 *There is a cat under the desk.*   §Watashi wa áni yori mittsú shita désu. 私は兄より三つ下です。 *I'm three years younger than my older brother.*

shitabírame 舌鮃；舌平目 *sole (fish)*

[ni] shitagatte ～に従って *consequently; accordingly; therefore; so*

shitaga·u [vi shitagawanai; shitagatta] 従う *comply with; follow*   §chūkoku ni shitagau 忠告に従う *comply with a warning*   §hō ni shitagau 法に従う *abide by the law*   §kenryokúsha ni shitagau 権力者に従う *obey the authorities*   §shūkan ni shitagau 習慣に従う *follow custom*

shitagi 下着 *underclothes; underwear*

shitagókoro 下心 *ulterior motive*

shitai 死体 *dead body; corpse; carcass*   §shitai íki 死体遺棄 *abandonment of a dead body*   §shitai anchisho 死体安置所 *morgue*

shitajiki ni nár·u [vi -naránai; -nátta] 下敷きになる *be crushed (under)*   §Kodomo wa kuruma no shitajiki ni nátte shimatta. 子供は車の下敷きになってしまった。 *The child was run over by a car.*

shitajiki ni suru [vt] 下敷きにする *use as a draft*   §Watashi no kono án o shitajiki ni shite kentō-shite kudasái. 私のこの案を下敷きにして検

討して下さい。 *Use my proposal as a draft and think on it.*

shitaku 仕度；支度 *preparation* ⑧shokuji no shitaku 食事の支度 *meal preparation* ⑧gaishutsu no shitaku 外出の支度 *preparation for going out* ——**shitaku-suru** [*vt*] 支度する *prepare*

shitamachi 下町 *low-lying, working-class neighborhoods (traditional shopping and entertainment district)* ⑧shitamachi chííki 下町地域 *plebeian districts* ⑧shitamachifū 下町風 *plebeian* ⑧shitamachi kátagi 下町気質 *spirit of the common people; downtown spirit*

shitashí·i [*adj* shitashiku nái; shitáshikatta] *親しい (be) close; friendly; intimate* ⑧Watashi ní wa shitashíi yūjin ga inai. 私には親しい友人がいない。 *I have no close friends.* ——**shitáshiku** 親しく *friendly; intimately*

shitashimi 親しみ *intimacy; familiarity*

shitáshisa 親しさ *familiarity; intimacy*

shitatárazu [no] 舌足らず（の）*tongue-tied; cryptic* ⑧Ishihara no búnshō wa shitatárazu desu. 石原の文章は舌足らずです。 *Ishihara's writing is cryptic.*

shitatár·u [*vi* shitataránai; shitatátta] 滴る *drip; trickle* ⑧Áse ga hitai kara shitatátte iru. 汗が額から滴っている。 *Sweat is dripping from my brow.*

shitate 仕立て *tailoring; sewing* ⑧shitateya 仕立て屋 *a tailor* ⑧shitateóroshi 仕立て下ろし *brand-new* ⑧Kono fukú wa shitate ga íi. この服は仕立てがいい。 *These clothes are well-made.*

shitatsúzumi o útsu 舌鼓を打つ *smack (one's) lips; make a hearty meal of*

shitá·u [*vt* shitawánai; shitátta] 慕う *yearn for; long for; adore; idolize* ⑧Kodomo wa senséi o shitátte iru. 子供は先生を慕っている。 *The child adores the teacher.*

shitei 指定 *appointment; designation; assignment* ⑧shitéiseki 指定席 *reserved seat* ⑧shitei no jikan 指定の時間 *the designated time* —— **shitei-suru** [*vt*] 指定する *designate; indicate* ⑧Kyokuchō wa káigi no basho o shitei-shimáshita. 局長は会議の場所を指定しました。 *The director designated the place for the meeting.*

shiteki-suru [*vt*] 指摘する *identify; point out* ⑧kettén o shiteki-suru 欠点を指摘する *point out defects*

shiten 支店 *branch store; branch office*

shiten 視点 *perspective; viewpoint; point of view* ⑧Kono shiten kara mondai o kangáete miyố. この視点から問題を考えてみよう。 *Let's consider the problem from this point of view.*

shíto 使徒 *apostle* ⑧heiwa no shíto 平和の使徒 *an apostle of peace*

shítoshito [to] しとしと（と）*softly; gently* ⑧Áme ga shítoshito fútte iru. 雨がしとしと降っている。 *The rain is falling gently.*

shitóyaka [na] 淑やか（な）*feminine; graceful; modest; polite*

&shitóyaka na josei 淑やかな女性 *a graceful woman*

shitsu 質 *quality* & Ryṓ yóri shitsu ga taisetsu desu. 量より質が大切です。*Quality is more important than quantity.*

shitsubō 失望 *disappointment* ——**shitsubō-suru** [*vi*] 失望する *be disappointed; give up hope; be discouraged*

shitsúdo 湿度 *humidity* &Shitsúdo ga takái. 湿度が高い。*Humidity is high.*

shitsugyō 失業 *unemployment* &shitsugyṓsha 失業者 *unemployed person* &shitsugyṓritsu 失業率 *unemployment rate* &shitsugyō hóken 失業保険 *unemployment insurance* &shitsugyō téate 失業手当 *unemployment compensation*

shitsuke 躾 *upbringing; home discipline; training* &Ryṓshin wa shitsuke ga kibishíi desu. 両親は躾が厳しいです。*My parents are strict on discipline.*

shitsumon 質問 *question* &shitsumon ōtō káigi 質問応答会議 *question-and-answer session* &Náni ka shitsumon ga arimásu ka? 何か質問がありますか？ *Do you have any questions?* &Shitsumon-shité mo íi desu ka? 質問してもいいですか？ *May I ask a question?*

shitsumu jíkan 執務時間 *office hours*

shitsúnai 室内 *indoors* &shitsunai pū́ru 室内プール *indoor pool* &shitsunáigaku 室内楽 *chamber music* &shitsunai gákudan 室内楽団 *chamber music orchestra*

shitsúrei [na] 失礼（な） *discourteous; impolite* &Hito o yubi-sásu no wa shitsúrei desu. 人を指差すのは失礼です。*It is impolite to point at people.* &Shitsúrei desu ga, dóchira-sama désu ka? 失礼ですが、どちら様ですか？ *Excuse me, but who is calling?* <*formal*> &Shitsúrei shimásu. 失礼します。*Excuse me (for leaving now).* &Shitsúrei-shimashita. 失礼しました。*Forgive me!*

shitsuren-suru [*vi*] 失恋する *be disappointed in love*

shitto 嫉妬 *jealousy* ——**shitto-bukái** [*adj* shitto-búkaku nái; shitto-búkakatta] 嫉妬深い *(be) jealous* &Tsúma wa shitto-bukái. 妻は嫉妬深い。*My wife's very jealous.* ——**shitto-suru** [*vi*] 嫉妬する *be jealous* &Watashi wa kánai ni shitto-shite iru. 私は家内に嫉妬している。*I'm jealous of my wife.*

shiwa 皺 *wrinkle*

shíya 視野 *range of vision; (one's) view* &shíya ni háiru 視野に入る *come into view; come in sight* &shíya ni ireru 視野に入れる *bring into (someone's) field of vision* &Fújita-san wa shíya ga semái. 藤田さんは視野が狭い。*Ms. Fujita takes a narrow view of things.*

shiyákusho 市役所 *city hall*

shiyōnin 使用人 *employee; servant* &koyṓsha to shiyōnin 雇用者と使用人 *employer and employee*

shiyū 私有 *private ownership* &shiyū no 私有の *privately owned*

  §shiyū záisan 私有財産 *private property*

shízan 死産 *stillbirth*

shizen 自然 *nature*   §shizen génshō 自然現象 *natural phenomenon*   §shizen hássei 自然発生 *spontaneous generation*   §shizen hógo 自然保護 *environmental protection*   §shizen kágaku 自然科学 *natural science*   §shizénkai 自然界 *the natural world*   §shizénshoku 自然食 *natural food; health food*   §shizen shúgi 自然主義 *naturalism*   §shizen sūhai 自然崇拝 *nature worship*   §shizen tóta 自然淘汰 *natural selection* ——**shizenteki [na]** 自然的（な）*natural; unaffected* ——**shizen ni** 自然に *naturally; instinctively; spontaneously; of its own (volition)*

shízuka [na] 静か（な）*still; quiet* ——**shízuka ni** 静かに *quietly*   §Shízuka ni shite kudasái. 静かにして下さい。*Be quiet, please!*

shizukésa 静けさ *quiet; tranquillity*

shizukú 滴 *drop (of liquid)*   §Noki kara shizukú ga tárete iru. 軒から滴が垂れている。*Water is dripping from the eaves.*

shizumarikáer·u [*vi* shizumarikaeránai; shizumarikáetta] 静まり返る *become completely silent; become deathly still*

shizumár·u [*vi* shizumaránai; shizumátta] 静まる *become quiet; grow still*   §Sáwagi ga kyū ni shizumátta. 騒ぎが急に静まった。*The commotion suddenly died down.*

shizume·ru [*vt* shizumenai; shizumeta] 沈める *sink (something); submerge*   §fúne o shizumeru 船を沈める *sink a ship*   §sófā ni mi o shizumeru ソファーに身を沈める *sink onto a sofa*

shizum·u [*vi* shizumanai; shizunda] 沈む *sink*   §kimochi ga shizumu 気持ちが沈む *feel depressed; feel low*   §Táiyō ga nishi ni shizumu. 太陽が西に沈む。*The sun sinks in the west.*   §Bōfū de fúne ga shizunda. 暴風雨で船が沈んだ。*The ship sank in a storm.*

sho- 初〜 *first-*   §shohan 初版 *first edition*   §shotáimen 初対面 *first meeting*   §shóka 初夏 *early summer*

shó 賞 *a prize; a reward*   §Nōberú-shō ノーベル賞 *Nobel Prize*

shó- 小〜 *small size*   §shōgékijō 小劇場 *little theater*   §Shō Ájia 小アジア *Asia Minor*

shó- 省〜 *conservation of*   §shō enérugí 省エネルギー *energy conservation*

-shó 〜章 *chapter*   §jússhō yónsetsu 十章四節 *chapter ten, section four*

shóbai 商売 *business; trade*   §mizushóbai 水商売 *the entertainment business, including bars, cabarets, etc.*   §Uchi no shóbai wa nikúya desu. 家の商売は肉屋です。*Our business is running a meat store.*

shóbatsu 処罰 *sanction; penalty; punishment*   §Káre wa hō o yabútte shóbatsu o úketa. 彼は法を破って処罰を受けた。*He broke the law and was punished for it.*

shōbén 小便 *urine; piss*   §ne-shōbén 寝小便 *wetting the bed*   §Tachishóben wa mittomo nái. 立小便はみっともない。*It's unseemly to piss in the open.* ——**shōbén-suru** [*vi*] 小便する *urinate; piss*

shōbō 消防 *fire fighting* ❧shōbōsho 消防署 *fire station; fire department* ❧shōbōsha 消防車 *fire engine* ❧shōbōshi 消防士 *fire fighter* ❧shōbōtai 消防隊 *fire brigade*

shóbu 勝負 *victory; decision; a match; a game* ❧shóbu ni kátsu 勝負に勝つ *win the game* ——**shóbu-suru** [*vt*] 勝負する *play; have a game*

shōbun 処分 *disposal; dispositon (of)* ——**shóbun-suru** [*vt*] 処分する *dispose of; take care of* ❧Tamatta hón o shóbun-shimáshita. 溜まった本を処分しました。*I got rid of all the books that had accumulated.*

shóchi 処置 *a measure; a step; action* ——**shóchi-suru** [*vt*] 処置する *deal with; take care of* ❧kizuguchi o shóchi-suru 傷口を処置する *take care of a wound*

shōchi 承知 *consent; compliance* ——**shōchi-suru** [*vt*] 承知する *agree to; comply with; accept; acknowledge* ❧Go-irai no kén ni tsúite shōchi-itashimáshita. ご依頼の件について承知いたしました。*I accept your request. <formal>*

shōchō 象徴 *symbol* ❧Háto wa heiwa no shōchō désu. 鳩は平和の象徴です。*The dove is a symbol of peace.* ——**shōchōteki** [**na**] 象徴的(な) *symbolic*

shōdaku 承諾 *acceptance; consent; agreement* ❧shōdakusho 承諾書 *letter of agreement* ❧shōdaku o éru 承諾を得る *get (someone's) consent* ——**shōdaku-suru** [*vt*] 承諾する *accept; consent (to)*

shōdō 衝動 *impulse; urge* ❧shōdō ni karareru 衝動にかられる *act on impulse* ——**shōdōteki** [**na**] 衝動的(な) *impulsive*

shōdoku 消毒 *disinfection; sterilization* ❧shōdokúzai 消毒剤 *disinfectant* ——**shōdoku-suru** [*vt*] 消毒する *disinfect*

shōga 生姜 *ginger*

shógai 生涯 *lifetime; career* ❧shógai no omoide 生涯の思い出 *lifelong memory* ❧shógai no shigoto 生涯の仕事 *lifetwork*

shōgai 傷害 *injury; bodily harm* ❧shōgai hóken 傷害保険 *accident insurance*

shōgai 障害 *obstacle; barrier; snag*

shōgákkō 小学校 *elementary school*

shōgakukin 奨学金 *scholarship; grant* ❧shōgaku shíkin 奨学資金 *scholarship fund*

[o-]shōgatsu (お)正月 *New Year's ; January*

shōgeki 衝撃 *shock* ❧shōgeki o ataeru 衝撃を与える *give a shock* ❧shōgeki o ukéru 衝撃を受ける *receive a shock* ❧tsuitotsu no shōgeki 追突の衝撃 *shock of collision* ❧shōgekíha 衝撃波 *a shock wave* ❧shákai ni shōgeki o ataeru jíken 社会に衝撃を与える事件 *an incident that shocked society*

shōgen 証言 *testimony; witness* ——**shōgen-suru** [vt] 証言する *testify; give witness (to)* ❊hōtei de shōgen-suru 法廷で証言する *give evidence in court*

shōgun 将軍 *shogun; generalissimo*

shṓgyō 商業 *commerce* ❊shōgyō chíiki 商業地域 *commercial district* ——**shṓgyō no** 商業の *commercial*

shōheki 障壁 *barrier* ❊kotoba no shōheki o norikoéru 言葉の障壁を乗り越える *overcome the language barrier*

shōhi 消費 *consumption; spending* ❊shōhi shákai 消費社会 *a consumer society* ❊shōhísha 消費者 *consumer* ❊shōhízai 消費財 *consumer goods* ❊shōhízei 消費税 *consumption tax* ——**shōhi-suru** [vt] 消費する *consume; spend* ❊dénryoku o shōhi-suru 電力を消費する *consume electricity*

shōhin 賞品 *a prize* ❊shōhin o morau 賞品を貰う *receive a prize*

shohōsen 処方箋 *prescription (for medicine)*

shōhyō 商標 *trademark; brand* ❊tōroku shóhyō 登録商標 *registered trademark*

shōji 障子 *sliding translucent paper door*

shōjíki 正直 *honesty* ——**shōjíki na** 正直な *honest; upright* ❊Masao-chan wa shōjíki na shōnen desu. 正男ちゃんは正直な少年です。 *Masao is an honest young man.* ——**shōjíki ni** 正直に *honestly; frankly; straightforwardly* ❊Shōjíki ni itte, watashi wa kono shigoto ga kirai désu. 正直に言って、わたしはこの仕事が嫌いです。 *To be honest, I don't like this work.*

shōji·ru [vi/vt shōjinai; shōjita] 生じる *give rise to; arise ; happen; occur* ❊Nammon ga shōjite shimatta. 難問が生じてしまった。 *A knotty problem came up.*

shōjo 処女 *virgin; maiden* ❊shojósaku 処女作 *maiden work; first work*

shōka 消化 *digestion* ❊shōka fúryō 消化不良 *indigestion* ❊shōka kíkan 消化器官 *digestive tract* ❊shōkazai 消化剤 *a digestive* ——**shōka-suru** [vt] 消化する *digest*

shōka 消火 *fire extinguishing; fire fighting* ❊shōkáki 消火器 *fire extinguisher* ❊shōkasen 消火栓 *fireplug; hydrant* ❊shōka ni ataru 消火に当たる *fight a fire* ——**shōka-suru** [vt] 消火する *put out a fire*

shōkai 紹介 *introduction* ❊shōkaijō 紹介状 *a letter of introduction* ❊jiko shókai 自己紹介 *self-introduction* ——**shōkai-suru** [vt] 紹介する *introduce* ❊Ryṓshin ni Tádashi-san o shōkai-shimáshita. 両親に匡さんを紹介しました。 *I introduced Tadashi to my parents.*

shōken 証券 *bond; securities* ❊shōken-gáisha 証券会社 *securities company* ❊shōken torihikijo 証券取引所 *stock exchange*

shoki 書記 *clerk; secretary* ❊shokíchō 書記長 *secretary general*

shokkaku 触覚 *(sense of) touch*

shokki 食器 *dishes; dinner set; tableware* §shokki aráiki 食器洗い機 *dishwasher*

shōko 証拠 *proof; evidence; testimony* §shōko fujúbun 証拠不十分 *insufficient evidence* §ugokánu shōko 動かぬ証拠 *irrefutable evidence* §Rón yori shōko. 論より証拠. *Proof is better than argument. <set phrase>*

shōkō 将校 *military officer; commissioned officer*

shōkō 商工 *commerce and industry* §Shōkō Kaigisho 商工会議所 *Chamber of Commerce and Industry*

shókoku 諸国 *various countries* §Kōtáishi to Kōtaishíhi wa Ajia shókoku o hōmon-saremáshita. 皇太子と皇太子妃はアジア諸国を訪問されました。 *The crown prince and princess visited various Asian countries. <formal>*

shoku 職 *job; position; employment* §shokuba 職場 *workplace*

shokúbutsu 植物 *plant; vegetation* §shokubutsúen 植物園 *botanical garden* §shokubutsúgaku 植物学 *botany* §shokubutsu níngen 植物人間 *a (human) vegetable* §shokubutsúshitsu 植物質 *vegetable matter* §shokubutsúyu 植物油 *vegetable oil*

shokudō 食道 *esophagus*

shokudō 食堂 *dining room* §shokudōsha 食堂車 *dining car*

shokúgyō 職業 *occupation; business* §shokugyō anteisho 職業安定所 *unemployment agency* §shokugyō gákkō 職業学校 *vocational school* §shokugyójin 職業人 *a business person* §shokugyō kyóiku 職業教育 *professional training* §Otōsan no shokúgyō wa nán desu ka? お父さんの職業は何ですか？ *What is your father's occupation?* —— **shokugyōteki [na]** 職業的 （な） *professional*

shokúin 職員 *personnel; employee* §shokuínroku 職員録 *personnel directory* §seiki shokúin 正規職員 *regular employee* §rinji shokúin 臨時職員 *temporary employee*

shokuji 食事 *meal* §shokuji o tsukúru 食事を作る *fix a meal* —— **shokuji-suru** [vi] 食事する *eat; dine*

shokumínchi 植民地 *colony*

shokuryōhin 食料品 *foodstuff; groceries*

shokuryō kíki 食糧危機；食料危機 *food crisis*

shokuséikatsu 食生活 *daily diet* §yútaka na shoku-séikatsu 豊かな食生活 *a rich diet* §Shokuséikatsu ga midárete iru. 食生活が乱れている。 *I have bad eating habits.*

shokutaku 食卓 *dining table*

shokutsū 食通 *a gourmet*

shokuyoku 食欲 *appetite* §shokuyoku ga áru 食欲がある *have an appetite* §shokuyoku o sosoru 食欲をそそる *stimulate (one's) appetite* §shokuyoku o okósu 食欲を起こす *whet (one's) appetite*

shōkyaku 焼却 *incineration* §shōkyakujo 焼却所 *garbage disposal* *plant* ❊shōkyakúro 焼却炉 *incinerator*

shōkyokusei 消極性 *passivity* ——**shōkyokuteki [na]** 消極的（な）*passive; negative* ❊Káre wa súbete ni táishite shōkyokuteki désu. 彼は全てに対して消極的です。*He's negative about everything.*

shōmei 照明 *lighting; illumination* ❊yakan shōmei 夜間照明 *night illumination* ❊chokusetsu shōmei 直接照明 *direct lighting* ❊kansetsu shōmei 間接照明 *indirect lighting* ❊butai shōmei 舞台照明 *stage lighting*

shōmei 証明 *proof; evidence* ❊shōmeisho 証明書 *certificate* ❊aribai shōmei アリバイ証明 *proof of an alibi* ——**shōmei-suru** [vt] 証明する *prove; certify; testify to; reveal* ❊téiri o shōmei-suru 定理を証明する *prove a theory*

shōmén 正面 *face-on; the front* ❊shōmen génkan 正面玄関 *front entrance* ❊shōmen kanránseki 正面観覧席 *grandstand; front-row seat* ❊shōmen shótotsu 正面衝突 *head-on collision*

shómin 庶民 *the people; the populace* ❊Ano seijika wa totemo shominteki desu. あの政治家はとても庶民的です。*That politician has real popular appeal.*

shōmóhin 消耗品 *articles of consumption; expendables*

shómu 商務 *commercial affairs* ❊shōmu chókan 商務長官 *secretary of commerce (US)*

shōnen 少年 *a youth* ❊shōnen híkō 少年非行 *juvenile delinquency* ❊shōnen jídai 少年時代 *(period of) youth* ❊shōnen zásshi 少年雑誌 *juvenile magazine*

shōnika 小児科 *pediatrics* ❊shōniká'i 小児科医 *pediatrician*

shōnin 商人 *merchant*

shōnin 承認 *acknowledgment; consent; approval* ❊kókka no shōnin o éru 国家の承認を得る *receive government approval* ——**shōnin-suru** [vt] 承認する *recognize; admit; approve* ❊aitékoku o shōnin-suru 相手国を承認する *recognize another country*

shōnin 証人 *witness* ❊shōnin ni náru 証人になる *become a witness* ❊shōnin o tanómu 証人を頼む *summon a witness* ❊shōnin ni tátsu 証人に立つ *stand witness (to)*

shōnin 昇任 *promotion (in rank)*

shoppá·i [adj shoppáku nái; shoppákatta] しょっぱい *(be) salty*

shórai 将来 *future* ❊Shórai no yumé wa nán desu ka? 将来の夢は何ですか。*What's your dream for the future?*

shōrei 奨励 *encouragement; incentive* ❊chochiku no shōrei 貯蓄の奨励 *an incentive for saving* ——**shōrei-suru** [vt] 奨励する *encourage; stimulate; promote* ❊kagaku gíjutsu no hatten o shōrei-suru 科学技術の発展を奨励する *promote the advancement of science and technology*

shóri 勝利 *victory; triumph; conquest* ❊shōrísha 勝利者 *winner*

§shṓri o éru 勝利を得る *gain a victory* §shṓri o osaméru 勝利を収める *clinch a victory*

shorui 書類 *document* §jūyō shórui 重要書類 *important documents*

shōryaku 省略 *abbreviation; omission* ——**shōryaku-suru** [*vt*] 省略する *cut; delete; abridge; shorten* §hanashí o shōryaku-suru 話を省略する *shorten a speech*

shōryō no 少量の *a little; a small amount of*

shosai 書斎 *study; den*

shōsai 詳細 *details; particulars* ——**shōsai [na]** 詳細（な）*detailed* §shōsai na setsumei 詳細な説明 *a detailed explanation*

shōsetsu 小説 *fiction; a novel; a short story* §shōsetsuka 小説家 *author; novelist* §chōhen shṓsetsu 長編小説 *full-length novel* §shishṓsetsu 私小説 *an "I" novel* §suiri shṓsetsu 推理小説 *mystery (detective) story*

shṓsha 商社 *business firm; trading company*

shōshin 昇進 *promotion (in rank); advancement* ——**shōshin-suru** [*vi*] 昇進する *be promoted*

shoshínsha 初心者 *beginner*

shōsoku 消息 *information; news* §shōsokúsuji 消息筋 *information sources* §shōsoku o tátsu 消息を絶つ *cut off information; stop correspondence*

shōsū́ 少数 *small number; minority* §shōsū mínzoku 少数民族 *minority ethnic group* §shōsū íken 少数意見 *minority opinion*

shōsū́ten 小数点 *decimal point*

shṓtai 招待 *invitation* §shōtaijō 招待状 *(written) invitation* §shōtáikyaku 招待客 *invited guest* ——**shṓtai-suru** [*vt*] 招待する *invite* §Búka o wága-ya ni shṓtai-shiyṓ. 部下をわが家に招待しよう。*I'll invite my staff to my home.*

shṓtai 正体 *true form; character* §shṓtai o arawásu 正体を現わす *reveal (one's) true colors* §shṓtai mo náku yóu 正体もなく酔う *get blind drunk*

shotáimen 初対面 *first meeting* §Kyṓ, futarí wa shotáimen desu. 今日、二人は初対面です。*They (those two) are meeting for the first time today.*

shṓten 商店 *shop; store* §shōténgai 商店街 *a shopping street*

shṓten 焦点 *focus* §shōten kyóri 焦点距離 *focal distance* §shṓten ga áu 焦点が合う *be in focus* §shṓten o awaséru 焦点を合わせる *adjust the focus* §Kázoku no wadai no shṓten wa musuko no kekkon móndai deshita. 家族の話題の焦点は息子の結婚問題でした。*The family's conversation focused on the son's marriage.*

shotoku 所得 *personal income* §shotokúzei 所得税 *income tax* §kokumin shótoku 国民所得 *national income*

shōtotsu 衝突 *collision* §shōtotsu jíko 衝突事故 *collision accident*

————**shōtotsu-suru** [vi] 衝突する *collide; clash; conflict*

Shōwa 昭和 *Showa era (1926-1989)*

shoyō [na] 所要（な）*necessary; required* ⁸shoyō na jōkén 所要な条件 *necessary conditions.*

shōyō de 商用で *on business* ⁸Shōyō de Amerika ni ikimásu. 商用でアメリカに行きます。 *I'm going to America on business.*

shoyū 所有 *ownership; possession* ⁸shoyūbutsu 所有物 *possessions* ⁸shoyūchi 所有地 *(one's) personally owned land* ⁸shoyūken 所有権 *right of ownership* ——**shoyū-suru** [vt] 所有する *own; possess*

shōyu 醤油；正油 *soy sauce*

shozai 所在 *whereabouts* ⁸sekinin no shozai o akíraka ni suru 責任の所在を明らかにする *make clear where the blame lies*

shōzō 肖像 *portrait; icon* ⁸shōzōga 肖像画 *a portrait*

shozoku 所属 *attached; belonging (to)* ——**shozoku-suru** [vi] 所属する *belong to* ⁸Watashi wa dono seitō ní mo shozoku-shite inai. 私はどの政党にも所属していない。 *I don't belong to any political party.*

shū 週 *week* ⁸shūmatsu 週末 *weekend* ⁸shū itsuka-sei 週五日制 *five-day workweek*

-shū ～州 *state of~* ⁸Arizoná-shū アリゾナ州 *the state of Arizona*

shūbi 守備 *defense* ⁸shūbi o katameru 守備を固める *strengthen the defense*

shūbun 秋分 *autumnal equinox* ⁸Shūbun no Hí 秋分の日 *Autumnal Equinox (national holiday)*

shūchi no tōri 周知の通り *as you know* ⁸Ketsuron ni tsúite wa shūchi no tōri desu. 結論については周知の通りです。 *You already know what the conclusion is.*

shuchō 主張 *claim; assertion* ——**shuchō-suru** [vt] 主張する *insist on; assert; make a strong claim for* ⁸kénri o shuchō-suru 権利を主張する *assert (one's) right* ⁸Kénri wa hakkíri to shuchō-shita hő ga íi. 権利ははっきりと主張した方がいい。 *One should clearly assert one's rights.*

shūchū 集中 *concentration; centralization* ⁸shūchū kőza 集中講座 *an intensive course* ⁸shūchűryoku 集中力 *ability to concentrate* ——**shūchū-suru** [vi] 集中する *concentrate on* ⁸Jibun no shigoto ni shūchū-shinasái. 自分の仕事に集中しなさい。 *Concentrate on your own work.*

shudai 主題 *theme; topic; subject* ⁸Kono éiga wa shudai ga hakkíri shinai. この映画は主題がはっきりしない。 *The subject of this movie is not clear.*

shúdan 手段 *means; device; way* ⁸Kono mondai o kaiketsu-suru shúdan ga mitsukaranai. この問題を解決する手段が見つからない。 *We can't find a way to solve this problem.*

shūdan 集団 *group; body* ⁸shūdan séikatsu 集団生活 *communal living*

🔹shūdan shúgi 集団主義 *collectivism* — —**shūdanteki [na]** 集団的（な） *collective; group-oriented* 🔹Nihonjín wa shūdanteki dá to iwareru. 日本人は集団的だと言われる。 *Japanese are said to be group-oriented.*

shuei 守衛 *a guard*

shūeki 収益 *earnings; profits; proceeds* 🔹Sono charitī íbento dé no shūeki wa sukunákatta. そのチャリティーイベントでの収益は少なかった。 *The proceeds from the charity event were small.*

shúfu 主婦 *housewife* 🔹sengyō shúfu 専業主婦 *full-time housewife* 🔹kengyō shúfu 兼業主婦 *part-time housewife*

shúgei 手芸 *handicraft; manual arts* 🔹shugéihin 手芸品 *handicraft articles*

shúgi 主義 *doctrine; ism; principle* 🔹shakai shúgi 社会主義 *socialism* 🔹shihon shúgi 資本主義 *capitalism* 🔹shúgi o mamóru 主義を守る *keep one's principles*

Shūgíin 衆議院 *House of Representatives (J)* 🔹Shūgiin gíin 衆議院議員 *member of the House of Representatives*

shúgo 主語 *subject (Gram)* 🔹Kono bún wa shúgo ga shōryaku-sarete imásu. この文は主語が省略されています。 *The subject of this sentence has been omitted.*

shūgō 集合 *meeting; assembly* 🔹shūgō basho 集合場所 *meeting place* 🔹shūgō jíkan 集合時間 *meeting time* — —**shūgō-suru** 集合する [vi] *gather; meet; assemble* 🔹Dantai wa éki ni shūgō-suru. 団体は駅に集合する。 *The group will meet at the station.*

shúha 宗派 *religious sect; religious branch*

shúi [no] 周囲（の） *circumference; surroundings* 🔹Shúi no hitó ni méiwaku o kaketáku nái. 周囲の人に迷惑をかけたくない。 *I don't want to bother people around me.* 🔹Kono iké wa shúi ga sán-kiro áru. この池は周囲が三キロある。 *This pond is three kilometers in circumference.*

shúji 習字 *calligraphy; penmanship*

shújin 主人 *husband; master; boss (of a shop)* 🔹shujínkō 主人公 *hero; leading actor / actress* 🔹go-shújin ご主人 *(another's) husband* 🔹shujinyaku 主人役 *host; hostess* 🔹Shújin wa íma, rúsu ni shite orimásu. 主人は今、留守にしております。 *My husband's not home right now.* <formal> 🔹Go-shújin wa go-zaitaku deshó ka? ご主人はご在宅でしょうか？ *Is your husband home?* <formal>

shūjin 囚人 *prisoner*

shújutsu 手術 *operation; surgery* 🔹shújutsu o ukéru 手術を受ける *receive surgery* 🔹shújutsu o kuwaeru 手術を加える *perform surgery*

shūkai 集会 *meeting; assembly; gathering* 🔹shūkai no jiyú 集会の自由 *freedom of assembly.*

shūkaku 収穫 *harvest; crop* ❊Kotoshi wa kome no shūkaku ga ōi sō desu. 今年は米の収穫が多いそうです。 *They say the rice harvest will be big this year.*

shūkan 週間 *week*

shūkan 習慣 *custom; convention; practice* ❊Sékai ni wa iroiro na shūkan ga áru. 世界にはいろいろな習慣がある。 *There are various customs in the world.*

shūkánshi 週刊誌 *weekly (magazine)*

shukanteki [na] 主観的（な）*subjective* ❊Kore wa watashi no shukanteki na íken desu. これは私の主観的な意見です。 *This is my subjective opinion.*

shuken 主権 *sovereignty* ❊kokumin shúken 国民主権 *sovereignty of the people*

shūketsu 終結 *conclusion; end; a closing (down)* ——**shūketsu-suru** [vi] 終結する *end; close; terminate* ❊Sensō ga shūketsu-shita. 戦争が終結した。 *The war ended.*

shūkin 集金 *bill collecting* ❊shūkín-in 集金員 *bill collector* ——**shūkin-suru** [vt] 集金する *collect payment*

shukketsu 出血 *hemorrhage; bleeding* ❊Shukketsu o tomeru kótó ga dekínakatta. 出血を止めることが出来なかった。 *I couldn't stop the bleeding.* ——**shukketsu-suru** [vi] 出血する *bleed* ❊shukketsu daisábisu 出血大サービス *bargain sale; "sacrifice" sale*

shukkin 出勤 *going to work* ——**shukkin-suru** [vi] 出勤する *go to work*

shukudai 宿題 *assignment; homework* ❊shukudai o dásu 宿題を出す *give homework*

shukuden 祝電 *congratulatory telegram*

shukufuku 祝福 *blessing; benediction* ——**shukufuku-suru** [vt] 祝福する *bless; give a blessing (to)* ❊Shímpu wa futarí no kekkon o shukufuku-shimáshita. 神父は二人の結婚を祝福しました。 *The priest blessed their marriage.*

shukuhaku 宿泊 *lodging; staying the night* ❊shukuhakúryō 宿泊料 *room charge* ❊shukuhaku shísetsu 宿泊施設 *lodgings; accommodations* ——**shukuhaku-suru** [vi] 宿泊する *stay the night; lodge*

shukuji 祝辞 *congratulatory address*

shukujitsu 祝日 *(national) holiday*

shukumei 宿命 *fate; destiny; karma* ❊shukuméiron 宿命論 *fatalism* ❊shukumei rónsha 宿命論者 *fatalist* ❊Kō náru kótó ga watashi no shukumei ná n desu. こうなることが私の宿命なんです。 *It's my fate that things turned out this way.* ——**shukumeiteki [na]** 宿命的（な）*destined; predetermined* ❊Kamiyama to Kázuko-san wa shukumeiteki na deai o shita. 神山と和子さんは宿命的な出会いをした。 *Fate* *drew Kamiyama and Kazuko together.* ——**shukumeiteki ni** 宿命的に *in a way determined by fate*

shukúsha 宿舎 *lodging; quarters*

shukushō 縮小 *reduction (in size)* ——**shukushō-suru** [vt] 縮小する *reduce (in size)* ❀Keikaku no kíbo o shukushō-shinákereba yosan ga tarinaku narimásu. 計画の規模を縮小しなければ予算が足りなくなります。 *If we don't scale down the project, the budget won't cover it.*

shúkyō 宗教 *religion* ——**shūkyōteki** [na] 宗教的（な）*religious* ❀shūkyōteki kyōshínsha 宗教的狂信者 *a religious fanatic* ❀shūkyōteki na kōi 宗教的な行為 *a religious act*

shūmai 焼売；シューマイ *Chinese shao-mai (dumplings)*

shūmatsu 週末 *weekend*

shūmatsu 終末 *the end of the world; the apocalypse* ❀shūmatsúron 終末論 *eschatology*

shumbun 春分 *vernal equinox* ❀Shumbun no Hi 春分の日 *Vernal Equinox (national holiday)*

shúmi 趣味 *hobby; interest; taste* ❀Watashi no shúmi wa górufu desu. 私の趣味はゴルフです。 *My hobby's golf.* ❀Miyamoto-san wa fukú no shúmi ga íi. 宮本さんは服の趣味がいい。 *Miyamoto has good taste in clothes.*

shunga 春画 *pornographic picture; pornography*

shúngiku 春菊 *edible chrysanthemum leaves*

shunin 主任 *director (of a program); supervisor* ❀gemba shúnin 現場主任 *foreman; work-site supervisor* ❀shunin bengóshi 主任弁護士 *chief attorney*

shūnin 就任 *inauguration; installation* ❀shūnin énzetsu 就任演説 *inaugural address* ——**shūnin-suru** [vi] 就任する *install (to office); take office* ❀Mondéru-shi ga árata ni zainichi Amerika táishi ni shūnin-saremáshita. モンデール氏が新たに在日アメリカ大使に就任されました。 *Mondale was again installed as US ambassador to Japan.*

shunkan 瞬間 *moment; instant* ❀ketteiteki shunkan 決定的瞬間 *the decisive moment* ——**shunkan** [ni] 瞬間（に）*at the moment (of)* ❀Watashi o míta shunkan ni, Miyuki-san wa nigedashite shimatta. 私を見た瞬間に、美由紀さんは逃げ出してしまった。 *The moment she saw me, Miyuki ran away.*

shunō káidan 首脳会談 *summit conference*

shūnyū 収入 *revenue; income* ❀shūnyū ínshi 収入印紙 *revenue stamp* ❀Shúnyú wa dono gúrai desu ka? 収入はどのぐらいですか。 *About how much do you make?*

shuppan 出帆 *sailing; departure* ——**shuppan-suru** [vi] 出帆する *sail*

shuppan 出版 *publication* ❀shuppámbutsu 出版物 *a publication* ❀shuppánsha 出版社 *publishing company; publisher* ——**shuppan-suru** [vi] 出版する *publish*

shuppatsu 出発 *departure; start* 🔸shuppatsu jíkoku 出発時刻 *time of departure* ——**shuppatsu-suru** [*vi*] 出発する *depart; leave; set off (on a journey)*

shuppi 出費 *expenses* 🔸Shuppi o kiritsumenákereba kakei ga hatan-shite shimau. 出費を切り詰めなければ家計が破綻してしまう。 *If we don't cut expenses we'll not be able to make ends meet at home.*

shúri 修理 *repair* 🔸shūrikō 修理工 *mechanic* ——**shúri-suru** [*vt*] 修理する *repair; fix* 🔸Tokei o shúri-shite moratta. 時計を修理してもらった。 *I had my watch repaired.*

shúrui 種類 *sort; type; species; variety* 🔸Kō itta shúrui no hón o mótte imásu ka? こういった種類の本を持っていますか？ *Do you have this type of book?* 🔸Kono futatsú wa shúrui ga onaji désu. この二つは種類が同じです。 *These two are of the same species.*

shuryō 狩猟 *hunting; shooting* 🔸shuryōka 狩猟家 *a hunter* 🔸shuryō ni iku 狩猟に行く *go hunting*

shusai 主催 *sponsorship; auspices* 🔸shusáisha 主催者 *sponsor* 🔸shusai tóshi 主催都市 *host city* ——**shusai-suru** [*vt*] 主催する *sponsor*

shúsai 秀才 *brilliant person; talented person*

shusei [no] 守勢（の）*defensive* 🔸shusei ni tátsu 守勢に立つ *be on the defensive*

shūsei 修正 *correction; amendment; revision* 🔸shūséian 修正案 *draft amendment* 🔸shūséieki 修正液 *correction fluid; white-out* ——**shūsei-suru** [*vt*] 修正する *correct; amend; revise* 🔸Kimi no rombun wa ichíbu shūsei-shita hố ga íi. 君の論文は一部修正した方がいい。 *You ought to revise some sections of your paper.*

shúshi 趣旨；主旨 *main point; theme; focus; aim; purport* 🔸Anáta no rombun no shúshi ga yóku ríkai-dekimasén. あなたの論文の趣旨がよく理解できません。 *I can't quite grasp the point of your thesis.*

shūshínkei 終身刑 *life imprisonment; life sentence*

shushō 首相 *prime minister* 🔸shushō kántei 首相官邸 *prime minister's residence*

shūshoku 就職 *employment* 🔸shūshokú-guchi 就職口 *job opening* 🔸shūshokúnan 就職難 *difficulty in finding a job* 🔸shūshoku shíken 就職試験 *employment examination* 🔸shūshoku no yosō 就職の予想 *job prospects* 🔸shūshoku o mōshikómu 就職を申し込む *apply for work* ——**shūshoku-suru** [*vi*] 就職する *be employed* 🔸Imōtó wa shímbunsha ni shūshoku-shimáshita. 妹は新聞社に就職しました。 *My younger sister got a job with a newspaper company.*

shushoku 主食 *staple food* 🔸Nihonjín no shushoku wa komé desu. 日本人の主食は米です。 *The staple food of Japanese is rice.*

shūshū-suru [*vt*] 収集する *collect; gather* 🔸Watashi wa kitte o shūshū-shite imásu. 私は切手を収集しています。 *I collect stamps.*

shussan 出産 *birth* ❚shussánritsu 出産率 *birth rate* ❚shussan (*or* susshō) tódoke 出産（出生）届け *register of birth* ——**shussan-suru** [*vt*] 出産する *give birth*

shusse 出世 *success in life; achievement; getting ahead; promotion* ❚shussésaku 出世作 *work that establishes a reputation* ——**shusse-suru** [*vi*] 出世する *succeed; make a name for oneself* ❚Otto wa shusse-suru koto bákari kangáete iru. 夫は出世することばかり考えている。 *My husband thinks only of getting ahead.*

shusseki 出席 *attendance* ❚shussekí-bo 出席簿 *attendance record* ❚shussekísha 出席者 *a person present* ❚shusseki o tóru 出席を取る *take attendance* ——**shusseki-suru** [*vi*] 出席する *attend* ❚Kyố wa zen'in ga shusseki-shite iru. 今日は全員が出席している。 *Today everyone is in attendance.*

shusshin 出身 *origin* ❚shusshínchi 出身地 *birthplace* ❚shusshínkō 出身校 *alma mater* ❚Chichí wa Tōdai no shusshin desu. 父は東大の出身です。 *My father is a graduate of Tokyo University.*

shúsu 繻子 *satin*

shutai 主体 *subject* ❚shutaisei 主体性 *identity; individuality; independence* ——**shutaiteki [na]** 主体的（な）*subjective; independent* ——**shutaiteki ni** 主体的に *subjectively; individually*

shutchō 出張 *business trip* ❚shutchōjo 出張所 *branch office* ——**shutchō-suru** [*vi*] 出張する *travel on business* ❚Watashi wa ashita Séndai ni shutchō-shimásu. あたしは明日仙台に出張します。 *Tomorrow I'm going to Sendai on business.*

shúto 首都 *capital* ❚shutóken 首都圏 *the capital region*

shú to shite 主として *principally; chiefly; mainly* ❚Kyố no káigi de wa shú to shite tsugí no purojékuto ni tsúite tốron-shita. 今日の会議では主として次のプロジェクトについて討論した。 *At the meeting today we mainly discussed the next project.*

shutsuen 出演 *appearance; performance* ❚shutsuénsha 出演者 *performer* ❚shutsuénryō 出演料 *performance fee* ——**shutsuen-suru** [*vi*] 出演する *appear; act (in a play)* ❚térebi bángumi ni shutsuen-suru テレビ番組に出演する *appear on a TV program*

shutsugen-suru [*vi*] 出現する *appear; make an appearance* ❚Yuki-ótoko ga shutsugen-shita tte hontố désu ka? 雪男が出現したって本当ですか？ *Is it true that the Abominable Snowman was seen?*

shúwa 手話 *sign language*

shuyaku 主役 *leading role (play / music)* ❚Masaru wa gakkō no géki de shuyaku o enjimásu. 勝は学校の劇で主役を演じます。 *Masaru has the lead in the school play.*

shuyō 腫瘍 *tumor* ❚nō shúyō 脳腫瘍 *brain tumor* ❚akusei shúyō 悪性腫瘍 *malignant tumor*

shuyō [na] 主要（な）*main; central; principal; major* ❚shuyō jímbutsu

主要人物 *central figure*   ⑧shuyō sángyō 主要産業 *principal industry*   ⑧shuyō tóshi 主要都市 *major city*

shūyō 収容 *accommodating; admitting; taking in*   ⑧shūyōjo 収容所 *concentration camp; internment center*   ⑧hōryo shūyōjo 捕虜収容所 *prison camp*   ⑧nammin shūyōjo 難民収容所 *refugee camp* —— **shūyō-suru** [*vt*] 収容する *accommodate; admit; take in*

shuzai 取材 *gathering information; field trip*   ⑧shuzai kísha 取材記者 *investigative reporter* —— **shuzai-suru** [*vt*] 取材する *gather data; cover (a story)*   ⑧Kore wa densetsu ni shuzai-shita shōsetsu désu. これは伝説に取材した小説です。 *This is a novel based on legends I researched.*

shúzoku 種族 *tribe*

sō そう *thus; so*   ⑧Sō shite kudasái. そうして下さい。 *Please do so.*   ⑧Sō itte kudasái. そう言って下さい。 *Please say that.*   ⑧Sō iu hitó wa shirimasén. そういう人は知りません。 *I don't know such a person.*

sō 層 *layer*   ⑧chisō 地層 *layer of soil*   ⑧dansō 断層 *(earthquake) fault*   ⑧kōsō 高層 *upper stratum*   ⑧kōsō bíru 高層ビル *high-rise building*   ⑧Ano káshu no fán wa sō ga atsui. あの歌手のファンは層が厚い。 *That singer's fans are from every age range.*

sō; sóryo 僧；僧侶 *priest (Budd)*

soaku [*na*] 粗悪（な）*inferior*   ⑧Soaku na sū́tsu o kawasarete shimatta. 粗悪なスーツを買わされてしまった。 *I was sold an inferior suit.*

sōan 草案 *a draft (proposal)*   ⑧Atarashíi jōrei no sōan ga máda dekiagaranai. 新しい条例の草案がまだ出来上がらない。 *The draft ofr the new ordinance is not ready yet.*

sóba [*ni*] 傍；側（に）*beside; near (physical proximity)*   ⑧Ginkō no sóba ni yūbínkyoku ga áru. 銀行の傍に郵便局がある。 *There is a post office near (next to) the bank.*   ⑧Watashi no sóba ni yotte goran. 私の傍に寄ってごらん。 *Come over here by me.* <*fem*>

sóba 蕎麦 *buckwheat; buckwheat noodles*   ⑧sobáya 蕎麦屋 *a noodle shop*

sōba 相場 *exchange rate*   ⑧Kyṓ no sōba wa íkura kashira? 今日の相場はいくらかしら。 *I wonder what the (yen-dollar) exchange rate is today.* <*fem*>

sobakásu そばかす *freckles*   ⑧sobakasu bíjin そばかす美人 *a freckle-faced beauty*

sōbetsu 送別 *send-off*   ⑧sōbetsúkai 送別会 *farewell party*

sobié·ru [*vi* sobiénai; sobiéta] そびえる *tower; rise above*   ⑧Kyōkai no tṓ ga tákaku sobiéte imásu. 教会の塔が高くそびえています。 *The church steeple towers high (above other buildings).*

soboku [*na*] 素朴（な）*simple; plain; naive*   ⑧soboku na aji 素朴な味 *plain flavor*   ⑧soboku na kurashikata 素朴な暮らし方 *a simple life*

sochira そちら *there; that direction; you* §Shújin wa sochira ni ukagatte orimásu ka? 主人はそちらに伺っておりますか？ *Is my husband there? <formal>* §Sochira no go-íken wa ikága desu ka? そちらの意見はいかがですか？ *What is your opinion? <formal>*

sōdai [na] 壮大（な）*grand; magnificent; spectacular* §Sono kaihatsu-gáisha wa sōdai na keikaku o tátete iru. その開発会社は壮大な計画を立てている。 *The development company is making a grand plan.*

sōdan 相談 *consultation* §sōdan'yaku 相談役 *advisor; counselor* §sōdan áite 相談相手 *a person one can talk things over with* §sōdan ni noru 相談に乗る *hear (someone) out; listen to one* ——**sōdan-suru** [vi] 相談する *confer; consult*

sodaté·ru [vt sodaténai; sodáteta] 育てる *grow (something); rear (someone); raise* §Watashi no shúmi wa rán o sodatéru kotó desu. 私の趣味は蘭を育てることです。 *My hobby is raising orchids.*

sodáts·u [vi sodatánai; sodátta] 育つ *grow; grow up; reach maturity; be brought up* §Watashi wa Minami Áfurika de sodátta. 私は南アフリカで育った。 *I grew up in South Africa.*

sode 袖 *sleeve* §nagasode [no] 長袖（の）*long-sleeved* §hansode [no] 半袖（の）*short-sleeved* §sodenashi [no] 袖なし（の）*sleeveless* §sode o makuru 袖を捲る *roll up (one's) sleeves*

sṓdō 騒動 *strife; confusion; disturbance; riot* §o-ie sṓdō お家騒動 *family strife* §gakkō sṓdō 学校騒動 *school disturbance* §sṓdō o okósu 騒動を起こす *cause a riot*

soegi 添え木；副え木 *splint*

soe·ru [vt soenai; soeta] 添える；副える *lend; add* §kuchi o soeru 口を添える *add on (to what someone has said)* §Watashi wa ónshi ni tegami o soete kinenhin o okutta. 私は恩師に手紙を添えて記念品を送った。 *I sent my former teacher a memento along with a letter.* §Tsúma wa kangófu o soete chichí o sanpo-saseta. 妻は看護婦を添えて父を散歩させた。 *My wife got my father to take a walk accompanied by a nurse.*

sófu 祖父 *(one's own) grandfather*

sogai-suru 疎外する *be estranged; avoid (meeting someone)* §Watashi wa ítsumo mawari no hitó kara sogai-sarete iru yṓ ni kanjite iru. 私はいつも回りの人から疎外されているように感じている。 *I always feel I'm being avoided by people around me.*

sōgankyō 双眼鏡 *binoculars*

sōgen 草原 *prairie; plain*

sōgi 争議 *a dispute; trouble; strike* §rōdō sōgi 労働争議 *a labor dispute*

sōgi 葬儀 *funeral* §sōgiya 葬儀屋 *funeral home; funeral parlor; mortician* §sōgísha 葬儀社 *mortuary*

sṓgo [no] 相互（の）*mutual* §sōgo fújo 相互扶助 *mutual aid* §sōgo gínkō 相互銀行 *mutual loan and savings bank* 🔹sōgo ríkai 相互理解 *mutual understanding* ――**sōgo ni** 相互に *mutually*

sōgō 総合；綜合 *consolidation; synthesis* 🔹sōgō byōin 総合病院 *general hospital* 🔹sōgō dáigaku 総合大学 *university* 🔹sōgō kéikaku 総合計画 *general (overall) plan* 🔹sōgōron 総合論 *synthesis*

sōgū 遭遇 *confrontation; encounter* 🔹Ónshi ni nijūnen-buri ni sōgū-shita。恩師に二十年ぶりに遭遇した。*I ran across a teacher I hadn't seen in twenty years.*

sōi 相違 *disparity; difference* 🔹íken no sōi 意見の相違 *a difference of opinion*

sōji 掃除 *cleaning* ――**sōji-suru** [vt] 掃除する *clean*

sójō 僧正 *abbot (Budd)*

sōjū 操縦 *handling (an airplane)* 🔹sōjúseki 操縦席 *pilot seat* 🔹sōjúshi 操縦士 *airplane pilot* ――**sōjū-suru** [vt] 操縦する *pilot (a plane)*

sōkai 総会 *general assembly* 🔹kabunushi sókai 株主総会 *stockholders' meeting* 🔹teirei sókai 定例総会 *regular general assembly* 🔹rinji sókai 臨時総会 *extraordinary general assembly*

sōkai [na] 爽快（な）*invigorating; exhilarating* 🔹Kyō wa ása kara sōkai na kíbun desu。今日は朝から爽快な気分です。*I've felt exhilarated since this morning.*

sōkei [na] 早計（な）*premature* 🔹Íma koko de ketsuron o dásu no wa sōkei desu。今ここで結論を出すのは早計です。*It would be premature to come to a conclusion here and now.*

sokki 速記 *shorthand* 🔹Kokkai no sokkíroku 国会の速記録 *the secretary's minutes of the Diet meeting*

sokkúri [na] そっくり（な）*identical; all; entirely* 🔹Musume-san wa o-kásan ni sokkúri desu。娘さんはお母さんにそっくりです。*Your daughter is the spitting image of her mother.* 🔹Akisu ni hōseki o sokkúri nusumárete shimatta。空き巣に宝石をそっくり盗まれてしまった。*While I was away all of my jewelry was stolen.*

soko そこ *there [near listener]* 🔹Soko de nání shiteru no? そこで何してるの？*What are you doing there? <fem>* 🔹Soko ni éki ga arimásu。そこに駅があります。*The station is there.*

soko 底 *bottom* 🔹úmi no soko 海の底 *the bottom of the ocean* 🔹kutsu no soko 靴の底 *the sole of a shoe*

sóko 倉庫 *warehouse; storehouse*

sokobie 底冷え *chilling to the bone* 🔹Hokkáidō no fuyú wa sokobie suru hodo samúi desu。北海道の冬は底冷えするほど寒いです。*Hokkaido winters are so cold you're chilled to the bone.*

sokoná·u [vt sokonawánai; sokonátta] 損なう *harm; damage; ruin* 🔹kenkō o sokonáu 健康を損なう *ruin (one's) health*

-sokonau ～損なう *miss doing; fail to do* 🔹densha ni norisokonau 電車

に乗り損なう *miss a train*

sōkṓsha 装甲車 *armored vehicle*

sokubai 即売 *on-the-spot sale*

sokubaku 束縛 *restriction; constraint* ——**sokubaku-suru** [vt] 束縛する *restrict; constrain* ⑧katei ni sokubaku-sareru 家庭に束縛される *be tied to (one's) family*

sókudo 速度 *speed* ⑧hannō sókudo 反応速度 *reaction time* ⑧sókudo o ageru 速度を上げる *increase speed* ⑧sókudo o sagéru 速度を下げる *decrease speed* ⑧sókudo o otósu 速度を落とす *slow down*

sokumen 側面 *angle; side; side view* ⑧sokuménzu 側面図 *side view; profile* ⑧sokumen kara énjo-suru 側面から援助する *(to) support from the side* ⑧Mondai wa ṓku no sokumen kara mínákereba ikenai. 問題は多くの側面から見なければいけない。 *We must look at the problem from many angles.*

sokuseki 即席 *on-the-spot* ⑧sokuseki no supíchi 即席のスピーチ *an impromptu speech*

sokushi 即死 *instant death* ——**sokushi-suru** [vi] 即死する *die instantly* ⑧Yūjin wa jidṓsha jíko de sokushi-shita. 友人は自動車事故で即死した。 *My friend died instantly in a car accident.*

sokushin 促進 *promotion; acceleration* ——**sokushin-suru** [vi] 促進する *promote; step up; quicken* ⑧sangyō no shinkō o sokushin-suru 産業の振興を促進する *promote the development of industry*

sokutatsu 速達 *express mail; special delivery* ⑧sokutatsu ryṓkin 速達料金 *special delivery fee* ⑧Kono tegami o sokutatsu de okutte kudasái. この手紙を速達で送って下さい。 *Send this letter by special delivery, please.*

sōkyū ni; sakkyū ni 早急に *quickly; right away* ⑧Kono shigoto o sōkyū ni shóri suru yṓ ni! この仕事を早急に処理するように。 *See that this business is taken care of right away!*

somar·u [vi somaranai; somatta] 染まる *be dyed; be colored* ⑧áku ni somaru 悪に染まる *be tainted by evil* ⑧Sóra ga yūhi ni somatta. 空が夕日に染まった。 *The sky was colored by the sunset.*

sómatsu [na] 粗末（な） *coarse; crude; plain; rustic; rough* ⑧sómatsu na kimono 粗末な着物 *a shabby kimono* ⑧sómatsu na shokuji 粗末な食事 *plain food*

some·ru [vt somenai; someta] 染める *(to) dye* ⑧hṓo o someru 頬を染める *turn red; blush* ⑧kamí o someru 髪を染める *dye (one's) hair* ⑧nuno o someru 布を染める *dye cloth*

somúk·u [vi somukánai; somúita] 背く *go against; act contrary to; rise (turn) against* ⑧hō ni somúku 法に背く *act contrary to the law* ⑧yó ni somúku 世に背く *turn against the world*

són 損 *loss* ⑧Sore o káu no wa són desu. それを買うのは損です。 *You'd take a loss buying that.* ——**són-suru** [vi] 損する *lose; suffer a* *loss*

sonaé·ru [*vt* sonaénai; sonáeta] 備える *provide; prepare* ❊Taifú ni sonáete toranjisutā-rájio to kaichū déntō o yói-shita. 台風に備えてトランジスターラジオと懐中電灯を用意した。*Preparing for the typhoon, I made ready a transistor radio and a flashlight.*

sonchō 尊重 *esteem; respect (for a thing)* ❊jinken sónchō 人権尊重 *respect for human rights* ❊kósei no sonchō 個性の尊重 *respect for individuality* ――**sonchō-suru** [*vt*] 尊重する *respect*

sonkei 尊敬 *respect (for a person); deference* ❊sonkei o haráu 尊敬を払う *pay respect* ❊sonkei no nén o idáku 尊敬の念を抱く *have respect for* ――**sonkei-suru** [*vt*] 尊敬する *respect* ❊Watashi wa chichí no ikikáta o sonkei-shite imásu. 私は父の生き方を尊敬しています。*I respect my father's way of life.*

sonna そんな *such; that kind of* [*designating a person or thing known to both the speaker and listener*] ❊sonna tóki ni wa そんな時には *at such times* ❊Sonna kotó o itté wa ikemasén. そんなことを言ってはいけません。*You mustn't say such a thing.* ――**sonna ni** そんなに *to that extent; such* ❊Sonna ni supído o dasánai de! そんなにスピードを出さないで。*Don't drive so fast!*

sono その *that* [*designating a thing near listener or known by both speaker and listener*] ❊Sono mádo o akete kudasái. その窓を開けて下さい。*Please open that window.* ❊Sono hí wa totemo áme ga tsúyokatta. その日はとても雨が強かった。*On that day it rained hard.* ❊Sono tóri desu. その通りです。*As you say!; That's right.*

sono áto; sono go その後 *after that*

sono kóro その頃 *about that time*

sono mamá そのまま *as is* ❊Sono mamá ni shite óite kudasái. そのままにしておいて下さい。*Leave things just as they are.*

sonó ta その他 *in addition and others*

sono uchi [ni] そのうち（に） *soon; before long; one of these days* ❊Sono uchi kánojo mo arawaréru deshō. そのうち彼女も現われるでしょう。*She'll show up before long.* **sono ué** その上 *above and beyond; besides; in addition* ❊Yamamoto-kun wa atamá ga íi, sono ué supótsu mo bannō da. 山本君は頭がいい、その上スポーツも万能だ。*Yamamoto's smart, and on top of that, he's good at all sports.* <*masc*>

sōnyū-suru [*vt*] 挿入する *insert; put in*

sonzai 存在 *being; existence* ――**sonzai-suru** [*vi*] 存在する *exist* ❊Uchūjin wa sonzai-shinai yo. 宇宙人は存在しないよ。*Alien creatures don't exist!*

sōon 騒音 *noise* ❊sōon bōshi 騒音防止 *noise prevention* ❊sōon kógai 騒音公害 *noise pollution*

sōpurándo ソープランド *"soapland" (bathhouse brothel)*

sóra 空 *sky*

sore それ *that* [*an object located nearer hearer than speaker, or information shared by speaker and hearer*]

sore dókoro ka それどころか *on the contrary; far from* 🔹"Minamino-san wa sore o kiite yorokobimáshita ka?" "Sore dókoro ka okoridáshita yo!" 「南野さんはそれを聞いて喜びましたか？」「それどころか、怒り出したよ。」 *"Was Minamino happy to hear that?" "Far from it. She got angry."*

sore hodo それ程 *not so; so much* [*with neg*] 🔹Mondai wa sore hodo muzukáshiku nákatta. 問題はそれ程難しくなかった。 *The questions weren't so hard.*

sore já... それじゃ〜 *well then...; then* 🔹Sore já, mata ashita! それじゃ、また明日！ *Well, I'll see you tomorrow!*

sore kara それから *afterward; and then*

Sore máde desu. それまでです。 *That's it.* (*or That's the extent of it / There's nothing more to be said.*)

sore ni それに *in addition; also* 🔹Kyő wa atsúi desu né. Sore ni kaze mo nái desu né. 今日は暑いですね、それに風もないですね。 *It's hot today, isn't it? Also, there's no wind.*

soréra no それらの *those*

soré·ru [*vi* sorénai; sóreta] 逸れる *turn away; miss the mark* 🔹Taifǘ wa Nihón o sórete Chōsen hántō ni jōriku-shita rashíi. 台風は日本を逸れて朝鮮半島に上陸したらしい。 *The typhoon seems to have turned away from Japan and landed on the Korean peninsula.*

soretómo それとも *or; or else* 🔹Kono hón wa anáta no desu ka, soretómo Okada-san no désu ka? この本はあなたのですか、それとも岡田さんのですか？ *Is this your book, or is it Okada's?*

sorézore それぞれ *each; severally; respectively* 🔹Nímotsu wa sorézore kimerareta basho ni oite kudasái. 荷物はそれぞれ決められた場所に置いて下さい。 *Put your bags in your respective assigned places.*

sóri そり *sled*

sōri dáijin 総理大臣 *prime minister*

sōritsu 創立 *establishment* 🔹sōritsúsha 創立者 *founder* ——**sōritsu-suru** [*vt*] 創立する *found; establish*

soroban 算盤 *abacus*

soroé·ru [*vt* soroénai; soróeta] 揃える *arrange; put in order; make even* 🔹Nágasa o soróete kíru yō ni. 長さを揃えて切るように。 *Cut it (my hair) so that it will all be the same length.* 🔹Kóe o soróete utaimashǒ. 声を揃えて歌いましょう。 *Let's all sing together.* 🔹Tốten wa shốhin o hốfu ni soróete imasu. 当店は商品を豊富に揃えています。 *This store is well stocked with merchandise.*

soroi 揃い *a set* 🔹soroi no chawan 揃いの茶碗 *a set of tea cups* 🔹O-matsuri de minna o-soroi no yukata o kite iru. お祭りでみんなお揃いの浴衣を着ている。 *At the festival, everyone is wearing the same style* yukata.

sórosoro [to] そろそろ（と）*soon; slowly; little by little*

sorótte 揃って *all; everyone; in unison* ❀Kázoku sorótte ryokō ni ikimásu. 家族揃って旅行に行きます。*The whole family is going on a trip together.*

soró·u [*vi* sorowánai; sorótta] 揃う *be even; be arranged; be in order* ❀Zairyō wa zémbu sorótte imasu. 材料は全部揃っています。*The materials are all in order.*

sór·u [*vt* soránai; sótta] 剃る *shave* ❀Hige o máinichi sótte imasu ka? 髭を毎日剃っていますか？*Do you shave every day?*

sór·u [*vi* soránai; sótta] 反る *warp; bend* ❀Kono íta wa kansō-shite sótte iru. この板は乾燥して反っている。*This board is dried out and warped.*

sóryo 僧侶 *Buddhist priest*

sósa 操作 *operation; management; manipulation* ❀chōbo no sósa 帳簿の操作 *juggling the books* ❀shikin sósa 資金操作 *money management* ——**sósa-suru** [*vt*] 操作する *operate; manage; manipulate* ❀Kono kikái o jōzú ni sósa-shite kudasái. この機械を上手に操作して下さい。*Be careful how you operate this machine.*

sōsaku 捜索 *a search* ❀kataku sōsaku 家宅捜索 *house search* ❀sōsakutai 捜索隊 *search party* ——**sōsaku-suru** [*vt*] 捜索する *search; look for* ❀Yukue fúmei no kodomo o keisatsu wa sōsaku-shite iru. 行方不明の子供を警察は捜索している。*The police are searching for the missing child.*

sósen 祖先 *ancestor*

sóshiki 組織 *organization* ❀minkan sóshiki 民間組織 *private organization* ——**sóshiki-suru** [*vt*] 組織する *organize* ❀Borántia o sóshiki-suru no wa muzukashíi. ボランティアを組織するのは難しい。*It is difficult to organize volunteers.* ——**soshikiteki [na]** 組織的（な）*systematic* ❀Sono dantai wa tsúne ni soshikiteki na katsudō o shite iru. その団体は常に組織的な活動をしている。*That group always acts in a systematic way.*

[o-]sōshiki（お）葬式 *funeral* ❀sōshiki o itonámu 葬式を営む *conduct a funeral* ❀sōshiki ni sanretsu-suru 葬式に参列する *attend a funeral*

sōshísha 創始者 *founder; organizer*

soshite そして *and then; and* ❀Shingapóru wa átsuku soshite shítsudo mo takái. シンガポールは暑くそして湿度も高い。*Singapore is hot, and the humidity is high.*

soshitsu 素質 *(one's) nature; character; quality; aptitude; the makings (to become)* ❀Musuko ní wa ongakuka no soshitsu ga arisṓ desu. 息子には音楽家の素質がありそうです。*It looks like my son has the makings of a musician.*

sōshitsu 喪失 *loss*   ❽jishin sőshitsu 自信喪失 *loss of confidence*   ❽kioku sőshitsu 記憶喪失 *loss of memory* ——**sōshitsu-suru** [*vt*] 喪失する *lose; forfeit*   ❽Musuko wa íkutsu mo no daigaku nyűshi ni óchite, sukkári jishin o sōshitsu-shite shimatta. 息子はいくつもの大学入試に落ちて、すっかり自信を喪失してしまった。 *My son failed the entrance exams for a number of universities and completely lost confidence.*

soshō 訴訟 *lawsuit*   ❽keiji sóshō 刑事訴訟 *a criminal suit*   ❽soshō o okósu 訴訟を起こす *sue (someone); file suit*

sōsho 草書 *"grass writing" (cursive style of writing Japanese)*

sōshoku 装飾 *decoration; ornament*   ❽sōshokuhin 装飾品 *an ornament*   ❽shitsunai sőshoku 室内装飾 *interior decoration* ——**sōshoku-suru** [*vt*] 装飾する *decorate*

sosog·u [*vt* sosoganai; sosoida] 注ぐ *pour; flow*   ❽námida o sosogu 涙を注ぐ *pour forth tears*   ❽chikará o sosogu 力を注ぐ *focus effort*   ❽hí ni abura o sosogu 火に油を注ぐ *pour oil on a fire*   ❽Kawá ga úmi ni sosoide iru. 川が海に注いでいる。 *The river flows into the sea.*

sosokkashí·i [*adj* sosokkáshiku nái; sosokkáshikatta] そそっかしい *(be) careless; hasty*   ❽Tsúma wa sosokkáshikute ítsumo shippai-bákari shite iru. 妻はそそっかしくていつも失敗ばかりしている。 *My wife is careless and is always fouling up.*

sotchoku [*na*] 率直（な）*frank*   ❽sotchoku na hitó 率直な人 *a frank person* ——**shotchoku ni** 率直に *frankly*   ❽Kyő wa watashi no kimochi o sotchoku ni iwasete moraimásu. 今日は私の気持ちを率直に言わせてもらいます。 *Today I'm going to speak frankly.*

sóto 外 *outside*   ❽uchi to sóto 家と外 *inside and outside; us and them*   ❽Sóto de asobi-nasái. 外で遊びなさい。 *Play outside.*

sōtō [*no*] 相当（の）*quite; considerable* ——**sōtō ni** 相当に *considerably; rather*   ❽sōtō ni kurushíi 相当に苦しい *rather painful* ——**sōtō-suru** [*vi*] 相当する *be equivalent to; correspond to*   ❽Nihongo no kana wa arufabétto ni sōtō-suru. 日本語のかなはアルファベットに相当する。 *Japanese kana correspond to the alphabet.*

sotsugyō 卒業 *graduation*   ❽sotsugyősei 卒業生 *alumna; alumnus*   ❽sotsugyőshiki 卒業式 *graduation ceremony*   ❽sotsugyő shősho 卒業証書 *diploma* ——**sotsugyō-suru** [*vi/vt*] 卒業する *graduate*

[ni] sotte 〜沿って *along...; beside...; alongside (of)...*   ❽Kawá ni sotte kokudó ga tőtte iru. 川に沿って国道が通っている。 *The highway runs alongside the river.*

sotto そっと *lightly; stealthily; quietly; softly*   ❽sotto shinobikómu そっと忍び込む *sneak in quietly*   ❽Sotto shite óite! そっとしておいて！ *Leave the matter alone! (or Keep quiet!)*

so·u [*vi* sowanai; sotta] 沿う；副う *follow alongside; go along*   ❽Go-kibő ni sou yō dóryoku-shimasu. ご希望に沿うよう努力します。 *I* *will try to do as you wish.*

sówasowa そわそわ *restlessly* ——**sówasowa-suru** [vi] そわそわする *be nervous; be fidgety* 💲Musumé wa kyō wa hajímete no déto de ása kara sówasowa-shite ochitsukanai. 娘は今日は初めてのデートで朝からそわそわして落ち着かない。 *Today my daughter is going on her first date, so she's been on edge and unable to settle down ever since this morning.*

soyókaze そよ風；微風 *breeze*

sóyosoyo [to] そよそよ（と）*softly; gently* 💲Harúkaze ga sóyosoyo to fúite kokochiyói. 春風がそよそよと吹いて心地よい。 *A soft spring breeze is blowing; it feels nice.*

sózan 早産 *premature birth*

sōzen to suru 騒然とする *be noisy; be confused; be bedlam* 💲sōzen to shita káigi 騒然とした会議 *a noisy meeting*

sōzō 想像 *imagination* 💲sōzṓryoku 想像力 *power of imagination* 💲Kirin wa sōzō-jṓ no dōbutsu desu. キリンは想像上の動物です。 *The kirin is an imaginary animal.* ——**sōzō-suru** [vt] 想像する *imagine*

sōzō 創造 *creation* 💲sōzṓsha 創造者 *creator* 💲sōzṓsei 創造性 *creativity* 💲ténchi sōzō 天地創造 *the creation of heaven and earth* ——**sōzō-suru** [vt] 創造する *create* 💲Sakka wa ṓku no risōteki na jímbutsu o sōzō-shita. 作家は多くの理想的な人物を創造した。 *The writer created many ideal characters.*

sōzoku 相続 *inheritance* 💲sōzokunin 相続人 *heir* 💲sōzoku záisan 相続財産 *inheritance* ——**sōzoku-suru** [vt] 相続する *inherit* 💲Chichí wa sófu no záisan o sōzoku-shimáshita. 父は祖父の財産を相続しました。 *My father inherited my grandfather's wealth.*

sōzōshí·i [adj sōzōshíku nái; sōzōshíkatta] 騒々しい *(be) noisy*

sōzōshísa 騒々しさ *noise* 💲machi no sōzōshísa 町の騒々しさ *city noise*

su 巣 *nest; (spider) web* 💲súbako 巣箱 *birdhouse; a (bee-) hive* 💲futarí no ái no su 二人の愛の巣 *a love nest*

sú 酢 *vinegar*

sū- 数～ *several; a few* 💲sūnin 数人 *several people* 💲Kyṓ wa kyaku wa sūnin dake datta. 今日は客は数人だけだった。 *There were only a few customers today.* 💲Kyṓ wa sūkai denwa ga átta. 今日は数回電話があった。 *There were several phone calls today.*

subarashí·i [adj subaráshiku nái; subaráshikatta] 素晴しい *(be) wonderful; remarkable* 💲Kimi wa hontō ni subaráshíi josei da. 君は本当に素晴しい女性だ。 *You're a remarkable woman. <masc>*

subayá·i [adj subayáku nái; subayákatta] 素早い *(be) quick; rapid; nimble* ——**subayáku** 素早く *quickly; nimbly* 💲Nakátani-san wa tosshin-shite kúru kuruma kara subayáku mi o kawashita. 中谷さんは突進して来る車から素早く身を交わした。 *Nakatani quickly jumped* *out of the way of the oncoming car.*

-sube 〜術 *a way; a means (to)...* 🔹Násu sube ga nái. 為す術がない。 *There's nothing I can do about it.*

suberídai 滑り台 *(playground) slide*

subér·u [*vi* suberánai; subétta] 滑る *slide; slip; ski* 🔹Ashí ga subétte kegá o shita. 足が滑って怪我をした。 *I slipped and hurt myself.* 🔹Chokkákkō de shámen o subétta. 直滑降で斜面を滑った。 *I skied straight down the slope.*

subesube [to] すべすべ（と）*smooth; slippery; velvety* ——**subesube-suru** [*vi*] すべすべする *(be) smooth; slippery; velvety* 🔹Josei no háda wa subesube-shite iru. 女性の肌はすべすべしている。 *A woman's skin is smooth.*

súbete [no] 全て（の）*every; all; everything* 🔹Watashi wa kánojo no súbete o áishite iru yo. 私は彼女の全てを愛しているよ。 *I love everything about her.*

súde ni 既に *already* 🔹Sonó hito nara súde ni shitte imásu yo. その人なら既に知っていますよ。 *If that's who you mean, I already know her.*

-sue 〜末 *end (of)* 🔹suekko 末っ子 *the last child (of a family)* 🔹toshi no sue 年の末 *the end of the year* 🔹Kúshin no sue ni yattó kansei-shita. 苦心の末にやっと完成した。 *With a lot of effort, I finally completed it.*

sue·ru [*vt* suenai; sueta] 据える *place; set; lay; put; appoint* 🔹Térebi o tana ni suemáshita. テレビを棚に据えました。 *I put the TV on the shelf.*

suetsuke·ru [*vt* suetsukenai; suetsuketa] 据え付ける *install; set; fix* 🔹Reizóko o daidokoro ni suetsukete moratta. 冷蔵庫を台所に据え付けてもらった。 *We had a refrigerator installed in the kitchen.*

sūgaku 数学 *mathematics*

súgao 素顔 *true face; face without make-up*

súgata 姿 *figure; form* 🔹Dare no súgata mo miénai. 誰の姿も見えない。 *I can't see anyone.* 🔹Machi no súgata ga ippen-shite shimatta. 町の姿が一変してしまった。 *The town's appearance was completely changed.*

sugi 杉 *Japanese cedar; cryptomeria*

-sugi 〜過ぎ *after...; past...* 🔹Íma yójinijuppúnsugi desu. 今四時二十分過ぎです。 *It's now twenty minutes past four.*

sugí·ru [*vi/vt* suginái; súgita] 過ぎる *pass; go beyond* 🔹Shōténgai o sugíru to hashí ni demásu. 商店街を過ぎると橋に出ます。 *When you get beyond the shopping street you'll come to a bridge.* 🔹Yakusoku no jikan o súgite shimatta. 約束の時間を過ぎてしまった。 *I was late for my appointment.* 🔹Míeko-san wa omae ní wa súgita jitsú ni íi nyóbō da. 美枝子さんはお前には過ぎた実にいい女房だ。 *Mieko is really a good wife; too good for you.* <*masc*>

-sugíru ～過ぎる *in excess (of)* §Á tabesúgichatta. ああ、食べ過ぎちゃった。*Oh, I ate too much.*

sugó·i [*adj* súgoku nái; súgokatta] 凄い *(be) great; terrific; terrible; awful* §Sugói métsuki de niramáreta. 凄い目つきで睨まれた。*I was looked at in an awful way.* **(or He / She looked at me in an awful way.)** —— **sugóku** 凄く *terrifically; very; awfully* §Kánojo wa sugóku kírei da. 彼女は凄くきれいだ。*She's awfully pretty.* <*masc*>

sugós·u [*vt* sugosánai; sugóshita] 過ごす *spend (time); get through* §Sono hí sono hí o nán to ka sugóshite iru. その日その日を何とか過ごしている。*Somehow I manage to get through each day, one at a time.* §Kotoshi wa natsu-yásumi o Karúizawa de sugoshimásu. 今年は夏休みを軽井沢で過ごします。*This year I'm going to spend my summer vacation at Karuizawa.*

súgu 直ぐ *right away; soon* §Súgu iku yó. 直ぐ行くよ。*I'm going (there) right now.* §Súgu okóru hito wa kirai desu. 直ぐ怒る人は嫌いです。*I don't like people who get angry quickly.*

suguré·ru [*vi* sugurénai; sugúreta] 優れる；勝れる *be better (than); be superior (to)* §Motoki-san wa tōsha de sugúreta gyōseki o tsukurimáshita. 元木さんは当社で優れた業績を作りました。*Ms. Motoki has an outstanding record in this company.* §Kaoiro ga sugurénai. 顔色が優れない。*You don't look so well.* §Kono dezáin wa máe no yóri sugúrete iru. このデザインは前のより優れている。*This design is better than the former one.*

sūhai 崇拝 *worship* §gūzō súhai 偶像崇拝 *idol worship* —— **sūhai-suru** [*vt*] 崇拝する *worship* §Naporeon wa eiyū to shite sūhai-sarete iru. ナポレオンは英雄として崇拝されている。*Napoléon Bonaparte is worshipped as a hero.*

suibaku 水爆 *hydrogen bomb*

suichoku [no] 垂直 （の） *perpendicular*

suichū báre 水中バレー *water ballet*

suidō 水道 *(city) water* §suidókyoku 水道局 *water department* §suidóya 水道屋 *plumber*

suigin 水銀 *mercury* §suigin chúdoku 水銀中毒 *mercury poisoning*

suigara 吸い殻 *cigarette butt*

suihei [no] 水平 （の） *level; horizontal* §suiheisen 水平線 *the horizon; a horizontal line*

súi 水位 *water level* §Shūchū gōu no eikyō de kawa no súi-i ga agatte iru. 集中豪雨の影響で川の水位が上がっている。*The water level of the river has risen because of the localized downpour.*

suijóki 水蒸気 *steam; vapor*

suijun 水準 *a level; standard* §suijúnki 水準器 *carpenter's level* §Saikin dé wa seikatsu súijun ga tákaku nátte iru. 最近では生活水準が高くなっている。*Recently the living standard has risen.*

suika 西瓜 *watermelon*

suikō 遂行 *execution; carrying out; fulfilling* ——**suikō-suru** [vt] 遂行する *fulfill* ⑧Nímmu o kakujitsu ni suikō-subeshi. 任務を確実に遂行すべし。 *You must execute your duties to the letter.*

suikóm·u [vt suikómánai; suikónda] 吸い込む *inhale; suck in (up)* ⑧Sanso kyūnyúki kara sánso o suikónda. 酸素吸入器から酸素を吸い込んだ。 *I breathed oxygen from the ozygen inhaler.*

suimin 睡眠 *sleep* ⑧suimin-búsoku 睡眠不足 *lack of sleep* ⑧suimín yaku 睡眠薬 *sleeping pill*

suirai 水雷 *torpedo* ⑧suiraitei 水雷艇 *torpedo boat*

súren 睡蓮 *water lily*

súiryoku 水力 *water power* ⑧suiryoku hátsuden 水力発電 *water power generator*

suisai 水彩 *watercolor* ⑧suisaiga 水彩画 *watercolor painting* ⑧suisai énogu 水彩絵の具 *watercolors (paints)*

suisámbutsu 水産物 *marine products* ⑧Suisánchō 水産庁 *Fisheries Agency*

suisei 彗星 *comet*

Suisei 水星 *the planet Mercury*

suisen 水仙 *narcissus*

suisen 推薦 *recommendation* ⑧suisensho 推薦書 *letter of recommendation* ——**suisen-suru** [vt] 推薦する *recommend* ⑧Watashi wa Miyata-san o watashi no kōnin ni suisen-shita. 私は宮田さんを私の後任に推薦した。 *I recommended Ms. Miyata as my successor.*

súisha 水車 *waterwheel*

suishitsu ósen 水質汚染 *water pollution*

súishō 水晶 *quartz; crystal* ⑧suishō-dókei 水晶時計 *a quartz watch* ⑧súishō no péndanto 水晶のペンダント *crystal pendant*

suishōtai 水晶体 *eye lens*

súiso 水素 *hydrogen*

suisoku 推測 *a guess* ——**suisoku-suru** [vt] 推測する *guess; conjecture* ⑧Hyakunen-go no chikyū no jōtai ga suisoku-dekimásu ka? 百年後の地球の状態が推測できますか？ *Can you conjecture what the earth will be like a century from now?*

suitai 衰退 *decline; decay* ——**suitai-suru** [vi] 衰退する *decline; decay* ⑧Búmmei wa suitai-shite iku. 文明は衰退していく。 *Civilizations decline.*

suitei 推定 *deduction; supposition* ——**suitei-suru** [vt] 推定する *suppose; presume; deduce* ⑧Keisatsu wa Asáhara o satsujin hánnin to suitei-shite sósa-shite iru. 警察は麻原を殺人犯人と推定して捜査している。 *The police are investigating Asahara on the supposition that he is guilty of murder.*

suitō-gákari 出納係 *teller; cashier*

suitorí-gami 吸取紙 *blotter; blotting paper*

suitór·u [*vt* suitoránai; suitótta] 吸い取る *blot; soak up*   🞂Shihonka wa rōdṓsha no umidáshita rijun o katappashi kara suitótte iku. 資本家は労働者の生み出した利潤を片っ端から吸い取っていく。 *Profits generated by workers are immediately soaked up by capitalists.*

Suiyṓbi 水曜日 *Wednesday*

suizṓkukan 水族館 *aquarium*

súji 筋 *tendon; line; theme; plot*   🞂Niku no súji o tóreba yawarákaku náru. 肉の筋を取れば柔らかくなる。 *If you remove the tendons from the meat it will be more tender.*   🞂Watashi wa Genji no súji no shusshin désu. 私は源氏の筋の出身です。 *I am a descendent of the Genji clan.*   🞂Kore wa táshika na súji kara no jōhō desu. これは確かな筋からの情報です。 *This information is from a reliable source.*   🞂monogátari no súji 物語の筋 *the plot of a story*

sūji 数字 *numeral; a figure*

sujigaki 筋書 *outline; summary*   🞂Kōshō wa sujigaki-dṓri ni susunda. 交渉は筋書通りに進んだ。 *Negotiations followed the outline exactly.*

sujiko 筋子 *salmon roe*

sujímichi 筋道 *reason; logic; the thread (of a story)*   🞂Sujímichi o kichín to tátete setsumei-shinai to wakari-zurái desu yó. 筋道をきちんと立てて説明しないと分かりづらいですよ。 *If you don't explain it logically and coherently it's difficult to understand.*

sujimúkai 筋向かい *across the street; catercornered from here*   🞂Sujimúkai no ié to wa tsukiái ga arimasén. 筋向かいの家とは付き合いがありません。 *I have no contact with the people in the house diagonally across the street.*

sukébei [na] 助平（な） *lewd; lecher*   🞂sukebei kónjō 助平根性 *lewd nature*

sukí [na] 好き（な） *like; be fond of*   🞂Sakana ga sukí desu ka? 魚が好きですか。 *Do you like fish?*   🞂Sukí na daké tótte kudasái. 好きなだけ取って下さい。 *Take as many as you like.*

suki 隙 *an opening; opportunity*   🞂Kéndō de wa aite no suki o nerau kotó ga daijí desu. 剣道では相手の隙を狙うことが大事です。 *In kendo it's important to watch for openings in an opponent's defense.* ——**suki ni** 隙に *upon the opportunity of; taking advantage of the fact that...*

sukikírai 好き嫌い *preference; likes and dislikes*   🞂Sánsai no musuko wa sukikírai ga hageshíi desu. 三歳の息子は好き嫌いが激しいです。 *My three-year-old son has strong likes and dislikes.*

sukín スキン *condom*

sukkári [to] すっかり（と） *completely*   🞂Shukudai o sukkári wasurete ita. 宿題をすっかり忘れていた。 *I completely forgot my homework.*   🞂Sukkári aki ráshiku nátte kimáshita. すっかり秋らしくなってきま

した。 *It really seems like fall now.*

sukkíri [to] すっきり（と）*neatly; clearly; pat* ❊Máda byōki ga sukkíri naótte inai. まだ病気がすっきり直っていない。*I still haven't completely recovered from my illness.* ——**sukkíri-suru** [*vi*] すっきりする *be refreshed; be clear; be neat* ❊Kánojo wa ítsumo sukkíri-shita fukú o kite iru. 彼女はいつもすっきりした服を着ている。*She always dresses neatly.* ❊Kyō wa atamá ga sukkíri-shinai. 今日は頭がすっきりしない。*My head's not clear today.*

sukóshi 少し *few; a little; slight* ❊Mō sukóshi o-kane ga hoshíi. もう少しお金がほしい。*I'd like to have a little more money.* ❊Sukoshi daké de ma ni aimásu. 少しだけで間に合います。*Just a little will do.* ——**sukoshi mo** [*with neg*] 少しも *not...at all; none at all* ❊Senséi no hanashí wa sukoshi mo wakaránakatta. 先生の話は少しも分からなかった。*I didn't understand anything the teacher said.*

sukóyaka [na] 健やか（な）*healthy* ❊Sukóyaka na nikutai ní wa sukóyaka na séishin ga yadorimásu. 健やかな肉体には健やかな精神が宿ります。*In a healthy body resides a healthy mind.* ——**sukóyaka ni** 健やかに *healthily* ❊Akambō wa sukóyaka ni sodátte imásu. 赤ん坊は健やかに育っています。*The baby is growing healthily.*

suk·u [*vi* sukanai; suita] 空く；透く *be empty; be open* ❊Densha wa ángai suite ita. 電車は案外空いていた。*The train was surprisingly uncrowded.* ❊Hará ga suite tamaranai! 腹が空いてたまらない。*I'm so hungry I can't stand it!*

sukui 救い *help; rescue*

sukunákutomo 少なくとも *at least* ❊Kono shigoto ga owaru máde, sukunákutomo isshúkan wa kakarimásu. この仕事が終わるまで少なくとも一週間はかかります。*It'll take at least a week before this work is done.*

suk·u [*vt* sukuwanai; sukutta] 救う *save* ❊San Sū Chī jóshi wa kuni o sukutta eiyū no hítori desu. サン・スー・チー女史は国を救った英雄の一人です。*Sang Suu Kyi is a hero who saved her country.* ❊Watashi no nayamí o sukutte kudasái. 私の悩みを救って下さい。*Save me from my distress.*

sumás·u [*vt* sumásánai; sumáshita] 済ます *finish* ❊Kaikei wa mō sumashimáshita yo. 会計はもう済ましましたよ。*I have already paid the bill.* ——**(de) sumasé·ru** [*caus* sumasénai; sumáseta] （で）済ませる *make do with* ❊O-híru wa ariawase de sumasemashó. お昼は有り合わせで済ませましょう。*For lunch we'll make do with leftovers.*

sumáto [na] スマート（な）*slender; stylish* ❊Éiko-san wa saikin sumáto ni narimáshita. 栄子さんは最近スマートになりました。*Eiko has lost some weight recently.* ❊Sono wanpísu wa totemo sumáto na dezáin desu ne. そのワンピースはとてもスマートなデザインですね。*The design of that dress is really chic, isn't it.*

sumí 炭 *charcoal*

sumí 墨 *india ink* 🔸 sumie 墨絵 *a black and white ink painting*

súmi 隅 *corner (of a room)* 🔸 Heya no súmi ni piano ga áru. 部屋の隅に
ピアノがある。*There's a piano in the corner of the room.*

sumikóm·u [*vi* sumikómánai; sumikónda] 住み込む *live in (at one's
place of work)* 🔸 sumikomi jūgyōin 住み込み従業員 *live-in
employee*

Sumimasén ga... 済みませんが... *Excuse me, but...; I'm sorry, but...*
🔸 Sumimasén ga, ryōgae-shite itadakemasén ka? 済みませんが、両替
していただけませんか。*Excuse me. Would you change this bill,
please?*

Sumimasén (deshita)! 済みません（でした）。*I'm sorry (for what I
did)!*

sumire 菫 *violet (flower)*

sumō 相撲 *Japanese style wrestling* 🔸 sumōtori 相撲取り *sumo wrestler*
🔸 sumō o tóru 相撲を取る *(to) do (or play) sumo; wrestle*

sumomo 李 *plum*

sumpō 寸法 *measurement; plan* 🔸 Uesuto no sumpō o hakátte kuremasén
ka? ウエストの寸法を測ってくれませんか？*Would you take my
waist measurement?* 🔸 Chikái uchi ni itte miyṓ to iu sumpō da. 近いう
ちに行ってみようという寸法だ。*I plan to try to go in the near
future.* <*masc*>

súm·u [*vi* sumánai; súnda] 住む *live; dwell* 🔸 Watashi wa Nihón ni
yonjūnen-chíkaku súnde imásu. 私は日本に四十年近く住んでいま
す。*I've lived in Japan for nearly forty years.* 🔸 "Súmeba miyako" tó
wa yóku itta monó desu. 「住めば都」とはよく言ったもので
す。*"If you live there, it's the best spot on earth," is well put.*

súm·u [*vi* sumánai; súnda] 済む *to finish; be through with* 🔸 Shikén ga
súnde hotto shite iru tokoró desu. 試験が済んでほっとしているとこ
ろです。*Exams are over and I'm relieved.* 🔸 Súnda kotó o tóyakaku iú
no wa yameyṓ. 済んだことをとやかく言うのは止めよう。*Stop
complaining about what's over and done with.* 🔸 Kore de súmu to
omóu no? これで済むと思うの？*Do you think you've seen the end of
this?* <*fem*>

súm·u [*vi* sumánai; súnda] 澄む；清む *be clear; clarified* 🔸 Mizuúmi
no mizu ga súnde imásu. 湖の水が澄んでいます。*The lake is clear.*
🔸 Kánojo wa kóe ga súnde iru. 彼女は声が澄んでいる。*Her voice is
(crystal) clear.* 🔸 Súnda atamá de kangae-nasái. 澄んだ頭で考えなさ
い。*Think with a clear head.*

suna 砂 *sand* 🔸 sunaba 砂場 *sandbox* 🔸 sunahama 砂浜 *sandy beach*

súnao [na] 素直（な）*obedient; frank; plain; straightforward* 🔸 Uchi no
ko wa minna súnao desu. うちの子はみんな素直です。*All my
children are obedient.* 🔸 Kánojo wa súnao na jí o kakimásu. 彼女は素

直な字を書きます。*Her writing is plain.* ——**súnao ni** 素直に *obediently; simply* §Chūkoku wa súnao ni kikinasái. 忠告は素直に 聞きなさい。*Listen obediently to the advice.*

sunappó·i [*adj* sunappóku nái; sunappókatta] 砂っぽい *(be) sandy*

sunáwachi 即ち *that is; that is to say; namely*

suné すね *shin* §Yūjin no Tágami wa suné ni kizu o mótte iru. 友人の 田上はすねに傷をもっている。*My friend Tagami has a scar on his shin.* §suné o kajíru すねをかじる *to sponge off of*

suné·ru [*vi/ vt* sunénai; súneta] 拗ねる *be sulky; be cynical* §Gósai no musumé wa súgu ni súnete nakidásu. 五歳の娘は直ぐに拗ねて泣き 出す。*Our five-year-old daughter sulks and cries at the slightest thing.* §Yó o súnete íkita tokoro de nan no toku mo nái. 世を拗ねて生きたと ころで何の得もない。*Nothing is gained by being cynical.*

súpā スーパー *supermarket*

supána スパナ *wrench*

suponji スポンジ *foam rubber*

suppádaka [no] すっ裸（の）*(stark-) naked* §Ákachan wa suppádaka de mizuásobi o tanoshínde iru. 赤ちゃんはすっ裸で水遊びを楽しん でいる。*The baby is enjoying playing in the water naked.*

suppá·i [*adj* suppáku nái; suppákatta] 酸っぱい *(be) sour; acidic* §Watashi wa suppái monó wa taberaremasén. 私は酸っぱいものは食 べられません。*I can't eat sour (acidic) foods.*

-súra 〜すら *even~* §Daigakúsei de súra dekínai mondai o ano chūgakúsei ga tóita. 大学生ですらできない問題をあの中学生が解 いた。*That middle-school student solved a problem even a university student couldn't do.*

súrasura [to] すらすら（と）*fluently; smoothly* §Doitsú-go o súrasura to yómu ドイツ語をすらすらと読む *read German fluently* §Kōshō ga súrasura hakonde keiyaku ni kogitsuketa. 交渉がすらすら運んで契 約にこぎつけた。*Negotiations went smoothly and an agreement was reached.*

surechiga·u [*vi* surechigawanai; surechigatta] 擦れ違う *pass each other* §Nobori-dénsha to kudari-dénsha ga Mitaká-eki de surechigatta. 上り 電車と下り電車が三鷹駅で擦れ違った。*The inbound and outbound trains passed each other at Mitaka station.* §Dómo gíron ga surechigatte kamiawanai. どうも議論が擦れ違って噛み合わない。 *The arguments don't mesh; they pass each other by.*

súri 掏摸 *pickpocket*

surikire·ru [*vi* surikirenai; surikireta] 擦り切れる *(be) threadbare; worn out* §Zubón no suso ga surikirete shimatta. ズボンの裾が擦り切れ てしまった。*The hem of these pants is worn out.*

surimúk·u [*vt* surimukánai; surimúita] 擦り剥く *skin; graze; scrape* §Koronde hiza o surimúita. 転んで膝を擦り剥いた。*I fell and* *skinned my knee.*

suritsuke·ru [*vt* suritsukenai; suritsuketa] 擦り付ける *rub against; rub on* §Inú ga hana o watashi no karada ni suritsukete kíta. 犬が鼻を私に擦り付けてきた。*My dog rubbed its nose on me.*

suru [*vi / vt* shinai; shita] する *do* §Suru kotó wa nani mo nái. することは何もない。*I have nothing to do.* §Kenkyū o máinichi shite iru. 研究を毎日している。*I'm doing research every day.*

súr·u [*vt* suránai; sútta] 刷る *print* §Íma, watashítachi wa gakkyū shímbun o sútte iru. 今、私たちは学級新聞を刷っている。*Now we are printing a class newspaper.*

súr·u [*vt* suránai; sútta] 掏る *to pickpocket* §Saifu o surárete shimatta rashíi. 財布を掏られてしまったらしい。*It seems my wallet was pickpocketed.*

surudó·i [*adj* surúdoku nái; surúdokatta] 鋭い *(be) pointed; sharp; keen* §surudói métsuki 鋭い目つき *sharp eyes* §Kono hōchō no hasaki wa surudói wa. この包丁の刃先は鋭いわ。*This kitchen knife is sharp.* <*fem*> §Kimi wa surudói kansatsú-ryoku o mótte iru né. 君は鋭い観察力を持っているね。*You certainly have keen powers of observation.* <*masc*>

súrusuru [to] するする（と） *easily; smoothly; slippery* §Sono josei wa súrusuru to óbi o tóita. その女性はするすると帯を解いた。*The lady slipped off her obi.* §Sáru wa súrusuru to kí o nobotte itta. 猿はするすると木を登っていった。*The monkey scampered nimbly up the tree.*

suru to すると *then; and then; thereupon* §Ojīsan wa yamá ni shibakari ni ikimáshita. Suru to mishiranu hitó ni deaimáshita. おじいさんは芝刈りに行きました。すると見知らぬ人に出会いました。*The old man went to the mountain to gather wood and there he met a stranger.*

[o-]súshi 寿司 *sushi (vinegar-flavored rice, usually served with raw fish and garnished with wasabi, or Japanese horseradish)*

sushi-zume [no] 鮨詰めの *crowded; jam-packed* §sushi-zume no dénsha 鮨詰めの電車 *a jam-packed train*

suso 裾 *hem; skirt* §susono 裾野 *the foot of a mountain* §suso o matsuru 裾をまつる *take up a hem*

súsu 煤 *soot*

susug·u [*vt* susuganai; susuida] 濯ぐ；漱ぐ *rinse; wash out* §Senzai de aráttára shikkári susuide kudasái. 洗剤で洗ったらしっかり濯いで下さい。*When you wash clothes with detergent, rinse them well.*

susume·ru [*vt* susumenai; susumeta] 進める；奨める *urge; advance* §héi o susumeru 兵を進める *advance (one's) troops* §hanashí o susumeru 話を進める *proceed with talks*

susume·ru [*vt* susumenai; susumeta] 勧める；薦める *recommend; encourage* §gakusei no jihatsuteki kenkyū o susumeru 学生の自発的研究を勧める *encourage students to do independent research*

§Watashi wa kōnin ni Mórita-san o susumeta. 私は後任に森田さんを勧めた。*I recommended Mr. Morita as my successor.*

susum·u [*vi* susumanai; susunda] 進む *advance; take the initiative* §Musuko wa konogoro susunde benkyō-suru yṓ ni nátta. 息子はこの頃進んで勉強するようになった。*Recently my son has begun to study on his own initiative.* §Háha no byōjō ga susunde iru yṓ da. 母の病状が進んでいるようだ。*My mother's condition (of the disease) seems advanced.*

susur·u [*vt* susuranai; susutta] 啜る *sip; slurp* §Cha o susutte nómu no wa mittomo-nái. 茶をすすって飲むのはみっともない。*It's inelegant to slurp one's tea.*

[gasorin] sutándo （ガソリン）スタンド *gasoline station*

sutando スタンド *table lamp*

sutare·ru [*vi* sutarenai; sutareta] 廃れる *go out of date; be out of fashion; come to ruin* §Sutareta fūshū ni imada ni kodawáru no wa okashíi. 廃れた風習に今だにこだわるのはおかしい。*It's odd to stick to such antiquated customs.* §Sore dé wa otokó ga sutareru zó. それでは男が廃れるぞ。*That's an unmanly thing to do!* <*masc*>

suteki [na] 素敵（な） *excellent; splendid; great; wonderful; gorgeous* §Sono sḗtā wa suteki da wa. そのセーターは素敵だわ。*That's a gorgeous sweater.* <*fem*> §Hamanaka-san wa suteki na hitó desu. 浜中さんは素敵な人です。*Ms. Hamanaka is a wonderful person.*

suténresu ステンレス *stainless steel*

sute·ru [*vt* sutenai; suteta] 捨てる *discard; throw away; abandon* §gomí o suteru ごみを捨てる *throw out garbage* §mizu o suteru 水を捨てる *drain the water* §Kikuchi wa kázoku o sutete déte itta. 菊池は家族を捨てて出て行った。*Kikuchi abandoned his family and left (home).*

súto スト *a strike; walkout* §súto o uchikiru ストを打ち切る *call off a strike*

sutṓbu ストーブ *heater* §gasu sutṓbu ガスストーブ *gas heater* §sekiyu sutṓbu 石油ストーブ *kerosene heater*

sūtto すうっと *quickly; silently; suddenly* §Michiru ga me no máe ni sūtto arawáreta no de bikkúri-shita. ミチルが目の前にすうっと現われたのでびっくりした。*Michiru startled me when he appeared before me without making a noise.* ——**sūtto-suru** [*vi*] すうっとする *feel relieved* §Zutsū ga sátte sūtto-shita. 頭痛が去ってすうっとした。*My headache went away and I felt fine.*

su·u [*vt* suwanai; sutta] 吸う *suck; smoke* §kū́ki o suu 空気を吸う *suck in air* §Hachi ga hana no mítsu o sutte iru. 蜂が花の密を吸っている。*Bees suck nectar from flowers.* §Tabako o sutté wa ikemasén. 煙草を吸ってはいけません。*You mustn't smoke cigarettes.*

suwar·u [vi suwaranai; suwatta] 座る *sit; sit (Japanese-style)*

súyasuya [to] すやすや（と）*(sleep) quietly; peacefully; calmly* 🔹Ákachan ga súyasuya to nemutte imásu. 赤ちゃんがすやすやと眠っています。 *The baby is sleeping peacefully.*

suzu 鈴 *(small) bell*

suzuki 鱸 *sea bass (fish)*

suzume 雀 *sparrow* 🔹suzume no námida 雀の涙 *a tiny amount* <set phrase>

suzumébachi 雀蜂 *hornet*

suzunari 鈴なり *hang in clusters* 🔹Budō ga suzunari ni minótte iru. 葡萄が鈴なりに実っている。 *Grapes are hanging in clusters.*

suzúran 鈴蘭 *lily-of-the-valley*

suzushí·i [adj suzúshiku nái; suzúshikatta] 涼しい *(be) cool* 🔹Suzushíi kaze ga fúite imásu. 涼しい風が吹いています。 *A cool breeze is blowing.*

T

tá 田 *rice paddy* 🔹taue 田植え *rice planting*

ta [no] 他（の）*another; other; others* 🔹tafúken 他府県 *other prefectures* 🔹sonó ta その他 *and others*

-ta 〜た [past tense suffix] 🔹Dono haná mo minna kírei datta. どの花もみんなきれいだった。 *All the flowers were beautiful.* 🔹Háha wa totemo génki deshita. 母はとても元気でした。 *Mother was very well.* 🔹Sono éiga wa omoshírokatta. その映画は面白かった。 *That movie was interesting.*

tába 束 *bundle; bunch* 🔹hanatába 花束 *a bouquet of flowers*

tabako たばこ；煙草 *tobacco; cigarettes* 🔹tabakoya 煙草屋 *tobacco store (shop)* 🔹tabako o suu たばこを吸う *smoke* 🔹tabako o yameru たばこを止める *quit smoking; give up cigarettes*

tabané·ru [vt tabanénai; tabáneta] 束ねる *bundle; tie up* 🔹furushímbun o tabanéru 古新聞を束ねる *bundle up old newspapers* 🔹Kamí o ushiro de tabánete kuremasén ka? 髪を後ろで束ねてくれませんか。 *Would you tie up my hair in a bun, please?*

tabehốdai 食べ放題 *"All you can eat!"*

tabemóno 食べ物 *food* 🔹Tabemóno wa ainiku nani mo arimasén. 食べ物はあいにく何もありません。 *I'm afraid there's nothing to eat.*

tabé·ru [vt tabénai; tábeta] 食べる *eat* 🔹Késa náni tábeta no? 今朝何食べたの？ *What did you have for breakfast? <fem>*

tabí 旅 *a trip; travel* 🔹Tabí wa michizure, yó wa násake. 旅は道連れ世は情け。 *On a trip, a companion; in the world, kindness. <set phrase>*

-tabí ni 〜度に *every time...* 🔸Tsúma wa káigai ni ryokō-suru tabí ni miyage o takusan katte kimásu. 妻は海外に旅行する度に土産をたくさん買ってきます。*Every time my wife takes a trip abroad, she buys lots of souvenirs.*

tabitabi 度々 *often; frequently* 🔸Yūta-kun wa tabitabi shukudai o wasuremásu. 雄太君は度々宿題を忘れます。*Yūta frequently forgets (to do) his homework.*

tabō [na] 多忙な *busy* 🔸Nihonjín wa tabō na máinichi o okutte iru. 日本人は多忙な毎日を送っている。*Japanese live busy lives.*

tábun 多分 *probably* 🔸Ashitá wa tábun haréru deshō. 明日は多分晴れるでしょう。*Tomorrow will probably be fair.*

-tachi 〜たち；達 [*pronoun plu suffix, rarely with nouns*] 🔸kimitachi 君たち *you (all)* 🔸bókutachi 僕達 *we* 🔸kodomotachi 子供たち *children*

tachiagár·u [*vi* tachiagaránai; tachiagátta] 立ち上がる *stand up; make / take a stand; act* 🔸Nagái aida netakiri dátta sóbo ga kyō yatto béddo kara tachiagáru kotó ga dekimáshita. 長い間寝たきりだった祖母が今日やっとベッドから立ち上がることができました。*Today, my grandmother, who has been bedridden for a long time, was able to get out of bed.* 🔸Nammin kyūsai ni séifu wa tachiagáru kettei o shita. 難民救済に政府は立ち上がる決定をした。*The government decided to take a stand (on the question of whether or not) to rescue refugees.*

tachibá 立場 *standpoint; place; position* 🔸Hito no tachibá ni nátte kangáete goran. 人の立場になって考えてごらん。*Try thinking about it from another person's standpoint.*

tachidomar·u [*vi* tachidomaranai; tachidomatta] 立ち止まる *stop walking* 🔸Otoko no hitó wa tachidomatte tabako ni hí o tsúketa. 男の人は立ち止まって煙草に火をつけた。*A man stopped and lit a cigarette.*

Tachiiri kinshi. 立ち入り禁止。*No trespassing.*

tachimachi 忽ち *in an instant; immediately; suddenly* 🔸Atarashii arubamu wa tachimachi urikírete shimatta. 新しいアルバムは忽ち売り切れてしまった。*The new album sold out immediately.*

tachimíseki 立ち見席 *standing room*

tachinaori 立ち直り *recovery; recovering; bouncing back* 🔸tachinaori ga hayái 立ち直りが早い *quick at recovering (from an illness or shock)*

tachinaór·u [*vi* tachinaoránai; tachinaótta] 立ち直る *recover; bounce back* 🔸byōki kara tachinaóru 病気から立ち直る *recover from a sickness* 🔸Tamotsu-san wa tōsan no dageki kara súgu tachinaorimáshita. 保さんは倒産の打撃からすぐ立ち直りました。*Tamotsu soon recovered from the blow of bankruptcy.* 🔸Kaisha no gyōseki wa tachinaótte iru. 会社の業績は立ち直っている。*The* *company's business has recovered.*

tachinók·u [*vi* tachinokánai; tachinóita] 立ち退く *leave; evacuate*
§Shakuchi no kígen ga kíreta no de tachinóite atarashíi tochi o katta. 借地の期限が切れたので立ち退いて新しい土地を買った。*The lease on the rented land expired, so I left and bought a new lot.*

táda 只 *free of charge* §Táda hodo takái monó wa nái. 只ほど高いものはない。*Nothing is more expensive than (what's called) "free." <set phrase>*

táda 唯 *only; just* §Aitsu wa yahári táda no hitó datta na. あいつはやはり唯の人だったな。*He was only human after all.*

tádachi ni 直ちに *immediately; right away* §Tádachi ni shuppatsu-shiyó. 直ちに出発しよう。*Let's leave right away.*

tadáima 只今 *just now; right now* §Buchō wa tadáima denwa-chū desu. 部長は只今電話中です。*The chief is on the phone just now.*

Tadaimá! ただいま。*I'm home! <set phrase>*

tadashí·i [*adj* tadáshiku nái; tadáshikatta] 正しい *(be) correct; accurate; right* §tadashíi jikan 正しい時間 *the correct time* §Senséi no iu kotó ga ítsumo tadashíi to wa kagiránai. 先生の言うことがいつも正しいとは限らない。*What the teacher says is not always right.* —— **tadáshiku** 正しく *correctly; accurately* §Nihongo o tadáshiku hatsuon-shite kudasái. 日本語を正しく発音して下さい。*Pronounce Japanese correctly.*

tadás·u [*vt* tadasánai; tadáshita] 正す *correct; rectify* §Machigái wa súgu ni tadáshita hō ga íi. 間違いは直ぐに正した方がいい。*One ought to correct a mistake right away.*

tadayó·u [*vi* tadayowánai; tadayótta] 漂う *drift; float; hang in the air* §Fúne ga hōkō o ushinatte úmi ni tadayótte iru. 船が方向を失って海に漂っている。*The ship lost its course and is drifting at sea.* §Átari ichimen ni sénkō no niói ga tadayótte imasu. 辺り一面に線香の匂いが漂っています。*The air is filled with the smell of incense.*

tadóshi 他動詞 *transitive verb (Gram)*

taema [no] nái 絶え間（の）ない *constant* §taemanái dóryoku 絶え間ない努力*constant effort*

taé·ru [*vi* taénai; táeta] 耐える；堪える *endure; bear; put up with* §Kono átsusa ni wa kore íjō taerarénai. この暑さにはこれ以上耐えられない。*I can't bear this heat anymore.*

taé·ru [*vi* taénai; táeta] 絶える *come to an end; end* §Tennen kinénbutsu no tóki wa yagate táete shimaimásu. 天然記念物の「鴇」はやがて絶えてしまいます。*The Japanese crested ibis, designated as a natural treasure, will eventually become extinct.*

táezu 絶えず *unceasingly; constantly; always; all the time; without stopping* §Kono iké wa táezu mizu ga wakidéte imasu. この池は絶えず水が湧き出ています。*This pond is constantly fed by an artesian* *spring.*

tagai ni 互いに *mutually* ❸Kázoku wa tagai ni tasukeáu monó desu yó. 家族は互いに助け合うものですよ。 *Family members should (mutually) help each other.*

tagayás·u [*vt* tagayásánai; tagayáshita] 耕す *cultivate; plow* ❸Nihón de wa tá ya hataké o kikái de tagayásu nóka ga fúete kita. 日本では田や畑を機械で耕す農家が増えてきた。 *An increasing number of farmers in Japan plow their rice paddies and fields with machinery.*

tahó 他方 *on the other hand* ❸Sansei ga ói. Tahó de wa hantai íken mo áru. 賛成が多い。他方では反対意見もある。 *The majority are in favor. On the other hand, there are opposing opinions.*

tái 鯛 *sea bream (fish)*

tai- 耐～ *resistant to—* ❸tainetsu no 耐熱の *heatproof; heat-resistant* ❸taishin no 耐震の *earthquake-proof*

tai- 対～ *against; versus; anti-* ❸taikū misáiru 対空ミサイル *anti-aircraft missile* ❸taisenshá hō 対戦車砲 *antitank gun* ❸Nihón tai Róshia no barēbóru-jíai 日本対ロシアのバレーボール試合 *the Japan-versus-Russia volleyball game*

-tai ～たい [*v: desiderative suffix*] ❸Ashita mo górufu ga shitái. 明日もゴルフがしたい。 *I want to play golf again tomorrow.* ❸Ninjin wa tabétaku nái. 人参は食べたくない。 *I don't want to eat (the) carrots.*

táibatsu 体罰 *corporal punishment*

táido 態度 *attitude* ❸Miyuki-chan wa jugyō táido ga totemo íi. みゆきちゃんは授業態度がとてもいい。 *Miyuki's attitude in class is very good.*

taifū 台風 *typhoon*

taigū 待遇 *treatment; handling; pay* ❸tsutome no taigū káizen 勤めの待遇改善 *improvement of employment terms* ❸Watashi no kaisha wa taigū ga amari yóku nái. 私の会社は待遇があまり良くない。 *The pay at my company isn't very good.*

taigyō 大業 *great work; major undertaking*

taihai 退廃 *decadence* ❸búnka no taihai 文化の退廃 *the decadence of a culture* ——**taihaiteki [na]** 退廃的（な）*decadent* ❸taihaiteki na kangaekata 退廃的な考え方 *a decadent manner of thinking.* ——**taihai-suru** [*vi*] 退廃する *become decadent*

Taihéiyō 太平洋 *Pacific Ocean*

taihen [na] 大変（な）*very; awful; exceedingly; terrible; serious* ❸Taihen na shigoto ga yatto owatta. 大変な仕事がやっと終わった。 *That awful job is finally over.* ❸Kono natsú wa taihen atsúi. この夏は大変暑い。 *This summer it's very hot.*

táiho 逮捕 *an arrest* ❸taihojō 逮捕状 *arrest warrant* ——**táiho-suru** [*vt*] 逮捕する *arrest; take into custody* ❸Ano satsujin yōgísha wa yatto táiho-saremáshita. あの殺人容疑者はやっと逮捕されました。 *The murder suspect was finally arrested.*

taihō 大砲 *cannon*

táiiku 体育 *physical education* 🔹taiikúkan 体育館 *gymnasium* 🔹taiiku shísetsu 体育施設 *physical education facilities*

taiin 退院 *leaving a hospital* ——**taiin-suru** [vi] 退院する *leave a hospital* 🔹Sono kanja wa ashita taiin-shimásu. その患者は明日退院します。 *That patient is leaving the hospital tomorrow.*

táiji 胎児 *embryo; fetus*

táiji 退治 *subjugation; eradication* ——**táiji-suru** [vt] 退治する *defeat; get rid of* 🔹Nezumi o táiji-shimashő. 鼠を退治しましょう。 *Let's get rid of the rats.*

taijō hőshin 帯状疱疹 *shingles; (Tech) herpes zoster*

taijū 体重 *(body) weight* 🔹taijū ga fuéru 体重が増える *gain weight*

taikai 大会 *convention; assembly* 🔹benron táikai 弁論大会 *debate meet* 🔹marason táikai マラソン大会 *marathon race* 🔹rinji táikai 臨時大会 *extraordinary assembly* 🔹teiki táikai 定期大会 *regular assembly*

taikaku 体格 *physique; (physical) constitution* 🔹gasshíri-shita taikaku がっしりした体格 *a stout physique* 🔹Yamáshita-san wa taikaku ga íi. 山下さんは体格がいい。 *Yamashita has a good build.*

taiken 体験 *personal experience* 🔹taikéndan 体験談 *relating (one's) experiences* 🔹Máruta-san wa shigoto no taiken o hanáshite kuremáshita. 丸田さんは仕事の体験を話してくれました。 *Mr. Maruta told me of his work experience.* ——**taiken-suru** [vt] 体験する *experience* 🔹Saikin, fushigi na kotó o taiken-shita. 最近、不思議なことを体験した。 *I had a strange experience recently.*

taiketsu 対決 *confrontation; showdown* ——**taiketsu-suru** [vi] 対決する *confront; be in confrontation*

táiki 大気 *atmosphere; air* 🔹taikíken 大気圏 *the atmosphere* 🔹taiki ósen 大気汚染 *air pollution*

taikin 大金 *great wealth; large sum of money* 🔹Taikin o hatáite kono é o kaimáshita. 大金をはたいてこの絵を買いました。 *I paid a fortune for this painting.*

taikō 対抗 *opposition; rivalry* ——**taikō-suru** [vi] 対抗する *oppose; go against*

taikősha 対向車 *oncoming car*

taikutsu 退屈 *boring; boredom* 🔹Kono terebi bángumi wa taikutsu da wa. このテレビ番組は退屈だわ。 *This TV show is boring <fem>* ——**taikutsu na** 退屈な *tedious; boring* 🔹taikutsu na hitó 退屈な人 *a boring person.* ——**taikutsu-suru** [vi] 退屈する *be bored; be tired of* 🔹Iínchō no supíchi no nágasa ni sankásha wa minna taikutsu-shimáshita. 委員長のスピーチの長さに参加者はみんな退屈しました。 *Everyone became bored because the chairperson's* *speech was so long.*

taiman 怠慢 *negligence; procrastination* ❧Aoki-san wa shókumu taiman de jōshi ni shikarareta. 青木さんは職務怠慢で上司に叱られた。 *Ms. Aoki was reprimanded by her boss for negligence on the job.* ——
  taiman na 怠慢な *negligent; neglectful; lazy* ❧taiman na gakusei 怠慢な学生 *a lazy student*

táimatsu 松明 *torch* ❧táimatsu o tomósu 松明を灯す *light a torch*

taimu rekōdā タイムレコーダー *time clock* ❧taimu rekōdā o ósu タイムレコーダーを押す *punch the time clock*

taionkei 体温計 *thermometer (for taking body temperature)*

taipu yōshi タイプ用紙 *typing paper*

taira [na] 平ら（な） *flat; even* ❧taira na tochi 平らな土地 *flat land*

tairiku 大陸 *continent* ❧Afurika táiriku アフリカ大陸 *the African continent* ❧tairikú-dana 大陸棚 *continental shelf* ——**tairikuteki na** 大陸的な *open-minded; broad-minded* ❧Kánojo no seikaku wa tairikuteki désu. 彼女の性格は大陸的です。 *She is open-minded.*

tairitsu 対立 *opposition; confrontation; mutual antagonism* ❧tairitsu kōho 対立候補 *opposition candidate*——**tairitsu-suru** [vi] 対立する *be opposed (to each other)* ❧Kigyō-gawa to jūmin-gawa no íken wa hagéshiku tairitsu-shite imásu. 企業側と住民側の意見は激しく対立しています。 *The opinions of the corporation and the residents are violently opposed.*

tairyō 大量 *large quantity* ❧tairyō shítsugyō 大量失業 *mass unemployment*

táiryoku 体力 *physical strength; power* ❧tairyoku tésuto 体力テスト *test of physical strength* ❧Háha wa táiryoku ga otoróete kite imasu. 母は体力が衰えてきています。 *Mother's strength is failing.*

taisa 大佐 *colonel*

taisaku 対策 *a measure; a countermeasure* ❧Hikō bōshi no taisaku o kinkyū ni kōjinákereba narimasén. 非行防止の対策を緊急に講じなければなりません。 *We must take emergency measures to prevent delinquency.*

taisei 体制 *organization; system; structure* ❧shakai táisei 社会体制 *social structure* ❧keizai táisei 経済体制 *economic structure* ❧seiji táisei 政治体制 *political system*

Taiséiyō 大西洋 *Atlantic Ocean*

taisetsu [na] 大切（な） *valuable; important* ❧Kazoku ryókō wa wágaya no taisetsu na nenjū győji desu. 家族旅行はわが家の大切な年中行事です。 *Our family trip is our most important event of the year.* ——
  taisetsu ni 大切に *carefully; with care* ❧Taisetsu ni atsukatte kudasái. 大切に扱って下さい。 *Handle it carefully.*

táishi 大使 *ambassador* ❧taishíkan 大使館 *embassy* ❧Chū-Bei Nihon táishi 駐米日本大使 *Japanese ambassador to America*

táishita 大した *very; terrific; significant; important; major; great; outstanding* ❸Anó hito wa táishita hitó da. あの人は大した人だ。 *That person is outstanding. <masc>* ❸Táishita kotó wa nái. 大した事はない。 *It's not a big deal.*

táishite 大して *not very much; not significantly* ❸Kyō wa táishite sámuku nái. 今日は大して寒くない。 *It's not very cold today.*

[ni] táishite 〜に対して *as opposed to...; over against...; with regard to* ❸Kita Chōsén wa kaku gíwaku ni táishite, kōshiki no kaitō o shite inai. 北朝鮮は核疑惑に対して公式の回答をしていない。 *North Korea has not made a public response with regard to the suspicions about its nuclear capability.*

taishō 対象 *an object; objective; subject; topic* ❸kenkyū no taishō 研究の対象 *research subject*

táishō 大将 *general (army); admiral (navy)*

taishō 対照 *a contrast* ——**taishōteki [na]** 対照的（な） *contrastive* ❸Kimi to bóku to wa taishōteki na íken o mótte iru. 君と僕とは対照的な意見を持っている。 *You and I hold opposite opinions. <masc>* ——**taishōteki ni** 対照的に *contrastively* ——**taishō-suru** [*vi / vt*] 対照する *contrast* ❸A to B to o taishō-shite goran. AとBとを対照してごらん。 *Contrast A and B.*

taishō 対称 *symmetry* ❸sáyū taishō no tatemóno 左右対称の建物 *a symmetrical building (left and right)* ——**taishōteki [na]** 対称的（な） *symmetrical* ❸A to B no zukei wa taishōteki désu. AとBの図形は対称的です。 *The figures A and B are symmetrical.*

Taishō jídai 大正時代 *Taishō era (1912–26)*

taishoku 退職 *retirement* ❸taishokukin 退職金 *retirement benefit* ——**taishoku-suru** [*vi*] 退職する *retire* ❸Watashi wa rokujūgó-sai de taishoku-shimásu. 私は65歳で退職します。 *I'm going to retire at sixty-five.*

taishū 大衆 *the general public; the masses* ❸taishū búngaku 大衆文学 *popular literature* ❸taishūgyo 大衆魚 *common fish* ❸taishūka 大衆化 *popularization* ❸taishū shókudō 大衆食堂 *public eatery* ❸taishūsei 大衆性 *popularity* ——**taishūteki [na]** 大衆的（な） *popular*

taisō 体操 *gymnastics; physical exercise; calisthenics* ❸kikai táisō 器械体操 *apparatus gymnastics* ❸taisóbu 体操部 *gymnastic club* ❸biyō táisō 美容体操 *shape-up calesthenics*

táisō [na] 大層（な） *rather; big; great; excellent* ❸Kyō wa táisō atsúi. 今日は大層暑い。 *It's rather hot today.* ❸Táisō na motenashi o arígatō gozaimáshita. 大層なもてなしをありがとうございました。 *Thank you for your excellent hospitality. <formal>*

taitei 大抵 *usually; generally; in general* ❸Watashi wa taitei jūichíji ni wa futon ni hairimásu. 私は大抵十一時には布団に入ります。 *I* *usually go to bed at eleven o'clock.* ——**taitei no** 大抵（の）*most of; a great deal of; ordinary* ❂Taitei no hitó ni wa kono mondai ga tokénai. 大抵の人にはこの問題が解けない。*Most people cannot solve this problem.*

taiwa 対話 *dialogue; talking; conversation*

taiyaku 大役 *major role; great responsibility* ❂Yakusha ni nátte hajímete taiyaku ga mawatte kíta. 役者になって初めて大役が回って来た。*I received my first major role since becoming an actor.* ❂Kono yố na taiyaku o ōsetsukai, tsutsushínde o-uke-itashimásu. このような大役を仰せ遣い、慎んでお受け致します。*I humbly accept this great responsibility. <formal>*

táiyō 太陽 *the sun; solar* ❂taiyō dénchi 太陽電池 *solar battery* ❂taiyō enérugī 太陽エネルギー *solar energy* ❂taiyōkei 太陽系 *the solar system* ❂taiyōtō 太陽灯 *sunlamp* ❂taiyốreki 太陽暦 *the solar calendar*

taizai 滞在 *(period of) stay* ——**taizai-suru** [vi] 滞在する *stay* ❂Rósu ni wa dono kurai taizai-suru tsumori désu ka? ロスにはどのくらい滞在するつもりですか。*How long do you plan to stay in Los Angeles?*

taka 鷹 *a hawk*

takabúr·u [vi] takaburánai; takabútta] 高ぶる；昂る *be excited; be proud; be haughty* ❂Shínkei ga takabútte nemuremasén. 神経が昂って眠れません。*My nerves are so on edge I can't sleep.* ❂Hashimoto-san wa ítsumo táido ga takabútte iru. 橋本さんはいつも態度が高ぶっている。*Mr. Hashimoto always has a haughty attitude.*

taká·i [adj tákaku nái; tákakatta] 高い *(be) high; tall; expensive* ❂Eberésuto wa sékai de ichíban takái yamá desu. エベレストは世界で一番高い山です。*Everest is the highest mountain in the world.* ❂Otōtó wa bóku yori nisénchi sé ga takái. 弟は僕よりニセンチ背が高い。*My younger brother is two centimeters taller than me. <masc>* ❂Nikú wa takái desu ne. 肉は高いですね。*Meat is expensive, isn't it?* ——**tákaku** [adv] 高く *high* ❂Tori ga sóra tákaku tonde imásu. 鳥が空高く飛んでいます。*The bird is flying high (in the sky).*

takamár·u [vi takamaránai; takamátta] 高まる *rise; mount; grow loud* ❂Minshu shúgi o motoméru minshū no kóe ga takamátte imásu. 民主主義を求める民衆の声が高まっています。*The people's cry for democracy is growing loud.*

takamé·ru [vt takaménai; takámeta] 高める *raise; enhance; promote*

taká 宝 *treasure* ❂takaramóno 宝物 *a treasure* ❂takará kuji 宝くじ *public lottery* ❂takara ságashi 宝探し *treasure hunt* ❂takará no mochigusare 宝の持ち腐れ *an unused treasure; a waste of talent <set phrase>*

tákasa 高さ *height*

také 丈 *length; height; stature* ❂Uwagi no také ga tsumátte shimatta. 上

着の丈が詰まってしまった。 *This jacket shrunk!* §Kokóro no také o tsukúshite... *心の丈を尽くして〜 With all my heart...*

take 竹 *bamboo* §takenoko 竹の子 *bamboo shoot* §takeuma 竹馬 *stilts* §takeyabu 竹薮 *bamboo thicket*

taki 滝 *waterfall* §takitsubo 滝壺 *waterfall basin*

takibi 焚き火 *bonfire; open fire*

takkyū 卓球 *table tennis; pingpong*

táko 蛸 *octopus* §takoashi háisen 蛸足配線 *multiple electric cords to one outlet*

táko 凧 *kite (toy)* §Takoáge o shiyō. 凧上げをしよう。 *Let's fly a kite.*

[o-]taku (お)宅 *house; home* §o-taku お宅 *another's house (or home); you* §O-taku ni ukagawasete itadaité mo íi desu ka? お宅に伺わせて頂いてもいいですか。 *May I visit you at home?<formal>* §O-tsuide no sétsu wa taku ní mo o-yori kudasái. おついでの節は宅にもお寄り下さい。 *If you are in the neighborhood please come and visit us. <formal>*

tak·u [vt takanai; taita] 炊く *cook* §Góhan o taite óite kudasái! ご飯を炊いておいて下さい。 *Please cook the rice.*

takujō 卓上 *tabletop* §takujō keisánki 卓上計算機 *tabletop calculator* §takujō níkki 卓上日記 *desk calendar* §takujō sutándo 卓上スタンド *desk lamp*

takumashí·i [adj takumáshiku nái; takumáshikatta] 逞しい *be robust; sturdy; powerfully built* §Watashi wa takumashíi dansei ni akogarete imásu. 私は逞しい男性に憧れています。 *I'm attracted to strong men.* §Morímoto-san wa tokidoki shōrai e no sōzō o takumáshiku shite iru. 森本さんは時々、将来への想像を逞しくしている。 *Mr. Morimoto sometimes has big dreams about the future.*

takumi [na] 巧み（な）*clever; skillful* §Anó shokunin no tesábaki wa takumi da. あの職人の手捌きは巧みだ。 *That craftsman does beautiful handwork. <masc>* ——**takumi ni** 巧みに *cleverly; skillfully* §Ano sērusúman wa shinséihin o takumi ni urikónde iru. あのセールスマンは新製品を巧みに売り込んでいる。 *The salesman is cleverly pushing his new product.*

takurám·u [vt takuramánai; takuránda] 企む *scheme; maneuver; mastermind* §Imbō o takuránde irú no wa dáre ka? 陰謀を企んでいるのは誰か。 *Who is it that's masterminding the plot?*

takusán [no] 沢山（の）*many; a lot; much* §Kotoshi wa takusán no gakusei ga nyūgaku-shite kíta. 今年は沢山の学生が入学してきた。 *This year many students enrolled.* §Kyō wa shukudai ga takusan áru. 今日は宿題が沢山ある。 *Today I have a lot of homework to do.*

takús·u [vt takusánai; takúshita] 託す *entrust; leave to someone's charge; commit (to)* §Kotozuke o takúshite kimáshita. 言付けを託してきました。 *I left a message.*

takuwaé·ru [*vt* takuwaénai; takuwáeta] 蓄える *save; hoard; lay by; store up* ❀chíshiki o takuwaéru 知識を蓄える *store up knowledge* ❀hige o takuwaéru 髭を蓄える *let one's beard grow*

tamá 玉 *ball*

tamá 弾 *bullet*

tamá 珠 *bead*

tama [no] たま（の）*rare; occasional* ❀Tama no yasumí ni wa ié de nombíri shimásu. たまの休みには家でのんびりします。*The few holidays I have, I stay home and relax.* ——**tama ni** たまに *infrequently; occasionally; seldom* ❀Takémura-san wa tama ni piano o hikimásu. 竹村さんはたまにピアノを弾きます。*Ms. Takemura plays the piano occasionally.*

tamamono 賜；賜物 *gift* ❀Kámi no tamamono 神の賜物 *a gift from God*

tamanégi 玉葱 *(round) onion*

tamaranai [*adj* tamaranaku nái; tamaranákatta] 堪らない *(be) unbearable; intolerable; too much; unable to stand* ❀Ítakute tamaranai. 痛くて堪らない。*It hurts so much I can't stand it.* ❀Kono hón wa omoshírokute tamaranai. この本は面白くて堪らない。*This book is unbearably funny.*

tamar·u [*vi* tamaranai; tamatta] 溜まる *accumulate; build up* ❀Tana no ué ni hokori ga tamatte iru yó. 棚の上に埃が溜まっているよ。*Dust has accumulated on top of the shelf.* ❀Watashi no chokin wa daibu tamatta. 私の貯金は大分溜まった。*My savings have built up quite a bit.*

támashii 魂 *soul*

tamatama たまたま *by chance; unexpectedly* ❀Watashi wa tamatama sono jíko o mokugeki-shite shimatta. 私はたまたまその事故を目撃してしまった。*By chance I witnessed the accident.*

tambo 田圃 *rice paddy* ❀tambómichi 田圃道 *path between rice paddies*

-tamé ni ～為に *for the sake of; because* ❀Kenkō no tamé ni tabako no suisugi ni chúi-shimashố. 健康の為に煙草の吸い過ぎに注意しましょう。*For your health's sake, be careful not to smoke too much.* ❀Watashi ga puropốzu o kotowátta tamé ni, káre wa hoka no onna to kekkon-shite shimatta. 私がプロポーズを断わった為に、彼は他の女と結婚してしまった。*Because I turned down his proposal, he married another woman.*

tamé ni náru 為になる *be good for (one); be useful* ❀Kono hón wa kimi no tamé ni náru yo. この本は君の為になるよ。*This is a good book for you to read.*

tamerá·u [*vt* tamerawánai; tamerátta] 躊躇う *waver; hesitate* ❀Áni wa mố yonjússai ni náru no ni, máda kekkon o tamerátte imasu. 兄はもう四十歳になるのに、まだ結婚を躊躇っています。*My older* *brother's already forty, but he's still hesitant about getting married.*

tame·ru [*vt* tamenai; tameta] 溜める；貯める *save; store up; build up; accumulate* ❸Ryokō híyō o tamete imásu. 旅行費用を貯めています。*I'm saving up for a trip.*

tamés·u [*vt* tamesánai; taméshita] 試す *test; examine* ❸kikai o taméshite miru 機械を試してみる *test a machine*

tamóts·u [*vt* tamotánai; tamótta] 保つ *keep; preserve; maintain* ❸Bukka no antei o tamótsu tamé ni séifu wa dóryoku-shite iru. 物価の安定を保つために政府は努力している。*The government is striving to keep living costs stable.*

tampaku; tampakúshitsu 蛋白；蛋白質 *protein*

támpaku [na] 淡白（な）*plain; simple; bland* ❸Minagawa-san wa totemo támpaku desu. 皆川さんはとても淡白です。*Mr. Minagawa is an unaffected man.* ❸Kono ajitsuke wa totemo támpaku desu. この味付けはとても淡白です。*The flavor is very bland.*

tampen shōsetsu 短編小説 *short story; short novel*

támpo 担保 *collateral; security (for a loan)*

támpopo 蒲公英 *dandelion*

tan 痰 *phlegm*

tana 棚 *shelf* ❸hóndana 本棚 *bookshelf*

Tanabata 七夕 *Tanabata Festival; the Star Festival (July 7)*

tanchō [na] 単調（な）*monotonous* ❸tanchō na seikatsu 単調な生活 *a monotonous life* ❸Kono mérodī wa totemo tanchō désu. このメロディーはとても単調です。*This melody is very monotonous.*

tandoku [no] 単独（の）*solo; single; solitary; independent; individual* ❸tandoku káiken 単独会見 *exclusive interview* ❸Ensoku de tandoku kōdō wa kinshi-sarete imásu. 遠足で単独行動は禁止されています。*We don't permit people to go their own way on excursions.*

táne 種 *seed* ❸táne o maku 種を蒔く *plant seeds* ❸shimpai no táne 心配の種 *a cause for worry* ❸Hanashi no táne ga nakunatta. 話の種がなくなった。*I can't think of anything to say.*

tanebi 種火 *pilot light (for a gas appliance)*

tango 単語 *a word; an individual word*

tán'i 単位 *academic unit of credit; unit of measurement* ❸jūryō tán'i 重量単位 *unit of weight* ❸Kongákki no tán'i ga tarinai. 今学期の単位が足りない。*I don't have enough units this term.*

taní 谷 *valley*

tanin 他人 *stranger* ❸tanin no soráni 他人の空似 *a chance resemblance* ❸tanin gyōgi 他人行儀 *acting like a stranger* ❸Watashi wa tanín átsukai-sareta. 私は他人扱いされた。*I was treated like a stranger.*

tanjíkan [no] 短時間（の）*brief (span of time)* ❸Watashi wa tanjíkan no kúnren o úketa. 私は短時間の訓練を受けた。*I received training for* *a brief period.* ——**tanjíkan de** 短時間で *in a short time; quickly*

tanjōbi 誕生日 *birthday*

tanjun [na] 単純（な）*simple; uncomplicated*

tánka 担架 *stretcher*

tanken 探検 *exploration* ❀tankenka 探検家 *an explorer* ❀tankentai 探検隊 *an exploration party* ——**tanken-suru** [vt] 探検する *explore*

tánki [na] 短気（な）*short-tempered* ❀tánki o okósu 短気を起こす *lose one's temper* ❀Shújin wa totemo tánki desu. 主人はとても短気です。*My husband is very short-tempered.*

tánnaru 単なる *a mere; only* ❀tánnaru itazura 単なる悪戯 *a mere prank*

tánni 単に *merely* ❀Tánni waratta máde de, kimi o baka ni suru tsumori wa nákatta. 単に笑ったまでで、君を馬鹿にするつもりはなかった。*I merely laughed; I didn't mean to make fun of you.*

tannō 胆嚢 *gall bladder*

tanomoshí·i [adj tanomóshiku nái; tanomóshikatta] 頼もしい *(be) reliable; responsible* ❀Takao-san wa totemo tanomoshíi hitó desu. 高尾さんはとても頼もしい人です。*Mr. Takao is very reliable.*

tanóm·u [vt tanománai; tanónda] 頼む *request; ask (for)* ❀Watashi wa shin'yū ni shakkín o tanónda. 私は親友に借金を頼んだ。*I asked a close friend for a loan.* ❀"Dare ni mo iwanáide" to tanomáreta. 「誰にも言わないで」と頼まれた。*I was asked not to tell anyone.*

tanoshíge ni 楽しげに *merrily; happily* ❀Kodomótachi wa tanoshíge ni utá o utatte iru. 子供たちは楽しげに歌を歌っている。*The children are singing merrily.*

tanoshí·i [adj tanóshiku nái; tanóshikatta] 楽しい *(be) happy; enjoyable; fun* ❀Pátī wa tanóshikatta desu ka? パーティーは楽しかったですか。*Was the party fun?* —— **tanóshiku** 楽しく *merrily; happily* ❀Watashi wa tanóshiku ikitái. 私は楽しく生きたい。*I want to enjoy life. (lit: I want to live happily.)*

tanoshími 楽しみ *pleasure; enjoyment; fun* ❀Patchiwáku wa tsúma no yúiitsu no tanoshími desu. パッチワークは妻の唯一の楽しみです。*Patchwork is my wife's only enjoyment.* ——**tanoshími ni suru** 楽しみにする *look forward to* ❀Kaigai ryókō o tanoshími ni shite iru. 海外旅行を楽しみにしている。*I'm looking forward to my trip abroad.*

tanoshím·u [vt tanoshímánai; tanoshínda] 楽しむ *enjoy; have fun* ❀Watashi to kánai wa kinō myújikaru o míte tanoshínda. 私と家内は昨日ミュージカルを見て楽しんだ。*My wife and I enjoyed watching a musical yesterday.*

tansei 嘆声 *a sigh*

tanshuku 短縮 *abbreviation; truncation; shortening* ❀tanshuku dáiaru 短縮ダイアル *speed dialing* ❀tanshuku júgyō 短縮授業 *a shortened lecture* ——**tanshuku-suru** [vt] 短縮する *abbreviate; shorten*

§Kono búnshō o mótto tanshuku-shite goran. この文章をもっと短縮してごらん。 *Try shortening this sentence some more.*

tánso 炭素 *carbon (element)*

tansu 箪笥 *chest of drawers*   §ishō-dánsu 衣装箪笥 *chest of drawers for kimono*   §yōfuku-dánsu 洋服箪笥 *wardrobe*

tansú 単数 *singular (gram)*

tantei 探偵 *detective*   §tantei shōsetsu 探偵小説 *a detective story*   §shiritsu tántei 私立探偵 *private detective*

tanteki [na] 端的（な）*direct; point-blank; frank; bare*   §tanteki na jíjitsu 端的な事実 *the bare facts* ——**tanteki ni** 端的に *frankly; directly; succinctly*   §Tanteki ni iéba gyámburu wa ihō désu. 端的に言えばギャンブルは違法です。 *To put it plainly, gambling is illegal.*

tantō 担当 *in charge*   §tantōsha 担当者 *person in charge* ——**tantō-suru** [vt] 担当する *take charge of; be responsible for*   §Kóndo no purojékuto wa Ogímoto-san ga tantō-shimásu. 今度のプロジェクトは荻本さんが担当します。 *Ms. Ogimoto will be in charge of the next project.*

taoré·ru [vi] taorénai; taóreta] 倒れる *fall; collapse; topple*   §Obásan ga totsuzen michibata ni taóreta. お婆さんが突然道端に倒れた。 *An old lady suddenly collapsed at the side of the road.*

taós·u [vt] taosánai; taóshita] 倒す *throw down; bring down; topple; knock over*   §Kodomo wa tsumazuite sekiyu sutóbu o taóshite shimaimáshita. 子供はつまづいて石油ストーブを倒してしまいました。 *My child tripped and knocked over the kerosene stove.*

tappúri たっぷり *all of; a lot; fully; enough; plenty*   §Jikan ga tappúri aru yo. 時間がたっぷりあるよ。 *There's plenty of time.*   §Tōsuto ni bátā o tappúri nutte kudasái. トーストにバターをたっぷり塗って下さい。 *Spread plenty of butter on the toast.*

tára 鱈 *cod*   §tarako 鱈子 *cod roe*

-tára 〜たら [conditional suffix]   §Amerika e ittára hagaki o kudasái. アメリカへ行ったら葉書を下さい。 *If you go to America, send me a postcard.*   §Sono éiga ga omoshírokattára oshiete kudasái. その映画が面白かったら教えて下さい。 *If the movie's interesting, let me know.*

tarai 盥 *washtub*

taré·ru [vi] tarénai; táreta] 垂れる *hang down; droop; dangle; drip*

-tari... -tari (suru) 〜たり〜たり〜（する）*alternate between ... and ...*   §Kóndo no pátī de wa tábetari nóndari odottári dekimásu. 今度のパーティーでは食べたり飲んだり踊ったりできます。 *At the party we'll be able to eat, drink, and dance.*

tari·ru [vi] tarinai; tarita] 足りる *be enough; suffice*

taru 樽 *barrel*

tarum·u [vi] tarumanai; tarunda] 弛む *be slack; be loose; sag; relax*

❧Rōpu ga tarunde iru. ロープが弛んでいる。 *The rope is slack.*
❧Nemuku nátte mé no kawá ga tarundé kita. 眠くなって目の皮が弛んできた。 *I'm so sleepy my eyelids are drooping.*

taryō 多量 *abundance; excess* ——**taryō ni** 多量に *abundantly; excessively* ❧Hayashi-san wa totsuzen taryō ni chi o háite nyūin-shimáshita. 林さんは突然多量に血を吐いて入院しました。 *Ms. Hayashi suddenly spit up a great deal of blood and was hospitalized.*

táshika 確か *sure; certain; definite* ——**táshika na** 確かな *reliable; firm; secure* ——**táshika ni** 確かに *securely; certainly; definitely*

tashikamé·ru [*vt* tashikaménai; tashikámeta] 確かめる *make certain; make sure; verify* ❧Há'isha no yoyaku no jikan o tashikámete kudasái. 歯医者の予約の時間を確かめて下さい。 *Please verify the time of my dentist's appointment.*

tashízan 足し算 *addition* (Math)

tashō 多少 *some; somewhat; more or less; a few* ❧Kore kará wa seikatsu ga tashō rakú ni narimásu. これからは生活が多少楽になります。 *From now on my life will be somewhat easier.*

tasogare 黄昏 *twilight*

tassei 達成 *achievement; attainment; accomplishment* ——**tassei-suru** [*vt*] 達成する *achieve; accomplish; attain* ❧Yatto mokuhyō o tassei-suru kotó ga dékita. やっと目標を達成することができた。 *I finally was able to attain my goal.*

tassur·u [*vi* tasshinai; tasshita] 達する *reach; arrive at; come up to* ❧Táku-kun no seiseki wa yatto heikínten ni tasshimáshita. 拓君の成績はやっと平均点に達しました。 *Taku's grades finally came up to average.*

tas·u [*vt* tasanai; tashita] 足す *add to; supply; make up for; supplement; perform; do* ❧Ofúro ni mizu o tashite óite ne! お風呂に水を足しておいてね！ *Add water to the bath, OK?* <*fem*> ❧Yō o tashi ni chótto dekakete kimásu. 用を足しにちょっと出かけて来ます。 *I'm going out a minute to do an errand.*

tasū 多数 *several; many; numbers of; majority* ❧tasūketsu 多数決 *majority decision* ❧tasū íken 多数意見 *majority opinion* ❧shísha tasū 死者多数 *numerous fatalities*

tasukár·u [*vi* tasukaránai; tasukátta] 助かる *be helped; be rescued; be saved; survive* ❧Dangan ga sórete tasukátta. 弾丸が逸れて助かった。 *The bullet missed me and I was saved.* ❧Yóku hataraite kurerú no de tasukáru yo. よく働いてくれるので助かるよ。 *You're a great help because you work hard.*

tasuké 助け *help; rescue* ❧Keganin wa tasuké o motomemáshita ga minná wa shirán-kao o shite imáshita. 怪我人は助けを求めましたが、みんなは知らん顔をしていました。 *The injured cried for help but everyone ignored them.* ❧Kimi no chūkoku wa tasuké ni naru yo. 君

の忠告は助けになるよ。*Your advice will be a great help.*

tasuké·ru [*vt* tasukénai; tasúketa] 助ける *rescue; save; help* 8Uráshima Tárō wa kodomótachi ni ijimerarete iru káme o tasukemáshita. 浦島太郎は子供たちに苛められている亀を助けました。*Urashima Tarō rescued the turtle that was being tormented by the children.* 8Watashi wa chichí no shigoto o tasúkete imásu. 私は父の仕事を助けています。*I'm helping my father with his work.*

tatae·ru [*vt* tataenai; tataeta] 称える；賛える *praise* 8Chichí wa naganen no kōseki o tataeráreta. 父は永年の功績を称えられた。*My father was praised for his many years of service.*

tatakai 戦い *battle; war; fight* 8tatakai ni kátsu 戦いに勝つ *win a battle* 8tatakai ni makeru 戦いに負ける *lose a battle*

tatakau [*vt* tatakawanai; tatakatta] 戦う；闘う *fight; battle; make war* 8yámai to tatakau 病と闘う *fight against a disease* 8Amerika wa Dóitsu to tatakatta. アメリカはドイツと戦った。*America fought against Germany.*

tatakiwár·u [*vt* tatakiwaránai; tatakiwátta] 叩き割る *break (something) by striking (it)* 8Suika o mekákushi de tatakiwátte asonda. 西瓜を目隠しで叩き割って遊んだ。*We played a game where we broke open watermelons by striking them blindfolded.*

taták·u [*vt* tatakánai; tatáita] 叩く *tap; knock; beat; spank* 8dóramu o tatáku ドラムを叩く *beat a drum* 8Shiawase nára té o tatakṓ. 幸せなら手を叩こう。*If you're happy, clap your hands.* 8Kodomo wa otṓsan ni oshiri o tatakáreta. 子供はお父さんにお尻を叩かれた。*The children were spanked by their father.*

tatami 畳 *woven straw mat flooring*

tatamu [*vt* tatamanai; tatanda] 畳む *fold* 8tatamíisu 畳み椅子 *folding chair* 8hankáchi o yottsú ni tatande kudasái. ハンカチを四つに畳んで下さい。*Fold the handkerchiefs into quarters.*

tátari 祟り *evil curse; retribution*

tatazúm·u [*vi* tatazumánai; tatazúnda] 佇む *loiter; linger; stop (for a while)* 8Mishiranu hitó ga denchū no káge ni tatazúnde iru. 見知らぬ人が電柱の陰にたたずんでいる。*There's a strange man loitering in the shadow of a power pole.*

táte 盾；楯 *shield*

táte [no] 縦（の） *perpendicular; vertical* 8táte no sén 縦の線 *perpendicular line*

-tate [no] 〜立て（の） *fresh; just made* 8araitate no shátsu 洗い立てのシャツ *a freshly laundered shirt* 8yakitate no pán 焼き立てのパン *freshly baked bread*

tategami 鬣 *mane* 8raion no tategami ライオンの鬣 *a lion's mane*

tatemae 建て前；立て前 *principle; official position; outward stance* 8honne to tatemae 本音と建て前 *underlying motive and outward stance*

tatémono 建物 *building*

tatenaos·u [*vt* tatenaosanai; tatenaoshita] 立て直す；建て直す *rebuild; reconstruct* §keikaku o tatenaosu 計画を立て直す *reformulate plans* §Kono terá wa káji de yakete, nochí ni tatenaosáreta. この寺は火事で焼けて、後に建て直された。 *This temple was burned and later rebuilt.*

taté·ru [*vt* taténai; táteta] 建てる *build; erect* §uchi o taté·ru 家を建てる *build a house*

taté·ru [*vt* taténai; táteta] 立てる *stand (something) up; erect; hoist; plan* §keikaku o taté·ru 計画を立てる *form a plan* §hatá o taté·ru 旗を立てる *hoist a flag* §kóe o taté·ru 声を立てる *raise one's voice* §ocha o taté·ru お茶を立てる *brew tea*

tatoe...te mo 例え〜ても *even if; although* §Tatoe ashita netsú ga átte mo kanarazu ikimásu. 例え明日熱があっても必ず行きます。 *Even if I have a fever tomorrow I'm going.*

tatóeba 例えば *for example*

tatoebánashi 譬え話；喩え話 *parable; allegory*

tatoé·ru [*vi / vt* tatoénai; tatóeta] 譬える；喩える *liken (to); compare (to)* §Shíro wa yuki, áka wa ringo, bíjin wa haná ni tatoeraremásu. 白は雪、赤はりんご、美人は花にたとえられます。 *White is likened to snow, red to apples, and a beautiful woman to a flower.*

tatsu 竜；龍 *dragon*

táts·u [*vi* taténai; tátta] 経つ *elapse; go by; pass* §Mó sanjíkan tátta. もう三時間経った。 *Already three hours has passed.*

táts·u [*vi* taténai; tátta] 立つ *stand (up); arise; rise; start out* §Sá tátte kudasái. さあ、立って下さい。 *OK, stand up.* §Entotsu kara kemuri ga tátte iru. 煙突から煙が立っている。 *Smoke is rising from the chimney.* §Ashita watashi wa tabí ni tachimásu. 明日私は旅に立ちます。 *Tomorrow I'm starting on a trip.*

tatsumaki 竜巻 *tornado; whirlwind; twister*

tatsu no otoshigo 竜の落とし子 *seahorse*

tatta たった *just; only* §Sankásha wa tatta kore daké? 参加者はたったこれだけ？ *Are these the only participants?*

tayasú·i [*adj* tayásuku nái; tayásukatta] たやすい *(be) easy; simple* — **tayásuku** たやすく *easily; without difficulty*

táyori 便り *news; word; correspondence* §Uchi kara táyori ga átta. 家から便りがあった。 *I got news from home.*

táyori ni 頼りに *relying on; helped by; depending on* §Ojíisan wa tsúe o táyori ni arúite imásu. おじいさんは杖を頼りに歩いています。 *The old man is walking with the help of a cane.* §Kimi wa táyori ni naránai. 君は頼りにならない。 *I can't depend on you.* <*masc*>

tayoriná·i [*adj* tayorináku nái; tayorinákatta] 頼りない *(be) helpless; unreliable* §Uchi ní wa tayorinái kodomo ga sannín mo imásu. 家には

頼りない子供が三人もいます。 *I have three helpless children at home.* §Sono hanashí wa tayorinái ne. その話は頼りないね。 *That story is unreliable.* ——**tayorinása** 頼りなさ *helplessness*

tayór·u [*vi* / *vt* tayoránai; tayótta] 頼る *rely on; depend on* §Káre wa máda keizaiteki ni oyá ni tayótte iru. 彼はまだ経済的に親に頼っている。 *Financially he still depends on his parents.*

tazuna 手綱 *reins; bridle* §tazuna sábaki 手綱捌き *handling the reins*

tazuné·ru [*vt* tazunénai; tazuneta] 尋ねる；訊ねる *inquire after; ask; search for* §michi o tazunéru 道を尋ねる *ask the way.*

tazuné·ru [*vt* tazunénai; tazuneta] 訪ねる *visit; call on* §Sensei no otaku o tazunemáshita. 先生のお宅を訪ねました。 *I visited my teacher's house.*

té 手 *hand; arm* §té o ageru 手を上げる *raise (one's) hand* §té ni ireru 手に入れる *get hold of; acquire; buy* §té ga tarinai 手が足りない *be short of hands* §té ga kakáru 手がかかる *require effort (or time / attention)* §té o útsu 手を打つ *act; take a measure; strike a bargain* §Watashi no kodomo wa totemo té ga kakarimásu. 私の子供はとても手がかかります。 *My children require a lot of attention.* §Hoka no té o kangáete mimashō. 他の手を考えてみましょう。 *Let's try thinking of another way (to do it).* §Kono hen de té o uchimasén ka? この辺で手を打ちませんか。 *Shall we settle on these terms?*

[o-]teárai (お)手洗い *washroom; lavatory; toilet*

téashi 手足 *arms and legs; limbs*

teatari shídai ni 手当り次第に *at random; whatever comes to hand*

téate 手当 *fringe benefits; aid; allowance* §fuyō téate 扶養手当 *dependency allowance* §ōkyū téate 応急手当 *first aid*

tebanás·u [*vt* tebanásánai; tebanáshita] 手放す *part with; let go of; let alone* §Kore wa chichí no katami ná no de, tebanásu kotó wa dekimasén. これは父の形見なので、手放すことはできまん。 *This is a keepsake from my father; I can't part with it.*

tébiki 手引き *handbook*

tebori 手彫り *hand carving*

tebúkuro 手袋 *glove*

tēburú kake テーブル掛け *tablecloth*

techō 手帳 *notebook; schedule*

tédate 手立て *device; means; measure* §Kono keikaku o jikkō ni utsúsu tédate o kangaeyō. この計画を実行に移す手立てを考えよう。 *Let's think about means for implementing this plan.*

tegákari 手がかり *clue* §Hánnin no tegákari ga mattaku tsukámete inai. 犯人の手掛かりが全く掴めていない。 *They haven't been able to find a single clue to the (identity of the) criminal.*

tegami 手紙 *letter* §tegami o káku 手紙を書く *write a letter*

tegata 手形 *(bank) draft; bill; note*

tegoro [na] 手頃（な）*handy; convenient; suitable; moderate* ❂tegoro na ōkisa 手頃な大きさ *a handy size* ❂tegoro na nedan 手頃な値段 *a moderate price*

téhai 手配 *arrangement; preparations; (police) search order* ❂shimei tehainin 指名手配人 *most wanted criminal* ——**téhai-suru** [vt] 手配する *arrange; prepare* ❂Kuruma o téhai-shite kudasái. 車を手配して下さい。*Arrange a car for me, please.*

tehón 手本 *a copy; model; example* ❂shūji no tehón 習字の手本 *calligraphy copybook* ❂Dō yattára íi ka tehón o shiméshite kudasái. どうやったらいいか手本を示して下さい。*Show me (an example of) how to do it.*

teian 提案 *proposal; motion; suggestion* ❂Teian wa shōnin-sareta. 提案は承認された。*The motion passed.* ❂Kokkai wa yotōgíin no teian o ukeireta. 国会は与党議員の提案を受け入れた。*The Diet passed the bill presented by the government (ruling) party.* ——**teian-suru** [vt] 提案する *propose; make a motion; suggest*

teiden 停電 *power failure*

téido 程度 *degree; extent; level* ❂áru téido made ある程度まで *to a certain extent* ❂Tōkyō Dáigaku wa watashi ní wa téido ga takasugimásu. 東京大学は私には程度が高過ぎます。*Tokyo University is too high a level for me.*

teien 庭園 *garden*

teigaku 停学 *suspension from school* ❂Wakabáyashi-san wa kōsoku o yabútte teigaku shóbun ni nátta. 若林さんは校則を破って停学処分になった。*Wakabayashi broke the school regulations and was suspended.*

téigi 定義 *definition* ——**téigi-suru** [vt] 定義する *define* ❂Tsugí no kotobá o téigi-shite kudasái. 次の言葉を定義して下さい。*Define the following word(s).*

teika 定価 *list price*

téiki [no] 定期（の）*regular; fixed term; periodical* ❂teiki táikai 定期大会 *regular convention (or conference)* ❂teikíken 定期券 *(train / bus) pass* ❂teikiyókin 定期預金 *fixed deposit* ❂teiki shíken 定期試験 *periodical exams* ——**teikiteki ni** 定期的に *regularly; periodically* ❂Sono kōkyō dántai wa teikiteki ni kenshū ryókō ga arimásu. その公共団体は定期的に研修旅行があります。*That public organization takes regular training trips.*

teikíatsu 低気圧 *low atmospheric pressure*

teikō 抵抗 *resistance; reservation* ❂Shanai kara omowánu teikō ga átta. 社内から思わぬ抵抗があった。*There was unexpected resistance from within the company.* ❂Anáta no kōdō ní wa teikō ga áru. あなたの行動には抵抗がある。*I have reservations about what you did.* ——**teikō-suru** [vt] 抵抗する *resist* ❂Minshu séiryoku wa gunji séiken ni teikō-shite iru. 民主勢力は軍事政権に抵抗している。*Democratic* *forces are resisting the military government.*

teikoku [no] 帝国（の）*imperial* ⑧teikoku shúgi 帝国主義 *imperialism*

teikyō 提供 *sponsorship; providing; furnishing; offering; donation* ⑧Kono bangumi wa A-gáisha no teikyō de o-okuri-shimáshita. この番組はA会社の提供でお送りました。*This program is brought to you by "A" Company.* ——**teikyō-suru** [vt] 提供する *sponsor; provide; furnish; offer; donate*

téinei [na] 丁寧（な）*polite; careful* ⑧teineigo 丁寧語 *polite language* ⑧Másako-san wa kotoba-zúkai ga téinei desu. 雅子さんは言葉遣いが丁寧です。*Masako's language is polite.* ——**téinei ni** 丁寧に *politely; carefully* ⑧Gakusei wa téinei ni heyá o katazúkete kureta. 学生は丁寧に部屋を片付けてくれた。*The students carefully straightened up the room.*

teinéisa 丁寧さ *politeness*

teinen 定年 *retirement* ⑧teinen taishoku nénrei 定年退職年齢 *mandatory retirement age*

teiō sékkai 帝王切開 *caesarean section*

teiré 手入れ *taking care; maintenance; police raid* ⑧teiré no ıkıtodóita niwa 手入れの行き届いた庭 *a well-kept garden* ⑧bakuchiyádo ni teiré o suru 博打宿に手入れをする *make a raid on a gambling den* ——**teiré-suru** [vt] 手入れする *take care of; maintain*

teirei no 定例の *regular; fixed* ⑧Teirei kákugi ga hirakárete iru. 定例閣議が開かれている。*A regular cabinet meeting is in session.*

téiri 定理 *theorem (Math)* ⑧Pitagórasu no téiri ピタゴラスの定理 *the Pythagorean theorem*

teiryō búnseki 定量分析 *quantitative analysis*

teiryūjo 停留所 *bus stop*

teisatsu 偵察 *reconnaissance* ——**teisatsu-suru** [vt] 偵察する *scout; reconnoiter* ⑧teki no ugokí o teisatsu-suru 敵の動きを偵察する *reconnoiter the movements of the enemy*

teisei 訂正 *correction* ——**teisei-suru** [vt] 訂正する *revise; correct* ⑧goyaku o teisei-suru 誤訳を訂正する *correct a mistranslation*

teisei búnseki 定性分析 *qualitative analysis*

teisen 停戦 *cease-fire*

teisha 停車 *(vehicle) stopping* ⑧Teisha Kinshí! 停車禁止。*Stopping Forbidden!* ——**teisha-suru** [vi] 停車する *stop; stop at* ⑧Tokkyū réssha wa kono éki ni nifúnkan teisha-shimásu. 特急列車はこの駅に２分間停車します。*The express train stops at this station for two minutes.*

teishi 停止 *stopping* ⑧kyū téishi 急停止 *sudden stop* ⑧ichiji téishi 一時停止 *momentary stop* ——**teishi-suru** [vt] 停止する *stop* ⑧Sono hón no hakkō o teishi-sareta. その本の発行を停止された。

Publication of the book was stopped.

teishō 提唱 *proposal; advocacy* ——**teishō-suru** [vt] 提唱する *propose; advocate* ❽Hiroshima shímin wa sekái ni mukete kakujíkken no haizetsu o teishō-shite iru. 広島市民は世界にむけて核実験の廃絶を提唱している。 *The citizens of Hiroshima are advocating the abolition of nuclear testing.*

teishoku 停職 *suspension from (one's) job* ❽Mudan kékkin ga tsuzuite teishoku ni nátta. 無断欠勤が続いて停職になった。 *She was suspended for repeated unexcused absences from work.*

teishoku 定食 *set menu*

téishu 亭主 *husband; head of household*

teishutsu 提出 *submission; presentation* ——**teishutsu-suru** [vt] 提出する *submit; hand in; present* ❽Watashi wa senséi ni repóto o teishutsu-shimáshita. 私は先生にレポートを提出しました。 *I handed in my report to the teacher.*

teisóshiki 定礎式 *ceremony for laying the cornerstone*

teitaku 邸宅 *mansion*

teitetsu 蹄鉄 *horseshoe*

teitō 抵当 *mortgage* ❽teitóken 抵当権 *(holder of) a mortgage* ❽Shakkín no támpo ni tochi o teitō ni ireta. 借金の担保に土地を抵当に入れた。 *I mortgaged my property as security for the loan.*

téjina 手品 *magic* ❽tejináshi 手品師 *a magician*

teki 敵 *enemy*

-teki 〜滴 *a drop (of liquid)* ❽suiteki 水滴 *a drop of water* ❽Máiasa megúsuri o ni-san-teki sáshite kudasái. 毎朝、目薬を二、三滴差して下さい。 *Apply two or three drops of eye medicine every morning.*

tékido [no] 適度（の） *moderate* ❽tékido no óndo 適度の温度 *moderate temperature*

tekiō 適応 *adaptation* ——**tekiō-suru** [vi] 適応する *adapt (to); apply; use* ❽Watashi wa dónna kankyō dé mo tekiō-suru kotó ga dekimásu. 私はどんな環境でも適応することができます。 *I can adapt to any environment.*

tekisei kákaku 適正価格 *fair price*

tekisetsu [na] 適切（な） *appropriate; fitting* ❽tekisetsu na jogen 適切な助言 *fitting advice*

tekisúru [vi tekishinái; tekíshita] 適する *fit; suit; be fit for; be good for* ❽Watashi wa íma no shigoto ga tekíshite imásu. 私は今の仕事が適しています。 *The job I have now suits me.*

tekitō [na] 適当（な） *appropriate; suitable* ——**tekitō ni** 適当に *appropriately; suitably*

tekkai 撤回 *withdrawal; retraction* ❽Sono hōan no tekkai o motoméru kóe ga agatta. その法案の撤回を求める声が上がった。 *A call was raised for the withdrawal of the bill.* ——**tekkai-suru** [vt] 撤回する

withdraw; retract §hatsugen o tekkai-suru 発言を撤回する *retract a statement*.

tekkan 鉄管 *iron pipe*

téko 挺子 *lever* §tekoire-suru 挺子入れする *support; bolster* §Aitsu wa ichido kimetára téko de mo ugokánai. あいつは一度決めたら挺子でも動かない。 *Once he's made up his mind, you couldn't budge him (lit: you couldn't move him with a lever).* <*masc*>

tékubi 手首 *wrist*

temá 手間 *time and effort; trouble; labor* §temá ga kakáru 手間がかかる *(be) timeconsuming*

temae 手前 *just before; this side of; out of consideration for; I* <*humble*> §Gínkō no temae de tomete kudasái. 銀行の手前で止めて下さい。 *Stop this side of the bank.* §Séken no temae ga átte, katte wa yurusarénai. 世間の手前があって、勝手は許されない。 *You can't just do as you please in (the face of) society.* §Temae-dómo no misé de wa tekisei kákaku de hambai-shite orimásu. 手前どもの店では適正価格で販売しております。 *Prices in our stores are reasonable.* <*formal*>

temáneki 手招き *beckoning; motioning (with the hand for someone to come)* ——**temáneki-suru** [*vi*] 手招きする *beckon; motion to come* §Hágino-san wa watashi o mikakete temáneki-shite kureta. 萩野さんは私を見かけて手招きしてくれた。 *Ms. Hagino saw me and motioned to me (to come).*

temmondai 天文台 *astronomical observatory*

temmongaku 天文学 *astronomy*

-té mo íi ～てもいい *may (do); be OK to (do)* §Shichaku-shité mo íi desu ka? 試着してもいいですか？ *May I try it on?* §Sono kudámono o tabéte mo íi desu yo. その果物を食べてもいいですよ。 *You may eat that fruit.*

temotó ni 手元に；手許に *at hand; beside (one); nearby* §Kodomo o ítsumade mo temotó ni oite okitái. 子供をいつまでも手元に置いておきたい。 *I want to have my children always nearby.* §Íma temotó ni o-kane ga arimasén. 今、手元にお金がありません。 *I don't have any money at present.*

tempuku 転覆 *an overthrow; subversion; downfall* ——**tempuku-suru** [*vi*] 転覆する *capsize; overturn; subvert* §Asase ni noriágete gyosen ga tempuku-shita. 浅瀬に乗り上げて漁船が転覆した。 *The fishing ship ran aground on a shoal and capsized.* §Yátō wa seiken o tempuku-saseyó to ugóite iru. 野党は政権を転覆させようと動いている。 *The opposition parties moved to overthrow the party in power.*

tempura 天麩羅 *deep-fried food*

ten 点 *dot; point; score (on a test); a matter* §ten o útsu 点を打つ *mark with a dot* §íi ten o tóru いい点を取る *get a good grade* §Gakunen héikin wa nanajū-go tén desu. 学年平均は75点です。 *The average score for this grade level is 75 (points).* ❖Kono ten dé wa minná no íken ga itchi-shita. この点ではみんなの意見が一致した。 *Everyone agreed on this point.*

tén 天 *heaven*

tenagédan 手投げ弾 *hand grenade*

téngoku 天国 *paradise; heaven*

tengu 天狗 *long-nosed goblin*

tenímotsu 手荷物 *hand luggage* ❖tenímotsu ichiji azukarisho 手荷物一時預かり所 *baggage room; checkroom* ❖Tenímotsu o azukátte itadakemásu ka? 手荷物を預かって頂けますか? *Would you check my bags, please?*

ten'in 店員 *salesperson; salesclerk*

tenji 展示 *display; exhibition* ❖tenjíkai 展示会 *an exhibition* ❖tenjijō 展示場 *exhibition hall* ——**tenji-suru** [vt] 展示する *display* ❖Sono tenjijō ní wa watashi no sakuhin ga tenji-shite áru. その展示場には私の作品が展示してある。 *My work is on display in that exhibition hall.*

tenjō 天井 *ceiling*

tenka 点火 *ignition; lighting* ——**tenka-suru** [vi] 点火する *ignite; set fire (to)*

ténka 天下 *the whole world; everything under heaven; the realm* ❖ténka o tóru 天下を取る *take power; bring the whole country under (one's) rule*

tenkai 展開 *development; expansion* ——**tenkai-suru** [vi / vt] 展開する *develop; spread; evolve; expand* ❖gíron o tenkai-suru 議論を展開する *expand (the scope of) a discussion* ❖Gánka ni daisōgen ga tenkai-shite ita. 眼下に大草原が展開していた。 *A great plain spread out before us.*

tenkan 転換 *transformation; change* ❖kibun ténkan 気分転換 *change of mood* ❖hōkō ténkan 方向転換 *change of direction* ——**tenkan-suru** [vi] 転換する *turn; change; transform* ❖Wadai ga hyakuhachijūdo tenkan-shita. 話題が180度転換した。 *The discussion took a 180-degree turn.*

tenkei 典型 *model; pattern* ——**tenkeiteki [na]** 典型的（な）*typical* ❖Kono ié wa tenkeiteki na Nihon yōshiki desu. この家は典型的な日本様式です。 *This is a typical Japanese-style house.*

tenken 点検 *inspection; a check* ——**tenken-suru** [vt] 点検する *inspect; examine* ❖Jidōsha wa teikiteki ni tenken-suru hitsuyō ga áru. 自動車は定期的に点検する必要がある。 *It is necessary to inspect an automobile periodically.*

ténki 天気 *weather* ❖tenkízu 天気図 *weather map; weather chart* ❖Ténki wa yóku narisō desu. 天気は良くなりそうです。 *It looks like the weather's going to get better.*

tenkin 転勤 *(job) transfer* ——**tenkin-suru** [*vi*] 転勤する *transfer*
  §Watashi wa Ōsaka shíten ni tenkin-shimáshita. 私は大阪支店に転勤
しました。*I transferred to the Osaka branch office.*

tenkō 転向 *(political) conversion*   §kyōsanshugi kara no tenkōsha 共産
主義からの転向者 *a convert from communism*——**tenkō-suru** [*vi*]
転向する *convert; change over*

ténkyo 転居 *removal; change of residence* ——**ténkyo-suru** [*vi*] 転居す
る *move; change (one's) address*   §Watashitachi wa kóndo Tōkyō
kara Kanágawa ni ténkyo-suru kotó ni nátta. 私たちは今度東京から神
奈川に転居することになった。*We're going to move from Tokyo to
Kanagawa.*

tennen [no] 天然（の）*natural*   §tennen gásu 天然ガス *natural gas*
  §tennen kinémbutsu 天然記念物 *natural monument*   §tennénshoku
天然色 *natural color*   §tennen páma 天然パーマ *natural wave (in
the hair)*   §tennen shígen 天然資源 *natural resources*

tennentō 天然痘 *smallpox*

tennō 天皇 *emperor*   §Tennō Héika 天皇陛下 *His Imperial Majesty;
the (Japanese) Emperor*   §Tennō Kōgō Ryōhéika 天皇皇后両陛下
Their Majesties the Emperor and Empress

Tennōsei 天王星 *Uranus*

ténnyo 天女 *heavenly being; angel*

tenóhira 掌 *palm (of the hand)*

tenránkai 展覧会 *exhibition*

tensai 天才 *genius; talent*   §Éjison wa hatsumei no tensai déshita. エジ
ソンは発明の天才でした。*Edison was a genius at invention.* ——
tensaiteki [na] 天才的（な）*talented; gifted*   §tensaiteki na
baiorinísuto 天才的なバイオリニスト *a gifted violinist*

ténshi 天使 *angel*   §byákui no ténshi 白衣の天使 *an angel in white (a
nurse)*

tentómushi 天道虫 *ladybug; ladybird*

tenugui 手拭い *face towel; hand towel*   §tenuguíkake 手拭い掛け
towel rack

teochi 手落ち *omission; oversight*

teókure 手遅れ *too late; not in time*   §teókure ni náru 手遅れになる *be
too late; fail to (do) in time*   §Íma kara de wa mō teókure desu. 今から
ではもう手遅れです。*It's too late now.*

teonó 手斧 *hatchet*

teppan 鉄板 *iron sheet; iron plate; griddle*

teppén 天辺 *top; summit*

teppō 鉄砲 *gun*

[o-]terá （お）寺 *Buddhist temple*

terás·u [*vt* terasánai; terashíta] 照らす *shine on; light up; illuminate*
  §Tōdai wa asase o terashimásu. 灯台は浅瀬を照らします。*The*

lighthouse lights up the shallows.

térebi テレビ *TV*   §terebi bángumi テレビ番組 *television program* §terebi káiken テレビ会見 *television interview*

terebín-yu テレビン油 *turpentine*

teré·ru [*vi* terénai; téreta] 照れる *be shy; be embarrassed*   §Watashi wa hitomae de homérarete térete shimatta. 私は人前で褒められて照れてしまった。*I was embarrassed when I was praised publicly.*

tesakí 手先 *the fingers; hands*   §Tesakí ga furuete iru 手先が震えている。*My hand's shaking.*   §Watashi wa tesakí ga kíyō desu. 私は手先が器用です。*I'm good with my hands.*

tesei [no] 手製（の）*handmade; homemade*   §tesei no kéki 手製のケーキ *homemade cake*

tesō 手相 *lines of the palm*   §tesō o míru 手相を見る *read (one's) palm*

tesú 手数 *trouble; burden*   §tesúryō 手数料 *handling charge; fee*   §O-tesū désu ga, kono tegami o kakitome de dáshite kudasaimasén ka? お手数ですが、この手紙を書留で出して下さいませんか。*I hate to trouble you, but would you mind sending this letter by registered mail?*

tesurí 手摺 *handrail; railing; bannister*

tetsu 鉄 *steel; iron*   §tetsubō 鉄棒 *iron rod; iron bar*

tetsudái 手伝い *help; assistance*   §o-tétsudai-san お手伝いさん *maid*   §Kyō wa ie no tetsudái ga áru. 今日は家の手伝いがある。*I have to help at home today.*

tetsudá·u [*vt* tetsudawánai; tetsudátta] 手伝う *help; assist; aid*   §Kyō wa ichinichi háha no shigoto o tetsudaimásu. 今日は一日、母の仕事を手伝います。*I'm helping mother (with her work) all day today.*

tetsudō 鉄道 *railway; railroad*   §tetsudō jíko 鉄道事故 *a railroad accident*

tetsúgaku 哲学 *philosophy*   §tetsugakúsha 哲学者 *philosopher*

tetsuya 徹夜 *all night through*   §tetsuya no keikai 徹夜の警戒 *all-night vigil*   §Yūbé wa tetsuya de benkyō-shimáshita. 夕べは徹夜で勉強しました。*Last night I studied all night long.*

tetteiteki [na] 徹底的（な）*thorough*   §tetteiteki na shirabe 徹底的な調べ *a thorough investigation* ——**tetteiteki ni** 徹底的に *thoroughly*

tezáiku 手細工 *handicraft*

tezáwari 手触り *the feel (of something)*

to 戸 *sliding door* (J)

to と *and* [*conjunction for nouns or noun phrases*]   §Watashi wa bánana to míkan ga sukí desu. 私はバナナとみかんが好きです。*I like bananas and tangerines.*

to と [*particle: quotation marker*]   §"Ashitá wa gakkō wa arimasén" to senséi ga iimáshita. 「明日は学校はありません」と先生が言いました。*The teacher said, "Tomorrow there is no school."*

to と [*particle: adverb marker*]   §sássa to さっさと *quickly; promptly*

❽kichínto きちんと *neatly; precisely*

to と *with* **❽Watashi wa Mốri-san to ténisu o shimásu.** 私は毛利さんと
テニスをします。 *I play tennis with Mr. Mori.*

tố 十 *ten (when counting objects)*

tố 塔 *steeple; tower; pagoda*

tobaku 賭博 *gambling*

tobas·u [*vt* tobasanai; tobashita] 飛ばす *make fly; skip over; leave out*
❽Kodomótachi ga kamihikốki o tobashite imásu. 子供たちが紙飛行機
を飛ばしています。 *Children are flying paper planes.* **❽Tsuyói kaze
ga kamban o tobashita.** 強い風が看板を飛ばした。 *A strong wind
blew away the sign board.* **❽Muzukashíi mondai wa tobashité mo íi
desu,** 難しい問題は飛ばしてもいいです。 *It's all right to skip the
difficult problems.*

tốben 答弁 *an answer; a reply* **❽tōben gíjutsu** 答弁技術 *answer tactics
(or skill)*

tobiagár·u [*vi* tobiagaránai; tobiagátta] 跳び上がる *jump up*

tobidás·u [*vi* tobidasánai; tobidashíta] 飛び出す *run out; dart out* **❽Dốro
ni kyū ni tobidásu to kiken desu.** 道路に急に飛び出すと危険です。
It's dangerous to run out into the street.

tobiishi 飛び石 *stepping stone* **❽tobiishi rénkyū** 飛び石連休 *"stepping-
stone holidays" (holidays every other day, as during "Golden Week")*

tobokế·ru [*vi* tobokénai; tobóketa] 恍ける；惚ける *pretend not to know;
play dumb* **❽Tobốkete mo muda da.** 恍けても無駄だ。 *It'll do no
good to pretend you don't know.* **toboshí·i** [*adj* tobóshiku nái;
tobóshikatta] 乏しい *(be) scarce; short of; deficient in; poor in*
❽Nihón wa tennen shígen ga toboshíi. 日本は天然資源が乏しい。
Japan is deficient in natural resources. **❽Kốhira-san wa bengóshi no
keiken ga toboshíi.** 小平さんは弁護士の経験が乏しい。 *Ms. Kohira
is short on legal experience.*

tob·u [*vi* tobanai; tonda] 跳ぶ *jump*

tob·u [*vi* tobanai; tonda] 飛ぶ *fly; rush* **❽Watashi wa Nyūyốku kéiyu de
Bosúton ni tobimásu.** 私はニューヨーク経由でボストンに飛びま
す。 *I'm flying to Boston by way of New York.* **❽Watashi wa nyū́su o
kiite, tonde kimáshita.** 私はニュースを聞いて飛んで来ました。 *I
heard the news and rushed right here.*

tốbun 当分 *for the present; for a while; for the time being* **❽Tốbun no
aida ié o rúsu ni shimasu.** 当分の間、家を留守にします。 *I'm going
to be away from home for a while.*

tốchaku 到着 *arrival* **❽tōchaku róbī** 到着ロビー *arrival lobby*
❽tōchaku jíkoku 到着時刻 *arrival time* **――tốchaku-suru** [*vi*] 到着
する *arrive* **❽teikoku ni tōchaku-suru** 定刻に到着する *arrive on
schedule*

tochi 土地 *land; lot; real estate* **❽tochi báibai** 土地売買 *dealing in real* *estate*

tōchi 統治 *reign; rule* ——**tōchi-suru** [*vt*] *to reign; rule; be in control of*　❧Kita Mariana Shótō wa kokuren ga tōchi-shite imásu. 北マリアナ諸島は国連が統治しています。 *The U.N. administers the Northern Mariana Islands.*

tóchō 都庁 *metropolitan government (office)*　❧Tōkyō Tóchō 東京都庁 *Tokyo Metropolitan Government*

tōchō 登頂 *reaching the (mountain) summit*　❧Sono sangakutai wa tōchō ni seikō-shimáshita. その山岳隊は登頂に成功しました。 *The mountain-climbing party succeeded in reaching the summit.*

tōchō-suru [*vt*] 盗聴する *tap (a telephone)*　❧Kono denwa, tōchō-sarenái kashira? この電話、盗聴されないかしら。 *I wonder if this telephone is tapped. <fem>*

tochū [de] 途中（で） *en route; on the way; halfway through*　❧shigoto o tochū de sabóru 仕事を途中でサボる *quit a job halfway through.*　❧Watashi wa uchi ni káeru tochū desu. 私は家に帰る途中です。 *I'm on my way home.*

tōdai 灯台 *lighthouse*

todana 戸棚 *cupboard*

todoké 届け *registry; registration; notice*　❧shusshō tódoke 出生届け *birth registration*　❧kesseki tódoke 欠席届け *notice of absence*

todoké·ru [*vt* todokénai; todóketa] 届ける *deliver*　❧Píza o san-chōme ni-bánchi no Fujíhashi ni todókete kudasái. ピザを３丁目２番地の藤橋に届けて下さい。 *Deliver a pizza to Fujihashi at No. 2, 3-chōme, please.*

todók·u [*vi* todokánai; todóita] 届く *arrive; be delivered; reach (to)*　❧Watashi no tegami ga todóita? 私の手紙が届いた？ *Did my letter arrive?*　❧Musuko wa ōkiku nátte tenjō ni té ga todokisō desu yo. 息子は大きくなって天井に手が届きそうですよ。 *My son's gotten so tall he can almost reach the ceiling.*

todomár·u [*vi* todomaránai; todomátta] 留まる *stay*　❧Watashi wa shōkaku ga miokurare, íma no chíi ni todomáru koto ni nátta. 私は昇格が見送られ、今の地位に留まることになった。 *I was passed over for a promotion, so I'm to stay at my present position.*

tōgárashi 唐辛子 *chili; hot pepper; cayenne pepper*

togár·u [*vi* togaránai; togátta] 尖る *be sharp; be pointed*　❧togátta hári 尖った針 *a sharp needle*　❧Kimi, sonna ni togáru na yo. 君そんなに尖るなよ。 *Don't get your dander up. <masc>*

togé 刺 *thorn; splinter*　❧bara no togé 薔薇の刺 *rosebush thorn*　❧Yubí ni togé o sáshite shimatta. 指に刺を刺してしまった。 *I have a splinter (stuck) in my finger.*

tōge 峠 *mountain pass; crisis*　❧tōge o kosu 峠を越す *cross over a pass*　❧byōki no tōge 病気の峠 *the crisis of an illness*

tŏgi 討議 *discussion* ——**tŏgi-suru** [*vt*] 討議する *discuss* §Uriage baizō kéikaku ni tsúite zén-shain de tŏgi-shite iru. 売り上げ倍増計画 について全社員で討議している。 *All the employees are discussing the company's plans for doubling sales.*

tóg·u [*vt* togánai; tóida] 研ぐ *sharpen; whet* §hōchō o tógu 包丁を研 ぐ *sharpen a kitchen knife*

tóguchi 戸口 *doorway; door*

tohō mo nái 途方もない *absurd; ludicrous*

tohō ni kureru 途方に暮れる *be at a loss; become perplexed*

tōhyō 投票 *a vote; ballot* §tōhyōbi 投票日 *election day* §tōhyōjo 投 票所 *polling place; the polls* §tōhyō yóshi 投票用紙 *a ballot* —— **tōhyō-suru** [*vi*] 投票する *vote; cast a ballot*

tō·i [*adj* tōkunái; tókatta] 遠い *(be) far; distant* §Gakkō wa tōku nái. 学 校は遠くない。 *The school isn't far.* §tōi shinseki 遠い親戚 *a distant relative* §Chichí wa sukóshi mimí ga tōi désu. 父は少し耳が 遠いです。 *Dad's a little hard of hearing.*

toiawase 問い合わせ *inquiry*

toiawasé·ru [*vt* toiawasénai; toiawáseta] 問い合わせる *inquire; ask* §Ashita no shūgō basho o toiawaseyó. 明日の集合場所を問い合わせ よう。 *I'll inquire about tomorrow's meeting place.*

toiki 吐息 *a sigh; long breath*

tōitsu 統一 *unification* ——**tōitsu-suru** [*vt*] 統一する *unify; standardize* §Kamehameha Daiō wa Háwai o tōitsu-shimáshita. カメハメハ大王は ハワイを統一しました。 *King Kamehameha unified Hawaii.*

toitsumé·ru [*vt* toitsuménai; toitsúmeta] 問い詰める *question; interrogate; cross-examine* §Kéiji wa higēsha ni sono hi no aribai o toitsumemáshita. 刑事は被疑者にその日のアリバイを問い詰めま した。 *The police detective interrogated the suspect concerning his alibi for that day.*

tŏji 当時 *at that time; then* §Tŏji no Nihon no jinkō wa íma hodo dé wa arimasén deshita. 当時の日本の人口は今ほどではありませんでし た。 *At that time Japan's population was not as great as it is today.*

tojikomór·u [*vi* tojikománai; tojikomótta] 閉じ籠る *shut oneself in; be confined* §Musumé wa heyá ni tojikomorimáshita. 娘は部屋に閉じ 籠りました。 *My daughter shut herself up in her room.*

tojímari 戸締り *shutting of doors and windows* ——**tojímari-suru** [*vt*] 戸締りする *lock up; close all doors and windows*

tojí·ru [*vt* tojínai; tójita] 閉じる *close; fasten* §Sá, hón o tójite goran. Soshite mé mo tójite goran. さあ本を閉じてごらん。 そして目も閉 じてごらん。 *Now, close your books. And then, close your eyes also.*

tōjō 登場 *appearance* §shintōjō 新登場 *new appearance (of a product)* ——**tōjō-suru** [*vi*] 登場する *appear; come on the scene* §Ano káshu wa yóku térebi ni tōjō-shimásu. あの歌手はよくテレビに登場

します。 *That singer often appears on TV*

tóka とか *and / or* 　§Sukóshi wa tabéru toka nómu toka shinai to génki ni naránai wa yo. 少しは食べるとか飲むとかしないと元気にならないわよ。 *If you don't eat or drink a little you won't get well.* \<fem>

tōka 十日 *tenth of the month; ten days*

tokai 都会 *city* 　§tokaika 都会化 *urbanization* 　§tokai séikatsu 都会生活 *city life* ——**tokai no** 都会の *metropolitan; urban* 　§tokai no zattō 都会の雑踏 *urban congestion*

tokás·u [*vt* tokasánai; tokáshita] 溶かす *dissolve; melt; thaw* 　§Kusuri o mizu ni tokáshite nomimáshita. 薬を水に溶かして飲みました。 *I dissolved the medicine in water and drank it.* 　§Kōnetsu wa kínzoku o tokashimásu. 高熱は金属を溶かします。 *High temperature will melt metal.*

tokei 時計 *clock; watch* 　§tokeidai 時計台 *clock tower* 　§tokeiya 時計屋 *a watch store*

tōkei 統計 *statistics*

tokekóm·u [*vi* tokekománai; tokekónda] 溶け込む *melt into; get into; be involved in* 　§kimochi ga tokekómu 気持ちが溶け込む *to empathize with* 　§Kono mizuúmi ni wa yūgai bússhitsu ga tokekónde iru. この湖には有害物質が溶け込んでいる。 *This lake contains harmful substances.*

toké·ru [*vi* tokénai; tóketa] 溶ける *dissolve; melt; thaw* 　§Háru ni náru to mizuúmi no kōri ga tokéru. 春になると湖の氷が溶ける。 *When spring comes, the ice on the lake will melt.* 　§Kono busshitsu wa mizu ni tokéru. この物質は水に溶ける。 *This substance dissolves in water.*

tokí 時 *time* 　§tokí ga nagaréru 時が流れる *time flows by* 　§tokí ga tátsu 時が経つ *time passes* 　§tokí o tsubusu 時を潰す *kill time*

-tóki ～時 *when* 　§Hón o yómu toki, mégane o kakéru. 本を読む時、眼鏡をかける。 *I wear glasses when I read.*

tóki 陶器 *ceramics; pottery; chinaware*

tōki 投機 *speculation* ——**tōki-suru** [*vt*] 投機する *speculate*

tokidoki 時々 *sometimes; now and then*

tokken 特権 *special privilege; franchise* 　§tokken káikyū 特権階級 *the privileged class*

tókkyo 特許 *a patent; concession; franchise* 　§tókkyo o tóru 特許を取る ˉ(to) patent 　§tokkyóchō 特許庁 *patent office* 　§tokkyoken shingíkai 特許権審議会 *patent (protection) council*

toko 床 *bed* 　§toko ni tsúku 床につく *go to bed*

tokonoma 床の間 *decorative alcove (in Japanese houses)*

tokoró 所 *place; location* 　§Koko wa J.F. Kénedī ga umareta tokoró desu. ここはJ.F. ケネディーが生まれた所です。 *This is the place where J.F. Kennedy was born.*

tokoró de ところで *by the way; Well, ...* 　§Tokoró de ashita no tsugō wa ikága deshō ka? ところで明日の都合はいかがでしょうか。 *By the way, how does tomorrow suit you?*

-tokoró desu. ～ところです。 *at the point of (doing); about to (do)* ⑧Íma denwa o shiyŏ to shita tokoró desu. 今電話をしようとしたところです。 *I was just about to telephone (you).* ⑧Kyō no fukushū o shite iru tokoró desu. 今日の復習をしているところです。 *We're just now reviewing today's lesson.* ⑧Íma chōdo shukudai ga owatta tokoró desu. 今ちょうど宿題が終わったところです。 *I have just finished doing my homework.*

tokoya 床屋 *barbershop* ⑧tokoyasan 床屋さん *barber*

toku 得 *advantage; a bargain* ⑧toku o suru 得をする *benefit; profit by* ⑧Yásuku shite moratte toku o shitá no. 安くして貰って得をしたの。 *They sold it to me cheap; I got a bargain.* <fem>

tók·u [vt tokánai; tóita] 解く *untie; unravel; solve* ⑧gokai o tóku 誤解 を解く *resolve a misunderstanding* ⑧Nazo ga tokáreta. 謎が解かれ た。 *The riddle was solved.*

tōkú [no] 遠く（の） *distant; far off; far away; a long way* ⑧Tōkú no shinrui yóri chíkaku no tanin. 遠くの親類より近くの他人。 *Better a stranger who is near than a relative far away.* <set phrase>

tokubetsu [na/ no] 特別（な／の） *special; particular* ⑧tokubetsu káikei 特別会計 *special account* ⑧tokubetsu bángumi 特別番組 *a special (TV / radio) program* ⑧Tokubetsu no riyū wa arimasén. 特別 の理由はありません。 *I have no special reason.* ——**tokubetsu ni** 特 別に *especially; in particular* ⑧Kono fukú wa kyŏ no tamé ni tokubetsu ni atsuraemáshita. この服は今日のために特別に誂えまし た。 *I had this dress made especially for today.*

tokuchō 特徴 *special characteristic; special feature; distinction* ⑧Yoshimi-san wa tokuchō no áru kaodachi o shite imasu. 良美さんは 特徴のある顔だちをしています。 *Yoshimi has distinctive (facial) features.*

tokúi [na] 得意（な） *good at; one's specialty* ⑧Arai-san wa Doitsugo ga tokúi desu. 荒井さんはドイツ語が得意です。 *German is Ms. Arai's specialty.* ——**tokuí ni náru** 得意になる *become stuck up* ⑧Komamura-san wa homéru to súgu tokúi ni náru yo. 駒村さんは褒め るとすぐ得意になるよ。 *If you praise Mr. Komamura it goes right to his head.*

tokuigao de 得意顔で *triumphantly; with a smug expression* ⑧Masaru wa tokuigao de tsuri no séika o hōkoku shité kita. 勝は得意顔で釣の成果 を報告してきた。 *Masaru came in and smugly told us about the fish he had caught.*

[o-]tokui-san （お）得意さん *special customer*

tokuisei 特異性 *idiosyncrasy; distinguishing characteristic* ⑧Hito to tá no dōbutsu tó no tokuisei wa nán desu ka? ヒトと他の動物との特異

性は何ですか。 *What is it that distinguishes human beings from other animals?*

tóku ni 特に *particularly; especially* 🞵Kotoshi no natsú wa tóku ni atsúi ne. 今年の夏は特に暑いね。 *Summer this year is especially hot, isn't it?*

tokurei 特例 *exception; special case*

tokushu [na] 特殊（な）*special type; characteristic; peculiar* 🞵Hayashi-san wa kokuren no náka de tokushu na nímmu ni tsúite imasu. 林さんは国連の中で特殊な任務に就いています。 *Mr. Hayashi holds a special office in the United Nations.*

tokutei no 特定の *fixed; established; specific* ——**tokutei-suru** [vt] 特定する *fix; settle on; establish*

tŏkyoku 当局 *the authorities; the officials (in charge)* 🞵Kono mondai wa daigaku tŏkyoku ga kaiketsu-subéki desu. この問題は大学当局が解決すべきです。 *This is a problem that should be settled by the university officials.*

tomadó·u [vi tomadowánai; tomadótta] 戸惑う *be puzzled; be at a loss; be perplexed* 🞵Totsuzen no shitsumon ni tomadótte shimatta. 突然の質問に戸惑ってしまった。 *The sudden question left me at a loss.*

tomar·u [vi tomaranai; tomatta] 止まる *stop; halt* 🞵Máe no kuruma ga kyū ni tomarimáshita. 前の車が急に止まりました。 *The car ahead stopped suddenly.* 🞵Kono tokei wa tomatte imásu. この時計は止まっています。 *This watch has stopped.*

tomar·u [vi tomaranai; tomatta] 泊まる *stay; stop over; lodge (at)* 🞵hóteru ni tomaru ホテルに泊まる *stay at a hotel* 🞵Ié ni senshū kara shinseki no monó ga tomatte imásu. 家に先週から親戚の者が泊まっています。 *We've had relatives staying with us since last week.*

tombo 蜻蛉 *dragonfly*

tome·ru [vt tomenai; tometa] 止める *turn off; stop* 🞵Gásu no motosen o tomemáshita. ガスの元栓を止めました。 *I turned off the main gas outlet.* 🞵Ie no máe de kuruma o tomemáshita. 家の前で車を止めました。 *I stopped the car in front of the house.*

tome·ru [vt tomenai; tometa] 留める *fasten; button; pin; fix; tack* 🞵Musumé wa aidoru káshu no shashin o heya no kabe ni tomemáshita. 娘はアイドル歌手の写真を部屋の壁に留めました。 *My daughter tacked her favorite pop singer's photograph on the wall in her room.*

tome·ru [vt tomenai; tometa] 停める *secure* 🞵Fúne o hatoba ni tomenasái. 船を波止場に停めなさい。 *Secure the boat to the pier.*

tómi 富 *wealth*

tomodachi 友達 *friend* 🞵tomodachi ni náru 友達になる *become friends; make friends with*

tomogui 共食い *eating one another; cannibalism*

tómokaku ともかく *at any rate; anyhow; anyway* 🞵Tómokaku shikén wa owatta! ともかく試験は終わった。 *Well, anyway, the test's over!*

tomoná·u [*vt* tomonawánai; tomonátta] 伴う *accompany; involve; have a concomitant* ❽Sono jikken wa kiken o tomonaimásu. その実験は危険を伴います。 *That experiment involves danger.*

tomo ni 共に *together; collectively*

tōmórokoshi 玉蜀黍 *corn*

tomós·u [*vt* tomosánai; tomóshita] 灯す；点す *light (a fire)* ❽akari o tomósu 灯りを灯す *light a lantern*

tónai 都内 *inside Tokyo City* ❽Watashi wa tónai ni súnde imasu. 私は都内に住んでいます。 *I live in Tokyo City proper.*

tōnan 盗難 *theft; robbery* ❾Rusu-chū ni tōnan ni átte shimatta. 留守中に盗難に合ってしまった。 *While I was out my house was burglarized.*

tōnan 東南 *southeast* ❾Tōnan Ájia 東南アジア *Southeast Asia*

tonari 隣 *next to; next door* ❽tonari no hitótachi 隣の人たち *the people next door* ❽tonari no heyá 隣の部屋 *adjacent room* ❽Tonari ni suwattémo íi desu ka? 隣に座ってもいいですか？ *May I sit next to you?*

tonde mo nái とんでもない *surprising; shocking; absurd; preposterous; inconceivable* ❽Tonde mo nái koto ga ókite shimaimáshita. とんでもないことが起きてしまいました。 *Something inconceivable happened.* ❽"Dōmo arígatō gozaimáshita." "Íe, tonde mo arimasén." 「どうも有難うございました。」「いいえ、とんでもありません。」 *"Thank you very much." "Don't mention it."*

tónikaku とにかく *anyhow; at any rate; in any case* ❽Tónikaku mō ichido yatte goran. とにかくもう一度やってごらん。 *Anyhow, try again.*

tonkatsu とんカツ *pork cutlet*

ton'ya 問屋 *wholesaler; wholesale dealer*

tōnyōbyō 糖尿病 *diabetes*

tōnyū 豆乳 *soybean milk*

toppa 突破 *breakthrough* ——**toppa-suru** [*vt*] 突破する *exceed; break through* ❽nankan o toppa-suru 難関を突破する *overcome difficulties* ❽Wágasha no uriage wa kotoshi nichōen o toppa-shita. 我が社の売り上げは今年二兆円を突破した。 *This year our company's sales exceeded ¥2 trillion.*

toraé·ru [*vt* toraénai; toráeta] 捕える；捉える *capture; seize; take; take hold of; catch* ❽Hánnin o toráeta. 犯人を捕えた。 *They caught the criminal.* ❽Rēdā ga tekikan o toráeta. レーダーが敵艦を捕えた。 *The radar picked up the enemy ship.* ❽Torae-kata ga chigau kéredo, kimi to bóku to wa onaji kotó o mondai ni shite iru n da yo. 捉え方が違うけれど、君と僕とは同じことを問題にしているんだよ。 *We may not look at it the same way, but you and I see the same thing as a problem. <masc>*

torámpu トランプ *playing cards*

toré·ru [*vi* torénai; tóreta] 取れる *come off; be removed; be separated from* 🞕Botan ga tórete shimatta. ボタンが取れてしまった。 *The button came off.* 🞕Koshi no itamí ga tórete kimáshita. 腰の痛みが取れてきました。 *My backache's gone.*

toré·ru [*vi* torénai; tóreta] 取れる *be obtained; harvest* 🞕Sakana ga tóreta? 魚がとれた？ *Did you catch any fish?* 🞕Kotoshi wa komé ga takusan tore-ső desu. 今年は米が沢山獲れそうです。 *It looks like we'll harvest a lot of rice this year.*

tori 鳥 *bird* 🞕torikago 鳥籠 *birdcage*

tōri 通り *street* 🞕tōri ni ménshite 通りに面して *facing the street* 🞕Tōri de yūjin ni aimáshita. 通りで友人に会いました。 *I met a friend on the street.*

tōrí 通り *coming and going; passing along* 🞕Kono kōsáten wa kuruma no tōrí ga hageshíi desu. この交差点は車の通りが激しいです。 *The traffic at this intersection is fierce.*

-tőri [ni] ～通り（に）*just as; exactly* 🞕Ítsumo no tōri watashi wa rokúji ni okimáshita. いつものとおり私は６時に起きました。 *As always, I got up at six.* 🞕Oya no iu tőri ni shinasái. 親の言うとおりにしなさい。 *Do as your parents say.*

toriáezu 取り敢えず *for the time being; at once; hastily* 🞕Toriáezu kore de daiyō-shite kudasái. とりあえずこれで代用して下さい。 *For the time being, use this as a substitute.* 🞕Toriáezu uchikin o harátte okimáshita. とりあえず内金を払っておきました。 *I paid the down payment right away.*

toriage·ru [*vt* toriagenai; toriageta] 取り上げる *take up; discuss; take away; deliver (a baby)* 🞕juwáki o toriageru 受話器を取り上げる *pick up the receiver* 🞕mondai o toriageru 問題を取り上げる *take up (or discuss) a problem* 🞕Tsukue no náka ni kakúshite oita manga o senséi ni toriageráreta. 机の中に隠しておいた漫画を先生に取り上げられた。 *The comic book I had hidden in my desk was taken away by the teacher.* 🞕Samba-san ga ákachan o toriageta. 産婆さんが赤ちゃんを取り上げた。 *A midwife delivered the baby.*

toriatsukai 取り扱い *treatment; handling; usage* 🞕Toriatsukai Chūi. 取り扱い注意。 *Handle With Care.* ——**toriatsuka·u** [*vt* toriatsukawanai; toriatsukatta] 取り扱う *handle; take charge of* 🞕Ano yōhínten de wa burando mono wa toriatsukatte imasén. あの洋品店ではブランド物は取り扱っていません。 *That clothing store doesn't handle brand-name goods.*

toridas·u [*vt* toridasanai; toridashita] 取り出す *take out; pick out; extract* 🞕Otokó wa pokétto kara jūen-dama o toridashita. 男はポケットから十円玉を取り出した。 *The man took a ten-yen coin from his pocket.*

toride 砦 *fort*

torié 取り柄 *redeeming quality; merit*   🔸Kóyama ni wa nan no torié mo nái. 小山には何の取り柄もない。 *Mr. Koyama hasn't a single redeeming quality.*

torihada 鳥肌 *gooseflesh; goose pimples*   🔸Kówakute torihada ga tátte imasu. 怖くて鳥肌が立っています。 *I'm so scared I've got goose pimples.*

torihazus·u [*vt* torihazusanai; torihazushita] 取り外す *take away; remove; detach*   🔸Kono kankisen wa torihazusemásu. この換気扇は取り外せます。 *This ventilation fan can be detached.*

toríhiki 取り引き *trade; exchange; transaction*   🔸Ano misé to wa toríhiki ga áru. あの店とは取り引きがある。 *We have dealings with that store.* —— **toríhiki-suru** [*vi / vt*] 取り引きする *do business with; deal with*

torii 鳥居 *(Shinto shrine) gateway*

toriire·ru [*vt* toriirenai; toriireta] 取り入れる；獲り入れる *include; incorporate; take in; harvest*   🔸shūkakúbutsu o toriireru 収穫物を取り入れる *harvest crops*   🔸Áme ga fútte kita no de sentakumono o toriireta. 雨が降ってきたので洗濯物を取り入れた。 *It started to rain, so I brought in the wash.*   🔸Anáta no íken o toriireru kotó ni shimásu. あなたの意見を取り入れることにします。 *We'll include your opinion.*

torikae·ru [*vt* torikaenai; torikaeta] 取り替える *renew; replace; exchange; swap*   🔸oshíme o torikaeru おしめを取り替える *change a diaper*   🔸Shin'ichi wa manga o kinen kítte to torikaeta. 伸一は漫画を記念切手と取り替えた。 *Shin'ichi swapped his comic books for memorial stamps.*

torikakar·u [*vi* torikakaranai; torikakatta] 取りかかる *begin; set about; set to work*   🔸Súgu ni shigoto ni torikakarinasái. 直ぐに仕事に取りかかりなさい。 *Get to work right away.*

tōrikakár·u [*vi* tōrikakaránai; tōrikakátta] 通りかかる *pass by; happen to come along*   🔸Soko o tōrikakátta tóki, itamí o uttáete mogáite iru josei ni aimáshita. そこを通りかかった時、痛みを訴えてもがいている女性に会いました。 *As I was passing by there, I came across a woman who was groaning in pain.*

torikeshi 取り消し *cancellation; retraction; withdrawal*

torikes·u [*vt* torikesanai; torikeshita] 取り消す *cancel; withdraw*   🔸Hóteru no yoyaku o torikeshimashō ka? ホテルの予約を取り消しましょうか？ *Shall we cancel the hotel reservation?*

torikó 虜 *captive; prisoner*   🔸kói no toríkó 恋の虜 *a prisoner of love*   🔸toríkó ni náru 虜になる *become a prisoner; be captured*

torikowás·u [*vt* torikowasánai; torikowáshita] 取り壊す *demolish; tear down; raze*   🔸Sono furúi bíru wa torikowasáreru kotó ni narimáshita. その古いビルは取り壊されることになりました。 *That old building* *is going to be torn down.*

torikum·u [*vt* torikumanai; torikunda] 取り組む *deal with; take on; face (in a ring)* §Yoneyama-san wa aráta na kenkyū kádai ni torikunde imásu. 米山さんは新たな研究課題に取り組んでいます。 *Mr. Yoneyama is taking on a new research project.*

torimak·u [*vt* torimakanai; torimaita] 取り巻く *surround; hem in* §Kasai gémba o őku no yajiuma ga torimaita. 火災現場を多くの野次馬が取り巻いた。 *Many spectators surrounded the scene of the fire.*

toriniku 鶏肉 *chicken meat; poultry*

torinokos·u [*vt* torinokosanai; torinokoshita] 取り残す *leave behind* §Íshi wa ten'i-shita gansáibō o torinokoshite shújutsu o chūshi-shita. 医師は転移した癌細胞を取り残して手術を中止した。 *The doctor halted the operation and left the cancer, which had already begun to spread.*

torinozok·u [*vt* torinozokanai; torinozoita] 取り除く *eliminate; remove; set apart* §Jimoto no hitótachi wa kaigan ni suterareta akikan ya gomí o kírei ni torinozokimáshita. 地元の人たちは海岸に捨てられた空き缶やごみをきれいに取り除きました。 *The residents removed all the empty cans and trash discarded on the beach.*

tōrinuke·ru [*vi* tōrinukenai; tōrinuketa] 通り抜ける *pass through* §Watashítachi wa mori o tōrinukete chikámichi o shita. 私たちは森を通り抜けて近道をした。 *We took a shortcut through the forest.*

torishimar·u [*vt* torishimaranai; torishimatta] 取り締まる *control; oversee; manage* §Keisatsu wa supído íhan o torishimatte iru. 警察はスピード違反を取り締まっている。 *The police control speed violations.*

torishirabe 取り調べ *investigation; examination*

torishirabe·ru [*vt* torishirabenai; torishirabeta] 取り調べる *investigate; examine* §Kéiji wa yōgísha o kuwáshiku torishirabete iru. 刑事は容疑者を詳しく取り調べている。 *The police detectives are thoroughly examining the suspect.*

toritsuke·ru [*vt* toritsukenai; toritsuketa] 取り付ける *install; equip* §Kabe ni dénki no súitchi o toritsukemáshita. 壁に電気のスイッチを取り付けました。 *I installed a light switch on the wall.* §Watashi wa jóshi kara ryōkai o toritsukete orimásu. 私は上司から了解を取り付けております。 *I have the boss's approval.*

tōrō 灯篭 *(garden) lantern*

torobi とろ火 *low fire; simmering flame*

tōroku 登録 *registration; record* §tōroku shóhyō 登録商標 *registered trademark* ――**tōroku-suru** [*vt*] 登録する *register* §namae o tōroku-suru 名前を登録する *register one's name*

tóron 討論 *a debate* §tōrónkai 討論会 *debate meeting* ――**tóron-suru** [*vt*] 討論する *debate; discuss*

tór·u [*vt* toránai; tótta] 取る *take; take away; obtain; pick; interpret; seize; receive* ❸kane o tóru 金を取る *steal money* ❸Imōtó no té o tótte michi o watarimáshita. 妹の手を取って道を渡りました。*I took my little sister's hand and crossed the street.* ❸Ane wa tsúi ni hakushígō o torimáshita. 姉は遂に博士号を取りました。*My older sister finally received her Ph.D.* ❸Shió o tótte kudasái. 塩を取って下さい。*Please pass the salt.*

tór·u [*vi / vt* tōránai; tótta] 通る *go through; pass* ❸Kono básu wa Shibuya o tōrimásu ka? このバスは渋谷を通りますか。*Does this bus go through Shibuya?* ❸Shūshoku shíken ni tōrimáshita. 就職試験に通りました。*I passed the employment exam.*

tóryō 塗料 *paints; paint goods*

tōsei 当世 *the present (age)* ❸Tōsei no wakámono wa otokó da ka onná da ka wakaránai kakkō o shite iru monó da nā. 当世の若者は男だか女だか分からない格好をしているものだなあ。*The way young people dress these days, you can't tell whether they're boys or girls!* <masc>

tōsei 統制 *regulation; control* ❸tōsei kéizai 統制経済 *controlled (planned) economy* ——**tōsei-suru** [*vt*] 統制する *regulate; control* ❸Kono kuní de wa imada ni genron ga tōsei-sarete iru. この国では未だに言論が統制されている。*There is still little freedom of speech in this country.*

tōsen 当選 *election victory* ——**tōsen-suru** [*vi*] 当選する *be elected; win the prize* ❸Tsúma ga fujinkáichō ni tōsen-shimáshita. 妻が婦人会長に当選しました。*My wife was elected president of the women's society.*

toshí 年 *one's age; year* ❸toshí o tóru 年をとる *get older* ❸O-toshí wa o-ikutsu desu ka? お年はおいくつですか。*How old are you?* ❸Yói o-toshí o o-mukae kudasái. 良いお年をお迎え下さい。*Have a Happy New Year.* <formal>

tóshi 都市 *city; cities; towns and cities; urban center* ❸toshi kéikaku 都市計画 *city planning* ❸toshi móndai 都市問題 *urban problem* ❸toshi séikatsu 都市生活 *urban life* ——**toshika-suru** [*vt*] 都市化する *urbanize*

tóshi 闘志 *fighting spirit; determination* ❸Otōtó wa juken ni mukete tóshi mamman desu. 弟は受験に向けて闘志満々です。*My younger brother is facing his entrance exams with determination.*

tōshi 投資 *investment* ❸tōshi shíntaku 投資信託 *investment trust* ——**tōshi-suru** [*vt*] 投資する *invest* ❸kabu ni hyakuman'en o tōshi-suru 株に百万円を投資する *invest one million yen in stocks*

toshigoro 年頃 *puberty; be of age; age range* ❸Nakayama-san ní wa toshigoro no musume-san ga imásu. 中山さんには年ごろの娘さんがいます。*Mr. Nakayama has a daughter who is of age.* ❸Watashítachi wa hóbo onaji toshigoro desu. 私たちはほぼ同じ年ごろです。*We're* *about the same age.*

toshishita no 年下の *younger*

tōshi-suru [vi] 凍死する *freeze to death*

to shite として *as; for* ❀Sátō-san wa tsúyaku to shite dōkō-shimáshita. 佐藤さんは通訳として同行しました。 *Ms. Sato accompanied me as interpreter.* ❀Watashi to shité wa mō nani mo iu kotó wa nái. 私としてはもう何も言うことはない。 *As for me, I have nothing to say.*

-tōshite 〜通して *through; by means of* ❀Kimono o tōshite háda made nurete shimatta. 着物を通して肌まで濡れてしまった。 *I'm wet through to the skin.* ❀Myámmā de wa tsúyaku o tōshite o-hanashi o shimáshita. ミャンマーでは通訳を通してお話をしました。 *In Myanmar I spoke through an interpreter.*

toshitótta 年とった *elderly* ❀toshitótta ryōshin 年とった両親 *elderly parents*

toshiue no 年上の *older*

toshiyorí 年寄り *elderly person; old person*

tōshóran 投書欄 *readers' column; letters to the editor*

tōshu 投手 *(baseball) pitcher*

tōsō 闘争 *conflict; strife; struggle* ――**tōsō-suru** [vi] 闘争する *struggle; fight*

tōsō 逃走 *an escape; flight* ――**tōsō-suru** [vi] 逃走する *escape; flee* ❀Hánnin wa kuruma o nusúnde tōsō-shita. 犯人は車を盗んで逃走した。 *The criminal stole a car and escaped.*

-totan ni 〜途端に *just as...; just at the moment; in the act of* ❀Ié o déta totan ni áme ga furidashimáshita. 家を出た途端に雨が降り出しました。 *Just as I left home it started to rain.*

tōtei 到底 *not...at all; absolutely; by any possibility; hardly* ❀Náni o yatte mo kimi ní wa tōtei kanawánai ya. 何をやっても君には到底かなわないや。 *There's no way I can get the best of you.* <masc>

totemo とても *very*

tōtō とうとう *in the end; at last; finally* ❀Káyama-san wa tōtō kónakatta. 加山さんはとうとう来なかった。 *In the end, Ms. Kayama didn't come.* ❀Naganen no dóryoku no kekka, tōtō seikō-shimáshita. 永年の努力の結果、とうとう成功しました。 *As a result of many years of effort, I finally succeeded.*

totonoé·ru [vt] totonoénai; totonóeta] 整える *put things in order; prepare for; arrange* ❀Fukú o ima no uchi ni totonóete okimashō. 服を今のうちに整えておきましょう。 *I'll get my clothes ready while there's time.* ❀Taichō o tsúne ni totonóete okú no wa igai to muzukashíi. 体調を常に整えておくのは意外と難しい。 *It's surprisingly difficult to always stay in shape.*

totsuzen 突然 *suddenly; unexpectedly* ❀totsuzen hén'i 突然変異 *a mutation* ❀Básu wa totsuzen tomarimáshita. バスは突然止まりまし

た。 *The bus stopped suddenly.*

totte 取っ手 *a handle; knob*

[ni] tótte 〜 (に) とって *to; for; in the opinion of* ❂Watashi ni tótte Masáhiko-san wa kakegae no nái hitó nan desu. 私にとって雅彦さんはかけがえのない人なんです。 *Masahiko is indispensable to me.*

tótte ok·u [vt tótte okanai; tótte oita] 取っておく *keep; save; put aside*

tōwaku 当惑 *perplexity; embarrassment* ——**tōwaku-suru** [vi] 当惑する *be perplexed; be embarrassed*

Tōyō 東洋 *the East; Orient* ❂Tōyōjin 東洋人 *an (East) Asian; an Oriental* ❂Tōyō bíjutsu 東洋美術 *(East) Asian art* ❂Tōyō búmmei 東洋文明 *Far Eastern civilization*

tōyu 灯油 *fuel oil; kerosene*

tōza 当座 *the present; the time being* ❂tōza yókin 当座預金 *checking account*

tōzakár·u [vi tōzakaránai; tōzakátta] 遠ざかる *be distant; be far from* ❂Kiteki no otó ga tōzakátte iku. 汽笛の音が遠ざかって行く。 *The train whistle fades into the distance.* ❂Koko no tokoro Saitō-san to Tátsuno-san wa tōzakátte imasu. ここのところ斎藤さんと立野さんは遠ざかっています。 *Lately, Saito and Tatsuno have drifted apart.*

tōzaké·ru [vt tōzakénai; tōzaketa] 遠ざける *keep away; prevent from approaching; refrain from associating with*

tozan 登山 *mountain climbing* ❂tozanka 登山家 *a mountaineer*

tōzen [no] 当然 (の) *matter of course; expected; reasonable; (something) taken for granted* ❂Minná ga sō iú no wa tōzen desu. みんながそう言うのは当然です。 *It's reasonable that everyone would say so.*

tsúba; tsubakí 唾 *saliva; spittle* ❂tsúba o háku 唾を吐く *(to) spit* ❂HIV úirusu wa tsubakí kara kansen-suru koto wa arimasén. HIVウイルスは唾から感染することはありません。 *HIV is not contracted from saliva.*

tsúbaki 椿 *camellia* ❂kantsúbaki 寒椿 *winter camellia* ❂tsubaki ábura 椿油 *camellia oil*

tsubame 燕 *swallow (bird)*

tsubo 壺 *jar; pot* ❂Kore wa seiji no tsubo désu. これは青磁の壺です。 *This is a celadon jar.*

tsubo 坪 *a unit of area (3.954 sq. yds.)*

tsubomí 蕾 ; 莟 *(flower) bud*

tsúbu 粒 *a grain; a drop*

tsubure·ru [vi tsuburenai; tsubureta] 潰れる *be crushed; be smashed; be destroyed* ❂Tamágo ga tsuberete shimatta. 卵が潰れてしまった。 *The eggs were crushed.*

tsubus·u [vt tsubusanai; tsubushita] 潰す *crush; smash; squash* ❂jikan o tsubusu 時間を潰す *kill time*

tsubuyák·u [vi tsubuyakánai; tsubuyáita] 呟く *mutter; murmur*

tsuchí 土 *earth; soil; ground*

tsūchi 通知 *notification; information* ——**tsūchi-suru** [vt] 通知する *notify; report* §Kuwashíi koto wa áto de tsūchi-shimasu. 詳しいことは後で通知します。 *We will report the details to you later.*

tsūchō 通帳 *bankbook; passbook* §yokin tsūchō 預金通帳 *savings account book*

tsudoi 集い *meeting; gathering*

tsūdoku-suru [vt] 通読する *peruse; read (a book) from cover to cover* §Kono rombun o hitotōri tsūdoku-shite óita yo. この論文を一通り通読しておいたよ。 *I read the entire thesis through once.*

tsúe 杖 *cane; staff* §tsúe o tsúku 杖をつく *use a cane*

tsūgaku 通学 *attending school; commuting to school* ——**tsūgaku-suru** [vi] 通学する *attend school; commute to school* §Musuko wa básu de tsūgaku-shite iru. 息子はバスで通学している。 *My son takes the bus to school.*

tsuge·ru [vt tsugenai; tsugeta] 告げる *tell; inform; let know*

tsugí [no] 次（の） *the following; next* §Tsugí no básu ni norimashő. 次のバスに乗りましょう。 *Let's take the next bus.* §Tsugí ni náni o shimashő ka? 次に何をしましょうか。 *What shall we do next?*

tsugí tsugi [ni] 次々（に） *one (right) after the other; successively* §Tsugí tsugi ni keganin ga básu kara orosaremáshita. 次々に怪我人がバスから降ろされました。 *One after another the injured were taken from the bus.*

tsugō 都合 *convenience; conditions; circumstances* §Shigoto no tsugő de shusseki dekimasén deshita. 仕事の都合で出席できませんでした。 *I wasn't able to attend because of my work.*

tsug·u [vt tsuganai; tsuida] 注ぐ *pour* §"Ói, bíru o tsuide kureru kai?" 「おーい、ビールを注いでくれるかい？」 *"Hey! Will you pour me some beer?"* <masc>

tsug·u [vt tsuganai; tsuida] 継ぐ *succeed to; inherit* §Ken'ichi wa chichí no áto o tsuide shachō ni nátta. 健一は父の後を継いで、社長になった。 *Ken'ichi succeeded his father and became president of the company.*

tsuguná·u [vt tsugunawánai; tsugunátta] 償う *compensate for; make amends for; recompense; pay reparations* §Nihon séifu wa kátsute shinryaku-shita kuníguni ni táishite jūbún tsugunátta to omoimásu ka? 日本政府はかつて侵略した国々に対して充分償ったと思いますか。 *Do you think Japan has made sufficient amends to the countries she invaded?*

tsui 対 *a pair*

tsúi つい *just; only; carelessly* §Gomen nasái. Tsúi wasurete. ごめんなさい。つい忘れて。 *I'm sorry. I just forgot (to do it).*

tsuide ni 序でに *along the way; at the same time* §Kaimono ni iku

tsuide ni kono tegami o dáshite kite kurenai? 買い物に行く序でにこ
の手紙を出して来てくれない? *On your way to the store would you
mail this letter for me?*

tsuihō 追放 *banishment; eviction* ——**tsuihō-suru** [vt] 追放する
banish; evict; deport 8Fuhō námmin wa tsuihō-saremáshita. 不法難
民は追放されました。*The illegal immigrants were deported.*

tsuika 追加 *addition; addendum* 8tsuika ryṓkin 追加料金 *additional
costs* ——**tsuika-suru** [vt] 追加する *add (to); supplement* 8O-súshi
o mō ichinin-mae tsuika-shite kudasái. お寿司をもう一人前追加して
下さい。*Add another serving of sushi, please.*

tsuikyū 追及 *a search; pursuit; inquiry* ——**tsuikyū-suru** [vt] 追及する
search; pursue; inquire into

tsúi ni 遂に *at last; finally; in the end* 8Tsúi ni kansei-shita zo! 遂に完
成したぞ! *I finally finished it! <masc>*

tsuinin 追認 *ratification; confirmation* ——**tsuinin-suru** [vt] 追認する
ratify; confirm

tsuiraku 墜落 *a fall; (plane) crash* 8tsuiraku jíko 墜落事故 *a plane
crash* ——**tsuiraku-suru** [vi] 墜落する *fall; crash* 8Hikṓki ga úmi
ni tsuiraku-shita. 飛行機が海に墜落した。*The plane crashed into the
ocean.*

tsuiseki-suru [vt] 追跡する *pursue; chase* 8Sūdai no patókā ga shirói
kuruma o tsuiseki-shite iru. 数台のパトカーが白い車を追跡してい
る。*Several police cars are pursuing a white car.*

tsuitachí 一日 *first day of the month*

[ni] tsúite 〜 (に) ついて *concerning; about* 8Sono kotó ni tsúite dṓ
omoimásu ka. その事についてどう思いますか? *What do you think
about that?*

tsúite ik·u [vi tsúite ikanai; tsúite itta] 付いて行く *accompany; keep up
with; go along with (an idea)* 8O-saki ni itte kudasái. Áto kara tsúite
ikimásu kara. お先に行って下さい。後から付いて行きますから。
Go on ahead. I'll follow along later.

tsuitotsu 追突 *rear-end collision* ——**tsuitotsu-suru** [vi] 追突する
crash into from behind

tsuiyás·u [vt tsuiyasanai; tsuiyáshita] 費やす *spend; expend* 8Watashi
wa kyūjitsu o górufu de tsuiyáshite imasu. 私は休日をゴルフで費や
しています。*I spend my holidays playing golf.*

tsūji·ru [vi tsūjinai; tsūjita] 通じる *connect with; go (to); be well
acquainted with* 8Kono michi wa Pári ni tsūjite iru. この道はパリに
通じている。*This road connects (or goes) to Paris.* 8Denwa ga
tsūjinákatta. 電話が通じなかった。*The call didn't go through.*
8Futarí wa hanashí ga tsūjinai. 二人は話が通じない。*They (the two)
cannot communicate.* ——**[o] tsūjite** (を) 通じて *through;
throughout* 8Ano kátā wa Nihon zénkoku o tsūjite yūmei na dezáinā

desu. あの方は日本全国を通じて有名なデザイナーです。 *That person is a famous designer throughout Japan.*

tsūjō [no] 通常（の） *ordinary; common; general* ⊗tsūjō kókkai 通常国会 *ordinary Diet session* ⊗tsūjō héiki 通常兵器 *conventional weapon*

tsuká 塚 *mound; tumulus*

tsū́ka 通貨 *currency; money* ⊗tsū́ka no antei 通貨の安定 *currency stabilization* ⊗tsū́ka no bōchō 通貨の膨張 *inflation of currency* ⊗tsūka kíki 通貨危機 *monetary crisis*

tsukaé·ru [vi tsukaénai; tsukáeta] 仕える *serve* ⊗kámi ni tsukaéru 神に仕える *serve God* ⊗oyá ni tsukaéru 親に仕える *serve (one's) parents*

[o-]tsukai （お）遣い *errand; mission; message* ⊗musuko ni o-tsukai o tanómu 息子にお遣いを頼む *request (one's) son to run an errand* ⊗o-tsukai ni iku お遣いに行く *go on an errand*

tsukaihatás·u [vt tsukaihatasánai; tsukaihatáshita] 使い果たす *use up; squander* ⊗kiryoku o tsukaihatásu 気力を使い果たす *use up all (one's) energy* ⊗Watashi wa arigane o zémbu tsukaihatáshite shimatta. 私は有り金を全部使い果たしてしまった。 *I squandered all the money I had.*

tsukaisute [no] 使い捨て（の） *disposable; throw-away* ⊗tsukaisute jídai 使い捨て時代 *the "disposable" era* ⊗tsukaisute kámera 使い捨てカメラ *disposable camera*

tsukaitsukús·u [vt tsukaitsukusánai; tsukaitsukúshita] 使い尽くす *use up; spend* ⊗séiryoku o tsukaitsukúsu 精力を使い尽くす *spend all (one's) energy*

tsukamae·ru [vt tsukamaenai; tsukamaeta] 捕まえる *take hold of; grab onto with (one's) hand; capture; catch; arrest*

tsukamar·u [vi / vt tsukamaranai; tsukamatta] 捕まる *take hold of; be caught* ⊗Rṓpu ni tsukamari nasái. ロープに捕まりなさい。 *Take hold of the rope.* ⊗Támiya-san wa supīdo íhan de tsukamatta. 田宮さんはスピード違反で捕まった。 *Ms. Tamiya was caught for speeding.*

tsukám·u [vt tsukamánai; tsukánda] 掴む *seize; take hold of; catch* ⊗hito no jakutén o tsukámu 人の弱点を掴む *discover someone's weak point* ⊗kikái o tsukámu 機会を掴む *seize an opportunity*

tsūkan-suru [vt] 痛感する *feel strongly about; feel intensely* ⊗Kónkai no kōshō dé wa jibun no chikara-búsoku o tsūkan-shimáshita. 今回の交渉では自分の力不足を痛感しました。 *In the negotiations this time I felt powerless.*

tsukaré 疲れ *tiredness; exhaustion; weariness*

tsukaré·ru [vi tsukarénai; tsukáreta] 疲れる *be tired* ⊗Tsukárete arukénai. 疲れて歩けない。 *I'm too tired to walk.* ⊗Kyṓ wa totemo tsukáreta. 今日はとても疲れた。 *I'm really tired today.*

tsukarekír·u [*vi* tsukarekiránai; tsukarekítta] 疲れ切る *be exhausted; be worn out*

tsuka·u [*vt* tsukawanai; tsukatta] 使う *use* ❸Kono denwa o tsukatte mo íi desu ka? この電話を使ってもいいですか。*May I use this telephone?*

tsuké 付け *charge account; credit; bill of sale* ❸Kyṓ no kaimono wa tsuké ni shite óite kudasái. 今日の買い物は付けにしておいて下さい。*Charge these things to my account.*

tsukemono 漬物 *pickles; vegetables pickled in salt, vinegar, or sake lees (J)*

tsuké·ru [*vt* tsukénai; tsúketa] 点ける *light (a stove); turn on (a light)* ❸Rájio o tsúkete kudasái. ラジオを点けて下さい。*Turn on the radio, please.*

tsuké·ru [*vt* tsukénai; tsúketa] 付ける *affix; attach; add; charge (put on one's bill)* ❸nikki o tsukéru 日記を付ける *keep a diary* ❸Jiténsha ni kagí o tsukemáshita. 自転車に鍵を付けました。*I put a lock on my bicycle.* ❸Mochimóno ni wa namae o tsúkete kudasái. 持ち物には名前を付けて下さい。*Attach your name to your personal effects.* ❸Shiharai wa shújin ni tsúkete oite kudasái. 支払いは主人に付けておいて下さい。*Charge it to my husband.*

tsukí 月 *moon* ❸o-tsuki-sáma お月さま *the moon* ❸tsuki ákari 月明り *moonlight* ❸tsukíyo 月夜 *a moonlit night*

tsukí 月 *month* ❸tsukí ni ichido 月に一度 *once a month*

-tsuki ～付き *including; with* ❸daidokoro-tsuki wan-rūmu mánshon 台所付きワンルームマンション *one-room apartment including kitchen* ❸furoku-tsuki zásshi 付録付き雑誌 *a magazine with supplement* ❸omake-tsuki kyárameru おまけ付きキャラメル *caramel candy with included gift*

tsukiai 付き合い *companion; keeping company (with)* ❸tsukiai no íi hito 付き合いのいい人 *a person who is easy to get along with* ❸Tanaka-san wa tsukiai ga hirói. 田中さんは付き合いが広い。*Mr. Tanaka has a wide circle of friends.*

tsukiatár·u [*vi* tsukiataránai; tsukiatátta] 突き当たる *run into; bump into; crash into* ❸Kono michi wa chūshajō ni tsukiatarimásu. この道は駐車場に突き当たります。*This street dead ends into a parking lot.* ❸Sono kuruma wa gādoréru ni tsukiatátta. その車はガードレールに突き当たった。*The car crashed into a guardrail.*

tsukiá·u [*vi* tsukiawánai; tsukiátta] 付き合う *accompany; keep company with; mix with* ❸Tómoko wa Yūsuke to tsukiátte iru. 友子は雄介と付き合っている。*Tomoko is keeping company with Yusuke.* ❸Kaimono ni tsukiátte kurenai? 買い物に付き合ってくれない？*Would you like to go shopping with me?* <fem>

tsūkin 通勤 *commuting to work; going to work* ❸tsūkin téiki 通勤定期

commuter pass ❸tsūkin dénsha 通勤電車 *commuter train* ❸tsūkínsha 通勤者 *commuter*

tsukisás·u [*vt* tsukisasánai; tsukisáshita] 突き刺す *pierce; penetrate; stab* ❸Otōtó wa nikú ni náifu o tsukisáshite tabéru. 弟は肉にナイフを突き刺して食べる。 *My (little) brother eats his meat by spearing it with his knife.*

tsukisoi 付き添い *attendant; private (practical) nurse* ❸Sono byōin ní wa tsukisoi no kangófu-san mo imáshita. その病院には付き添いの看護婦さんもいました。 *That hospital also has private nurses.*

tsukisó·u [*vi* tsukisowánai; tsukisótta] 付き添う *attend; accompany; wait upon* ❸Háha wa byōki no kodomo ni tsukisótte imasu. 母は病気の子供に付き添っています。 *My mother is attending a sick child.*

tsukitôr·u [*vi* tsukitōránai; tsukitótta] 突き通る *penetrate; pierce* ❸Urakágari no hári ga fuku no omoté made tsukitótte shimatta. 裏かがりの針が服の表まで突き通ってしまった。 *The stitches in the lining came through to the face of the garment.*

tsukkír·u [*vt* tsukkiránai; tsukkítta] 突っ切る *cross; run across; run through; cut across* ❸akashíngō o tsukkítte hashiru 赤信号を突っ切って走る *run a red light* ❸Guraundo o tsukkítte iku to chikámichi desu. グラウンドを突っ切って行くと近道です。 *You can take a shortcut by cutting across the playground.*

tsūkō 通行 *traffic* ❸tsūkōdomé 通行止め *a street closed to traffic; no entry* ❸tsūkōnin 通行人 *pedestrian; passerby* ❸ippō tsūkō 一方通行 *one-way traffic*

tsuk·u [*vi* tsukánai; tsúita] 点く *go on; come on; light; ignite* ❸Tonari no uchí ni akari ga tsukimáshita. 隣の家に明りが点きました。 *A light went on in the house next door.*   **tsúk·u** [*vi* tsukánai; tsúita] 付く *stick to; adhere; be connected with* ❸Waishatsu ni shimi ga tsúite imasu. ワイシャツに染みが付いています。 *There's a stain on my shirt.* ❸Sono tansu ní wa hikidashi ga itsútsu tsúite imasu. その箪笥には引き出しが5つ付いています。 *The dresser has five drawers.*

tsúk·u [*vi* tsukánai; tsúita] 着く *arrive; reach* ❸Sawano-san wa késa Tōkyó-eki ni tsukimáshita. 沢野さんは今朝東京駅に着きました。 *Ms. Sawano arrived this morning at Tokyo Station.*

tsukue 机 *desk*

tsukuró·u [*vt* tsukurowánai; tsukurótta] 繕う *repair; mend; patch; darn* ❸Háha wa kutsúshita no aná o tsukurótte kuremásu. 母は靴下の穴を繕ってくれます。 *Mother darns my socks.*

tsukúr·u [*vt* tsukuránai; tsukútta] 作る *make* ❸góhan o tsukúru ご飯を作る *fix a meal; cook dinner* ❸Bíru wa múgi kara tsukurimásu. ビールは麦から作ります。 *Beer is made from barley.*

tsukúr·u [*vt* tsukuránai; tsukútta] 造る *create* ❸mú kara tsukuru 無から造る *create from nothing*

tsukúzuku つくづく *seriously; carefully* ❖tsukúzuku kanjiru つくづく感じる *feel keenly*

tsúma 妻 *(one's own) wife*

tsumam·u [*vt* tsumamanai; tsumanda] 摘む *pick (with fingers); pinch* ❖Hidói niói ni hana o tsumamimáshita. ひどい臭いに鼻を摘みました。 *I had to hold my nose, it smelled so bad!* ❖Edamame wa tsumande tabéru hō ga umái. 枝豆は摘んで食べる方が旨い。 *Edamame taste better when you eat them with your fingers. <masc>*

tsumarána·i [*adj* tsumaránaku nái; tsumaránakatta] つまらない *(be) uninteresting; dull; boring; trivial* ❖tsumaránai koto つまらないこと *a trivial matter.* ❖Kono hón wa mattaku tsumaránai. この本は全くつまらない。 *This book is really boring.*

tsúmari つまり *that is (to say); after all; to put it simply; briefly* ❖Tsúmari, kimi wa shitsuren-shita waké da ne! つまり、君は失恋した訳だね。 *In other words, you got dumped, right? <masc>*

tsumár·u [*vi* tsumaránai; tsumátta] 詰まる *clog; stop up; become jammed; choke* ❖Gesui ga tsumátte iru. 下水が詰まっている。 *The drain's stopped up.* ❖Kaban ní wa o-miyage ga takusan tsumátte imasu. 鞄にはお土産が沢山詰まっています。 *My bag is packed with gifts.*

tsumazuk·u [*vi* tsumazukanai; tsumazuita] 躓く *stumble; trip up; fail* ❖Watashi wa tsumazuite ashikúbi o nenza-shita. 私は躓いて足首を捻座した。 *I tripped and sprained my ankle.* ❖Jígyō ni tsumazuite shimatta. 事業につまずいてしまった。 *I failed on the project.*

tsúmbo 聾 *deaf person (offensive; preferred:* mimi no kikoenai hito*)*

tsume 爪 *nail; claw* ❖tsumekíri 爪切り *nail clipper* ❖tsumeyásuri 爪やすり *nail file*

tsumekom·u [*vt* tsumekomanai; tsumekonda] 詰め込む *cram (into)* ❖Kaban no náka ni náni mo ká mo tsumekonda. 鞄の中に何もかも詰め込んだ。 *I crammed everything into my suitcase.*

tsumeta·i [*adj* tsumetaku nái; tsumétakatta] 冷たい *cold (to the touch); chilly* ❖Sóto wa tsumetai kaze ga fúite iru. 外は冷たい風が吹いている。 *Outside, there's a cold wind blowing.* ❖Tsumetai nomimóno ga hoshíi. 冷たい飲み物がほしい。 *I want a cold drink.* ❖Sáchiko-san wa saikin watashi ni tsumetaku nátta wa. 幸子さんは最近私に冷たくなったわ。 *Sachiko has been cool toward me lately. <fem>*

tsúmi 罪 *sin; crime; guilt; a wrong* ❖tsúmi to bátsu 罪と罰 *crime and punishment* ❖tsumibitó 罪人 *sinner* ❖Hito o damásu no wa tsúmi desu. 人を騙すのは罪です。 *It's wrong to cheat others.*

tsumikasanar·u [*vi* tsumikasanaranai; tsumikasanatta] 積み重なる *pile up; be stacked* ❖Gūzen ga tsumikasanatta. 偶然が積み重なった。 *Coincidence piled on coincidence. (or There was a series of coincidences.)* ❖Yogoremono ga kago no náka ni tsumikasanatte iru.

汚れ物が篭の中に積み重なっている。 *Dirty clothes are piled up in the basket.*

tsumini 積み荷 *load; freight; cargo*

tsumitate 積立て *savings; reserve* §tsumitatekin 積立金 *reserve fund*

tsumori つもり *intention; plan* §Ashitá wa górufu ni ikú tsumori désu. 明日はゴルフに行くつもりです。 *I plan to go golfing tomorrow.*

tsumór·u [*vi* tsumóranai; tsumótta] 積もる *accumulate; be piled up* §yukí ga tsumóru 雪が積もる *snow piles up* §hokori ga tsumóru 埃が積もる *dust accumulates*

tsum·u [*vt* tsumanai; tsunda] 積む *load; put on* §torákku ni komé o tsumu トラックに米を積む *load rice onto a truck* §Kodomo wa mokuhen o tsunde asonde iru. 子供は木片を積んで遊んでいる。 *The children are playing with blocks, piling one on top of the other.*

tsumugigúruma 紡ぎ車 *spinning wheel*

tsuná 綱 *cord; line; rope; hawser* §tsunáhiki 綱引き *tug-of-war*

tsunagar·u [*vi* tsunagaranai; tsunagatta] 繋がる *be bound; be tied; be joined* §Igirisu to Furansu ga kaitei tónneru de tsunagarimáshita. イギリスとフランスが海底トンネルで繋がりました。 *England and France were joined by a tunnel under the sea.*

tsunag·u [*vt* tsunaganai; tsunaida] 繋ぐ *tie; fasten; connect* §Níhon no rópu o tsunaide kudasái. 二本のロープを繋いで下さい。 *Tie the two ropes together, please.* §Minna té o tsunaide arukimashô. みんな手を繋いで歩きましょう。 *Let's all walk hand-in-hand.*

tsunami 津波 *tidal wave*

tsúne no 常の *constant; ordinary* ——**tsune ni** 常に *constantly; always* §Sófu wa tsúne ni génki desu. 祖父は常に元気です。 *My grandfather is always in good health.* §Chichí wa ása no sampo o tsúne to shite iru. 父は朝の散歩を常としている。 *Dad always takes a walk in the morning.*

tsunér·u [*vt* tsunéranai; tsunétta] つねる *pinch* §Yumé de wa nái ka to jibun no hóho o tsunétte mimáshita. 夢ではないかと自分の頬をつねってみました。 *I pinched myself (lit., my cheek) to make sure it wasn't a dream.*

tsunó 角 *horn; antler*

tsuppariai 突っ張り合い *thrusting attack (sumo)*

tsuppár·u [*vi / vt* tsupparánai; tsuppátta] 突っ張る *strain; stretch* §Kínniku ga tsuppátte iru. 筋肉が突っ張っている。 *The muscle is strained.*

tsura·i [*adj* tsuraku nái; tsurákatta] 辛い *(be) painful; hard; trying* §Hayáoki wa tsurai. 早起きは辛い。 *Getting up early is hard.* §Tsurai mé ni bákari áu. 辛い目にばかり合う。 *I get nothing but hard knocks.*

tsuranúk·u [*vt* tsuranukánai; tsuranúita] 貫く *run (pass) through;*

penetrate   §Yá wa mato o tsuranúita. 矢は的を貫いた。 *The arrow penetrated the target.*   §Kono kawá wa machí o tsuranúite úmi ni sosoide imasu. この川は町を貫いて海に注いでいます。 *This river runs through the town to the ocean.*

tsurara 氷柱 *icicle*

tsure 連れ *companion*   §Tabisaki de tsure o mitsukemáshita. 旅先で連れを見つけました。 *I made some friends while I was traveling.*

tsure·ru [*vt* tsurenai; tsureta] 連れる *travel with as (one's) companion*   §tsurete iku 連れて行く *take (a person) along*

[ni] tsurete 〜に連れて *as; with; in consequence of; in proportion to*   §Toshí ga tátsu ni tsuret e háha no shí no kanashimi ga usuráide kita. 年が経つに連れて母の死の悲しみが薄らいできた。 *As the years passed, my sorrow over my mother's death diminished.*

tsuri 釣り *fishing; angling*   §tsuribari 釣り針 *fishhook*   §tsuribori 釣り堀 *fish pond*   tsurizao 釣り竿 *fishing pole; fishing rod*

[o-]tsuri お釣 *change (after payment is tendered)*   §O-tsuri ga tarinai. お釣りが足りない。 *This isn't the right change. (or There isn't enough change.)*

tsuriai 釣り合い *balance; equilibrium*

tsúro 通路 *passageway; aisle; corridor*

tsúru 鶴 *crane (bird)*

tsurú 蔓 *vine*

tsurúhashi 鶴嘴 *a pick; pickaxe*

tsurushiagé·ru [*vt* tsurushiagénai; tsurushiágeta] 吊し上げる *subject to a kangaroo court; impeach; hang up*   §Minná ga yotté takatte hitóri no otokó o tsurushiágeta. みんなが寄って集って一人の男を吊し上げた。 *Everyone ganged up on the man and subjected him to a kangaroo court.*

tsúrutsuru つるつる *slippery; smooth; greasy*   §tsurutsuru no atamá つるつるの頭 *bald-headed*   §tsúrutsuru subéru つるつる滑る *slip; ski; skate* ——**tsúrutsuru-suru** つるつるする *be slippery; be smooth; be greasy*

tsūshin 通信 *(written) correspondence; communication; news*   §tsūshin éisei 通信衛星 *communications satellite*   §tsūshin hámbai 通信販売 *mail-order business*   §tsūshin kyóiku 通信教育 *correspondence school*   §tsūshínsha 通信社 *news agency*

tsutá 蔦 *ivy*

tsutae·ru [*vt* tsutaenai; tsutaeta] 伝える *pass on (information); communicate; convey*   §Sono shirase o minná ni tsutaemashita その知らせをみんなに伝えました。 *I passed the information on to everyone.*   §Dő wa denki o tsutaeru. 銅は電気を伝える。 *Copper conducts electricity.*

tsutaná·i [*adj* tsutanáku nái; tsutanákatta] 拙い *(be) poor; clumsy;*

awkward   ❈tsutanái é 拙い絵 *a poor painting*

tsutawar·u [*vi* tsutawaranai; tsutawatta] 伝わる *be handed down; be transmitted; spread; be introduced (to)*   ❈Sono uwasa wa machi-jū ni tsutawarimáshita. その噂は町中に伝わりました。 *The rumor spread through the town.*   ❈Netsú wa dōsen o tsutawarimásu. 熱は銅線を伝わります。 *Heat is conducted through copper wire.*

tsutomé 勤め；務め *work; activity; duty*   ❈tsutomenin 勤め人 *business person; worker; employee*   ❈tsutomesaki 勤め先 *(one's) place of work*   ❈tsutomé o hatásu 務めを果たす *fulfill one's duty*

tsutomé·ru [*vi / vt* tsutoménai; tsutómeta] 勤める *be employed; work*   ❈Miyázaki-san wa depáto ni tsutómete imasu. 宮崎さんはデパートに勤めています。 *Ms. Miyazaki works in a department store.*

tsutomé·ru [*vi* tsutoménai; tsutómeta] 務める *serve (in a role / in a post)*   ❈Sóbo wa daigíshi no hísho o tsutómete imashita. 祖母は代議士の秘書を務めていました。 *My grandmother served as secretary for a Diet member.*

tsutomé·ru [*vi* tsutoménai; tsutómeta] 努める *do (one's) best; try hard*   ❈Máinichi, dáietto-suru yǒ ni tsutómete imasu. 毎日、ダイエットするように努めています。 *I'm trying hard to diet every day.*

tsutsúji つつじ *azalea; rhododendron*

tsutsúm·u [*vt* tsutsúmánai; tsutsúnda] 包む *wrap; pack; bundle (up)*   ❈Kore o tsutsúnde kudasái. これを包んで下さい。 *Wrap it (up), please.*

tsutsushím·u [*vt* tsutsushímánai; tsutsushínda] 慎む *be careful about; be prudent about; refrain from; abstain from*   ❈kotobá o tsutsushímu 言葉を慎む *be careful about (one's) words*   ❈tabako o tsutsushímu 煙草を慎む *refrain from smoking*

tsuya 艶 *polish; shine; luster*   ❈migaite tsuya o dásu 磨いて艶を出す *bring out the shine by polishing*   ❈Sono kóe ni tsuya ga áru. その声に艶がある。 *There's polish (or refinement) to that voice.*

[o-]tsúya （お）通夜 *a wake; vigil*

tsǔyaku 通訳 *interpreter; oral interpretation*   ❈dōji tsǔyaku 同時通訳 *simultaneous interpretation* ——**tsǔyaku-suru** [*vt*] 通訳する *interpret (orally)*

tsuyó·i [*adj* tsúyoku nái; tsúyokatta] 強い *(be) strong; powerful; hard*   ❈Tsuyói áme ga fútte iru. 強い雨が降っている。 *It's raining hard.*   ❈Dóa o tsúyoku hīite kudasái. ドアを強く引いて下さい。 *Pull hard on the door (to open it).*   ❈Musuko wa kenka ga tsuyói. 息子は喧嘩が強い。 *My son is strong in a fight.*   ❈Sóbo wa rekishi ni tsuyói. 祖母は歴史に強い。 *Grandmother is very good in history.*

tsuyomár·u [*vi* tsuyomaránai; tsuyomátta] 強まる *grow strong*   ❈Taifū ga chikazuki, amaashi ga tsuyomátte kita. 台風が近づき、雨脚が強まってきた。 *The rainfall has increased in intensity with the approach of* *the typhoon.*

tsuyomé·ru [*vt* tsuyoménai; tsuyómeta] 強める *strengthen; intensify; emphasize* ▪Yamada wa góki o tsuyómete iyótte kita. 山田は語気を強めて言い寄ってきた。 *Yamada came at me, raising his voice.*

tsúyu 露 *dew*

tsuyu 梅雨 *rainy season*

[o-]tsúyu （お）汁 *soup; broth*

tsūzoku gógen 通俗語源 *folk etymology*

tsuzuke·ru [*vt* tsuzukenai; tsuzuketa] 続ける *continue; go on (with); carry on* ▪Áki ni nihongo no réssun o tsuzukemásu ka? 秋に日本語のレッスンを続けますか？ *Are you going to continue Japanese lessons in the fall?*

ni] tsuzuite 〜に続いて *in the wake of; following on; following after* ▪Kōchō-senséi no hanashí ni tsuzuite PTA káichō no hanashi ga hajimarimáshita. 校長先生の話に続いて、PTA 会長の話が始まりました。 *After the principal spoke, the PTA chairperson began her speech.*

-tsuzúke·ru 〜続ける *keep on (doing)...* ▪Sákki kara térebi o mitsuzúkete iru. さっきからテレビを見続けている。 *I've been watching television continuously for some time.*

tsuzuki 続き *continuation*

tsuzuk·u [*vi* tsuzukanai; tsuzuita] 続く *continue* ▪Áme ga isshúkan mo tsuzuite iru. 雨が一週間も続いている。 *It's been raining a week.* ▪Kono michi wa mukō made tsuzuite iru. この道は向こうまで続いている。 *This road continues on (beyond).*

tsuzura 葛籠 *woven bamboo trunk*

tsuzurí 綴り *spelling*

tsuzur·u [*vt* tsuzuranai; tsuzutta] 綴る *spell* ▪Mishishíppī tte dó tsuzurimásu ka? ミシシッピーってどう綴りますか？ *How do you spell Mississippi?*

U

ú 鵜 *cormorant* ▪ukai 鵜飼 *cormorant fishing*

úba 乳母 *wet nurse; nurse; nanny*

ubagúruma 乳母車 *baby carriage*

ubá·u [*vt* ubawánai; ubátta] 奪う *rob; deprive of; take* ▪ínochi o ubáu 命を奪う *take a life; kill* ▪jiyú o ubáu 自由を奪う *usurp (one's) freedom* ▪Tōríma wa watashi no handobággu o ubátte nigemáshita. 通り魔は私のハンドバッグを奪って逃げました。 *A purse-snatcher grabbed my handbag and ran.*

uchi うち；内 *inside; within* ▪kokoro no uchi 心のうち *inside the* *heart*   8 Yashiki no uchi ní wa katte ni háitte wa ikemasén. 屋敷のうちには勝手に入ってはいけません。 *You must not enter this estate without permission.*

uchi 家 *house; home*

uchiage·ru [*vt* uchiagenai; uchiageta] 打ち上げる *launch; set off*   8 rokétto o uchiageru ロケットを打ち上げる *launch a rocket*   8 Gaiya ni furai o uchiageta. 外野にフライを打ち上げた。 *I hit a fly to the outfield.*

uchiake·ru [*vt* uchiakenai; uchiaketa] 打ち明ける *confess; open up; confide (in someone)*   8 Tanókura wa watashi ni káre no minoue-bánashi o sukkári uchiaketa. 田野倉は私に彼の身の上話をすっかり打ち明けた。 *Tanokura opened up to me completely about his personal problems.*

uchiawase 打ち合わせ *arrangement; consultation*   8 Kyó wa gógo kara uchiawase ga áru. 今日は午後から打ち合わせがある。 *I have a consultation this afternoon.*

uchiawase·ru [*vt* uchiawasenai; uchiawaseta] 打ち合わせる *make arrangements; talk over; strike against*   8 Watashi to Ueda-san wa ashita no káigi ni tsuite uchiawaseta. 私と上田さんは明日の会議について打ち合わせた。 *Ueda and I talked over tomorrow's meeting.*   8 Tetsu to ishí o uchiawasete hí o okóshita. 鉄と石を打ち合わせて火を起こした。 *I struck metal against a stone and started a fire.*

uchigawa 内側 *the inside; the inner part*

uchikats·u [*vi* uchikatanai; uchikatta] 打ち勝つ *overcome; conquer*   8 kurushimi ni uchikatsu 苦しみに打ち勝つ *overcome suffering*

uchikeshi 打ち消し *denial; negation; negative (Gram)*

uchikes·u [*vt* uchikesanai; uchikeshita] 打ち消す *deny; retract; negate*   8 Sono déma o uchikesanai to taihen na kotó ni náru yo. そのデマを打ち消さないと大変な事になるよ。 *If we don't deny that false rumor there'll be terrible consequences.*

uchiki [na] 内気（な）*shy; bashful; timid; introverted*   8 Tsúma wa uchiki de hitomae ni déru no o iyagátte iru. 妻は内気で人前に出るのを嫌がっている。 *My wife is shy; she doesn't like to appear in front of people.*

uchikir·u [*vt* uchikiranai; uchikitta] 打ち切る *bring to a close; discontinue*   8 Sono bangumi wa uchikirareru kotó ni nátta. その番組は打ち切られることになった。 *That program is to be discontinued.*

uchimata 内股 *inner thigh*   8 uchimata [no] 内股（の）*pigeon-toed*   8 uchimata gōyaku 内股膏薬 *opportunistic; an opportunist*

-uchi ni ～うちに *while*   8 Áme ga furánai uchi ni kaerimashó. 雨が降らないうちに帰りましょう。 *Let's go home while it's still not raining.*

uchi no 家の *mine; ours*   8 uchi no kaisha うちの会社 *my company*   8 Uchi no monó o sōdan-shité kara kimemásu. 家の者と相談してから

決めます。*I'll talk it over at home and then decide.*

uchinuk·u [*vt* uchinukanai; uchinuita] 打ち抜く *pierce; penetrate* §Kugi ga kabe o uchinuite-shimatta. 釘が壁を打ち抜いてしまった。*The nail went right through the wall.*

uchitoke·ru [*vi* uchitokenai; uchitoketa] 打ち解ける *be at home with; get along with; be frank with; open up to* ——**uchitokenai** 打ち解けない *be reserved; be standoffish* §Tsúma no tsureko wa nakanaka watashi ni uchitokenai. 妻の連れ子はなかなか私に打ち解けない。*My wife's child (by another husband) is very standoffish with me.*

uchíwa 団扇 *(round, flat) fan*

uchiwa 内輪 *within the family* §uchiwa-bánashi 内輪話 *domestic talk* §uchiwa no mondai 内輪の問題 *a family matter*

uchiwake 内訳 *details; items* §Kono ryōshūsho no uchiwake o oshiete kudasái. この領収書の内訳を教えて下さい。*Please itemize this bill.*

uchiyabúr·u [*vt* uchiyaburánai; uchiyabútta] 打ち破る *break down; defeat; smash* §furúi shūkan o uchiyabúru 古い習慣を打ち破る *break with old customs*

úchū 宇宙 *universe; outer space* §uchū́jin 宇宙人 *an alien* §uchūsen 宇宙船 *spaceship* §uchū hikṓshi 宇宙飛行士 *astronaut*

udé 腕 *arm; ability* §Udé o ótchatta. 腕を折っちゃった。*I broke my arm.* §ude-dókei 腕時計 *wristwatch* §udé o ageru 腕を上げる *perfect (one's) skill*

udemae 腕前 *skill* §Kimi no udemae o mísete moraṓ. 君の腕前を見せてもらおう。*Show me what you can do.*

udewa 腕輪 *bracelet*

údo 独活 udo *(plant); (Tech) Aralia cordata* §údo no taiboku 独活の大木 *a big lummox; a clumsy person <set phrase>*

udon うどん *noodles* §udon'ya うどん屋 *noodle shop*

ue 上 *above; on; up* §ue no kodomo 上の子供 *the older child* §Ue ni agarimásu. 上に上がります。*Going up!* §Néko wa tsukue no ue ni imásu yo. 猫は机の上にいますよ。*The cat's on top of the table!*

uejini 飢死 *death from starvation* ——**uejini-suru** [*vi*] 飢死する *starve to death*

ueki 植木 *potted plant* §uekíbachi 植木鉢 *flowerpot* §uekiya[-san] 植木屋（さん） *gardener*

ue·ru [*vt* uenai; ueta] 植える *plant* §Niwa ni kusábana o ueta. 庭に草花を植えた。*I planted flowers in the garden.*

ué·ru [*vi* uénai; úeta] 飢える *starve; go hungry* §chíshiki ni uéru 知識に飢える *be starved for knowledge*

ugai-suru [*vi*] うがいする *gargle; rinse (one's) mouth* §shiómizu de ugai-suru 塩水でうがいする *gargle with salt water*

ugokás·u [*vt* ugokasánai; ugokáshita] 動かす *move; transport; haul*

ugokí 動き *movement; motion; change* ❽shákai no ugokí 社会の動き *social change*

ugók·u [*vi* ugokánai; ugóita] 動く *move; change* ❽Kuruma ga hitoride ni ugóite shimatta. 車がひとりでに動いてしまった。*The car moved by itself.* ❽Yonónaka ga hagéshiku ugóite iru. 世の中が激しく動いている。*The world is changing fast.*

ugúisu 鶯 *Japanese bush warbler*

uji 蛆 *maggot*

új·i 氏 *clan* ❽ujigami 氏神 *tutelary deity; local god (Shintō)* ❽ujiko 氏子 *people under protection of a local god (Shintō)* ❽Új i yori sodachi 氏より育ち *Upbringing is more important than family (or blood). <set phrase>*

ukabe·ru [*vt* ukabenai; ukabeta] 浮かべる *float; sail* ❽mé ni námida o ukabenágara 目に涙を浮かべながら *with tears in one's eyes* ❽Mokei no fúne o púru ni ukabeta. 模型の船をプールに浮かべた。 *They floated their model ships in the pool.*

ukab·u [*vi* ukabanai; ukanda] 浮かぶ *float; come to the surface; occur to (one)* ❽Hikōsen ga sóra ni ukande iru. 飛行船が空に浮かんでいる。 *A blimp is floating in the sky.* ❽Meian ga ukanda. 名案が浮かんだ。 *A brilliant idea occurred to me.*

ukaga·u [*vt* ukagawanai; ukagatta] 伺う *inquire; call at; visit* ❽Chótto ukagaimásu ga... ちょっと伺いますが... *May I ask...? <formal>* ❽O-taku ni ukagatté mo yoroshíi deshō ka? お宅に伺ってもよろしいでしょうか。 *May I call on you at your home? <formal>*

ukai 迂回 *detour; roundabout way* ❽ukáiro 迂回路 *a detour*

ukár·u [*vi* ukaránai; ukátta] 受かる *pass; succeed in* ❽shiken ni ukáru 試験に受かる *pass an examination*

ukea·u [*vt* ukeawanai; ukeatta] 請け合う *assure; guarantee*

ukeire·ru [*vt* ukeirenai; ukeireta] 受け入れる *accept; receive; agree to* ❽Nammin o ukeireru júmbi ga okurete iru. 難民を受け入れる準備が遅れている。 *Preparations to receive refugees are behind schedule.* ❽Rōdṓsha no yōkyū wa ukeireráreta. 労働者の要求は受け入れられた。 *The demands of the laborers were met.*

ukemí [no] 受け身（の）*passive; passive voice (Gram)* ❽Anáta no táido wa ítsumo ukemí da wa. あなたの態度はいつも受け身だわ。 *Your attitude is always passive. <fem>*

ukemochi 受け持ち *charge; responsibility* ❽Záimu ni tsúite wa watashi no ukemochi désu. 財務については私の受け持ちです。 *Finances are my responsibility.*

ukemots·u [*vt* ukemotanai; ukemotta] 受け持つ *take charge of; be in charge of* ❽Watashi wa shōgaku rokunénsei o ukemotte iru. 私は小学六年生を受け持っている。 *I'm in charge of the sixth grade.*

uké·ru [*vt* ukénai; úketa] 受ける *receive; accept; catch* ❽kói o ukéru

好意を受ける *accept a favor* §tegami o ukéru 手紙を受ける *receive a letter* §bōru o gurốbu de ukéru ボールをグローブで受ける *catch a ball with a glove*

uketamawár·u [*vt* uketamawaránai; uketamawátta] 承る *hear; be told; know; understand* §Go-íken o uketamawaritáku zonjimásu. ご意見を承りたく存じます。 *I'd like to hear your opinion.* <*formal*> §Go-yōmei o uketamawarimásu. ご用命を承ります。 *We are at your service.* <*formal*>

uketori 受取 *a receipt* §Uketori o itadakemásu ka? 受取を頂けますか。 *May I have a receipt?*

uketorinin 受取人 *addressee*

uketor·u [*vt* uketoranai; uketotta] 受け取る *receive; get; accept* §dáikin o uketoru 代金を受け取る *receive payment* §Kánojo kara no tegami o uketotta. 彼女からの手紙を受け取った。 *I got a letter from her.*

uketsug·u [*vt* uketsuganai; uketsuida] 受け継ぐ *succeed to; inherit; take over* §Chíchi no shigoto o uketsugu kotó ni shita. 父の仕事を受け継ぐことにした。 *I decided to take over my father's business.*

uketsuke 受付 *information desk; reception room; receptionist*

uketsuke·ru [*vt* uketsukenai; uketsuketa] 受け付ける *receive; accept* §Nyūgaku gánsho no mōshikomi wa asú made uketsukemásu. 入学願書の申込は明日まで受け付けます。 *We will accept applications for enrollment until tomorrow.* §Watashi wa kōsei bússhitsu o uketsukenai. 私は抗生物質を受け付けない。 *I can't take antibiotics.*

ukézara 受け皿 *saucer; receptacle* §chawan to ukézara 茶碗と受け皿 *cups and saucers*

úki 雨期；雨季 *wet season; rainy season*

uki 浮き *a float; cork* §ukibúkuro 浮き袋 *an air float (for swimming)*

ukihashi 浮き橋 *floating bridge*

úkiuki [to] 浮き浮き（と）*buoyantly; with a light heart* ——**úkiuki-suru** [*vi*] 浮き浮きする *float on air* §Káre kara puropốzu-sarete Chíeko wa úkiuki-shite iru. 彼からプロポーズされて智恵子は浮き浮きしている。 *Since he proposed to her Chieko has been on a cloud.*

ukíyo 浮世 *the transitory world (lit: floating world)* §ukiyóe 浮世絵 *Edo-period woodblock prints* §ukiyo no wazurawashisa 浮世のわずらわしさ *worldly cares*

ukkári うっかり *carelessly; inadvertently* ——**ukkári-suru** [*vi*] うっかりする *be careless; be forgetful; be absent-minded* §Ukkári-shite watashi wa dénsha o norikóshite shimatta. うっかりして私は電車を乗り越してしまった。 *I was absent-minded and rode the train beyond my stop.*

uk·u [*vi* ukanai; uita] 浮く *float* §Shitai ga kawá ni uite ita. 死体が川に浮いていた。 *A body was floating in the river.*

umá 馬 *horse* §umagoya 馬小屋 *stable*

umá·i [adj úmaku nái; úmakatta] 旨い (be) sweet; delicious; skillful; good <masc> ❅Kono ryōri wa totemo umái. この料理はとても旨い。 This food is really good. ❅Umái kangáe ga ukanda. うまい考えが浮かんだ。 I had a good idea. ❅Kimi wa utá ga umái. 君は歌がうまい。 You sing well! <masc>

umamí 旨み (good) taste; flavor ❅Kōmúin nante umamí no nái shigoto da. 公務員なんて旨みのない仕事だ。 A civil servant's job is drab. <masc>

umare 生まれ birth; origin; descent; lineage ❅Watashi wa Gogatsu úmare desu. 私は五月生まれです。 I was born in May. ❅Yosíkawa wa umare ga yóku nái. 吉川は生まれがよくない。 Yoshikawa doesn't come from a good family.

umarekawár·u [vi umarekawaránai; umarekawátta] 生まれ変わる start (life) over again; be reborn ❅Tsugí ni umarekawáru tóki ni wa onná ga íi na. 次に生まれ変わる時には女がいいな。 When I'm reborn it would be nice to be a woman. <masc>

umare·ru [vi umarenai; umareta] 生まれる；産まれる be born

umaretsuki 生まれつき by nature; naturally; from birth ❅Káre wa umaretsuki karada ga yowái. 彼は生まれつき体が弱い。 He's been sickly all his life.

umar·u [vi umaranai; umatta] 埋る be buried; be filled (in) ❅Ketsuin ga umatta. 欠員が埋った。 All personnel openings are filled.

ume 梅 Japanese apricot; plum ❅umeboshi 梅干し pickled Japanese apricot ❅umeshu 梅酒 a liqueur of alcohol, Japanese apricots, and sugar

ume·ru [vt umenai; umeta] 埋める bury; fill in ❅aná o umeru 穴を埋める fill in a hole ❅Akaji o umerú no wa taihen da. 赤字を埋めるのは大変だ。 It's hard to make up a deficit.

umetaté-chi 埋立地 land-fill; reclaimed land

umetaté·ru [vt umetaténai; umetáta] 埋め立てる reclaim a tract of land from the sea ❅Kono wán o umetátete kūkō o kensetsu-suru keikaku ga áru. この湾を埋め立てて空港を建設する計画がある。 There is a plan to fill in this bay and make an airport.

úmi 海 ocean ❅umibe 海辺 the beach; seashore

úmmei 運命 fate; destiny ❅umméi-ron 運命論 fatalism ❅ummei-rónsha 運命論者 a fatalist

um·u [vt umanai; unda] 生む；産む bear; give birth to ❅Tsúma wa futago o umimáshita. 妻は双子を産みました。 My wife gave birth to twins. ❅Watashitachi no dóryoku wa yói kekka o unda. 私たちの努力はよい結果を生んだ。 Our efforts produced good results.

úm·u [vi umánai; únda] 膿む fester; form pus ❅Kizuguchi ga únde itái. 傷口が膿んで痛い。 The wound has festered and hurts.

ún 運 luck; fate; destiny; chance ❅ún ga íi 運がいい be lucky ❅ún ga warúi 運が悪い be unlucky ❅Ún ga muite kíta. 運が向いてきた。

Fortune smiled on me.

ún. うん *yes; O.K.*

unagas·u [*vt* unagasanai; unagashita] 促す *urge; press; nudge* 🔹Senséi wa nándo mo séito ni chūi o unagashita. 先生は何度も生徒に注意を促した。 *The teacher cautioned the pupils over and over to be careful.*

unagi 鰻 *eel*

unarí 唸り *a groan; a roar* 🔹Mótā wa ōkina unarí o hasshite iru. モーターは大きな唸りを発している。 *The motor let out a big roar.*

unár·u [*vi* unaránai; unátta] 唸る *groan; growl; roar* 🔹Béddo de unátte irú no wa dáre ka na? ベッドで唸っているのは誰かな。 *Who is that groaning in bed? <masc>*

unasare·ru [*vi* unasarenai; unasareta] うなされる *have a nightmare* 🔹Kánai wa náni ka unasarete iru yō da. 家内は何かうなされているようだ。 *My wife seems to be having a nightmare.*

unazuk·u [*vi* unazukanai; unazuita] 頷く *nod; assent to* 🔹Watashi no hatsugen ni minná wa unazuita. 私の発言にみんなは頷いた。 *Everyone nodded in agreement with what I said.*

únchin 運賃 *freight expense; fare*

undō 運動 *movement; exercise; motion; campaign* 🔹undōkai 運動会 *athletic meet* 🔹undōjō 運動場 *athletic field* 🔹undō shínkei 運動神経 *motor nerve* 🔹senkyo úndō 選挙運動 *election campaign* 🔹shakai úndō 社会運動 *a social movement* ——**undō-suru** [*vi*] 運動する *start a movement; exercise* 🔹Nánika undō-shite imásu ka? 何か運動していますか。 *Are you doing some kind of exercise?*

undōgutsu 運動靴 *sneakers; sport shoes*

un'ei 運営 *management; operation* 🔹Kokkai ún'ei wa muzukáshiku nátte iru. 国会運営は難しくなっている。 *Management of the Diet has become difficult.* ——**un'ei-suru** [*vt*] 運営する *manage; operate* 🔹gakkō o un'ei-suru 学校を運営する *run a school*

únga 運河 *canal*

úni 雲丹 ; 海胆 *sea urchin*

unnun 云々 *and so forth; such-and-such* ——**unnun-suru** [*vt*] 云々する *go on and on*

unsō 運送 *transportation; transit* 🔹unsógyō 運送業 *transportation industry* 🔹unsōya 運送屋 *movers; moving company*

unten 運転 *driving; operation* 🔹unténshi 運転士 *(professional) driver* 🔹unténshu 運転手 *chauffeur; driver* 🔹unten shíkin 運転資金 *operating fund; a fund to cover operating expenses* ——**unten-suru** [*vt*] 運転する *drive; operate* 🔹kuruma o unten-suru 車を運転する *drive a car*

únto うんと *a great deal; a lot* 🔹Zṓ wa únto dekákatta yo! 象はうんとでかかったよ。 *The elephant was really big.*

unubore·ru [*vi* unuborenai; unuboreta] 自惚れる *be conceited; be vain; be* *stuck up* ❽Ishikawa-kun wa hánsamu de atamá ga íi to omótte unborete iru. 石川君はハンサムで頭がいいと思って自惚れている。 *Ishikawa's stuck up; he thinks he's so handsome and smart.*

ún'yu 運輸 *transportation* ❽Un'yúshō 運輸省 *Ministry of Transportation*

unzári [na] うんざり（な）*disgusting; boring* ——**unzári-suru** [vi] うんざりする *be disgusted; be fed up (with)* ❽Séito wa kōchō-sénsei no maido no nagái hanashí ni unzári-shite iru. 生徒は校長先生の毎度の長い話にうんざりしている。 *The students are fed up with the principal's frequent long-winded lectures.*

uo 魚 *fish* ❽uo íchiba 魚市場 *fish market*

uókka ウオッカ *vodka*

urá 裏 *the back; back yard; reverse side; wrong side* ❽urabyóshi 裏表紙 *back cover* ❽uramon 裏門 *back gate* ❽uraguchi 裏口 *back door* ❽uraniwa 裏庭 *back yard* ❽uradóri 裏通り *alley; back street*

urá; uraji 裏；裏地 *lining* ❽Uraji wa sáten ga íi. 裏地はサテンがいい。 *Satin would be good for the lining.*

uragáes·u [vt uragaesánai; uragáeshita] 裏返す *turn over; turn inside out* ❽Shátsu o uragáeshite hóshite kudasái. シャツを裏返して干して下さい。 *Turn the shirts inside out and then hang them out to dry.*

uragaki 裏書き *endorsement* ——**uragaki-suru** [vt] 裏書きする *endorse* ❽Kogítte ni uragaki-shite kudasái. 小切手に裏書きして下さい。 *Endorse the check, please.*

uragiri 裏切り *treachery; betrayal* ❽uragiri kói 裏切り行為 *an act of treachery* ❽uragirimono 裏切り者 *traitor*

uragír·u [vt uragiránai; uragítta] 裏切る *betray* ❽Tanaka-san wa watashi o uragítta. 田中さんは私を裏切った。 *Tanaka betrayed me.*

uragoe 裏声 *falsetto*

uragoshi 裏漉し *strainer*

urameshí·i [adj uraméshiku nái; uraméshikatta] 恨めしい *(be) resentful; hateful; reproachful; bitter* ❽Yome no tsumetai shiuchi ga urameshíi. 嫁の冷たい仕打ちが恨めしい。 *I resent my daughter-in-law's cool behavior.*

uramí 恨み *a grudge* ❽uramí o harásu 恨みを晴らす *avenge oneself; settle a score* ❽uramí o idáku 恨みを抱く *hold a grudge* ❽hito no uramí o kaú 人の恨みを買う *make an enemy* ——**urám·u** [vt uramánai; uránda] 恨む *resent; begrudge; bear a grudge; hate*

uranai 占い *fortune-telling; divination* ❽uranáishi 占い師 *fortune-teller* ❽hoshi uránai 星占い *astrology* ❽tesō uránai 手相占い *palmreading*

urayamashí·i [adj urayamáshiku nái; urayamáshikatta] 羨ましい *(be) envious; jealous of* ❽O-kane no áru hitó ga urayamashíi. お金のある

人が羨ましい。 *I envy a person who has money.*

urayám·u [*vt* urayamánai; urayánda] 羨む *envy* ❊Anó hito o urayánde mo shikata ga nái. あの人を羨んでも仕方がない。 *It will do no good to envy her.*

urazuke 裏付け *backing; support; proof; substantiation* ❊urazuke sósa 裏付け捜査 *investigation of proof*

urazuké·ru [*vt* urazukénai; urazúketa] 裏付ける *back up; support*

uréi 憂い *grief; distress; sorrow*

ure·ru [*vi* urenai; ureta] 売れる *sell; be sold* ❊Kono seihin wa yóku urete iru. この製品はよく売れている。 *This product is selling well.*

uré·ru [*vi* urénai; úreta] 熟れる *ripen* ❊Bánana ga yóku úrete iru. バナナがよく熟れている。 *The bananas are very ripe.*

ureshigár·u [*vi / vt* ureshigaránai; ureshigátta] 嬉しがる *be delighted; happy* [*not used with first person*]

ureshí·i [*adj* uréshiku nái; uréshikatta] 嬉しい *(be) glad; happy; delighted* ❊Buchō ni nárete ureshíi. 部長になれて嬉しい。 *I'm glad I got to be section chief.*

úri 瓜 *melon* ❊úri futatsú 瓜二つ *like two melons (or like two peas in a pod)* <set phrase>

uriage 売り上げ *proceeds* ❊uriagé-daka 売り上げ高 *proceeds* ❊Kyó no uriage wa dō datta? 今日の売り上げはどうだった？ *How much did we take in today?*

uriba 売り場 *sales counter; department; sales place* ❊kagu úriba 家具売り場 *furniture department* ❊keshōhin úriba 化粧品売り場 *cosmetics counter*

uridashi 売り出し *sale; bargain sale* ❊saimatsu ō-úridashi 歳末大売り出し *big year-end sale*

urikire 売り切れ *sold out* ❊Eiji shímbun wa urikire désu. 英字新聞は売り切れです。 *The English newspapers are sold out.*

urikiré·ru [*vi* urikirénai; urikíreta] 売り切れる *be sold out*

urimono 売り物 *item for sale*

uriya 売り家 *house for sale*

uroko 鱗 *(fish) scales* ❊uroko-gúmo 鱗雲 *cirrocumulus clouds* ❊Mé kara uroko ga óchita. 目から鱗が落ちた。 *The scales fell from my eyes. (or My eyes were opened.)* <set phrase>

urotsuk·u [*vi* urotsukanai; urotsuita] うろつく *loiter; wander about* ❊Sákki kara ayashii otokó ga kono átari o urotsuite iru. さっきから怪しい男がこの辺りをうろついている。 *A strange man has been loitering about this vicinity.*

úrouro-suru [*vi*] うろうろする *be idle; wander; be confused* ❊Obásan ga michi ni mayótte úrouro-shite iru. お婆さんが道に迷ってうろうろしている。 *An old lady lost her way and is wandering about confused.*

ur·u [*vt* uranai; utta] 売る *sell* ❊tochi o uru 土地を売る *sell land*

⠀⠀⠀8kenka o uru 喧嘩を売る　*start a fight*　8abura o uru 油を売る *waste time* *<set phrase>*

urúdoshi 閏年 *leap year*

urusá·i [*adj* urúsaku nái; urúsakatta] 煩い *(be) annoying; troublesome; bothersome; noisy*　8Kuruma no hashíru otó ga urusákute nemurenai. 車の走る音が煩くて眠れない。 *Cars going by are so noisy I can't sleep.*　8Uchi no oyaji wa urusái. うちの親父は煩い。 *My old man is strict.* *<masc>*

urushi 漆 *lacquer*

úryō 雨量 *rainfall*

usagi 兎 *rabbit*

usetsu 右折 *right-hand turn* ——**usetsu-suru** [*vi / vt*] 右折する *turn right*　8Tsugí no shingō o usetsu-shite kudasái. 次の信号を右折して下さい。 *Turn right at the next traffic light.*

ushi 牛 *cow; cattle*

ushiná·u [*vt* ushinawanai; ushinatta] 失う *lose*　8ki o ushinau 気を失う *faint; lose consciousness*　8o-kane o ushinau お金を失う *lose money*　8kikái o ushinau 機会を失う *miss (one's) chance*　8chíi mo meisei mo ushinau 地位も名声も失う *lose both (one's) position and reputation*

ushiro 後ろ *the back; rear; behind; in back of*　8ushiro kara 後ろから *from behind*　8Ushiro o muité wa ikemasén. 後ろを向いてはいけません。 *You must not look back.*

úso 嘘 *a lie; falsehood*　8usótsuki 嘘つき *a liar*　8úso o tsúku 嘘をつく *tell a lie*　8Usótsuki wa dorobō no hajimari. 嘘つきは泥棒の始まり。 *Telling lies is the start of a thief.* *<set phrase>*

usu- 薄～ *light...; faint...*　8usuchairo 薄茶色 *tan*　8usumurásaki 薄紫 *light purple*　8usubi 薄日 *thin sunlight*　8usugéshō 薄化粧 *light makeup*　8usugumori 薄曇り *slightly cloudy*　8usugurái 薄暗い *dim*

usu·i [*adj* usuku nái; usúkatta] 薄い *(be) thin; light; weak*　8Aji ga usui. 味が薄い。 *The flavor is weak.*　8Kánojo wa nínjō ga usui. 彼女は人情が薄い。 *She's cold-hearted.*　8Kono pan-kéki wa usu-sugíru このパンケーキは薄過ぎる。 *These pancakes are too thin.* ——**usuku** 薄く *thinly; lightly; faintly*

usuji no 薄地の *sheer (material)*

usume·ru [*vt* usumenai; usumeta] 薄める *dilute; water down; weaken*　8aji o usumeru 味を薄める *weaken the flavor*　8iró o usumeru 色を薄める *lighten the color*

usuppera [na] 薄っぺら（な）*flimsy; shallow; superficial*　8usuppera na hito 薄っぺらな人 *a shallow person*

utá·i 歌 *song*

utagai 疑い *a doubt; suspicion*　8utagai o harásu 疑いを晴らす *allay suspicion*

utaga·u [*vt* utagawanai; utagatta] 疑う *doubt; be doubtful of; be suspicious; suspect* ⊗Jibun no mé o utagatta. 自分の目を疑った。*I doubted my own eyes!*

utagawashí·i [*adj* utagawáshiku nái; utagawáshikatta] 疑わしい *(be) questionable; doubtful*

utai 謡 *Noh song (recitation)*

uta·u [*vt* utawanai; utatta] 歌う *sing; chant; recite* ⊗Utá o utaimashō. 歌を歌いましょう。*Let's sing a song.*

utchari うっちゃり *sumo maneuver (throwing the opponent out at the edge of the ring)*

útouto [to] うとうと（と）*drowsily* ——**útouto-suru** [*vi*] うとうとする *fall off (to sleep); doze; be drowsy*

úts·u [*vt* uténai; útta] 打つ *strike; hit* ⊗haetataki de útsu はえたたきで打つ *hit with a fly swatter* ⊗muné o útsu hanashí 胸を打つ話 *a story that touches the heart.* ⊗Sono jōkén de té o utō. その条件で手を打とう。*I'll do it under those conditions.*

utsubuse うつ伏せ; 俯せ *lying on one's stomach* ⊗Utsubuse de nerú to rakú da yo! うつぶせで寝ると楽だよ。*It's more comfortable to sleep on your stomach.*

utsubús·u [*vi* utsubusánai; utsubúshita] うつ伏す; 俯す *lie face down; lie on one's stomach; lie prone*

utsubyō 鬱病 *(mental / nervous) depression*

utsukushí·i [*adj* utsukúshiku nái; utsukúshikatta] 美しい *(be) beautiful* ——**utsukúshiku** 美しく *beautifully; charmingly*

utsukushísa 美しさ *beauty; charm*

utsumúk·u [*vi* utsumukánai; utsumúita] 俯く *hang (one's) head; look down* ⊗Mómoko wa ítsumo utsumúite arúku. 桃子はいつもうつむいて歩く。*Momoko always walks with her eyes on the ground.*

utsurikawari 移り変わり *change; transition* ⊗Yonónaka no utsurikawari wa memagurushíi. 世の中の移り変わりはめまぐるしい。*The changes in the world make your head spin.*

utsurikawár·u [*vi* utsurikawaránai; utsurikawátta] 移り変わる *change; shift*

utsúr·u [*vi* utsuránai; utsútta] 映る *be reflected (in); reflect* ⊗Tsukí wa iké ni utsútte iru. 月は池に映っている。*The moon is reflected in the pond.*

utsúr·u [*vi* utsuránai; utsútta] 移る *move; change* ⊗kokóro ga utsúru 心が移る *have a change of heart* ⊗tokí ga utsúru 時が移る *time goes by* ⊗Byōki ga utsútte iru 病気が移っている。*The sickness is catching.*

utsushí 写し *a copy* ⊗Jūminhyō no utsushí ga hitsuyō désu. 住民票の写しが必要です。*A copy of your residence card is necessary.*

utsús·u [*vt* utsusánai; utsúshita] 写す *copy; make a copy; take a photo*

§Tanin no tōan o utsúshite wa ikemasén. 他人の答案を写してはいけません。 *You must not copy other's answers.*

utsús·u [vt utsusánai; utsúshita] 移す *move; transfer; carry* §Piano o tonari no heyá ni utsúshite kudasái. ピアノを隣の部屋に移して下さい。 *Move the piano into the other room.*

utsutsu [to] うつうつ（と）；鬱々（と）*depressed; in low spirits* §Shimpai-goto ga áru sei ka, utsuutsu to shite supótsu o tanoshiménai. 心配事があるせいか、鬱々としてスポーツが楽しめない。 *Something must be on his mind because he's depressed and can't enjoy sports.* ——**útsu utsu-suru** [vi] 鬱々する *be depressed*

utsuwa 器 *vessel; container; caliber* §utsuwa ga chīsái 器が小さい *the container is small; a small-minded person* §Anó hito wa dáijin ni náru utsuwa dé wa nái. あの人は大臣になる器ではない。 *He's not qualified to be a cabinet minister.*

uttae·ru [vt uttaenai; uttaeta] 訴える *accuse; sue; appeal to* §ryóshiki ni uttaeru 良識に訴える *appeal to (one's) conscience* §mé ni uttaeru pósutā 目に訴えるポスター *a poster that catches the eye*

uttóri-suru [vi] うっとりする *be fascinated by* §Kánojo no amári no utsukushísa ni uttóri-shite shimatta. 彼女のあまりの美しさにうっとりしてしまった。 *I was fascinated by her fabulous beauty.*

uwa- 上～ *upper* §uwaago 上顎 *upper jaw; roof of the mouth* §uwa-ba 上歯 *upper teeth* §uwabe 上辺 *surface; outside; appearance* §uwagi 上着 *coat; jacket* §uwagúsuri 上薬 *(pottery) glaze*

uwaki 浮気 *infidelity; fickleness* ——**uwaki-suru** [vi] 浮気する *be unfaithful* §Shújin wa dómo uwaki-shite iru ráshii. 主人はどうも浮気しているらしい。 *It seems my husband is being unfaithful.*

uwamawár·u [vi uwamawaránai; uwamawátta] 上回る *exceed; be over (above)* §Kotoshi no uriage wa yosó o uwamawátte iru. 今年の売り上げは予想を上回っている。 *This year's sales are beyond what we predicted.*

uwasa 噂 *rumor* §uwasa ga tátsu 噂が立つ *rumors arise*

uyamá·u [vt uyamawánai; uyamátta] 敬う *respect; honor; worship*

úyoku 右翼 *right wing*

úyouyo うようよ *in swarms* ——**úyouyo-suru** [vi] うようよする *be swarming with; be crowded (with)* §Ari ga úyouyo-shite iru. 蟻がうようよしている。 *It's swarming with ants.*

uzú(maki) 渦（巻き）*whirlpool* §hito no uzú 人の渦 *a whirlpool of people* §arasói no uzú ni makikomaréru 争いの渦に巻き込まれる *be dragged into the whirlpool of a conflict*

uzura 鶉 *quail*

úzuuzu-suru [vi] うずうずする *be itching (to do something); be impatient* §Kodomo wa asobi ni ikitákute úzuuzu-shite iru. 子どもは遊びに行きたくてうずうずしている。 *The children are itching to go out to play.*

W

wa は [particle: subject / topic marker] §Zṓ wa hana ga nagái. 象は鼻が長い。 *The elephant has a long trunk.*

wa わ (emphatic sentence-final particle) <fem> §Watashi mo ikitái wa. 私も行きたいわ。 *I want to go too!* <fem>

wá 和 *harmony; accord*

wá 輪；環 *circle; ring; link; loop* §Wá ni natte narabimashṓ. 輪になって並びましょう。 *Let's form a circle.*

-wa 〜羽 [classifier for birds and rabbits]

wabí 侘 *an aesthetic term for "taste for the simple and quiet"*

[o-]wabi （お）詫び *apology* §O-wabi no kotobá mo arimasén. お詫びの言葉もありません。 *I can't tell you how sorry I am.* ——**owabi-suru** [vi / vt] お詫びする *apologize* §Gobusata o o-wabi-shimásu. ご無沙汰をお詫びします。 *I apologize for not keeping in touch.*

wabi·ru [vt wabinai; wabita] 詫びる *apologize*

wabishí·i [adj wabíshiku nái; wabíshikatta] 侘しい (be) lonely; desolate; miserable §wabishíi kakkō 侘しい格好 *a forlorn figure (of a person)* §Káre wa wabishíi gaikoku-gúrashi ni shūshífu o útte, kikoku-shita. 彼は侘しい外国暮らしに終止符を打って帰国した。 *He put an end to his lonely sojourn in the foreign country and returned to his native land.*

wabun 和文 *Japanese writing*

wadai 話題 *topic; subject (of conversation)* §Kánojo wa wadai ga hōfu desu. 彼女は話題が豊富です。 *She's conversant on many subjects.*

Wa-Ei 和英 *Japanese and English* §Wa-Ei jíten 和英辞典 *Japanese-English dictionary*

wafū 和風 *Japanese style* §wafū dorésshingu 和風ドレッシング *Japanese-style salad dressing*

wafuku 和服 *Japanese clothing*

wagamáma [na] わがまま（な）*selfish; willful; self-indulgent* ——**wagamáma ni** わがままに *willfully; self-centeredly*

wagáshi 和菓子 *Japanese-style confection*

wagō 和合 *harmony; accord; concord*

wagomu 輪ゴム *rubber band*

wáiro 賄賂 *a bribe; bribery*

waisetsu [na] 猥褻（な）*indecent; obscene*

waishatsu ワイシャツ *shirt*

wái wai [to] わいわい（と）*noisily; clamorously; vociferously* §Wái wai iwarete watashi wa yatto késsshin-shita. わいわい言われて私はやっと決心した。 *Everyone made such a fuss I finally made a decision.*

wájutsu 話術 *the art of telling a story*

wáka 和歌 *Japanese thirty-one-syllable poem*

wákaba 若葉 *young leaves*

wakachiá·u [*vt* wakachiawánai; wakachiátta] 分かち合う *share; divide*

wakagáer·u [*vi* wakagaeránai; wakagáetta] 若返る *grow younger*
§Buráun-shi wa nennen wakagáette iru yố desu. ブラウン氏は年々若
返っているようです。 *Mr. Brown seems to grow younger year by
year.*

wakai 和解 *reconciliation* ——**wakai-suru** [*vi*] 和解する *reconcile*
§Oyako kánkei wa háha no byōki o kikkake ni wakai-shita. 父子関係は
母の病気をきっかけに和解した。 *Through the mother's illness,
father and son were reconciled to each other.*

waká·i [*adj* wákaku nái; wákakatta] 若い *(be) young; small; low*
§kangae ga wakái 考えが若い *an immature idea* §wakái bangố 若
い番号 *a low number* §Wakái hitó wa génki de urayamashíi. 若い人
は元気で羨ましい。 *I envy the energy of young people.* ——**wákaku**
若く *youthful* §Kánojo wa toshi no wari ni wákaku miéru ne. 彼女は
年の割に若く見えるね。 *She looks young for her age. <fem>*

wakaré·ru [*vi* wakarénai; wákareta] 別れる *be separated; divided;
branch off; part from; diverge* §Nijūnen tsuresotta fūfu ga wakaréru
kotó ni nátta. 二十年連れ添った夫婦が別れることになった。 *The
couple who have been together for twenty years are going to separate.*
§Koko de michi ga futatsú ni wakárete iru. ここで道が二つに別れて
いる。 *The road forks here.* §Watashi to tsúma to no íken ga wakárete
shimatta. 私と妻との意見が別れてしまった。 *My wife's opinion and
my own are divided.*

wakarikír·u [*vi* wakarikiránai; wakarikítta] 分かり切る *be plain; be
evident* ——**wakarikítta** (attr) 分かり切った *plain; evident; obvious*

wakár·u [*vi* wakaránai; wakátta] 分かる *understand; see; know*
§Hánnin ga wakátta. 犯人が分かった。 *The culprit was identified.*
§Eigo ga yóku wakaránai. 英語がよく分からない。 *I don't
understand English well.* §Kimi wa wakaránai hitó da ne. 君は分か
らない人だね。 *I don't understand you. <masc>*

wákasa 若さ *youth; youthfulness*

wakasagi 公魚 *pond smelt (a freshwater fish)*

wakas·u [*vt* wakasanai; wakashita] 沸かす；湧かす *boil (water); heat
(the bath); make hot; excite; breed* §Fúro o wakashi-súgichatta. 風呂
を沸かし過ぎちゃった。 *I made the bath too hot.* §Sono shiai wa
kanshū o wakashite shimatta. その試合は観衆を湧かしてしまった。
The game excited the spectators. §Bushố-shite shirami o wakashite
shimatta. 無精して虱を湧かしてしまった。 *Because of lack of
sanitation, the place bred lice.*

wakawakashí·i [*adj* wakawakáshiku nái; wakawakáshikatta] 若々しい
(be) youthful; young

wáke 訳 *reason; cause; meaning* §Kono kotoba no wáke ga
wakarimasén. この言葉の訳がわかりません。 *I don't understand the*

meaning of this word.   **§**Sore nára okóru wáke da. それなら怒る訳だ。 *If that's so, there's reason to get mad.*

wakea·u [vt wakeawanai; wakeatta] 分け合う *share (with)*   **§**mōké o wakeau 儲けを分け合う *share the proceeds*

wakegi 冬葱 *scallion*

wakemae 分け前 *share (of something); portion*   **§**Watashi no wakemae wa dono kurai ni náru no? 私の分け前はどのくらいになるの。 *I wonder what my share will be. <fem>*

wakeme 分け目 *dividing line; part in the hair*

wáke ni (wa) ikanai 訳にはいかない *can't very well...; can't get by without... <idiom>*   **§**Oshieru wáke ni wa ikanai yo. 教える訳にはいかないよ。 *I can't very well tell you.*

waké·ru [vt wakénai; wáketa] 分ける *divide; part; separate; distinguish*   **§**futatsu ni wakéru 二つに分ける *divide in half*   **§**okashi o wákete taberu おかしを分けて食べる *divide the sweets and eat them*

wakí 脇 *the side; by (at) the side of; beside*   **§**Watashi no wakí ni suwari-nasái. 私の脇にすわりなさい。 *Sit beside me.*   **§**hanashí o wakí ni sorásu 話を脇に逸らす *digress from the subject*

wakidé·ru [vi wakidénai; wakidéta] 沸き出る；湧き出る *gush forth; spurt*   **§**Iwa no sukima kara izumi ga wakidéte iru. 岩の隙間から泉が湧き出ている。 *A spring is gushing through a gap in the rocks.*   **§**Yūki ga wakidéta. 勇気が湧き出た。 *I had a spurt of courage.*

wakige 脇毛 *underarm hair*

wakimí 脇見 *looking to the side*   **§**wakimi únten 脇見運転 *inattentive driving; looking to the side while driving* ——**wakimí-suru** [vi] 脇見する *look aside*

wakimichi わき道；脇道 *bypath; branch road; digression*   **§**wakimichi e soréru 脇道へ逸れる *go astray; wander from the path; beat about the bush*

wakinóshita 脇の下 *underarm; armpit*

wak·u [vi wakanai; waita] 沸く；湧く *boil; become hot; gush out; spring up*   **§**O-yu ga wakimáshita yo! お湯が沸きましたよ。 *The water's boiling!*   **§**Gíron ga waite iru. 議論が沸いている。 *The argument has become heated.*

wakú 枠 *framework; frame*   **§**wakugumi 枠組み *framework*   **§**Kono kíji o tensen no wakú de kakonde okó. この記事を点線の枠で囲んでおこう。 *I'll enclose this article in dotted lines.*   **§**Kimi no íken wa wakú ni hamatte ite shinsemmi ga nái. 君の意見は枠にはまっていて新鮮味がない。 *Your opinion conforms to the (usual) framework; there's nothing new (about it).*

wakusei 惑星 *planet*

wákuwaku [to] わくわく（と） *excitedly; nervously; on edge* ——**wákuwaku-suru** [vi] わくわくする *be nervous; be excited; be keyed* up; be trembling 🖗Watashi wa wákuwaku-shinágara musumé no nyūshi háppyō o machimáshita. 私はわくわくしながら娘の入試発表を待ちました。*I waited on pins and needles for the results of my daughter's entrance exam.*

wamekigóe 喚き声 *a scream*

wamék·u [vi wamekánai; waméita] 喚く *scream; yell*

wampaku [na] 腕白（な）*naughty; mischievous; unruly* 🖗Uchi no ko wa wampaku désu. うちの子は腕白です。*My child is full of mischief.* 🖗Wampaku-zákari no ko o sodatéru no wa taihen désu. 腕白盛りの子を育てるのは大変です。*It's awful rearing an unruly child.*

wampísu ワンピース *one-piece dress*

[o-]wan （お）碗；（お）椀 *bowl* 🖗gohan-jáwan ご飯茶碗 *a rice bowl*

wán 湾 *bay; gulf; inlet* 🖗Tōkyōwan 東京湾 *Tokyo Bay*

wána 罠 *a trap; a snare* 🖗wána ni kakáru 罠にかかる *be caught in a trap* 🖗wána o kakéru 罠をかける *set a trap*

wáni 鰐 *alligator* 🖗wanigawa 鰐皮 *alligator skin*

wán-wan わんわん *bow-wow* 🖗Inú wa wánwan nakimásu. 犬はわんわん鳴きます。*A dog barks "bow-wow."*

wáon 和音 *chord*

wápuro ワープロ *abbr for "word processor"*

wára 藁 *straw* 🖗warabuki yáne 藁葺き屋根 *straw-thatched roof*

wárabi 蕨 *bracken*

warai 笑い *a smile; a laugh* 🖗warai o osaéru 笑いを抑える *suppress a laugh*

waraigóe 笑い声 *laughter*

wara·u [vi warawanai; waratta] 笑う *laugh; smile*

wareme 割れ目 *gash; fissure; crack* 🖗Garasu mádo ni wareme ga háitte iru. ガラス窓に割れ目が入っている。*There's a crack in the window.*

waremono 割れ物 *breakable; fragile article; broken article*

ware·ru [vi warenai; wareta] 割れる *crack; break; split; be broken (in pieces)*

wareware 我々 *we*

wariai 割合 *ratio; rate; proportion; percentage* ——**wariai [ni]** 割合（に）*comparatively* 🖗Tésuto wa wariai ni yóku dekita. テストは割合によく出来た。*I did comparatively well on the test.*

wariate 割り当て *allotment; quota*

wariaté·ru [vt wariaténai; wariáteta] 割り当てる *assign; allot* 🖗Kónsāto no chíketto o gojū-mai uru yō ni wariateráreta. コンサートのチケットを五十枚売るように割り当てられた。*We were each assigned fifty concert tickets to sell.*

waribashi 割り箸 *disposable wooden chopsticks*

waribiki 割引 *discount; reduction* 🖗Waribiki ga arimásu ka? 割引があ

りますか。 *Do you give a discount?*

warikan 割り勘 *equal split; go Dutch; Dutch treat* ❛Kyṓ no shokujidai wa gónin de warikan ni shiyṓ. 今日の食事代は五人の割り勘にしよう。 *Let's split the cost of today's meals among the five of us.*

warikítte 割り切って *decisively* ❛Warikítte kōshō-suru shíka nái. 割り切って交渉するしかない。 *There's nothing to do but (sit down and) talk this through.*

warikóm·u [*vi* warikómánai; warikónda] 割り込む *cut; break* ❛retsu ni warikómu 列に割り込む *cut in line* ❛hanashí ni warikómu 話に割り込む *interrupt (break into) a conversation*

warízan 割り算 *division (Math)*

war·u [*vt* waranai; watta] 割る *break; crack; divide; cut* ❛ringo o futatsú ni waru りんごを二つに割る *cut an apple in half* ❛Otóshite koppu o watte shimatta. 落としてコップを割ってしまった。 *I dropped the cup and broke it.* ❛Kenka no chūsai ni watte háitta. けんかの仲裁に割って入った。 *I broke in to arbitrate the fight.* ❛Uísukī o watte nómu. ウイスキーを割って飲んだ。 *I mix water with my whisky.*

warugí 悪気 *offense; malice; ill will; evil intent* ❛Káre wa warugí no nái hito desu. 彼は悪気のない人です。 *He is a person without malice.*

warú·i [*adj* wáruku nái; wárukatta] 悪い *(be) bad; wrong; evil; wicked* ❛warúi kusé 悪い癖 *bad habit* ❛Kono shóhin wa hinshitsu ga warúi. この商品は品質が悪い。 *The quality of these goods is poor.* ❛Káre wa warúi koto bákari shite iru. 彼は悪い事ばかりしている。 *He's always doing something bad.* ❛Sonna kotó o shitára anó hito ni warúi. そんなことをしたらあの人に悪い。 *If I did that, I would be wronging him.*

warúkuchi; warúguchi 悪口 *abuse; bad-mouthing; slander* ❛Kánojo wa ítsumo watashi no warúkuchi bákari itte iru. 彼女はいつも私の悪口ばかり言っている。 *She always says only bad things about me.*

wásabi 山葵 *Japanese horseradish*

washitsu 和室 *Japanese-style room*

washoku 和食 *Japanese cuisine*

wasuremono 忘れ物 *something left behind; lost article*

wasureppó·i [*adj* wasureppóku nái; wasureppókatta] 忘れっぽい *(be) forgetful* ❛Watashi wa toshi no séi ka saikin wasureppóku nátte kita. 私は年のせいか最近忘れっぽくなってきた。 *Maybe it's because I'm getting old, but recently I have become forgetful.*

wasure·ru [*vt* wasurenai; wasureta] 忘れる *forget* ❛Ítsu made mo kúyokuyo-surú na yo. Sonna kotó wa mṓ wasureró yo. いつまでもくよくよするなよ。そんなことはもう忘れろよ。 *Don't keep moping about it. Forget it!* <*masc*>

watá 綿 *cotton (wool); cotton plant*

watakushi 私 *I; me <formal>*

watarídori 渡り鳥 *migratory bird*

watar·u [vt wataranai; watatta] 渡る *go over; cross*   ❽michi o wataru 道 を渡る *cross the street*   ❽Horie Ken'ichi wa yótto de Taihéiyō o watatta. 堀江謙一はヨットで太平洋を渡った。 *Horie Ken'ichi crossed the Pacific in a sailboat.*

watar·u [vi wataranai; watatta] 亘る *range (over); extend*   ❽Shushō wa yojíkan ni wataru dai-nétsuben o furutta. 首相は四時間に亘る大熱弁 を奮った。 *The prime minister delivered an impassioned speech lasting four hours.*

watashi 私 *I; me*   ❽watashítachi 私たち *we; us*   ❽Watashi wa Amerikájin desu. 私はアメリカ人です。 *I am an American.*   ❽Watashi wa gakusei désu. 私は学生です。 *I am a student.*

watashítachi no 私たちの *our*

watas·u [vt watasanai; watashita] 渡す *pass across; hand; hand over; surrender*   ❽Heya no kagí o watashite oku yó. 部屋の鍵を渡してお くよ。 *I'll give you the key to my room.*

wayaku 和訳 *Japanese translation*

wazá 技 *skill; art; technique*

wazá 業 *deed; act*

wáza to わざと *on purpose; intentionally; deliberately*   ❽wáza to makeru わざと負ける *lose on purpose; deliberately lose*

wazawai 災い *an evil; misfortune; troubles*   ❽Wazawai o manéku yó na kotó wa surú na yó! 災いを招くようなことはするなよ。 *Don't do anything that will cause (lit: invite) trouble!*   ❽Wazawai o ténjite fukú to násu. 災いを転じて福となす。 *Turn a misfortune into a blessing.* <set phrase>

wázawaza わざわざ *purposely; on purpose; specially*   ❽Wázawaza oide kudasátte arígatō. わざわざおいで下さってありがとう。 *Thank you for taking the time to come.* <formal>

wázuka [na] 僅か（な）*a few; a little; a mere*   ❽Nokori no kane wa wázuka shika nái. 残りの金は僅かしかない。 *There's only a little money left.* ——**wázuka ni** 僅かに *only; merely; just*

wazurai 煩い；思い *sickness; suffering; trouble; anxiety*   ❽Hito no yó wa nán to wazurai no ói kotó ka? 人の世は何と煩いの多いことか。 *How full of suffering is the life of human beings.*

wazura·u [vt wazurawanai; wazuratta] 煩う *suffer from; have trouble with; be ill*   ❽gán o wasurau 癌を煩う *suffer with cancer*

wazurawashí·i [adj wazurawáshiku nái; wazurawáshikatta] 煩わしい *(be) troublesome; annoying; vexatious*   ❽Imin tetsúzuki wa jitsú ni wazurawashíi. 移民手続きは実に煩わしい。 *Immigration procedures are troublesome.*

Y

ya や _and [conjunctive between nouns or noun phrases; inclusive]_

ya 矢 _arrow_ ❊yumi to ya 弓と矢 _bow and arrow_

Yá! やあ。 _Hi!_ ❊Yá, génki? やあ、元気？ _Hi! How are you?_ _<informal>_

yabái [adj yabaku nái; yábakatta] やばい _dangerous; illegal; shady; dubious_ ❊Konna tokoro o mitsukattara yabái! こんなところを見つかったらやばい。 _It wouldn't do to be caught in a place like this!_ _<informal>_

yaban [na] 野蛮（な） _barbarous; savage; uncivilized_ ❊bumméijin ni kagítte yaban na kối o kurikaeshimásu. 文明人に限って野蛮な行為を繰り返します。 _It's civilized people that keep repeating uncivilized acts._

yabu 藪 _thicket; a scrub; shrubbery_ ❊take yabu 竹薮 _bamboo thicket_ ❊yabu kará bō 薮から棒 _a bolt from the blue <set phrase>_ ❊yabu hebi 薮蛇 _something best left alone (lit: snakes in a thicket) <set phrase>_

yabure 破れ _a tear; a rent; a rupture; a breach_

yabure kábure 破れかぶれ _desperation; recklessness_ ❊yabure kábure ni náru 破れかぶれになる _be driven to desperation_

yaburé·ru [vi yaburénai; yabúreta] 破れる _tear; burst; be torn_ ❊Kamí ga yabúreta. 紙が破れた。 _The paper tore._ ❊Yumé ga yabúreta. 夢が破れた。 _The dream vanished._ ❊Kiroku ga yabúrareta. 記録が破られた。 _The record was broken._

yabúr·u [vt yaburánai; yabútta] 破る _tear; break; destroy; beat (in a match)_ ❊heiwa o yabúru 平和を破る _destroy the peace_ ❊hōritsu o yabúru 法律を破る _break the law_ ❊shōji o yabúru 障子を破る _tear the shoji_

yáchin 家賃 _house rent; rental fee_

yachō 野鳥 _wild bird_

yádo 宿 _inn; sleeping place; lodging_ ❊yadochō 宿帳 _hotel registry_ ❊yadonashi no hitó 宿無しの人 _a homeless person_

yadokari 宿借り；寄居虫 _hermit crab_

yadorígi 宿り木；寄生木 _mistletoe; parasitic plant_

yaezákura 八重桜 _double-flowered cherry blossom_

yágai 野外 _outside; outdoor; the open air_ ❊yagáigeki 野外劇 _open-air theater_ ❊yagai kónsāto 野外コンサート _outdoor concert_

yagate やがて _soon; presently; before long; eventually_ ❊Otto wa yagate kúru deshố. 夫はやがて来るでしょう。 _My husband will come before long._

yági 山羊 _goat_

yágu 夜具 _bedding_

yagura 櫓 _tower; turret_ ❊hinomi yágura 火の見櫓 _fire tower_

yagurumasō 矢車草 *cornflower; bachelor's button*

yahári やはり *as expected; still; all the same; also* ❧Yahári watashi no itta tóri ni nátta deshō? やはり私の言った通りになったでしょう? *It was just as I said (it would be), wasn't it?*

yáji 野次 *jeering; hooting* ——**yajír·u** [*vt* yajiránai; yajítta] 野次る *hoot (down); jeer* ❧Kōénsha o yajítte irú no wa dáre da! 講演者を野次っているのは誰だ。 *Who is that jeering the speaker?* <*masc*>

yajírushi 矢印 *arrow (symbol)*

yajiuma 野次馬 *curious spectator; crowd; onlooker*

yajū 野獣 *beast; wild animal*

yakamashí·i [*adj* yakamashíku nái; yakamashíkatta] 喧しい *(be) noisy; clamorous; boisterous; severe (with); critical; choosy* ❧Kōji no otó ga yakamashíkute nemurenai. 工事の音が喧しくて眠れない。 *The construction work's so noisy I can't sleep.* ❧Keisatsu ga yakamashíi kara ki o tsukéro! 警察がやかましいから気をつけろ! *Be careful! The police are tough (they won't let you get by with anything).* <*masc*>

yakan 夜間 *at night; night time* ❧yakan éigyō 夜間営業 *night-time business*

yakan 薬缶 *teakettle*

yakata 館；屋形 *mansion; manor house* ❧yakata-búne 屋形船 *a pleasure boat*

yáke ni やけに *desperately; unreasonably; terribly; exceptionally* ❧Kyō wa yáke ni múshimushi-suru na! 今日はやけにむしむしするな。 *It's terribly humid today!* <*masc*>

yakeato 焼け跡 *ruins (site) of a fire*

yakedo 火傷 *a burn; a scald*

yakei 夜景 *night view* ❧Hónkon wa hyakuman-doru no yakei to iwarete iru. 香港は百万ドルの夜景と言われている。 *Hong Kong is said to have a million-dollar night view.*

yake·ru [*vi* yakenai; yaketa] 焼ける *be burned down; be baked; be toasted; be burned; be sunburnt* ❧Ié ga yakete shimatta. 家が焼けてしまった。 *The house burned down.* ❧Mochi ga yakete iru. 餅が焼けている。 *The mochi (rice cake) is toasted.*

yaki- 焼き〜；焼〜 *baked; grilled* ❧yakiniku 焼肉 *grilled meat* ❧yakiimo 焼芋 *baked sweet potatoes* ❧yakiríngo 焼りんご *baked apples* ❧yakidófu 焼豆腐 *broiled tofu*

yakiba 焼き場 *crematorium*

yakimóchi 焼き餅 *jealousy* ❧yakimóchi o yakú 焼き餅を焼く *be jealous*

yakimono 焼き物 *pottery; earthenware* ❧yakimonóshi 焼き物師 *potter*

yákkai [na] 厄介（な）*embarrassing; troublesome; onerous; annoying* ❧Yákkai na mondai ga ókite shimatta. 厄介な問題が起きてしまった。 *An annoying problem has arisen.* ❧Yákkai o kákete sumimasén.

厄介をかけてすみません。*I'm sorry to have caused you trouble.*

yakkyoku 薬局 *pharmacy*

yak·u [*vt* yakanai; yaita] 焼く *burn; bake; toast; roast; broil* §kamikúzu o yaku 紙屑を焼く *burn trash paper* §pán o yaku パンを焼く *bake (or toast) bread* §nikú o yaku 肉を焼く *broil (or roast) meat*

yáku 約 *about* §Tōkyō kara Ōsaka máde shinkánsen de yáku sanjíkan de ikimásu. 東京から大阪まで新幹線で約三時間で行きます。*You can go from Tokyo to Osaka by the bullet train in about three hours.*

yakú 役 *role (e.g. in a play); part* §yakú o furu 役を振る *assign parts (in a play); assign responsibilities* §yakú ni tátsu 役に立つ *be helpful; be useful; be handy* §yakuzuki 役付き *a person in a responsible position* §Watashi wa kyō hajímete serifu no áru yakú ga tsúita. 私は今日初めて台詞のある役がついた。*Today I got a speaking part for the first time.*

yakuba 役場 *town office* §mura yákuba 村役場 *village office* §machi yákuba 町役場 *town office*

yakúbi 厄日 *evil (or unlucky) day*

yakuhárai 厄払い *exorcist* §yakuhárai o suru 厄払いをする *exorcise; drive out demons*

yakuhin 薬品 *medicine; pharmaceutical supplies* §kagaku yákuhin 化学薬品 *chemical(s)* §kampō yákuhin 漢方薬品 *Chinese medicine*

yakúin 役員 *officer; person in charge* §kyōkai yakuin 教会役員 *church officer* §dantai yakuin 団体役員 *club leader*

yakumé 役目 *duty; responsibility; role; function; office* §Hito ní wa sorézore sono hito nari no yakumé ga áru. 人にはそれぞれその人なりの役目がある。*Everyone has his own role.*

yakumí 薬味 *spices; flavor; seasoning; condiments* §Yakumí ga yóku kiite iru. 薬味がよく利いている。*You can taste the spices (in this).* §Yakumí o yóku kikasete kudasái. 薬味をよく利かせて下さい。*Season well.*

yakunin 役人 *government official; public officer* §yakunin kónjō 役人根性 *bureaucratic mentality*

yakusha 役者 *actor (in traditional Japanese theater)* §senryō yákusha 千両役者 *a star; a headliner* §Yakusha ga sorótte iru. 役者が揃っている。*The principal participants have gathered.*

yakushó 役所 *government office* §shiyákusho 市役所 *city hall* §ku-yákusho 区役所 *ward office*

yakusō 薬草 *medicinal herb*

yakusoku 約束 *agreement; date; promise; appointment* §yakusoku o mamóru 約束を守る *keep a promise* §kuchi yákusoku 口約束 *a verbal agreement* ——**yakusoku-suru** [*vt*] 約束する *promise; make an appointment*

yakús·u [*vt* yakusánai; yakúshita] 訳す *translate* §Koten o gendaigo ni

yakúsu no wa muzukashíi. 古典を現代語に訳すのは難しい。 *It's difficult to translate classics into contemporary language.*
yakuwari 役割 *part (in a play); role; responsibility; duty; function* §yakuwari o hatásu 役割を果たす *perform one's function* §Kúrabu de no hitorihitóri no yakuwari o kimemashṓ. クラブでの一人一人の役割を決めましょう。 *Let's decide on the responsibility of each club member.*
yakuzai 薬剤 *medicine; drug* §yakuzáishi 薬剤師 *pharmacist; druggist*
yákyoku 夜曲 *serenade*
yakyū 野球 *baseball*
yamá 山 *mountain* §yamáyama 山々 *mountains*
yamaárashi 山嵐 *porcupine*
yamabato 山鳩 *turtledove*
yamabiko 山彦 *an echo*
yamábushi 山伏 *ascetic mountain priest*
yámai 病 *disease; illness* §Yámai wa ki kara. 病は気から。 *The mind rules the body. <set phrase>*
yamaimo 山芋 *Japanese yam*
yama kaji 山火事 *forest fire*
yamámichi 山道 *mountain path (**or** road)*
yamamori 山盛り *heaping (of food)*
yamaneko 山猫 *wildcat* §yamaneko súto 山猫スト *a wildcat strike*
yamanote 山の手 *hilly residential section of Tokyo; the Bluff (Yokohama)*
yamashí·i [*adj* yamashíku nái; yamashíkatta] やましい *(be) ashamed; have a guilty feeling* §Watashi ní wa nánra yamashíi tokoró wa arimasén. 私には何らやましいところはありません。 *I don't feel at all guilty; my conscience is clear.*
Yámato 大和；倭 *Japan (old name)* §Yamato-dámashii 大和魂 *Japanese spirit*
yame·ru [*vt* yamenai; yameta] 止める；辞める *quit; cease; end; stop* §tabako o yameru 煙草を止める *quit smoking* §shigoto o yameru 仕事を辞める *quit one's job.*
yami 闇 *darkness* §yamíyo 闇夜 *a moonless night* §yami no yó 闇の世 *Hades*
yamome 寡 *widow* §otoko yamome 男やもめ *widower*
yam·u [*vi* yamanai; yanda] 止む *cease; stop* §Áme ga yanda. 雨が止んだ。 *The rain's stopped.*
yamuoénai やむを得ない *(be) unavoidable; inevitable; beyond (one's) control*
yanagi 柳 *willow* §yanagi no íto 柳の糸 *drooping branches of a willow tree* §yanagi ni kazé 柳に風 *listening passively (lit: willow in the wind) <set phrase>* §Yanagi no shita ni ítsumo dojō wa inai. 柳の下にいつもどじょうはいない。 *Good luck doesn't always repeat itself.*

<set phrase>

yáne 屋根 *roof* §yane-zútai ni 屋根伝いに *from roof to roof* §yaneura-beya 屋根裏部屋 *attic room*

yaní 脂 *resin; gum; tar* §matsuyani 松脂 *pine resin*

yánushi 家主 *landlady; landlord*

yaochō 八百長 *rigging (a match); a put-up job; fixed (match)* §yaochō-jíai 八百長試合 *a fixed (or rigged) match*

yaoya(-san) 八百屋（さん）*vegetable (-fruit) shop* §yaoya-san 八百屋さん *greengrocer*

yappári *(see yahári)*

-yára やら～ *and; or; and so forth* §Kinō wa kodomo ga nakú yara sawágu yara de taihen dátta. 昨日は子供が泣くやら騒ぐやらで大変だった。 *Yesterday was awful with the children crying and making a racket all day long.*

Yáre yare! やれやれ！ *Thank God!; Well, well!; That's over, thank God!*

yari 槍 *spear* §yarinage 槍投げ *javelin throwing (contest)*

yarikata やり方 *way of doing* §Amimóno no yarikata ga wakarimasén. 編物のやり方が分かりません。 *I don't know how to knit.*

yarikiréna·i [*adj* yarikirénaku nái; yarikirénakatta] 遣り切れない *(be) unbearable; can't stand* §Tonari no káppuru wa urusákute yarikirénai. 隣のカップルは煩くて遣り切れない。 *The couple next door are so noisy I can't stand it.*

yarinaós·u [*vt* yarinaosánai; yarinaóshita] やり直す *do over again; try again* §Kimí, kono keisan machigátte iru yo! Súgu yarinaósu yố ni! 君、この計算間違っているよ！直ぐやり直すように！ *You've made a mistake on this calculation. Do it again, right away!* <masc>

yarisugí·ru [*vt* yarisugínai; yarisúgita] やり過ぎる *overdo* §Nándemo yarisúgite wa ikenai. 何でもやり過ぎてはいけない。 *Nothing should be overdone. (Everything in moderation.)*

yarítori 遣り取り *give and take; exchange* §Watashítachi wa hageshíku íken no yarítori o shita. 私たちは激しく意見の遣り取りをした。 *We exchanged opinions heatedly.*

yarō 野郎 *fellow; guy* <masc>

yar·u [*vt* yaranai; yatta] 遣る；やる *do; play (tennis / golf / etc.); send; give* §Ténisu o yarố ze! テニスをやろうぜ！ *Let's play tennis.* <masc> §Musúme o daigaku ni yatta. 娘を大学に遣った。 *I sent my daughter to college.* <masc> §Kodomo ni kozúkai o yatta. 子どもに小遣いをやった。 *I gave the children some spending money.* <masc> §Haná ni mizu o yatta. 花に水をやった。 *I watered the plants.*

yasai 野菜 *vegetable*

yasashi·i [*adj* yasashiku nái; yasashíkatta] 易しい *(be) easy; plain; simple*

yasashi·i [*adj* yasashiku nái; yasashíkatta] 優しい *(be) gentle; sweet;*

tender; kind

yasashísa 優しさ *tenderness; delicacy*

yasei [no] 野生 （の） *wild; untamed* 🔹yasei dőbutsu 野生動物 *wild animal* 🔹yaseimi 野性味 *an air of roughness*

yase·ru [vi yasenai; yaseta] 痩せる *become thin; lose weight* 🔹Yabe-san wa yasete iru. 矢部さんは痩せている。 *Yabe is thin.* (*or Yabe has lost weight.*)

yáshi やし *palm tree*

yashikí 屋敷；邸 *estate; mansion; residence*

yáshin 野心 *ambition; aspiration; desire* 🔹yáshin mamman 野心満々 *full of ambition* 🔹yashinka 野心家 *an ambitious person* 🔹yáshin o idáku 野心を抱く *have ambition* ——**yashinteki [na]** 野心的（な） *ambitious*

yashina·u [vt yashinawanai; yashinatta] 養う *rear; bring up; support; cultivate; develop* 🔹Watashi wa kázoku o yashinawanákereba naránai. 私は家族を養わなければならない。 *I have to support my family.* 🔹kiryoku o yashinau 気力を養う *develop spiritual strength*

yashiro 社 *Shinto shrine*

yasō 野草 *wild plants*

yasú·i [adj yásuku nái; yasúkatta] 安い *(be) cheap; inexpensive*

-yasui 〜易い *easy to (do)* 🔹Kono kusuri wa nomiyasui. この薬は飲み易い。 *This medicine is easy to swallow.* 🔹Kono séito wa totemo oshieyasúi. この生徒はとても教えやすい。 *This student is easy to teach.*

yasumí 休み *rest; holiday* 🔹yasumí o tóru 休みを取る *take a holiday.*

[O-]yasumi nasái. お休みなさい。 *Good night!*

yasumono 安物 *cheap article* 🔹Yasumonó kai no zeni úshinai. 安物買いの銭失い。 *Wasting money by buying cheap things (Penny wise and pound foolish).* <set phrase>

yasúm·u [vt yasumánai; yasúnda] 休む *rest; retire; go to bed; be absent from; take a holiday (or day off)* 🔹Sukóshi yasúnde kara matá hajimeyő. 少し休んでからまた始めよう。 *Let's rest a while and then begin again.* 🔹Mő osói kara yasumő ka? もう遅いから休もうか。 *It's late; let's go to bed.*

yasuppó·i [adj yasuppóku nái; yasuppókatta] 安っぽい *(be) cheap; cheap-looking* 🔹Kono dóresu wa yasuppói ne. このドレスは安っぽいね。 *This dress looks cheap, doesn't it?* <fem>

yasuri やすり *a file; rasp* 🔹kamiyásuri 紙やすり *sandpaper*

yasuyásu [to] 易々（と） *easily; effortlessly* 🔹kónnan na shigoto o yasuyásu to yaru 困難な仕事を易々とやる *perform a difficult task with ease*

yátai 屋台 *a festival float; a stage for dancing; a street stall* 🔹yátai o hiku 屋台を引く *pull a float* 🔹yatái mise 屋台店 *a street stall*

yatara [na] やたら（な）*indiscriminate; haphazard; at random* §Yatara na kotó wa iu wáke ni wa ikanai. やたらなことは言う訳にはいかない。 *It wouldn't do for me to just shoot my mouth off.* ——**yatara ni** やたらに *indiscriminately; recklessly; randomly; wildly* §Yatara ni tobimawáru na! やたらに跳び回るな。 *Don't jump around so wildly. <masc>*

yátō 野党 *opposition (political) party* §yótō to yátō 与党と野党 *the government and opposition parties*

yatoinin 雇い人 *employee*

yatóinushi 雇い主 *employer*

yató·u [vt yatowánai; yatótta] 雇う *employ; hire*

yátsu 奴 *fellow; chap; guy; he (him) <masc>*

yatsuré·ru [vi yatsurénai; yatsúreta] やつれる *grow thin; be haggard; be worn out* §Anó hito, byōki káshira. Yatsúrete iru wa. あの人、病気かしら。やつれているわ。 *I wonder if she's ill; she's (so) thin. <fem>*

yatto やっと *at last; at length; finally; just* §Yatto kansei-shita. やっと完成した。 *I finally finished it.* §Shūden ni yatto maniátta. 終電にやっと間にあった。 *I just made the last train.*

yattoko やっとこ *pliers; pincers*

yattsú 八つ *eight (when counting things)*

yattsuké·ru [vt yattsukénai; yattsúketa] やっつける *do away with; beat; defeat; kill; finish off* §Kyōjū ni kono shigoto o yattsukeyó. 今日中にこの仕事をやっつけよう。 *Let's finish off this work today.* §Aitsu o yattsúkete yaró. あいつをやっつけてやろう。 *I'll take care of him. <masc>*

yawaragé·ru [vt yawaragénai; yawarageta] 和らげる *soften; assuage; relax* §shōgeki o yawarageru 衝撃を和らげる *soften a blow*

yawarág·u [vi yawaragánai; yawaráida] 和らぐ *be softened; be assuaged* §Kimi to issho ni irú to kimochi ga yawaráide kúru yo. 君と一緒にいると気持ちが和らいで来るよ。 *When I'm with you I feel relaxed. <masc>*

yawaráka na 柔らかな *soft; gentle; mild; tender* §yawaráka na futon 柔らかな布団 *a soft futon* §Minamoto-san wa monogoshi ga yawaráka desu. 源さんは物腰が柔らかです。 *Minamoto's movements (and expressions) are gentle.*

yawaraká·i [adj yawarakáku nái; yawarakákatta] 柔らかい *(be) soft; gentle; easy; mild; tender; pliant* §yawarakái hanashí 柔らかい話 *a talk that's easy to follow.* §Tōfu wa yawarakái. 豆腐は柔らかい。 *Tofu is soft.* §Kono nikú wa yawarakái. この肉は柔らかい。 *This meat is tender.* ——**yawarakáku** 柔らかく *gently; tenderly*

yáya やや *somewhat; to some extent; rather* §Kyó wa yáya samúi. 今日はやや寒い。 *It's rather cold today.*

yo よ *(sentence-ending particle; emphatic)* ▪ Háyaku tábeta hō ga íi yo. 早く食べた方がいいよ。 *You'd better hurry up and eat!*

yó 世 *the world; society; the age* ▪ yó no owari made 世の終わりまで *to the end of the world* ▪ yó ni shirárete iru 世に知られている *famous; known to the world* ▪ yó o suteru 世を捨てる *abandon the world* ▪ ano yó あの世 *the other world; the world after death*

yó 用 *business; errand* ▪ Kyō wa yó ga arimásu. 今日は用があります。 *I have an errand (to do) today.* ▪ Watashi wa kaisha no yó de Kyūshū ni ikimásu. 私は会社の用で九州に行きます。 *I'm going to Kyushu on company business.*

yó [na] ～様（な）*like; as; seems to be* ▪ Áme ga fúru yó desu ne. 雨が降るようですね。 *It looks like rain.* ▪ Watashi wa Ishikawa-san no yó na hitó ga sukí desu. 私は石川さんのような人が好きです。 *I like a person like Ishikawa.* ——**yó ni** ～様に *as if; in such-and-such a manner* ▪ Tori no yó ni sóra o tobetára nā. 鳥のように空を飛べたらなあ。 *If only I could fly like a bird.* <masc> ▪ Watashi wa ítsumo no yó ni góji ni shokuba o déta. 私はいつものように五時に職場を出た。 *As always, I left work at 5:00 o'clock.*

yoaké 夜明け *dawn; daybreak*

yóbi 予備 *preparation; a spare; in reserve* ▪ yobi chíshiki 予備知識 *prior knowledge* ▪ yobikō 予備校 *preparatory school* ▪ yobi sénkyo 予備選挙 *preliminary election* ▪ yóbi no o-kane 予備のお金 *reserve (or emergency) money*

yóbi; -yóbi 曜日 *day of the week* ▪ Getsuyóbi 月曜日 *Monday* ▪ Suiyóbi 水曜日 *Wednesday* ▪ Kyō wa nanyóbi desu ka? 今日は何曜日ですか? *What day (of the week) is it today?*

yobidashi 呼び出し *a call; a summons* ▪ Kaisha kara kyū ni yobidashi ga kakátta. 会社から急に呼び出しがかかった。 *I got an emergency call to go to my office.*

yobidás·u [vt yobidasánai; yobidáshita] 呼び出す *call; convene* ▪ Nogi san o denwá-guchi ni yobidáshite ikadakemasén ka? 野木さんを電話口に呼び出して頂けませんか。 *Would you call Ms. Nogi to the phone, please?* <formal>

yobō 予防 *prevention* ▪ yobō chūsha 予防注射 *vaccination; preventive injection* ▪ kasai yóbō 火災予防 *fire prevention* ——**yobō-suru** [vt] 予防する *prevent; guard against* ▪ uirusu kánsen o yobō-suru ウイルス感染を予防する *guard against being infected with a virus*

yōbō 要望 *a request* ▪ Kimi no yōbō ní wa kotaerarénai. 君の要望には応えられない。 *I cannot comply with your request.* ——**yōbō-suru** [vt] 要望する *request* ▪ Netakiri-rōjin é no hōmu-hérupā no haken o tó ni yōbō-shite iru. 寝たきり老人へのホームヘルパーの派遣を都に要望している。 *We are requesting the city to provide a home-helper service for bedridden old people.*

yob·u [vt yobanai; yonda] 呼ぶ *call; invite; name* §Tákushī o yonde kudasái. タクシーを呼んで下さい。 *Call a taxi, please.* §Senséi ga yonde iru yo. 先生が呼んでいるよ。 *The teacher's calling you.* §Máda "máma" to yonde kurenái wa. まだ「ママ」と呼んでくれないわ。 *She still doesn't call me "mama."* <fem> §Ōta-san o shokuji ni yobimáshita. 大田さんを食事に呼びました。 *I invited Ota to dinner.*

yobun 余分 *excess; extra; spare; superabundance; surplus* §Yobun na nímotsu wa motánai yố ni. 余分な荷物は持たないように。 *Make sure you don't have excess baggage.*

yóchi 予知 *foreknowledge; prediction* §yochi nóryoku 予知能力 *ability to predict* §jishin yochi sóchi 地震予知装置 *earthquake prediction device* ——**yóchi-suru** [vt] 予知する *know in advance; predict; foresee*

yóchi 余地 *space; room; margin; freedom* §Koko ni kuruma o ichídai tomeru yóchi ga áru. ここに車を一台停める余地がある。 *There's room to park a car here.*

yōchíen 幼稚園 *kindergarten*

yóchiyochi [to] よちよち（と） *toddling; with tottering steps* §Akambō ga yóchiyochi arukidáshita. 赤ん坊がよちよち歩き出した。 *The baby began to toddle.*

yōchū 幼虫 *larva; chrysalis*

yodan 余談 *digression*

yodan 予断 *prediction; prophecy* §Chíchi no byōjō wa máda yodan o yurusánai. 父の病状はまだ予断を許さない。 *No prognosis can be given on my father's condition.* ——**yodan-suru** [vt] 予断する *presuppose; suppose*

yodare 涎 *slobber; saliva* §yodarékake 涎かけ *a bib*

yōdochínki ヨードチンキ *iodine*

yodóm·u [vi yodománai; yodónda] 淀む；澱む *stagnate; be sluggish* §Sono kawá wa gomí de yodónde iru. その川はごみで澱んでいる。 *The river is stopped up with garbage.*

yodōshi 夜通し *all night; through the night* §Watashi wa yodōshi háha no kámbyō o shita. 私は夜通し母の看病をした。 *I looked after my sick mother all through the night.*

yōeki 溶液 *(liquid) solution*

yōfū 洋風 *foreign; Western style* §yōfū kénchiku 洋風建築 *Western-style building*

yōfuku 洋服 *clothes (Western style)* §yōfuku-dánsu 洋服箪笥 *chest of drawers*

yōga 洋画 *Western painting*

yógan 溶岩 *(molten) lava*

yogen 予言 *prophecy* §yogénsha 予言者 *a prophet* ——**yogen-suru**

[*vt*] 予言する *predict; prophesy*

yōgísha 容疑者 *a suspect*

yōgo 用語 *technical term* §yōgo káisetsu 用語解説 *glossary* §igaku yốgo 医学用語 *medical terminology*

yogore 汚れ *stain; spot; smudge* §Yogore ga ochínai. 汚れが落ちない。 *The spot won't come out.* §Kono yogore o otóshite kudasái. この汚れ を落として下さい。 *Remove this stain, please.*

yogore·ru [*vi* yogorenai; yogoreta] 汚れる *be dirty; be soiled; be contaminated* §Kōjố no haikíbutsu de kawá ga yogoreta. 工場の廃棄 物で川が汚れた。 *The river was contaminated with waste from the factory.*

yogos·u [*vt* yogosanai; yogoshita] 汚す *soil; dirty; stain; contaminate* §Heyá o yogasanáide ne. 部屋を汚さないでね。 *Don't make the room dirty.* §Hanzai ni té o yogoshite shimatta. 犯罪に手を汚してしまっ た。 *He stained his hands with crime.*

yōgu 用具 *tool; implement; equipment* §undō yốgu 運動用具 *athletic equipment* §daidokoro yốgu 台所用具 *kitchen utensils*

yōgyojō 養魚場 *fish hatchery*

yohaku 余白 *blank (space); margin* §yohaku o nokósu 余白を残す *leave a margin*

yōhin 用品 *outfit; implement; supplies; articles* §jimu yốhin 事務用品 *office supplies*

yohō 予報 *a forecast* §tenki yóhō 天気予報 *weather forecast*

yohodo 余程 *very; much; considerably; a great deal* §Ōtomo-san wa yohodo komátte iru rashíi. 大友さんは余程困っているらしい。 *Ōtomo seems to be in a rather bad situation.*

yoi 酔い *inebriety; drunkenness* §yoi ga mawaru 酔いが回る *get drunk* §yoi ga saméru 酔いが醒める *become sober* §yoi o samásu 酔いを 醒ます *sober up*

yối 用意 *preparation* §hijō no tóki no yối 非常の時の用意 *preparations for an emergency* ——**yối-suru** [*vt*] 用意する *prepare; get ready for* §Kánai wa íma, shokuji no yối o shite imásu. 家内は 今、食事の用意をしています。 *My wife is preparing the meal now.*

yōi 容易 *ease* ——**yōi na** 容易な *easy* ——**yōi ni** 容易に *easily* §Sono mondai wa yōi ni kaiketsu-dekíru. その問題は容易に解決でき る。 *That problem can be solved easily.*

yōiku 養育 *upbringing; fostering* ——**yōiku-suru** [*vt*] 養育する *rear; bring up; foster* §Kodomo o yōiku-surú no wa taihen désu. 子どもを 養育するのは大変です。 *It's quite a job rearing children.*

Yóisho! よいしょ。 [*interjection*] *Heave ho!*

yōji 楊枝; 楊子 *toothpick*

yốji 幼児 *infancy*

yốjin 用心 *caution* §hi no yốjin 火の用心 *taking precaution against* fires   **yōjímbō** 用心棒 *security guard; bodyguard* ——**yōjin-suru** [*vi*] 用心する *be careful; take care*

yōjin-buká·i [*adj* -búkaku nái; -bukákatta] 用心深い *(be) cautious; careful; vigilant*

yojír·u [*vt* yojiránai; yojítta] よじる *twist*   **Himo o yojítte goran.** 紐をよじってごらん。 *Twist the string.*   **hara no kawá o yojítte warau** 腹の皮をよじって笑う *double up with laughter* <set phrase> (*see also* **nejíru**)

yójo 養女 *adopted daughter*

yóka 余暇 *spare time; free time; leisure*

yōka 八日 *the eighth of the month; eight days*

yokan 予感 *foreboding; presentiment* ——**yokan-suru** [*vt*] 予感する *have a premonition; have a hunch*   **Watashi wa fukô na jínsei o yokan-shite iru.** 私は不幸な人生を予感している。 *I have a premonition that my life is going to be unhappy.*

yókan 羊羹 *sweet jelly made from beans*   **mizu yókan** 水羊羹 *soft yōkan*

yokei na 余計な *too many (much); excessive; unnecessary*   **yokei na monó** 余計な物 *unnecessary item(s); superfluous things*   **Yokei na o-séwa wa yakanáide kure!** 余計なお世話は焼かないでくれ！ *Thanks, but no thanks!* <masc>

yōkén 用件 *business; matter; condition*   **Kyô wa jūyō na yōkén de ukagaimáshita.** 今日は重要な用件で伺いました。 *I came today on an important matter.*

yoké·ru [*vt* yokénai; yóketa] 避ける *dodge; avoid; make way for*   **Mizutamari o yókete tôtte kudasái.** 水溜まりを避けて通って下さい。 *Avoid the puddle and go (or come) on.*

yóki 容器 *vessel; container*   **pori-yóki** ポリ容器 *plastic container*

yóki 予期 *expectation; anticipation*   **Yóki ni hánshite musuko wa nyūshi ni shippai-shita.** 予期に反して息子は入試に失敗した。 *Contrary to our expectations, our son failed the entrance examination.* ——**yóki-suru** [*vi / vt*] 予期する *expect; anticipate*   **yóki-senu dekígoto** 予期せぬ出来事 *an unanticipated occurrence*

yóki na 陽気な *cheerful; happy; lively; merry; gay; sunny; jolly*   **yōki na hitó** 陽気な人 *a cheerful person* ——**yōki ni** 陽気に *cheerfully; happily*   **O-matsuri de minná ga yóki ni sawáide iru.** お祭りでみんなが陽気に騒いでいる。 *At the festival everyone is having a merry time.*

yokin 預金 *a deposit (of money); savings*   **futsû yókin** 普通預金 *ordinary savings account*   **tōza yókin** 当座預金 *savings (or checking) account*   **yokin tsûchō** 預金通帳 *savings account book* ——**yokin-suru** [*vt*] 預金する *save; deposit (money)*

yokka 四日 *the fourth of the month; four days*

yokkyū 欲求 *craving; desire; a want*   §yokkyū fúman 欲求不満 *frustration; unsatisfied desire*

yoko 横 *side; width; breadth; horizontal direction* ——**yoko ni** 横に *on the side; sideways; horizontally*   §Térebi no yoko ni denwa ga áru. テレビの横に電話がある。 *The telephone is beside the TV.*   §Yoko ni náttemo íi desu ka? 横になってもいいですか。 *Is it all right if I lie down?*

yokobai 横這い *crawling sideways* —— **yokobai-suru** [vi] 横這いする *crawl sideways (like a crab); level off*   §Bukka wa yokobai jōtai desu. 物価は横這い状態です。 *Commodity prices haven't changed much.*

yokogaki 横書き *horizontal writing (as English)* ——**yokogaki-suru** [vt] 横書きする *write horizontally*

yokogao 横顔 *profile*   §Kánojo no yokogao wa kawaíi. 彼女の横顔は可愛い。 *She has a cute profile.*   §Sōri dáijin no yokogao ni furetai. 総理大臣の横顔に触れたい。 *I'd like to get a different (a more personal) perspective on the prime minister.*

yokogír·u [vt yokogíranai; yokogítta] 横切る *cut across; cross*   §Fumikiri o yokogíru toki, chūi-shite kudasái. 踏切を横切る時、注意して下さい。 *When you go over the RR crossing be careful.*   §Me no máe o supótsú-kā ga sugói supído de yokogítte itta. 目の前をスポーツカーが凄いスピードで横切って行った。 *A sports car cut across right in front of me going at a terrific speed.*

yokoku 予告 *previous announcement; advance notice*   §yokokuhen 予告編 *preview of a fillm* ——**yokoku-suru** [vt] 予告する *announce beforehand*

yokomoji 横文字 *horizontal writing; a Western language*

yokomuki 横向き *sideways; facing to the side*

yokoóyogi 横泳ぎ *sidestroke*

yokos·u [vt yokosanai; yokoshita] 寄越す *send (over); give*   §Kane o yokose! 金をよこせ！ *Hand over your money!* <masc>   §Kodomo o inaka e hítóri de yokoshi-nasái yo. 子供を田舎へ一人でよこしなさいよ。 *Send the child to visit us in the country by himself.*

yokotawár·u [vi yokotawaránai; yokotawátta] 横たわる *lie down; stretch out*   §Byōnin wa béddo ni yokotawátte iru. 病人はベッドに横たわっている。 *The sick person is stretched out on the bed.*

yokozuna 横綱 *sumo grand champion*

yóku よく *often*   §Watashi no kázoku wa yóku gaishoku-suru. 私の家族はよく外食する。 *Our family eats out often.*

yokú 欲 *lust; desire; greed; covetousness*   §yokú no fukái hitó 欲の深い人 *a greedy person*

yokubarí 欲張り *greedy person; miser*   §Musumé wa ítsumo yokubari-bákari iu. 娘はいつも欲張りばかり言う。 *My daughter's always asking for things.*

yokubō 欲望 *desire; ambition* ❧Yokubō ní wa mitáshite íi mono, warúi mono ga áru. 欲望には満たしていいもの、悪いものがある。 *There are some ambitions that are good to fulfil; some that are bad.*

yokujō 浴場 *bathing room*

yokusei-suru [*vt*] 抑制する *control; check; suppress; inhibit* ❧Bukka jōshō o yokusei-suru séido ga nái. 物価上昇を抑制する制度がない。 *There is no system to control rising prices.*

yokusō 浴槽 *bathtub*

yokuyō 抑揚 *intonation; inflection*

yōkyū 要求 *a demand; require; a need; a claim* ——**yōkyū-suru** [*vt*] 要求する *demand; require; need; claim* ❧Rōdṓsha wa chin'age o yōkyū-shite iru. 労働者は賃上げを要求している。 *Workers are demanding a raise.*

yōma 洋間 *Western-style room*

yome 嫁 *bride; daughter-in-law* ❧o-yome-san お嫁さん *the bride* ❧yomeiri 嫁入り *wedding; marriage* ❧yome ni iku 嫁に行く *get married; become a bride*

yómi [no kuni] 黄泉（の国） *the realm of the dead; Hades*

yomigaer·u [*vi* yomigaeranai; yomigaetta] 蘇る；甦る *return to life; revive; be resurrected* ❧Kioku ga yomigaetta! 記憶が蘇った! *Now I remember!*

yomíkaki 読み書き *reading and writing*

yomimóno 読み物 *reading matter* ❧Náni ka karui yomimóno ga yomitái. 何か軽い読み物が読みたい。 *I'd like something light to read.*

yōmō 羊毛 *wool*

yóm·u [*vt* yománai; yónda] 読む *read* ❧hón o yómu 本を読む *read a book* ❧hito no shínchū o yómu 人の心中を読む *read a person's mind*

yōmúin 用務員 *janitor*

yón 四；4 *four (the numeral)*

yonaká 夜中 *the middle of the night; in the dead of night*

yondokoroná·i [*adj* yondokoronáku nái; yondokoronákatta] 拠無い *(be) unavoidable; necessary; urgent* ❧Ashitá wa yondokoronái yōji de kaisha o yasumásete morau. 明日は拠無い用事で会社を休ませてもらう。 *I'll have to take tomorrow off from work because of some urgent business.*

yonónaka 世の中 *the world; society; the age* ❧sawagashíi yonónaka 騒がしい世の中 *turbulent world*

yopparai 酔っ払い *drunk person* ❧Densha no náka de yopparai ni karamárete komátta. 電車の中で酔っ払いに絡まれて困った。 *I had trouble with a drunk who came at me on the train.*

yoppara·u [*vi* yopparawanai; yopparatta] 酔っ払う *be (become) intoxicated* ❧Hisashiburi ni sake o nónde yopparatte shimatta. 久し振

りに酒を飲んで酔っ払ってしまった。 *I drank sake for the first time in a long time and ended up getting drunk.*

yōran 要覧 *an outline; a survey; manual*

yōrei 用例 *example; instance*

yóri (mo) より（も）*(more) than* ❡Táiyō wa tsukí yori mo háruka ni ōkíi. 太陽は月よりも遥かに大きい。 *The sun is far bigger than the moon.*

-yori 寄り～ *toward...* ❡Umi-yori no michi o tótte ikó. 海寄りの道を通って行こう。 *Let's take the ocean (side) road.*

yoridokoro 拠り所 *grounds; authority; source* ❡Kokoro no yoridokoro ga hoshíi. 心の拠り所が欲しい。 *I want something to set my mind at ease.*

yorigonomi-suru [vt] 選り好みする *pick and choose*

yorikakár·u [vi yorikakaránai; yorikakátta] 寄り掛かる *lean against; depend on* ❡Sono kabe ni yorikakátte wa damé. Penki nuritate désu yo. その壁に寄り掛かっては駄目。ペンキ塗り立てですよ。 *Don't lean against this wall. It's just been painted. <fem>*

yorikir·u [vt yorikiranai; yorikitta] 寄り切る *push out of the ring (in sumo)*

yorimichi 寄り道 *a stop on the way* ——**yorimichi-suru** [vi] 寄り道する *tarry on the way; stop by* ❡Kinō no hōkago, yorimichi-shite éiga o mí ni itta. 昨日の放課後、寄り道して映画を見に行った。 *Yesterday after school I stopped on the way home to see a movie.*

yoriso·u [vi yorisowánai; yorisótta] 寄り添う *draw close to; snuggle up to* ❡Futári wa yorisótte yó o akashita.. 二人は寄り添って世を明かした。 *The couple passed the night snuggled up to each other..*

yoroi 鎧 *armor*

yōrōin 養老院 *old people's home*

yorokobashí·i [adj yorokobashíku nái; yorokobashíkatta] 喜ばしい；悦ばしい *(be) delighted; happy; pleasant*

yorokobi 喜び *joy; delight*

yorokób·u [vi yorokobánai; yorokónda] 喜ぶ *be pleased; be glad to; be happy* ❡Ryōshin wa futarí no kekkon o kokoró kara yorokónde iru. 両親は二人の結婚を心から喜んでいる。 *Both parents are pleased with the marriage.* ——**yorokónde** 喜んで *willingly* ❡Káre wa yorokónde tetsudátte kureta. 彼は喜んで手伝ってくれた。 *He willingly helped me.* ——**yorokobásu** [caus] 喜ばす *please (someone)* ❡Ojísan obásan o yorokobásu no wa ureshíi desu. お祖父さんお祖母さんを喜ばすのは嬉しいです。 *I enjoy pleasing grandfather and grandmother.*

yoromék·u [vi yoromekánai; yoroméita] よろめく *stagger; reel; have an affair* ❡ishí ni tsumazuite yoroméku 石につまづいてよろめく *stumble over a rock and stagger* ❡hitozuma ni kokoró ga yoroméku 人

妻に心がよろめく　*have an affair with a married woman*

yóron 世論　*public opinion*　§yoron chốsa 世論調査　*public opinion survey*　§yóron ni uttaéru 世論に訴える　*appeal to public opinion*

Yōróppa ヨーロッパ　*Europe*

yoroshí·i [*adj* yoróshiku nái; yoróshikatta] 宜しい　*(be) good; all right*

Yoroshiku onegai-shimásu. 宜しくお願いします。*Please (do it for me); It's a pleasure to meet you. <set phrase>*

yóroyoro to よろよろと　*wobbly; totteringly*　——**yóroyoro-suru** [*vi*] よろよろする　*totter; stagger*

yóru 夜　*night*

yor·u [*vi* yoranai; yotta] 寄る　*draw near; approach*　§Mínami wa watashi no sóba ni yotte kíta. 南は私の傍に寄って来た。*Minami came up beside me.*

[ni] yoru to 〜に因ると　*according to...*　§Tenki yóhō ni yoru to ashitá wa haréru số desu. 天気予報によると明日は晴れるそうです。*According to the weather report, tomorrow will be fair.*

yōryố 容量　*capacity*

yósa 良さ　*merit; virtue; good (quality)*　§Másako-san wa kao ni hitogara no yósa ga arawárete iru. 正子さんは顔に人柄の良さが表われている。*Masako's good character shows in her face.*

yōsai 洋裁　*dressmaking*

yosan 予算　*an estimate; budget*　§yosan hénsei 予算編成　*budget compiling*

yōsan 養蚕　*raising silkworms; sericulture*

yose 寄席　*vaudeville theater (J)*

yoseatsumé·ru [*vt* yoseatsuménai; yoseatsuméta] 寄せ集める　*gather; collect; put together*　§Hagire o yoseatsuméte patchiwáku no kússhon o tsukurimáshita. 端切れを寄せ集めてパッチワークのクッションを作りました。*I collected scraps and made a patchwork cushion.*

yosegi-záiku 寄せ木細工　*wooden mosaic handicraft*

yōsei 妖精　*fairy; elf*

yōsei 要請　*a demand; a request; requirement*　——**yōsei-suru** [*vt*] 要請する　*request; demand; require; requisition*

yose·ru [*vt* yosenai; yoseta] 寄せる　*bring (someone or something) close; move aside; gather together; visit; send (a letter)*　§miken ni shiwa o yoseru 眉間に皺を寄せる　*wrinkle one's brow*　§Tsukue o súmi ni yosete kudasái. 机を隅に寄せて下さい。*Move the desk over into the corner.*

yōsetsu 溶接　*welding*　§denki yốsetsu 電気溶接　*electric welding*

Yóshi! よし。*All right!; O.K.*　§Yóshi, watashi ni makáshite kure! 良し、私に任してくれ！*All right! Leave it to me! <masc>*

yōshi 用紙　*a form (to be filled out)*　§genkō yốshi 原稿用紙　*manuscript paper*　§shinsei yốshi 申請用紙　*application form*　§tōan yốshi 答案

用紙 *answer sheet*

yōshi 養子 *adopted (male) child* ❚yōshi éngumi 養子縁組 *adoption marriage (**or** adopting the husband of one's daughter)* ❚yōshi o mukaeru 養子を迎える *adopt a child*

yoshíashi 善し悪し *good and bad; merits and demerits* ❚Shōjiki-sugíru no mo yoshíashi desu. 正直すぎるのも善し悪しです。 *Being too honest has its merits and demerits.*

yōshiki 様式 *form; style* ❚Kono tatemóno wa goshikku yōshiki desu. この建物はゴシック様式です。 *This building is in gothic style.*

yoshin 余震 *aftershock; after quake*

yōsho 洋書 *foreign book*

yōshoku 養殖 *culturing; raising; breeding* ❚yōshoku shínju 養殖真珠 *cultured pearl* ——**yōshoku-suru** [vt] 養殖する *culture; breed; rear* ❚Sono iké de wa unagi o yōshoku-shite iru. その池では鰻を養殖している。 *They're raising eel in that pond.*

yōshoku 洋食 *Western food*

yoshū 予習 *study in advance; preparation* ——**yoshū-suru** [vt] 予習する *prepare in advance*

yōshu 洋酒 *foreign alcoholic drinks*

yosó [no] 他所（の）*other; outside* ❚Yosó no hito ní wa minna kūrā ga áru noni... 他所の人にはみんなクーラーがあるのに。 *Other people have air conditioning, (so why don't we?)* ——**yosó de** 他所で *elsewhere*

yosō 予想 *expectation; anticipation* ❚yosōgai 予想外 *unexpected; unanticipated* ❚yosō ga taténai 予想が立たない *be unpredictable* ——**yosō-suru** [vt] 予想する *expect; anticipate; imagine* ❚Futarí no shōrai o yosō-suru no wa muzukashíi. 二人の将来を予想するのは難しい。 *It's difficult to imagine what the future of that couple will be.*

yōso 要素 *element; factor; feature* ❚Kono busshitsu no kōsei yōso wa nán desu ka? この物質の構成要素は何ですか。 *What are the constituent elements of this substance?*

yosó·u [vt yosōwánai; yosótta] 装う *wear; be dressed in; pretend; disguise* ❚heiki o yosóu 平気を装う *pretend to be calm* ❚mi o yosóu 身を装う *adorn oneself* ❚tanin o yosóu 他人を装う *act like strangers*

yosoyososhí·i [adj yosoyososhíku nái; yosoyososhíkatta] よそよそしい *(be) standoffish; indifferent; distant* ❚Aitsu tó wa nagái tsukíai ná no ni imada ni yosoyososhíi. あいつとは長い付き合いなのに未だによそよそしい。 *I've known him a long time but he's still standoffish.*

yōsu 様子 *state of affairs; situation* ❚yōsu o ukagau 様子を窺う *look into things; inquire into a situation* ❚Áme ga furisō na yōsu désu. 雨が降りそうな様子です。 *It looks like rain.*

yōsui 用水 *tap water; water for irrigation; city water* ❚yōsúiken 用水権

water rights   §bōka yósui 防火用水 *fire prevention water*   §kangai
yósui 灌漑用水 *irrigation water*

yōsúru ni 要するに *In short...; In the last analysis...*   §Yōsúru ni sekinin
wa kimi ni áru yo. 要するに責任は君にあるよ。 *All things
considered, you're responsible. <masc>*

yotei 予定 *plan; program; schedule*   §yoteihyō 予定表 *a schedule*
§Máda yotei ga tatánai. まだ予定が立たない。 *The schedule's not yet
set.* ——**yotei-suru** [*vt*] 予定する *plan; schedule; arrange ahead*
§Ashitá wa gógo kara káigi o yotei-shite imásu. 明日は午後から会議
を予定しています。 *We've scheduled a meeting for tomorrow
afternoon.*

yotén 要点 *the point; the gist (of a matter); the essentials*   §Yōtén o
hanáshite kudasái. 要点を話して下さい。 *Tell me the gist.*

yótsu 四つ *four (when counting things)*

yōtsū 腰痛 *backache; pain in the lower back*

yotsukado 四つ角 *crossroads; street corner*

yotsumbai 四つん這い *crawling; on all fours*

[ni] yotte 〜に依って *depending on...*   §Watashítachi wa rōdō ni yotte
shotoku o éte iru. 私たちは労働によって所得を得ている。 *We are
paid depending on our work.*

yótto ヨット *sailboat; yacht*

yó·u [*vi* yowánai; yótta] 酔う *get drunk; get seasick*   §Fúne ni yótte
shimatta. 船に酔ってしまった。 *I got seasick.*   §Norimono ni yóu
node ryokō wa kirai da. 乗り物に酔うので旅行は嫌いだ。 *I don't
like to travel because I get motion sickness. <masc>*

yó wa- 要は〜 *In short...*   §Yó wa watashi ni o-kane o kashite kuré to iu
kotó da ne? 要は私にお金を貸してくれということだね。 *In short,
you're asking me to lend you some money, right? <masc>*

yowabi 弱火 *low burner; weak flame*   §Yowabi de sanjúppun nikónde
kudasái. 弱火で三十分煮込んで下さい。 *Boil over a low flame for
thirty minutes.*

yowá·i [*adi* yówaku nái; yowákatta] 弱い *(be) weak; frail; feeble*
§Watashi wa karada ga yowái. 私は体が弱い。 *I'm physically weak.*
§Watashi wa sūgaku ni yowái. 私は数学に弱い。 *I'm weak in math.*
§Watashi wa ame ni yowái. 私は飴に弱い。 *I have a weakness for
candy.*

yowaki [na] 弱気（な） *timidity; timid; frail; lacking courage*

yowamé·ru [*vt* yowaménai; yowámeta] 弱める *attenuate; make weak;
enfeeble*   §Gásu no hí o yowámete kudasái. ガスの火を弱めて下さ
い。 *Turn down the gas.*

yowámushi 弱虫 *coward*

yowár·u [*vi* yowaránai; yowátta] 弱る *be (or become) weak; weaken*
§Saikin karada ga yowátte kita. 最近、体が弱ってきた。 *These days I*

feel weak.

yówasa 弱さ *weakness*

yoyaku 予約 *previous engagement; reservation; subscription* §yoyakú-seki 予約席 *reserved seat* ——**yoyaku-suru** [*vt*] 予約する *subscribe to; make a reservation* §Kónsāto no chíketto o yoyaku-shite okimásu. コンサートのチケットを予約しておきます。*I'll make reservations for the concert.*

yōyaku 要約 *summary* ——**yōyaku-suru** [*vt*] 要約する *summarize* §Kimi no komento o yonhyaku-ji ínai ni yōyaku-shite goran. 君のコメントを四百字以内に要約してごらん。*Summarize your comments in four hundred words or less.* <*masc*>

yoyū 余裕 *room; margin* §Jikan no yoyū ga nái. 時間の余裕がない。*I have no time to spare.* §Séki ni máda yoyū ga áru. 席にまだ余裕がある。*There are still vacant seats.* §Káre wa ítsumo yoyū o mísete iru. 彼はいつも余裕を見せている。*He always keeps his composure.*

[o-]yu (お) 湯 *hot water* §yuágari 湯上がり *after (taking) a bath* §O-fúro no o-yu ga waita. お風呂のお湯が沸いた。*The bath is ready.* (**or** *The water for the bath is hot.)*

yū́ 優 *"A" grade; excellent*

yūai 友愛 *friendship; fellowship*

yūbé 夕べ *evening*

yūbé 昨夜 *last night; yesterday evening*

yūben 雄弁 *eloquence* ——**yūben na** 雄弁な *eloquent* §yūbenka 雄弁家 *an eloquent speaker; a powerful orator*

yubí 指 *finger; toe* §oyayubi 親指 *thumb; big toe* §hitosashíyubi 人さし指 *index finger* §nakáyubi 中指 *middle finger* §koyubí 小指 *little finger; little toe*

yū́bi 優美 *grace; charm* ——**yūbi [na]** 優美（な）*graceful; elegant; refined* §yū́bi na odori 優美な踊り *a graceful dance*

yūbin 郵便 *mail* §yūbin bángō 郵便番号 *postal code* §yūbin fúrikae 郵便振替 *postal transfer* §yūbínkyoku 郵便局 *post office* §yūbin'ya-[san] 郵便屋（さん）*mail carrier* §yūbin háitatsu 郵便配達 *a mail carrier; mailman; mail delivery*

yubiníngyō 指人形 *(hand) puppet*

yubisás·u [*vt* yubisasánai; yubisáshita] 指差す *point at; indicate* §Hito o yubisáshite wa ikenai. 人を指差してはいけない。 *You mustn't point at people.*

yubiwa 指輪；指環 *a ring* §kekkon yúbiwa 結婚指輪 *wedding band*

yūbō [na] 有望（な）*promising; hopeful* §Anáta no shṓrai wa yūbō desu. あなたの将来は有望です。*You have a promising future.*

yūbokúmin 遊牧民 *nomads*

yū́bune 湯船 *bathtub*

yūdachi 夕立ち *(sudden) shower*

yūdai [na] 雄大（な）*elegant; grand*　§Me no máe ni yūdai na keikan ga hirogatte ita. 目の前に雄大な景観が広がっていた。 *A grand view spread out before me.*

yudan 油断 *inattention; negligence* ——**yudan-suru** [vi] 油断する *let up (one's) guard; be negligent*　§Yudan-suru to shippai-suru yo. 油断すると失敗するよ。 *If you're off your guard, you'll fail.*

yudané·ru [vt] yudanénai; yudáneta] 委ねる *relinquish; give to another's care; entrust*　§Watashi ga ichídai de kizúita jígyō o kodomótachi ni yudanéru kotó ni shita. 私が一代で築いた事業を子どもたちに委ねることにした。 *I decided to leave my lifetime's work to my children.*

Yudayájin ユダヤ人 *a Jew*

Yudayakyō ユダヤ教 *Judaism*

yuden 油田 *oil field*

yudé·ru [vt] yudénai; yúdeta] 茹でる *boil (in water)*

yūdoku [na] 有毒（な）*poisonous*　§yūdoku gásu 有毒ガス *poison gas*

yué 故 *reason; cause; circumstances*　§Ámachi wa hitoatari ga yói yué ni hyōban ga íi. 天池は人当たりがよい故に評判がいい。 *Amachi has a good reputation because he's sociable.*

yūeki [na] 有益（な）*useful; beneficial; instructive*

yūénchi 遊園地 *playground; amusement park; recreation area*

yūetsu 優越 *superiority* ——**yūetsúkan** 優越感 *superiority complex*

yúfuku [na] 裕福（な）*affluent; wealthy*　§yúfuki ni náru 裕福になる *become wealthy*　§Kánai wa yúfuku na katei ni sodátta. 家内は裕福な家庭に育った。 *My wife grew up in a wealthy family.*

yúga 優雅 *grace; elegance* ——**yúga na** 優雅な *graceful; elegant*　§Kono hóteru no róbī wa yúga na fun'íki ga áru. このホテルのロビーは優雅な雰囲気がある。 *This hotel lobby has an elegant atmosphere.*

yūgai 有害 *harmfulness; noxiousness* ——**yūgai na** 有害な *harmful; noxious*　§yūgai bússhitsu 有害物質 *a noxious substance*

yugame·ru [vt] yugamenai; yugameta] 歪める *distort; warp; twist; contort*　§Jíjitsu o yugamete wa ikenai. 事実を歪めてはいけない。 *One must not distort the facts.*　§Kanja wa itamí ni kuchi o yugamete táete iru 患者は痛みに口を歪めて耐えている *The patient grimaced and endured the pain.*

yugam·u [vi] yugamanai; yuganda] 歪む *be distorted; be twisted; be contorted; be warped*　§Mégane no furēmu ga yugande kao ni awánaku nátta. 眼鏡のフレームが歪んで顔に合わなくなった。 *My glasses are twisted and no longer fit my face.*　§seikaku no yuganda hitó 性格の歪んだ人 *a person with a warped personality.*

yūgata 夕方 *evening; dusk*

yúge 湯気 *vapor; steam*

yūgen-gáisha 有限会社 *limited corporation; company*

yúgi 遊戯 *game; pastime; amusement*

yūgō 融合 *fusion; unity; harmony* &kaku yūgō 核融合 *nuclear fusion* ——**yūgō-suru** [*vi*] 融合する *fuse; unite; merge*

yūhan 夕飯 *supper; evening meal*

yūhi 夕日；夕陽 *evening sun; setting sun*

yūígi na 有意義な *significant; interesting; full of meaning* &Kyō no gakushūkai wa totemo yūígi deshita. 今日の学習会はとても有意義でした。 *The (academic) meeting today was very interesting.*

yuigon 遺言 *last will and testament* &yuigonjō 遺言状 *a will*

yúiitsu [no] 唯一（の） *only; sole; one* &Otto no yúiitsu no torié wa kenkō na kotó kashira. 夫の唯一の取り柄は健康なことかしら。 *Is my husbands' sole redeeming feature his good health, I wonder?* <fem>

yuinō 結納 *exchange of betrothal presents* &yuinōkin 結納金 *betrothal gift (money)*

yūjo 遊女 *courtesan; (licensed) prostitute*

yūjō 友情 *friendship* &Futarí wa atsui yūjō de musubarete iru. 二人は厚い友情で結ばれている。 *The two were joined by a warm feeling of friendship.*

yuka 床 *floor*

yúkai [na] 愉快（な） *pleasant; happy; cheerful; delightful; fun*

yūkai 誘拐 *abduction; kidnapping* ——**yūkai-suru** [*vt*] 誘拐する *kidnap* &Musumé ga yūkai-sarete minoshirokin o yōkyū-sarete iru. 娘が誘拐されて身代金を要求されている。 *My daughter was kidnapped and they're demanding ransom.*

Yúkai deshita! 愉快でした。*It was fun!*

yūkan [na] 勇敢（な） *brave; courage; heroic* ——**yūkan ni** 勇敢に *bravely; courageously; heroically* &Heitai wa kuni no tamé ni yūkan ni tatakatta. 兵隊は国のために勇敢に戦った。 *The soldiers fought bravely for their country.*

yukashí-i [*adj* yukashíku nái; yukashíkatta] 床しい *(be) sweet; charming; gentle; refined; tasteful* &Náoko-san wa totemo yukashíi hitogara désu. 尚子さんはとても床しい人柄です。 *Naoko has a very sweet personality.*

yukata 浴衣 *informal cotton kimono*

yūkei [no] 有形（の） *tangible; visible* &yūkei bunkázai 有形文化財 *tangible cultural treasure* &yūkei shísan 有形資産 *tangible assets*

yuketsu 輸血 *(blood) transfusion* ——**yuketsu-suru** [*vt*] 輸血する *give a blood transfusion*

yukí 雪 *snow* &yuki no kesshō 雪の結晶 *snow crystal* &yukígutsu 雪靴 *snowshoes* &yukidáruma 雪達磨；雪だるま *snowman*

-yuki ～行き *bound for...* &Watashi wa Sanfuranshisuko-yuki no hikōki ni norimásu. 私はサンフランシスコ行きの飛行機に乗ります。 *I'm taking a plane bound for San Francisco.*

yúki 勇気 *courage; bravery; boldness; drive* &yūki o dásu 勇気を出す

show courage ❽yúki o ushinau 勇気を失う *lose courage* ❽Watashi ní wa sore o suru yúki ga nái. 私にはそれをする勇気がない。*I don't have the courage to do that.*

yūki 有機 *organic* ❽yūki kágaku 有機化学 *organic chemistry* ❽yūki kagóbutsu 有機化合物 *an organic compound* ❽yūkitai 有機体 *an organism*

yukidoke 雪解け *slush; melting snow*

yukidomari 行き止まり *end of a street; dead end; blind alley; an impasse*

yūkizuké·ru [*vi* -zukénai; -zúketa] 勇気づける *encourage; embolden*

yukizumari 行き詰まり *a deadlock*

yukizumár·u [*vi* yukizumaránai; yukizumátta] 行き詰まる *reach a deadlock; come to the end* ❽Keikaku wa yukizumátte shimatta. 計画 は行き詰まってしまった。*The plan came to a standstill.*

yukkúri [**to**] ゆっくり（と）*slowly; leisurely* ❽Kyő wa jikan o kákete yukkúri to oishii monó o tsukurő. 今日は時間をかけてゆっくりと美 味しいものを作ろう。*Today I'm going to take my time and prepare something delicious.* ❽Dőzo go-yukkúri! どうぞ、ごゆっくり。 *Please take your time. <set phrase>*

yūkō 有効 *effectiveness; validity* ——**yūkō na** 有効な *effective* ❽yūkō séibun 有効成分 *effective ingredients* ❽yūkō kíkan 有効期間 *validity period* ❽Pasupőto no yūkō kígen ga kírete iru. パスポートの 有効期限が切れている。*My passport's no longer valid.* ——**yūkō ni** 有効に *effectively*

yūkō 友好 *friendship; goodwill* ——**yūkōteki [na]** 友好的（な） *friendly* ——**yūkōteki ni** 友好的に *friendly* ❽Torukójin wa Nihonjín ni táishite yūkōteki desu. トルコ人は日本人に対して友好的です。 *Turks are friendly to Japanese.*

yuk·u 行く *go*

yukue 行方 *(one's) whereabouts* ❽yukue fúmei 行方不明 *whereabouts unknown; missing* ❽Nihón no yukue wa dő naru no deshő ka? 日本の 行方はどうなるのでしょうか。*Where is Japan headed?*

yumé 夢 *a dream* ❽yumé o míru 夢を見る *(to) dream*

yūmei [na] 有名（な）*noted; famous; well known; distinguished* ❽yūméijin 有名人 *celebrity* ❽Róndon wa kiri de yūmei désu. ロン ドンは霧で有名です。*London is known for its fog.*

yumí 弓 *a bow (archery / violin)*

yúmoa ユーモア *humor*

yūnō [na] 有能（な）*capable* ❽Yūnō na jinzai ga mitsukaranai. 有能な 人材が見つからない。*I can't find capable personnel.*

yunomi 湯飲み；湯呑み *teacup (J)*

yunyū 輸入 *an import* ❽yunyūhin 輸入品 *imported goods* ❽yunyū chőka 輸入超過 *an excess of imports* ——**yunyū-suru** [*vt*] 輸入する *import* ❽Endaka de őku no gaikoku séihin ga yunyū-sarete iru. 円高

で多くの外国製品が輸入されている。*Because of the high value of yen, many foreign products are imported.*

yurag·u [*vi* yuraganai; yuraida] 揺らぐ *swing; sway; tremble* ❦Futarí no dansei kara puropŏzu-sarete Noriko no kokoró wa yuraide iru. 二人の男からプロポーズされて、紀子の心は揺らいでいる。*Noriko was proposed to by two men and now she's vacillating between them.*

yurai 由来 *origin; genesis; provenance* ❦Kono kottŏhin no yurai ga shiritái. この骨董品の由来が知りたい。*I'd like to know the provenance of this antique.*

yurameˊk·u [*vi* yuramekánai; yuraméita] 揺らめく *flicker; blink; quiver; sway* ❦Kawamo ni hokage ga yuraméite iru. 川面に火影が揺らめいている。*The reflection of a light is flickering on the surface of the river.*

yūransen 遊覧船 *pleasure boat; sight-seeing boat*

yúrei 幽霊 *ghost; apparition*

yure·ru [*vi* yurenai; yureta] 揺れる *shake; sway; rock; roll; swing* ❦Ōkaze de kí no eda ga yurete iru. 大風で木の枝が揺れている。*Tree limbs are shaking in the heavy wind.*

yuri 百合 *lily*

yúri [na] 有利（な）*profitable; advantageous* ❦Kōshō de Támura wa wága-sha ni yŭri na jŏkén o hikidáshita. 交渉で田村はわが社に有利な条件を引き出した。*In the negotiations, Tamura managed to get (lit: extracted) advantageous terms for our company.*

yurikago 揺り籠 *cradle*

yurú·i [*adj* yúruku nái; yurúkatta] 緩い *(be) loose; lenient; lax; gentle* ❦Bín no futa ga yurúi yo. 瓶の蓋が緩いよ。*The cap to the bottle is loose.* ❦Yurúi noborizaka désu. 緩い上り坂です。*It's a gentle slope.* ❦Saikin, keisatsu no torishimari ga yúruku nátta. 最近、警察の取り締まりが緩くなった。*Lately police control has been lax.*

yuruméˊ·ru [*vt* yuruménai; yúrumeta] 緩める *loosen; unbend* ❦Shīto-béruto o yurúmete mo íi desu yó. シートベルトを緩めてもいいですか。*It's OK to loosen your seat belt.*

yurúm·u [*vi* yurumánai; yurúnda] 緩む *be loose; loosen; become slack; let up* ❦Sámusa ga yurúnde kite iru. 寒さが緩んできている。*The cold weather has let up.* ❦Shigoto ni nárete ki ga yurúnde-kita. 仕事に慣れて気が緩んできた。*Lately I've gotten used to my work and am more relaxed.*

yurushí 許し *forgiveness; pardon*

yurús·u [*vt* yurusánai; yurúshita] 許す *permit; let; forgive; pardon* ❦Yurúshite kudasái. 許して下さい。*Please forgive me.*

yurúyaka na 緩やかな *loose; leninent; generous; easy; gentle* ❦Jinkō zōkáritsu wa yurúyaka na kắbu o egáite iru. 人口増加率は緩やかなカーブを描いている。*The population percentage shows a slight* *increase.* ——**yurúyaka ni** 緩やかに *gently; leniently* §Kōsoku o yurúyaka ni shite hoshíi to iu séito kara no kóe ga agatte iru. 校則を緩やかにしてほしいという生徒からの声が上がっている。 *Students are demanding that school regulations be more lenient.*

yūryoku [na] 有力（な）*strong; powerful; leading; influential* §yūryokúsha 有力者 *an influential person* §Kóndo no sénkyo de yūryoku na taikṓba ga arawáreta. 今度の選挙で有力な対抗馬が現われた。 *In this election a strong opposition candidate is running.*

Yūséishō 郵政省 *Ministry of Posts and Telecommunications*

yūsen 優先 *priority* §yūsénken 優先権 *precedence; first claim (on)* §saiyūsen 最優先 *top priority* §yūsénkabu 優先株 *preferred stock* ——**yūsen-suru** [vt] 優先する *have priority; have precedence*

yū́shi 有志 *a volunteer* §Yū́shi o tsunótte kái o kessei-shita. 有志を募って会を結成した。 *We solicited volunteers and organized a club.*

yūshi 融資 *financing; a loan* §Watashi no kaisha wa ginkō no yūshi o úkete iru. 私の会社は銀行の融資を受けている。 *My company receives financing from the bank.*

yūshi-gáisha 融資会社 *finance company*

yūshō 優勝 *championship* §yūshṓki 優勝旗 *the pennant* §yūshōsen 優勝戦 *championship match* ——**yūshō-suru** [vi] 優勝する *win a victory* §Uchi no kōkō wa yakyū táikai de yūshō-shita. うちの高校は野球大会で優勝した。 *My high school won the baseball tournament.*

yūshoku 夕食 *evening meal; supper; dinner*

yūshū [na] 優秀（な）*superior; excellent* §Kánojo wa yūshū na gakusei désu. 彼女は優秀な学生です。 *She is a superior student.*

yushutsu 輸出 *an export* §yushutsúzei 輸出税 *export duty* ——**yushutsu-suru** [vt] 輸出する *export* §Nihón wa genryṓ o yunyū-shite, kakōhin o yushutsu-shite iru. 日本人は原料を輸入して、加工品を輸出している。 *Japan imports raw materials and exports finished products.*

yusō 輸送 *transportation; transport; conveyance* §yusō shúdan 輸送手段 *transportation facilities* ——**yusō-suru** [vt] 輸送する *transport; carry; ship*

yūsō 郵送 *mail* §yūsṓryō 郵送料 *mailing charge* ——**yūsō-suru** [vt] 郵送する *mail; send by mail*

yusur·u [vt yusuranai; yusutta] 強請る *blackmail; extort money*

yútaka [na] 豊か（な）*abundant; plentiful; ample; rich; well off* §Keiken yútaka na pairótto no sōjū nára anshin da wa. 経験豊かなパイロットの操縦なら安心だわ。 *I feel safe with a pilot who has plenty of experience.* <fem>

yutámpo 湯たんぽ *hot-water bottle* (J)

yūtán Uターン *U-turn* ——**yūtán-suru** [vi] Uターンする *return to one's home town* §Nagái koto Tōkyō de seikatsu-shite itá ga, kóndo yūtán-shite furúsato de shigoto o suru kotó ni shita. 長いこと東京で生活していたが、今度Uターンして故郷で仕事をすることにした。 *I lived in Tokyo for a long time, but now I'm going to make a U-turn and work in my home town.*

yutori ゆとり *margin; room for expansion; space* ❽Yutori no áru seikatsu ni akogarete iru. ゆとりのある生活に憧れている。 *I long for a life where there's room to breathe.* ❽Kono shímen wa máda yutori ga áru. この紙面はまだゆとりがある。 *There's still space on this paper.*

yūutsu [na] 憂鬱 (な) *gloom; melancholy* ❽yūtsúkan 憂鬱感 *melancholy* ❽yūtsúshitsu 憂鬱質 *a melancholic temperament* ❽Máinichi áme bakari de yūutsu na kíbun desu. 毎日雨ばかりで憂鬱な気分です。 *Rain every day makes me feel melancholy.*

yuwaé·ru [vt yuwaénai; yuwáete] *tie; fasten* ❽Kono himo o yuwáete kudasái. この紐を結わえて下さい。 *Tie this string, please.*

yuwákashi 湯沸かし *teakettle*

yuwakashíki 湯沸かし器 *hot-water heater*

yūwaku 誘惑 *temptation* ❽yūwaku ni kátsu 誘惑に勝つ *overcome temptation* ❽yūwaku to tatakau 誘惑と戦う *fight temptation* —— **yūwaku-suru** [vt] 誘惑する *tempt; seduce* ❽Chūnen no fujin wa hátachi no hánsamu na seinen o yūwaku-shita. 中年の婦人は二十歳のハンサムな青年を誘惑した。 *The middle-aged woman seduced a handsome 20-year-old.*

yūyake 夕焼け *evening glow ; sunset*

yúyo 猶予 *postponement* ❽shikkō yúyo 執行猶予 *postponement of enforcement* —— **yúyo-suru** [vt] 猶予する *give time (to)* ❽Shakkín no hensai o áto isshūkan yúyo-shite kudasái. 借金の返済をあと一週間猶予して下さい。 *Please postpone the repayment of the loan by a week.*

yuyushí·i [adj yuyushíku nái; yuyushíkatta] 由々しい *(be) serious; grave* ❽Kore wa yuyushíi jítai ni narisó da. これは由々しい事態になりそうだ。 *This promises to become a serious situation.*

yūzū 融通 *accommodation; advance (of money)* ❽yūzū tégata 融通手形 *a promissory note* ❽yūzū ga kiku 融通がきく *flexible* —— **yūzū-suru** [vt] 融通する *accommodate; advance* ❽Sumimasén ga, sukóshi o-kane o yūzū-shite moraemasén ka? すみませんが、少しお金を融通してもらえませんか。 *I'm sorry, but could you lend me a little money?*

yuzur·u [vt yuzuranai; yuzutta] 譲る *yield; hand over; cede* ❽Michi o yuzutte kudasái. 道を譲って下さい。 *Let me pass, please*

Z

zabúton 座布団 *flat, rectangular cushion for sitting on the floor*

zadánkai 座談会 *panel discussion ; talk session*

zagane 座金 *(metal) washer*

-zai ～罪 *crime; sin*   §sōránzai 騒乱罪 *(illegal) riot*   §satsujinzai 殺人罪 *murder; homicide*

záiaku 罪悪 *guilt; sin*

zaibatsu 財閥 *prewar Japanese business conglomerate*

zaikai 財界 *financial circles*

zaiko 在庫 *stores; stock*   §zaikohin 在庫品 *goods in stock*   §zaiko séiri 在庫整理 *stock inventory*

zaimoku 材木 *lumber; wood; timber*

záimu 財務 *financial affairs*   §zaimuka 財務課 *finance department*

zainin 罪人 *a convict*

zairyŏ 材料 *(raw) materials; ingredient(s)*   §karē no zairyŏ カレーの材料 *ingredients for making curry*

záisan 財産 *property; estate; fortune*   §zaisanka 財産家 *a person of wealth*   §zaisan mókuroku 財産目録 *property inventory*   §zaisan shótoku 財産所得 *property income*

zaisei 財政 *public finance; fiscal policy*

zaiseki-suru [vi] 在籍する *be enrolled; registered (in school)*   §Watashi wa máda kono daigaku ni zaiseki-shite imásu. 私はまだこの大学に在籍しています。 *I'm still enrolled in this university.*

zaishitsu 在室 *in (one's office)*   §Buchŏ wa máda zaishitsu-chū désu. 部長はまだ在室中です。 *The division chief is still in her office.*

zaishoku kíkan 在職期間 *term of office; period of service*

zakkaya 雑貨屋 *general store; grocer*

zakki yŏshi 雑記用紙 *scratch paper*

zákkubaran [na] ざっくばらん（な）*frank; open; candid* ── **zákkubaran ni** ざっくばらんに *outspoken; frankly*   §Tátsuno wa jibun no himitsu o zákkubaran ni katatte kureta. 龍野は自分の秘密をざっくばらんに語ってくれた。*Tatsuno frankly told her secret.*

zákuro 石榴；柘榴 *pomegranate (tree)*

Zamā míro! ざまあ見ろ。 *Serves you right!* <impolite>

zandaka 残高 *(bank) balance; remainder*

zánge 懺悔 *repentance; confession (Cath)* ──**zánge-suru** 懺悔する *repent*

zangyaku [na] 残虐（な）*brutal; cruel*   §zangyaku na kŏi 残虐な行為 *a cruel deed*

zangyŏ 残業 *overtime work*   §zangyŏ téate 残業手当 *overtime pay* ── **zangyŏ-suru** [vi] 残業する *work overtime*   §Sengetsu watashi wa gojū-jíkan mo zangyŏ-shita. 先月私は五十時間も残業しました。*I worked overtime fifty hours last month.*

zánkin 残金 *remainder of money; balance*

zankoku 残酷 *cruelty; brutality* ——**zankoku na** 残酷な *cruel; brutal; inhuman; harsh* ⚑zankoku na jíken 残酷な事件 *brutal incident;*

zannén [na] 残念（な）*regrettable; disappointing; too bad* ⚑Anó hito ni mố aénai no ga zannén desu. あの人にもう会えないのが残念です。 *It's too bad I'm not going to be able to see him again.* ——**zannen nágara...** 残念ながら～ *regrettably; I'm sorry, but...* ⚑Zannen nágara kónkai no dōsốkai wa kesseki-sasete kudasái. 残念ながら今回の同窓会は欠席させて下さい。*I'm sorry, but I'll have to miss the alumni meeting this time.*

zansatsu 惨殺 *brutal murder; butchery*

zansetsu 残雪 *remaining snow*

zánsho 残暑 *remaining heat of summer*

zappi 雑費 *miscellaneous expense; petty expenses* ⚑Seikatsúhi no náka de zappi wa igai to kakáru monó desu. 生活費の中で雑費は意外とかかるものです。*Miscellaneous expenses make up a surprising amount of the cost of living.*

zaragami 更紙 *rough paper; pulp paper*

zarazara [na / no / to] ざらざら（な／の／と）*rough; sandy* ——**zárazara-suru** [vi] ざらざらする *feel rough* ⚑Shitá ga zárazara-shite iru. 舌がざらざらしている。*My tongue feels rough.*

zarigani ざりがに *crawfish; crayfish*

zaru 笊 *bamboo basket*

zaseki 座席 *a seat* ⚑zaseki bangó 座席番号 *seat number*

zasetsu-suru [vi] 挫折する *be frustrated; be baffled (by); fail* ⚑Jígyō o kakudai-suru keikaku wa zasetsu-shite shimátta. 事業を拡大する計画は挫折してしまった。*The plans to expand the business failed.*

zashō-suru [vi] 座礁する *run aground; be stranded*

zasshi 雑誌 *magazine; journal; periodical*

zasshu 雑種 *mixed breed; a mutt (dog)*

zasshū́nyū 雑収入 *miscellaneous income*

zassō 雑草 *weed*

zatsudan 雑談 *a chat; gossip* ——**zatsudan-suru** [vi] 雑談する *have a chat (with)* ⚑Jugyōchū, zatsudan-shité wa ikemasén. 授業中、雑談してはいけません。*During class, students must not chat with each other.*

zatsuekífu 雑役夫 *handyman; odd jobber*

zatsuon 雑音 *noise; static; interference*

zatto ざっと *roughly; approximately; offhand* ⚑Anáta no kenkyū rómbun ni zatto mé o tōshimáshita. あなたの研究論文にざっと目を通しました。*I looked over your research paper briefly.*

zawameki ざわめき *commotion; a stir; noise* ⚑Kốshi ga danjó ni tátta totan, ốki na zawameki ga agatta. 講師が壇上に立った途端、大きなざわめきが上がった。*Just as the lecturer stepped to the podium there* *was a great commotion.*

zawaméku ざわめく [*vi* zawamekánai; zawaméita] *be noisy*

zázā [to] ざあざあ（と）*pouring rain* §Áme ga zázā fútte iru. 雨がざあざあ降っている。*It's pouring.*

zazen 座禅 *sitting in meditation* (Budd)

zéhi 是非 *right and wrong; propriety; by all means; at any cost* §Toshíhaku no zéhi ni tsúite kentō-shimashố. 都市博の是非について検討しましょう。*We will look into the pros and cons of the city fair.* §Zéhi, o-ai-shitái. 是非、お会いしたい。*I must see you.*

zeikin 税金 *tax* §zeikin o osaméru 税金を納める *pay taxes* §chokusetsúzei 直接税 *direct tax* §kansetsúzei 間接税 *indirect tax* §kanzei 関税 *customs duty* §menzei 免税 *duty free* §shotokúzei 所得税 *income tax* §zeikan 税関 *customs; customs office* §zeimúsho 税務署 *tax office*

zeitakú 贅沢 *luxury* §Zeitakú ni kurashitái. 贅沢に暮らしたい。*I'd like to live in luxury.* §Zeitakú ga mi o horobósu 贅沢が身を滅ぼす。*Luxury destroys the body.* <set phrase> ——**zeitakú na** 贅沢な *luxurious; extravagant*

zekkō-suru 絶交する [*vi / vt*] *break off with; cut connection with; put an end to* §Michio to Míchiko wa jūnénrai no tsukiái o zekkō-shita. 道夫と路子は十年来の付き合いを絶交した。*Michio and Michiko put a period to their ten-year relationship.*

zémbu 前部 *front part* §Kuruma no zémbu ni ijō ga áru. 車の前部に異常がある。*There's something wrong with the front end of the car.*

zémbu 全部 *all; in all; altogether; everything* §Zémbu wakátta. 全部分かった。*I understand everything.* §Zémbu de íkura desu ka? 全部でいくらですか。*How much is it altogether?*

zembun 全文 *whole sentence; full text* §Watashi no sakubun wa zembun naosáreta. 私の作文は全文直された。*Every bit of my essay was corrected.*

zemmen 前面 *front; façade*

zemmenteki [na] 全面的（な）*totally; completely* §Sono jísho wa zemmenteki ni kaitei-sareta. その辞書は全面的に改訂された。*That dictionary was completely revised.*

zemmetsu-suru [*vi*] 全滅する *be annihilated* §Teki wa zemmetsu-shita. 敵は全滅した。*The enemy was annihilated.*

zén 善 *good* §zén to áku 善と悪 *good and evil*

zén- 前 ～ *the former...* §zénshushố 前首相 *the former prime minister*

[o-]zen （お）膳 *traditional one-person dining table* §zen o totonoéru 膳を整える *set the table* §zen ni mukau 膳に向かう *sit down to eat*

Zén 禅 *Zen sect* (Budd)

zénchi [no] 全知（の）*omniscient*

zenchíshi 前置詞 *preposition* (Gram)

zenchó 前兆 *omen; sign* ⚡Daijíshin no zenchō ga átta. 大地震の前兆があった。 *There were signs indicating the coming of the great earthquake.*

zéndai mimon 前代未聞 *unprecedented; never before heard of*

zen'ei 前衛 *avant-garde* ⚡zen'eiha 前衛派 *avant-garde coterie* ⚡Káre wa tsúne ni undō no zen'ei ni iru. 彼は常に運動の前衛にいる。 *He's always in the forefront of (any) movement.*

zengaku 全額 *total amount (of money)* ⚡Hokenkin ga zengaku shiharawáreta. 保険金が全額支払われた。 *I was paid the total amount of the insurance money.*

zengakúbu 前額部 *forehead*

zén'i 善意 *good intentions; favorable sense* ⚡Hito no zén'i wa shínjita hō ga íi. 人の善意は信じた方がいい。 *One ought to believe in others' good intentions.*

zenin 是認 *approval* ——**zenin-suru** [vt] 是認する *approve* ⚡Watashi no teian wa kónkai mo zenin-sareta. 私の提案は今回も是認された。 *Again my motion was approved.*

zenjitsu 前日 *the previous day; the day before* ⚡Shukkoku no zenjitsu ni nátte, ryoken ga kírete irú no ni kizúita. 出国の前日になって、旅券が切れているのに気付いた。 *The day before my trip I discovered my passport had expired.*

zénjutsu no 前述の *the aforesaid; above-mentioned* ⚡Ketsuron wa zénjutsu no tōri desu. 結論は前述の通りです。 *The conclusion is as stated above.*

zénkai 前回 *the time before; last time* ⚡Kónkai wa zénkai no shippai o kurikaesánakatta. 今回は前回の失敗を繰り返さなかった。 *This time I didn't repeat the same mistake I made before.*

zénki 前期 *first term (in school); first half (of a business year)* ⚡zenki shíken 前期試験 *first-term exam* ⚡Edo jídai zénki 江戸時代前期 *early Edo period*

zenkō 善行 *good conduct; good deed* ⚡zenkō o tsumú 善行を積む *keep on doing good deeds*

zénkoku 全国 *the entire country*

zennō [no] 全能 (の) *omnipotent* ⚡Kámi wa zennō désu. 神は全能です。 *God is omnipotent.*

zenrei 前例 *precedent; previous instance* ⚡Zenrei ni nottóri hándan-suru. 前例に則り判断する。 *I will judge following precedent.*

zenritsusen 前立腺 *prostate gland*

zénryaku 前略 *Dispensing with the preliminaries... (abbreviated salutation to a letter)*

zenryoku 全力 *all (one's) effort* ⚡zenryoku o tsukusu 全力を尽くす *do (one's) best; expend every effort*

zensai 前菜 *hors d'oeuvre*

zénse 前世 *a former life; previous existence* §zénse no mukúi 前世の報い *retribution for (actions in) a former life*

zénsha 前者 *the former* §Kó'sha yóri zénsha no íken no hō ga watashi no kangáe ni chikái ki ga suru. 後者より前者の意見の方が私の考えに近い気がする。*I feel my opinion is closer to the former than to the latter.*

zenshin másui 全身麻酔 *general anesthesia*

zenshin-suru [vi] 前進する *advance; go forward* §Chúgoku no minshu shúgi wa jūnenmáe ni kurabete zenshin-shite iru. 中国の民主主義は十年前に比べて前進している。*Compared to ten years ago, Chinese democracy has progressed.*

zenshō 全焼 *completely burned* §Káji de wágaya wa zenshō-shita. 火事でわが家は全焼した。*My home burned to the ground.*

zensoku 喘息 *asthma*

zenson-suru [vi / vt] 全損する *be a total loss; lose entirely; total (a car)*

zentai [no] 全体（の）*the whole* §zentai shúgi 全体主義 *totalitarianism* §zentai o miwatasu 全体を見渡す *look over the whole*

zentei 前提 *prerequisite; premise* §zentei jóken 前提条件 *prerequisite condition* §Watashi o jogai-suru kotó o zentei ni gíron-shite kudasái. 私を除外することを前提に議論して下さい。*Please discuss it on the premise that I am not involved.*

zénto 前途 *the future; prospects* §zénto tanan 前途多難 *troubles ahead* §zénto yūbō na gakusei 前途有望な学生 *a promising student*

zenzen 全然 *all; entirely; (not) at all* §Eigo wa zenzen hanasemasén. 英語は全然話せません。*I can't speak English at all.*

zenzénjitsu 前々日 *the day before yesterday*

zeppan 絶版 *out of print*

zeppeki 絶壁 *precipice*

zetchō 絶頂 *the top; height; climax; peak* §zetchóki 絶頂期 *peak period* §ninki no zetchō 人気の絶頂 *peak of (one's) popularity*

zetsubō 絶望 *despair; loss of hope* ——**zetsubōteki [na]** 絶望的（な）*hopeless* ——**zetsubōteki ni** 絶望的に *hopelessly* ——**zetsubō-suru** [vi] 絶望する *despair; give up hope* §Jínsei ni zetsubō-surú no wa máda hayái. 人生に絶望するのはまだ早い。*It's too early to give up on life.*

zetsumetsú 絶滅 *extinction* §zetsumetsushu 絶滅種 *extinct species*

zettai ni 絶対に *absolutely; positively* §zettai óndo 絶対温度 *absolute temperature* §zettai-shúgi 絶対主義 *absolutism* §zettai tasú 絶対多数 *absolute majority* §Zettai ni káre o yurusánai wa! 絶対に彼を許さないわ。*I absolutely will not forgive him.* *<fem>*

zo ぞ *(sentence-ending particle: emphatic) <masc>*

zó 像 *statue* §buronzú-zō ブロンズ像 *a bronze statue* §butsuzō 仏像 *a Buddhist statue*

zṓ 象 *elephant*

zṓchiku 増築 *building extension* ——**zṓchiku-suru** [vt] 増築する *extend a building*

zṓdai 増大 *an increase* ——**zṓdai-suru** [vi] 増大する *increase* ❸Fuan ga zṓdai-shite iru. 不安が増大している。*Anxiety is increasing.*

zṓen 造園 *landscape gardening*

zṓgaku 増額 *increase in amount (of money)* ❸Yosan wa zṓgaku ni nátta. 予算は増額になった。*The budget was increased.*

zṓgan 象眼 *damascene* ❸zṓgan-záiku 象眼細工 *inlay*

zṓge 象牙 *ivory*

zṓka 増加 *an increase* ❸Tṓkyṓ no jinkṓ wa máda zṓka o tadótte iru. 東京の人口はまだ増加を辿っている。*Tokyo's population is still on the increase.* ——**zṓka-suru** [vi] 増加する *increase*

zṓkei bíjutsu 造形美術 *plastic arts*

zṓkin 雑巾 *cleaning cloth*

-zoku ～族 *tribe; family; kin* ❸kázoku 家族 *a family* ❸ichízoku 一族 *one family* ❸búzoku 部族 *a tribe* ❸gorufúzoku ゴルフ族 *golfers* ❸bōsṓzoku 暴走族 *motorcycle gang; hotrodders*

zoku 俗 *customs; manners; worldliness; common; vulgar* ❸shúzoku 習俗 *manners and customs* ❸zokujin 俗人 *a layman* ❸zoku ni iwarete iru... 俗に言われている *commonly called...* ❸zokugo 俗語 *slang*

zoku-súru [vi] 属する *belong to; come under the category of* ❸Nihón wa Ajiáshū ni zokú-shite iru. 日本はアジア州に属している。*Japan belongs to Asia.*

zokuzoku [to] 続々（と）*one after the other* ❸Gaikoku séihin ga zokuzoku to nyūka-shite iru. 外国製品が続々と入荷している。*Foreign products are flooding the market.*

zókuzoku-suru [vi] ぞくぞくする *feel chilly; shiver* ❸Netsu no séi ka senaka ga zókuzoku-shite iru. 熱のせいか背中がぞくぞくしている。*I guess I have a fever; my back feels chilly.*

[o-]zōni （お）雑煮 *rice cakes (mochi) boiled with vegetables (New Year's treat)*

zonjí·ru [vt] zonjínai; zónjita 存じる *know* <formal> ❸Sono katá o zónjite orimásu. その方を存じております。*I know that person.* <formal>

zonzái [na] ぞんざい（な）*careless; sloppy; crude; rude* ❸Káre no hanashiburi wa zonzái da. 彼の話ぶりはぞんざいだ。*His manner of speaking is rude.* <masc>

zṓo 憎悪 *hatred; abhorrence; detestation*

zórozoro [to] ぞろぞろ（と）*in great numbers; in a stream* ❸ṓzéi no tsūkínkyaku ga éki kara zórozoro to déte kimáshita. 大勢の通勤客が駅からぞろぞろと出てきました。*A crowd of commuters streamed out of the station.*

zōsen 造船 *shipbuilding* ❷zōsen kōjō 造船工場 *ship factory* ❷zōsen-gáisha 造船会社 *a shipbuilding company* ❷zōséngyō 造船業 *shipbuilding industry*

zōtei 贈呈 *gift; presentation* ——**zōtei-suru** [vt] 贈呈する *present as a gift*

zótto-suru [vi] ぞっとする *shudder; shiver; be horrified* ❷Sono hanashí o kiite zotto-shimáshita. その話を聞いて、ぞっとしました。*When I heard that, I was horrified.*

zōwai 贈賄 *a bribe*

zu 図 *picture; plan; figure; map; diagram* ❷zuan 図案 *a design; sketch* ❷zumen 図面 *a sketch; blueprint* ❷zukei 図形 *a diagram* ❷zúga 図画 *drawing; painting; picture* ❷zuhyō 図表 *diagram; chart*

zubári [to] ずばり（と）*straight; frank; as it is* ❷sono monó zubári そのものずばり *just as it is* ❷zubári to kíru ずばりと切る *cut clean through* ❷Itái kotó o zubári to itte nokéru. 痛いことをずばりと言ってのける。*He tells it like it is, even if it hurts.*

zubón ズボン *trousers; slacks; pants*

zubunure [ni] ずぶ濡れ（に）*wet through; drenched* ❷Hageshíi áme ga kyū ni furidashite, zubunure ni nátte shimatta. 激しい雨が急に降り出して、ずぶ濡れになってしまった。*It suddenly started to rain hard and I got drenched.*

zubutó·i [adj zubútoku nái; zubútokatta] 図太い *(be) bold; impudent; presumptuous*

zudón [to] ずどん（と）*with a bang* ❷Taihō kara tamá ga zudón to tobidáshita. 大砲から弾がずどんと飛び出した。*The cannonball was fired from the cannon with a bang.*

zugáikotsu 頭蓋骨 *skull; cranium*

zúibun [na] 随分（な）*very; extremely; fairly* ❷Zúibun to matásáreta. 随分と待たされた。*I was kept waiting a long time!*

zuihitsu 随筆 *essay; miscellany; random notes* ❷zuihitsuka 随筆家 *an essayist*

-zuke 〜付け *dated...* ❷Kyō ni nátte sengetsu no hatsuka-zuke no tegami ga todóita. 今日になって先月の二十日付けの手紙が届いた。*Today, finally, a letter dated the 20th of last month arrived.*

zúkezuke i·u [vt -iwanai; -itta] ずけずけ言う *speak bluntly; blurt out* ❷Tsúma wa aite kamawázu zúkezuke monó o iú. 妻は相手構わずずけずけものを言う。*My wife blurts out whatever she wants to say to anyone without caring who it is.*

zukínzukin ずきんずきん *throb*

zúkizuki ずきずき *throb* ❷Atamá ga zúkizuki itái. 頭がずきずき痛い。*My head's throbbing.*

zúkku ズック *canvas cloth*

-zumé 〜詰（め）*packed with; packed in* ❷kanzumé 缶詰 *canned goods*

❧binzumé ビン詰 *bottled goods*   ❧fukurozumé 袋詰 *packaged goods*

zúnō 頭脳 *brains; the head*

zúnzun ずんずん *quickly; rapidly*   ❧Shigoto ga zúnzun susunde iru. 仕事がずんずん進んでいる。 *Work is proceeding rapidly.*

zurári [to] ずらり（と）*in a row; lined up*   ❧Kyōshitsu ní wa kodomo no nafuda ga zurári to kakátte iru. 教室には子供の名札がずらりと掛かっている。 *In the classroom, the children's name tags hang neatly in a row.*

zuré ずれ *discrepancy; a lag; aberration*   ❧jikan no zuré 時間のずれ *a lag in time*   ❧Watashi to kimi tó de wa kangáe ni zuré ga áru. 私と君とでは考えにずれがある。 *There's a discrepancy between your way of thinking and mine.* <masc>

zuré·ru [vi zurénai; zúreta] ずれる *slip out of position*   ❧Pinto ga zúrete ita. ピントがずれていた。 *It was out of focus.*   ❧Ítsumo anáta wa rónten ga zúrete iru. いつもあなたは論点がずれている。 *Your logic is always a little off.* <fem>

zurú·i [adj zúruku nái; zúrukatta] 狡い *(be) dishonest; cunning; crafty; sly*   ❧zurúi kangáe ずるい考え *a dishonest idea; a sly idea*

zurusŏ [na] 狡そう（な）*sly, cunning, or crafty in manner or appearance*   ❧Káre wa zurusŏ na kao o shite iru. 彼はずるそうな顔をしている。 *He looks like he's got something up his sleeve..*

zúruzuru [to] ずるずる（と）*slippery*   ❧Kígen o zúruzuru to hikinobáshite wa ikenai. 期限をずるずると引き延ばしてはいけない。 *You can't keep on extending the time limit.*   ❧Kánojo wa suso o zúruzuru hikizutte iru. 彼女は裾をずるずる引きずっている。 *She's trailing the hem of her skirt.*

zushín [to] ずしん（と）*with a thud*

zutazuta ni ずたずたに *shred; tear to pieces*   ❧Watashi no kokóro wa zutazuta ni sareta. 私の心はずたずたにされた。 *My heart was torn to pieces.*

-zútsu 〜ずつ *each; per*   ❧Hitotsu-zútsu kotáete kudasái. 一つずつ答えて下さい。 *Answer (them) one by one.*

zutsū 頭痛 *headache*

zutto ずっと *all the time; all through; throughout; far; direct*   ❧zutto mukó ずっと向こう *far away; far beyond; way over there*   ❧Zutto mukashi no kotó da kedo... ずっと昔のことだけど... *It happened a long time ago, but...*

zūzūshí·i [adj zūzūshíku nái; zūzūshíkatta] 図々しい *(be) impudent; shameless; brazen*

zūzūshísa 図々しさ *impudence; shamelessness*   ❧Káre no zūzūshísa ga tamaranaku iyá desu! 彼の図々しさがたまらなく嫌です。 *I can't stand his impudence!*

Appendix A
Date Conversion Table, 1868 to 2000

Meiji 明治

1868	**Meiji 1**	1879 ... 12		1890 ... 23		1901 ... 34	
1869 ... 2		1880 ... 13		1891 ... 24		1902 ... 35	
1870 ... 3		1881 ... 14		1892 ... 25		1903 ... 36	
1871 ... 4		1882 ... 15		1893 ... 26		1904 ... 37	
1872 ... 5		1883 ... 16		1894 ... 27		1905 ... 38	
1873 ... 6		1884 ... 17		1895 ... 28		1906 ... 39	
1874 ... 7		1885 ... 18		1896 ... 29		1907 ... 40	
1875 ... 8		1886 ... 19		1897 ... 30		1908 ... 41	
1876 ... 9		1887 ... 20		1898 ... 31		1909 ... 42	
1877 ... 10		1888 ... 21		1899 ... 32		1910 ... 43	
1878 ... 11		1889 ... 22		1900 ... 33		1911 ... 44	
						1912 ... **45**	

Taishō 大正

1912	**Taishō 1**	1916 ... 5		1920 ... 9		1924 ... 13	
1913 ... 2		1917 ... 6		1921 ... 10		1925 ... 14	
1914 ... 3		1918 ... 7		1922 ... 11		**1926** ... **15**	
1915 ... 4		1919 ... 8		1923 ... 12			

Shōwa 昭和

1926	**Shōwa 1**	1942 ... 17		1958 ... 33		1974 ... 49	
1927 ... 2		1943 ... 18		1959 ... 34		1975 ... 50	
1928 ... 3		1944 ... 19		1960 ... 35		1976 ... 51	
1929 ... 4		1945 ... 20		1961 ... 36		1977 ... 52	
1930 ... 5		1946 ... 21		1962 ... 37		1978 ... 53	
1931 ... 6		1947 ... 22		1963 ... 38		1979 ... 54	
1932 ... 7		1948 ... 23		1964 ... 39		1980 ... 55	
1933 ... 8		1949 ... 24		1965 ... 40		1981 ... 56	
1934 ... 9		1950 ... 25		1966 ... 41		1982 ... 57	
1935 ... 10		1951 ... 26		1967 ... 42		1983 ... 58	
1936 ... 11		1952 ... 27		1968 ... 43		1984 ... 59	
1937 ... 12		1953 ... 28		1969 ... 44		1985 ... 60	
1938 ... 13		1954 ... 29		1970 ... 45		1986 ... 61	
1939 ... 14		1955 ... 30		1971 ... 46		1987 ... 62	
1940 ... 15		1956 ... 31		1972 ... 47		1988 ... 63	
1941 ... 16		1957 ... 32		1973 ... 48		**1989** ... **64**	

Heisei 平成

1989	**Heisei 1**	1992 ... 4		1995 ... 7		1998 ... 10	
1990 ... 2		1993 ... 5		1996 ... 8		1999 ... (11)	
1991 ... 3		1994 ... 6		1997 ... 9		2000 ... (12)	

Appendix B
Classifiers

There are two separate systems for counting things in Japanese: (1) native Japanese numerals (for quantities of up to ten) supplemented by Chinese-derived numerals (for quantities of more than ten) and (2) counters, a Japanese or Chinese-derived numeral plus a classifier.

Many things may be counted with the two numeral systems. Still others traditionally have classifiers associated with them. For instance, the classifier for cylindrical things such as pencils or cans of beer is *hon*. Sheets of paper, slices of bread, and shirts—all thin and flat things—are counted with the classifier *mai*. Animate things, such as people, dogs, cats, horses, birds, and so on, are always counted with a numeral plus classifier.

The principal classifiers in use today are given in the following table. If you cannot find the appropriate classifier, count with the native Japanese numeral system up to ten, and the Chinese-derived numeral system beyond; for quantities of up to ten, native Japanese numerals are provided at the very top of the table.

When used in a sentence, the counter normally follows the thing one is counting; for example, "There are three children." *Kodomo ga* (children) *sannin* (three persons) *imasu* (are). When the counter is used alone as a noun, it is not followed by a particle; for example, "Give me one sheet [of paper]." *Ichimai* (one sheet [of paper]) *kudasai* (please).

Classifiers

Numerals	1 hitótsu	2 futátsu	3 mittsu	4 yottsu	5 itsútsu
animals -*hiki* (small, 4-legged)	ippiki	nihiki	sámbiki	yónhiki	góhiki
birds -*wa*	ichíwa	níwa	sánwa	yónwa	gówa
books -*satsu*	issatsu	nísatsu	sánsatsu	yónsatsu	gosatsu
bunches -*taba*	hitótaba	futátaba	mítaba	yóntaba	gótaba
days -*nichi*	ichinichi	futsuka	mikka	yokka	itsuka
dishes -*sara*	hitósara	futásara	mísara	yónsara	gósara
fruit -*ko*	íkko	níko	sánko	yónko	góko
glassfuls -*hai*	íppai	níhai	sámbai	yónhai	gohai
hours -*jikan*	ichijíkan	nijíkan	sanjíkan	yonjíkan	gojíkan
houses -*ken*	íkken	níken	sánken	yónken	goken
machines -*dai*	ichídai	nídai	sándai	yóndai	godai
minutes -*fun*	íppun	nífun	sámun	yónfun	gofun
months -*kagetsu*	ikkágetsu	nikágetsu	sankagetsu	yonkágetsu	gokágetsu
pairs -*soku*	issoku	nísoku	sánzoku	yónsoku	gósoku
pencils -*hon*	íppon	níhon	sámbon	yónhon	gohon
people -*nin*	hitóri	futari	sannín	yonín	gonín
sheets -*mai*	ichímai	nímai	sámmai	yómmai	gomai
building floors -*kai*	ikkai	nikai	sangai	yonkai	gokai
times -*do*	ichido	nido	sando	yondo	godo
years -*nen*	ichínen	nínen	sannen	yonen	gonen

6	7	8	9	10	
muttsu	*nanátsu*	*yattsu*	*kokónotsu*	*tō*	Numerals
roppiki	*nanáhiki*	*happiki*	*kyū́hiki*	*juppiki*	-hiki
rokúwa	*nanáwa*	*hachíwa*	*kyū́wa*	*jū́wa*	-wa
rokúsatsu	*nanásatsu*	*hassatsu*	*kyū́satsu*	*jussatsu*	-satsu
rokutába	*nanátaba*	*hachitába*	*kyū́taba*	*juttába*	-taba
muika	*nanoka*	*yōka*	*kokonoka*	*tōka*	-nichi
rokusára	*nanásara*	*hachisára*	*kyū́sara*	*jússara*	-sara
rókko	*nanáko*	*háchiko*	*kyū́ko*	*júkko*	-ko
róppai	*nanáhai*	*hachíhai*	*kyū́hai*	*júppai*	-hai
rokujíkan	*nanajíkan*	*hachijíkan*	*kyū́jikan*	*jūjíkan*	-jikan
rókken	*nan'ken*	*hakken*	*kyū́ken*	*júkklen*	-ken
rokúdai	*nanádai*	*hachídai*	*kyū́dai*	*jū́dai*	-dai
róppun	*nan'fun*	*hachífun*	*kyū́fun*	*júppun*	-fun
rokkágetsu	*nanakágetsu*	*hakkágetsu*	*kyūkágetsu*	*jukkágetsu*	-kagetsu
rokusoku	*nanásoku*	*hassóku*	*kyū́soku*	*jussoku*	-soku
róppon	*nanáhon*	*hachíhon*	*kyū́hon*	*júppon*	-hon
rokúnin	*nanánin*	*hachínin*	*kyū́nin*	*jū́nin*	-nin
rokúmai	*nanámai*	*hachímai*	*kyū́mai*	*jū́mai*	-mai
rokkai	*nanakai*	*hachikai*	*kyū́kai*	*jukkai*	-kai
rokudo	*nanado*	*hachido*	*kyūdo*	*jūdo*	-do
rokúnen	*nanánen*	*hachínen*	*kyū́nen*	*jū́nen*	-nen

The "weathermark" identifies this book as a production of Weatherhill, Inc., publishers of fine books on Asia and the Pacific.